HANDBOOK OF THE INTERNATIONAL POLITICAL ECONOMY OF GOVERNANCE

HANDBOOKS OF RESEARCH ON INTERNATIONAL POLITICAL ECONOMY

Series Editors: Matthew Watson, *Department of Politics and International Studies, University of Warwick, Coventry, UK* and Benjamin J. Cohen, *Louis G. Lancaster Professor of International Political Economy, University of California, Santa Barbara, USA*

This highly original *Handbook* series offers a unique appraisal of the state-of-the-art of research in International Political Economy (IPE). Consisting of original contributions by leading authorities, *Handbooks* in the series provide comprehensive overviews of the very latest research within key areas of IPE. Taking a thematic approach, emphasis is placed on both expanding current debate and indicating the likely research agenda for the future. Each *Handbook* forms a prestigious and high quality work of lasting significance. The *Handbooks* will encompass arguments from both the British and American schools of IPE to give a comprehensive overview of the debates and research positions in each key area of interest, as well as offering a space for those who feel that their work fits neither designation easily. Taking a genuinely international approach these *Handbooks* are designed to inform as well as to contribute to current debates.

Handbook of the International Political Economy of Governance

Edited by

Anthony Payne

Professor of Politics, University of Sheffield, UK

Nicola Phillips

Professor of Political Economy, University of Sheffield, UK

HANDBOOKS OF RESEARCH ON INTERNATIONAL POLITICAL ECONOMY

Edward Elgar
Cheltenham, UK • Northampton, MA, USA

Published by
Edward Elgar Publishing Limited
The Lypiatts
15 Lansdown Road
Cheltenham
Glos GL50 2JA
UK

Edward Elgar Publishing, Inc.
William Pratt House
9 Dewey Court
Northampton
Massachusetts 01060
USA

A catalogue record for this book
is available from the British Library

Library of Congress Control Number: 2013949796

This book is available electronically in the ElgarOnline.com
Social and Political Science Subject Collection, E-ISBN 978 0 85793 348 5

ISBN 978 0 85793 347 8 (cased)

Typeset by Servis Filmsetting Ltd, Stockport, Cheshire
Printed and bound in Great Britain by T.J. International Ltd, Padstow

Contents

Contributors

Andrew Baker is a Reader in the School of Politics, International Studies and Philosophy at Queen's University Belfast, UK.

James Brassett is a Reader in International Political Economy at the University of Warwick, UK.

Brendan Carey recently completed a PhD in the School of Politics, International Studies and Philosophy at Queen's University Belfast, UK.

Philip G. Cerny is a Professor Emeritus of Politics and Global Affairs at the University of Manchester, UK, and Rutgers University, USA.

Jennifer Clapp is a Professor and Canada Research Chair in Global Food Security and Sustainability at the University of Waterloo, Canada.

Liam Clegg is a Lecturer in International Relations at the University of York, UK.

Niheer Dasandi is a Research Fellow with the Developmental Leadership Programme, based at University College London, UK.

Lorraine Elliott is a Professor of International Relations at the Australian National University.

Andrew Gamble is a Professor of Politics at the University of Cambridge, UK.

Andrew Geddes is a Professor of Politics at the University of Sheffield, UK.

Sophie Harman is a Senior Lecturer in the School of Politics and International Relations, Queen Mary, University of London, UK.

Colin Hay is a Professor of Government and Comparative Public Policy at Sciences Po, Paris, and an Affiliate Professor of Political Analysis at the University of Sheffield, UK.

Matthew J. Hoffmann is an Associate Professor of Political Science at the University of Toronto, Canada.

David Hudson is a Senior Lecturer in Political Economy at University College London, UK.

Peter Knorringa is a Professor of Private Sector & Development, International Institute of Social Studies, Erasmus University Rotterdam, The Netherlands.

Frederick W. Mayer is a Professor of Political Science, Public Policy and the Environment at Duke University, USA.

Georg Menz is a Professor in Political Economy and Jean Monnet Chair in European Integration, Goldsmiths, University of London, UK.

Manuela Moschella is an Assistant Professor in Political Science at the University of Turin, Italy.

Valbona Muzaka is a Senior Lecturer in International Political Economy at King's College London, UK.

Peter Newell is a Professor of International Relations at the University of Sussex, UK.

Anthony Payne is a Professor of Politics at the University of Sheffield, UK.

Nicola Phillips is a Professor of Political Economy at the University of Sheffield, UK.

Tony Porter is a Professor in the Department of Political Science, McMaster University, Canada.

Ben Richardson is an Assistant Professor in International Political Economy, University of Warwick, UK.

Jean-Philippe Thérien is a Professor in the Department of Political Science at the Université de Montréal, Canada.

Jacqui True is a Professor of Politics and International Relations at Monash University, Australia.

Eleni Tsingou is an Assistant Professor of International Political Economy at the Copenhagen Business School, Denmark.

Geoffrey R.D. Underhill is a Professor of International Governance at the University of Amsterdam, The Netherlands.

Rorden Wilkinson is a Professor of International Political Economy at the University of Manchester, UK.

Introduction: the international political economy of governance

Nicola Phillips and Anthony Payne

It is almost too easy to introduce a book of this sort by invoking yet again the ubiquity that the term 'governance' has achieved across the social sciences since the 1990s, including in international political economy (IPE). Like all buzzwords and intellectual fashions, this ubiquity has been enabled in spite of voluminous expressions of unease with the concept of governance: many hundreds of pages in academic books and journals have been given over to worrying about whether it is merely a vacuous concept that adds little to our understanding of world politics and political economy, or in fact provides us with sharper analytical tools with which to carve out an understanding of contemporary global change. It is not our collective purpose here to pick our way once again through those longstanding debates, nor to orient the book around another defence (or otherwise) of the centrality of the concept of governance to our field of study. We want instead to do something rather different: to look forward and call for a 'refreshing' of debates and ways of thinking about governance in IPE, and to assemble some of the best and most innovative research in this area to advance ideas about how this can and should be achieved.

On what basis do we make this claim that the study of governance in IPE stands in need of refreshing? Part of an answer lies in a claim that, traditionally, IPE has arguably done less well in developing distinctive contributions to the study of governance than some other sub-fields, notably, the sub-fields of public policy and international relations (IR). In the mid-2000s, the IPE literature on governance could reasonably be thought of as 'at best embryonic' (Payne 2005: 70), notwithstanding the fact that embedded within IPE were to be found indispensable resources for the broader study of governance. International political economists have always been very clear that in order to understand the politics, or agency, of governance, one must first grasp the structural context which gives rise to this politics and which in turn it shapes. From that central premise have sprung bodies of vibrant research in IPE on the manner in which the global political economy is being and should be governed, much of which is reflected amply in the pages of this volume. We find it nevertheless appropriate to advance the claim that there remains much to be done in order to identify empirically and understand theoretically the wide range of emergent patterns of governance in the global political economy, and it is in this constructive spirit that we call here for a redoubling of our collective efforts.

Yet it is abundantly clear that this is not an easy task. Patterns of governance in the global political economy are themselves unstable, continually in flux, in some cases merely embryonic, in others longstanding but fragile, and so on. James Rosenau indicated in the mid-1990s that the emerging system of governance – which he and others saw in terms of the disaggregation and dispersion of authority in the international system – was an 'unfinished story' (Rosenau 1995: 39). The same could be said of the 2010s, but it is of course appropriate to ask why one would expect it to be otherwise. The 'story' of global change, and the systems put in place to govern this process, have always been and are inevitably going to be in a condition of continual flux and evolution, even if some become entrenched over a more extended period of time than others.

Yet Rosenau's formulation also points us, perhaps unintentionally on his part, to the primary grounds on which we claim that a 'refreshing' of the study of governance is now needed. Over the 1990s and the 2000s, when governance became a mainstay of many sub-fields, including IPE, the task was conceived essentially as one of understanding what kind of world order would be put in place by the processes that were perceived to be under way. On the latter, we felt that we had a reasonably firm grip: they were associated with the myriad processes of globalisation, themselves structured by the 'hegemonies' of neoliberal ideology, global (financial) markets and the United States. Thus debates centred on understanding the layers of governance that were built on these foundations, and the 'projects' of governance through which they were entrenched – the changing role of states in governance and the shift to the primacy of markets, emergent forms of global or supranational governance 'beyond the state', the manner in which power was refracted through international organisations, the varying modes of governance which were put in place to facilitate the 'neoliberalisation' of global and national economies, the disaggregation of political authority, and so on. The point is, simply, that we thought we knew what we were dealing with in terms of the core structural, ideological and political forces at play, and the questions related mainly to what sort of world order they would yield in the short and medium terms.

We suggest, however, that these unquestionably vibrant and interesting debates, albeit far from completed, have now been loosened from their moorings by a range of trends and events in the global political economy, such that the foundations of the study of governance now stand in need of re-examination. One would immediately think in this respect of the crises in the Anglo-American and Eurozone economies which took hold in the late 2000s, the fall-out from which, at the time of writing, is still in full flow. We are still, of course, a long way from having the perspective necessary for understanding the longer-term consequences of the crises, but a range of questions have already become pertinent relating to such matters as their impact on the ideological foundations of the contemporary world order, the Anglo-American dominance of the global political economy, and the direction of the relationship between different forms of political control and the operations of global markets. One would also think of the longer-term processes by which a range of 'rising powers' are actually or potentially disrupting structures of power and forms of authority in the global political economy, and possibly sowing the ideological, political and economic seeds of very different patterns of governance from those which we associated with the heyday of neoliberal global governance. The nature of political resistance and civil society activism has also come to assume distinctive forms which challenge much of what we thought we knew in the 1990s and 2000s about the nature of power and political control.

The list could go on, and indeed will go on as we advance through the chapters collected here. The point that needs to be made in this introductory context is, simply, that many of the assumptions that anchored the study of governance in IPE over the 1990s and 2000s have been shaken loose, and that its conceptual foundations are now more fragile, and in some cases distinctly unsteady. This is not to say that the entire edifice of governance debates needs to be razed to the ground. It is simply to suggest that we need to take seriously the intriguing and important processes of change that have occurred, and are occurring, in the global political economy, and think afresh about how the study of governance needs to evolve in order to accommodate the associated conceptual, theoretical and empirical challenges that are now laid before us.

We seek to take a step in this direction with this volume. It is organised in two parts. The first, which we have referred to as the international political economy of governance, takes up four themes which we consider to be foundational to the study of governance, both as it has developed and as it needs to develop in the future. These relate to the underpinning ideologies of governance, the levels at which governance is articulated, the actors involved in governance, and the ethical questions associated with governance. In the remainder of this Introduction, we justify this thematic framing for the volume, exploring in a preliminary way how the case for a 'refreshing' of the study of governance manifests itself in these four areas. The authors of the chapters in Part I of the volume then pick up each of these areas in turn, not in order simply to survey the 'state of the debate', but to advance their own distinctive 'takes' on the questions and thereby contribute to the next phase of scholarship on these themes.

Moving, as it were, from the international political economy of governance to the governance of the international political economy, the chapters in Part II are then charged with addressing the patterns of governance which prevail in particular arenas and issue areas. The authors were invited to consider their contributions in the light of the four framing themes we set out, and indeed all four themes emerge strongly and resonate in varied and distinctive ways across the wide range of arenas and patterns of governance that the authors consider. The Conclusion, finally, pulls together some of the key insights offered into contemporary dynamics in the four thematic areas, and considers how these insights can be mobilised in refreshing the study of governance.

IDEOLOGIES OF GOVERNANCE

One of the most notable contributions of IPE to the study of governance has been its claim that all forms and projects of governance are intrinsically ideological. Much more than approaches to governance that have emerged from the fields of, say, international relations or public policy, by its nature IPE has been alert to the centrality of ideas and ideologies in constituting the structures of the global political economy, and to the ideological purposes that are served by particular projects of governance that have emerged in the contemporary era. These have been captured most notably in critical traditions in IPE, finding early expression in the work of Robert Cox and Susan Strange, among others. Cox (1983: 168) was concerned with the ways in which the material and ideological dimensions of power were 'always bound together, mutually reinforcing one another, and not reducible one to the other' and advanced the admittedly slippery concept of a *nébuleuse* to refer to the ideological forces which shaped the contemporary world order. Ideology is, in short, a governance structure in itself – in the formulation of Stephen Gill (1995) or Andrew Gamble (2001), the 'constitution' which itself 'governs' world politics and development. In a slightly different mould, Strange (1988) referred more commonly to the role of ideas, captured in the notion of a 'knowledge' structure, again as one of the dimensions of power which underpinned and shaped the contemporary international political economy. The point is that the focus on the ideologies of governance was embedded in IPE scholarship from the time that IPE began to shape itself as a field of study. Those early insights have been expanded and developed vigorously in subsequent work, often distilled into the shorthand form of a concern with neoliberalism, especially in critical strands of IPE. The concept of neoliberalism has provided a device for understanding not only the direction of economic change and the content and outcomes of the economic strategies of governments and international organisations, but also, more broadly, the ideological forces and structures of political power which have driven forwards a particular conception of the relationship between markets, states and societies in the contemporary period.

However, this is not to say that these insights into the ideological character of governance have been taken up fully enough across the terrain of governance debates, within IPE or outside it. A good deal of the literature, despite its considerable value, has continued to privilege an agency-centred approach to governance (focusing on actors, multilateral institutions, global civil society, bargaining and collective action), without due attention to the material and ideological structures which themselves govern the global political economy and shape 'the way things are usually done' (Cox 1981: 152). It has also tended to focus on particular projects of governance without addressing sufficiently their ideological underpinnings and, more to the point, ideological purposes. In much of the literature, global governance has thus been understood as an activity, where the core of the study of global governance is properly a focus on 'purposive acts', rather than 'tacit arrangements' (Finkelstein 1995: 4–5). The problem, as Craig Murphy (2000: 796) usefully complained, has been the consequent inability of many approaches to global governance, even those with a critical orientation, to account for 'why so much of this creative movement in world politics seems to have added up to the supremacy of the neoliberal agenda both within and across states'. By extension, the issue is not only that much of the global governance literature neglects the issue of ideology, but also that global governance presented itself as ideologically neutral. It is this shroud of neutrality that, as Anthony Payne (2005) has argued, obscures the key point that global governance is in essence an ideological project which aims to sustain a particular, neoliberal, world order.

The contributors to this volume seek purposefully to remove this shroud of neutrality. They collectively set out to expose the manner in which ideological forces themselves govern the global political economy, the ideological and ideational underpinnings of particular projects of governance, and the ideological purposes that are served by those projects. As we have observed, for much of the 1990s and 2000s the concept of neoliberalism provided the theoretical, conceptual and empirical anchor for much of the literature on governance in IPE, whether critical in its orientation or attached to orthodox approaches relying on neoclassical or neoliberal theory. Yet there is a sense in which we now need to question the assumptions about the structural 'hegemony' of neoliberalism that we have become used to deploying in attempting to understand the ideological forces shaping governance. One reason for this is a growing perception that the ideological power of neoliberalism is on the wane, weakened by a combination of its poor and, in some contexts, disastrous record in promoting growth and development around the world, the crises of the Anglo-American model and the Eurozone project from the late

2000s onwards, and the apparent emergence of alternative ideologies of governance associated with the growing power of economies which have conspicuously eschewed a neoliberal development model.

All of these contentions are the subject of vibrant debate, which is reflected in many of the contributions to this volume. Yet, whether or not it is deemed premature, or just plain wrong, to think that we are moving beyond neoliberalism, we need at least to ask if we are now in a situation in which an unbending reliance on the concept of neoliberalism as a theoretical and empirical anchor still serves us well in capturing the direction and complexities of contemporary governance.

LEVELS OF GOVERNANCE

In IPE, as in the many other fields in which the study of governance occupies an important place, the notion that governance operates at a variety of 'levels' is so basic an assumption that it scarcely needs to be articulated. Many approaches to governance have featured a distinct nation-state-centrism, concerning themselves with how particular national polities, economies and societies are governed, by both national states and other actors within national boundaries. Much of the impetus towards breaking out of those nationalist shackles emerged from European Union (EU) studies, specifically in the development of the concept of 'multi-level governance' (Hooghe and Marks 2001; Bache and Flinders 2004), which sought to capture the complexities of a regional arena in which governance occurred beyond the nation-state, and the relationship between the regional, national and subnational levels in the articulation of governance in the setting of the EU. IPE and, to a lesser extent, IR were similarly fertile beds for the development of perspectives on international, transnational and global levels of governance, where again the core questions revolved around how to conceptualise governance 'above' and 'beyond' national states. In this sense, developments in the study of governance spoke very directly to longstanding methodological and theoretical debates in the social sciences concerning 'levels of analysis', and indeed have been pivotal in pushing those debates forward.

The difficulty has been that the different sub-fields hosting the study of governance have tended to confine themselves to a particular 'level', such that, for example, IPE has focused its energies mostly on 'global governance', EU studies on supranational and regional governance in that particular setting, and comparative political economy or public policy on the national level. Admittedly, in one sense, this is overstating the case, inasmuch as none of these approaches should be accused of having an entirely myopic focus on its corresponding level of governance. Comparative political economy and public policy approaches could not fail to accommodate the idea that there are influences on governance and policy that emanate from beyond the national polity or economy; similarly EU studies has been preoccupied with the relationship between supranational governance and governance within member-states and member economies. Yet it is nevertheless fair to say that a division of labour persists between various fields and sub-fields, and that we have collectively done less well at understanding the interactions between levels of governance than at identifying the levels at which governance is articulated. Part of the problem, however, is that the question has been framed precisely in those terms – as being about interactions between levels, retaining a notion that they are in some sense discrete – rather than as being about how to understand the ways that levels of governance are intrinsically enmeshed.

We suggest that there is scope for refreshing debates about governance on these grounds, and specifically that understanding governance across different levels is the direction in which we need collectively to move. Analytically, it is probably inescapable that we will retain an idea of levels of analysis, and that our various sub-fields will be more concerned with some levels than others. Nevertheless, there is clearly space for a more considered treatment of the dynamics of governance across levels than we have hitherto developed. This comment applies as much to IPE as any other sub-field, inasmuch as our focus on global and transnational forms of governance can fairly be said to have neglected the manner in which these arenas and forms of governance are intrinsically constituted by governance at other levels. Put differently, the focus has tended to rest with the ways in which governance at the global and transnational levels has implications for governance at other (particularly national and subnational) levels, but much less attention has been directed to the dynamics of constitution (and contradiction) flowing in the other direction, except perhaps where those dynamics emanate from the forces associated with the power of the United States and its partners. Thus the contributors to this volume seek not only to explore empirically how governance in particular arenas operates at different levels – in, above, below and beyond national states and economies – but also to consider the question of how, in particular contexts, we can begin to understand and conceptualise governance across levels.

ACTORS AND AGENCY IN GOVERNANCE

One of the conceptual and empirical mainstays of the study of governance is the idea that the activity of governance is no longer the preserve of national states. As well as being pushed downwards, upwards and outwards to different spatial levels, authority and agency have dispersed to a wide range of actors at and across all these levels. Ranging from credit rating agencies or non-governmental organisations to multilateral institutions or transnational criminal networks and mafias, the core questions concern who possesses and exercises agency, what those forms of agency look like, and of what sort of new or emerging world order they are the harbingers. A shift to 'polycentric' governance has been one interpretation (Scholte 2004); Philip Cerny (2010) has advanced the notion of 'transnational neopluralism'; others have spoken of a 'new medievalism' (Ruggie 1993) or a 'new transgovernmentalism' (Slaughter 1997). All different in their theoretical and empirical significance, the common theme is a desire to understand the consequences of the dispersion and reconfiguration of agency and authority for governance in the global political economy.

A large number of specific avenues of enquiry have emerged as part and parcel of this endeavour. One has been the empirical investigation and mapping of who these new actors are and what they do (Wilkinson 2002). Another significant track of governance research has sought not to lose sight of national states. Here the starting point has been, with variations on the theme, a contention that states have been subject to a thorough reorganisation and that state power likewise has been intrinsically reconfigured. Hence there has emerged an enormous array of conceptually tantalising concepts, from the 'competition state' (Cerny 1997) or the 'disaggregated state' (Slaughter 2004), to the 'internationalisation of the state' (Cox 1987), 'leaner, meaner' forms of state-ness (Evans 1997) or the 'Schumpeterian post-national workfare regime' (Jessop 2002). A third key focus, among many others, has been the increasing salience of private actors and private forms of governance, and the question of how the relationship between public and private authority in the contemporary world should be understood (Cutler et al. 1999; Hall and Biersteker 2002; Dingwerth 2008; Nölke and Graz 2008). These themes of continuing relevance are all picked up energetically in the chapters collected in this volume.

However, the chapters also reflect on the new challenges that have been presented to us by contemporary events, which, we suggest, should prompt a 'refreshing' or re-examination of some of our assumptions. The financial and economic crisis since the late 2000s has been particularly important in this respect, providing the context and impetus for what appears to be a rather new configuration of agency, and redrawing once again the contours of the relationship between public and private authority. The days when we could easily, and rather lazily, speak of a 'privatisation' or 'marketisation' of political and economic authority are clearly receding, as we witness a distinctly uneasy and fragile process of renegotiating the complex relationship between public and private authority and the interaction between public and private spheres of governance. For those interested in the politics and agency of resistance, furthermore, this uneasy relationship has provided both a focal point and an impetus to new forms of political engagement, whether domestically in electoral arenas (where those exist) or more broadly through new protest movements. In short, the quickly changing landscape of agency, and by extension authority, is – or should be – pushing us to reflect on and re-examine the ways in which we handle these concepts in governance debates.

ETHICAL ISSUES IN GOVERNANCE

Our fourth theme refers to a set of questions which has become pervasive in governance research: these address the normative and ethical issues associated with governance in general and with particular projects of governance more specifically. By identifying the theme in this way, we refer to a wide array of approaches and concerns. Perhaps the most salient has been the preoccupation with the related issues of legitimacy, accountability, representation and inclusion, which take their cue most obviously from a contention that governance in all arenas other than democratic national polities suffers intrinsically from a 'democratic deficit'. The question which IPE scholarship has addressed vigorously in this respect concerns how we can think about a legitimate form of global governance, which exhibits the characteristics of democracy, in the absence of democratically delegated and centralised authority (*Review of International Political Economy* 2011). The focus thus falls on the ethical content of particular kinds of governance, and the ethical implications of the shift of authority and agency out of the hands of national states associated with the processes of disaggregation and dispersion that we described earlier.

One of the problems associated with this strand of literature is that it is too often assumed that the national states in question are democratic; in other words, that they are essentially modelled on Western ideas of liberal democracy. This inevitably shapes (and skews) the ways in which research agendas on governance are defined. It is also assumed that the national states which feature in governance debates conform with the associated types and extent of 'statehood'; clearly, the questions are sharply different when we turn our attention to governance in areas of 'limited statehood' (Börzel and Risse 2010). These complaints aside, it is the case that one of the most vibrant avenues of governance research in recent years, in IPE as elsewhere, has taken ethical questions as its central preoccupation.

It seems obvious to us, indeed, that ethics both are – and should be – becoming ever more pervasive as a core concern across IPE scholarship (Brassett and Holmes 2010). While we have been used to thinking about questions of, for example, global financial governance and its 'democratic deficit', we are now compelled to range much more widely over the ethical terrain associated with particular forms and arenas of governance. The ethics of banking are constantly in the spotlight in popular debate, as are corporate scandals and business behaviour in general, as well as the deep imbrication of national governments, supranational authorities and a range of other actors in patterns of governance that most of us would deem to be deeply unethical. Similarly, the distributional consequences of particular forms and projects of governance have long preoccupied scholars in the field, ranging widely from concerns with global poverty and inequality to questions of labour standards, the possibilities for fair(er) trade and production, or what a form of 'global justice' might look like.

Ethical considerations run as a leitmotif through this volume, picked up in the chapters in different ways across a wide range of arenas and issue areas. Yet we also get a clear sense of the ways in which, as in the other themes we have identified, the parameters of our concerns might need begin to shift. The scholarship focusing on what a legitimate form of global governance might look like, as just one example, may well need to grapple much more with the fact that many actually or potentially powerful 'new' actors in global governance do not carry with them the same, established, deeply ingrained ideas about liberal democratic governance as those actors who or which have traditionally dominated. What is apparent, amidst a rapidly changing political-economic landscape, is that the force of ethical and normative questions remains undiminished, and indeed is perhaps ever stronger than ever, in IPE debates on governance in all its forms.

REFERENCES

Bache, Ian and Matthew Flinders (eds) (2004), *Multi-Level Governance*, Oxford: Oxford University Press.
Börzel, Tanya A. and Thomas Risse (2010), 'Governance without a state: can it work?', *Regulation and Governance*, **4**, 113–34.
Brassett, James and Christopher Holmes (2010), 'International political economy and the question of ethics', *Review of International Political Economy*, **17** (3), 425–53.
Cerny, Philip G. (1997), 'Paradoxes of the competition state: the dynamics of political globalisation', *Government and Opposition*, **32** (2), 251–74.
Cerny, Philip G. (2010), *Rethinking World Politics: A Theory of Transnational Neopluralism*, Oxford: Oxford University Press.
Cox, Robert W. (1981), 'Social forces, states and world orders: beyond international relations theory', *Millennium: Journal of International Studies*, **10** (2), 126–55.
Cox, Robert W. (1983), 'Gramsci, hegemony and international relations: an essay in method', *Millennium: Journal of International Studies*, **12** (2), 162–75.

Cox, Robert W. (1987), *Production, Power, and World Order: Social Forces in the Making of History*, New York: Columbia University Press.

Cutler, A. Claire, Virginia Haufler and Tony Porter (eds) (1999), *Private Authority and International Affairs*, Albany, NY: State University of New York Press.

Dingwerth, Klaus (2008), 'Private transnational governance and the developing world', *International Studies Quarterly*, **52**, 607–34.

Evans, Peter (1997), 'The eclipse of the state? Reflections on stateness in an era of globalization', *World Politics*, **50** (1), 62–87.

Finkelstein, Lawrence S. (1995), 'What is global governance?', *Global Governance*, **1** (4), 367–72.

Gamble, Andrew (2001), 'Neo-liberalism', *Capital and Class*, **75**, 127–34.

Gill, Stephen (1995), 'Globalisation, market civilisation, and disciplinary neo-liberalism', *Millennium: Journal of International Studies*, **24** (3), 399–423.

Hall, Rodney Bruce and Thomas J. Biersteker (eds) (2002), *The Emergence of Private Authority in Global Governance*, Cambridge: Cambridge University Press.

Hooghe, Liesbet and Gary Marks (2001), *Multi-Level Governance and European Integration*, Lanham, MD: Rowman & Littlefield.

Jessop, Bob (2002), *The Future of the Capitalist State*, Cambridge: Polity Press.

Murphy, Craig N. (2000), 'Global governance: poorly done and poorly understood', *International Affairs*, **76** (4), 789–803.

Nölke, Andreas and Jean-Christophe Graz (eds) (2008), *Transnational Private Governance and its Limits*, London: Routledge.

Payne, Anthony (2005), 'The study of governance in a global political economy', in Nicola Phillips (ed.), *Globalizing International Political Economy*, Basingstoke: Palgrave Macmillan, pp. 55–81.

Review of International Political Economy (2011), Special Issue on 'Legitimacy and Global Governance', **18** (1).

Rosenau, James N. (1995), 'Governance in the twenty-first century', *Global Governance*, **1** (1), 13–43.

Ruggie, John Gerard (1993), 'Territoriality and beyond: problematizing modernity in international relations', *International Organization*, **47** (1), 139–74.

Scholte, Jan Aart (2004), 'Globalization and governance: from statism to polycentrism', CSGR Working Paper 130/04, University of Warwick, February.

Slaughter, Anne-Marie (1997), 'The real new world order', *Foreign Affairs*, **76** (5), 183–97.

Slaughter, Anne-Marie (2004), *A New World Order*, Princeton, NJ: Princeton University Press.

Strange, Susan (1988), *States and Markets*, London: Pinter.

Wilkinson, Rorden (2002), 'Global governance: a preliminary interrogation', in Rorden Wilkinson and Steve Hughes (eds), *Global Governance: Critical Perspectives*, London: Routledge, pp. 1–13.

PART I

THE INTERNATIONAL POLITICAL ECONOMY OF GOVERNANCE

1 Ideologies of governance
Andrew Gamble

The ideological character of the contemporary governance of the international system has been shaped by many factors, but principally by the interests and ideology of the United States (US) after it became the leading world power in 1945, and additionally by the traditions of economic liberalism which go back to discourses, contexts and institutions developed in the eighteenth and nineteenth centuries, at a time when Britain was the rising and then leading power. Both will be discussed in this chapter. The international system combines the international economy and the international state system, and states remain core actors in both (Thompson 2008). As the most powerful player in the international system, the United States has played a major part in creating and sustaining the evolving system of rules which has governed the international system. Its ideological preferences have been fairly prominently displayed, and for alternatives to succeed they have first had to gain US approval. The United States however is not the sole source of governance in the international system. The three main modes of governance – markets, hierarchies and networks (Thompson et al. 1991) – create structures with their own logic and consequences, which put constraints on the United States as well as on other states in the international system. These structures are not neutral but have their own ideological character, creating a predisposition to particular kinds of solutions. These different modes of governance can be found in all actual forms of governance, but the way in which they are combined varies. The preference for market forms of governance in both the private and the public sectors is one of the distinguishing hallmarks of contemporary governance and its specific ideological character.

IDEOLOGY AND GOVERNANCE

Governance has been interpreted and defined in many different ways (Rhodes 1996; Bevir 2009; Rosenau 2006; Pierre and Peters 2000). In its original meaning it signified the action or manner of government and, by extension, the office, function or power of governing. In the seventeenth century it also came to denote the method of management, and system of regulations used to govern a state, an association, a household or a person. Inseparable from these early meanings of governance is an idea of order, of how the manner or mode in which government is conducted contributes to stability and prosperity and civil peace, or their opposites. The consequences of the quality of governance for human societies are profound, as starkly expressed in the frescoes depicting the allegory of good and bad government by Lorenzetti in the Palazzo Pubblico in Siena. Governance is not a dry technical question, but goes to the heart of how order is established and sustained in human societies and, therefore, what a good society is. Even when governance is presented purely as a set of procedures this still implies a substantive conception of the good. Ideology is therefore not a contingent but a necessary part of governance, because modes of governance are distinguished by their differing ideological assumptions. They have to be constructed and sustained through discourse and argument, which contain judgements about how the world is, how it works and how it might be.

Ideology can also be analysed at many levels, and comes in many forms, from the articulations of grand theory to the popular common sense deployed in the media. It is wrong to think of ideology as more or less fixed coherent doctrines or world-views. Ideologies are rather clusters or families of ideas which frequently overlap and, as Michael Freeden (1996) has shown, are best distinguished one from another by examining which ideas are treated as core and which as peripheral. Ideologies are an indispensable part of modern politics, the common currency of political argument, and as a result they have a protean character. They are highly adaptable, constantly evolving, incorporating new elements and borrowing from elsewhere, redefining their terms, and subtly changing the meaning of some of their core concepts. Ideologies are not owned by anybody, but should rather be thought of as sets of resources which individuals and groups use to make sense of the world and to make choices (Harris 1968).

Contemporary governance is extremely complex because of the interconnected and interdependent nature of modern social systems. There are many different kinds of institutions which require governing. Some are extremely local and small in scale; others have a global reach and operate transnationally (Rosenau 2006). The existence of such diversity sets up persistent problems of coordination, so that there needs to be both governance at the micro level of institutions and governance at the macro level of the system. Very little of this is designed or planned; it emerges through responses to particular circumstances, and the exploitation of particular advantages by states, corporations or other actors. What results is a patchwork of rules and institutions which are sometimes dignified with the name of global governance, but which generally fall far short of that. This is partly because there is no one integrated global economy or global society to be the object of governance, and there tend to be competing ideas of governance, which makes the development of a set of common rules difficult (Rupert 2000; Phillips 2005). But the impulse to impose a relative order on international affairs is a powerful one, and it is a project which has been pursued at various times by a great power acting consciously or unconsciously as a hegemon (Gilpin and Gilpin 2001). No such project could succeed if the aim was to impose uniformity upon the rest of the world or force convergence to a single pattern favoured by the hegemonic power. But the ideological character of contemporary governance shows itself in the aspiration to impose a greater degree of uniformity and convergence on the rest of the world than would otherwise exist. This can be justified as delivering a public good (Kindleberger 1986) or criticised as serving a particular set of interests (Harvey 2003). Seen from different perspectives, both interpretations are true, because this is how governance works. It involves the making of ideological choices and the advancing of moral claims. It seeks to establish rules that are not only efficient in the outcomes they deliver, but which are also considered right and legitimate. A system of governance is most successful when the normative and practical assumptions underlying it are not challenged, but are just accepted as common sense, the way things are, or the way things have always been. The deep conservatism in all human beings is a glue that holds societies together, but this is harder to bring about in modern society because of the extent and pace of change, which constantly dissolves existing relationships and forces individuals, groups and whole societies to adjust the way they live

(Oakeshott 1961). Even here, however, the most radical change tends to be followed by periods of consolidation and attempts to make the change seem normal and consensual, as though it had always existed.

Governance can be seen at its simplest in relation to associations of various kinds. It provides a set of rules which defines the aims of the association, establishes the offices for carrying them out and lays down how the holders of these offices should be selected, what their duties are and how they are to be made accountable for what they do. Such rules prescribe behaviour, set limits, create expectations and establish benchmarks. They may be the result of deliberation amongst the members or they can be imposed from above, but whatever their origin they determine what is legitimate by crystallising or reflecting particular ideas and interests. The adoption of rules to facilitate their governance transforms associations into institutions, which then take on a life of their own and confront the individual as an established order, constraining what individuals can and cannot do by defining the nature of the possible and the desirable. All human institutions in this way have both practical and imaginative foundations. Their governance can be defined through formal constitutions, but will also depend on a much looser set of arrangements resting on traditions, conventions and precedents.

States are associations, but very complex ones. As associations they have their own governance rules, but they also sit in judgement on the governance rules of others. Their task is to endorse, sustain, reform and occasionally formulate and impose the governance rules for the multitude of associations within their jurisdiction, and also to coordinate their activities. Modern states assert sovereignty, which means exclusive jurisdiction over a territory and the monopoly of legitimate violence, and at the same time claim to represent their citizens in several different ways (Runciman and Vieira 2008). This has been done by identifying the state with the nation and by appealing to popular sovereignty and the general will. Both are compatible with authoritarian forms of rule, but gradually democratic interpretations of both have strengthened, particularly in advanced economies, although democracies in the sense defined by Western agencies are still in a minority among the member-states of the United Nations (Economist Intelligence Unit 2011). Representation in the modern state is indirect since the people cannot govern themselves, but the state acts in their name and is assumed to possess a single will and personality. This unitary character of state sovereignty (even in federal constitutions) is one of the modern state's distinguishing characteristics.

Modern states, however, have never been self-contained islands. They have emerged as major players in a new kind of international economy over the last 300 years, which has encouraged ever greater economic interdependence, the organisation of transnational markets and a transnational division of labour, and unprecedented flows of labour, capital and goods across the world. This economy has destroyed self-sufficiency and made all communities to a greater or lesser extent dependent upon the world market. The problem for this new international economic system is precisely how order can be established and sustained in a world in which political authority is fragmented into competing nation-states (Wallerstein 1974). Markets may appear spontaneous and evolutionary, but they require certain kinds of support which they themselves cannot provide. The intervention of states is essential for markets to survive, and free markets even more so (O'Neill 1998; Plant 2010). At the international level there is no global sovereign that automatically guarantees that kind of order, so the problem of who is to establish, enforce and change the rules of governance at a global level is an acute one.

All forms of governance are normative in the sense that they reflect particular beliefs and values and contain explicit or implicit judgements about what is good and what is bad, what is appropriate and what is inappropriate (Bevir 2009). Their ideological character can be implicit or very explicit. The latter is most apparent when a regime adopts a rigid ideological doctrine, as the Soviet Union did with Marxism-Leninism. But more often the ideological character is implicit, although still just as essential. Ideologies have always played a major role in shaping contemporary governance of the international economy, making possible international orders and making the rules of such orders seem like common sense (Cox 1987, 1996). Such orders depend upon the role played by leading states, so it is often their ideologies which become translated to the international sphere and become accepted as the new common sense. World orders are not guaranteed, and in the past they have frequently broken down. The extent to which the writ of the leading power runs throughout the whole of the international state system will vary, depending on the strength of other powers, and the degree to which the leading power can offer genuine public goods which others acknowledge as public goods and is prepared to bear the cost of providing them. Real hegemonic power emerges when the leading state does not have to rely on its military or its economic power to impose the rules it favours, but finds that these rules are willingly adopted by other states, because they perceive benefits to themselves from doing so. This is how ideology becomes translated into the idiom of common sense. What was originally a clear political choice becomes treated as an immutable and uncontroversial aspect of the way things are.

THE HERITAGE OF ECONOMIC LIBERALISM

In the twentieth century the rise of the United States, and its assumption of international leadership, helped consolidate and extend liberalism as the dominant ideology of the modern era. It followed the long period of British ascendancy in the nineteenth century. The liberal world order which Britain had helped to create and sustain was thought by many to be terminally wounded by the effects of the First World War, the Great Crash and the Great Depression, which saw the final end of attempts to resuscitate the gold standard. But economic liberalism revived under US leadership after 1945. There were many differences from the liberal order established by Britain (O'Brien 2003), but it was still recognisably liberal. Other visions of world order, whether national-protectionist, fascist or socialist, which in the 1930s seemed set to triumph, were pushed back, at least in the areas of the world dominated by the United States. There was a new flourishing of the tradition of economic liberalism, the dominant form of which became known as 'neoliberalism'.

The defining characteristic of economic liberalism is its preoccupation with the way in which the economy is organised. Friedrich Hayek (1944: 68) summed up this central idea when he said that 'to be controlled in our economic pursuits means to be . . . controlled in everything'. The essential criterion of value for economic liberals is the individual. The preferences, interests and liberty of individuals take priority over everything else. The self-regulating spontaneous order of the market is the institution which must be protected above all other institutions if that principle is to be respected. Arguments that we now recognise as economic liberal arguments were increasingly commonplace in the eighteenth century, not least in the writings of the English and Scottish schools of political economy, but economic liberalism was not formulated as an ideology until the rise of modern liberal political parties and a specific liberal political economy in the nineteenth century, organised around the principles of laissez-faire, sound money and free trade.

Ideas do not exist in a vacuum, but arise in particular contexts, and even when they claim to be universal they commonly serve specific purposes. The ideas of liberal political economy were extremely important in legitimating and defining the new international order which was arising in the nineteenth century, with Britain at its centre. It laid down the principles which should guide public policy and inform the judgements of politicians and other public officials. It became distilled into a form of common sense, which became deeply impressed on the official mind in Britain and, by extension, in many of the other countries which participated in the liberal international order which Britain had fashioned. The rules of international governance it prescribed centred around how to preserve the gold standard and therefore sound public finances in every nation, how to promote free trade to achieve the greatest possible economic growth and peaceful intercourse, and how to encourage governments to limit themselves to securing internal order and external defence, raising taxes for these purposes and for these purposes alone.

At the heart of this conception was an imagined order, based on the great engine of the division of labour and accumulation of capital of nineteenth-century capitalism, which came to be regarded as a social invention as miraculous in its way as the flow of technical inventions which it made possible and put to such productive use. So remarkable was the transformation of the international economy in the century from the end of the Napoleonic Wars to the outbreak of the First World War that economic liberals came to believe strongly that there should be no unnecessary interference in this great spontaneous mechanism which had been set in motion. The key political symbol of this commitment was free trade, which was far more than just a fiscal policy. It stood for a whole set of beliefs about how the relationships between states, markets and households should be regulated in a modern economy, and not just at national level, but at international level too (Trentmann 2008). Here was a set of rules for international governance, to which Britain largely adhered, although different rules applied for the colonial territories. Many other countries followed Britain's lead.

There were dissenters and critics. Those too weak to resist were forcibly incorporated in the empire of free trade for their own good and protection (Gallagher and Robinson 1953). Others were won over by the force of argument and their own material interests. But there were others who were strong enough to resist Britain on both ideological and practical grounds. Germany and the United States, in particular, in the last decades of the nineteenth century imposed very high tariffs against British goods in order to protect their own developing industries from British competition. Economic liberalism began to break down as an international doctrine of governance because so many countries began to flout its prescriptions and Britain had no means to enforce it. Similarly many countries abandoned laissez-faire as a guide to domestic policy, preferring to create strong developmental states to push forward industrial progress to make their industries compete with and surpass the leading industries in Britain. The gold standard and the rules of sound finance fared better. These were institutionalised in the Treasuries of all the Great

Powers. British financial strength and stability throughout the nineteenth century was something all states still sought to emulate, and London remained the world's financial and commercial capital even after it was no longer the industrial capital.

EMBEDDED LIBERALISM

After the cataclysm of two world wars and the Great Depression, economic liberalism made a remarkable comeback. There was no return to a single unified international system. Instead the international state system was now bipolar, reflecting the division between the United States and the Soviet Union, each with their own respective sphere of influence. Within the US sphere the defeat of Germany and Japan made possible the resurrection of a new liberal international order, and a new pattern of governance to go with it. The initial plans were set out at Bretton Woods and subsequently amended in response to the development of the Cold War. The plan was predominantly a US plan, reflecting the political, military, financial and ideological dominance of the United States (Helleiner 1994; Frieden 2006). The United States was able to insist on the points it wanted, and veto those it did not. At first, its terms for helping its allies and its defeated enemies reconstruct their devastated economies were harsh. Only later, with the Marshall Plan and the agreement of a series of military alliances, including the North Atlantic Treaty Organization (NATO), did the position of the US soften. The security argument won over the economic argument. US credits combined with the big stimulus provided by high military spending to meet the Soviet threat helped lay the foundations for post-war recovery.

From the start the United States sought to create new rules for the international economy and the international state system reflecting American values and American interests. The United States had long seen itself as a rising new nation, untainted by the corruption and power politics of Europe, an anti-imperial and anti-colonial power which was on the side of all nations seeking self-determination. The strong strain of idealism in US foreign policy, articulated most forcefully by Woodrow Wilson at the end of the First World War, was rejected by the US Congress at the time, but it re-emerged still stronger after the experience of the Second World War and played a part in persuading many Americans that they had to shoulder a responsibility for spreading good governance to the rest of the world, helping other nations to adopt the institutions of liberal capitalism and democracy, and creating an institutional architecture for the development of international prosperity and international security. The strong instinct of isolationism and disengagement from world politics was overcome, displaced by other perspectives such as foreign policy realism which argued that the US could only protect its security, both economic and military, by becoming actively engaged in the governance of the rest of the world.

The American ideological tradition is a liberal tradition, in the original sense of the term. The United States lacked the ideological diversity which was common in Europe, failing to develop either a reactionary conservatism based on landowners and rural communities or a socialist labour movement (Hartz 1955). There were elements of both, but neither succeeded in mounting an effective challenge to the ascendancy of the dominant liberal consensus in the United States. By the middle of the twentieth century, having survived the Great Crash and the Great Depression, that consensus was consolidated by the strength of the US economy in the 1950s and the 1960s, which brought unprecedented standards of living to the majority of US citizens. The institutions of free market capitalism and constitutional government under the rule of law were confirmed as the incontestable foundational principles for good governance.

The new international regime which was to blossom spectacularly in the 1950s and 1960s became known retrospectively as 'embedded liberalism' (Ruggie 1982). Karl Polanyi had argued that the self-regulating market economy of the nineteenth century was a highly creative but also a very destructive force, and had become 'disembedded' from the wider society, eventually bringing forth strong political reaction and the imposition of regulation and control. Ruggie adapted this idea, suggesting that the new liberal international order created after 1945 differed from the one which had existed before 1914 because, this time, the economic liberalism of the system was concentrated at the international level in the form of qualified free trade and free movement of capital, whereas at the national level governments had made their own social compacts between capital and labour, resulting in the creation of some regimes, as in Sweden, with high levels of spending and taxation and government coordination of the economy. National ideological patterns differed, but there was a general acceptance of a much enlarged role for the state. Terms like the 'mixed economy' and 'managed capitalism' became commonplace. The softening of the ideological battles between the democratic left and the democratic right was much remarked, along with the virtual disappearance of the unemployment, mass poverty and the accentuated business cycle which had marked capitalism earlier and had made many doubt its future. Andrew Shonfield (1966) could write in *Modern Capitalism* that the very term 'capitalism' now seemed redundant. Some of this was ascribed to Keynesianism and the new readiness of governments to take responsibility for managing their economies; some of it to the social democratic compacts between labour and capital; and some of it to the new military spending (Baran and Sweezy 1968). Much of it, too, depended on the United States being able and willing to supply leadership and support and to construct a liberal international order which served its wider strategic, economic and ideological purposes (Gilpin and Gilpin 2001).

THE RISE OF NEOLIBERALISM

During this period of embedded liberalism a considerable revival of economic liberal thought took place, much of it celebratory of the new dispensation over which the United States presided, and which allowed for a range of different national solutions within the democratic camp. But this was also the period in which some of the currents which were later to shape neoliberalism were to emerge. Neoliberalism is part of the much older tradition of economic liberalism, but also has its own distinctive motifs. The term neoliberalism is a problematic one, because it is mainly a term which has been used by those who are critical of the policies and ideas associated with neoliberalism, and not by neoliberals themselves. In France, for example, the term neoliberalism is generally used pejoratively to denote specific characteristics of Anglo-American political economy, such as globalisation, deregulation, the promotion of finance and the policies pursued by the governments of Ronald Reagan and Margaret Thatcher. Many 'neoliberals' prefer labels such as classical liberal, market liberal, economic liberal, economic libertarian or simply conservative.

The original use of the term neoliberal was by German liberals of the ordoliberal school in the 1930s. Their critique was aimed at the anti-liberal policies of the Nazi regime, but also at the trend of German economic policy since Bismarck (Nicholls 1994; Turner 2008). They sought to reclaim older German liberal traditions which had become buried during the rise of the *Machtstaat* when the economy had become subordinate to the requirements of national power and competition with other nations. The national political economy of that period was voiced with great eloquence by Max Weber (1994) in his inaugural lecture at Freiburg. The ordoliberals sought, by contrast, a strict *Rechtstaat* of general rules which would forbid concentrations of economic power and ensure competition and a limited state. Its primary purpose was to ensure decentralisation of both economy and of politics. Many of the ideas of the ordoliberals were picked up after the war and helped to shape the political and economic thinking of Ludwig Erhard and other centre-right German politicians who constructed the social market economy as the new model which the Federal Republic of West Germany should follow. Strong emphasis was placed on governance rules which ensured sound finance, stable prices and market competition as the means to promote an export-led economic revival. Within the framework of the new Western liberal international economy this proved a highly successful formula for rebuilding West German prosperity.

The revival of economic liberalism was more muted elsewhere, other strands of liberalism favouring an extended role for the state being more prominent. A noteworthy gathering took place at a hotel on Mont Pelerin in 1947, organised by Hayek and bringing together many of the most prominent economic liberals from Europe and the United States, including many of the ordoliberals, as well as Milton Friedman, Lionel Robbins, Frank Knight and Ludwig von Mises. Compared with the positions that some of the participants were later to assume, the Mont Pelerin Society was at first rather a moderate body, grateful that the ideas of economic liberalism had survived at all (Jackson 2010). Indeed Ludwig von Mises stormed out of one meeting, declaring that his fellow members were no better than socialists.

Some of the ideas of economic liberalism may have revived after 1945, and Hayek may have dedicated himself to restating the foundations of a free society, based on the insights of classical liberalism, but there was no organised 'neoliberal movement' and economic liberals – such as Hayek who warned that even mild forms of social democracy were the first steps on a road to serfdom – did not make much impact. Much of the intellectual energy of the 1950s went into showing how the West could develop a democratic form of capitalism which could prove superior to the planned economies of the Soviet East, both in its ideological attractiveness and in its economic productivity. This meant that cooperation between the democratic left and right was important, and a consensus on the role of the state, and in particular on welfare spending, levels of taxation and trade union rights, was part of that compact in many countries. This limited the appeal of those economic liberals such as Hayek who warned of the dangers of the post-war compromise and wanted to reverse many of the gains that labour movements had made, advocating return to a purer form of economic liberalism. When Hayek published *The Constitution of Liberty* in 1960 he was discouraged that it received much less attention than *The Road to Serfdom* in 1944.

For the more developed nations in the Western economy the governance arrangements established at Bretton Woods had worked reasonably well, although they had to be adapted to changing circumstances and supplemented by emergency programmes such as Marshall Aid. Convertibility of currencies proved much more difficult than expected and was postponed until the second half of the 1950s for most countries. Trade expanded strongly, particularly through the 1950s and 1960s, and all the more developed economies experienced strong growth, high employment and low inflation. The gold exchange standard system based on the dollar provided an adequate financial framework, and might well have lasted longer had it not been for the pressures imposed on it by the United States. The monetary system of Bretton Woods with its elaborate system of pegs and permitted devaluations under certain circumstances did not survive, because the US refused to subject itself to its rules. The US moved rapidly from major creditor to major debtor because it needed to spend so much to sustain its extensive investment and military involvement overseas. The additional costs of the domestic Great Society programme in the 1960s imposed further burdens. The only way the US could afford its spending was to use its privileged position as the possessor of the one major international currency and issue more of it. Under the Bretton Woods system this required others, the surplus countries, to hold more dollars, which by the second half of the 1960s they were no longer willing to do. The Bretton Woods system of foreign exchange broke down temporarily in 1971, and then permanently in 1973. The United States unilaterally floated the dollar because it was not prepared to cut its spending to preserve the value of the dollar within the fixed exchange rate system. The unwillingness of countries in surplus to continue to amass dollars, rather than be paid in gold, forced the United States to abandon its support for this aspect of the Bretton Woods system. It endorsed instead a system of floating exchange rates in which the dollar was still the leading currency and the store of value for the international economy, and the international institutions – the International Monetary Fund (IMF), the World Bank, and the General Agreement on Tariffs and Trade (GATT) – were still dominated by the United States. The US was also still the largest and most productive economy, but the success of Japan and Germany, in particular, meant that the economic balance had shifted and the US was no longer as dominant in all spheres as it had been (Kennedy 1987; Schwartz 2010).

The end of the international monetary system established at Bretton Woods ushered in the era of neoliberal governance, because it necessitated new governance rules for the international economy to deal with the problems of debts and deficits in a system of floating exchange rates. Inflation had begun to increase in the second half of the 1960s and, with the end of the financial discipline imposed by the gold exchange standard, it began to accelerate, first in the form of a commodity price boom but soon translating into rising prices and wages. The situation was made much worse by the opportunistic decision by the Organisation of Petroleum Exporting Countries (OPEC) in 1973 to use its market power to extract higher rents from the international economy by hiking the price of oil. The oil shocks tipped the international economy into a generalised recession while inflation continued to accelerate. The combination of high inflation and high unemployment produced a period of 'stagflation' and painful restructuring of national economies. The national Keynesianism of the long boom was seen as having no answers for this novel combination of problems, and instead monetarist theories now gained the ascendancy.

At a technical level monetarism offered a set of macroeconomic techniques for managing and stabilising the international economy in a period of floating exchange rates. It abandoned the responsibility of governments for employment and growth and made the control of inflation the priority. It did so by urging all governments to achieve a strict control of the money supply, articulating firm monetary targets and sticking to them whatever the short-term effects on employment and growth. The political and ideological significance of this change was that it redefined the relationship between the state and the market, thereby withdrawing legitimacy from national Keynesian solutions if they could not be made compatible with the overriding requirement for financial stability. In this way the embedded liberalism of the previous period was gradually dismantled because it was seen as no longer affordable. What became established in its place was the idea that conforming to the requirements of the international market was now what governments must do if their national economies were to survive and prosper.

The extent of this change should not be exaggerated. The international economy remained a liberal international order presided over by the United States. What changed were some of the governance principles by which the US sought to exercise control and stabilise this economy. The ideological shift was important in allowing certain economic liberal ideas to acquire greater influence than they had hitherto achieved. An ideological offensive developed against Keynesianism and social democracy, in which some of this argument was technical – the best way to restrain inflation – but the substance was political and ideological, and concerned the size and scope of the state. The 1970s was a period of, at best, slow growth and great economic uncertainty. It led to fierce distributional struggles between labour and capital over the share of wages and profits in national income but also over the social wage, the benefits distributed to citizens through the tax system. The legitimacy of democratic capitalism had been based in part on a significant extension of the social wage in many countries, but now both the affordability and desirability of this were brought into question. Economic liberalism had been making some ground since the 1960s through the activities of free market think tanks, such as the Institute for Economic Affairs, the Heritage Foundation, the Cato Institute and the American Enterprise Association. In the 1970s there was an increasing ferment of these ideas and much cross-fertilisation with conservative ideas. The conjunction of these two ideological traditions formed a 'New Right', which was economically liberal and socially conservative. Advocates of the New Right sought large reductions in public spending, the curbing of trade union rights, together with controls on immigration, a crackdown on crime and heightened national security (Hoover and Plant 1988).

Many of the more developed economies in the Western international economy became politically deadlocked in the 1970s, which made finding compromises difficult and increased political polarisation as problems mounted. The key arbiter, however, remained the United States. The decisive political event was the election of Ronald Reagan as President in 1980, which confirmed the ascendancy of New Right ideas and the final abandonment of the ambitions enshrined in the Great Society programme of the 1960s. Although the policies of the Reagan administration were very contradictory, important steps were made in fashioning and imposing the new governance rules which became designated as neoliberalism (Harvey 2005). Although it was nourished by the ideas of old and new economic liberals who became prominent once more in the 1970s, neoliberalism was never simply the application of the ideas of classical economic liberalism. In many respects the neoliberal policy regime which emerged disappointed many of its strongest ideological supporters. The extended state remained in being and continued to increase. Daniel Bell (1985) identified the forces pressing for an extended state as the rise of a normative economic policy, which Keynesianism had sanctioned, the priority attached to investment in science and technology, and the remorseless spread of the entitlement culture. Neoliberalism had greatest success in limiting and even reversing the growth of the state in the first area, but not in the other two, and even the first was put in question by the 2008 financial crash.

The distinctive feature of neoliberalism as a new set of governance rules for the international economy was the manner in which it drew on mainstream liberal economics to derive a set of techniques which could be incorporated into policy-making. This was something which had been developing for a while, but it now became institutionalised and a dominant feature of the policy process. Central to it was the use of econometric modelling and cost–benefit analysis. The neoclassical synthesis which emerged in economics challenged the Keynesian legacy and gradually stripped economics of all its remaining historical, political, sociological and philosophical features, simplifying it into an abstract and analytically powerful technique for analysing the dynamics of choice and incentives in markets under very restricted assumptions. The ideological assumption of this kind of positive economics was that the market could be studied as though it was completely disembedded from politics, society and culture, and that by doing so highly relevant knowledge for public policy could be derived.

Neoliberalism in this technical sense at times seems rather distant from the traditional concerns of liberal political economy, but it agrees with their fundamental postulate: that the aim of public policy is primarily to enable the market rather than to limit it, and that there is a presumption in favour of market logic and market solutions for any public policy problem. The importance of neoliberalism is that these assumptions became ingrained in the policy process as practical techniques, rather than as normative assumptions. They have been distilled into a simple technical language which makes economic advice essential in the analysis of any public-policy problem, with the result that economists, together with lawyers, stand as gatekeepers in the policy process determining what counts as evidence and a credible argument.

The importance of this for governance is that this expertise has been deployed in developing a particularly elaborate set of rules and guidelines for the operation of this new neoliberal regime. The triumph of neoliberal governance is sometimes presented as the latest stage in the Polanyian double movement, the disembedding of the market after its re-embedding in the Keynesian era. But this disembedding has taken place in conjunction with a very active state. The paradox of neoliberalism goes beyond the free economy and the strong state of ordoliberalism. The ordoliberals wanted the state to be strong to ensure the conditions in which the market could be free. The state had to have the capacity to intervene to break up any concentrations, whether of labour or capital, which threatened the working of competition and the free flow of goods and services. It needed to be strong to break the resistance of organised interest groups and compel all agents to operate within the rules of the market order.

Contemporary neoliberals do not simply want a strong state; they want an active state to reconfigure not just the relationship between the state and the market, but also the nature of the state and the public sector itself. In Marxist terminology neoliberals believe in extending commodification into every sphere of the private and public sector. The application of the techniques of economic analysis to every human relationship and activity is the hallmark of this approach. Neoliberals seek to refine the notion of economic calculus, estimating the costs and benefits involved in every transaction. It is a logical extension of the utilitarian approach so important in the historical development of economic reasoning. This kind of economics is about economising, doing more with less, seeking out the most efficient use of resources, assuming that the only rational motivation individuals can have is to derive the most benefit at the least cost from every activity. Utilitarianism is not the whole of classical liberalism, only a strand within it. Yet in the course of the development of economics it has managed to become the core of the discipline, gradually expelling all other elements as extraneous and irrelevant. The power of the analytical techniques which economics has developed using an a priori deductive technique and parsimonious assumptions has given it increasing status and authority within all forms of public organisation, even as its broader ability to explain economic events has dwindled. Its practical value has continued to rise primarily because it is able to give definite answers to a range of important practical questions, such as whether governments should decide for or against a particular investment proposal.

Neoliberalism is deeply infused with the techniques of modern economic analysis, which have accordingly become rather detached from liberal political economy. Many of the great twentieth-century figures in liberal political economy, including Hayek, maintained serious objections to the methodology of modern economic analysis (Caldwell 2004). Joseph Schumpeter understood this point when he separated normative political economy from positive economic analysis. Some of the most prominent neoliberal economists, including Milton Friedman (1962), have also been advocates of key principles of liberal political economy, but have never accepted the validity of Austrian economic analysis, or indeed of any approach which did not utilise positive economics. For many of the economic liberals of the Mont Pelerin Society, neoliberalism meant new approaches within the perspective of classical economic liberalism. Neoliberalism in the 1980s became dominant, however, less because of the adoption of classical economic liberalism than because of the usefulness of the techniques which economists could provide to governments.

This technical aspect of neoliberalism has often been underrated in many treatments of it. It is distinct from earlier forms of neoliberalism and makes it a particular kind of ideology, one which claims to be stripped of all normative assumptions but which in fact contains normative assumptions which are unexamined and treated as starting points in the analysis. Most important of these are, firstly, assumptions about the priority of the market economy and of market exchange over all other institutional arrangements and social practices; and, secondly, assumptions about the applicability of market reasoning to all public-policy questions. It has been the incorporation of these assumptions into the governance rules of the neoliberal era which has been one of its defining features. This kind of neoliberal thinking deliberately cuts itself off from historical understanding of the contexts in which action takes place. It has no use for history, either its own history as a discipline, or the history of political and economic institutions. This is what it makes it so valuable as a technique.

This helps to resolve one of the great paradoxes of neoliberal governance. Despite all the rhetoric which accompanied the various political manifestations of the New Right in the 1970s and 1980s about the need to roll back the state and reverse the trend towards socialism, the actual achievements were rather modest. States and public sectors have everywhere been reorganised, but they have not shrunk. What neoliberalism has assisted is a change in governance rules for the international economy by supplying an apparently neutral language of efficiency, incentives, cost-effectiveness and competition. It has led to systematic changes in many different institutions in both the private and public sectors. These approaches aim both at reducing the scope of institutions outside the market, as well as reorganising public sector institutions to make them more transparent and accountable (Power 1997). Neoliberalism is for this reason strongly associated with the new public management and the spread of its principles to public sectors around the world. The audit and target culture, the experiments with quasi markets, the emphasis on process rather than substance, the adoption of new forms of regulation, the split between the government as a provider and the government as a purchaser – all these developments have come to define a particular set of governance rules which became firmly established in the neoliberal era.

THE PHASES OF NEOLIBERALISM

Neoliberalism as the latest ideological form of economic liberalism has been adapted to different contexts for the governance of the international system. The Washington Consensus in the 1980s was succeeded by the 'Post-Washington Consensus' in the 1990s, and then by the present period of policy inertia and political gridlock after the financial crash. In the 1980s the reconfiguring of the governance rules which the international institutions applied to countries needing assistance led to the elaboration of a set of instruments for policy reform, known as the Washington Consensus, partly because so many of the international institutions had their headquarters in Washington. These instruments included fiscal discipline, privatisation, deregulation, import liberalisation, competitive currencies and a preference for spending cuts rather than tax increases to deal with fiscal deficits (Williamson 1989). They reflected the model of the economy which it was taken for granted was the only possible model for developing countries, and indeed developed countries, to adopt. The Washington Consensus was never formally proclaimed or embodied in a particular document. It did not need to be. The consensus arose because so many of the individuals staffing the key international agencies saw the world in the same way and adopted the same ideological assumptions about the priority which should be given to markets because of their superiority as a mechanism of allocating resources.

The principles of the Washington Consensus appeared vindicated once Soviet communism collapsed. The central planning principles on which it had been based had become increasingly discredited and did not pose a threat to economic liberal principles. More subtly, what the removal of the Soviet Union as an ideological competitor did was also to remove legitimacy and credibility from political and economic alternatives to free market capitalism. The existence of the Soviet Union appeared to suggest that there was an alternative, but with the Soviet Union gone the ideological underpinnings of many other alternatives disappeared too. From social democracy in Western Europe to developmental states in Asia and protectionist regimes in Africa, the fight against neoliberalism was weakened, and new political coalitions came forward arguing that the best policy was to work within the constraints of neoliberalism, and seek, accordingly, the best possible accommodation with the liberal international economy. This meant accepting the governance rules and conditionality on which the international agencies insisted. There had always been a strong belief in the superiority of the US model and in the priority which should be given to markets, but there had been some willingness to incorporate local differences into the model. From the 1980s onwards there was much less willingness to accept compromises of this kind and there emerged a belief that the right institutions and the right policies should be imposed on as many countries as possible. The international community should oblige everyone to sign up to the same rules, since that was in everyone's interest.

The Washington Consensus in its extreme form lasted for about a decade, but then it began to weaken. Numerous objections began to be raised to it, and counter-movements developed as the full implications of the new governance rules became apparent (Payne 2005). The strong sense that capitalism had been 'unleashed' in the 1980s and 1990s inspired some of the wilder formulations of hyper-globalisation, but also brought increasing resistance to the growing inequality in the world economy. The emergence of new rising powers allowed the developing nations to begin to resist more effectively some of the outcomes in the World Trade Organization (WTO) and to propose alternatives. The changes led some to argue that a new Post-Washington Consensus had emerged (Stiglitz 2002), one which reflected the shifting balance of power between states, as well as the rise of China, India and Brazil. The Post-Washington Consensus put much more emphasis on the need for and obligation of the rich countries to provide foreign aid and take the lead in combating climate change. Underlying these shifts was the conception that the international system could not just be conceived as a borderless market; it also should be conceived as an embryonic state, and governance rules adjusted to reflect that fact. The Post-Washington Consensus gave greater priority to social investment to boost human capital and infrastructure and to create the conditions for successful market economies. The emphasis was still, however, on market economies. It was less an alternative to the Washington Consensus than a modification of it (Rupert 2000). There was very little impetus to change the institutional architecture of the Post-Washington Consensus. The governance rules continued to reflect the dominance of the same few great powers. The WTO saw the greatest change because of the new negotiating strength of some of the rising powers, but as a result it quickly became deadlocked in the Doha Round negotiations. The World Bank and the IMF remained under the control of the United States and its allies. There was no suggestion that the US was willing to relinquish that control (Frieden 2006).

In sum, the key governance institutions of the international economy remained dominated by Washington. This demonstrated the limits of economic liberalism. The international system remained one shaped by the interests of its most powerful states, and international markets could only flourish so long as those states, and in particular the United States, willed it. Neoliberalism rose to prominence when it did because, politically, it helped achieve some key objectives of US policy-makers. It legitimised a number of shifts in the way the international economy was governed – for example, the shift from fixed to floating exchange rates – which were seen as essential by the Americans.

The third phase of neoliberalism opened in 2008 with the Great Financial Crash.

This brought an abrupt halt to the boom of the previous two decades and plunged the Western economy into a steep recession. There was speculation for a time that the crisis was so serious that it would leave neoliberalism discredited and force a radical reshaping of economic policy and governance. Four years after the crash this had not yet happened. Neoliberalism proved remarkably resilient, and strong pressure was applied to restore the governance arrangements of the past decade as quickly as possible. The state had intervened strongly to prevent a complete collapse of the financial system, but this was presented as a temporary measure, justified by the extraordinary events of 2008, and not signalling any development of a new interventionist role for the state and new forms of hierarchical governance in general. Neoliberals and Keynesians both agreed that the financial authorities should not make the mistakes of the 1929 crash, and turn the crash into a slump. Fiscal conservatives thought differently and criticised the bailouts, but their views did not prevail.

Since the crash a fierce ideological battle has broken out over who was most to blame for it and how a lasting recovery can be built. There is dispute over whether the best solution should be a sharp contraction in the size of the state to match at least the contraction of the economy, or whether there should be instead a permanent expansion of the state. The crash has highlighted some flaws in the financial model of growth which dominated the economic boom of the previous two decades and led to calls in some countries for a rebalancing of activity towards manufacturing. There have been proposals too for a new financial architecture to reduce the chances of such a financial crash ever happening again, including the possible separation of retail banking from investment banking. But there are few moves to question the fundamental character of contemporary governance or its predominant ideological character, the priority accorded to market forms of governance and coordination.

One reason for this may lie in the extent to which the ideological character of contemporary governance does not manifest itself only at the macro level of the rules for governance of the international system. It is also visible at the micro level. The spread of markets and the ideas and values associated with them have affected corporate and family households, as well as the organisation of the public household. One of the fundamental ideas of economic liberalism has been the idea of the tax state, the argument that the state and its spending are parasitic upon the private sector, which is the sole source of wealth. This divides the population into makers and takers, the latter being all those employed by the state and dependent upon the state for benefits. The tax state expands so long as its fiscal base is secure and legitimate, and it provides funds for many different kinds of special interests which lobby government relentlessly to win its support. Following a crisis, however, when the economy plunges into recession the fiscal base contracts, while public spending, particularly in the era of the welfare state, automatically expands because of the swelling number of claimants. Spending cuts are demanded to reduce the size of the public sector so that it is at least no greater proportionately than it was before the crisis. But the tendency of the tax state to grow increases the part of the economy which is deemed parasitic rather than wealth-creating and adds to pressure within democracies for the interests of those dependent upon the state to be reflected in the policies governments pursue. The politics of austerity is about redistributing wealth and income back to the private sector and those who control property and investment, making it profitable once more to invest and restore the economy to growth.

Neoliberalism, from this perspective, is the latest version of economic liberalism which seeks to find ways to police the boundaries between the public and the private, between the state and the market, and to ensure that in moments of crisis these fundamental relations are not breached. The contradiction in this position is that the state and the public household have assumed an increasingly important role as one of the drivers of economic growth and the development of the productive economy. Cutting back the state, and particularly spending on infrastructure, which always tends to be the first target in periods of retrenchment, threatens to prolong the slump and postpone recovery. In most governance arrangements the states and their public households are recognised for their contribution to the health of the economy. But the dominant ideological argument continues to suggest the opposite: that states are inefficient, wasteful and a burden on the productive economy which should be minimised as much as possible. Contemporary governance requires more than markets in order to perform the complex tasks required for the smooth functioning of the international system, but ideologically it is important for the default position always to be that markets take priority.

Similar considerations apply to companies and private households. Networks and hierarchies are the modes of governance which tend to govern these spheres, but markets increasingly penetrate both, and the dominant neoliberal narrative has conceptualised both spheres in terms of markets. Firms, for example, have been analysed as a nexus of contracts (Easterbrook and Fischel 1991), dissolving the problem of owners and managers, or managers and workers, groups with distinct roles and interests. Instead the firm is theorised as a setting for the interaction of individuals with various bundles of property rights (Parkinson et al. 2000). In such a world, power conceived in traditional zero-sum terms no longer exists (Crouch 2011). Everything is reduced to considerations of efficiency and incentives. The underlying assumption is that, so long as markets are open and competitive, then equilibrium outcomes which are Pareto-optimal emerge spontaneously. If markets are not competitive, or if the outcomes mean the accumulation of power, rent-seeking and conflict, the causes are to be sought in the application of bad governance rules which allow economic relations to become politicised. In this lexicon bad governance rules are those which do not have as their fundamental aim the guaranteeing of open and competitive markets.

There have even been some attempts to theorise the family as a nexus of contracts, providing economic explanations for love, marriage, divorce and child-rearing (Becker 1981). In relation to ideologies of governance the family is subordinate to the requirements of the market, playing a supportive role rather than challenging it. Families become problematic if the networks they generate invade the sphere of the market and sustain clientelist practices, subverting competition. From a neoliberal perspective the role of families is to sustain and support their individual members and fit them for the work and occupational roles they need to perform. They are also an important provider of unpaid welfare and domestic labour, charges which might otherwise fall on the tax state. As markets and industry developed, families gradually lost their economic functions and the size of the basic family unit tended to shrink.

For families to play a full role in sustaining markets and market modes of governance they also need to become centres for the inculcation of values and attitudes which are friendly rather than hostile to markets and the way markets work. Since most family relationships are altruistic and solidaristic, rather than based on pecuniary advantage and self-interest, they tend to sustain a set of values and attitudes which are not the same as those demanded in a market order. Private households also inculcate attitudes to budgeting and the allocation of resources which involve hierarchy and planning rather than market allocation through competition and price. But private households still perform very important functions for neoliberal governance. Firstly, the analogy between the finances of the public household and the finances of the private household has become one of the most central and effective ideological tropes of economic liberalism. Its credibility was destroyed by Keynes, but it has never lost its popular appeal. Treating the two as directly analogous reinforces the message of the need for cuts and balancing the public budget, just as private households must balance their budgets. Secondly, the contemporary family in advanced economies has become increasingly the site for the consumption of a dazzling array of goods and services which the modern economy produces. One of the most significant of these has been financial services, in areas such as insurance, investment, mortgages, pensions, student loans and private health. The practice of making forms of loans and credit available to more and more citizens reinforces the need for all citizens to become financial subjects, market wise and market literate, organising their finances in ways that allow them to realise their goals. This 'financialisation' of everyday life reaches deep into families and their individual members, and helps make the logic of markets seem commonsense and irresistible, as well as greatly increasing levels of personal debt (Hobson and Seabrooke 2007; Langley 2008). Individuals increasingly want the goods which the modern economy supplies, and this makes them dependent upon the services which enable individuals to achieve them. The more individuals must act economically in order to operate effectively in a market society, the greater their disposition to see market processes and the rules which govern them as inevitable.

CONCLUSION

The ideology which infuses contemporary governance is not monolithic and has many internal contradictions which generate sites of resistance. But its power is also undeniable, and it is seen at its strongest in times of economic downturn and austerity. The ideology is embedded at many different levels and in many different institutions, and this is what makes radical alternatives to it seem so futile and utopian, because it is hard to imagine such a large overturning of the commonsense assumptions that underpin governance of so many different institutions. That is why resistance often takes the form of suggesting modifications and imposing barriers, to protect some spheres of social activity from subordination to the market. There have been many successes, but the strength of market ideology is now so deep-rooted that it can absorb even major external shocks such as the financial crash of 2008.

Economic liberalism, like all ideologies, has internal paradoxes and inconsistencies. It elevates the market above all other institutions and wants a politics-free world in which decisions are taken according to market logic rather than political logic. To achieve this, however, requires a very active state, and a political movement and ideology to underpin it. The separation of the state and the market which economic liberalism seeks is an illusion, and is revealed as such whenever there is a major crisis and the state is called upon to intervene and guarantee the market order. A politics-free world can only be secured through political means. Similarly, the universalism which economic liberalism has always claimed for its ideas has always depended on them being consistent with the national interests of the leading great power. Leading powers, however, like the United States, are never content to be bound by the rules which they apply to others, so the liberal form of governance which has prevailed in the international system since 1945 has always had both universal and national elements. The new rising powers challenge the existing dispensation and seek to modify or replace some of the existing governance rules. But, to do so effectively, it will not be enough for them to assert their national interests. They must also find a new ideology of governance in which to present their claims, a new model for ordering the international economy and the relationship between states. That is much harder to do, and there is little sign as yet that the era of economic liberalism is drawing to a close.

REFERENCES

Baran, Paul and Paul Sweezy (1968), *Monopoly Capital*, Harmondsworth: Penguin.
Becker, Gary (1981), *A Treatise on the Family*, Cambridge, MA: Harvard University Press.
Bell, Daniel (1985), 'The public household', in *The Cultural Contradictions of Capitalism*, London: Heinemann.
Bevir, Mark (2009), *Key Concepts in Governance*, London: Sage.
Caldwell, Bruce (2004), *Hayek's Challenge: An Intellectual Biography of F.A. Hayek*, Chicago, IL: Chicago University Press.
Cox, Robert (1987), *Production, Power, and World Order: Social Forces in the Making of History*, New York: Columbia University Press.
Cox, Robert (1996), *Approaches to World Order*, Cambridge: Cambridge University Press.
Crouch, Colin (2011), *The Strange Non-Death of Neo-Liberalism*, Cambridge: Polity.
Easterbrook, Frank and Daniel Fischel (1991), *The Economic Structure of Corporate Law*, Cambridge, MA: Harvard University Press.
Economist Intelligence Unit (2011), *The Democracy Index 2011*, London: *The Economist*.
Freeden, Michael (1996), *Ideologies and Political Theory: A Conceptual Approach*, Oxford: Clarendon.
Frieden, Jeffrey (2006), *The Fall and Rise of Global Capitalism*, New York: W.W. Norton.
Friedman, M. (1962), *Capitalism and Freedom*, Chicago, IL: Chicago University Press.
Gallagher, J. and R. Robinson (1953), 'The imperialism of free trade', *Economic History Review*, **21** (2), 296–306.
Gilpin, Robert and Jean Gilpin (2001), *Global Political Economy*, Princeton, NJ: Princeton University Press.
Harris, Nigel (1968), *Beliefs in Society*, London: Watts.
Hartz, L. (1955), *The Liberal Tradition in America: An Interpretation of American Political Thought since the Revolution*, New York: Harcourt, Brace.
Harvey, D. (2003), *The New Imperialism*, Oxford: Oxford University Press.
Harvey, D. (2005), *A Brief History of Neo-Liberalism*, Oxford: Oxford University Press.
Hayek, F.A. (1944), *The Road to Serfdom*, London: Routledge.
Hayek, F.A. (1960), *The Constitution of Liberty*, London: Routledge.
Helleiner, Eric (1994), *States and the Re-emergence of Global Finance: from Bretton Woods to the 1990s*, Ithaca, NY: Cornell University Press.
Hobson, John and Leonard Seabrooke (eds) (2007), *Everyday Politics of the World Economy*, Cambridge: Cambridge University Press.
Hoover, Kenneth and Raymond Plant (1988), *Conservative Capitalism in Britain and the United States: A Critical Appraisal*, London: Routledge.
Jackson, B. (2010), 'At the origins of neo-liberalism: the free economy and the strong state 1930–1947', *Historical Journal*, **53** (1), 129–51.
Kennedy, Paul (1987), *The Rise and Fall of the Great Powers*, New York: Random House.
Kindleberger, C.P. (1986), *The World in Depression*, Harmondsworth: Penguin.
Langley, Paul (2008), *The Everyday Life of Global Finance; Saving and Borrowing in Anglo-America*, Oxford: Oxford University Press.

Nicholls, A. (1994), *Freedom with Responsibility: The Social Market Economy in Germany, 1918–1963*, Oxford: Clarendon Press.
Oakeshott, Michael (1961), 'On being conservative', in *Rationalism in Politics*, London: Methuen.
O'Brien, Patrick (2003), 'The myth of Anglophone succession', *New Left Review*, **24**, 113–34.
O'Neill, John (1998), *The Market: Ethics, Knowledge and Politics*, London: Routledge.
Parkinson, John, Andrew Gamble and Gavin Kelly (eds) (2000), *The Political Economy of the Company*, London: Hart.
Payne, Anthony (2005), *The Global Politics of Unequal Development*, Basingstoke: Palgrave Macmillan.
Phillips, Nicola (ed.) (2005), *Globalising International Political Economy*, Basingstoke: Palgrave Macmillan.
Pierre, Jon and B. Guy Peters (2000), *Governance, Politics and the State*, Basingstoke: Macmillan.
Plant, Raymond (2010), *The Neo-Liberal State*, Oxford: Oxford University Press.
Power, Michael (1997), *The Audit Society: Rituals of Verification*, Oxford: Clarendon Press.
Rhodes, R.A.W. (1996), 'The new governance: governing without government', *Political Studies*, **44** (4), 652–67.
Rosenau, James N. (2006), *The Study of World Politics, Vol 2: Globalisation and Governance*, London: Routledge.
Ruggie, John (1982), 'International regimes, transactions and change: embedded liberalism in the postwar economic order', *International Organization*, **36** (2), 379–415.
Runciman, David and Monica Vieira (2008), *Representation*, Cambridge: Polity.
Rupert, Mark (2000), *Ideologies of Globalisation*, London: Routledge.
Schwartz, Herman (2010), *States versus Markets: The Emergence of a Global Economy*, Basingstoke: Palgrave Macmillan.
Shonfield, Andrew (1966), *Modern Capitalism: The Changing Balance of Public and Private Power*, London: Oxford University Press.
Stiglitz, Joseph (2002), *Globalisation and its Discontents*, London: Allen Lane.
Thompson, Grahame, Jennifer Frances, Rosalind Levacic and Jeremy C. Mitchell (eds) (1991), *Markets, Hierarchies and Networks*, London: Sage.
Thompson, Helen (2008), *Might, Right, Prosperity and Consent: Representative Democracy and the International Economy, 1919–1921*, Manchester: Manchester University Press.
Trentmann, Frank (2008), *Free Trade Nation: Commerce, Consumption and Civil Society in Modern Britain*, Oxford: Oxford University Press.
Turner, R. (2008), *Neo-Liberal Ideology: History, Concepts and Policies*, Edinburgh: Edinburgh University Press.
Wallerstein, Immanuel (1974), *The Modern World System*, New York: Academic Press.
Weber, Max (1994), 'The nation-state and economic policy', in Peter Lassman and Ronald Speirs (eds), *Weber: Political Writings*, Cambridge: Cambridge University Press, pp. 1–28.
Williamson, John (1989), 'What Washington means by policy reform', in J. Williamson (ed.), *Latin American Readjustment: How Much Has Happened*, Washington, DC: Institute for International Economics, pp. 7–20.

2   Levels of governance and their interaction
Colin Hay

This chapter seeks to introduce, in the most general terms, the concept of 'levels' within political economic analysis, reflecting on the stratified ontology of political economy on which it rests. The chapter develops an ontology of political economy, considering whether and to what extent it is accurate and/or useful to refer to political economic realities as presenting themselves to us in discrete stratified levels. In the process, alternatives to a stratified ontology are discussed, the debate about this in (economic) geography is reviewed and the implications for political economy are considered. Discussion then moves from the concept of levels in general to the question of the particular levels to which political economists make reference – in effect, to the specific levels which typically populate a stratified ontology (the local, the national, the international, the regional, the interregional and the global). The value of a stratified account of political economic systems and their development is considered and the implications are drawn out for an account of globalisation and its governance.

INTERROGATING INTERDEPENDENCE

Central to claims as to the distinctiveness of the political economic context in which we find ourselves today is the concept of interdependence. Indeed, if there is a single concept that captures the challenge that contemporary developments are seen to pose to conventional approaches to political economy, it is surely this. Yet interdependence is not a simple concept and has in fact become synonymous with a range of rather different claims. It is thus important from the outset to distinguish between what might be termed 'domain interdependence' – the interdependence of the political, the economic and the cultural as domains of the social; and what might be termed 'spatial interdependence' – the interdependence of spatial scales and levels of analysis. The latter is the core focus of this chapter. But, before exploring spatial interdependence in more detail, it is first important to establish what we mean by interdependence itself.

In the most basic and general terms interdependence might be understood as a relationship between two or (invariably) more factors, processes, variables, domains or, indeed, spatial scales characterised by reciprocal causation or, perhaps better, mutual conditioning (Baldwin 1990; Kroll 1993). Thus, if A, B and C are interdependent, then any change in B will result in a change in A and C, any change in A will result in a change in B and C, and any change in C will result in a change in A and B. In short, any change in one will result in a change in all of the others. Yet this is a necessary but not in itself sufficient condition of interdependence. For the relationship between A, B and C to be seen as genuinely interdependent a further condition must also hold: neither A, B nor C must be the clear driver (or determinant) of changes in the others. An example may serve to clarify the point. We might well have good evidence for suggesting that unemployment, inequality and levels of crime are related (generally, they are) (see, for instance, Krohn 1970; Hagan and Peterson 1995). But, if our understanding of that relationship is that the direction of causation runs consistently from unemployment via inequality to crime, then this is better seen as a relationship of dependence, rather than interdependence.

A more likely candidate for a genuinely interdependent set of relationships is that between levels of distrust in politicians (A), the projection of self-interested motives onto political actors (the tendency to see politicians as 'in it for themselves') (B), and evidence that we might take as consistent with the self-interested behaviour of political actors (C). Here, it is at least credible to think, a change in any one of these variables is likely to be reflected in a change in the other two (Hay 2007; Stoker 2006). Thus, if, for instance, we become more inclined to view our politicians as motivated by self-interest, we are less likely to trust them and more likely to read their behaviour in such instrumental terms (thereby confirming our initial hunch). By the same token, if we become more convinced of the probity of those we have elected (perhaps following an election in which we have unseated many previous incumbents), we are likely to be less inclined to project narrowly self-interested motives on to them and less likely to read their behaviour in such terms. The point is that there is no consistent direction of causation between these variables; it is just as likely that a change in A will result in a change in B and C as it is that a change in C will give rise to a change in A and B. And, as long as this remains the case, this is a relationship characterised by interdependence.

Defined in this way, interdependence is a neutral and descriptive concept – neither innately good nor innately bad. Yet interdependence is hardly likely to prove politically neutral, in the sense that relations which are interdependent (or acknowledged to be interdependent) are likely to be far less tractable and amenable to political intervention than those which are more clearly characterised (or seen to be characterised) by dependence. An age of interdependence is, then, likely to be one in which it is both rather more difficult to govern and rather more difficult for citizens to hold to account those who claim to govern (see also Jessop 1998; Rosenau and Czempiel 1992). These are themes to which we return.

But what of spatial interdependence more specifically? By this we refer to the interconnectedness (for some, the growing interconnectedness) of political and economic processes at different spatial scales; and, typically, to the idea that domestic dynamics are shaped (again, for many, increasingly by transnational or global factors and that transnational or global dynamics are shaped (increasingly) by domestic dynamics. It is this sense of the interdependence of outcomes at different levels of analysis or different spatial scales that is generally seen as the most profound challenge that real-world developments pose to conventional understandings of political economy. Here it is useful to examine in a more general way claims as to the greater extent and salience of spatial interdependence and the challenge this might be seen to pose to political economy.

In order to do so, however, it is first important to establish the range of contending claims associated with arguments about spatial interdependence. But, before even doing that, it is necessary to take a further step backwards and to establish what we mean by spatial interdependence specifically. Here again we are talking about reciprocal causation or mutual conditioning. But when it comes to spatial interdependence these relationships are stretched across geographical or territorial boundaries or between previously discrete spatial scales or levels of analysis. In other words, spatial interdependence is about global–local and local–global connections: situations in which, for instance, actions conceived within one jurisdiction have consequences (typically unintended consequences) within another jurisdiction or in which transnational processes, practices and dynamics condition or circumscribe domestic or local strategies (Swyngedouw 2004). Contemporary examples are rife, but certainly include the manifestly global consequences of the decisions of mortgage lenders in subprime markets in the United States for borrowers, investors and consumers around the world, and the cumulatively consequential character of individual consumer choices for our collective environmental security. As such examples perhaps already serve to indicate, spatial interdependence may well increase the scope and scale of the consequences of one's actions, but it is typically far from obviously empowering.

Such spatial interdependence is increasingly held to characterise the condition of the world economy, and is often treated as synonymous with the claim that we live in a world that is economically interdependent (see, for instance, Keohane and Nye 1977; Wagner 1988). But, once again, we need to proceed with caution. For, as a moment's reflection reveals, a series of mutually incompatible claims can be – and invariably are – made by authors seeking to establish the need to acknowledge and deal with such interdependence. Different authors undoubtedly do base their arguments on the greater attention we must devote to issues of spatial interdependence on different premises. But part of the problem here is that they are very rarely clear and explicit in declaring such assumptions. To guide us through this potential minefield, it is useful to think about the array of potential positions available to us. Though the following list is by no means completely exhaustive, we might start by differentiating between those arguing that: (1) spatial interdependence is a novel condition necessitating a new approach to political economy; (2) spatial interdependence may not be new per se, but we may be exposed to it to a significantly greater extent, again requiring a new approach to political economy; (3) spatial interdependence may be neither new nor more prevalent, but it may acquire, or have come to acquire, a greater salience which contemporary political economists need, as a consequence, to acknowledge; (4) spatial interdependence may not be novel, but its contemporary manifestations are different in character and kind to those we are accustomed to dealing with, requiring new modes and strategies of political economic analysis; (5) spatial interdependence (and the form it now takes) may be neither new, nor more prevalent nor more salient: in fact, it may be something of an illusion and an unhealthy distraction from dependence and the more traditional preoccupations of political economists; and (6) whether novel, more prevalent, more salient or none of these, the very idea of spatial interdependence and the sensitivity of political actors to it needs to be acknowledged by contemporary political analysts.

Interestingly, the first four of these positions – each of which suggests (albeit for rather different reasons) that spatial interdependence needs to be acknowledged by political economists far more than it has been to date – might be taken to imply the need to dissolve the typically entrenched subdisciplinary division of labour between domestic or comparative political economy on the one hand, and international political economy on the other (see, for instance, Gamble et al. 1996). For, if the parameters of domestic political economic choice are circumscribed to any significant extent by transnational trends, processes and governance mechanisms, and, conversely, if transnational trends, processes and governance mechanisms are themselves conditioned to any significant degree by domestic political dynamics, then an analytical division of labour which leads us to focus specifically on, and thereby privilege, either spatial scale to the exclusion of the other can only blind us to key drivers of political economic change. If, in other words, there are domestic conditions of existence of inter- and transnational dynamics, and vice versa, then what value is there in approaches which close off our capacity to explore them?

Yet, though appealingly simple, even this formulation is potentially problematic. For it reduces the problem of spatial interdependence in political economic analysis (and the systems described in such analysis), in effect, to a two-level game (between the domestic and the inter- or transnational) when things are in fact potentially far more complicated. And it is, moreover, to presume that domestic/comparative political economy is concerned exclusively with the national level, and international/global political economy with the para-national. The point is that very little traditional political economy explicitly denies the influence of inter- and/or transnational dynamics, and much of it acknowledges such influences quite openly (think of Adam Smith, Malthus or Marx, for instance). The converse is no less true of the (albeit) far more recent founding works of international political economy (think, for instance, of the work of Susan Strange 1970, 1988). But the more important point is that spatial interdependence is certainly not just about – and perhaps not even principally about – the long-acknowledged interplay between the domestic and the international, but about what is typically labelled the problem of multi-level governance (Hooghe 1996; Hooghe and Marks 2001; Bache and Flinders 2004). Spatial interdependence is about acknowledging, and ideally responding to, the interpenetration, interplay and mutual or co-determination – in short, the interdependence – of causal processes and mechanisms at a multiplicity of spatial scales or levels (Jessop 2008: Chapters 8 and 9).

Contemporary political economy is, then, in its concern to acknowledge and respond to the analytical and indeed practical challenges posed by multi-level governance, increasingly focused on the interplay between political and economic processes operative at a variety of spatial scales. In the process, it typically finds the need to differentiate between the local, the (sub-state) regional, the national, the (para-state) regional, the inter-regional and the transnational, the global or the planetary.[1] But what it all too rarely does is to reflect on the status of such categories. Is political-economic reality stratified in terms of discrete levels as such a conception typically implies and, even if so, how do we know that we have identified the right levels to make reference to in our analysis? It is to these ontological questions and their implications that I now turn directly.

THE SPATIAL ONTOLOGY OF POLITICAL ECONOMY

These, to be fair, are questions that contemporary political economists rarely consider explicitly. Though there is, of course, a now vast literature on multi-level governance (as well surveyed in Bache and Flinders 2004), the ontological status of the levels to which the analysts invoking such a conception make reference has not been a focus of discussion at all within that literature. And that is something of a problem. For there is nothing at all self-evident about the idea that political-economic space is stratified in terms of the existence of discrete and clearly demarcated (or demarcate-able) spatial levels or tiers: the local, the regional, the national, the international and the global, for instance.

Certainly no less compelling, and typically rather more compelling to those who have reflected systematically on such matters (see, for instance, Cox 1998; Cumbers et al. 2003; Delaney and Leitner 1997; Marston 2000), is that the spatial dimension of social, political and economic reality is not stratified at all. From this conception, social and political processes, whatever their specific spatio-geographic characteristics and capacities, do not exist as processes operative at specific spatial scales, levels or tiers. This does not make it wrong to refer to the local, the national or the global, say, as we invariably do, as distinct and discrete spatial scales; but it does make it important to reflect on precisely what we are doing when we make such an analytical move, and the potential distortion it might entail.

Before we consider that, it is perhaps important to consider first the ontological defence of the claim that social (or indeed political or economic) space is stratified. That defence is typically made by philosophical realists and relates to the concept of emergence. Emergence, as Andrew Sayer (2000: 12) puts it, can be said to exist in 'situations in which the conjunction of two or more features or aspects gives rise to new phenomena, which have properties which are irreducible to those of their constituents, even though the latter are necessary for their existence'. The classic example is the irreducibility of the properties of water to those of the hydrogen and oxygen molecules from which it is comprised. By extension, so the argument by analogy goes, the properties of the international order are irreducible to those of the states out of which that order is comprised just as, and in the same way as, the properties of water are irreducible to those of hydrogen and oxygen. This is a neat argument and it looks like a strong logical basis for the ontological distinctiveness of the international as distinct from the national and hence of ontological stratification (on the grounds of the irreducibility of the former to the latter). But we need to be careful here. For this is not necessarily a terribly good analogy and it is not necessarily strictly relevant either. Consider each point in turn. The analogy with water is not, in fact, an especially good one, since it is far more credible to see the properties of the international order as reducible at least in some sense to the conduct of states motivated nationally than it is to see the properties of water as some kind of additive product of those of its constituent molecules. Indeed, the claim that international politics is reducible to the conduct of states is the very basis of realism, perhaps still the single most influential theory of international relations (IR). Whether there is, then, an ontological difference in kind between the national and the international remains at least contestable in a way that is simply not the case with the chemical analogy to which Sayer and other realists point.

But, rather more significantly, even if it were accepted – as perhaps it is likely to be by most non-IR realists – that there is an ontological difference in kind between the international and the national (as polities or political economies), this need not imply that they constitute distinct spatial scales that are, in principle, discrete and themselves stratified. It might, for instance, be argued that at any spatial scale (if we allow ourselves to talk in such terms) there are likely to be traces of both international and national processes of causation (and many other things besides). As this suggests, even amongst those for whom it is uncontentious, the principle of emergence is by no means decisive in adjudicating the stratified nature of social ontology.

This perhaps suggests the value of an alternative position, one that would certainly seem compatible with the work a number of those political and economic geographers

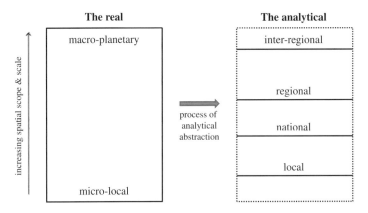

Figure 2.1   Ontological stratification as an analytical simplification

who have reflected most systematically on the ontological status of levels and the question of ontological stratification (see, for instance, Cox 1998; Cumbers et al. 2003; Delaney and Leitner 1997; Marston 2000). This is depicted schematically in Figure 2.1.

It might be termed the 'as if real-ist' position (Hay 2005). This acknowledges no ontological stratification of the social, seeing the spatial dimension of political and economic reality as an unstratified continuum stretching from the most micro and local to the most macro and planetary (whilst acknowledging that very few social and political processes are genuinely planetary in their scope and scale). But it nonetheless sees the potential analytical value in appealing to social, political and economic systems as if they were stratified in terms of the existence of distinct levels of structuration. These levels are not real per se, but 'as if real': they are the product of an analytical strategy designed to simplify and to aid the analysis of an ontologically more complex reality. As such, their value is purely analytical, to be gauged not in terms of the credibility of the claim that the levels to which they point are real, but in terms of the potential insight they offer.

But why might we think it useful to simplify a spatial ontology that we acknowledge to be more complex in this way? The answer is perhaps twofold: first, because it helps us to clarify and contextualise social, political and economic conduct; and, second, because this is typically how the social, political and economic actors we are interested in studying themselves orient their behaviour towards the environment in which they find themselves. Consider each point in turn. When we analyse political economic processes (indeed, any social processes) we invariably do so in terms of conduct (behaviour) and context (environment) – more conventionally agency and structure – and it is far easier to do so at one spatial level at a time (Giddens 1984). Thus, whilst we may increasingly acknowledge the need to recognise the spatially differentiated consequences of behaviour (by positing, for instance, local, national and transnational effects of discrete forms of conduct) and the spatially complex motivations informing such behaviour (as actors project the strategic consequences of their behaviour in spatially differentiated ways), it is far easier to build this up through a consideration of processes of structuration at a variety of different levels – as I seek to show in the next section. Second, and as already intimated, this is precisely how actors themselves typically orient their behaviour and their strategies towards the multiple environments in which they acknowledge themselves to be located and within which and with respect to which they seek to realise their intentions. Put slightly differently, actors seeking to realise their intentions, even when acutely aware that their behaviour may have a variety of different types of effect at different spatial scales, typically do so by thinking primarily of one spatial scale at a time.

THINKING IN LEVELS: STRATIFIED STRUCTURATION

So how might we go about generating analytical insights in contemporary political economy through the positing of 'as if real' stratified spatial levels? The short answer to that question is by conceiving of each level as a distinct process of structuration (Bryant and Jary 1991; Giddens 1984; Hay 1995): a dynamic system in which the conduct of actors and the context in which they find themselves are intimately and iteratively interlinked. In other words, we conceive of political-economic processes as operative at distinct spatial levels within each of which actors orient themselves strategically to the context in which they perceive themselves to be located and seek to realise specific goals and intentions.

Actors are here conceptualised as conscious, reflexive and strategic. They are intentional in the sense that they are assumed to act purposively in the attempt to realise their intentions and preferences. However, they may also act intuitively and/or out of habit. Nonetheless, even when acting routinely they are assumed to be able to render explicit their intentions and their motivations. Moreover, actors are assumed to monitor the immediate consequences of their actions, whether intuitively or more deliberately, and to be capable of monitoring the longer-term consequences of their actions. In so doing, they may come to modify, revise or reject their chosen means to realise their intentions as, indeed, they may also come to modify, revise or reject their original intentions and the conception of interest upon which they were predicated.

Agents are situated within a context about which they are assumed to know much and within which they act strategically. But the contexts in which actors find themselves are also selective of strategy in the sense that, given a specific context, only certain courses of strategic action are likely to see actors realise their intentions. Social, political and economic contexts are densely structured and highly contoured. As such, they present an unevenly distributed configuration of opportunity and constraint to actors.

This in a sense is fine – and now highly conventional – but it is to deal with the interplay of conduct and context, structure and agency, at only one level and as if all aspects of context are potentially subject to transformation by all actors. This is to exclude from the equation the crucial concept of power, understood here as the ability to shape the contexts within which others formulate strategy. We can, then, identify deeper levels of structuration relating to structures over which given strategic actors (within a particular time frame) have minimal impact or control; in short, a stratified social ontology. Such structural constraints (and the opportunities they imply) are effectively imposed by the actions of the (more) powerful (whether intentionally or unwittingly), setting the context for the (relatively) powerless. These might be considered non-appropriatable or nonaccessible levels of structure. They condition the possible range of strategies and actions within a specified social and political context, but are not immediately accessible to transformation by the agents that they embed within such a context.

This is a spatially stratified process in the sense that the product of the strategies and routine actions of ministers and other government officials typically become the structures which constrain and condition the actions of local authorities and local partnerships (inasmuch as they define a legal setting for their action). The actions of these bodies in turn set the context within which local businesses and local citizens themselves formulate strategic calculations and engage in strategic conduct. But, as this suggests, we must be careful here about attributing power in a totalising manner. If we are interested in the strategic investment decisions made by local businesses, then local authorities and other agents of local governance represent (more) powerful actors insofar as they frame significant aspects of the context within which such decisions are formulated. Yet, if we concentrate on the formulation of local economic development strategies, local business decisions, and the ways in which these are framed, represent aspects of the strategic terrain over which local governance networks have minimal influence. Power is relational (Jessop 1990, 2008). This stratified concept of structuration is depicted schematically in Figure 2.2.

At the highest levels of spatial stratification we are dealing with powerful agents

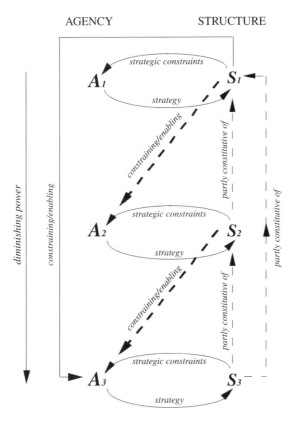

Figure 2.2   Stratified structuration

(A_1) able to project consequential strategies of significant spatial scope and scale. Such actions, like all social agency, take place within a context which is 'always already there' (S_1) and which favours certain strategies over others; a context which is itself the product of previous displays of agency. This imposes strategic constraints upon even the most powerful of actors (collective or individual). Nonetheless, the strategic conduct of such actors has the effect of transforming (however partially) the contours of that strategic context. The context even at this highest spatial level (S_1) is thus dynamic and constantly evolving. Its strategic selectivity is not, however, purely the product of the effects (intended and unintended) of the actions of the powerful. It is also shaped by the invariably unanticipated and contingent effects of the actions and interactions of the relatively powerless and those unable to project consequential strategies of significant spatial scope and scale. Thus, crucial aspects of the strategic selectivity of the terrain inhabited by the powerful include the likely reactions of the powerless to particular strategies, and their ability to mobilise strategic resources to empower themselves.

Nonetheless, from the vantage point of the less powerful (A_2, A_3), the structures of the state or of the global political economy appear as external constraints over which they can exercise minimal, if any, strategic or intentional influence. The powerless do not (by virtue of their powerlessness) exist as strategic actors able to make a decisive intervention on this terrain. The strategic context inhabited by less powerful strategic actors (like A_3) thus comprises accessible levels of structure amenable to strategic action (S_3) and non-accessible levels of structure beyond their immediate strategic reach (S_2, S_1). Power resides in the capacity (whether intentionally exercised or not) to transform aspects of the context in which other less powerful groups and individuals are constrained to formulate their strategies.

GLOBALISATION RECONSIDERED: A MULTI-LEVEL PERSPECTIVE

The implications of this kind of multi-level conceptualisation can be illustrated with respect to debates about globalisation. But, if we are to develop the above abstract account into one which might inform a consideration of the dynamics of the global political economy, what is first required is a theoretical apparatus capable of linking the relationships between agents and their structured contexts at a variety of spatial scales. This is developed schematically in Figure 2.3, in which different spatial scales (chosen on the basis of their potential heuristic utility) are treated as levels of structuration in the broader process of globalisation/counter-globalisation (as in Figure 2.2). The dynamics of the global political economy are captured in the complex and unpredictable interaction between these various levels of structuration.

Beginning at the level of subnational processes and economic dynamics we can identify a range of strategic actors (for instance, businesses, governmental and extra-governmental actors) formulating a variety of strategies (be they specific production–distribution regimes or economic growth strategies). If such strategies are to prove successful in their own terms, they must be oriented not only to the configuration of opportunity and constraint provided by the immediate subnational economic and political environment, but also to the broader national, regional and, indeed, global context. These higher levels of

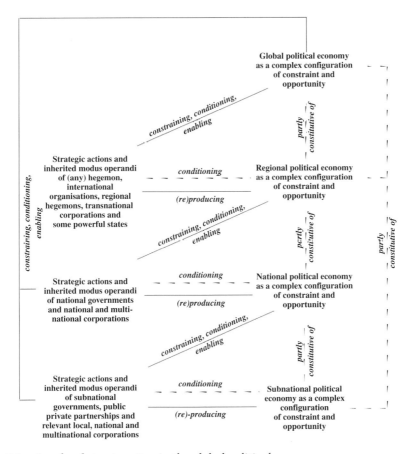

Figure 2.3   Levels of structuration in the global political economy

structuration are inaccessible to direct intervention by the subnational actors themselves, but nonetheless have a crucial bearing upon the strategic selectivity of the context in which they seek to realise their strategic intentions. Such actors can be assumed to have no privileged knowledge of the contours of the terrain they inhabit and, on the basis of partial information, may well come to misperceive the complex configuration of opportunity and constraint they face.

At higher levels of structuration (say, the national level) we can identify a range of potentially more influential actors, the effects of whose strategies may significantly alter the context in which, say, subnational actors operate. They too, however, must adapt their strategies to the environment in which they find themselves. Once again, that environment contains significant external constraints passed down to them from higher levels of structuration (say, those operating at regional and/or global spatial scales). These aspects of context are, consequently, not amenable to direct intervention by the actors themselves, becoming effectively external constraints. As at lower spatial scales, these actors have no privileged access to the contours of the strategic terrain they inhabit and will tend to adapt existing understandings of the operation of the system to their own situation and experience as a guide to formulating strategy in a changing environment.

At the very highest spatial scales (for instance, the global) something very interesting and significant occurs: we effectively run out of strategic actors capable of making decisive interventions at the level of the system itself. This raises a seeming paradox. For, if no strategic global actors can (as yet) be identified, how it is that we can speak meaningfully of a process of (global) structuration at all, let alone restore actors to the process of globalisation? The answer is to be found in unintended consequences. For, whilst there is a deficit of actors capable of purposively refashioning the global political economy itself, there are a whole host of actors capable of contributing unintentionally to a series of global processes, tendencies and counter-tendencies. Perhaps the classic example here is global environmental degradation. A complex array of subnational, national, multinational and transnational actors contribute, through the more or less unintended consequences of their actions, to a genuinely global structuration process: one of environmental degradation. Clearly, the potentially global significance of individual acts of ecological despoliation hardly empowers the actors involved, but it does nonetheless contribute to a global or planetary process. Moreover, in the absence of genuinely global governance mechanisms or alternative strategies for ensuring concerted global solutions to such global 'bads', little is likely to be done to counter such a tendency. This is perhaps a genuine sense in which we can speak of globalisation as a process without a (discrete) subject.

This observation has important implications for the attempt to restore active (and hence potentially accountable) subjects to a process of globalisation widely appealed to as a process without a subject; that is, to render governable globalisation. It suggests, in particular, the need to differentiate between: (1) genuine processes of globalisation in which, in the absence of genuinely global actors, developmental tendencies and counter-tendencies are generated and sustained through the unintended consequences of actions pursued consciously at lower spatial scales; and (2) processes pursued consciously by strategic actors at the national or regional level which are (falsely) appealed to as processes of globalisation. In this second case, restoring subjects to the process of globalisation may entail challenging the appeal made by politicians and commentators alike to globalisation as the proximate cause of political decisions pursued for strategic advantage at the national or regional level.

It is interesting at this point to note, however, that, although globalisation is frequently – and problematically – referred to as a process without a subject, it is rarely in the sense identified above. In the penultimate section of this chapter I examine the popular invocation of globalisation in such terms and turn to the broader question of restoring active subjects to the process of globalisation.

BRINGING THE SUBJECT BACK IN: STRUCTURE, AGENCY AND GLOBALISATION

Insofar as international political economists tend to speak of a structure–agency 'problem', it is because they think that they have a 'solution'. That solution invariably involves some claim to have identified a middle between the twin extremes of structural-ism and intentionalism (Adler 1997; Wendt 1999). Such middle ways have the obvious appeal of acknowledging the dynamic interaction of structure and agency, of context and conduct. Consequently, they tend to place the emphasis not upon the explication of deterministic structural logics or the identification of hegemonic intentional actors, but upon the elucidation of processes, in which structure and agent are intimately interwoven, over time. Given that globalisation is a process term, one might be forgiven for thinking that the analysis of globalisation naturally lends itself to a subtle and complex rendition of the structure–agency relationship to elucidate the causal mechanisms involved. Sadly, this has yet to prove the case.

This is because, whilst globalisation may masquerade as a process term in both the popular and academic vernacular, it tends to feature in both registers as a 'process without a subject'. It is, in short, a process to which no actors are linked, a process which rapidly becomes a deterministic logic of structural inevitability the closer one looks. Accordingly, the term 'globalisation', as used in most popular and academic debate, is an obfuscation, and a potentially dangerous one at that. For it tends to conjure a sense of inexorability, inevitability and immutability, mapping a path to an end-state (a condition of pure globalisation) never fully realised, yet always in the process of being realised. This represents a dangerous conflation of process and teleology which can only serve to hide the complex causal processes which generate the evidence frequently cited in support of the globalisation thesis.

To point to the dangers of appeals to globalisation as a causal process is not to insist that globalisation is a figment of the imagination. It is merely to suggest the need for considerable caution in the use of the term if we are not further to mystify phenomena which might genuinely be regarded as evidence of globalisation. The challenge posed by this chapter (not, it should be noted, an entirely novel one) is to build upon the foundations laid by the critique of earlier, more cavalier appeals to the notion of globalisation, to further unpack and demystify this 'process without a subject'. This in turn suggests that we should view globalisation not so much as a process or end-state but, at best, as a tendency to which counter-tendencies may be mobilised. Once viewed in such terms, the challenge is to reveal the dynamic and contingent articulation of processes in certain spatial contexts at certain moments in time to yield effects which might be understood as generating evidence of globalisation. Such scrutiny invariably reveals the causal significance of processes operating at spatial scales below the global and for which strategic political actors might be held accountable. Our aim, then, must be two-fold: (1) to explain the complex causation (often by appeal to logics of unintended consequence) of those genuine, if rare, processes of globalisation which escape the intentions of the actors involved; and (2) to demonstrate (where this is not the case) that key actors retain considerable control over what they choose to appeal to as a globalisation process which they claim to be powerless against.

If we are to do this, it is imperative that we reverse the conventional direction of causality appealed to in the academic literature as, indeed, in the popular discourse of globalisation. We must ask not what globalisation might explain, but how we might account for the phenomena widely identified as evidence of globalisation. If we are to resist and reject the deterministic appeal to a process without a subject, we seek to resist the temptation to refer to globalisation as an explanatory (or independent) variable. Within such a schema, the term 'globalisation' becomes little more than a convenient shorthand for a confluence of processes which might together be seen as constitutive of any observed (and, presumably, contingent) globalisation tendency. The existing literature has, to date, given far too limited attention to such genuine (causal) processes, such as financial liberalisation, to which actors might be linked directly. Financial liberalisation is, perhaps, a good example, for many accounts of globalisation's seeming 'logic of no alternative', of neoliberal convergence in effect, rely in the end on claims not of globalisation per se but of financial liberalisation and consequent heightened capital mobility. In such cases, appeal to the term 'globalisation' is, as suggested, quite simply an obfuscation: if the causal agent is the (quite conscious political) decision to engage in a process of financial liberalisation, why not call it as it is?

As I have sought to argue, there is no need to make essentialising and reifying assumptions about the effects, consequences or even the very existence of globalisation. For, insofar as globalisation can be identified, it is understood as a tendency: the contingent outcome of a confluence of specific processes that are themselves likely to be limited in space and time. Globalised outcomes and effects might then be the product of very different, indeed entirely independent, mechanisms and processes of causation (financial liberalisation, European integration and policy transfer, to identify merely three) that can only be obscured by appeal to a generic (and causal) logic of globalisation. Whilst problematising and interrogating the processes which underpin globalising tendencies, then, it is important to resist the temptation to appeal to globalisation itself as a causal factor or process working apparently independently of the actions, intentions and motivations of real subjects. It is precisely this appeal to causal processes without subjects that summons the logic of necessity and inevitability so often associated with the notion of globalisation.

If we are then to demystify globalisation, we must ensure that, in making what we think are causal arguments, we can identify the actors involved, thus giving due attention to the 'structuration' of globalising tendencies whilst rejecting structuralist or functionalist 'logics' operating over the heads or independently of social subjects.

It is only by paying careful attention to the problem of structure and agency in this way, dismissing accounts which privilege either structure or (far less frequently in analyses of globalisation) agency in the determination of outcomes, that the notion of globalisation might be used to open up and not merely to obfuscate the analysis of political economic change.

CONCLUSION: GOVERNANCE ACROSS LEVELS

Thus far I have focused considerable attention on the stratified nature of social and political reality and the analytical challenges posed by the attempt to develop a spatially sensitive political economy. In this, the final section of the chapter, it is important to draw out the implications of this for governance specifically. Governance might be understood here, quite simply, as the attempt to impose a common or collective purpose upon events; the process of seeking to steer, control, regulate or otherwise influence outcomes, thereby rendering them answerable to a common or collective purpose or good.

The crucial – and, in a sense, the obvious – point of this chapter is that multi-level governance or, as might be preferred, governance across levels, is both inherently complex (and more complex in kind than governance at a single level) and made necessary by the kinds of spatial interdependence that this chapter has sought to elucidate. It poses very considerable practical challenges, to which, arguably, we have yet to respond adequately.

As soon as we acknowledge that actions motivated by the desire to realise an intention at a specific spatial scale are likely to have consequences at other spatial scales, we become aware of the need for governance across levels. Consider the problem of debt. Here we typically acknowledge a potential fallacy of composition in our understanding of the consequences of indebtedness (Blyth 2013). If consumers or households are in debt, we invariably suggest that it is good for them to seek, as quickly as possible (and all things being equal), to begin to repay that debt. Yet, if we move up a level and reconsider the problem of private debt at a national level, we are likely to reach a rather different set of conclusions. What is good advice for the consumer or household (repay one's debt as soon as possible) is not necessarily good advice for the nation as a whole. For, as Keynesians in particular tend to emphasise, if we all cut our consumption to repay our debt at the same time, then we are likely to precipitate a massive drop in aggregate demand with serious knock-on consequences for economic output, employment, personal income and perhaps even indebtedness. There is a danger, in other words, that by ignoring the potential fallacy of composition of national debt – by deciding what to do about it by extrapolating from the rational course of action for the individual household facing debt – we threaten inadvertently to compound matters by creating a debt spiral. Rationality at the level of the unit (here the actor or household) may generate irrationality at the level of the system.

This, in essence, is the problem of governance; and the point is that it is a multi-level problem. For there is, in effect, a second fallacy of composition to which we might point here, one which arguably has crucial implications for our understanding of the global financial crisis and the problematic character of the turn to public austerity that it has prompted. The problem is that, at the level of the national economy and in a world of acknowledged economic interdependence, it may well no longer be quite so self-evident, as in the classical Keynesian position, that foregoing the repayment of debt whilst growth is resuscitated is the best course of action. The concern here is with the willingness of financial market actors to hold debt denominated in the currency of an economy that is single-handedly resisting, in the name of the collective national interest, repaying its debt (public or private). For, if other economies are writing down their debt, then financial market actors are likely to demand a higher rate of interest on debt denominated in the currency of a more intransigently indebted state. Here again there is a collective-action problem, since what is rational at the level of the individual state (the writing down of debt in the face of anxieties about speculative dynamics in financial markets) is likely to prove collectively irrational (suppressing aggregate global demand and threatening to prompt a global depression). The solution, or at least the potential solution, is again the same: governance – indeed, governance across levels. For what is required here is the coordination at a transnational level (amongst a community of indebted states) of behaviour at the national level (choices about the repayment or deferral of national debt are, in the end, national in character). As this suggests, this is not so much a question of governance at a higher level – global governance for instance – as it is a coordination problem across levels of governance (a combination of transnational coordination and national action is what it required). But, as this example perhaps already suggests, such governance across levels is not something we are very good at.

It is not difficult to see why. The problem, in essence, is one of both legitimacy and capacity. Citizens, as we know well, typically have more problems these days than once they did in accepting the probity and legitimacy of decisions made in the context of a formally democratic national polity (Hay 2007; Stoker 2006); unremarkably, they tend to be more suspicious still of decisions made at a transnational level in institutions which invariably make no claim to being democratic or representative in this way at all. Thus, whilst we may tend to be more accepting today of the idea that institutions of global coordination, global governance or, better perhaps, planetary governance across levels are necessary, we have yet to devise a set of such institutions and mechanisms capable of garnering even the modest (and deteriorating) legitimacy of national-level institutions. Partly as a consequence, and judging by the competences and capacities we have assigned them, we have tended to date not to place as much confidence in the institutions we have designed to perform such transnational coordinating functions as the significance of their roles might warrant. Thus, whilst we would seem to acknowledge increasingly the need for such institutions and the desirability for such institutions to be both legitimate and competent, we seem as yet to have little idea of what effective and democratic planetary governance across levels would even look like. To envisage, devise, design and build such institutions is perhaps the greatest single challenge the world faces today; one on which, arguably, its fate as a social, economic and ecosystem will depend.

NOTE

1. The term 'planetary' is typically not used in such debates about spatial stratification; and perhaps for good reason, since the distinction between the global and the planetary is not in essence a spatial one. It is none-theless an important one. I use it here to distinguish between processes (such as financial interdependence) whose geographical scope, scale and reach has the capacity to impact on all parts of the globe but whose influence is in practice highly uneven (which I term 'global') and those processes and issues (such as the sustainability of the planet as an ecosystem) which are inherently holistic and pertain to the planet as a system in a singular way (which I term 'planetary').

REFERENCES

Adler, Emanuel (1997), 'Seizing the middle ground: constructivism in world politics', *European Journal of International Relations*, **3** (3), 319–63.
Bache, Ian and Matthew Flinders (eds) (2004), *Multi-Level Governance*, Oxford: Oxford University Press.
Baldwin, David A. (1990), 'Interdependence and power: a conceptual analysis', *International Organization*, **34** (4), 471–506.
Blyth, Mark (2013), *Austerity: The History of a Dangerous Idea*, Oxford: Oxford University Press.
Bryant, Christopher G.A. and David Jary (eds) (1991), *Structuration Theory*, New York: Routledge.
Cox, Kevin (1998), 'Spaces of dependence, spaces of engagement and the politics of scale, or, looking for local politics', *Political Geography*, **17** (1), 1–23.
Cumbers, Andrew, Danny MacKinnon and Robert McMaster (2003), 'Institutions, power and space: assessing the limits to institutionalism in economic geography', *European Urban and Regional Studies*, **10** (4), 325–42.
Delaney, David and Helga Leitner (1997), 'The political construction of scale', *Political Geography*, **16** (2), 93–97.
Gamble, Andrew, Anthony Payne, Ankie Hoogvelt, Michael Dietrich and Michael Kenny (1996), 'Editorial: new political economy', *New Political Economy*, **1** (1), 5–11.

Giddens, Anthony (1984), *The Constitution of Society*, Cambridge: Polity Press.
Hagan, John and Ruth D. Peterson (eds) (1995), *Crime and Inequality*, Stanford, CA: Stanford University Press.
Hay, Colin (1995), 'Structure and agency', in D. Marsh and G. Stoker (eds), *Theory and Methods in Political Science*, Basingstoke: Palgrave Macmillan, pp. 189–206.
Hay, Colin (2005), 'Making hay . . . or clutching at ontological straws? Notes on realism, "as-if-realism" and actualism', *Politics*, **25** (1), 39–45.
Hay, Colin (2007), *Why We Hate Politics*, Cambridge: Polity Press.
Hooghe, Liesbet (ed.) (1996), *Cohesion Policy and European Integration: Building Multi-Level Governance*, Oxford: Oxford University Press.
Hooghe, Liesbet and Gary Marks (2001), *Multi-Level Governance and European Integration*, Lanham, MD: Rowman & Littlefield.
Jessop, Bob (1990), *State Theory*, Cambridge: Polity Press.
Jessop, Bob (1998), 'The rise of governance and the risks of failure: the case of economic development', *International Social Science Journal*, **50**, 29–45.
Jessop, Bob (2008), *State Power*, Cambridge: Polity Press.
Keohane, Robert O. and Joseph S. Nye, Jr (1977), *Power and Interdependence*, Boston, MA: Little Brown.
Krohn, Marvin D. (1970), 'Inequality, unemployment and crime: a cross-national analysis', *Sociological Quarterly*, **17** (3), 303–13.
Kroll, John A. (1993), 'The complexity of interdependence', *International Studies Quarterly*, **37** (3), 321–47.
Marston, Sallie A. (2000), 'The social construction of scale', *Progress in Human Geography*, **24** (2), 219–42.
Rosenau, James N. and Ernst-Otto Czempiel (eds) (1992), *Governance without Government: Order and Change in World Politics*, Cambridge: Cambridge University Press.
Sayer, Andrew (2000), *Realism and Social Science*, New York: Sage.
Stoker, Gerry (2006), *Why Politics Matters: Making Democracy Work*, Basingstoke: Palgrave Macmillan.
Strange, Susan (1970), 'International economics and international relations: a case of mutual neglect', *International Affairs*, **46** (2), 304–15.
Strange, Susan (1988), *States and Markets*, New York: Continuum.
Swyngedouw, Erik (2004), 'Globalisation or "glocalisation"? Networks, territories and rescaling', *Cambridge Review of International Affairs*, **17** (1), 25–48.
Wagner, R. Harrison (1988), 'Economic interdependence, bargaining power and political influence', *International Organization*, **42** (3), 461–83.
Wendt, Alexander (1999), *Social Theory of International Politics*, Cambridge: Cambridge University Press.

3 Transnational neopluralism and the process of governance

Philip G. Cerny

The concept of governance has undergone a number of significant changes since the late twentieth century. Indeed, I would argue that the word itself is characterised by a particular ambiguity that has run through the political and social sciences generally, not just international relations (IR) and international political economy (IPE), since their early development. That is, the distinction between institutions on the one hand, and processes on the other. 'Governance' has generally been taken to mean something different from, although inextricably intertwined with, 'government', an ambiguity represented by the title of Arthur F. Bentley's seminal work on pluralism, *The Process of Government*, just over a century ago (Bentley 1908). The very concept of 'governance' as it was previously used in political theory connoted not institutionalised structures nor more formal political processes, but informal practices, indirect forms of social control, and loose and fungible structures of power such as the 'self-organising networks' analysed by policy-network theorists (Rhodes 1996), economic sociologists, marketing specialists and some political economists (Thompson et al. 1991; Castells 1996; Henderson et al. 2002).

Therefore, while 'government' is about institutions, 'governance' is about the social and economic, as well as political, processes by which power and influence are put into practice, outcomes are shaped and decisions made and implemented, and broad social, political and economic trends managed and controlled by a range of actors. These actors may be working primarily within an established set of political or governmental institutions, which is how the traditional study of political science was framed in terms of 'political systems', but they are also working outside, below and cutting across those institutions. This is particularly important in a so-called 'globalising' world, where those institutions are increasingly in flux, challenged and eroded by transnational structural trends and the rise and fall of old and new categories of political, social and economic actors (Cerny 2000a). At the core of these processes, furthermore, is the interaction of two equally inextricably intertwined categories that are also at the core of the political and social sciences: the public and the private. Governance in a globalising world, like domestic politics but at a range of intersecting and overlapping structural levels, is about the hybridisation of the public and the private. While there is not space here to go into the public–private theoretical debate per se at any length (I have addressed this issue elsewhere: Cerny 1999, forthcoming), it is central not only to understanding the interaction of these levels, but also to analysing how power and influence are developed and exercised, or, as Robert Dahl so famously put it, 'who governs?' (Dahl 1961).

However, as the editors point out in the Introduction to this book, much of the work in international political economy that has used the word 'governance' has been about what has been mislabelled 'global governance'; that is, the development of: (1) international regimes, which are essentially intergovernmental institutions; (2) new kinds of interstate relations; and (3) changes to the state itself. In this sense, the concept of governance has not really extended beyond the traditional assumptions of international relations: that is, that IR and IPE are first and foremost about relations between states. Most work on IR and IPE still takes for granted that there are two distinct yet coexisting political processes and sets of institutions at work simultaneously in the modern world: domestic politics and international relations (Hollis and Smith 1990). The first takes place within established nation-states, and the second takes place as nation-states as political units (or 'unit actors': Waltz 1979) interact with each other. This is sometimes called the 'inside/outside distinction' (Walker 1993). This chapter argues that, on the contrary, globalisation is a political process that challenges the inside–outside distinction itself.

As mentioned above, since the early twentieth century, another key paradigm has been at work in the study of politics, although mainly limited to the domestic field. That paradigm is pluralism. Pluralism as a paradigm itself has a chequered history, challenged by other paradigms including Marxist class analysis, theories of elitism and corporatism, and the revival of sociological theories of the state in the tradition of Max Weber. For my purposes, however, the key development in the evolution of pluralism as a concept is the version called neopluralism (Lindblom 1977; McFarland 2004), which acknowledges the shortcomings in early versions of pluralist theory and proposes a more realistic version of the approach. In neopluralism, the outcomes of various political processes are determined in the last analysis not by the a priori existence of cohesive, vertically unified nation-states as such. Rather, they stem from the interaction of a range of individual and collective (group) actors below, outside, surrounding, cutting across and populating states and societies. These actors have very different kinds of social bonds, levels of social, economic and political power resources, understandings of how to use that power, material interests, normative values, political projects and, of course, the determination to pursue those interests, values and projects in a range of public and private arenas.

In other words, such actors are not equal, and some of them possess far more in the way of resources, clout and organisational coherence required to dominate outcomes. Lindblom (1977) in particular referred to 'the privileged position of business' in a neopluralist world. Such 'groups', as they are known in the literature – a version of which has been called 'group theory' (Truman 1951) – are the main source of both political stability and instability, continuity and change, repression and freedom, stagnation and progress. It is crucial, however, that they have differing and sometimes incompatible interests as well as common interests, that there are several (even many) of them, and that they engage in processes of conflict, competition and coalition-building in order to pursue those interests. Those processes take place within, outside, below and cutting across a range of 'structured fields of action' (Crozier and Friedberg 1977) that include, but are not limited to, the state or government.

In this pluralistic and/or neopluralistic political process, actors face a range not only of constraints but also of opportunities, embedded in those structured fields of action, to shape political outcomes, depending on how they operate within those constraints or how they seek, successfully or unsuccessfully, to transcend and/or transform them. But all of them depend upon the capacities of real-world, crosscutting 'interest' groups – including both 'sectional' (or 'material interest') and 'value' groups (Key 1953) – to manipulate constraints, to identify and take advantage of opportunities, and to shape new directions through processes of competition and coalition-building. What are new, however, are the rapidly growing transnational linkages among groups and the emergence of those increasingly influential, even powerful, cross-border sectional and value groups that are coming to dominate a growing range of crosscutting, uneven yet crucial, transnational political processes. These processes are not replacing nation-states as such. This is not a 'borderless world' (Ohmae 1990), but one of a multiplication of borders old and new, horizontal and vertical. Furthermore, they are crystallising into transnational webs of power. These webs and their interlocked strands of power and political action are continually and ever more rapidly expanding, intensifying and consolidating, becoming more and more densely interwoven as the new century advances.

States are themselves increasingly trapped in these webs. The most important movers and shakers are no longer simply domestic political forces, institutions and processes, whether in terms of economic interdependence, including multinational firms and global financial markets, as well as production, distribution and consumption chains; social interconnections, migration and the movement of people; relationships of violence and force (including terrorism); 'transgovernmental networks' cutting across governments; problem-solving 'epistemic communities'; technological change from the internet to a growing variety of human activities; ideological conflict and competition; and a whole range of other deep trends. Instead, the most influential actors are those who can coordinate their activities across borders, at multiple levels and multiple nodes of power, and are thus able to convince and/or bully governments, other competing actors, both public and private, and mass publics alike, thereby shaping in this process not merely transnational – even global – outcomes but also local and regional micro- and meso-politics too.

These new, unofficial borders are increasingly horizontal borders among 'interests', broadly defined. These include material interests, cultural identities and social values: economic sectors and markets; crosscutting social groupings, including classes and fractions of classes, ethnicities and religions; diverse parts of a 'disaggregated' state linked into 'transgovernmental networks' (Slaughter 2004); political pressure groups, value groups and social movements; and myriad other social, economic and political actors, both individual and collective, which increasingly operate on international, transnational and 'translocal' playing fields. This 'transnational neopluralism' is, however, a work in progress, continually shaping political action and institutional change and in turn itself being reshaped in a range of inextricably intertwined ways, and embedded by a process called 'structuration' that ultimately leads to institutional as well as behavioural change.

PLURALISM, GLOBALISATION AND GOVERNANCE

In a globalising world, therefore, political power itself is becoming more diffuse, refracted through an increasingly complex, prismatic structure of socio-economic forces and levels of governance, from the global interaction of transnational social movements and interest/pressure groupings, multinational corporations, financial markets, and the like, on the one hand, to the re-emergence of subnational and cross-national ethnic, religious and policy-oriented coalitions and conflicts of the type familiar in domestic-level political sociology, on the other (Cerny 2012). Governance is therefore being transformed into a 'polycentric' or 'multinucleated' global political system operating within the same geographical space, and/or overlapping spaces, in a way analogous to the emergence of coexisting and overlapping functional authorities in metropolitan areas and subnational regions (Ostrom et al. 1961).

The underlying governance problematic in such multilayered political systems is at least twofold. On the one hand, it becomes harder to maintain the boundaries which are necessary for the efficient 'packaging' of public or collective goods; and, in the second place, it becomes harder to determine what collective goods are demanded or required in the first place; that is, even to measure what is the 'preferred state of affairs' (Ostrom et al. 1961: 832–5; cf. Cerny 1999; Lowi 1964). On the other hand, state actors themselves paradoxically act in routine fashion to undermine the holistic and hierarchical character of traditional state sovereignty, authority or *potestas*, leading to a 'hollowing out of the state' (Jessop 1997). The international system of states as unit actors is thus being superseded by a much more diffuse, decentralised and crosscutting structural pattern, based on a revised version of Durkheim's division of labour (Durkheim 1893 [1933]: 405–6). Durkheim actually argued that there was no such thing as a genuine crosscutting international division of labour; he saw it as an almost wholly domestic phenomenon. However, as today's increasingly transnational division of labour expands, the kinds of things that states can do, and the constraints that derive from external pressures, are constantly changing. Different 'groups' are often interconnected with each other in complex ways that reflect diverse, even contrasting, identities and belongings, cutting across territory, class, gender, ethnicity, family ties and the like.

Without the state and its authoritative capacity to enforce the rules of the game, however, transnational complexity might at first seem to imply instability. Nevertheless, traditional pluralist theorists argued that, paradoxically, pluralism was actually a key stabilising factor in the modern world. For example, in Simmel's reformulation of Durkheim, pluralism and functional specialisation are in the last analysis stabilising, not destabilising. In a 'complex social structure', he argued, the roles and group memberships of individuals overlap with and cut across those of other individuals and groups – in the family, in employment, in friendships, in leisure activities, in communications, even in politics – creating a mutually reinforcing web of interactions cutting across potentially conflicting macro-groups such as economic classes (Simmel 1922 [1955]).

Stability therefore depends upon the overlapping and intertwining at the micro and meso levels of what would otherwise be destabilising conflicts, mitigating them and even making them cancel each other out, as argued by Lewis Coser (1956) in his classic updating of Simmel. In today's globalising world, overlapping memberships and crosscutting affiliations are spreading across an ever wider range of manifest and developed (complex, cohesive, differentiated, and so on) structural categories. This fluidity constitutes the basis not just for an international plurality of building blocks, but also for the crystallisation of new dynamic and pluralistic governance processes. However, their potential for stability is highly problematic, a theme I will return to at the end of this chapter.

INTEREST GROUPS AND THE GLOBALISATION PROCESS

In this changing environment, the stage is set for an increasingly active, accelerating and open process of interest group adjustment at several levels. At one level, the physical or material environmental bases of certain types of interest group association have been transformed by both technological change and greater awareness of the international and transnational interconnectedness of environmental and other issues. In particular, the multinationalisation of industry, the expansion of trade and the globalisation of financial markets, along with the development of a transnational consumer society, have transformed many of what Bentley (1908) called 'wealth groups' and V.O. Key (1953) called 'sectional groups' into transnational interest groups, operating across borders and involved in complex competition and coalition-building with each other, with state actors, with so-called 'global governance' regimes, and increasingly with mass publics. At another level, values and consciousness are also being transformed in the context of globalisation.

Within and across states, too, bureaucrats, politicians and other officials or 'state actors' have become more and more imbricated with groups of their counterparts in other countries through transgovernmental networks, policy communities and the like. In the economic sphere, post-Fordist forms of production based on flexibilisation have transformed 'techniques of industry', labour markets, finance and the like. And the rediscovery of ideas, not merely in terms of formal arguments but even more so in terms of discourses – whether constructivist discourses of institutional reconstruction or postmodernist discourses of multiple circuits of power – has transformed the every-day content of what Bentley called 'discussion groups' (as distinct from 'organisational groups'), as well as that of political actors and intellectuals, into forums for developing increasingly global or transnational understandings of the major challenges of the day, year or millennium – what I have elsewhere described as a post-Foucauldian *raison du monde* (Cerny 2010a).

At the same time, however, such changes also give rise to adaptive as well as transformational modes of behaviour. Therefore the particular shape a transformed international system is likely to take will be determined primarily by whether particular sets of groups – in particular, those competing groups led by 'institutional entrepreneurs' or 'change masters' (Kanter 1985) – are best able, either strategically or accidentally, to exploit the manifest and latent structural resources or political opportunity structures available to them most effectively in a period of flux. A key variable in explaining group-led change is thus the presence of strategically situated groups in a flawed and/or fluid structural context. Their presence constitutes a necessary but not sufficient condition of structural change.

This question is at the forefront of public consciousness at the time of writing, when a range of poorly coordinated national responses to the recent (and still current) global financial crisis raises fundamental questions about the capacity of either states or 'global governance' to cope with the most pressing issues of the day. Key sets of groups that have in the past been closely bound up with the territorial nation-state are increasingly experimenting with new forms of quasi-private regulation of their activities, especially in the context of neoliberal ideology and approaches to governance. Just as in domestic politics, those interest groups that are best endowed are not only the most involved in globalisation, but the most likely to succeed (Cerny 2010b).

And state actors themselves, once said to be 'captured' by large, well-organised domestic constituencies, are increasingly captured instead by transnationally linked sectors. These actors not only set state agencies and international regimes against each other – a process sometimes called 'venue shopping' (or 'forum shopping') or 'regulatory arbitrage' – in the desire to 'level the playing field' for their domestic clients in the wider world, but they also cause them simultaneously to try to network in an increasingly dense fashion with their peers in other states. Among the major losers are trade unions and other groups with few transnational linkages, although they are sometimes still in a position to demand and obtain compensatory side-payments from national governments.

Alongside these economic developments has come a range of meso- and micro-social and political developments. The rise of Marshall McLuhan's 'global village' (McLuhan 1964) has been paralleled (or, for some, even superseded) by a postmodernist fragmentation of cultures and societies, including the re-identification of societies as 'multicultural', emphasising shifting identities and loyalties, unravelling 'national culture societies' (Znaniecki 1952 [1973]) that were at the heart of the nation-state political project from Bismarck's *Kulturkampf* to postcolonial 'nation-building' (Bendix 1964). Major social movements and cause groups, furthermore, are increasingly focused on transnational issues, such as the environment, human rights, women's issues, the international banning of landmines, opposition to the holding of political prisoners, promoting 'sustainable development', eliminating poor countries' international debts and the like. Growing pressures for migration, along with new possibilities for international communication, have led to the growth of active diasporas as well as of 'global tribes' (Kotkin 1992). The end of the Cold War also unleashed a huge number of social and political demands which had previously been kept in ideological and political check. Whether change overall is fundamental and far-reaching enough to become paradigmatic change – that is, transformational change – will depend upon the balance of forces between sets of groups whose actions either continue to reinforce existing structural forms and practices or generate and reinforce new forms and practices.

And, finally, those alternative outcomes, or 'multiple equilibria', which may exist in theory and in the minds of key actors, may prove either too ambitious on the one hand, or too amorphous and fragmented on the other, to form an effective foundation for those groups' strategic or tactical calculations and for their pursuit of specific, coherent outcomes. As specific actors continually probe the potential for new ways to pursue their interests, the key driving force in this transformation and reconstruction will consist of transnationally linked group political actors engaging in crosscutting competition and coalition-building behaviour, exploiting the growing institutional loopholes of global politics, constructing new power games, creating new networks and changing people's perceptions of how world politics works, changing the parameters and dynamics of who gets, and should get, what, when and how.

GOVERNANCE AND THE TRANSNATIONALISATION OF ISSUES

The main variable propelling this process of change is usually seen to be the nature of the policy issues and challenges that face both states and international organisations today. These challenges include global economic growth, climate change and pollution, cross-border civil and insurgent wars, increasing relative inequality and the growing public salience of poverty and uneven development; not to mention a range of significant issues concerning particular transnationally networked economic and financial sectors, crosscutting transportation and infrastructure issues, technological changes with global implications, such as governing the internet, and the like. Operating in such a changing world is leading to new problems of management and control, what Lake has called 'the privatisation of governance' (Lake 1999; Kahler and Lake 2003) and others have identified as the emergence of 'private authority' in international affairs (Cutler et al. 1999; Ronit and Schneider 2000; Hall and Biersteker 2003). Institutions and formal processes of 'global governance' do not have the direct sanctioning power that has been at the core of state development and power in the modern era, especially in the form of Weber's 'monopoly of legitimate violence', whether domestic or international. In the meantime, the sovereignty of states is only partially and unevenly 'pooled' through the development of intergovernmental institutions and processes.

The increasing integration of transnational economic markets has led to the emergence of and increasing range of cross-border interest groups. In economic sectors characterised by the growing significance of multinational or transnational corporations, the ability of these corporations to coordinate their own actions across borders – whether in pressing for regulatory changes or playing off tax jurisdictions – is just the tip of the iceberg. Even small firms that seem ostensibly 'local' are not immune, being dependent upon 'foreign' raw materials, export markets, investment finance, migrant labour and the like, and both increasingly form nodes of wider networks and coordinate their actions. Less formal networks and more formal interaction among firms, 'private regimes', 'alliance capitalism' and the ability of non-state actors in general to develop a range of formal and informal interconnections, both economic and political, has led to significant degrees of policy transfer both across states and in terms of shaping the evolution of global governance more broadly (Higgott et al. 1999; Evans 2005). The linking of financial markets and institutions globally has led to far-reaching changes in market organisation, including cross-border mergers and convergence of market practices.

Significant issue-areas, such as accountancy, auditing and corporate governance, have witnessed ongoing negotiation processes among firms, private sector organisations representing particular industrial, financial and commercial sectors, as well as governments and international regimes, in order to reconcile conflicting standards and move toward a more level playing field (Mügge 2006). Furthermore, people of all social classes and groups are becoming enmeshed in international production processes, technological developments, markets and consumer preferences. In other words, the organisation of the world of work, once embedded in the Fordist factory system, increasingly depends upon flexible, complex transnational economic activities and circuits of political-economic power. Ordinary people in everyday life are growing more and more aware that their fates depend not so much on decisions taken at national level, but on wider developments and transformations at international, transnational and translocal levels (Hobson and Seabrooke 2007).

Indeed, even security, defence and war, since time immemorial the overwhelmingly predominant rationale for the state retaining and pursuing power, especially military power, in the international arena, are being reclaimed for the world as a whole; a qualitative leap beyond the rather crude and often stalemated twentieth-century notions of 'collective security' represented by the League of Nations and the United Nations (Pinker 2011; Goldstein 2011). Perhaps most salient of all, given the recent growth of concern with issues such as climate change and the increasingly obvious effects of global warming, have been environmental groups, which have come to occupy a central place among those who claim to represent people in general across borders, not only transcending the nation-state but also calling for global solutions to deal with a growing, imperative crisis.

In this context, normative values are being reassessed through the action of transnational cause groups. Among the most potent themes are human rights and human security. These groups have been successfully redefining two of the most important social and political issue-areas of the modern world for the traditional legitimation of nation-states themselves. Human rights – the international equivalent of civil rights, one of the most important value issue-areas where democratic states have in the past claimed to represent the most elemental underlying interests and values of their citizens – are now being internationalised. The pursuit of social justice and even social and economic redistribution, once the monopoly of the welfare state, are no longer limited to the arena or 'container' of the nation-state. These concerns have led to the rapid growth of 'transnational advocacy coalitions' (Keck and Sikkink 1998), now widely referred to as 'global civil society' and 'transnational social movements' (Tarrow 2005). Indeed, the increasingly 'splintered state' (Machin and Wright 1985) or 'disaggregated state' (Slaughter 2004) is itself caught up in horizontal cross-border power relationships too. In sum, world politics is coming to be increasingly characterised by what sociologists call 'functional differentiation': governance organised around different social, economic and political 'functions' or crosscutting issue-areas (Albert et al. 2013; Cerny 2013).

CHANGE AND TRANSFORMATION

Today a number of factors, including ethnic and religious ties, multiculturalism, transnational communities and the internationalisation of production, consumption and finance, have fostered the emergence of a vast range of alternative sources of economic advantage, political influence and social identity. These varied processes of change, although usually brought together under the label of globalisation, include the development of denser relations among states (internationalisation), growing below-the-border dealings cutting across states (transnationalisation), denser interactions among localities and regions ('translocalisation' or 'glocalisation') and the transformation of social, economic and political relations and processes at the domestic and local levels themselves – the macrocosm within the microcosm. More important than any one of these levels, however, are the interaction effects among them, which is where transnational neopluralism is most significant in shaping change.

This overall process of transformation, I suggest, has three main interlocking dimensions. The first and most obvious involves a change in the character of the state's domestic 'functions'; that is, its tasks, roles and activities. This involves first and foremost the way so-called 'public goods' are perceived, pursued and provided. In particular, the aim of social justice through redistribution and protectionism has been challenged and profoundly undermined by the marketisation and transnationalisation of the state's economic activities (and of the state itself) and by a new embedded financial orthodoxy (Cerny 1994a). These changes not only constrain the state in its economic policies, but also alter people's understanding of what politics is for, thereby challenging the political effectiveness of the very national liberal-democratic political systems which are supposed to represent what the people want.

The second dimension involves a fundamental reorientation of how states interact economically with each other. State actors are increasingly concerned with promoting the competitive advantages of particular production and service sectors in a more open and integrated world economy – the 'competition state' (Cerny 1990, 2000b, 2010a; Horsfall 2011) – not only in order to produce collective economic gains, but also to build new coalitions and expand the scope and reach of their own power and influence. In pursuing international competitiveness, state agencies closely linked with those economic sectors most closely integrated into the world economy increasingly accept, and indeed embrace, those complex interdependencies and transnational linkages thought to be the most promising sources of profitability and economic prosperity in a rapidly globalising world. States and state actors are increasingly agents of globalisation, rather than of resistance.

The third dimension concerns the relationship between structure and agency in general, in other words people; that is, between constraints embedded in existing structural and institutional rules, existing patterns of the distribution of resources and power, and existing practices and ways of doing things, on the one hand, and those individuals and groups who make tactical and strategic decisions, day-to-day or over the long term, that can alter or break those rules, patterns and practices, directly or indirectly, intentionally or unintentionally, on the other. Rather than continuing path-dependency, these effects generate multiple equilibria, creating the possibility of new 'branching points', thus opening the way to potential path modification and reconstruction of the system itself. It is crucial to identify these structural faults and explore the potential constraints and opportunities that actors may face in attempts to manipulate and reshape the structure of the system.

In this process, for example, the focus of the economic mission of the state has shifted considerably from its traditional concern with production and producer groups to one involving market structures and consumer groups, and from its understanding of the role of the state in general as a 'decommodifying agent' to that of a 'commodifying agent' (Cerny 1990); that is, concerned with making markets work better and more efficiently, rather than replacing them with new authoritative allocation mechanisms. Thus state actors have found their roles changing too, as the state has become more splintered and disaggregated. The crucial point, however, is that those tasks, roles and activities will not just be different, but rather that they will lose much of the overarching, macro-authoritative and superior normative philosophical character traditionally ascribed to the effective state, the good state and/or the just state. In the long run, state actors must adapt their own strategies to both perceived and material 'global realities', while other kinds of actors, economic and social, will play key roles too in restructuring the political arena.

HOW TRANSNATIONAL NEOPLURALISM WORKS

The central hypothesis entailed by the transnational neopluralist approach is that those actors who will be most effective at influencing and shaping politics and policy outcomes are those who possess the most transnationally interconnected resources, power and influence in a globalising world; that is, those who:

- perceive and define their goals, interests and values in international, transnational and translocal contexts, what might be called the ideational matrix;
- are able to build cross-border networks, coalitions and power bases among a range of potential allies and adversaries, or the political-sociological matrix; and
- are able to coordinate and organise their strategic action on a range of international, transnational and translocal scales in such a way as to pursue transnational policy agendas and institutional *bricolage*, the institutional matrix.

Globalisation in this sense not only constitutes a set of permissive conditions for the development of transnational pluralism and neopluralism; it also is itself increasingly constituted by the very political processes identified here. Jessop (2002) calls this aspect of political life 'strategic selectivity'. The strategies and tactics adopted by actors to cope with, control, manage and restructure political institutions, processes and practices determine what sort of globalisation we get. These strategies and tactics unfold at three levels.

The first level, the base, concerns such factors as: the distribution of resources in society; the kind of processes of production, distribution and exchange prevalent therein; the state of consciousness or the perception of interests, values and possibilities of the various individual and group actors; and the sorts of basic solidarities and alliances of a more political nature that emerge from all of these taken together.

The second level concerns what de Tocqueville called the character of intermediaries, or the openness or closure of political processes and coalitions that transform the raw material of the base into more specific political and economic resources within a narrower political process, sometimes called the power structure. How open or closed are elites? Do interests interact systematically with politicians and bureaucrats in a corporatist or neocorporatist fashion? What embedded alliances have evolved over time, and how open or flexible are they? Is public policy made by 'iron triangles', closed policy communities, wider policy networks, or transparent, competitive, pluralistic processes?

The third level concerns the structure of the institutional playing fields themselves, whether concentrated or diffused, unitary or fragmented, and the sorts of rules and practices that have evolved to coordinate different levels and/or pillars of the political system. Although some writers talk about the emergence of a global 'public sphere' (Germain 2001), the main thrust of the literature on globalisation is that globalisation makes such 'publicness' more problematic, thereby creating a need for a new politics of reshaping multi-level governance around various 'new architectures' that will recreate the 'public' either at a higher level or through a more complex network structure that crosses the public–private divide. Globalisation also involves the uneven multiplication of points of access and control. But shifting patterns with regard to economies of scale and scope do not provide conclusive evidence as to how this public–private hybrid will evolve.

Of course, multinational corporations hold a 'privileged position', as do financial market actors in an integrated, 24-hour global financial marketplace. But small and medium-sized enterprises also increasingly operate on a transnational scale, and it is even argued that globalisation is leading to a long-term Ricardian process of the equalisation of wages across the world (Kitching 2001). 'Old' groups have in many cases been able to parlay their existing resources into new profits by developing new investment strategies, such as restructuring and 'flexibilising' enterprises.

Perhaps more important, however, has been the emergence of 'new' groups of entrepreneurs, whether in countries that have traditionally encouraged such groups, such as the United States, or in those that have in the past suppressed or inhibited their activities, such as China and India (Baumol et al. 2007). The power of latent or potential groups or categories has been growing as well. Perhaps the most important of these is consumers, whose role in the allocation of resources has dramatically increased in contrast with that of more traditional producer groups. New categories of losers have been created as well, although in some cases these are groups that have already long been disenfranchised, suppressed or subsumed in authoritarian social hierarchies, such as tribes or clans. A dialectic of fractionalisation and reorganisation is therefore taking place that is analogous to the 'rearticulation of socio-political coalitions' that Spruyt (1994) identified with regard to the earlier transition from feudalism to the nation-state. The control of politics by pre-existing iron triangles, corporatist blocs or other dominant domestic policy coalitions is everywhere being challenged by diverse, more fluid coalitions at different levels of aggregation and organisation.

The single most important change in developed countries has probably been the growing predominance in economic policy-making of transnationally linked interest and value groups and the decline of nationally based, protectionist politics, despite the pressures of the current financial crisis. While it is always possible for geographically concentrated groups whose position is worsened by economic globalisation, such as workers displaced by import competition or by outsourcing, to organise resistance up to a point, the increasing imbrication of both small and large businesses in international markets, production chains and strategic alliances has tended to diffuse such effects more widely across the economy. Together with the combination of deskilling and reskilling of the workforce, and along with the flexibilisation of production methods and the long-term decline of national trade unions, it is becoming more and more difficult to organise politically effective resistance to globalisation as such.

Meanwhile, the restructuring of financial markets has drawn more sectors of the population into marketised finance, whether directly or indirectly through institutional investors such as pension funds, while traditional banking institutions have themselves become more marketised (Litan and Rauch 1998). In other words, the socio-political balance between what were once called 'national' and 'international' capitals has both blurred and shifted. There is little purely national capital left; a problem that has been exposed ever more starkly by the ongoing financial crisis. Indeed, recent attempts to reform financial regulation are increasingly facing obstacles stemming from the lack of a coherent transnational response.

The blurring of these traditional lines between what once formed the basis for the left–right divide at national level has switched the focus of group politics toward other kinds of linkages, whether the translocal restructuring of influence around multiculturalism and/or mutually exclusive but cross-border religious and ethnic identities, diaspora communities, world cities and the like, on the one hand, or the transnational/global reorganising of businesses and market structures around more extended networks, the development of epistemic communities of scientists and experts, the rapid growth of transnational advocacy coalitions and networks (non-governmental organisations, civil society, environmentalism, and so on), on the other.

'Left' and 'Right' are not opposites today, but are characterised by new forms of overlap and fragmentation. They are not only crosscut by convergent varieties of neo-liberalism – new 'valence issues' or common values held across the left–right divide (Campbell et al. 1960) – but are also divided within themselves over how to interpret, pursue and implement diverse goals. Long-term left/right blocs are giving way to mixed, complex and looser coalitions. Indeed, this process is running well ahead of consciousness of the implications of such changes, leading to political cognitive dissonance and, at times, to strange alliances that can distort preferences rather than effectively pursue them, as reflected in the support for the Republican Party in the United States by less-well-off 'social conservatives' since the Reagan era of the 1980s (Frank 2004).

Some dimensions of public and economic policy have increasingly become embedded and overdetermined: the reduction of barriers to trade and cross-border finance, the shift of government policy away from direct intervention toward regulation, the transformation of the state from the welfare state to the competition state, the expansion of mixed governance and the outsourcing of traditional governmental functions to private and/or mixed public–private providers, the flexibilisation of labour markets and so on (Cerny 2008). Across borders, more and more policy issue-areas are debated, competed over and reregulated in various mixed arenas of transnational regimes, global governance and transnational groups of private sector actors. In this context, actors themselves increasingly need to be able to operate on the basis of flexible response, shifting coalition-building and variable geometry in terms of both choosing short-term and/or long-term allies and developing policy strategies that involve the coordination of policy-making across borders.

The changing constellation of actors in a globalising world plus the increasing complexity of the structured field of action therefore creates opportunities for reactively and/or proactively restructuring the political playing field itself as particular problems and issues are confronted in practice, at all levels: micro, meso and macro. New patterns of influence and control are generated, from the fractionalisation and recasting of old alliances to the emergence and consolidation of new hierarchies, control mechanisms and unequal power structures. These processes of change will not be smooth or self-regulating. There will inevitably be the development of new inequalities, conflicts and destabilising events, interacting with old inequalities, conflicts and destabilising circumstances inherited from history, in a heady brew represented in its more extreme form by cross-border ethnic and religious conflicts and terrorism.

The evolution of globalisation, however, unlike Darwinist evolution, is not a random process of natural selection. It involves conscious actors, whether individuals or groups, who can interpret structural changes, multiple equilibria and opportunities creatively; change and refine their strategies; negotiate, bargain, build coalitions and mobilise their power resources in ongoing interactions with other actors; and – both in winning and in losing – affect and shape medium-term and long-term outcomes. I believe we are currently at a critical moment when alternative avenues of transformation are opening up. The globalisation process will continue to develop and expand, but it will be shaped more and more by the interaction of an expanding – pluralistic yet unequal – constellation of actors operating across increasingly diverse, 'multinucleated' transnational spaces, opening up a range of alternative outcomes and multiple equilibria.

OPPORTUNITIES AND CONSTRAINTS FOR TRANSNATIONAL NEOPLURALIST ACTORS

Because globalisation is most often seen as primarily an economic process, most of the literature on globalisation asserts that, by category, the key actors in terms of developing transnational linkages which have structurally transformational potential are economic actors. Of the main groups of economic actors, the least likely to take on the role of institutional entrepreneur thus far is the labour movement. Today, given the increasing significance of flexible manufacturing processes for large firms and the growing resort to flexible contracting and subcontracting among both large and small firms, including transnational strategic alliances, and other management practices, the potential collective power of labour has been greatly diminished. Nevertheless, the possibility of labour movements shifting their focus from collective industrial action of a Second Industrial Revolution type, to more widespread (if more fragmented) forms of social action in alliance with transnational social movements, may provide more potential for labour to participate in a transformative fashion in transnational structural change (Macdonald 2008; Evans 2007).

Another set of strategically situated economic actors includes owners and managers of multinational corporations. Whether at a localised, regionalised or genuinely transnational level, for example, owners and managers of high-technology firms large and small are often seen as taking on a collectively transformative role. Nevertheless, such actors are generally still dependent upon states and the state system for providing basic public goods, enforcing property rights and so on. In other words, the capacity of even the most cutting-edge multinational corporations, widely seen as the main 'carriers' of transnational capitalism since the 1970s, to live up to their structural potential is probably fairly limited at a strategic level.

Therefore probably the main group of economic actors that are most often seen as having the potential to become 'institutional entrepreneurs' on a wider scale are participants in global financial markets. Their (mainly indirect) ability to constrain macroeconomic and microeconomic policy, to engage in financial innovation, to seek out and exploit loopholes in regulatory systems, and to lobby politicians, plus their close links with government agencies which play an enforcement role, mean that the immediate transnational impact of their actions is evident both to them and, in turn, to other groups, including mass publics. This is particularly critical at the time of writing, as various political and institutional responses to the global financial crisis and recession have taken centre stage. Nevertheless, even financial market actors, especially investment bankers, are highly dependent on national governments for bailouts, recapitalisation and economic stimulus packages to promote recovery not only for national economies, but for the global economy too.

The main direct influence of economic transnationalisation in terms of actor behaviour will nevertheless be felt in two ways. First, we can identify the spread of an ideology of market globalisation through the mass media, the teaching of management in business schools, popular business literature (the 'airport bookshop' analysis of globalisation) and the like. Policy proposals around themes such as global financial regulation, in particular, are increasingly reinforcing this ideational trend in the current context of financial and economic crisis. This is sometimes referred to as 'intellectual capture'. Second, economic transnationalisation has had a wide-ranging indirect impact on other categories of agent. This is obvious in the case of political actors as they attempt to reconfigure forms of political authority to meet the challenge of transnationally rooted market failures and the demands of popular constituencies for the reassertion of political values, such as the 'public interest', in the face of the economic, social and indirect political power of economic actors. Neoliberal economic discourse is increasingly hegemonic despite the impact of, for example, the Occupy movement across the capitalist world.

The pressures on political actors, mainly state actors, to act as transnationalising institutional entrepreneurs are therefore likely to grow. Nevertheless, the capacity of state actors to act as institutional entrepreneurs in this way is extremely limited and uneven. At one level, of course, they can engage in institutional *bricolage*, attempting to empower and construct global governance regimes, in recent years most notably the Group of 20 (G20). Most of the time, however, such actors are bound by existing structural constraints, especially given the embeddedness of state institutions, which remain the main sources of legitimate political power despite trends of disaggregation and transnational policy innovation. At the same time, however, they suffer from a growing disillusionment with governments, politicians and bureaucrats generally. Traditional domestic pressure and interest groups, especially sectional pressure groups, are perceived less and less as parts of a positive-sum, pluralistic process of negotiating satisfactory compromises within the national political arena, and more and more as 'special interests', acting against the public interest, or free-riding on the collective actions of others.

With the splintering or disaggregation of the state, the crystallisation of more complex transnational opportunity structures and the development of transgovernmental networks, primarily domestically oriented interest and pressure groups are increasingly 'out of the loop', condemned to pursue politically problematic goals such as protectionism and open to marginalisation as obsolete representatives of the old left or the populist right. Transnationally linked interest groups are better able to use their influence at a number of different domestic and transnational levels at the same time, even playing state actors off against each other. At the same time, the capacity of political actors to act is still inextricably intertwined with the maintenance of state institutions and national discourses. Political actors are not about to try to deconstruct the state itself and design overtly supranational constitutional processes to replace it.

Paradoxically, in this situation, the overall weight of state interventionism in general tends to increase, often significantly, as states undertake enforcement functions on behalf of (especially) transnationally linked economic actors. The state is becoming a critical terrain of political conflict and coalition-building between forces favouring globalisation and those seeking to resist it. However, political actors will not be willing to undermine the state itself and thereby undermine the most significant single source of their own power. This fact is powerfully underpinned by the traditional role of the democratic state, wherein political actors have to be seen to be acting first and foremost on behalf of their domestic constituents if their actions are to be perceived as legitimate. When governmental leaders go home from major international meetings such as the

G20, they are immediately faced with such domestic pressures, making the transnationalisation of policy something that often has to be pursued surreptitiously and legitimated indirectly – or 'depoliticised' – especially when the light of crisis or disruptive change is shone on particular domestic sectors and interests (Roberts 2010).

Social actors are in a complex but potentially crucial position with regard to their capacity to reinforce and generate transnational structural change. There is emerging a new range of pressures from below. The proliferation of social actors on the international and transnational levels has been widely noted. The numbers and activities of such groups have grown in range, scale and scope. Some are more like traditional pressure or interest groups (Willetts 1982), adjusting the scale of their organisation to conform to the scale of problems facing particular categories of people in a global setting, especially sectional groups. However, more emphasis is placed today on the recent growth of transnational advocacy coalitions and social movements. In the first place, they specifically and intentionally target issues which are international and/or transnational in scope and pursue objectives which either are not being responded to, or cannot be effectively responded to, at national level because of the structural linkages among different levels and spaces (both territorial and virtual) and the constraints of domestic politics.

Another reason is that they can bring together and coordinate the actions of a range of coalition partners who would not normally be prepared to work closely with each other in a national setting for a variety of structural and historical reasons. Indeed, transnational cause groups can strategically 'whipsaw' policy-makers and sectional groups too, at local, national and international levels, going back and forth between applying traditional pressure-group tactics to government officials, organising local resistance and pursuing international or transnational media and other campaigns, as shown by a well-known case study of the Clayoquot and Great Bear rainforest campaigns in Canada (Krajnc 1999). In this context, then, social actors, mainly in the form of non-governmental organisations (NGOs) and 'new social movements', may be the most strategically situated actors of all and have the greatest potential leeway to imagine and to construct new forms of transnational structuration.

Nevertheless, there are still significant limitations to their scope and scale of action. The embeddedness of existing state and governmental institutions continues to constitute a major constraint. Furthermore, any kind of formal pluralist interest group must first of all focus on promoting its specific values and interests, often along the lines of what in the traditional interest and pressure group literature have been called 'single-issue pressure groups', rather than taking an overarching normative posture on the nature of the international system. Broad strategies based on the notion of a 'general (or public) interest' may actually dilute their activities and blunt their capacity to achieve their goals. Finally, they have limited and diverse bases of support. Therefore, there is unlikely to emerge a broad-based, public-interest-oriented 'global civil society' that would permit social actors to develop an overall structural impact of a kind that could transform the international system itself.

Transnational neopluralism can therefore be seen as creating new forms of feedback, path-dependency and the ratcheting-up of global politics and of globalisation itself. However, each set of actors faces not only promising opportunities, but also significant constraints in pursuing their group goals. Therefore, the result is not likely to be a coherent form of institutional selection, but rather an uneven process of politicking, bargaining, influence-seeking and the pursuit of self-interests in a classic neopluralist analytical context, veering between convergence and divergence, between a widening process of relatively stable horse-trading and bargaining on the one hand, and a neo-medieval 'durable disorder' (Minc 1993; Cerny 1998) on the other.

CONCLUSION: SCENARIOS OF CHANGE

Emerging patterns of transnational neopluralism can have a range of longer-term structural consequences for the governance of the international political economy and the international political economy of governance. This chapter has focused on underlying processes of change, but what kind of outcomes might be hypothesised to result from these processes? Given the increasingly open and nebulous character of system transformation, I have argued that the shape of the future will depend on the way strategically situated agents of all kinds shape that process, whether consciously or unwittingly. Given that there are multiple equilibria, only through a de facto process of structuration will a new structural pattern or patterns crystallise and consolidate. For this reason, I will outline four potential long-term scenarios of change.

The first scenario suggests that the structural developments outlined above do not entail a fundamental shift in the international system. From this perspective, globalising pressures merely trigger a range of adaptive behaviours on the part of strategically situated actors in each of the categories developed above who are still significantly constrained in their capacity to form effective transformative networks cutting across those categories. In such circumstances, it is likely that the key to understanding structural change (however limited) is most likely to rest with traditional political agents. Such agents, enmeshed in the deeply embedded nation-states system, would react to pressures for change by increasing the adaptive capacity of, for example, traditional forms of international cooperation, especially intergovernmental regimes, along with pressure on domestic actors to adapt as well.

At the same time, state-centric policy approaches – whether concerning environmental change, financial regulation, macroeconomic policy or social policy – will either permit emerging global challenges to be more or less effectively managed or at least provide sufficient 'band-aids' to prevent them spiralling out of control. These approaches include proponents of concepts such as the 'Beijing Consensus' and a turn to 'authoritarian liberalism' or 'state capitalism' (Bremmer 2010) in economic and development policy. This is what Hirst and Thompson (1999) called an 'inter-national' approach. I suggest that this approach has already been largely undermined by globalisation and transnationalisation. However, some, even many, of the most influential neopluralist interest groups may prefer this outcome, as it would allow them to expand their levers of control over key aspects of the globalisation process itself; for example, entrenching even further the clout of international financial market actors, leading to a growing de facto privatisation of international governance, while maintaining the ideological façade of democratic, or developmentalist, legitimacy and keeping domestic constituencies under control.

A second alternative scenario might be based on the predominance of transnational social movements and their ability to shape the agendas of other actors, both within and cutting across states. Two linked hypotheses can be raised again here: on the one hand, the development of a 'global civil society', based on common transnational norms and values, despite the limitations suggested earlier; and, on the other, the emergence of a cross-cutting genuine pluralism (or 'plurilateralism': Cerny 1993) as distinct from neo-pluralism. Held (1995), for example, has suggested some mixture of analogous develop-ments might well lead to the emergence of a transnational 'cosmopolitan democracy'. It might especially be the case that, should transnational social movements prove to be the predominant institutional entrepreneurs of the transnational structuration process, then a more complex, supranational process of 'mainstreaming' might well provide the glue for some form of de facto 'democratisation-without-the-state'. However, this remains a rosy scenario, an idealised state of affairs which it might be unwise to expect. Nevertheless, the crystallisation of a widening and deepening globalising rationality – what I have called a *raison du monde* – is likely to strengthen such value groups and permit them to increase their competitive and bargaining clout in a transnationalising, neopluralist governance process.

Third, however, the dominant image of transnationalisation and globalisation today, as suggested earlier, is still that of economic and business globalisation. Economic agents, through the transnational expansion of both markets and hierarchical (firm) structures and institutions, increasingly shape a range of key outcomes in terms of the allocation of both resources and values. Neoliberal ideology presents such developments as inevi-table; in Mrs Thatcher's famous phrase, 'There is no alternative'. Should transnational social movements prove more peripheral to the structuration process than a Polanyian 'double movement' might suggest, and should political actors and the state continue to act as promoters of globalisation and enforcement, then the governance structures of the twenty-first-century international system will be likely to reflect in a more direct and instrumental way than outlined in the first scenario the priorities of international capital. Without a world government or set of effective 'inter-national' (cooperative/ interstate) governance mechanisms, private economic regimes, such as internationalised financial markets and associations of transnationally active firms, large and small, are likely to shape the international system through their ability to channel investment flows and set cross-border prices for both capital and physical assets as well (Cerny 2000a). In this sense, the shape of the governance structures of such a system will merely mimic the structures of capital itself.

This raises a number of issues. In the first place, it has been suggested that capital cannot directly control society. Capitalists are concerned first and foremost with com-peting with each other, not with policing the system (which can eat up profits); and there is no collective mechanism, no 'ideal collective capitalist' to regulate the system in the interests of capital as a whole, other than the state (Holloway and Picciotto 1978). Nevertheless, indirect forms of control, for example through Gramscian cultural hegemony, may be more important than the state per se (especially in its limited guise as a 'nation-state'). Stephen Gill (1990, 2003, 2012), among others, sees the Trilateral Commission, the World Economic Forum (Davos) and other formal and informal networks among transnationally linked businessmen and their social and political allies as bearers of such an hegemony. Furthermore, it may be possible to hypothesise that, should transnational capital take a relatively holistic hegemonic form, then the interna-tional system of the twenty-first century will represent an even more truly liberal – or neoliberal – capitalist society in a way that no capitalist state has ever been able to.

Private sector-based mechanisms of control at a transnational level may indeed replace the state as a 'committee of the whole bourgeoisie'.

However, the crystallisation of other forms of international capital can also be envisaged, reflecting an unequal distribution of power or representation, perhaps among different economic sectors. For example, in the 1970s what essentially were cartels of hierarchically organised multinational corporations were thought by many on both sides of the political divide to be the form that international capital would take in the future. But in the world of dramatic international capital movements, especially since the 1980s, it is more often the financial markets which might be seen as exercising a 'sectoral hegemony' over the international system (Cerny 1994a, 1994b, 1996). In either case, however, any significant transfer of power or system control from political agents (via states) to economic agents would represent a fundamental change in the nature of governance.

A final scenario, which I have explored elsewhere (Cerny 1998, 2000a), is that exogenous pressures on the nation-state/states system, interacting with and exacerbating the tensions within that system, will cause that system to erode and weaken in key ways, but without providing enough in the way of structural resources to any category of agents (or combination of categories) to shape effectively the overarching transnational structuration process. In other words, no group or group of groups will be at the steering wheel of change in the international system, and competition between different groups will in turn undermine the capacity of any one of them to exercise such control. In such circumstances, the outcome might be what has been called 'neo-medievalism', or an 'archipelago' form of governance: a fluid, multilayered structure of overlapping and competing institutions, characterised by cultural flux, multiple and shifting identities and loyalties – a complex and uneven transnational multiculturalism – with different 'niches' at different levels for groups to focus their energies on. The medieval world was not a world of chaos; as noted above, it was a world of 'durable disorder' (Minc 1993).

Unless some coherent group of institutional entrepreneurs emerges to control and direct the process of transnational structuration, the medieval analogy may provide a better guide to understanding the international system in the twenty-first century than previous models involving states and the states system, both domestically and internationally. There is no reason in principle, after all, why 'governance' in this broad sense has to be tidy and logically coherent. The nation-state as such, and in particular the national industrial welfare state of the Second Industrial Revolution, may well be caught up in such wider, more complex webs, leading to increased uncertainty and possible disorder. At the same time, however, crosscutting neopluralist networks of economic, political and social agents would lead to an increase in the influence and power wielded by transnationally linked institutional entrepreneurs, some of whom will certainly attempt to transcend the limits of adaptive behaviour and develop new institutional strategies for transforming and reconstructing governance in this fluid, globalising world.

In each of these scenarios, then, we can see either an incremental or a much more rapid feedback process, based on actors' evolving strategies, behaviours and discourses, leading to a ratcheting-up of the globalisation process itself. However, the shape that process takes will differ depending on which actors – and coalitions of actors – develop the most influence and power to manipulate and mould particular outcomes within and across a range of critical issue-areas. The continuing development of international political economy as a transdisciplinary field is absolutely essential to our understanding of what is happening in the world today. Structural changes by themselves not only emerge from earlier processes of structuration, but are also ambiguous and amorphous in their ramifications for short-term events as well as for long-term transformation; they can lead to a range of alternative outcomes. IPE has been, and will continue to be, at the forefront of expanding our understanding of this process.

Therefore it is crucial that we analyse globalisation through competing paradigms, narratives and discourses. Unlike Darwinist evolution, globalisation is not a random process of selection. Nor can it be reduced pseudo-scientifically to predictable indicators by applying Ockham's razor to a data set, formula, equation or large-*n* study. It involves conscious actors, whether individuals or groups, who can interpret structural changes, alternative pathways and opportunities creatively and proactively; change and refine their strategies; negotiate, bargain, build coalitions and mobilise their power resources in ongoing interactions with other actors; and, both in winning and losing, affect and shape medium-term and long-term outcomes. Transnational neopluralism is a complex phenomenon that must be analysed and understood in its historical, structural and conjunctural complexity. However, by restoring political action and process to the centre of the stage, it may provide the best way to conceptualise the restructuring of governance during the rest of this century.

REFERENCES

Albert, Mathias, Barry Buzan and Michael Zürn (eds) (2013), *Bringing Sociology to IR: World Politics as Differentiation Theory*, Cambridge: Cambridge University Press.

Baumol, William J., Robert E. Litan and Carl J. Schramm (2007), *Good Capitalism, Bad Capitalism, and the Economics of Growth and Prosperity*, New Haven, CT: Yale University Press.

Bendix, Reinhard (1964), *Nation-Building and Citizenship*, Garden City, NY: Anchor Books.

Bentley, Arthur F. (1908), *The Process of Government*, Chicago, IL: University of Chicago Press.

Bremmer, Ian (2010), *The End of the Free Market: Who Wins the War Between States and Corporations?*, New York: Portfolio/Penguin.

Campbell, Angus, Philip E. Converse, Warren E. Miller and Donald E. Stokes (1960), *The American Voter*, New York: John Wiley & Sons.

Castells, Manuel (1996), *The Rise of the Network Society*, Oxford, UK and Cambridge, MA, USA: Blackwell.

Cerny, Philip G. (1990), *The Changing Architecture of Politics: Structure, Agency and the Future of the State*, London: Sage.

Cerny, Philip G. (1993), 'Plurilateralism: structural differentiation and functional conflict in the post-Cold War world order', *Millennium: Journal of International Studies*, **22** (1), 27–51.

Cerny, Philip G. (1994a), 'The infrastructure of the infrastructure? Toward "embedded financial orthodoxy" in the international political economy', in Barry Gills and Ronen Palan (eds), *Transcending the State–Global Divide: The Neostructuralist Agenda in International Relations*, Boulder, CO: Lynne Rienner, pp. 223–49.

Cerny, P.G. (1994b), 'The dynamics of financial globalization: technology, market structure and policy response', *Policy Sciences*, **27** (4), pp. 319–42.

Cerny, P.G. (1996), 'International finance and the erosion of state policy capacity', in Philip Gummett (ed.), *Globalization and Public Policy*, Cheltenham, UK and Brookfield, VT, USA: Edward Elgar, pp. 83–104.

Cerny, Philip G. (1998), 'Neomedievalism, civil wars and the new security dilemma: globalization as durable disorder', *Civil Wars*, **1** (1), 36–64.

Cerny, Philip G. (1999), 'Globalization, governance and complexity', in Aseem Prakash and Jeffrey A. Hart (eds), *Globalization and Governance*, London: Routledge, pp. 188–212.

Cerny, Philip G. (2000a), 'Political agency in a globalizing world: toward a structurational approach', *European Journal of International Relations*, **6** (4), 435–64.

Cerny, Philip G. (2000b), 'Restructuring the political arena: globalization and the paradoxes of the competition state', in Randall D. Germain (ed.), *Globalization and Its Critics: Perspectives from Political Economy*, London: Macmillan, pp. 117–38.

Cerny, Philip G. (2008), 'Embedding neoliberalism: the evolution of a hegemonic paradigm', *Journal of International Trade and Diplomacy*, **2** (1), 1–46.

Cerny, Philip G. (2010a), 'The competition state today: from *raison d'état* to *raison du monde*', *Policy Studies*, **4** (1), 5–21.

Cerny, Philip G. (2010b), *Rethinking World Politics: A Theory of Transnational Neopluralism*, New York, USA and Oxford, UK: Oxford University Press.

Cerny, Philip G. (2012), 'Globalization and the transformation of power', in Mark Haugaard and Kevin Ryan (eds), *Political Power: The Development of the Field*, Leverkusen/Opladen: Barbara Budrich for the International Political Science Association, Research Committee No. 36, Political Power, pp. 185–214.

Cerny, Philip G. (2013), 'Functional differentiation, globalization and the new transnational neopluralism', in Mathias Albert, Barry Buzan and Michael Zürn (eds), *Bringing Sociology to International Relations: World Politics as Differentiation Theory*, Cambridge: Cambridge University Press, pp. 205–27.

Cerny, Philip G. (forthcoming), 'Rethinking financial regulation: risk, club goods, and regulatory fatigue', in Thomas Oatley (ed.), *Handbook on International Monetary Relations*, Cheltenham, UK and Northampton, MA, USA: Edward Elgar.

Coser, Lewis A. (1956), *The Functions of Social Conflict*, London: Routledge & Kegan Paul.

Crozier, Michel and Erhard Friedberg (1977), *L'Acteur et le système: les contraintes de l'action collective*, Paris: Éditions du Seuil.

Cutler, A. Claire, Virginia Haufler and Tony Porter (eds) (1999), *Private Authority and International Affairs*, Albany, NY: State University of New York Press.

Dahl, Robert A. (1961), *Who Governs? Democracy and Power in the American City*, New Haven, CT: Yale University Press.

Durkheim, Emile (1893 [1933]), *The Division of Labor in Society*, trans. George Simpson, New York: Free Press, original French edition 1893.

Evans, Mark G. (2005), *Policy Transfer in Global Perspective*, Aldershot: Ashgate.

Evans, Peter (2007), 'Is it labor's turn to globalize? 21st century challenges and opportunities', paper presented to the Democracy and Development Seminar, Princeton Institute for International and Regional Studies, 24 October.

Frank, Thomas (2004), *What's the Matter with Kansas? How Conservatives Won the Heart of America*, New York: Henry Holt.

Germain, Randall D. (2001), 'Global financial governance and the problem of inclusion', *Global Governance*, **7** (4), 411–26.

Gill, Stephen (1990), *American Hegemony and the Trilateral Commission*, Cambridge: Cambridge University Press.

Gill, Stephen (2003), *Power and Resistance in the New World Order*, London: Palgrave Macmillan.

Gill, Stephen (2012), 'Towards a radical concept of praxis: imperial "common sense" versus the post-modern prince', *Millennium: Journal of International Studies*, **40** (3), 505–24.

Goldstein, Joshua S. (2011), *Winning the War on War: The Decline of Armed Conflict Worldwide*, New York: Dutton.

Hall, Rodney Bruce and Thomas J. Biersteker (eds) (2003), *The Emergence of Private Authority in Global Governance*, Cambridge: Cambridge University Press.

Held, David (1995), *Democracy and the Global Order: From the Modern State to Cosmopolitan Governance*, Cambridge: Polity Press.

Henderson, Jeffrey, Peter Dicken, Martin Hess, Neil Coe and Henry Wai-Chung Yeung (2002), 'Global production networks and the analysis of economic development', *Review of International Political Economy*, **9** (3), 436–64.

Higgott, Richard, Geoffrey R.D. Underhill and Andreas Bieler (eds) (1999), *Non-State Actors and Authority in the Global System*, London: Routledge.

Hirst, Paul and Grahame Thompson (1999), *Globalization in Question: The International Political Economy and the Possibilities of Governance*, 2nd edition, Cambridge: Polity Press.

Hobson, John M. and Leonard Seabrooke (eds) (2007), *Everyday Politics of the World Economy*, Cambridge: Cambridge University Press.

Hollis, Martin and Steve Smith (1990), *Explaining and Understanding International Relations*, Oxford: Clarendon Press.

Holloway, John and Sol Picciotto (eds) (1978), *State and Capital: A Marxist Debate*, London: Edward Arnold.

Horsfall, Daniel (2011), 'From competition state to competition states? An empirical exploration', PhD thesis, Department of Social Policy, University of York.

Jessop, Bob (1997), 'The future of the national state: erosion or reorganisation? Reflections on the West European case', paper presented at a conference on Globalisation: Critical Perspectives, University of Birmingham, 14–16 March.

Jessop, Bob (2002), *The Future of the Capitalist State*, Cambridge: Polity Press.

Kahler, Miles and David A. Lake (eds) (2003), *Governance in a Global Economy: Political Authority in Transition*, Princeton, NJ: Princeton University Press.

Kanter, Rosabeth Moss (1985), *The Change Masters: Innovation and Entrepreneurship in the American Corporation*, Glencoe, IL: Free Press.

Keck, Margaret E. and Kathryn Sikkink (1998), *Activists Beyond Borders: Advocacy Networks in International Politics*, Ithaca, NY: Cornell University Press.

Key, V.O., Jr (1953), *Politics, Parties, and Pressure Groups*, New York: Thomas Y. Crowell.

Kitching, Gavin (2001), *Seeking Social Justice Through Globalization: Escaping a Nationalist Perspective*, State College, PA: Pennsylvania State University Press.

Kotkin, Joel (1992), *Tribes: How Race, Religion and Identity Determine Success in the New Global Economy*, New York: Random House.

Krajnc, Anita (1999), 'Learning in British Columbia's Clayoquot and Great Bear rainforest campaigns: from public pressure to global civic politics', paper presented at the Annual Convention of the International Studies Association, Washington, DC, 16–20 February.

Lake, David A. (1999), 'Global governance: a relational contracting approach', in Aseem Prakash and Jeffrey A. Hart (eds), *Globalization and Governance*, London: Routledge, pp. 31–53.

Lindblom, Charles E. (1977), *Politics and Markets: The World's Political Economic Systems*, New York: Basic Books.

Litan, Robert E. and Jonathan Rauch (1998), *American Finance for the 21st Century*, Washington, DC: Brookings Institution Press.

Lowi, Theodore J. (1964), 'American business, public policy, case studies, and political theory', *World Politics*, **16** (4), 677–715.

Macdonald, Kate (2008), 'Global democracy for a partially joined-up world: toward a multi-level system of power, allegiance and democratic governance?', unpublished paper, London School of Economics and Political Science.

Machin, Howard and Vincent Wright (eds) (1985), *Economic Policy and Policy-Making under the Mitterrand Presidency, 1981–84*, London: Pinter.

McFarland, Andrew S. (2004), *Neopluralism: The Evolution of Political Process Theory*, Lawrence, KS: University of Kansas Press.

McLuhan, Marshall (1964), *Understanding Media: The Extensions of Man*, New York: McGraw Hill.

Minc, Alain (1993), *Le nouveau Moyen Âge*, Paris: Gallimard.

Mügge, Daniel (2006), 'Private–public puzzles: inter-firm competition and transnational private regulation', *New Political Economy*, **11** (2), 177–200.

Ohmae, Kenichi (1990), *The Borderless World: Power and Strategy in the Interlinked Economy*, Pensacola, FL: Ballinger Publishing.

Ostrom, Vincent, Charles M. Tiebout and Robert Warren (1961), 'The organization of government in metropolitan areas: a theoretical inquiry', *American Political Science Review*, **55** (3), 831–42.

Pinker, Steven (2011), *The Better Angels of Our Nature: The Decline of Violence in History and Its Causes*, New York: Viking Penguin.

Rhodes, R.A.W. (1996), 'The new governance: governing without government', *Political Studies*, **44** (4), 652–67.

Roberts, Alasdair (2010), *The Logic of Discipline: Global Capitalism and the Architecture of Government*, New York, USA and Oxford, UK: Oxford University Press.

Ronit, Karsten and Volker Schneider (eds) (2000), *Private Organizations in Global Politics*, London: Routledge.

Simmel, Georg (1922 [1955]), *Conflict and the Web of Group Affiliations*, New York: Free Press.

Slaughter, Anne-Marie (2004), *A New World Order*, Princeton, NJ: Princeton University Press.

Spruyt, Hendrik (1994), *The Sovereign State and Its Competitors: An Analysis of Systems Change*, Princeton, NJ: Princeton University Press.

Tarrow, Sidney (2005), *The New Transnational Activism*, Cambridge: Cambridge University Press.

Thompson, Graeme, Jennifer Frances, Rosalind Levačić and Jeremy C. Mitchell (eds) (1991), *Markets, Hierarchies and Networks: The Coordination of Social Life*, London, UK and Thousand Oaks, CA, USA: Sage.

Truman, David B. (1951), *The Governmental Process*, New York: Alfred A. Knopf.

Walker, R.B.J. (1993), *Inside/Outside: International Relations as Political Theory*, Cambridge: Cambridge University Press.

Waltz, Kenneth (1979), *Theory of International Politics*, Reading, MA: Addison-Wesley.

Willetts, Peter (ed.) (1982), *Pressure Groups in the Global System: The Transnational Relations of Issue-Orientated Non-Governmental Organizations*, New York: St Martin's Press.

Znaniecki, Florian (1952 [1973]), *Modern Nationalities: A Sociological Study*, Westport, CT: Greenwood Press.

4 The ethical dimensions of global governance
James Brassett

Global governance has steadily emerged as *the* background concept for thinking about a range of issues and practices in global politics. From finance to trade, environmental issues to health, and many pressing social concerns besides, global governance serves as a convenient – and constitutive – signifier for contemporary politics. Despite several rounds of well-weighted critiques of the content, purpose and form of global governance, the idea and practice has grown and adapted.

Part of the reason for this emergence, at least, is expedience. State-level policy-makers have encouraged their electorates to view a range of difficult issues as a – or the – primary concern of global governance. Witness the resurgence of the Group of 20 (G20) and the International Monetary Fund (IMF) during the period of the global financial crisis that began in the late 2000s. Equally, a number of international institutions have sought, often in times of crisis, to foster agendas of good governance on a global scale, whereby (apparently) neutral ideas such as transparency, human capital and community have become a key focus (as opposed to, say, domination via class, race or gender structures). In this way, the 'global' in global governance is always and already conceived as both spanning and ordering relations between levels.

The idea of global governance meets a widespread and pressing sense that globalisation entails certain political requirements for coordination, authority and legitimacy in complex and interconnected social contexts. To wit, it can be argued, complex times call for new ideological tropes and institutional buttresses to sustain liberal political economies (and their elites) into the next period. On this view, as the Introduction to this volume fairly underlines, global governance is part of a larger structural and ideological context that seeks to translate one set of power arrangements (neoliberalism, US-centrism, financialisation) into another (multi-polarity, new rising powers, and a blur between public and private forms of capitalism). For these reasons international political economy (IPE) stands at the forefront of disciplinary approaches to global governance that emphasise the related concerns of power and, indeed, ethics. How should the changing nature of global governance be addressed? What values might be fostered?

Critical IPE, in particular, is well placed to examine questions of power, with its emphasis on history, structure and agency, and value(s). It places in question the unchecked normative claims of global governance practitioners themselves, and it carries an ethics of engagement that goes beyond traditional academic imperatives to secure methods and maintain deliverables. Asking the question of power in global governance is at once a critique of existing arrangements and an anticipation of how they might be thought changeable.

If global governance is being constructed around – even in the name of – a particular set of power relations, it surely begs the critical question of who or what is left out. Indeed, I would argue, the animating insight of a broad spectrum of critical approaches to global governance is implicitly ethical, asking questions of justice, inclusion, reform (albeit from different perspectives). However, while critical IPE might be content with the 'implicit ethics' of analysing power-relations-as-contingent, there has been somewhat less emphasis on outlining a substantive ethical agenda to build into global governance. While the critical IPE of global governance may be implicitly ethical, to date there has been a paucity of explicit engagement with ethics or ethical theory. Important exceptions notwithstanding (Buchanan and Keohane, 2006; Murphy, 2000), the tendency has been to accept the disciplinary division whereby ethics is seen as a discrete realm of reflective thought that might supply reasons, but is largely irrelevant in terms of the hard-nosed political realities with which IPE is better acquainted.

Unfortunately, this silence can work both ways. While IPE has generally been slow to incorporate or engage with the insights of ethical theorists, it can be observed that political theorists – especially those of a Rawlsian persuasion – have sometimes 'assumed out of existence' the relevance of any structural context to theory or theorising. In this sense, a dialogue of the deaf can sometimes ensue (Higgott 2007).

For all its interdisciplinary intent, IPE has sidestepped a range of foundational questions over the content of terms such as 'justice' and 'democracy', even while such debates infuse the journals of cognate disciplines such as international relations (IR) and (even) economics. The tone seems to be that instances of injustice are pervasive and so ethical agendas should be understood as straightforward attempts to realise the amelioration of power relations (Murphy and Tooze 1996). Thus, a commitment to ethics – in an IPE sense – has tended to involve a commitment to the re-imagination of broadly social democratic objectives, often with a focal point such as global civil society or (currently) Occupy, and a theoretical buttress such as Keynes, Gramsci or Polanyi.

This is all good and well meaning, no doubt, but there is little attention paid to developing ethics as an open question, where multiple perspectives might be brought to bear, in a context where responsibility might entail the possibility of 'not acting' (Brassett and Holmes 2010). Moreover, without some level of acquaintance with the development and nuance of debates in ethical theory, IPE might overlook an emerging set of currents that contribute to and engage with the legitimation strategies of global governance per se. On this view, the emerging nexus between cosmopolitan, deliberative and/or Rawlsian theorists of global governance and the practitioners, institutions and activists they study is important and as yet barely articulated in the critical literature.

Vibrant debates on legitimacy, inclusion and global institutional reform are being conducted in elite institutions, funded by benefactors who claim global recognition. Prominent foundations, such as Carnegie and Ford, are supporting prominent global academics and producing policy relevant, ethically oriented publications such as *Ethics and International Affairs* and *Global Policy* in ways that suggest new ways of thinking about political engagement in IPE. For these reasons the subject of global governance is not only a question of ethics – where ethics is considered a critical device – but also, at the same time, a project that ethical theorists are centrally shaping in ways that IPE should reflect upon.

The aim of this chapter is to provide an overview, critique and reconstruction of the idea of global governance as an ethical question. While the argument is situated primarily within the disciplinary debates and literature of IPE, it nevertheless seeks to draw out a way of thinking about global governance that places it within, or at least renders the concept susceptible to, broader questions of ethics and 'the ethical'. In order to fix ideas, ethical questions might focus on a range of values or agendas such as justice, fairness, inclusion, equality or diversity. More critically, however, the idea of the ethical can be concerned with a deeper range of (related) ontological questions: who or what is left out of global governance? How are particular subjects of global governance thought and produced? And how might they be thought otherwise?

My central argument is that a more explicit (and open) discussion of ethics and ethical theory presents the chance to reinvigorate the climate of theoretical debate in IPE. Accepting the central tenets of critical IPE, a praxeological intent can be woven to a more democratic and democratising ethos of conversation (Brassett 2009). On this view, we might rethink the contours of political engagement as less about juxtaposing an 'ethical good' with a 'political bad', and more about the working-through of ethical possibilities and limits in creative fashion. A turn to ethics is not so much a departure from broader debates in the political economy of global governance as a working-through of the insights and intuitions of critical IPE, to foster a view of IPE as a continuous, open and reflective engagement on the terms of political possibility.

This argument is developed over three sections that seek to reflect on the emergence of a discourse of ethical global governance. The first section addresses a range of political theory-oriented approaches to global governance including liberal cosmopolitan and deliberative approaches, as well as radical democratic work. The next section then discusses a more performative set of propositions about ethical governance associated with the work of post-structural scholars. Performative arguments are sometimes set in ambiguous tension with the idea of ethics, since they can seem to preclude the very possibility of agency or judgement. The discussion highlights a number of reasons why we might move beyond such misconceptions. Finally, the third section makes the case for a pragmatic reconciliation between approaches by identifying a range of ways of thinking about critical political engagement beyond the fantasy of a singular and final answer on 'global ethics' (Brassett and Bulley 2007).

ETHICS AND GLOBAL GOVERNANCE

Recent years have seen a shift in the orientation of political theorists to address their subject in global perspective. From the publication of Charles Beitz's *Political Theory and International Relations* (1979), a trickle of articles and books has now turned into a torrent of publications that deal with what might be called 'global political theory' (*inter alia* Caney 2005; Cochran 1999; Habermas 2001; Held 1995; Held and McGrew 2002; Pogge 2002). While the ethical questions under consideration have remained fairly constant throughout – justice, democracy and equality – the ontology of global political theory has shifted somewhat. Previous discussions centred upon the question of 'international ethics', the stuff of which was states, their interrelations, and specific duties towards 'the poor'. Recent discussions emphasise global governance, global civil society, 'the global poor', and so on.

These (more traditional) political theoretic approaches to the ethics of global governance tend to proceed by highlighting a number of analytical dilemmas and output failures. The emphasis is very much on the reasoning that allows for particular forms of ethical judgement to be made. So, in analytical terms, a range of theorists have sought to identify how emerging practices of global governance constitute a direct challenge to (apparently) settled patterns of ethics; namely, sovereign accountability, popular democracy, and some association between authority and justice. This direction is important to consider because it seems to suggest that political theorists are acutely aware of the difficulty entailed in addressing such a broad question as 'ethical global governance'. Even if justice is an intensely contested concept , this should not distract from the equally difficult issue of whether and how structures of authority exist to uphold it (or not) on a global scale.

In terms of the output failings of global governance, it should also be noted that these are closely related to the analytical dilemmas discussed above. If structures of accountability and authority remain unclear then a question is permanently raised about what might be expected from various bodies and institutions. Witness the current and somewhat perplexing discussion over economic responsibility in the European Union (EU). Does responsibility lie with the member-states, the European Commission, the European Central Bank, or (as some might hope) the people? In situations of complex interdependence, pooled sovereignty and (seemingly) multiple channels of accountability, it is natural to assume that somebody, somewhere, will question the performance of a given element of global governance.

However, the output failings of global governance are more directly couched in terms of a number of common empirical issues. Statistics on wealth distribution, poverty-related mortality rates, intractable physical dilemmas such as environmental degradation, nuclear missile proliferation, and so forth, are the common agenda of global governance. That so many of these statistics point to ongoing failure means that, even in its emergent ambiguity, global governance is often tasked with 'solving the world's problems', an intuition that will be unpacked in subsequent sections.

Taking these points together – the analytical dilemma and the output failings – a common approach is to posit a framework of ethics and global governance, whereby both terms can be taken as settled ontological categories. Thus, it is argued, emerging practices of global governance pose a challenge to traditional patterns of ethical relations, while ethics, per se, provides a set of theoretical and affective resources for developing a critical account of global governance. While I want to problematise this effort to first separate and then reunite ethics and governance, especially in the next section, the pragmatist element of my argument would underline that such feats of conceptual narrative are, themselves, constitutive discourses in the world we engage, and therefore ripe for consideration.

Three broadly interrelated agendas of ethical global governance can be usefully engaged: cosmopolitanism, deliberative global governance and postmodern global democracy. What follows here draws on the work of key exponents of these various agendas – especially David Held, John Dryzek and Jan Aart Scholte – but cognate thinkers or theories will be flagged. While each of these approaches is clearly orientated towards the imagination of new forms of democracy, one of the strengths of these approaches is that their agendas necessarily overlap with, or allow space for, the development of other ethical values such as liberty, equality and diversity. This reflexive conception of ethics as plural, emergent, evolving, is a salutatory reminder that IPE finds itself within (and among) a host of academic agendas that never accepted the positivist separations between observer and observed, fact and value, ideas and reality;

agendas which have similarly sought to think of politics as a contingent and contestable process.

Cosmopolitanism

Cosmopolitanism has a long and venerable history in the philosophy of ethics. However, cosmopolitan thinkers are adept at updating and reorienting cosmopolitan intuitions for different historical periods. Thus, a cosmopolitan approach to global governance can be understood through the articulation of some straightforward and fairly direct assumptions. This brief section will introduce the basic concept of cosmopolitanism as a point of entry for consideration of further ethical approaches.

For cosmopolitans, ongoing changes in the extent and intensity of global social relations provoke a set of questions to state-centric political theory. How can national systems of social welfare survive when large global capital is in a position of unfettered mobility? Why do we retain national systems of accountability and legitimacy when it is increasingly global institutions that make the decisions? In this sense, a cosmopolitan approach works very much in the frame of ethics and global governance, using an empirical observation: the relative failure of governance (both national and global) to articulate a set of ethical responses. Often considered to be one of the foremost theorists of global democracy, David Held (1995: 21) expresses the dilemma as one which actually unravels previous conceptions of the congruence between territory, community and political legitimacy, and brings into question the very possibility of democracy.

As substantial areas of human activity are progressively organised on a global level, the fate of democracy and of the independent democratic nation-state, in particular, is fraught with difficulty. In this context, the meaning and place of democratic politics, and of the contending models of democracy, have to be rethought in relation to overlapping local, national, regional and global structures and processes.

Thus, cosmopolitanism pitches as a theory of global governance per se, seeking to render such processes according to some universal logic of ethics, be it accountability, representation or justice. The response is to articulate new forms of multi-level governance that promote or embody one of these values; in Held's case, maximal accountability and the inclusion of as many relevant actors as possible. For his part, Held has advocated a form of 'double democratisation' whereby democracy is interpreted not just as the deepening of democratic relations and practices within the national polity, but also the expansion of democratic practice at regional and global levels.

In this way, a stronger normative edge is brought to bear on the definition of global governance, whereby global governance can be rethought in critical liberal terms as something that should be accountable to law and affected democratic publics. While the cosmopolitan approach to global governance experienced a long period of popularity in the Industrial Relations (IR) textbooks, and a modest degree of recognition in sympathetic policy circles, it is also fair to say that a sustained period of critical reflection has dented some of its early strength. Two points stand out.

Firstly, the ambitious nature of the cosmopolitan argument has sometimes been portrayed as a weakness. Set against the traditional gamut of IR concerns for order, power and security, cosmopolitanism can sometimes appear slightly naive. Indeed, it is not uncommon for IR to render the pedagogy of cosmopolitanism within the broader – and rather hackneyed – dichotomy of idealism versus realism (Brassett 2008). On this view, for all its engagement with contemporary policy issues, cosmopolitanism sometimes gets placed in a category of utopian thought: well meaning, but unlikely.

Secondly, and perhaps more persuasively in critical terms, a number of Marxist-inspired thinkers have pointed to the curious slippage that occurs between ethics and market logic in cosmopolitan arguments (Jahn 2005). It is argued that a cosmopolitan approach, which begins as quite critical of the way globalisation has usurped the legitimacy of the nation-state, ultimately yields a perspective that endorses global capitalism with minor institutional amendments. Not only does the cosmopolitan argument risk failing to critique the excessive practices of global capitalism, on this view, but it may also risk entrenching them by contributing to the ideological legitimacy of global governance. At the very least, it can be suggested that the political agenda of cosmopolitan global governance requires unpacking to question how and why the concept of 'the global' is too often conflated with (apparently natural) market logics of spatial scale.

Despite this specific sociology of the cosmopolitan approach to global governance, it has clearly sketched a number of new horizons for thinking about global ethics. Indeed, it is worth noting that the cosmopolitan approach has overlapped with and energised a number of different currents within democratic thought in the global perspective. While such approaches would not necessarily claim the label 'cosmopolitan' for their work, it is clear that they nevertheless echo its central concerns and normative ambitions. Assumptions that are central to cosmopolitan thought – a global scale for ethics, the challenge of inclusion in global perspective and the question of founding the legitimacy of global governance – have formed a central problematic for subsequent authors to address.

Deliberative Global Governance

Despite the radical analytical ambitions of the cosmopolitan approach, critics have been drawn to stress the liberal, perhaps conservative, nature of its political ontology. In particular, the unchecked celebration of (multi-level) representative democracy has caused concern to a range of thinkers concerned with the substance of political deliberation. By this is meant that democracy is not just about allowing for choice, but also about the nature of the reasons provided. Is deliberation reasonable? Is deliberation ethical?

A range of approaches have sought to construct an image of deliberative global governance (Smith and Brassett 2008). Deliberation provides an interesting route into global governance because, on some interpretations, the 'ethic of deliberation' must be tied to the contingent and reflexive question of what global governance 'is' and what it 'should be'. Hence a number of authors associated with the idea of 'deliberative systems' have sought to develop an approach to deliberation that privileges the nature of discourse, rather than the site of discourse (Parkinson and Mansbridge 2012). For instance, while someone like John Dryzek works in a similar vein to cosmopolitanism, he holds back from essentialist arguments about what global governance 'is', precisely in order to think about how we might talk about it differently.

Dryzek identifies 'discourses' as the object of deliberation, and global civil society as the principal agent of deliberation. For him, deliberation is important because it potentially allows a means whereby agents can reflexively challenge the range of discourses that order and structure complex processes of global governance. As such, the political contestability of global governance is foregrounded. In line with cosmopolitanism, Dryzek (2006: 161) argues, 'democratic governance in the international system must . . . look very different from democratic government within states'. However, his primary concern is with the emergence of the concept of governance, per se, rather than any primary or exclusive association between globalisation and ethics.

Dryzek (1999: 33) accepts the idea that the international realm is best understood as embodying 'governance without government' (cf. Czempiel and Rosenau 1992). This means that it lacks the stable hierarchical structures or 'sovereign centres of power' that can be found in domestic democratic regimes. In the absence of this sort of 'government' the international order relies more on 'governance', defined as 'the creation and maintenance of order and the resolution of joint problems in the absence of . . . binding decision structures' (Dryzek 2000: 120). Against cosmopolitan arguments, he criticises the aspiration to recreate institutions of the nation-state at transnational and global levels, suggesting that such a move would merely replicate the vicissitudes of those institutions on a much larger scale: specifically problems of 'constitutional excess' and 'excessive administration'. Indeed, I find it to be an ongoing irony of global ethics that so many, often radical, political theorists get drawn into the celebration of what are essentially large bureaucracies.

Instead, and drawing on a novel interpretation of deliberative or 'discursive' democracy as a basis for his radical reformist agenda, Dryzek emphasises the key role that discourses play in shaping governance in the international system. He defines a discourse as 'a shared set of concepts, categories, and ideas that provide its adherents with a framework for making sense of situations, embodying judgements, assumptions, capabilities, dispositions, and intentions. It provides basic terms for analysis, debates, agreements, and disagreements' (Dryzek 2006: 1). Discourses can include examples such as market liberalism, globalisation, realism, sustainable development and human rights, but are not limited in terms of substance and the potential for people to contribute and speak.

On this view, it is argued that global policy agendas are somehow the product of contests between competing discourses. So, for instance, 'market liberalism' might be understood as a consequential discourse that is often criticised and contested by the 'anti-globalisation' discourse. The policy output of such products might then be some form of augmented, 'humanised' discourse, such as embedded liberalism or the Post-Washington Consensus (Dryzek 2006). Therefore, Dryzek argues, we should focus on democratising such discourses by opening them up to deliberative scrutiny: asking questions, providing reasons, hearing further critiques, and so on.

It is here perhaps that deliberation connects up most clearly with the concerns of critical IPE, oriented as it is to the de-naturalisation of the prevailing discourses of the market. If the focus of ethics could be the kinds of reasoning that underpin the political economy of governance, then the assumed naturalism of much that passes as global governance could form a point of entry for alternative viewpoints and possibilities.

Indeed, deliberative theorists contrast discursive democracy with those that emphasise high-level deliberation within institutions or formal processes of negotiation, such as the kind of deliberation that takes place between state representatives or within institutions such as the IMF or the World Trade Organization (WTO). Against this approach, Dryzek (2006: 27) 'looks to the potential for diffuse communication in the public sphere that generates public opinion that can in turn exercise political influence'. His hope is that civil society activists and non-governmental organisations can act as bearers of democratic values within transnational public spheres. They can perform this function insofar as they are able to criticise, contest and change the terms of dominant discourses or the balance of power between competing discourses. Civil society actors should contest discourses in such a way that they increase the scope for 'reflexive action' (Dryzek 2006: 115). This means that they educate publics about the nature and terms of dominant discourses, reveal their contingent and changeable nature, and encourage a process of critical reflection on their adequacy and acceptability.

In comparison to the model of cosmopolitan global governance, it is clear that a deliberative approach provides a more complex and nuanced picture of ethics and global governance. Instead of affirming existing market-centric logics of global governance, a deliberative approach is oriented towards the ongoing contest of such discourses. Rather than assume the site and substance of global ethics, it focuses attention toward the contingent exploration, negotiation and contest of global governance (its shape and practices). Indeed, many elements of deliberative global governance echo growing trends within critical IPE to celebrate the capacity of resistance by global civil society activists to shape the terms of political discourse in counter-hegemonic terms. However, as with all models of ethics and global governance – indeed all models of thought – there are a number of limitations which it might be instructive to reflect upon.

Firstly, the deliberative approach to global governance is somewhat nascent. Its empirical grounding is currently emerging and, while it is popular among political theorists, it is only just beginning to make headway into the fields of IR and IPE, which can perhaps claim a greater interest in the concept of global governance than most disciplines. Could one way forward be to orient deliberative approaches to the kinds of substantive debates about IPE embodied in, say, the discussions and publications of groups such as Occupy? Certainly, the capacity of reflexive action in IPE generated by such groups is palpable as they question the content and purpose of financial markets. Such dialogues are important and, as yet, barely articulated. The importance of uniting IPE expertise in global governance scholarship with the ethical ambitions of deliberative theorists seems an obvious goal in light of the proliferation of discourses on the ethics of financial governance.

Secondly, and anticipating the move to postmodern global democracies below, for all that a deliberative approach decentres our ontology of global governance, the same cannot be said for its understanding of deliberative ethics. As has been noted (Patomaki 2003; Vaughan-Williams 2007), when claiming to speak about a 'global' ethics, it is sadly ironic how so many agendas emerge from such a specific, Western tradition of political theory. Deliberative reasoning, it can be fairly noted, places heavy demands on the nature of speaking and listening that are both potentially exclusionary and, when woven to basic values of pluralism, might risk inscribing imperial fallacies of advanced/ reasonable versus backward/emotional–spiritual–sexual. It is notable, at least, how so many discussions of global ethics are conducted by Western, white, bourgeois, male scholars in privileged Anglophone universities, while the 'stuff' of global ethics is often carried out at several steps removed, both socially and geographically.

Postmodern Global Democracies

Following on from the critiques of cosmopolitanism and deliberative global govern-ance, there is a strain of scholarship that locates itself within widespread debates over the contestability of ethics and global governance. For his part, Jan Aart Scholte argues that cosmopolitan visions of global governance tend to replace the country-centrism of statism with a 'spatial globalism'. Thus ethical approaches to global governance orien-tate around:

> 'the global level' as an arena that is distinct from regional, national, local and immediate spheres of social relations. From such a perspective, global democracy becomes a question of bringing public participation and control to a global tier of regulation (such as the United Nations) . . . Yet democratic governance of global issues arguably needs to involve people not only as they walk the corridors of global organizations, but also as they live in households, workplaces, districts, provinces, countries and regions. (Scholte, forthcoming: 8)

On this view, we need to reimagine global governance in more radical terms, delinking from any essential focus on institutions, universal ethics or set of objectives. To do so would mean thinking of ethics and ontology as fundamentally entwined, and such a posi-tion holds profound implications for thinking about global governance. So, for instance, Scholte argues that many authors 'assume that "the demos" in global affairs mainly involves the human species as a single political community'. Against this view, he argues:

> Global problems do not always affect every human being on earth; nor do global developments affect all persons in the same ways and to the same extents. True, 'the people' in global politics might sometimes define themselves in universal terms when, say, climate change or infec-tious disease has potentially far-reaching consequences for every human inhabitant of earth. However, even on these occasions, differential impacts might prompt 'the people' in global democracy also to identify themselves partly on class, gender, racial or territorial lines. Then there are other circumstances in global politics where 'the people' might construct their interests and struggles in terms of age, caste, diaspora, disability, religious conviction or sexual orienta-tion. (Scholte, forthcoming: 8)

The important contribution of this line of thinking is to proffer the possibility that we might think of global governance in post-imperial terms, seeking to de-centre ethics and global governance by engaging with the critiques levelled against it. Such universalist pathologies in global governance clearly extend through the use of common languages, such as English, and the dominant frame of Western rationalism (seemingly used for organising all problems). But perhaps the two most glaring dilemmas for realising an ethical approach to global governance, in Scholte's view, are the diminished capacities for poor people actually to take part in democracy, and the failure to conceive of nature as an element within the world, rather than something inert for people to use.

For Scholte, an ethical approach to global governance must grapple with these and other complexities of global politics. It is not enough simply to re-articulate the scale of politics or somehow redirect (Western) logics of deliberation to global questions. Instead, the starting point for postmodern global democracy should be the very dilem-mas of thinking in 'transcalar' terms, reflecting on plural identities, promoting transcul-turality and assuming that material redistribution is a prerequisite of democracy. As such, the challenge of ethics and global governance is to work at multiple levels, listening to the propositions of diverse (often critical) voices, while articulating radical political agendas for the promotion of political agency.

Encapsulating many of the impulses of cosmopolitan and deliberative thinkers, postmodern global democracy seeks to reinvent their ambitions with reference to 'actually existing' practices of global democracy. Indeed, the inclination that we might learn more about global democracy from an indigenous tribe protesting against the construction of a dam, than from a group of educated white men (in chinos) discussing the finer points of Habermas, is disarmingly attractive. This plays to old pragmatist inclinations that democracy is something lived and made, not discovered through reflection. The praxeological dimension of postmodern global democracy is equally powerful: that we might better 'realise' global democracy, in some modest sense, by actually asking diverse people what they think global democracy should be, rather than imposing a model based on our own, limited, knowledge.

However, despite the clear attractiveness, there are limitations to the approach. For all that Scholte's argument moves impressively from critique to reconstruction, it is sometimes unclear why or how the different elements in the agenda hang together. It is just quite difficult to think about how (precisely) we might politicise different elements at the same time, or all elements at different times. For subjects who possess complex identities, it may be straightforward to think in transcalar terms, but for others maybe less so. Also, when members of a culture are speaking to members of another culture at different scales, it is hard to think about what is implied for outcomes. We might support the idea that different groups should engage in dialogue at different levels, but equally, perhaps, complex histories of violence in the modern world would surely qualify the mode and quality of dialogue. Moreover, and no doubt echoing the pluralism of the argument itself, there is nothing in being members of the same community, scale, faith, sex or tribe that suggests that two or more people will share any common opinion, so one wonders whether identifying such differences actually makes a difference.

Perhaps this is the point: democracy implies diversity. But then we are faced with the traditional question of democratic theory: what to do in cases of radical disagreement? What if humans will not renegotiate property rights to land, if the wealthy will not redistribute, if different cultures wish to remain exclusivist, and if analytically weak conceptions of global governance continue to prevail (as they do)? Despite the attractiveness of postmodern global democracy in analytical terms, there is simply a weight of political power and violence in global governance that is neither easily evinced by ethical agendas, nor absent in the genesis of ethics.

ETHICS AS GLOBAL GOVERNANCE?

So far the discussion of ethics and global governance has addressed a range of democratic approaches. The first section took an initial cut at the idea of global governance by thinking in terms of how ethical agendas – democratic, egalitarian, pluralist, and so on – could generate interesting lines of critical reconstruction. In particular, it was considered that a number of authors working in this frame emphasise the challenge of rethinking the questions of scale, inclusion and legitimacy in a global context.

For all that such authors used ethics to ask critical questions about global governance, however, there was a sense in which ethics, per se, could be taken as a relatively straight-forward set of ideas. Ethics was variously pitched as universality, deliberative freedom, or a radical form of postmodern praxis. In different ways, ethics was understood as a way of intervening in the IPE of global governance, moderating the terms of institution building, fleshing out the content of deliberations in the public sphere, and so forth. The implications for thinking about IPE more broadly might be to draw attention away from ongoing concerns with the definition of the economy in theory and practice, to develop a sensitivity to the production and negotiation of popular ideas about it, whether they contest its legitimacy, how they articulate alternatives. On the more radical view of postmodern global democracy, we might ask questions about how particular cases of inclusion (or not) in global governance rest on histories of racial, gendered or spatial otherness. Such an agenda might tie neatly with emerging discussions about everyday political economy (Hobson and Seabrooke 2007).

While such agendas pose important questions and political dilemmas that expand our repertoire of critical engagement in IPE, this section will take the discussion forward by looking to some alternative lines of thinking. For a range of authors working in a tradition of thought which draws variously from Nietszche, Foucault, Derrida and others, the epithet 'ethics' should be considered as perhaps the central question. How did we arrive at a separation between ethics and politics? What is permitted by this separation? Thus, post-structural scholars raise doubts over what is going on – perfomatively – in the idea that there is a realm of ethical reflection (read: good) that can somehow adjudicate, critique, diagnose and/or reform the 'real world' of politics (read: bad). Instead, such authors are concerned to ask questions such as: who is allowed to claim the title 'ethical'? What is done in the name of ethics? What is lost in this name?

For post-structural writers, ethics can take on a wholly different guise, less a realm of thought capable of reflexively 'improving' the world, and more an already existing constituent element in that world. So, for example, it is curious how we think of ethics as a way of reflecting on global governance, when global governance has always been infused with ethical discourses such as human rights, democracy and, indeed, justice. Thus, we might be better off thinking in terms of ethics as global governance. On this view, ethics is a constitutive force in social reality. Cosmopolitan thought has long worked to legitimate systems of global governance that many of those attracted to cosmopolitanism might wish to question. More critically, we might question how, and with what consequences, particular ethical subjects – individuals, consumers, 'the poor' – are constituted by ethical discourses of global governance. Numerous ethical agendas for global governance assume and nurture the idea of the reflexive liberal subject who is able to apply reason and exercise political agency. Thus, instead of asking how global governance might be ethically reformed to help the global poor, a post-structural perspective might be concerned with how that very question constructs a subject such as 'the poor' – as helpless, empty of political agency – and works to cement global governance (whatever that may be) as the political centre apparent.

Ethics as Global Governmentality

An important and currently underdeveloped route for unpicking the idea of ethics-as-global governance is provided in Foucault's concept of governmentality. While

Foucault's (2010) lectures on governmentality were not fully developed in his subsequent work, the concept has proved popular across the social sciences, and a number of authors have taken on the task of applying the concept of governmentality to the emergence and politics of global governance. This line of thought is concerned with the effects of discourses of global governance in terms of how they perform, or constitute, particular subjects, relationships and opportunities for change. While such a concern with detail, with the minutiae of functions and practices that allow for the emergence of global governance, may seem to turn away from ethics in a conventional sense – that of providing a critique and reconstruction of global governance – it is by no means devoid of possibilities for resistance and imaginative provocations to think and practise otherwise than existing logics of ethics and global governance allow.

Government is the 'conduct of conduct'. As Mitchell Dean (1999: 10) suggests, this can refer to several senses of government: direction, guidance and the calculations entailed; a moral concern with how one should 'conduct oneself'; self-direction; our behaviours. Often the idea of conduct is bound up with a larger logic which entails all meanings of conduct together. Witness the proliferation of codes of conduct in the global marketplace, as well as expectations regarding conduct by unspecified individuals, such as in matters of professional conduct, food production, sexual mores and so on. In this sense, ethics as a form of global governmentality points to the underlying links between dispositions, frameworks and surveillance (monitoring), operating at once at institutional, logical and individual levels. As Dean (1999: 12) describes:

> Notions of morality and ethics generally rest on an idea of self-government. They presume some conception of an autonomous, person capable of monitoring and regulating various aspects of their own conduct . . . Thus the notion of government extends to cover the way in which an individual questions his or her own conduct (or *problematizes* it) so that he or she may be better able to govern it. In other words government encompasses not only how we exercise authority over others, or how we govern abstract entities such as states and populations, but how we govern ourselves.

With such a rich and broad concept as governmentality it is perhaps easy to suggest a number of applications and case-studies that could bring value to the IPE of global governance. Important and interesting work has been concerned with the role of surveillance in the credit rating agencies, how data concerning the individual are collected throughout their lives enabling judgements on whether they should receive credit. Importantly, such work has also focused on how we govern ourselves, looking to how the emergence of modern financial subjects is congruent with a culture of attainment, where getting a good mortgage and buying a house (as an investment) are regarded as everyday signs of personal achievement (Langley 2008; also Langley 2010).

Equally, a range of studies have emphasised the close imbrications between ethics and the government of modern market subjects. So, for instance, the role of standards of ethical trade in disciplining Third World producers to reach certain ethical standards of production, distribution and employment has been highlighted (Hughes 2002). Interesting work is emerging on the constitution of ethical consumers who reflexively learn to choose products that concur with a certain logic of 'global ethics'. Usually such logics entail a spatial scale (the global), a moral goal (affirming the local) and an affective value (often the hopeful humanity of the consumer as read through the aesthetic of smiling indigenous children or farmers) (Brassett and Holmes 2010). As progenitors to the imaginative construction of global ethical relations, then, the concept of governmentality would therefore render such practices as manifestations of actually existing global governance: global governance as a lived experience.

On a different tack, Ole Jacob Sending and Iver B. Neumann (2006) look at how global governance works to legitimise itself. From the perspective of 'governmentality', they argue, the increasing role of non-state actors in shaping and carrying out global governance functions should not be seen as a zero-sum divide between states and non-governmental organisations, as is commonly the case in globalisation debates, but as an expression of a changing logic or rationality of government. For them, civil society is redefined from a passive object of government to be acted upon, into an entity that is both an object *and* a subject of government. In this way, the role of global civil society that was so celebrated by theorists of ethics and global governance considered in the previous section becomes a question mark: an element in the generalisation of logics and rationalities of global governance.

Consider, for instance, the way cosmopolitan and deliberative theorists narrate global civil society. It is presented as flexible, plural and multi-perspectival; its capacity to mediate between the local and the global is considered to be a potentially emancipatory quality, and its penchant for debate and disagreement a boon to democracy. From the point of view of governmentality, such values inscribe a particular subjectivity to global civil society so that it can become known and monitored, and so that it can ultimately monitor itself according to such values. For these reasons, perhaps, we become comfortable referring to distinctions between civil and uncivil society. More critically, the performance of such subjectivities has the effect of affirming the institutional model of cosmopolitan global governance, whereby civil society is produced as the legitimating monitor to the (apparently) sovereign centre of the institution. In Dryzek's more radical image, civil society is rephrased as the decentred and plural lifeblood of democracy, debating discourses that are either 'good' or 'bad', in order to have a 'consequence'. In both cases, an important source of legitimacy appears to reside 'outside' global governance, the 'inside' of which needs to be tamed. As Rob Walker (1993) has long argued, the delineation of boundaries between inside and outside is part of a modern fascination with defining away the terms of the political, reducing it to reproduction of existing limitations and deficiencies.

Drawing these ideas together, what is at stake in these debates is the politics of the possible in global governance. Binary oppositions between governance and civil society, and between ethical and unethical conduct, serve not only to frame debates in manageable terms, but also as important moments of what Foucault called 'problematisation', which 'develop the conditions in which possible responses can be given' (Foucault 1984). The specific form in which the problem is presented – such as ethics and global governance – will influence (or shape) which solutions are thought possible or impossible. As Foucault suggests, 'it is a question of trying to see how the different solutions to a problem have been constructed, but also how these different solutions result from a specific form of problematisation' (Foucault 1984). In short, ethics becomes a limit for thinking critically about the political possibilities of what we contingently refer to as global governance.

Such an approach has several implications. Firstly, we should consider how ethical arguments regarding global governance work to both regulate and foster market logics.

While arguments for better, more legitimate forms of governance might play on civilisational narratives of rendering markets 'safe' for the world, this is somewhat hubristic. It assumes ethics is something that can be added on to markets in an unproblematic manner. Perhaps the clearest examples of the genuine dilemmas that emerge can be found in agendas to foster environmental values in global markets (Newell 2008). Attempts to encourage sustainability through carbon emissions trading, for instance, have contributed to the further marketisation of the environment, with unclear consequences. Equally, the normative ambition to reduce carbon emissions through a move to biofuels has had the unintended effect of driving up demand for foods in a way that arguably prices out the world's poorest.

Secondly, we might question how the performance of particular cosmopolitan or deliberative arguments for legitimacy are actually a part of the problem. Such rationalities seek to manage contestability and reduce politics to process, revisability and opinion formation. By reducing global governance to a problem – who to include, what reasons to accept, how to adjudicate – we fail to question the performance of markets entailed and the identity of ethical subjects produced.

Finally, an intensely problematic element in the performance of ethical global governance is the assumption of a global scale as *the* legitimate site of politics. By placing the global scale as the central element, reducing discussion of ethics to form, function and process in relation to the global level, we unwittingly perform a number of market rationalities and subjectivities in global terms. For example, in the case of the Tobin Tax that has recently gained traction in debates about reforming the global financial sector, an ethical agenda is woven to the entrenchment of global finance. For all that the Tobin Tax seeks to rein in global finance, and draws huge popular support from apparently critical circles, the proposal works within – and actively affirms – monetarist assumptions of capital-account convertibility, mobile capital and cash-based approaches to ethical objectives (Brassett 2009).

Where do post-structural insights leave the discussion of ethical governance? For some within IPE, the ethical implication of post-structural thought is nihilism, a form of constant and withering critique that precludes agendas of improvement. The emphasis on power within the concept of governmentality, for instance, arguably works to undercut modern understandings of ethics as ameliorative: a way of intervening in existing power relations to support the 'left out', perhaps. If power is everywhere, even in ethics, then is there perhaps no way out? All that can be hoped for is different forms of power – a position often chided as relativist in ethical terms.

While such views are useful rhetorical devices for shoring up the modern project, there are a number of ways in which they curtail the possibilities for critical engagement. To mistake a critique of ethics for nihilism affirms that the only acceptable way of framing ethics is the modern. On the one hand, such a rhetorical move is clearly deployed so as to reduce the need to engage with the issues identified, not least the complicity of ethical agendas with violent practices, such as structural adjustment or debt. On the other hand, this form of rhetorical critique ignores the vast amount of theoretical work done within post-structural circles on issues of the responsibility to imagine new, less violent forms of ethical relation. True, such work cannot be easily couched within a blueprint agenda, with a neat tick list of goals. But proposals do exist, such as the suggestion of Jenny Edkins (2006) that famine should be redefined as a crime against humanity, an idea which clearly contests the accepted wisdom of global governance on such issues.

The issue is that such proposals work contingently. They are cautious about the potential for violence in assumptions about global governance. In this sense, the post-structural critique is oriented to the everyday. Thinking ethically is not simply about opposing one rationality with another – the 'good' versus the 'bad' – nor is it a process of reflection that identifies the 'truly just', be it 'the poor' or the 'working class' or 'humanity'. As Derrida (1992: 42) argues, 'when a responsibility is exercised in the order of the possible, it simply follows a direction and elaborates a program. It makes of action the applied consequence, the simple application of a knowledge or know-how. It makes of ethics and politics a technology.'

Instead, post-structural ethics are oriented to thinking differently about how everyday global governance can be imagined otherwise. This might be about small subversions, such as when protestors dress up as clowns to entertain the riot police sent to control them. It might be when the Space Hijackers put leaflets in Top Shop clothes, detailing the use of sweatshops by Top Shop (Rossdale 2010). Such acts do not propose a large agenda for making the world a better place, but instead they allow people to think differently about their place in relations of power and global governance.

CONCLUSION

To conclude, I want to draw together a few threads that might form the basis for developing a pragmatic approach to the ethical politics of global governance. Elements of the discussion may have raised difficult or uncomfortable questions, such as: is ethics really ethical as opposed to an embodiment of the kinds of power structures we favour or inhabit? Does ethical agency exist? In many ways, it is good to engage with the difficulty – indeed the (im)possibility – of ethics (Bulley 2010). The less we regard the ethics of global governance as a straightforward case of making the world a better place, the less likely we are to be drawn into the endless dichotomy between realism and Utopia (and between optimism and pessimism). From a pragmatic perspective, the task is to engage with the question of ethical responsibility in a world of diverse violence. On this view, nothing will solve all problems; all we can do is contingently engage. Thus, perhaps the best we can hope for is to foster a better conversation, where better is understood as more imaginative, less cruel, open to narratives of hope (Rorty 1989). In this way, we might start to see ethical approaches to global governance rather like attempts, among many others, to engage the world in less harmful ways.

A pragmatic approach to the ethics of global governance would regard the conversation as open and ongoing. While ethical agendas such as cosmopolitanism provide important vocabularies for addressing a range of dilemmas, post-structural arguments are correct to raise doubts over their limits. By 'limit', I do not mean the limit of their possibility. Rather, I refer to the idea of philosophical limits, that an agenda or idea constitutes a limit to our ability to think beyond it. Hence, I am attracted to vocabularies such as deliberation or postmodern global democracy, not because they trump cosmopolitanism, but because they raise the possibility of new questions and alternatives in the realm of global governance. Equally, by identifying new problems and limits, post-structural theorists identify challenges for thinking about the ethics of everyday global governance. So, for the discipline of IPE bent on method and agenda, the task may be to rediscover a spirit of engagement both politically and – strangely for such a diverse discipline – intellectually.

At one level, it may be a case of accepting that the big debates on ethical global governance are not going to go away. That they may be founded upon problematic separations hardly detracts from their constitutive significance. Thus, the responsibility to engage them, in the here and now, seems apparent. In banal terms, they raise important concerns to larger audiences in a way which invites further conversation. If the content of that conversation is critical in tone, then all to the good, not least as the larger debates are clearly more relevant in the corridors of power.

At another level, IPE should continue down the path, recently invigorated by cultural political economy, of engaging the everyday moral economies that sustain us. This might involve critiquing the subjectivities that are produced, or perhaps imagining them in slightly different (more progressive?) ways. But such agendas are not necessarily delinked from the larger debates. Rather they can be seen as commensurate on a spectrum of attempts. In short, there is no assurance to be had in schools or methods or even the specialism of ethics and global governance, and this only increases our responsibility to expand the contours of political engagement.

REFERENCES

Beitz, Charles (1979), *Political Theory and International Relations*, Princeton, NJ: Princeton University Press.
Brassett, J. (2008), 'Cosmopolitanism vs. terrorism? Discourses of ethical possibility before and after 7/7', *Millennium: Journal of International Studies*, **36** (2), 121–47.
Brassett, James (2009), 'A pragmatic approach to the Tobin Tax campaign: the politics of sentimental education', *European Journal of International Relations*, **15** (3), 447–76.
Brassett, J. and D. Bulley (2007), 'Ethics in world politics: cosmopolitanism and beyond?', *International Politics*, **44** (1), 1–18.
Brassett, James and Chris Holmes (2010), 'International political economy and the question of ethics', *Review of International Political Economy*, **17** (3), 425–53.
Buchanan, Allen and Robert O. Keohane (2006), 'The legitimacy of global governance institutions', *Ethics and International Affairs*, **20** (4), 405–37.
Bulley, Dan (2010), 'The politics of ethical foreign policy: a responsibility to protect whom?', *European Journal of International Relations*, **16** (3), 441–61.
Caney, S. (2005), *Justice Beyond Borders: A Global Political Theory*, Oxford: Oxford University Press.
Cochran, Molly (1999), *Normative Theory in International Relations: A Pragmatic Approach*, Cambridge: Cambridge University Press.
Czempiel, Ernst Otto and James N. Rosenau (1992), *Governance without Government: Order and Change in World Politics*, Cambridge: Cambridge University Press.
Dean, Mitchell (1999), *Governmentality: Power and Rule in Modern Society*, London: Sage.
Derrida, J. (1992), *The Other Heading: Reflections on Today's Europe*, Bloomington, IN: Indiana University Press.
Dryzek, J.S. (1999), 'Transnational democracy', *Journal of Political Philosophy*, **7** (1), 30–51.
Dryzek, J.S. (2000), *Deliberative Democracy and Beyond: Liberals, Critics, Contestations*, Oxford: Oxford University Press.
Dryzek, J.S. (2006), *Deliberative Global Politics: Discourse and Democracy in a Divided World*, Cambridge: Polity Press.
Edkins, Jenny (2006), 'The criminalisation of mass starvations: from natural disaster to crime against humanity', in Steven Devereux (ed.), *The New Famines: Why Famines Persist in an Era of Globalisation*, New York: Routledge, pp. 50–65.

Foucault, M. (1984), 'Polemics, politics and problematizations', interview conducted by Paul Rabinow, May, transcript available at: http://foucault.info/foucault/interview.html.

Foucault, M. (2010), *The Birth of Biopolitics: Lectures at the Collège de France, 1978–1979*, Basingstoke: Palgrave Macmillan.

Habermas, J. (2001), *The Postnational Constellation*, Cambridge: Polity Press.

Held, D. (1995), *Democracy and the Global Order: From the Modern State to Cosmopolitan Governance*, Cambridge: Polity Press.

Held, D. and A. McGrew (eds) (2002), *Governing Globalization: Power Authority and Global Governance*, Cambridge: Polity Press.

Higgott, Richard (2007), 'International political economy', in Robert Goodin, Phillip Pettit and Thomas Pogge (eds), *A Companion to Contemporary Political Philosophy*, 2nd edition, Oxford: Blackwell, pp. 153–82.

Hobson, John and Len Seabrooke (2007), *Everyday Politics of the World Economy*, Cambridge: Cambridge University Press.

Hughes, Alex (2002), 'Global commodity networks, ethical trade and governmentality', *Transactions of the Institute of British Geographers*, **26** (2), 390–406.

Jahn, B. (2005), 'Kant, Mill, and illiberal legacies in international affairs', *International Organization*, **59** (1), 177–207.

Langley, P. (2008), *The Everyday Life of Global Finance – Saving and Borrowing in Anglo-America*, Oxford: Oxford University Press

Langley, P. (2010), 'The performance of liquidity in the subprime mortgage crisis', *New Political Economy*, **15** (1), 71–89.

Murphy, C. (2000), 'Global governance: poorly done, poorly understood', *International Affairs*, **76** (4), 789–803.

Murphy, Craig N. and Roger Tooze (1996), 'The epistemology of poverty and the poverty of epistemology in IPE: mystery, blindness, and invisibility', *Millennium: Journal of International Studies*, **25** (4), 681–707.

Newell, Peter (2008), 'The political economy of global environmental governance', *Review of International Studies*, **34** (3), 507–29.

Parkinson, John and Jane Mansbridge (2012), *Deliberative Systems: Deliberative Democracy at the Large Scale*, Cambridge: Cambridge University Press.

Patomaki, H. (2003), 'Problems of democratizing global governance: time, space and the emancipatory process', *European Journal of International Relations*, **9** (3), 347–76.

Pogge, T. (2002), *World Poverty and Human Rights: Cosmopolitan Responsibilities and Reforms*, Cambridge: Polity Press.

Rorty, R. (1989), *Contingency, Irony and Solidarity*, Cambridge: Cambridge University Press.

Rossdale, C. (2010), 'Anarchy is what anarchists make of it: reclaiming the concept of agency in IR and security studies', *Millennium: Journal of International Relations*, **39** (2), 483–501.

Scholte, Jan Aart (forthcoming), 'Reinventing global democracy', *European Journal of International Relations*.

Sending, Ole Jacob and Iver B. Neumann (2006), 'Governance to governmentality: analyzing NGOs, states, and power', *International Studies Quarterly*, **50**, 651–672.

Smith, William and James Brassett (2008), 'Deliberation and global governance: liberal, cosmopolitan and critical perspectives', *Ethics and International Affairs*, **22** (1), 69–92.

Vaughan-Williams, N. (2007), 'Beyond a cosmopolitan ideal: the politics of singularity', *International Politics*, **44** (1), 107–24.

Walker, R.B.J. (1993), *Inside/Outside: International Relations as Political Theory*, Cambridge: Cambridge University Press.

PART II

THE GOVERNANCE OF THE INTERNATIONAL POLITICAL ECONOMY

5 Flexible 'G groups' and network governance in an era of uncertainty and experimentation
Andrew Baker and Brendan Carey

In 1998 a small group of advanced countries – the Group of Seven (G7) – determined the resolution and response to a financial crisis emanating from emerging economies (the so-called Asian financial crisis). Ten years later, in an almost exact reversal of that earlier pattern, a mixed group of advanced and emerging economies – the Group of Twenty (G20) – presided over the response to a financial crisis that began in the world's core North Atlantic financial centres. This apparent positional swap was a potent symbol of the way the governance of the international political economy had progressively changed during the first decade of the twenty-first century. The rise of the G20 and its displacement of the G7 (later G8) as the pre-eminent global economic governance forum provides a vivid illustration of how the status, standing and preponderance of advanced core countries has been challenged by a number of rising powers. At the Pittsburgh G20 leaders' summit of September 2009, a formal announcement was made that the G20 had moved from being a low-key network of finance ministry and central bank officials to a headline-grabbing leaders-level network: 'the world's premier forum for global economic cooperation' (G20 2009).

The term 'G groups' refers to a regular rhythm of meetings amongst groups of countries either at leaders' level (summits) or through a series of interactions between finance ministry and central bank personnel. Member countries seek to collaborate so as to influence or direct various aspects of the global economy and its constituent institutions. Usually, the 'G' is suffixed with a number, which is supposed to indicate the number of states which have membership of the group, although the G20 originally had 19 members and now has more than 20, while the G10 first had 11 and then 12 members. G groups have also operated as coalitions in international trade politics, most prominently the old 'quadrilateral' and more recently the trade G20, which is an exclusively developing-country grouping (Narlikar 2010). However, G groups first emerged in the field of international financial governance and this is where their role has been most prominent. Accordingly, this chapter focuses on the role of G groups in international financial governance and, in particular, on the movement from a G7/G8-dominated order to one in which the G20 assumes a central role.

G groups have shaped international financial governance for decades. Since 1962 the G10 group of central bankers and finance ministers has sought to manage the General Agreement to Borrow (GAB) of the International Monetary Fund (IMF). In 1971 it produced the Smithsonian agreement, which formally brought an end to the Bretton Woods exchange rate system. The very first meeting of what was to become the G7 leaders' summit in 1975 at Rambouillet, France, agreed the underlying principles of the new post-Bretton Woods regime of floating market-determined exchange rates and changed the IMF's articles of agreement (Baker 2006; Pauly 1997; James 1996; Putnam and Bayne 1987). Later, the G7 summit sought to pull the world economy out of recession by launching an ambitious coordinated international macroeconomic stimulus through the so-called 'Bonn locomotive strategy' of 1978 (Putnam and Henning 1989). The G5 finance ministers and central bankers negotiated the Plaza agreement in 1985 and its replacement, the G7, presided over the 1987 Louvre agreement (Funabashi 1988; Dobson 1991), with both seeking to provide some ad hoc management of the system of floating exchange rates through coordinated interventions to influence the value of the dollar. By the 1990s the G7 was launching a review of the existing global financial architecture and formulating the response to the Asian financial crisis of 1997–98, including creating a new G20 network of finance ministers and central bankers (Baker 2006; Soederberg 2004). The latter was subsequently expanded to include a leaders' process and was used to handle the collective international response to the dramatic financial meltdown of 2008 (Cooper 2010).

This potted history indicates that G groups have been responsible for many of the key landmark moments of collective international financial governance, authoring general principles and producing collective agreements. The inescapable conclusion is that G groups matter when it comes to international financial governance, but how and why they matter is less clear cut. We begin this chapter by elaborating the argument that they do indeed matter, dealing with objections that they are little more than an irrelevant sideshow, mere 'talking shops'. Second, we consider recent literature on G groups, particularly the 'club model politics' of Daniel Drezner (2007), which has become the dominant theoretical statement in the international relations literature of why states cluster into groups in the field of international financial governance. We outline why we think this approach is not well suited to explaining the political dynamics and role of contemporary G groups. Third, we go on to address the question of variance, which is evident in G group activities both by issue area and in terms of the level and type of interaction taking place within G group organisational hierarchies.

We use two cases – G20 discussions of IMF reform and international financial regulation – to develop two principal arguments. First, singular macro-conceptualisations of G groups are inadequate and misrepresent the type and form of governance that contemporary G groups represent, because the fundamental defining feature of G groups is that they are flexible and versatile, capable of morphing into different roles and performing different functions at different times. These different roles invariably involve different political dynamics that reflect contrasting rationales and objectives. This variance is overlooked in existing G group literature. In this chapter, we contrast the role and dynamics of G20 working groups with the exchanges between finance ministry and central bank deputies and with those between leaders. In the first case of IMF reform, the G20 acted as a 'circuit-breaker', enabling a seemingly intractable stand-off to be overcome, mainly through intense bargaining and negotiation over points of detail at senior levels. In the second case of financial regulation, working groups were more influential and a dynamic of brain-storming or puzzling was evident, involving the establishment of principles, priorities and agendas that were subsequently conveyed and signalled to other actors. Second, we use both cases to demonstrate that alignments and coalitions within the G20 have become considerably more fluid, varying across issue area and cutting across traditional developed/developing country boundaries. The conclusion then locates G20 activities in a broader context, relating them to the emerging literature on network governance and network making (Kahler 2009; Hafner-Burton et al. 2009). We argue that network making and coordination is itself an increasingly important governance activity in the international political economy of the twenty-first century, while a wider structural context of 'uncertainty' necessitates ongoing forms of 'governance experimentation' (Sabel 2004), of which the G20 itself is a form. At the same time, the G20 also seeks to orchestrate and oversee ongoing network-building activities.

WHY DO G GROUPS MATTER?

The most common objection to G groups is that they are little more than 'talking shops' (Cohen 2008) and are therefore largely inconsequential onlookers in governance reform (Dam 2010). Such objections are borne out of a realist or statist international relations ontology that defines the fundamentals of international political life in relation to an anarchic international system within which there is no overarching authority (Greico 1988). From this perspective, the problem of governments 'free-riding' (Snidal 1991; Barret 1999) in international agreements is omnipresent. Achieving state 'compliance' with internationally agreed objectives thus becomes the principal problem in international politics (Chayes and Chayes 1993; Kirton 2010). Consequently, the lack of legal status and structure of G groups and the absence of a conspicuous enforcement mechanism weakens them in an anarchic world of interest-driven great-power politics. In other words, the informality and flexibility of G groups is their fundamental weakness, given the nature of the international system. We argue exactly the opposite and suggest that informality and flexibility are the main strengths of G groups, that define their distinctive contribution to governance in the contemporary international political economy. Moreover, it is precisely because of this versatility and flexibility that political and bureaucratic elites find G group processes useful and why they continue to attach importance to them. In this sense, G groups represent a form of network governance; a non-hierarchical governance structure in which relations among actors are repeated and enduring, but where no one actor has the authority to arbitrate and resolve disputes that arise during exchanges (Podolny and Page 1998; Martinez-Diaz and Woods 2009). Appreciating how G groups function as a form of network governance, however, requires abandoning the realist and liberal moorings of much international relations theory and embracing an alternative ontology that adopts a different view of consequential and important political activity in the international system.

From our perspective, which in social science terms might be described as broadly constructivist, 'talking' and the act of deliberation matter, because economic ideas and understandings about how the world functions shape policy responses, define priorities and set the parameters and limits for feasible policy action (Risse 2000; Blyth 2002). The act of talking can result in shared understandings and approaches that evolve over time in ways that may not be immediately identifiable or measurable. These shared understandings provide an account of how the economic and financial world works and therefore define the nature of problems to be confronted and what to do about them (Blyth 2002). Inadvertently, therefore, the ongoing dialogue of G groups informs the act of interest calculation by individual G group members and helps to set priorities, objectives and strategies within a host of other governance settings in the international political economy, partially determining where important governance and policy work is conducted, as well as by whom and on what terms. Viewed through such a lens, issues of national compliance and enforcement become less central to G group activities.

Essentially, G groups perform three roles in the field of financial governance, although there is inevitably some overlap between these roles; they act as apex policy forums (Baker 2010), circuit-breakers and financial firefighters. Apex policy forums operate at the very highest levels of national officialdom. They have a global perspective, or remit, and seek to define priorities, directing, steering, framing and setting agendas, timetables and deadlines for work conducted elsewhere. Apex policy forum deliberations result in the release of statements or communiqués designed to convey a sense of consensus on priorities, agendas and broad policy orientation to other national authorities, markets, the financial press, as well as the array of other more specialist bodies and committees that constitute the current global financial architecture: the IMF, World Bank, Basle Committee on Banking Supervision (BCBS), Financial Stability Board (FSB) and others. When G groups perform the role of apex policy forum they essentially craft normative consensus about what the global financial system should look like, how it should function, and which values should inform its overall operation and organisation. This involves framing the conduct of international financial governance by diffusing objectives and priorities to other relevant bodies and determining the terms and content of financial governance discourse and debates.

Existing work (Baker 2008, 2010) has identified four powers that characterise apex policy forums. The first is a power of weighted resources. G groups bring together officials at the highest national levels in the finance ministries, central banks and offices of prime ministers and presidents of self-selecting groups of systemically significant countries, meaning that G groups represent and account for a concentration of the world's resources. For example, the G20 accounts for over 85 per cent of world gross domestic product (GDP), 80 per cent of world trade and 66 per cent of the world's population. What agreements they either reach, or fail to reach, on how the world's leading currencies are valued, and how exchange rate relationships should be managed and constituted, shape the structures of the world economy. Likewise, the G20 countries constitute the principal donors for the multilateral lending agencies, the IMF and the World Bank, accounting for 65.93 per cent and 65.49 per cent of the institutions' capital respectively. In other words, what the G20 can negotiate within itself in relation to shares of funds for these institutions determines the capital base, internal power structures and capability of the world's two leading multilateral donor agencies.

A second power is a power of instigation or initiation. G groups initiate proposals and set broad agendas and priorities for the wider institutional complex of international financial governance. Many of the more specialist regulatory committees and bodies charged with various functional aspects of financial governance are staffed by less senior officials from finance ministries, central banks and/or semi-autonomous regulatory agencies. This gives G groups significant directional capacity, because strategic meetings of senior figures from finance ministries, central banks and leaders' offices can catalyse the bureaucratic and technical capabilities of their respective institutions. They urge their bureaucracies to work together to share findings, experience and information (albeit within the context of agreed normative objectives). Sometimes, this involves G groups asking certain international bodies and networks to conduct work on their behalf and report back, whilst also setting a deadline for that work. Some of the best examples of this power of initiation occurred after the Asian financial crisis of the late 1990s. The G7 created the G20 and a new Financial Stability Forum (FSF), now the FSB, but also authored an approach to international financial governance designed to promote 'transparency' by launching 12 international financial codes and standards (Baker 2006). The aim of these standards and codes was to increase the available information to market participants based on a belief that this information would be rationally evaluated by investors (Blyth 2003). This was a de facto approval of an approach to financial governance based on 'a trilogy of greater transparency, more disclosure and more effective risk management by financial firms revolving around market prices', itself grounded in a belief that this was 'all that was required for the regulation of efficient financial markets' (Eatwell 2009). The G7's standards and codes exercise essentially institutionalised this approach to financial governance, with intensified multilateral surveillance revolving around the scrutiny of the 12 standards and codes through Reports on Observance of Standards and Codes (ROSCs – individual code assessments published on a country) and Financial Sector Assessment Programmes (FSAPs – all 12 codes assessed simultaneously across a single jurisdiction) becoming a mainstay of international financial governance during the 2000s.

Third is a power of endorsement. This involves official approval of the findings of more specialist networks and bodies that produce technical reports, such as the International Organization of Securities Commissions (IOSCO), the BCBS, the FSB and the IMF. Although G groups are selective in their endorsements, they rarely contest or reject the technical detail within the reports produced by these specialist bodies. However, evidence suggests that, if the proposals of specialist bodies are to enjoy political authority, the approval of G groups is essential. A combination of approval, publicity and promotional activities by high-profile G groups serves to energise and empower more specialised, technical, regulatory problem-solving networks and can give a sense of importance, prestige and urgency to their ongoing work (Baker 2009).

A fourth power is a power of veto, which essentially amounts to a capacity to stop certain things from happening. For example, the IMF's proposal to create a Sovereign Debt Restructuring Mechanism (SDRM) in the early 2000s required the approval of member countries to adjust the IMF's articles of agreement (Helleiner 2009). Once the G7 finance ministries and central banks rejected the SDRM proposal, its adoption became impossible. Likewise, if leading finance ministries and central banks reject a proposal for a loan, it would not be further discussed by the IMF's board of directors (Woods 2000). In short, apex policy forums set the parameters within which wider multilateral institutions operate and provide the political support necessary for their survival. Without the collective approval of leading figures involved in G groups, nothing in international financial governance can proceed. Proposals that are collectively opposed by G7 or G20 members are effectively vetoed or rejected.

In summary, therefore, G groups matter in their role as apex policy forums because they possess important framing powers that structure policy dialogue, shape agendas and effect how issues come to be understood and talked about internationally. This is a politically significant and contentious role as G groups essentially define how global financial governance challenges are to be understood and defined, as well as who has a legitimate right to participate.

A second G group role is as 'circuit-breakers' (De Brouwer and Yeaman 2007) in seemingly intractable standoffs outside more formal international financial institutions. The G20, for example, as a forum for dialogue between established liberal market economies and emerging economies, provides a much-needed space for 'frank and informal' (G20 2007) deliberation and contestation between a variety of cultural and value systems, allowing disagreements to be resolved and new understandings and alignments to be forged. G groups do this by building up personal relationships between their participants due to the informal nature of exchanges. We will explore this role as 'circuit-breaker' in a case-study exploring how the G20 has come to act as a de facto IMF executive board, although this role is also related to the power of weighted resources that G groups have as apex policy forums.

A third and final role entails G groups formulating high-level collective responses to financial crises, although this also overlaps with their roles as apex policy forums and circuit-breakers. The 'light' flexible nature of G groups as a series of informal exchanges and networks allows them to respond quickly without having to follow onerous bureaucratic procedure. Launching a programme of collective action from the highest levels of government in the most important countries can have reassuring effects on markets and domestic publics, which in turn can limit the spread of financial contagion across country borders and market segments. But this requires a speedy response, and the informality of G group processes does allow agreements to be formulated quickly. Throughout their history G groups have been chosen by political leaders to perform this vital firefighting role through both the collective provision of liquidity and the initiation of longer-term reform efforts and trajectories, evident most recently in the G7 response to the Asian financial crisis of the late 1990s and the G20 response to the financial meltdown of the late 2000s. Deputies involved in the G20 process from its inception openly admit that the channels of communication, interactions and relationships built up during the first part of the decade, which at the time seemed relatively inconsequential, were, in retrospect, 'important dress rehearsals' and 'fire drills' that facilitated a speedy collective response when it was really required following the financial catastrophe of 2008. Established personal relations meant that a collective speedy response could be mounted since participants were not coming to issues cold (confidential interviews with G20 Deputies, 2009 and 2010). Iterative policy drills of this sort are thus an important, if often hidden, G group function.

G7–G20 RELATIONS AND THE LIMITS OF CLUB MODEL POLITICS

Early literature on the G20, following its creation in 1999, largely focused on G7–G20 relations, perhaps unsurprisingly, given that the G20 was created by the G7 (Porter 2001; Germain 2001; Kirton et al. 2001; Kirton and von Furstenberg 2001; Martinez-Diaz 2007; Hajnal 2007; Beeson and Bell 2009). Most of this literature was concerned with considering whether the G20 required the G7 to secure wider G20 approval for its own governance initiatives. For example, Mark Beeson and Stephen Bell considered the role of developing countries in the G20 in terms of 'collectivist cooperation', whereby they participated in the G20 on a relatively equal footing, and contrasted this with 'hegemonic incorporation', whereby the G7 operated according to an 'incorporationist' rather than 'inclusionary' logic (Beeson and Bell 2009). A G20 characterised by hegemonic incorporation would suggest that the G20 is 'acting as a sounding board for reforms endorsed by the G7' (Culpeper 2000). Some fairly compelling empirical evidence based on communiqué analysis has been presented to demonstrate that a lot of G20 activities during the first 5–6 years of its existence involved approval, or endorsement, for G7 initiatives and preferences, leading to the conclusion that the G20 was not an effective vehicle for exercising developing-country influence on world affairs (Martinez-Diaz 2007).

Countries from outside of the G7 were invited to form a G20 by the G7 in 1999 in an admittedly rather arbitrary and ad hoc process that reputedly involved the US Treasury deputy, Tim Geithner, reading out a list over the telephone to his German counterpart. In this respect, during the early years of the G20 there was a clear division between old members and new members, conceived as 'invited guests'. At the same time, the G7 finance minister and central bank governors also continued to meet 3–4 times a year, compared to the G20's once a year. This greater momentum of contact amongst the G7, together with incumbency, meant that for the first half of the 2000s the G7 continued to operate as the premier G group. Consequently, the G7 versus the rest seemed to be the obvious and primary political cleavage within the G20. However, our interviews with officials involved in the G20 process reveal that contributions from non-G7 G20 members have grown over time, as they have learned to become more assertive and have grasped how to make G20 diplomacy work to their advantage (confidential interviews with South African and Indian officials, 2009 and 2010). Time, and becoming accustomed to G20 procedures, has therefore changed the dynamics of the G20 itself as a process. Recent contributions to the international relations literature have highlighted how networks themselves are dynamic forms of repeated and enduring interactions, which are not static but can change actors' perceptions and behaviour through education and socialisation. Such processes need to be further illuminated through the empirical application of theories of interaction and more rigorous analysis of network structure and effects (Hafner-Burton et al. 2009). In the case of the G20 there is certainly evidence that a process of evolution took place, which reached a crucial maturation point as the financial crisis of 2008–2009 unfolded, resulting in the G20 being promoted, as we have seen, to become the premier global economic governance forum from 2009 onwards.

The strongest theoretical statement of this 'G7 versus the Rest' position as constituting the major characteristic of international economic governance has been made by Daniel Drezner (2007) in his concept of 'club model politics', which has become one of the most influential theoretical statements in the North American international relations literature. Essentially, Drezner's argument can be broken down into three parts. First, developed countries bypass international financial institutions and design governance structures through the creation and utilisation of developed country clubs, such as the G7, the G10, the BCBS and the FSF, which ensure that 'decisions are made by powerful states behind closed doors' (Drezner 2007: 121). Second, powerful developed countries do this because they have rational incentives to create great-power clubs, so as to better control policy outcomes. Third, the primary cleavage in global financial governance is between developed and developing countries, because the adjustment costs relative to the benefits of financial regulatory coordination are significantly lower in developed countries than in developing countries. Due to the disparate preferences of its members as a mix of developed and developing countries, Drezner does not classify the G20 as a club.

The problem with Drezner's account is that it is too static and does not take sufficient account of how countries and their perceptions change and evolve as a consequence of their interactions with the international system and their participation in forms of network governance. Moreover, the club model begins to run into trouble when we begin to consider the rise of the G20 since the financial crash of 2008. The G20 not only was created by the G7, but the United States then chose it as the mechanism to handle the crisis when President Bush instigated the Washington G20 summit in November 2008, and when Treasury Secretary Tim Geithner announced that the G20 would become the premier global economic governance forum at the Pittsburgh summit in September 2009. In other words, the United States chose to pursue the global response to financial crisis in a setting other than a club forum, according to Drezner's own criteria, which is not something that the club model, on its own terms, would predict. Our position is that Drezner is right to suggest that the G20 is not a club, because of the heterogeneity of the perspectives and cultures represented. In that sense, rather than a club of narrow interests, the sheer variety of traditions, cultures, perspectives and values articulated within the G20 mean that it is at least a step in the direction towards a more 'plural world of co-existing civilisations ... based on an expectation of diversity with tolerance and a willingness to confront the frustrations of a search for consensus on diverse issues', as imagined by Robert Cox (2004: 320).

As the United States government took the lead in both creating and then promoting the G20, this raises the question of motivation. Earlier G20 scholarship perceptively pointed out that the G20 was originally motivated by a desire to achieve greater compliance with G7-authored objectives (Kirton et al. 2001; Kirton and von Furstenberg 2001). However, this was unlikely to remain either a static objective or a realistic aspiration over time, as the effects of repeated, enduring network interactions changed both G7 and non-G7 perceptions of the G20 over time. By 2006 the basic US Treasury Department position was that key G groups needed to represent more accurately the composition of the world economy and thus include large economies of systemic significance (Sobel and Steadman 2006). George Bush's turn to the G20 as the forum to formulate a collective response to the financial crisis of 2008 was therefore consistent with a position Treasury officials had been expressing for some time. A similar recognition of the need to make key fora more representative of the world economy by incorporating the biggest and most important national economies also informed and drove the move to expand the membership of the BCBS, IOSCO and the FSF to all G20 countries in the first half of 2009. The rise of the G20 suggests, therefore, that leading powers have been concerned with the effectiveness of the international governance machinery. Moreover, as we shall see in our first case-study, concern with effective and representative collective economic management has been consistently expressed in the US Treasury position on IMF quota reform (Sobel and Steadman 2006). The assumption that the principal cleavage in global financial governance is necessarily between developed and developing countries based on a simple calculation of the distribution of adjustment costs arising from international agreements is also questioned by the empirical record of the G20. Not only are leading states influenced by a more complex array of motivations than the club model allows for, but also the neat division between the so-called developed and developing world in multilateral governance settings is blurring (Payne 2005).

VARIABILITY IN FLEXIBLE G GROUPS

The variable nature and dynamics of contemporary G groups has largely been over-looked in the existing literature. This variability takes numerous forms. First, the G20 finance ministers' and central bank governors' network does not follow exactly the same pattern of interactions and dynamics as the leaders-level network, although the two are connected. For example, the finance ministry and central bank deputies' network at times resembles a 'think-tank' (Rubio-Marquez 2009), while the 'sherpas' network plays a bridging role between the leaders and finance ministry processes (Bayne 2004). There are also G20 chair delegations, G20 working groups and G20 study groups. When we refer to the G20, therefore, we are referring to a cluster of different but overlapping networks, some more transgovernmental, technical and collegiate in character, and others more intergovernmental in character based on political logics and interstate bargaining (Keohane and Nye 1974). Second, G group dynamics are also issue-specific. The ability of G groups to shift between different types of interaction and logics makes them particularly flexible forms of governance that reflect the multiple issues with which they deal. G groups, as 'informal mechanisms for dialogue', are bestowed with chameleon-like abilities to adapt their modes of operation and interaction depending on the nature of the issue being discussed. Third, the rise of so-called emerging economies is an ongoing and incremental process. In this respect, G20 members learn from and respond to one another over time, making alignment formation an inherently uneven, non-uniform process. G groups thus evolve over time, their nature and modes of operation continuously shifting to reflect new challenges. Network-building occurs incrementally, often out of sight, after the initial creation of new networks, with unintended consequences, changing perceptions and understandings and unfolding personal relationships. In what follows we seek to illuminate some of the variability at work in the recent operation of the G20 through the presentation of two case-studies.

Case 1: The G20 as a De Facto Non-resident Executive Board for the IMF

IMF reform first came onto the G20 agenda in a serious way when China chaired the G20 summit in 2005. Since then the G20 has arguably emerged as a de facto non-resident executive board for the IMF. G20 countries hold between 15 and 18 of the 24 seats on the IMF Executive Board at any one time and currently can cast between 60 per cent and 72 per cent of Executive Board votes on behalf of their constituencies. Frank and informal deliberations inside G20 meetings have contrasted with the stilted and often contentious nature of Executive Board and International Monetary and Financial Committee (IMFC) meetings (interviews with G20 insiders, 2009 and 2010). Because of this the G20 has been able to act as a 'circuit-breaker', overcoming stalemates and producing a partial redistribution of 'shares and chairs' in the IMF. Consequently, the content and nature of IMF reforms have been shaped and led by the G20, as much as by the Executive Board.

The Singapore resolution announced at the IMF's annual meeting in 2006 was formulated in prior G20 deliberations. It produced a 1.8 per cent ad hoc quota increase shared between China, South Korea, Mexico and Turkey, together with a more general shift in quota shares in the direction of developing countries of 2.2 per cent. This marked the start of a process of progressively increasing the representation of number of dynamic emerging market and developing countries (EMDCs). These reforms essentially mirrored those suggested by a G20 Troika report in 2005, at least in terms of scale and scope. Much of the complex bargaining surrounding these issues was handled in G20 deputies' meetings (confidential interview, G20 insider, September 2009). G20 summits in London and Pittsburgh also announced an intention to increase IMF resources in response to the financial crisis by 250 billion Special Drawing Rights (SDR) and $500 billion worth of loans through a New Agreement to Borrow (NAB), and a 5 per cent quota shift in favour of EMDCs. Key deadlocks in relation to these issues were also negotiated through the G20 process.

The key sticking point in these later discussions was that European leaders were unwilling to forego their over-represented position in the IMF in favour of rising Asia. The United States was willing to forego quota increases and even take a cut in its voting share, as long as it maintained the 15 per cent voting share required to veto changes to the Articles of Agreement. Meanwhile, large emerging economies showed a reluctance to lend to the IMF without significant movement on governance reforms. The G20 played a crucial role in surmounting these sticking points and delivering a 6 per cent quota shift, a mid-point between the 5 per cent agreed at the Pittsburgh summit and the 7 per cent shift demanded by the Brazil–Russia–India–China (BRIC) finance ministers in the run-up to Pittsburgh (BRIC 2009). Under half of this 6 per cent shift (2.6 per cent) was to come from 'advanced economies', the rest being taken from over-represented EMDCs (Bretton Woods Project 2010).

The longstanding deadlocks broken at the Gyeongju ministerial in 2010 were widely reported as the result of horse-trading between emerging market economies and G7 states regarding an urgent need to increase the IMF's capital pool (IMF 2010). But they also derived from a longer ongoing process of negotiation and tactical positioning by G20 state representatives inside G20 meetings over a number of years stretching back to 2005 (interviews with G20 insiders). Europe's over-representation involved eight permanent seats and one rotating seat on the Executive Board, potentially casting between 34 and 39 per cent of the IMF vote on behalf of their constituencies. No low-income country held a permanent seat on the Executive Board, while 45 sub-Saharan African countries shared two rotating executive directors and cast less than 5 per cent of the vote. According to the G20's own classifications, EMDCs held nine permanent and two rotating seats on the Executive Board, with a potential to cast between 24 and 32 per cent of the vote.

Breaking the impasse on Executive Board reform ultimately required that the US deploy what Edwin Truman (2006: 76) had described five years earlier as its 'nuclear option'. The IMF's Articles of Agreement stipulate a 20-member IMF Executive Board. The enlargement to 24 members needs to be approved every two years by the Board of Governors. Since the first expansion to 21 in 1978, gradual further expansion and approval has been a mere formality (Momani 2008). However, in August 2010, the US vetoed approval of the expanded Executive Board, which meant that agreement had to be reached before the end of October 2010. Hence the Gyeongju ministerial held on 23

October became the implicit deadline for the G20 to break the deadlock on 'share and chair' reform. Although the Europeans were the intended target of the US launch of this 'nuclear option', they would not have lost any seats on the Executive Board, had agreement not been reached. Rather, the Argentinean, Brazilian, Indian and rotating African chair would have been affected. Nevertheless, the impact of the US move was to build up the pressure on the Europeans from across the G20. The result was a compromise in which the US agreed to approve the 24-seat Executive Board in return for the Europeans agreeing to cede two seats to EMDCs.

The evidence presented here indicates that G20 positions on IMF governance are largely based on well-defined rational calculations of how to maximise voice, vote and influence within the Fund. The resulting form of interaction is a form of interest-based bargaining, with efforts to secure deals being driven by offering concessions and the adoption of tactical positions. Alignments in this process have not, however, followed a developed versus developing country pattern, but have in fact involved the US forming alignments with EMDCs in order to put pressure on Europe. What is most interesting here, therefore, is the position of the US. A desire to maximise voice and representation was kept in check and placed on hold, with the US displaying a willingness to see a minimal reduction in its shares in an effort to secure a more representative and better-financed IMF. In any event, unlike the club model of international financial politics, leading developed states were not able to identify common ground and definitely did not operate as a club in relation to the rest of the interstate system. This is not to say that the US will not continue to engage in the process of 'forum shopping' in attempts to realise preferences, but it does suggest that the G20 appears to allow for a more encompassing, cross-cutting and fluid set of alignments than the parsimony of the club model would entertain or predict.

Case 2: The G20's Regulatory Reform Agenda in an Era of Experimentation and Uncertainty

Whereas in the case of IMF reform the G20 fully engaged and acted as a circuit-breaker, in the case of financial regulatory reform it delegated the negotiation of detailed agreements, such as Basel III, to the BCBS and settled on formulating broader principles, priorities and agendas for other more specialist committees. Such an observation would suggest that G20 influence upon the area of financial regulation has been much less tangible than in the case of IMF reform, and has verged on the inconsequential, with the real action taking place in meetings of the BCBS and the FSB. There is a partial truth in this, but it is also an overstatement and G20 meetings did play a crucial role in placing financial regulation on a particular trajectory during 2008–09. Most importantly, the G20 approved and legitimised efforts to make regulation more 'macroprudential' and thus set in train a whole industry of research and knowledge generation in specialist international technical committees (Baker 2013). This is important because macroprudential ideas had spent most of the previous decade on the sidelines, confined to a few enthusiasts such as Claudio Borio, William White and other colleagues at the Basel-based Bank for International Settlements (BIS), as well as some outlying economists such as John Eatwell, Charles Goodhart, Martin Hellwing, Hyun Song Shin, Stephany Griffith-Jones, Jose Ocampo and industry figures such as Avinash Persaud. Such figures were largely lone voices during the financial boom of the 2000s. Their message made little headway with leading central bankers, particularly Alan Greenspan, who remained wedded on the whole to a simplified version of the so-called 'efficient markets' thesis that market actors, because of their rational interests, drive asset prices into equilibrium (Balizil and Schiessl 2009; Baker 2013).

In direct contradiction of many of the premises of efficient-market thinking (with its micro-foundations based on an assumption of the rational optimising behaviour of individual market participants), macroprudential thinking conceived of financial risk as a dynamic, systemic and endogenous property. This meant effective regulation had to involve top-down requirements and systemic monitoring, rather than bottom-up private risk-management systems revolving around market prices. The macroprudential case made allusions to the Keynesian notion of the fallacy of composition and drew inspiration from Hyman Minsky to make reference to 'pro-cyclicality' and 'herding' as characteristics of contemporary financial markets (Baker 2013), as well as seeing comparisons between financial systems and ecosystems and noting that complexity could engender fragility and have unintended consequences (Haldane and May 2010). In other words, accepting a macroprudential agenda, and seeking to make the construction of macroprudential regulatory regimes a political priority, was also a substantial intellectual sea change in the thinking driving international financial governance, which simply could not have taken hold without the political approval, endorsement and encouragement of the G20. Because the macroprudential agenda also made 'mitigating pro-cyclicality' one of its leading priorities, it also advocated instruments such as counter-cyclical buffers, leverage limits and a range of other policy tools that were previously off the table (Elliot 2011). At the same time it reignited the debate over capital controls, previously largely eschewed by, or denied to, regulators and official policy-makers (Grabel 2011). In short, the macroprudential turn offered to re-empower regulators by providing a basis and rationale for increased state intervention to curb and place limits on financial excesses.

This intellectual sea-change resulted in the previously marginalised Claudio Borio (2009) of the BIS pronouncing: 'we're all macroprudentialists now'. During the first half of 2009, G20 Working Group 1, 'Enhancing Sound Regulation and Strengthening Transparency', co-chaired by Canadian central bank G20 deputy Tiff Macklem and Indian central bank G20 deputy Rakesh Mohan, played a particularly prominent role in cementing this ideational shift (confidential correspondence between authors and leading international official). Working groups have become a staple of G20 exchanges and have been particularly important in driving the regulatory reform agenda, not least because this has involved a process of 'puzzling' to diagnose and understand the causes of the crisis and to advance blueprints for reform (interview with G20 insider, August 2009). As such, this process involves a 'brain-storming exercise', an exchange of ideas and a formulation of a consensus on the way forward. Given the heavy intellectual lifting required and the technical nature of many regulatory questions, working groups are well suited to addressing these questions. Working groups provide a valuable space for 'work-focused' dialogue, allowing for peer-to-peer exchange of policy ideas without participants falling back on well-oiled national positions (interview with G20 insider, September 2009). Working group outcomes and reports are then used as baselines to inform debates and help draft communiqués among deputies, ministers, 'sherpas' and leaders. Working groups also contribute to G20 network-building. They bring a range of public and private sector participants into G20 deliberations and consequently 'thicken' G20 networks. Working groups include not only G20 deputies, but also less senior officials, academics and other relevant public and private sector representatives. In this way, they temporarily expand the number of participants involved in G20 policy formulation. Working groups generally do not involve negotiation over points of detail, but rather perform a knowledge- or norm-generation function, defining broad priorities, approaches and agendas which are then taken forward in other settings, once ministers and leaders have approved their findings. In this respect, further more detailed analytical work and monitoring functions have now been delegated to the new FSB (particularly in the field of macroprudential policy), which the G20 is supposed to oversee and hold to account (Helleiner 2010).

The G20 began to promote a macroprudential approach to regulation following the Horsham Communique of March 2009, as the statement highlighted the need to 'mitigate pro-cyclicality' in the financial system. The G20 London summit subsequently charged the new FSB with the task of promoting and coordinating macroprudential policy, and the FSB has since written a number of updates on the evolving status of macroprudential knowledge and policy. Since 2010 the IMF, the BIS and the FSB, between them, have published over 20 analytical reports on developing macroprudential policies. While the G20 was instrumental in presiding over a key sea-change in regulatory philosophy by making macroprudential regulation a priority, the G20 itself has limited capacity to go much beyond this. Counter-cyclical macroprudential policy has to be implemented on a national basis (Warwick Commission 2009; Persaud 2010) and national politics and legislative processes, as Putnam's two-level game framework demonstrated, cannot be controlled by participants in G group processes (Putnam 1988). Nevertheless, even if building macroprudential policy nationally is likely to be a slow and arduous process, with legislators, parliamentarians and industry lobby-groups acting in ways that dilute provisions, the G20 has nevertheless presided over a startling shift to a macroprudential frame in the space of a little more than six months, from the first Washington Summit in late 2008 to the London and Pittsburgh summits of 2009. The consequence of this G20 activity is that a process of building macroprudential regulatory regimes has begun in the US, the European Union (EU) and the UK. The new Financial Stability Oversight Council (FSOC) in the US, the European Systemic Risk Board (ESRB) at the European Central Bank (ECB) and the Financial Policy Committee (FPC) at the Bank of England in the UK are all to be given some macroprudential powers and responsibilities. In addition, the research machinery of the global financial architecture is now focused on macroprudential analysis.

The macroprudential policy framework undoubtedly remains an issue of dispute across the G20. For example, US acceptance of the macroprudential approach, according to senior international officials, has always been 'half-hearted and 'quite partial', partly for 'philosophical' reasons relating to a faith in markets. This has resulted in far more focus on the 'too-big-to-fail' problem in respect of banks and far less emphasis on pro-cyclicality (Persaud 2010; confidential remarks to authors by senior international official, January 2012). Most pressure for a macroprudential shift within the G20 came from the UK, with support from Canada and other parts of Europe (Baker 2013; confidential remarks to authors by senior international official, January 2012). At the same time, macroprudential proposals found resonance with many Asian G20 countries, such as South Korea and India, precisely because they had used macroprudential policy instruments without actually ascribing that name to them (Borio 2011). One G20 member, Brazil, has used macroprudential rationales to justify the use of capital controls, even if the FSB has recently argued that these are not strictly a macroprudential policy instrument (Banco Centro do Brasil 2010; FSB et al. 2011). The G20's composition is therefore far more conducive to a more interventionist approach to financial regulation than the G7 had been pre-crash. At the same time, leading regulators in G7 states, such as the UK, appear to have undergone a conversion to macroprudential thinking. Given that G20 working groups were hugely important in providing the groundwork for this achievement, the dynamic at work relied on an exchange of ideas, or a 'logic of arguing' (Risse 2000), rather than the hard bargaining that prevailed in the case of IMF reform. The broader point here is that G groups are not characterised by a single dominant logic and indeed are able to morph into different roles depending on the issue and type and seniority of the network interactions taking place.

CONCLUSION: MAKING NETWORK GOVERNANCE

G groups represent a form of governance that is far from ideal. They are for example an inherently exclusive form of governance (Payne 2010; Keohane and Nye 2001), because by definition they have a restricted membership. At times, they can even produce a form of 'group-think' by restricting the range of perspectives heard in discussion, thus producing a form of 'enclave deliberation' that can result in a 'limited argument pool' becoming ensconced (Baker 2010; Sunstein 2002). The latter problem was particularly evident as the financial boom unfolded in core countries, when the G7 essentially endorsed a complacent vision of efficient financial markets. However, G groups also have strengths as a form of flexible network governance. This chapter has argued that these strengths are precisely what much North American international relations scholarship of a realist and liberal bent would regard as their weaknesses. Their strengths are in fact their informality and flexibility. This has been shown to facilitate personal relations and candid exchanges between key individuals, enabling them to respond quickly to crisis situations, adopt different roles and perform different functions at different times according to the issue at hand and the particular form or level of G group process in operation. For example, G groups have acted as 'circuit-breakers', negotiating deals and overcoming deadlocks, as in the case of IMF reform where the G20 acted as a de facto IMF executive board unhampered by the stilted, formal procedures of the official board. G groups can also act rapidly in crisis situations and perform the role of financial firefighters, formulating collective positions and strategies and dispensing and agreeing liquidity packages at times of financial distress. At other times, they can act as a 'steering committee' or an apex policy forum for the wider global financial architecture (Cooper 2010; Baker 2010), creating, diffusing and disseminating overarching norms, ideas and priorities, as we saw in the second case of the macroprudential ideational shift.

The existing literature has largely underestimated or neglected the diversity and flexibility which G groups display. The focus of academic research into G groups needs now to move away from a fixation with the 'G7 versus the Rest' relationship and deal with increasingly complex cross-cutting alignments that vary by issue area and reflect a form of network governance. A process of puzzling and experimentation is currently under way in relation to the internal politics of the G20, but also in relation to the content of policy proposals and the role of the process itself. Alignments vary across policy areas, but so too do the way G20 countries interact with one another in trying out new proposals and policy positions. Current G group interactions have been taking place in a context of uncertainty that has two sources. First, the financial crash of 2008 was a severe one and the reverberations are still unfolding, as is evident in the ongoing Eurozone crisis. The damage done by this crash to the long-term performance of core economies, especially heavily 'financialised' economies, remains uncertain and unpredictable. Second, international politics is being shaped by a discourse and wider belief that profound change in the nature of the global order is under way, represented by rising powers and the growing self-fulfilling prominence of the so-called BRIC (Brazil, Russia, India, China) economies. This sense that something momentous is under way was reinforced when the G20 replaced the G7/G8 as the premier forum for global economic governance. Yet the extent to which a tectonic shift in the world order is occurring, and what the rise of the BRIC countries really amounts to, remains shrouded in deep uncertainty. In a very real sense the members of the G20 are puzzling out what this means for themselves, in part through their ongoing exchanges. At the same time, the G20 itself is a novel form of governance bringing together states that are not natural allies, with very different cultures, values, ideologies and preferences. Liberal-market economies sit alongside coordinated market economies (Hall and Soskice 2001), developmental states (Weiss 1998; Wade 2003), a one-party state caught between a command economy and a market system, and a ruling monarchy with the characteristics of a *rentier* state, suggesting that a shift towards a more plural world of coexisting civilisations may be under way (Cox 2004).

In turn, the capacity of these very different societies to maintain cooperative relations remains uncertain, because the G20 represents a unique experiment in international governance. It is itself characterised by an ongoing form of experimentation as its networks allow for informal dialogue and interactions in which members try out positions, attempt to broker deals, discover what potential for common ground exists, but also exchange ideas and learn from one another. As political science and international relations scholarship increasingly embraces and incorporates the insights of formal network analysis, the G20 represents a fertile empirical case for research that seeks to demonstrate the causal mechanisms through which networks constrain and enable their members, the effects of network position on the behaviour of G20 members, their networks' resources, power relationships, and the mechanisms through which international norms are diffused (Hafner-Burton et al. 2009). In relation to this last point, it should be remembered that the G20 represents a series of interlocking core apex networks, operating within, but also crucially influencing and instigating, a wide array of governance networks. Understanding the G20 requires that closer attention be paid to the dynamic relations of its constituent networks and the broader series of evolving relationships it has with wider networks.

The biggest policy challenge presently facing the G20 is the management of currency relationships and global imbalances. The fate of the dollar is now partially determined by the management of Chinese surpluses and the reserve holdings of East Asian exporters and Middle East oil producers, which is one of the reasons for the progressive migration of exchange rate issues to the G20. Questions remain as to whether the G20 is too large and unwieldy a group to discuss these issues meaningfully. The US position to date has been to push for exchange rate adjustments involving the abandonment of competitive devaluation policies in Asia, whilst also encouraging surplus countries to rely less on export growth and more on domestic demand for growth by means of structural reforms in both Asia and Europe. This is a way of reducing the US current account deficit and its over-reliance on foreign capital inflows. Surplus countries, on the other hand, tend to see the issue in terms of reductions in the US fiscal deficit and movement towards a multipolar reserve currency system, with the dollar being gradually replaced by a basket of currencies comprised of the euro and renminbi, as well as the dollar (Eichengreen 2010). Russia, China, Brazil and the European Union all have begun to discuss and consider such a move. It is highly unlikely that the US will be willing to forego the privileges connected to being the issuer of the dominant world reserve currency, including macroeconomic autonomy and seigniorage. At the same time, the dollar's continued long-term status is now partially in the hands of non-traditional US allies, such as China, Russia and Middle Eastern countries, due to their significant dollar reserve holdings (Thompson 2007). Any shift towards an alternative multipolar currency system based on a rebalancing of global demand that involves increased consumption in surplus countries will therefore have to be a slow, managed one. Anything more rapid is likely to depreciate too rapidly the dollar reserve holdings of those very states calling for an alternative. Managing this process as a slow transition and overcoming potential stalemates will require continuous dialogue, debate and information exchange as to how this can be accomplished, as well as a constant focus on future national policy intentions. This is most likely to take place through the G20 process. As such, the crucial, practical future test for the G20 will be its capacity to resolve economic conflict and avoid beggar-thy-neighbour policies in the handling of this difficult issue.

REFERENCES

Baker, A. (2006), *The Group of Seven: Finance Ministries, Central Banks and Global Financial Governance*, Abingdon: Routledge.
Baker, A. (2008), 'Global monitor: the Group of Seven', *New Political Economy*, 13 (1), 103–15.
Baker, A. (2009), 'Deliberative equality and the transgovernmental politics of the global financial architecture', *Global Governance*, 15 (2), 195–218.
Baker, A. (2010), 'Deliberative international financial governance and Apex Policy Forums: where we are and where we should be headed', in G. Underhill, J. Blom and D. Mügge (eds), *Global Financial Integration Thirty Years On: From Reform to Crisis*, Cambridge: Cambridge University Press, pp. 58–73.
Baker, A. (2013), 'The new political economy of the macroprudential ideational shift', *New Political Economy*, 18 (1), 112–39.
Balizil, B. and M. Schiessl (2009), 'The man nobody wanted to hear: global banking economist warned of coming crisis', *Spiegel online*, 07/08, available at: http://www.spiegel.de/international/business/0,1518,635051,00.html.
Banco Centro do Brasil (2010), 'CMN and BC adopt measures of macroprudential nature', available at: http://www.bcb.gov.br/textonoticia.asp?codigo=2823&idpai=NEWS.
Barrett, S. (1999), 'A theory of full international cooperation', *Journal of Theoretical Politics*, 11 (4), 519-41.
Bayne, N. (2004), 'Are world leaders puppets or puppeteers? The Sherpas and decision making within the G7/G8 system', in B. Reneilda and B. Veerbeek (eds), *Decision Making Within International Organisations*, New York: Routledge/ECPR Studies in European Political Science, pp. 139–54.
Beeson, Mark and Stephen Bell (2009), 'The G-20 and international economic governance: hegemony, collectivism, or both?' *Global Governance*, 15, 67–86.

Blyth, M. (2002), *Great Transformations: Economic Ideas and Institutional Change in the Twenty First Century*, Cambridge: Cambridge University Press.

Blyth, M. (2003), 'The political power of financial ideas: transparency, risk and distribution in global finance', in J. Kirshner (ed.), *Monetary Orders: Ambiguous Economics, Ubiquitous Politics*, Ithaca, NY: Cornell University Press, pp. 239–59.

Borio, C. (2009), 'Implementing the macroprudential approach to financial regulation and supervision', Banque de France, *Financial Stability Review*, No.13, September.

Borio, C. (2011), 'Implementing a macroprudential framework: blending boldness and realism', *Capitalism and Society*, **6** (1), 1–23.

Bretton Woods Project (2010), 'Less than meets the eye: IMF reform fails to revolutionise the institution', 9 November, available at: http://www.brettonwoodsproject.org/art-567128 (accessed 1 October 2011).

BRIC (2009), 'Final communiqué of the Meeting of Finance ministers and Central Bank governors of the BRIC countries', London, 4 September, available at: http://www.brazil.org.uk/press/articles_files/20090904.html (accessed 1 October 2011).

Chayes, A. and A. Chayes (1993), 'On compliance,' *International Organization*, **47** (2), 175–205.

Cohen, B. (2008), 'The international monetary system: diffusion and ambiguity', *International Affairs*, **84** (3), 455–70.

Cooper, A. (2010), 'The G20 as an improvised crisis committee and/or a contested "steering committee" for the world', *International Affairs*, **86** (3), 741–57.

Cox, R. (2004), 'Beyond empire and terror: critical reflections on political economy and world order', *New Political Economy*, **9** (3), 307–23.

Culpeper, R. (2000), 'Systemic reform at a standstill: a flock of "gs" in search of global financial stability', G8 Governance Working Paper Series, available at: http://www.g7.utoronto.ca/g7/scholar/culpeper2000/index.html (accessed 1 June 2010).

Dam, K.W. (2010), 'The G20 and IMF governance reform', in C. Hahm and J. Mo (eds), *Proceedings of International Conference on G20 and Global Governance Reform*, 11–12 October, Asian Institute for Policy Studies, Seoul, pp. 49–57.

De Brouwer, G. and L. Yeaman (2007), 'Australia's G-20 host year: a Treasury perspective', *Economic Round-up* (Australian Treasury), Autumn, 29–45.

Dobson, W. (1991), *International Economic Policy Co-ordination: Requiem or Prologue?*, Washington, DC: Institute for International Economic Policy Co-ordination.

Drezner, D. (2007), *All Politics is Global: Explaining International Regulatory Regimes* Princeton, NJ: Princeton University Press.

Eatwell, J. (2009), 'Practical proposals for regulatory reform', in P. Subacchi and A. Monsarrat (eds), *New Ideas for the London Summit: Recommendations to the G20 Leaders*, London: Royal Institute for International Affairs, Chatham House, Atlantic Council, pp. 11–15.

Eichengreen, B. (2010), *Exorbitant Privilege: The Rise and Fall of the Dollar and the Future of the International Monetary System*, Oxford: Oxford University Press.

Elliot, D. (2011), 'Choosing among macroprudential tools', Brookings Institute, available at: http://www.brookings.edu/~/media/Files/rc/papers/2011/0607_macroprudential_tools_elliott/0607_macroprudential_tools_elliott.pdf (accessed 8 November 2011).

FSB, BCBS, IMF (2011), 'Macroprudential policy tools and frameworks', Progress Report to G20, 27 October.

Funabashi, Y. (1988), *Managing the Dollar: From the Plaza to the Louvre*, Washington, DC: Institute for International Economics.

G20 (2007). 'The Group of Twenty: a history', available at: http://www.g20.org/Documents/history_report_dm1.pdf (accessed 18 November 2009).

G20 (2009), 'Leader's declaration: the Pittsburgh Summit', Pittsburgh, 24–25 September, available at: http://www.g20.org/Documents/pittsburgh_summit_leaders_statement_250909.pdf (accessed 1 October 2011).

Germain, R. (2001), 'Global financial governance and the problem of inclusion', *Global Governance*, **7** (4), 411–26.

Grabel, I. (2011), 'Not your grandfather's IMF: global crisis, productive incoherence and developmental policy space', *Cambridge Journal of Economics*, **35**, 805–30.

Greico, J. (1988), 'Anarchy and the limits of cooperation: a realist critique of the newest liberal institutionalism', *International Organization*, **42** (3), 485–507.

Hafner-Burton, E., M. Kahler and A. Montgomery (2009), 'Network analysis for international relations', *International Organization*, **63**, 559–92.

Hajnal, P. (2007), *The G8 System and the G20: Evolution, Role and Documentation*, Aldershot: Ashgate.

Haldane, A. and R. May (2011), 'Systemic risk in banking ecosystems', *Nature*, 469, 351–5.

Hall, P. and D. Soskice (2001), 'An introduction to varieties of capitalism', in P. Hall and D. Soskice (eds), *Varieties of Capitalism*, Oxford: Oxford University, pp. 1–70.

Helleiner, E. (2009), 'Filling a hole in global financial governance? The politics of regulating sovereign debt restructuring', in N. Mattli and N. Woods (eds), *The Politics of Global Regulation*, Princeton, NJ: Princeton University Press, pp. 89–119.

Helleiner, E. (2010), 'What role for the new Financial Stability Board? The politics of international standards after the crisis', *Global Policy*, **1** (3), 282–90.

International Monetary Fund (IMF) (2010), 'G-20 ministers agree "historic" reforms in IMF governance', *IMF Survey Magazine Online*, available at: http://www.imf.org/external/pubs/ft/survey/so/2010/NEW102310A.htm (accessed 1 October 2011).

James, H. (1996), *International Monetary Cooperation Since Bretton Woods*, Oxford: Oxford University Press.

Kahler, M. (ed). (2009), *Networked Politics: Agency, Power and Governance*, Ithaca, NY: Cornell University Press.

Keohane, R. and J. Nye (1974), 'Transgovernmental relations and international organizations', *World Politics*, **27** (1), 39–62.

Keohane, R. and J. Nye (2001), 'Between centralization and fragmentation: the club model of multilateral cooperation and problems of democratic legitimacy', Kennedy School of Government Working Paper No. 01-004, February.

Kirton, J. (2010), 'Multilateral organizations and G8 governance: a framework for analysis', in J. Kirton, M. Larionova and P. Savona (eds), *Making Global Economic Governance Effective: Hard and Soft Law Institutions*, Aldershot: Ashgate, pp. 23–42.

Kirton, J., J. Daniels and A. Freytag (eds) (2001), *Guiding Global Order: G8 Governance in the Twenty-First Century*, Aldershot: Ashgate.

Kirton, J. and G. von Furstenberg (eds) (2001), *New Directions in Global Economic Governance: Managing Globalisation in the Twenty-First Century*, Aldershot: Ashgate.

Martinez-Diaz, Leonardo (2007), 'The G20 after eight years: how effective a vehicle for developing country influence?' Brookings Global Economy and Development Working Paper No. 12, October, avalable at: http://www.brookings.edu/events/1998/0414global-economics.aspx (accessed 6 January 2011).

Martinez-Diaz, L. and N. Woods (2009), 'Introduction: developing countries in a networked global order,' in N. Woods and L. Martinez-Diaz (eds), *Networks of Influence? Developing Countries in a Networked Global Order*, Oxford: Oxford University Press, pp. 1–18.

Momani, B. (2008), 'Getting a seat at the IMF Executive Board table', paper submitted for consideration to *Political Economy of International Organizations*, Ascona, Switzerland, 3–8 February, available at: http://www.cis.ethz.ch/events/past_events/PEIO2008/Momani_Getting.IMF.Seat (accessed 1 October 2011).

Narlikar, A. (2010), 'New powers in the club: the challenges of global trade governance', *International Affairs*, **86** (3), 717–28.

Pauly, L. (1997), *Who Elected the Bankers? Surveillance and Control in the World Economy*, Ithaca, NY: Cornell University Press.

Payne, A. (2005), *The Global Politics of Unequal Development*, Basingstoke: Palgrave.

Payne, A. (2010), 'How many Gs are there in "global governance" after the crisis? The perspectives of the "marginal majority" of the world's states', *International Affairs*, **86** (3), 729–40.

Persaud, A. (2010), 'The locus of financial regulation: home versus host', *International Affairs*, **86** (3), 637–46.

Podolny, J. and K. Page (1998), 'Network forms of organization', *Annual Review of Sociology*, **24**, 57–76.

Porter, Tony (2001), 'The democratic deficit in the institutional arrangements for regulating global finance', *Global Governance*, **7**, 427–39.

Putnam, R. (1988), 'Diplomacy and domestic politics: the logic of two-level games', *International Organization*, **42** (3), 427–60.

Putnam, R. and N. Bayne (1987), *Hanging Together: Co-operation and Conflict in the Seven Power Summits*, London: Sage.

Putnam, R. and R. Henning (1989), 'The Bonn Summit of 1989: a case study in co-ordination', in R. Cooper (ed.), *Can Nations Agree? Issues in International Economic Cooperation*, Washington, DC: Brookings Institution, pp. 12–140.

Risse, T. (2000), 'Let's argue!': Communicative action in world politics', *International Organization*, **54** (1), 1–39.

Rubio-Marquez, V. (2009), 'The G20: a practitioner's perspective', in N. Woods and L. Martinez-Diaz (eds), *Networks of Influence? Developing Countries in a Networked Global Order*, Oxford: Oxford University Press, pp. 19–38.

Sabel, C. (2004), 'Beyond principal–agent governance: experimentalist organizations, learning and accountability', in E. Engelen and M. Sie Dihan Ho (eds), *De Staat van de Democratie*, WRR Verkenning 3, Amsterdam: Amsterdam University Press, pp. 173–95.

Snidal, D. (1991), 'Relative gains and the pattern of international cooperation', *American Political Science Review*, **85** (3), 701–26.

Sobel, M. and L. Stedman (2006), 'The evolution of the G7 and economic policy coordination', Occasional Paper No. 3, Department of the Treasury, Office of International Finance.

Soederberg, S. (2004), *The Politics of the New International Financial Architecture: Reimposing Neoliberal Dominance in the Global South*, London: Zed.

Sunstein, C. (2002), 'The law of group polarization,' *Journal of Political Philosophy*, **10** (2), 175–95.

Thompson, H. (2007), 'Debt and power: the United States' debt in historical perspective', *International Relations*, **21** (3), 305–28.

Truman, E. (ed.) (2006), 'Reforming the IMF for the 21st century', Washington, DC: Peterson Institute.

Wade, R. (2003), *Governing the Market: Economic Theory and the Role of Government in East Asian Industrialization*, Princeton, NJ: Princeton University Press.

Warwick Commission (2009), 'The Warwick Commission on international financial reform: in praise of unlevel playing fields', December, Coventry: University of Warwick.

Weiss, L. (1998), *The Myth of the Powerless State*, Ithaca, NY. Cornell University Press.

Woods, N. (2000), 'Making the IMF and World Bank more accountable', *International Affairs*, **77** (1), 83–100.

6 The International Monetary Fund and the governance of international surveillance
Manuela Moschella

'Financial crisis: a hardy perennial': this is not just the title of the introductory chapter of Robert Aliber and Charles Kindleberger's *Manias, Panic and Crashes* (2011), but also an eloquent reminder of one of the distinct features of financial markets, namely, their inherently unstable nature (Minsky 1986). As the global financial crisis of the late 2000s vividly reminded us, during the upward trend of the business cycle, markets are prone to euphoric behaviour that fuels asset and property bubbles. The latter burst as soon as the business cycle deteriorates to the point where debts exceed what borrowers can pay off from their incoming revenues.

Recognising the perennial nature of financial instability, domestic political systems have over time developed several governance arrangements that are meant to circumscribe the effects of financial instability. These arrangements include prudential regulatory regimes, financial safety nets, and legal and accounting procedures. Similar efforts have been undertaken at the global level, where several governance arrangements exist which aim at minimising the likelihood of crisis and ensuring that those crises which do occur do not become systemic. These arrangements, which include both formal institutions and informal social practices, span those designed to prevent the eruption of crises – including surveillance mechanisms, prudential rules and procedures for regulatory cooperation and harmonisation – and those mainly designed to manage crises once they occur, such as the provisions that govern the functioning of the global financial safety net.

This chapter focuses on a specific set of governance arrangements that has been developed with the aim of contributing to global financial stability: namely, the arrangements which preside over the international monitoring of national economic policies. Specifically, my purpose is to assess the changes that have taken place in the governance framework for surveillance in the aftermath of the global financial crisis of the late 2000s. Particular attention will be devoted to analysing the surveillance tasks that the International Monetary Fund (IMF) performs. Indeed, the monitoring, with associated policy advice, of national economic and financial policies is at the heart of that institution's responsibilities.[1] In particular, one of the Fund's key tasks is that of 'help[ing] head off risks to international monetary and financial stability, alert[ing] the institution's 187 member countries to potential risks and vulnerabilities, and advis[ing] them of needed policy adjustments' (IMF 2007). The IMF thus provides a privileged perspective from which to identify some key developments in the policy area of surveillance by shedding light on 'the political architecture for global capital markets' (Pauly 1997: 8).

Distinguishing among the procedural, instrumental and ideational dimensions of governance frameworks, the chapter argues that three main post-crisis trends are emerging in IMF surveillance. The first is increased collaboration with other official regulatory bodies, in particular with the newly created Financial Stability Board (FSB). The second is the deepening of financial sector surveillance (FSS) within the framework of a macro-financial approach to global surveillance (Moschella 2011; Baker 2012). The third concerns the way in which the crisis has called into question the previously dominant views that markets are self-stabilising, and that emerging market economies – and not advanced economies – are the primary source of risk and should therefore be the main target of international surveillance.

Before proceeding, some clarifications are in order. To start with, this chapter is not meant to provide an assessment of the effectiveness of the post-crisis changes in IMF surveillance as compared to the pre-crisis ones. In other words, its purpose is not to evaluate whether the transformations in the conduct of surveillance will lead the IMF to be more effective than in the past. Nor does the chapter deal with the issue of democratic deficits in the governance arrangements under examination. Instead, its purpose is to bring to the surface some of the most important changes that have resulted from the contemporary global financial crisis in order to reflect on their transformative potential for global financial governance at large.

I develop my argument in three steps. First, I tease out some of the conceptual underpinnings of financial governance and introduce the key features of the pre-crisis surveillance governance framework. Second, I trace the changes that have taken place since the start of the crisis in 2007. Finally, I summarise the findings and reflect on their implications for global financial governance and for the challenges that IMF is expected to confront in the near future.

GOVERNING FINANCIAL STABILITY: THREE GOVERNANCE DIMENSIONS AND PRE-CRISIS TRENDS

Although international financial stability may at first glance appear as a technical matter that is remote from citizens' most pressing concerns, this is clearly not the case. Episodes of distress in global financial markets, including those that arise from poor domestic policies or international capital withdrawals, may destroy the capacity of the domestic financial sector to generate credit for activities such as consumption and investment. The resulting impact on the real economy, in terms of output loss and unemployment, can be severe and long-lasting, as the global financial crisis has once again vividly confirmed. In light of these considerations, it is therefore not surprising that financial stability is usually considered as a public good (Kindleberger 1973) and that states, regulatory authorities and even market participants devote considerable time and resources to designing international rules and institutions that can mitigate the tendency of financial turmoil to spill across borders (Abdelal 2007; Baker 2006; Kapstein 1994; Pauly 1997; Porter 2005; Singer 2007).

The IMF and its monitoring of national economic policies have long played a primary role in the governance framework that aims at preventing financial instability and managing crises once they occur. As conceived in the aftermath of the Second World War, the global governance framework was based on a clear code of conduct that set up the rules that national authorities were expected to follow. Under the par-valued exchange rate system, the international monitoring of the Fund consisted in the application of these rules of conduct, meaning that national policies were judged in terms of their consistency with the agreed par values. With the break-up of the Bretton Woods system in the 1970s, however, the rule-based system of global surveillance gave way to a discretion-based system in which the IMF's assessment of national policies was no longer exclusively anchored to the stability of currencies' par values. With the abandonment of the fixed exchange rate system, and the integration of world financial markets and associated challenges (Helleiner 1994), the assessment of the consistency of national policies with the international financial stability commitment became a much more discretionary and complicated task.

In order to analyse the main characteristics of global surveillance in the period that preceded the crisis of the late 2000s, it is important to identify a metric for such a judgement. In this connection, I break up the concept of governance into three dimensions that refer to the process through which policy solutions to specific problems are produced, the instruments through these solutions are achieved and, finally, the core beliefs that actors widely share on how to govern a specific issue area. In what follows, I focus on each dimension in turn and exemplify them through the analysis of the pre-crisis governance framework in the area of global surveillance.

First, governance systems vary according to the modalities through which policy solutions are taken or political action is exercised. A key dimension here is the number of actors that are involved in the decision-making process or in the delivery of a specific course of action. For instance, it is plausible to conceive of governance systems as varying along a continuum that ranges from centralised to fragmented. Whereas the former are characterised by the prevalence of one actor over the others, the latter are based on the collaboration of several actors for either adopting policies or carrying out the necessary political action to solve the specific problems of the governance area.

In the case of the global surveillance framework, the IMF has long occupied a primary position in the governance of this issue area. The central role of the Fund was maintained even in the aftermath of the collapse of the Bretton Woods system, when the Fund's responsibilities changed from those of an enforcer of member countries' observance of exchange-rate rules to those of an overseer of individual countries' exchange rate policies (Guitiàn 1992: 6). Since the early 1990s, however, several international and regional bodies have assumed increasing importance in the conduct of surveillance activity. Along with the IMF and the traditional surveillance functions exercised by the Bank for International Settlements (BIS) and the Organisation for Economic Co-operation and Development (OECD), a more prominent role has progressively been played by groups such as the Group of 20 (G20), regional economic groups, the FSB, and regional- and country-specific financial stability risk boards.

The growing relevance of these bodies and the attendant fragmentation of the governance framework can be explained by the shortcomings of the Fund's surveillance, which were brought to the surface by the emerging market crises of the 1990s (Independent Evaluation Office 2004, 2005; IMF 1999; Moschella 2010). The Fund repeatedly failed in identifying and warning about the incipient risks to global financial stability.[2] The complexity and interconnections that characterise today's global financial markets are also helpful in explaining the increasing dispersion of supervisory powers among several international bodies. Since an effective surveillance needs to make sense of macro-financial linkages and linkages across sectors and countries, up-to-date data and analyses are needed on domestic regulatory and supervisory structures, as well as on various market segments. No single organisation or regulatory body can be expected successfully to collect and analyse all the relevant information. The division of surveillance functions across several bodies can therefore increase the effectiveness of this important activity, even though one of the unintended consequences could be duplications of work (Schinasi and Truman 2010).

Second, governance systems also vary in terms of the instruments that are used to achieve the stated goal of a policy decision. In this connection, it is plausible to think of governance systems as varying along a spectrum that ranges from the use of hard-law instruments to the use of soft-law instruments. That is to say, whereas some governance systems may be characterised by strong enforcement mechanisms, others are based on instruments such as persuasion and cooperation. The latter may be attractive for national governments that want to limit sovereignty losses. In contrast, governance systems based on hard law imply delegation of 'authority for interpreting and implementing the law' (Abbott and Snidal 2000: 421–2), which refers to precise, legally binding obligations.

The distinction between hard and soft instruments has been useful in examining multilateral surveillance activities such as those that the OECD regularly carries out. In particular, it has been noted that surveillance can be associated with two different sets of instruments. The first are coercive instruments, which induce the fear of being punished. The use of economic sanctions and financial pressures belongs to this category of surveillance instruments. The second are instruments based on persuasion and moral pressures, including shaming, ridiculing and exclusion (Marcussen 2004: 13).

Next to their degree of stringency, surveillance instruments can also be distinguished according to the target of policy analysis and advice. That is to say, some surveillance instruments focus on assessing domestic macroeconomic management, while others are more tailored to assessing the robustness of regulatory, supervisory and crisis management systems. As for the IMF, the original core of the Fund surveillance was macroeconomic analysis. The IMF has traditionally analysed and provided advice on issues such as the choice of the exchange rate and the consistency between the regime of fiscal and monetary policy. In contrast, financial sector issues largely fell outside the purview of its monitoring activity, at least until the mid-1990s (Gola and Spadafora 2009). The limited attention devoted to financial sector issues is largely attributable to the characteristics of the IMF as an economic organisation. In particular, both the composition of its staff, which is primarily recruited from the macroeconomics profession (Momani 2005), and the institutional mandate that govern the Fund's activities, have oriented the focus of surveillance towards macroeconomic factors (Moschella 2012b).

From the early 1990s onwards, however, the range of IMF surveillance instruments has been significantly expanded to include financial sector issues. Member countries' policies to develop the domestic financial sector, and ensure sound governance and risk management in financial institutions, have been increasingly included in the Fund's analyses. Several factors contributed to the expansion of IMF surveillance towards financial sector surveillance (FSS), including the growing integration of global financial markets and the attendant recognition of the risks that such integration entails, as exemplified in the financial crises of the 1990s (Gola and Spadafora 2009; James 1995; Moschella 2011). However, the development of financial sector analyses has not been an automatic and rapid process, with the result that FSS was still a work-in-progress process when the global financial crisis burst (Moschella 2012b). One of the negative implications of the poor development of FSS within the Fund has been the organisation's failure to spot the severe risks and vulnerabilities that were building up in the global financial system from 2004 to 2007. Indeed, staff continued to focus on factors such as global imbalances and disorderly dollar decline as the key risks to global stability, largely failing to identify the risks building up in the financial sector where in fact the crisis burst (Independent Evaluation Office 2011).

Finally, it is possible to distinguish different kinds of governance arrangements and trace their evolution over time by focusing on the core beliefs that inform the conduct of a specific area of activity. Indeed, each policy area is characterised by the presence of a deep core of fundamental norms and beliefs which are regarded as widely shared in a policy community (Sabatier and Jenkins-Smith 1993). Core beliefs are distinct from policy solutions or strategies in that they identify basic normative preferences (Steinmo 2003). That is to say, core beliefs provide agents with not only a 'scientific', but also a 'normative' account of how a polity or a specific policy sector is expected to operate, defining 'what the common end of collective action should in fact be' (Blyth 2002: 38; Berman 1998: 29).

Some distinctive beliefs characterised the governance of the policy area of global surveillance in the run-up to the global financial crisis. Specifically, one of the hallmarks of the pre-crisis financial governance was the widespread faith in financial markets as a stabilising and efficient mechanism to ensure global stability and thereby mitigate the risks associated with the integration of world's capital markets (Baker 2012; Helleiner et al. 2009). This specific world-view of financial markets emphasised their self-stabilising quality by virtue of their rational efficiency and capacity to process and respond to information (Best 2010; Blyth 2003). Since private actors were regarded as having a comparative informational and expertise advantage over public authorities, the latter tended to delegate traditional governmental functions to the former. For instance, in the area of market regulation, Adrienne Heritier and Dirk Lehmkuhl (2011) have found that governments tend to rely more frequently on self-regulation by sectoral experts, particularly in areas of highly complex issues of market regulation. The belief in the stabilising role of the markets and in their superior informational set had important policy implications for the conduct of surveillance.

To start with, the widespread faith in markets as agents of financial stability led to the conclusion that the 'right' purpose of international surveillance should have been that of enhancing transparency (see also Best 2005). Increased information would have allowed market participants to make more informed and rational investment decisions, enabling them to discipline those countries judged to be following inappropriate policies and therefore ensure global financial stability. The belief in the self-stabilising quality of markets also led to the reliance on market discipline as an instrument to enforce global surveillance. Indeed, it is possible to say that one the most important pre-crisis trends was the partial privatisation of global surveillance activity as part of a broader trend towards the involvement of the private sector in global economic and financial governance (Cutler et al. 1999; Graz and Nölke 2008; Hall and Biersteker 2002).

This is particularly evident in the standards and codes initiative which followed the Asian financial crisis. The logic that underpinned this initiative was that international financial standards might be of help to promote good economic policies and transparency and therefore contribute to international financial stability (Financial Stability Forum 2001, 2000). Nevertheless, it was also widely believed that the success of the international standardisation initiative was closely dependent on the involvement of the private sector (Mosley 2003). If market participants had assessed countries' performance against internationally recognised standards in their investment decisions, thereby pricing capital on the record of compliance with international standards, the threats to international financial stability would have been reduced (Fischer 1999). The initiative consequently delegated the international monitoring of domestic policies to the private sector by giving it the task of assessing domestic policies against globally defined standards and enforcing them, 'as non-compliance would send negative signals to the international financial community, resulting in possible capital flight and investment strike' (Soederberg 2003: 13).

Finally, it is interesting to note that another core belief of the pre-crisis governance framework was the assumption that the main threat to global financial stability would have emanated from vulnerabilities in the domestic financial system of emerging market countries. This belief was nurtured by the experience of the Asian crisis. The fact that weaknesses in domestic financial sectors – substantial foreign borrowing by the private sector and a weak and overexposed banking system – significantly contributed to the severity of the 1997 crisis strengthened the position of those who argued that the focus of international surveillance should shift towards the assessment of the domestic financial systems of emerging market countries (see Eichengreen 1999; Goldstein 1999; Kenen 2001). One of the most visible implications of this belief was that the aforementioned international financial standard initiative was directed at the diffusion of international financial standards, modelled upon those of the Western countries (Mosley 2010: 738). The expectation was that the diffusion of the standards developed in the advanced economies would have diminished the probability of a crisis in an emerging country with the attendant global contagion.

In short, the governance of global surveillance in the late 1990s was staked on the premise that the main risk to the global economy was likely to materialise in the domestic financial system of emerging market countries. Hence, these countries were encouraged to bring their domestic financial systems in line with those of the advanced countries by following internationally recognised standards of financial conduct. In other words, it was 'implicitly assumed that [Western] regulatory systems had been operating efficiently' (Walter 2008: 22, 24). The unleashing of the global financial crisis proved these assumptions wrong. The Western world expected the crisis to erupt in a developing country, whereas in fact it erupted in the most sophisticated financial market in the world. In what follows, I trace what has changed in the governance framework as a result of the crisis, using as a benchmark the three dimensions just outlined.

EMERGING POST-CRISIS GOVERNANCE FORMS

The global financial crisis, like most of the other crises that preceded it, has dramatically shown the challenges that global surveillance faces in light of the integration and complexity of the world's financial markets. The IMF failed to identify the risks that were building up in the global financial system and to provide clear warnings to spur remedial political action. Specifically, the IMF performed poorly in identifying the risks that were building up in the US housing sector, as well as those in the global financial system as a whole, as the result of the securitisation of mortgages and the reliance on the shadow banking system (Independent Evaluation Office 2011). Likewise, it proved unable to appreciate the channels of global financial contagion and their implications for the real economy. These problems, which were not unique to the IMF but common to most of the international bodies tasked with surveillance responsibilities, were compounded by severe blind spots in the data available to financial regulators and supervisors. For instance, there have been serious information gaps about the quality of securitised instruments and the global interconnections of financial institutions via derivative transactions (Financial Stability Board and IMF 2009).

Faced with its weaknesses, the Fund has started an in-house reflection on the key elements of its surveillance strategy (IMF 2009b, 2010a, 2011b) and embarked on a process of reform to improve its activities. At the same time, the Fund has been called on to expand its surveillance repertoire by the Group of 20 (G20) leaders and has been involved in new surveillance initiatives with other international bodies. Let us assess these changes against the three governance dimensions identified in the previous section.

First, in relation to the process through which policy solutions are produced, one of the consequences of the post-crisis reform process has been increased collaboration between the IMF and other regulatory bodies, namely, the G20 Leaders and the FSB. The IMF has been asked to expand its monitoring activities by assessing the compatibility of the G20 countries' national economic policies with the objective of achieving strong, sustainable and balanced growth within the framework of the Mutual Assessment Programme (MAP). The Fund has also been involved in a number of surveillance activities carried out in conjunction with the FSB, which include the IMF–FSB Data Initiative and the Early Warning Exercise (EWE).

The Data Initiative aims at redressing one of the problems experienced during the crisis, namely, the lack of information on key financial sector vulnerabilities relevant for financial stability analysis. Indeed, at the height of the crisis, it became clear that there were scarcely any data available on the level of borrowing outside the traditional banking system, exposures taken through complex instruments, or the cross-border linkages of financial institutions. As a result, measuring risks deriving from maturity transformation or assessing the extent to which financial institutions and markets were interconnected proved very difficult. The IMF–FSB Data Initiative has thus started identifying the main gaps that need to be covered, as well as the lead international agency that will take responsibility for collecting the relevant data for each area (Clegg and Moschella 2013). The EWE, in turn, is an attempt to signal trends that could make markets or countries vulnerable to unanticipated events. It is meant to analyse vulnerabilities in depth, focusing on channels of transmission and contagion (IMF 2010b: 10). Both the IMF–FSB Data Initiative and the EWE were expressly mandated by the G20 leaders, respectively in April 2009 and November 2008.

These joint initiatives confirm one of the key pre-crisis trends, namely, the dispersion of surveillance responsibilities in the governance framework among several international bodies. This is also particularly evident in the new functions attributed to the FSB (Griffith-Jones et al. 2010; Helleiner 2010; Moschella 2012a). Indeed, one of the main changes associated with the transformation of the Financial Stability Forum (FSF) into the FSB in April 2009 was the enhancement of the monitoring functions attributed to the new body. In addition to the tasks that had already been mandated to the FSF – to assess vulnerabilities affecting the financial system, identify and oversee action needed to address them, and promote coordination and information exchange among authorities responsible for financial stability – the FSB has been tasked with the responsibilities of: (1) monitoring and advising on market developments and their implications for regulatory policy; (2) advising on and monitoring best practice in meeting regulatory standards; and (3) undertaking joint strategic reviews of the policy development work of the international standard-setter bodies (SSBs) to ensure their work is timely, coordinated, focused on priorities and addressing gaps (Article 2 of the FSB Charter).[3]

The FSB has also been tasked with the responsibility of conducting a programme of peer reviews, consisting of both thematic reviews and country reviews. Whereas thematic reviews focus on the implementation across the FSB membership of the financial standards developed by SSBs and analyse areas important for global financial stability, country reviews focus on the implementation and effectiveness of regulatory, supervisory or other financial sector policies in a specific FSB member jurisdiction. Country reviews are also conducted in cooperation with the international financial institutions in that they examine the steps taken or planned by national authorities to address the recommendations contained in the IMF–World Bank Financial Sector Assessment Program (FSAP) and Reports on the Observance of Standards and Codes (ROSCs). In short, the bulk of the new functions delegated to the FSB revolve around those of an enhanced monitoring of global stability and domestic regulatory and financial policies, therefore creating the conditions for potential duplication of work with the IMF.

Second, in terms of the instruments through which global surveillance is conducted, the post-crisis debate and reforms indicate a twofold development. To start with, there is a persistent reluctance to rely on hard measures to ensure compliance with the recommended policy advice.[4] That is to say, there have been no serious attempts at strengthening the corrective arm of global surveillance. Rather, in the 2011 Triennial Surveillance Review, the IMF emphasised 'the heavy premium' that its membership places 'on the cooperative nature of the institution', therefore rejecting the use of sanctions or other hard-quality instruments to enforce compliance with surveillance recommendations (IMF 2011a: 11). The reluctance to embrace hard measures to enforce the findings of global surveillance is also evident in the workings of the FSB. Specifically, in spite of the expansion of the FSB's responsibilities in enforcing compliance with international standards, the procedure for addressing the consequences of non-compliance has not been clarified (Helleiner 2010: 18). The decision-making rules that have been designed for the Plenary, which is the FSB decision-making body, constitute a further problem for the enforcement of global surveillance. In particular, the Plenary operates on the basis of consensus, meaning that a decision is considered adopted if no voting member opposes it or actively votes against it if given the opportunity. Here the potential problem is that the required unanimity implied in the consensus rule may weaken the FSB's capacity to enforce members' compliance with their commitments to undergo peer reviews and implement international financial standards. Indeed, it is hard to see how a non-complying jurisdiction will have its membership revoked if a consensual decision is needed in the Plenary (see also Baker 2010: 22; Helleiner 2010: 11; Moschella 2012a).

Furthermore, the post-crisis debate and reforms indicate renewed efforts in integrating financial sector issues into regular surveillance. These are exemplified in a number of policy initiatives. For instance, the IMF's financial stability assessments under the Financial Sector Assessment Program (FSAP) have been made mandatory for 25 members with systemically important financial sectors in an explicit recognition of the devastating implications that financial regulatory issues can have for global stability and economic well-being. The IMF has launched the vulnerability exercise for advanced and emerging market economies (VEA and VEE) and low-income countries (LICs) alike. The EWE the Fund conducts with the FSB is a further example of the way in which the Fund is strengthening its oversight of financial sector issues. Indeed, in the attempt to detect vulnerabilities to global financial stability, the EWE incorporates measures of common distress across global financial institutions and non-financial firms, as well as across sovereigns and asset markets (such as equity and credit markets) and data on cross-border bank exposures (IMF 2010b: 16).

Next to the focus on financial sector issues, the post-crisis debate and reforms also indicate strengthened efforts in deepening understanding of the links between financial and real activity and refining analysis of interconnectedness (IMF 2012). In short, the Fund is reorienting the focus of its surveillance instruments towards a macrofinancial or systemic approach (Moschella 2011). As the IMF (2012: 4) puts it: 'Recognizing the increased interconnectedness among countries and financial markets, there is a need for a more systemic focus, as well as a more integrated approach to macrofinancial policies, at the global level.'

In other words, IMF surveillance instruments have been refocused to the task of 'connecting the dots' in order to improve the organisation's understanding of the spillovers from highly interconnected financial centres, institutions and markets. To achieve this goal, the Fund has launched spillover reports for systematically important countries, including the United States, China, Japan, the Eurozone countries and the United Kingdom. That is to say, it has developed assessments of the international impact of the policies of the world's five largest economies. The increased attention towards spillovers in surveillance activity is further evident in the Decision on Bilateral and Multilateral Surveillance adopted by the Fund's Executive Board in July 2012; that is, the Integrated Surveillance Decision (ISD). Under the new Decision, if spillovers from a member's policies are considered to have the potential to undermine global economic and financial stability, these policies need to be discussed with the member within the Fund's bilateral surveillance (ISD paragraphs 22(iii)(b), 22(iv), 22 (vii)). The reorientation towards systemic surveillance is further evident in the design of the EWE, which 'aims to "connect the dots" between different risks, uncovering the scope for potential spillovers, and to understand their systemic impact . . . focusing on channels of transmission and contagion' (IMF 2010b: 10). The Fund is aware of the need to combine more effectively the findings of its bilateral and multilateral surveillance to deepen its understanding of the links between financial and real activity (IMF 2011b).

Finally, and closely connected to the transformations described thus far, the crisis seems to have brought about some important changes at the level of the belief system. In particular, the IMF's efforts at building a macrofinancial approach to surveillance point to a new understanding of what is the most appropriate focus of the policies of this area (Moschella 2011). In particular, similar to the shift towards macroprudential regulation that is taking place in international supervisory bodies such as the BIS and the

FSB (Baker 2012), the shift in the IMF suggests that the focus of international surveillance should no longer be confined to that of enhancing transparency and information to the markets, based on the belief that the private sector 'knows best' how to contribute to global financial stability (Kodres and Narain 2010: 4). Rather, the focus of international surveillance should be on the markets themselves. As the IMF unmistakeably puts it in one of the documents in which it investigates the causes of the crisis, the financial turmoil revealed that 'market discipline failed as optimism prevailed, due diligence was outsourced to credit rating agencies, and a financial sector compensation system based on short-term profits reinforced the momentum for risk taking' (IMF 2009a: 2; also de Laroisiére 2009; Financial Services Authority 2009).

Next to the emerging change in the belief in market discipline, the crisis and the attendant reforms to surveillance activities within and outside the IMF suggest another area where pre-crisis beliefs have at least been shaken. While it was widely believed that the international surveillance should focus primarily on the domestic financial systems in emerging market countries, one of the lessons of the crisis has been that such a limited focus was not helpful to the maintenance of global financial stability. Indeed, advanced economies constituted a primary source of risk, not only for the eruption of the crisis but also for its contagion, primarily via the financial channels. As the IMF (2011c: 15) puts it, 'the experience of the crisis suggests that more effective advanced economy regulation and supervision – consistent with international standards – would not only have better supported domestic stability, but would also have helped make capital flows safer'. As a result, many of the surveillance reforms have explicitly been targeted at reinforcing the surveillance over advanced economies. The Fund's vulnerability exercise for advanced economies, as well as the systemic spillover reports, are among the clearest examples in this regard. To these, we can certainly add the G20 surveillance exercise and the FSB peer review processes.

In summary, in the aftermath of the global financial crisis major changes have taken place in the conduct of IMF surveillance. These changes relate to the collaboration with other international bodies tasked with surveillance functions, the nature of the instruments used in the exercise of these functions and the core beliefs that guide them. The conclusions to the chapter now reflect on the implications of these findings for the evolution of both the IMF and global financial governance.

CONCLUSIONS

It is widely recognised that an external shock, such as a financial crisis, is likely to act as a catalyst for institutional change. The global financial crisis has been no exception, with 'change' touted as the catchword in the international financial governance debate (Moschella and Tsingou 2013). This chapter has engaged with the question of change in the aftermath of the crisis by focusing on the adjustments that have taken place in the governance arrangements that preside over the conduct of surveillance, particularly as they affect IMF surveillance.

The findings suggest some important implications for both global financial governance and the IMF. From a global perspective, the evidence lends support to existing propositions that the global financial crisis has the potential to generate a profound reorientation in the philosophy that underpins global financial regulation and supervision (Baker 2012; Foot and Walter 2011: 249; Germain 2010; Pagliari 2012; for a more sceptical view, see Broome et al. 2012). Although the initial response to the global financial crisis reiterated the need to rely on greater transparency, disclosure and improved risk management as the most appropriate responses to the financial turmoil (Best 2010), the debate has since shifted to the question of how to strengthen public sector initiatives, be they the improvement of IMF surveillance or the creation of new international bodies such as the FSB. Of course, this does not imply that market discipline has disappeared from the philosophy that underpins processes of global surveillance. More narrowly, the post-crisis debate and the new macrofinancial or systemic approach to surveillance imply a higher degree of intervention by public authorities and a shift away from an excessive reliance on the principles of market discipline (e.g. IMF et al. 2009).

As for the IMF, the changes that are documented in this chapter indicate the emergence of at least three challenges for the organisation. First, the progressive fragmentation of international surveillance calls for the establishment of mechanisms of cooperation among the many institutions involved. For instance, as noted earlier, the strengthened surveillance role for the FSB risks creating tensions and duplication of work with the IMF. This development thus requires the establishment of an appropriate division of labour and mechanisms of inter-institutional collaboration (Draghi and Strauss-Khan 2008). In the conduct of the EWE, agreement has been reached that the IMF will lead the work on macroeconomic and macrofinancial vulnerabilities, while the FSB will take the lead on vulnerabilities and regulatory challenges in the financial sector (IMF 2010b: 4).

Second, the rejection of a more robust framework for surveillance – including potential sanctions on countries for non-compliance with the Fund's recommendations – casts doubt on the potential of the IMF's procedures of multilateral surveillance to induce change (for an alternative approach to sanctions, see Palais Royale Initiative 2011; Truman 2010). As has often been noted (Broome and Seabrooke 2007; Lombardi and Woods 2008), IMF surveillance is severely limited by the inherent voluntarism of soft law, which is unable to oblige reluctant governments to change their policies.

Finally, the post-crisis changes to IMF surveillance pose important efficiency and legitimacy challenges that derive from the shift towards a systemic surveillance approach (Moschella 2012b). As for the efficiency challenge, a question can be raised regarding whether the Fund's organisational culture is ready for the complexities associated with conduct of systemic surveillance. For instance, it has been repeatedly noted that poor financial expertise has prevented the Fund from developing fully formed understandings of the relationship between financial sector weaknesses and global macroeconomic and financial stability on several occasions (e.g. IMF 1999; Moschella 2011). This pattern was replicated in the run-up to the global financial crisis. Indeed, the dominant macroeconomic expertise of IMF staff helps explain why, in spite of the alarm bell sounded by the crises of the 1990s, staff continued to focus on factors such as global imbalances and disorderly dollar decline as the key risks to global stability, largely failing to take action to address the risks building up in the financial sector (Independent Evaluation Office 2011). Within the IMF, these problems are well known (IMF 2011b), as reflected in the Action Plan for Surveillance, where the Managing Director calls for increased use of financial sector expertise in Article IV consultations, to be achieved by assigning a financial expert to each Article IV team for countries with systemically important financial sectors and for countries with mounting financial vulnerabilities, as well as by deepening internal training on these issues (IMF 2012: 8).

Furthermore, a major concern surrounds the ability of the IMF to collect the relevant data to conduct systemic surveillance (Moschella 2012b). Indeed, systemic surveillance entails taking into consideration not only government policies but also the activities of those actors that form the financial system, including large financial institutions, counterparties and asset managers. The problem for the IMF is that having access to this information would require the organisation to request its members to report data that they are not currently obliged to report.[5] The IMF is well aware of these shortcomings. For instance, in a background paper to the proposal to give the Fund the role of a systemic supervisor, it acknowledges that, 'although financial network analysis is increasingly recognised as a priority, the limited availability of data is a major challenge. Progress in mapping the international financial network is most advanced in banking, based on data collected by the BIS . . . But in other areas, there are substantial data gaps' (IMF 2010c: 9). In particular, the most serious gaps concern data-related exposures and maturities in debt securities and derivatives markets, foreign exchange markets and international equity markets. Data are not only missing. In other cases, data do exist but not in a useable form. This is particularly the case for networks involving decentralised over-the-counter (OTC) markets where intermediaries typically know their own exposures but not those of counterparties. However, this discussion is not meant to suggest that the IMF does not have – and is not able to develop – the analytical skills to undertake a through surveillance of the global financial system, as some commentators imply (Bossone 2009). The problem is more simply that the reforms that are taking place in IMF surveillance are at the limits of the Fund's expertise and resources, raising the question of whether the organisation is up to the task.

Finally, next to efficiency challenges there are also legitimacy challenges, associated with the shift to a macrofinancial or systemic approach to surveillance. Exploiting the discretion accorded to the Fund in the conduct of surveillance, the Fund is suggesting incorporating systemic surveillance into its mandate by changing its staff's operational practices and adjusting existing instruments. In other words, no formal change to the Fund's Articles of Agreement is envisaged and the discussion on a Multilateral Surveillance Decision, which would help clarify the scope and modalities of the new surveillance, is staked on the premise that such a decision is not proposed for adoption – at this stage, at least (IMF 2010a: 6). However, switching to systemic surveillance without a formal mandate cannot but aggravate the crisis of legitimacy of the organisation, especially in light of the scope of the proposed reform. That is to say, the lack of legalisation of IMF reform risks compromising the legitimacy of the organisation (see Beetham 1991: 17–21), undermining the very effectiveness of the proposed reform. Indeed, developing an approach to financial supervision that is premised on the assumption that domestic financial sector policies should be judged in terms of their spillover effects for other countries requires significant political support, since members, at least in principle, agree to adjust their financial policies not for the sake of their domestic economy but for the well-being of the international system. Hence, in the absence of the necessary political support, a change in the Fund's mode of surveillance is unlikely to be fully implemented, making the overall project of reforming IMF surveillance less successful than its designers believe it will be.

NOTES

1. Of course, surveillance is not the only task the IMF performs. The provision of financial assistance to members facing a fundamental disequilibrium in their balance of payments and the provision of technical assistance are the other main activities that the Fund regularly discharges. Nevertheless, according to some commentators, these other tasks can be considered modalities of surveillance from other perspectives (see, for instance, Guitiàn 1992: 22–5).
2. The global financial crisis has been no exception here. As will be clarified at greater length below, the IMF – as most other international observers – failed to clearly identify the signs of the incipient risks to global financial stability and to elicit action from global policy-makers (Independent Evaluation Office 2011).
3. The other tasks attributed to the FSB are those of setting guidelines for the establishment of supervisory colleges; managing contingency planning for cross-border crisis management; and collaborating with the IMF to conduct Early Warning Exercises.
4. An exception to this trend is represented by the surveillance reforms in Europe, where the European Union (EU) Commission has advanced proposals that include fines and other penalties for countries that deviate from the recommendations issued under the EU multilateral surveillance exercise.
5. Although under Article IV, Section 3(b) member countries have an obligation to provide the Fund with the information needed to conduct bilateral surveillance over exchange rate policies, Article VIII, Section 5 clarifies that members are under no obligation to provide information 'in such detail that the affairs of individuals or corporations are disclosed'.

REFERENCES

Abbott, Kenneth W. and Duncan Snidal (2000), 'Hard and soft law in international governance', *International Organization*, **54** (3), 421–56.
Abdelal, Rawi (2007), *Capital Rules: The Construction of Global Finance*, Cambridge, MA: Harvard University Press.
Aliber, Robert Z. and Charles P. Kindleberger (2011), *Manias, Panics, and Crashes, 6th edition*, Basingstoke: Palgrave Macmillan.
Baker, Andrew (2006), *The Group of Seven: Finance Ministries, Central Banks and Global Financial Governance*, London: Routledge.
Baker, Andrew (2010), 'Mandate, accountability and decision-making issues to be faced by the Financial Stability Board', in Stephany Griffith-Jones, Eric Helleiner and Ngaire Woods (eds), *The Financial Stability Board: An Effective Fourth Pillar of Global Economic Governance?*, Waterloo, Ontario: Centre for International Governance Innovation (CIGI), pp. 19–22.
Baker, Andrew (2012), 'The new political economy of the macroprudential ideational shift', *New Political Economy*, **18** (1), 112–39.
Beetham, David (1991), *The Legitimation of Power*, Basingstoke: Palgrave Macmillan.
Berman, Sheri (1998), *The Social Democratic Moment: Ideas and Politics in the Making of Interwar Europe*, Cambridge, MA: Harvard University Press.
Best, Jacqueline (2005), *The Limits of Transparency: Ambiguity and the History of International Finance*, Ithaca, NY: Cornell University Press.
Best, Jacqueline (2010), 'The limits of financial risk management: or what we didn't learn from the Asian crisis', *New Political Economy*, **15** (1), 29–49.
Blyth, Mark (2002), *Great Transformations: Economic Ideas and Institutional Change in the Twentieth Century*, Cambridge: Cambridge University Press.
Blyth, Mark (2003), 'The political power of financial ideas: transparency, risk, and distribution in global finance', in Jonathan Kirshner (ed.), *Monetary Orders: Ambiguous Economics, Ubiquitous Politics*, Ithaca, NY: Cornell University Press, pp. 239–59.
Bossone, Biagio (2009), 'The IMF, the US subprime crisis, and global financial governance', 3 February, available at: http://www.voxeu.org/index.php?q=node/2973.
Broome, André and Leonard Seabrooke (2007), 'Seeing like the IMF: institutional change in small open economies', *Review of International Political Economy*, **14** (4), 576–601.
Broome, André, Liam Clegg and Lena Rethel (2012), 'Global governance and the politics of crisis', *Global Society*, **26** (1), 3–17.
Clegg, Liam and Manuela Moschella (2013), 'The managers of information: international organizations,

data, and financial stability', in T. Porter (ed.), *Transnational Financial Regulation after the Crisis*, London: Routledge, pp. 50–71.

Cutler, Claire A., Virginia Haufler and Tony Porter (eds) (1999), *Private Authority and International Affairs*, Albany, NY: State University of New York Press.

de Laroisiére, Jacques (2009), 'The High Level Group on Financial Supervision in the EU', Brussels, 25 February.

Draghi, Mario and Dominique Strauss-Khan (2008), 'Letter to the Minister and Governors of the G20', 13 November.

Eichengreen, Barry (1999), *Towards a New International Financial Architecture: A Practical Post-Asia Agenda*, Washington, DC: Institute for International Economics.

Financial Services Authority (2009), 'The Turner Review: a regulatory response to the global banking crisis'.

Financial Stability Board and IMF (2009), 'The financial crisis and information gaps – report to the G-20 finance ministers and central bank governors', 29 October.

Financial Stability Forum (2000), 'Issues paper of the Task Force on Implementation of Standards', 25–26 March.

Financial Stability Forum (2001), 'Final report of the Follow-Up Group on Incentives to Foster Implementation of Standards', meeting of the Financial Stability Forum, 6–7 September.

Fischer, Stanley (1999), *The Financial Crisis in Emerging Markets: Lessons for Eastern Europe and Asia*, comments prepared for delivery at the East-West Institute conference, New York, 23 April.

Foot, Rosemary and Andrew Walter (2011), *China, the United States, and Global Order*, Cambridge: Cambridge University Press.

Germain, Randall (2010), *Global Politics and Financial Governance*, Basingstoke: Palgrave Macmillan.

Gola, Carlo and Francesco Spadafora (2009), 'Financial sector surveillance and the IMF', IMF Working Papers WP/09/247.

Goldstein, Morris (1999), *Safeguarding Prosperity in a Global Financial System: The Future International Financial Architecture*, Washington, DC: Institute of International Economics.

Graz, J.-C. and A. Nölke (2008), *Transnational Private Governance and Its Limits*, London: Routledge.

Griffith-Jones, Stephany, Eric Helleiner and Ngaire Woods (eds) (2010), *The Financial Stability Board: An Effective Fourth Pillar of Global Economic Governance?* Waterloo: Centre for International Governance Innovation (CIGI).

Guitiàn, Manuel (1992), *The Unique Nature of the Responsibilities of the International Monetary Fund*, Washington, DC: International Monetary Fund.

Hall, Rodney Bruce and Thomas J. Biersteker (eds) (2002), *The Emergence of Private Authority in Global Governance*, Cambridge: Cambridge University Press.

Helleiner, Eric (1994), *States and the Reemergence of Global Finance: From Bretton Woods to the 1990s*, Ithaca, NY, USA and London, UK: Cornell University Press.

Helleiner, Eric (2010), 'The Financial Stability Board and international standards', Centre for International Governance Innovation (CIGI) G20 Papers, June (1).

Helleiner, Eric, Stefano Pagliari and Hubert Zimmermann (eds) (2009), *Global Finance in Crisis: The Politics of International Regulatory Change*, London: Routledge.

Héritier, Adrienne and Dirk Lehmkuhl (2011), 'Governing in the shadow of hierarchy: new modes of governance in regulation', in Adrienne Héritier and Martin Rhodes (eds), *New Modes of Governance in Europe*, Basingstoke: Palgrave Macmillan, pp. 48–74.

IMF (1999), *External Evaluation of IMF Surveillance: Report by a Group of Independent Experts*, Washington, DC: International Monetary Fund.

IMF (2007), *Bilateral Surveillance over Members' Policies Executive Board Decision*, 15 June, Washington, DC: International Monetary Fund.

IMF (2009a), *Initial Lessons of the Crisis*, Washington, DC: International Monetary Fund.

IMF (2009b), 'Initial lessons of the crisis for the global architecture and the IMF', in *Prepared by the Strategy, Policy, and Review Department*, Washington, DC: International Monetary Fund.

IMF (2010a), *Review of the Fund's Mandate – Follow-Up on Modernizing Surveillance*, 30 July, Washington, DC: International Monetary Fund.

IMF (2010b), *The IMF–FSB Early Warning Exercise: Design and Methological Toolkit*, September, Washington, DC: International Monetary Fund.

IMF (2010c), *Financial Sector Surveillance and the Mandate of the Fund*, 19 March, Washington, DC: International Monetary Fund.

IMF (2011a), *2011 Triennial Surveillance Review – Review of the 2007 Surveillance Decision and the Broader Legal Framework for Surveillance*, 26 August, Washington, DC: International Monetary Fund.

IMF (2011b), *2011 Triennial Surveillance Review – Overview Paper*, 29 August, Washington, DC: International Monetary Fund.

IMF (2011c), *The Multilateral Aspects of Policies Affecting Capital Flows*, 13 October, Washington, DC: International Monetary Fund.

IMF (2012), *The IMF's Financial Surveillance Work*, 12 April, Washington, DC: International Monetary Fund.

IMF, Bank for International Settlements and the Financial Stability Board (2009), *Guidance to Assess the Systemic Importance of Financial Institutions, Markets and Instruments: Initial Considerations*, October.

Independent Evaluation Office (2004), 'The IMF and recent capital account crises: Indonesia, Korea, and Brazil', Evaluation Report, Washington, DC: Independent Evaluation Office.

Independent Evaluation Office (2005), 'The IMF's approach to capital account liberalization', Evaluation Report, Washington, DC: International Monetary Fund.

Independent Evaluation Office (2011), *IMF Performance in the Run-Up to the Financial and Economic Crisis: IMF Surveillance in 2004–07*, Washington, DC: International Monetary Fund.

James, Harold (1995), 'The historical development of the principle of surveillance', *IMF Staff Papers*, **42** (4), 762–91.

Kapstein, Ethan B. (1994), *Governing the Global Economy: International Finance and the State*, Cambridge, MA: Harvard University Press.

Kenen, Peter B. (2001), *The International Financial Architecture: What's New? What's Missing?* Washington, DC: Institute of International Economics.

Kindleberger, Charles (1973), *The World in Depression, 1929–1939*, Berkeley, CA: University of California Press.

Kodres, Laura and Aditya Narain (2010), 'Redesigning the contours of the future financial system', IMF Staff Position Note, Washington, DC: International Monetary Fund.

Lombardi, Domenico and Ngaire Woods (2008), 'The politics of influence: an analysis of IMF surveillance', *Review of International Political Economy*, **15** (5), 711–39.

Marcussen, Martin (2004), 'Multilateral surveillance and the OECD: playing the idea game', in Klaus Armingeon and Michelle Beyeler (eds), *The OECD and European Welfare States*, Cheltenham, UK and Northampton, MA, USA: Edward Elgar, pp. 13–31.

Minsky, Hyman P. (1986), *Stabilizing an Unstable Economy*, New Haven, CT: Yale University Press.

Momani, Bessma (2005), 'Recruiting and diversifying IMF technocrats', *Global Society*, **19** (2), 167–87.

Moschella, Manuela (2010), *Governing Risk: The IMF and Global Financial Crises*, Basingstoke: Palgrave Macmillan.

Moschella, Manuela (2011), 'Lagged learning and the response to equilibrium shock: the global financial crisis and IMF surveillance', *Journal of Public Policy*, **31** (2), 1–21.

Moschella, Manuela (2012a), 'Designing the Financial Stability Board: a theoretical investigation of mandate, discretion, and membership', *Journal of International Relations and Development*, doi: 10.1057/jird.2012.10.

Moschella, Manuela (2012b), 'IMF surveillance in crisis: the past, present, and future of the reform process', *Global Society*, **26** (1), 46–60.

Moschella, Manuela and Eleni Tsingou (eds) (2013), *Explaining Incremental Change in Global Financial Governance*, Colchester: ECPR Press.

Mosley, Layna (2003), 'Attempting global standards: national governments, international finance, and the IMF data regime', *Review of International Political Economy*, **10** (2), 331–62.

Mosley, Layna (2010), 'Regulating globally, implementing locally: the financial codes and standards effort', *Review of International Political Economy*, **17** (4), 724–61.

Pagliari, Stefano (2012), 'Who governs finance? The shifting public–private divide in the regulation of derivatives, rating agencies and hedge funds', *European Law Journal*, **18** (1), 44–61.

Palais Royale Initiative (2011), 'Reform of the International Monetary System: a cooperative approach for the twenty first century', report, 8 February.

Pauly, Louis W. (1997), *Who Elected the Bankers? Surveillance and Control in the World Economy*, Ithaca, NY: Cornell University Press.

Porter, Tony (2005), *Globalization and Finance*, Cambridge: Polity Press.

Sabatier, Paul and Hank Jenkins-Smith (eds) (1993), *Policy Learning and Policy Change: An Advocacy Coalition Approach*, Boulder, CO: Westview Press.

Schinasi, Garry J. and Edwin M. Truman (2010), Reform of the global financial architecture', Working Paper Series of the Peterson Institute for International Economics, WP 10-14.

Singer, David A (2007), *Regulating Capital: Setting Standards for the International Financial System*, Ithaca, NY: Cornell University Press.

Soederberg, Susanne (2003), 'The promotion of "Anglo-American" corporate governance in the South: who benefits from the new international standard?', *Third World Quarterly*, **24** (1), 7–27.

Steinmo, Sven (2003), 'The evolution of policy ideas: tax policy in the 20th century', *British Journal of Politics and International Relations*, **5** (2), 206–36.

Truman, Edwin M. (2010), 'Strengthening IMF surveillance: a comprehensive proposal', PIIE Policy Brief.

Walter, Andrew (2008), *Governing Finance: East Asia's Adoption of International Standards*, Ithaca, NY: Cornell University Press.

7 Private actors in the governance of global finance after the global crisis of 2008

Tony Porter

In the first stages of the global financial crisis of 2008 it seemed likely that the crisis would result in greatly reduced power for private business actors. As *Fortune* magazine put it, 'politically speaking, corporate America – most of which has nothing to do with the Wall Street mess – has been summarily dethroned. And it will be a long slog back' (Easton 2008). Yet by 2011 there were numerous indicators, at least in the United States, that financial firms had regained their power remarkably quickly. Bank profitability and bonuses had been restored while the rest of the economy languished. Almost no bankers had been prosecuted for wrongdoing. US President Barack Obama had appointed William Daley of JP Morgan Chase as his chief of staff to improve his relationship with Wall Street. What is more, rivers of lobbying money were flowing into Washington to turn back regulatory initiatives. Indeed, at a closed door meeting about implementing one of the new financial regulations, the head of the main financial lobby group was reported as having 'barked orders to surprised Congressional staff members, urging them to delay the rule, according to two people who attended. He acted like someone running the meeting, they said, rather than like an invited guest' (Protess 2011).

This chapter argues that, despite these signs of an apparent rebound in the power of private financial actors, there has been a significant but incremental shift away from unconstrained private power, while public authority has been enhanced. It illustrates this shift by examining the role of private actors in transnational regulatory developments in some detail, focusing especially on the role of firms in the Basel III banking standards, which were endorsed by the Group of 20 (G20) leaders in November 2010, and on initiatives to regulate derivatives and credit rating agencies (CRAs). This shift away from unconstrained private power does not primarily involve the replacement of private governance by public governance. It instead involves an increase in the public accountability of private financial actors which continue to play prominent roles in global financial governance. The shift is not uniform across governance settings, but rather varies greatly due to the distinctive characteristics of these settings and the continuing conflicts and uncertainties over the direction of change. This complexity is consistent with the four themes that are identified in the Introduction to this volume. Complexity can obscure the significance of the detail of transnational regulatory developments: if we only focus on more visible expressions of private power, such as those discussed in the previous paragraph, we can overstate the extent of this power.

The complex, private and transnational character of global financial flows means that adjustments in their governance, if they are to have any practical effect, must engage with transnational and private governance mechanisms that are a long distance from traditional national rule-making processes. To be successful, states can no longer simply issue commands, but instead must work with, mobilise and constrain vastly complex assemblages of activities that may have considerable autonomy and varying purposes. These activities may or may not be amenable to alignment with the public interest. Indeed, it is no longer clear that the force of governmental rules primarily starts with the state and moves down a chain of command, since change can be an interactive process that may start in some other parts of the assemblages that are involved. To a significant degree, the political relations between public and private actors have shifted from the type of more traditional national-level developments that were noted in the first paragraph above, to detailed contestations over the shaping of micro-level private and transnational practices that are quite far from traditional rule-making processes. To the extent that this is happening, it modifies the story told by those who only emphasise the capture of national political processes by business interests (Johnson and Kwak 2010; Lessig 2011) and runs counter to those who expected nation-states and national political processes to reassert their pre-eminence at a time of crisis (on different approaches to this question, see Helleiner and Pagliari 2011).

The chapter starts by expanding on these conceptual points, and then examines developments in transnational financial governance to assess their relevance. It analyses the role of private actors in one of the most important developments, the Basel III package of reworked bank capital standards that has been developed at the Basel Committee on Banking Supervision (BCBS), the main international grouping of G20 bank regulators. Basel III is the primary transnational response to the perceived need to alter the conduct of banks after the crisis. The chapter also examines more briefly two other related key reform initiatives: derivatives and credit rating. These represent a different type of private sector involvement in governance, since in both cases private sector institutions represent more collective private governance mechanisms than the Basel III case. However, the similarities across the three cases are striking: in each case private actors continue to enjoy considerable autonomy, but regulatory reform has constrained this autonomy and increased private actors' accountability. I am definitely not claiming that private power is adequately constrained in its interactions with the public sector. For instance, as vividly conveyed in work by Lessig (2011) and Hacker and Pierson (2010), the types of problems cited in the chapter's opening paragraph are symptomatic of a systematic money-driven corruption of the US political process that is destructive for the public interest in financial governance and other policy areas. However, if a more appropriate public–private relationship is to be created, it is important not only to consider failures, but also to examine how smaller successes in increasing private accountability work, such as the ones that are evident in transnational financial governance.

ASSESSING THE POWER OF PRIVATE FINANCIAL ACTORS: CONCEPTUAL ISSUES

There has been a long history of worrying about the power of banks and other financial actors. This has included analysis that conceptualises this power as emanating from the oligarchic structure in contemporary capitalism of the financial sector itself, as discussed, for instance, by US Supreme Court Justice Louis Brandeis, Russian revolutionary Vladimir Lenin and many others a century ago, or the more recent multidimensional process of financialisation (Epstein 2005; Froud et al. 2006), which includes the globalisation of financial flows, the greater prominence of capital markets and shareholder interests in corporate governance, the increased individual responsibility for financial security and, more generally, the increased presence of financial practices in all aspects of daily life. There is also a long tradition of analysing the way that states can amplify the power of financial actors, such as when the US or other powerful states aggressively promote the interests of their financial firms in international settings, perhaps to enhance the power of those states by enriching the economies they govern, or when states and regulators are captured by financial actors. Capture can occur, for example, through campaign financing, revolving doors where officials move back and forth between government and business, bribery of regulators, or 'intellectual capture', where studies or ideas financed by the industry unduly shape rule-making processes (Baker 2010; Davies 2010; Pagliari 2012).

Much of this analysis of the power of financial actors has focused especially on the national level but there has been recognition of an international dimension as well, such as when a nation-state works to promote the international power of finance, or when international finance subverts the power of nation-states. A more recent area of conceptual work, which is the focus of this chapter, has been the more complex entanglements and interactions between transnational public institutions and transnational private financial actors, shifting the locus of public–private interaction from the nation-state to transnational networks.

There is now a very large toolbox of concepts that can be used to analyse these transnational public–private interactions, with some variation in what they emphasise. For instance, 'private authority' emphasises the relative autonomy of private transnational rulemaking processes (Cutler et al. 1999; Hansen and Salskov-Iversen 2008); 'global governmentality' emphasises the interaction between larger-scale political rationalities and particular practices that extend far beyond states (Larner and Walters 2004); 'regulatory capitalism' emphasises the upswing in regulation that has accompanied neoliberalism (Levi-Faur 2005); the 'disaggregated state' emphasises the centrality of government officials in transnational networks (Slaughter 2004); the 'new constitutionalism' emphasises the encoding of private sector interests in international law (Gill 2003); 'international practices' emphasise the interaction of humans and objects in competent performances that extend beyond the state (Adler and Pouliot 2011); 'non-state market-driven governance' emphasises market-compatible social and environmental initiatives such as the certifications reflected in the ISEAL Alliance (Cashore 2002);[1] 'regime complexity' (Alter and Meunier 2009) and 'orchestration' (Abbott and Snidal 2009) emphasise states' strategies with regard to overlapping international regimes; and 'assemblages' (Ong and Collier 2005; Sassen 2006) emphasise the way that relatively autonomous clusters of public or private rules can combine to produce transnational governance in particular policy areas. Overall, this literature convincingly demonstrates that international affairs are about a great deal more than the interstate relations that were traditionally the focus of the analysis and study of international relations and law.

Elsewhere I have highlighted four overlapping factors that make transnational networks sufficiently robust to exercise independent influence over rule-making (Porter 2011). This independent influence is generally ignored or dismissed by approaches that see nation-states and national political processes as the only places where meaningful rules can be developed. The first of the four factors is the constitutive role of ideas. Ideas can certainly be formulated in transnational networks, and to the extent that they constitute new rules they can have an independent effect (Finnemore and Sikkink 1998). The second factor is the reinforcement of the effects of ideas through their entanglement with material objects. Some objects can be transnational, such as electronic networks that cross borders or documents that circulate internationally. This integration of ideas and materiality can make the operations of transnational networks more robust. The third factor is functionality: an increasing number of tasks, particularly at the global level, are motivated by shared concerns about solving a particular problem or technical task, rather than competing for national advantage, and this can help consolidate the authority of transnational networks. Path-dependence is the fourth factor: once interactions are channelled through a transnational network it can be costly to shift them elsewhere, and the repeated use of the network further reinforces this. Overall, since power has shifted away from the state and often involves the enrolment of relatively autonomous networks of transitional activities that continue to have distinct purposes, transnational networks can play a much more important role than if rules always originated in legislatures or other national political processes which had the power simply to force the addressees of the rules to comply.

To understand the interaction of public and private in transnational networks it is important not to rely on simplistic dualisms that always associate the public with states and the private with business. If regulators are captured by business interests, or if they act to promote their own private interests, they should be seen as closer to the private side of the public–private continuum than their formal location in the state might suggest. Similarly firms, business associations or markets can shift towards the public end of the continuum if they sustain public interests or spaces, such as when an internet provider helps citizens evade censorship and develop shared policy preferences and demands. We therefore need criteria for 'publicness' and the public interest that are not dependent on the type of institution with which they are associated.[2] Since any discursive claim to represent the public interest can always be contested, and since the substance of policies is always changing, it is useful to focus on the procedures that might be expected to produce outcomes that are in the public interest, rather than judging policies by some absolute standard of values. Mattli and Woods (2009) make this point, and then usefully develop such procedures. They divide these procedures into an institutional supply side and a societal demand side. On the supply side they identify inclusiveness, openness, transparency, fairness and accessibility. On the demand side they identify the need for information, supporting interests (such as non-governmental organisations, NGOs; or firms that help mobilise a public) and ideas (to motivate support and propose feasible actions).

These conceptual points set the stage for an analysis of the shifting balance between public and private in transnational networks. Contrary to approaches that assume from the start that only national policies matter, and that transnational institutions do not, we can assess variations in public and private influences in transnational networks, and then consider their relevance for policy. By more fully incorporating transnational networks, the analysis becomes more complex than if we only focused on a particular national policy. Indeed, it is impossible in this chapter to analyse both transnational developments and national-level developments in all the nation-states that participate in these networks. Yet there are three reasons why a focus on transnational developments can be valuable in assessing whether the power of private financial actors has changed in the aftermath of the 2007–08 financial crisis. First, transnational agreements are an aggregated or negotiated expression of the global status of financial reforms, taking into account variations in the strength of preferences and power across nation-states. Second, given the globalised character of finance, there are many reforms that are highly unlikely to be implemented unilaterally on a national level, mainly because doing so would put any country that acted unilaterally at a competitive disadvantage. Third, much like international human rights law, international financial agreements can create mechanisms of accountability that push states and firms to comply with the international consensus that the rules represent. As long as we continue to be alert to the way that international agreements can fail to be implemented nationally, they are useful in evaluating the state of play of financial reforms. The next section undertakes such an evaluation, drawing on the conceptual points made in this section.

PRIVATE ACTORS IN THE TRANSNATIONAL GOVERNANCE OF FINANCE: BEFORE AND AFTER THE CRISIS

This section starts with the most important transnational development in the regulation of banks: Basel III. It then more briefly considers the cases of the governance of derivatives and credit rating. Due to space limitations, some important transnational reform initiatives are only mentioned in passing, if at all, including the problem of institutions that are 'too big to fail', cross-border insolvency regimes, executive compensation, accounting standards, macroprudential regulation and corporate governance. The idea of a coordinated tax on financial transactions or institutions, which was rejected by the G20 in 2010 but continues to be discussed, particularly in the European Union, is also not addressed in detail. Nevertheless, the areas of reform that are discussed are sufficiently important to support the chapter's contention that there has been a significant incremental increase in the level of accountability of private actors since the crisis of 2008. The Basel III case illustrates the reshaping of relatively autonomous private governance practices within individual banks. The derivatives and credit rating cases involve more collective private governance mechanisms.

Basel III

Basel III builds on the two previous capital adequacy agreements developed at the Basel Committee on Banking Supervision.[3] The first 1988 Basel Accord established agreed standards for bank capital adequacy, specifying the amount of capital banks needed to hold against their risk-weighted assets. Since capital absorbs losses and is expensive, increasing it relative to assets, such as loans, will make insolvency less likely and restrain growth. The first Basel Accord was designed to rein in excessively risky expansion of bank lending while offsetting the downward pressure on standards through coordinated implementation in all the jurisdictions of the BCBS member-states, together constituting most global markets. At that time, and until 2008, the Basel Committee membership was restricted to regulators representing 12 of the countries with the largest banks. Most other jurisdictions also adopted the standards, encouraged by market pressures favouring adequately capitalised banks, and by peer pressure exerted through a set of regional bank regulatory bodies associated with the BCBS. During the financial crisis the membership of the BCBS was expanded to more closely match the G20's.

For its time, the 1988 Accord was an unusually complicated agreement by which jointly to alter the regulation of international banks. However, it was soon seen by the industry and regulators as too simple for the multiple, complex risks that banks were managing, and in response a long process of revision was launched, culminating in a far more detailed Basel II Accord agreed in 2004 and in the process of being implemented when the 2008 crisis began. Noteworthy new features of Basel II included rules allowing banks to use their internal risk models in calculating their required levels of capital, new charges for operational risk, and a new reliance on credit ratings in the assessment of the riskiness of assets. Critics have argued that Basel II served the interests of the large transnational banks, not the public interest (Claessens and Underhill 2010; Barth and Caprio 2006; Baker 2010; Lall 2010). The reliance on private sector risk management mechanisms seemed to critics to be an abdication of responsibility on the part of regulators. This impression is reinforced by the privileged role played in the development of Basel II by the Institute of International Finance, the main global lobby group for those banks, which proposed the idea of banks relying on their own risk management systems. As well, the largest banks that had the capacity to develop these risk management systems enjoyed reduced capital requirements relative to their competitors which still relied on the simpler Basel I procedure. However, Young (2012) has argued persuasively that, despite their extensive access, private sector actors were not able to achieve all their goals with their efforts to influence Basel II.

Basel III builds directly on Basel II. The main features of Basel III include more stringent and clearer standards on what will be allowed to count as bank capital; a simpler leverage ratio linking assets and capital to offset the complexity of Basel II, to act as a counter-cyclical tool; stronger liquidity requirements to prevent the evaporation of liquidity that had occurred during the crisis; and new rules to begin to integrate the shadow banking system that had developed around securitisation. These last proposals, for instance, included the requirement that banks hold capital against risks in their trading books and risks associated with the quasi-independent entities created by banks to produce securitised debt. The Basel III measures are to be phased in on varying time frames, with some key aspects due only in 2019.

What does Basel III tell us about the changing influence of private sector actors in financial governance after the 2008 crisis? As argued in the previous section, in order to answer this question we need to go beyond simply identifying business actors as private, and state actors as public, measuring which are more prominent. Instead, we need to look more carefully at the specific procedures and their effects on accountability.

In contemporary financial markets, a key aspect of accountability involves the allocation of risk. Much of the work of these markets involves taking responsibility for risk in exchange for a payment. This is most familiar in insurance, but a similar exchange occurs when a bank takes the risk of lending long-term for a homeowner's mortgage and charges more for doing so than it pays to depositors who supply the funds that are used for the mortgage, but take on none of the risk. In this traditional form of lending, banks supply the risk-monitoring and risk management capacities that can legitimise, on economic efficiency grounds, the profits they earn on the spread between the depositors' interest rates and the mortgage rate. More generally, when a financial actor borrows and then invests in a riskier activity, this is called leverage, since it can amplify the gains or losses from a financial actor's own stake in that investment. In the case of securities markets, the bank does not play an intermediating role, and investors receive returns on the securities that are supposed to reflect the risk of the investment. In derivatives markets the risk can be traded separately from the loan or security that the derivative contract references. For instance, a credit default swap (CDS) trades the risk that a borrower will default, and that trade is detached from that borrower's original debt contract. In all these examples there is an ever-present possibility that financial actors will receive payments that are supposed to reflect the risk that they are taking on, while they instead avoid their responsibility for this risk, for instance by having the government bail them out when it comes time to pay, or by obscuring the risk and shifting it to other actors.

This type of accountability problem was pervasive in and central to the financial crisis of 2008. For instance, in the lead-up to the crisis the American International Group (AIG), the largest insurance company in the US at the time, took on vast amounts of risk though CDS contracts, receiving lucrative payments, but was not able to honour those contracts when the defaults that the contracts were supposed to insure against occurred. AIG received the largest federal bailout in US history, US$182 billion, and this helped pay off its contracts, with the aim of preventing its problems spreading to other firms. Throughout the financial sector countless executives and traders walked off with huge bonuses, leaving their firms with the losses associated with the risks that had generated the revenue for those bonuses. Overall, the financial sector enjoyed years of extraordinarily high profitability that was supposed to reflect the efficiency of its risk management contributions, when risks were in fact not managed, imposing disastrously heavy costs on the rest of society.

All the provisions of Basel III aim to address these risk management and risk accountability problems. The amount of capital in the form of common equity that banks must hold relative to assets was increased from 2 per cent to at least 7 per cent (including a 4.5 per cent minimum and a 2.5 per cent capital conservation buffer which, if used, will trigger restrictions, including on dividend payouts and bonuses). This means that the holders of that equity, who are the owners of the bank, have more of their own funds at risk, available to cover losses. Attempts to require this capital to be correlated with the risk associated with the bank's assets, such as loans, had already been a feature of Basel I and II, but in Basel III new sets of assets associated with the shadow banking system were brought into the calculations. The calculations used to estimate the risk associated with various assets were modified to incorporate risks under conditions of stress similar to the 2008 crisis, rather than the calmer periods that Basel II used as a baseline. Risk weightings for exposures to financial firms were increased relative to exposures to other types of counterparties. More capital is required for exposure to the securitised products that were at the heart of the 2008 crisis. The creation for the first time of an internationally agreed simple leverage ratio attempts to backstop the risk of failure of the complex set of calculations involved in the more detailed risk-weighted capital-asset calculations.

The new liquidity rules require banks to hold enough liquid assets (such as cash or government bonds that can be traded under almost any circumstances) to see them through periods of instability, such as the 2008 crisis when liquidity evaporated as financial actors lacked enough trust to trade with one another. More specifically, a

Liquidity Coverage Ratio requires that a bank have enough liquid assets to cover the net cash outflows estimated to occur over thirty days of extreme stress. A second measure, a Net Stable Funding Ratio, requires that a bank have enough stable funding to cover its needs over a one-year period of extreme stress. This aims to correct the problem of banks relying on very short-term low-cost funding (such as overnight borrowing from other banks) to fund much riskier long-term investments (such as securitised mortgage products). During the crisis such short-term funding evaporated along with the trust that sustained it.

In the wake of the crisis the Basel Committee, the Financial Stability Board (FSB) and the G20 were also involved in developing other similar mechanisms to address risk management problems. These included measures to impose higher capital charges on financial institutions that were deemed 'too big to fail', labelled 'globally systemically important financial institutions' (G-SIFIs). During a crisis these G-SIFIs are so big or interconnected that governments can be forced to bail them out if they get into trouble (FSB 2011b). By 2013 new rules developed at the FSB had been endorsed by the G20 and were in the process of being implemented. This is a particularly significant restriction of private power. In 2012 the FSB published a set of recommendations for strengthening the oversight and regulation of the vast 'shadow banking system', which carried out credit intermediation activities outside the formal regulated banking system prior to the crisis. The recommendations included improving monitoring and information sharing, increasing the capital requirements for bank exposures to the shadow banking system, and new restrictions on shadow banking activities such as money market funds or securitisations (FSB 2012a). The general enthusiasm among policy-makers and regulators for 'macro-prudential regulation' has been an indication of a heightened sense of responsibility for the public interest in systemic stability (Baker 2012).

The provisions of Basel III, like any international agreements, are only meaningful if they are implemented, and if they require changes that would not already have occurred in their absence. The agreed timetable for implementation extends to 2019, and thus the fate of Basel III will not be entirely clear until that date. Nevertheless, there are strong indications that Basel III will be implemented to a significant degree, and that it will strongly alter the conduct of banks in ways that would not occur in its absence. To echo the wording at the beginning of this chapter, Basel III is a significant but incremental shift away from unconstrained private power, and an enhancement of private accountability and public authority.

A sign of the seriousness with which Basel III is being taken is the monitoring process initiated by the BCBS in September 2011, which 'is intended to provide additional incentives for member jurisdictions to fully implement the standards within the agreed timelines' (BCBS 2011: 1) and will thus review the details of national measures to assess their consistency with Basel III. For instance, its October 2011 'Progress report on Basel III implementation' focused on the standards for capital quality and quantity, and established four categories: (1) 'Draft regulation not published'; (2) 'Draft regulation published'; (3) 'Final rule published'; and (4) 'Final rule in force'. It then coded the progress of the 28 member jurisdictions. All jurisdictions except Argentina, Indonesia and Russia are scored at 4 for Basel II, although China, Turkey and the US are running parallel systems, with not all banks subject to the standards. The scores for implementation of standards for securitisation and the trading book, which were agreed in July

2009, averaged out at 2.8.[4] The average score for Basel III implementation was 1.5. The overall picture, then, is a slow and uneven but forward-moving sequential process of implementation of Basel I, II and III. The FSB has also stepped up its monitoring of the implementation of reforms.

A significant aspect of the Basel III implementation was the European Commission's work to transpose it into a revised Capital Requirements Directive, labeled 'CRD IV'.[5] CRD IV entered into force on 17 July 2013. An important and controversial aspect of the European Union's (EU) Basel III implementation is that many of the most important rules, including those on the quantity and quality of capital, leverage and liquidity, take the form of a Regulation, which automatically becomes law in member-states, unlike the previous CRD, which as a Directive required implementing legislation at the national level, allowing variation. This lack of discretion does not necessarily strengthen demands on banks. For instance, the UK authorities wished to implement higher capital requirements and most likely will not be able to do so, although discretion to impose higher charges in particular banks to address risks identified by supervisors, or in the counter-cyclical buffer provisions, is permitted by CRD IV (James and Forde 2011). Indeed, the International Monetary Fund (IMF) criticised the Commission for this setting of the maximum at the minimum specified by Basel III, as well as aspects of CRD IV which were laxer (Egenter 2011). In some cases CRD IV is stricter or more specific than Basel III, and in other cases the reverse is the case.

Firms that provide consulting or legal services to banks have assessed the impact on banks as very significant. Moody's (2011: 3), while noting the evolutionary character of the shift from Basel II to III, noted that the impact of Basel III 'should not be underestimated, because it will drive significant challenges that need to be understood and addressed'. McKinsey (2010) estimated that European banks will have to raise €1.1 trillion of Tier 1 capital, €1.3 trillion of short-term liquidity, and €2.3 trillion of long-term funding by 2019 as a result of Basel III, with comparable US figures of US$870 billion, US$800 billion and US$3.2 trillion. This does not include the impact of rules on G-SIFIs. This is estimated to reduce return on equity by 4 per cent in Europe and 3 per cent in the US, although this may be mitigated by various procedural changes, some of which, like more reliance on central counterparties, are consistent with the intent of the reform: 'broadly speaking, it seems unlikely at this time that the industry can regain its pre-Basel III profitability levels' (McKinsey 2010: 13). The impact is especially pronounced for activities that were central to the crisis: 'capital markets and trading businesses may be massively curtailed due to the new capital and funding requirements' (McKinsey 2010: 17). The task of implementation is characterised as 'monumental' (McKinsey 2010: 2). The operational costs of implementation for a mid-sized European bank are estimated at between €45 million and €70 million (McKinsey 2010: 22). Although implementation extends to 2019, reporting deadlines and market expectations are more accelerated and can require banks to begin implementation immediately. Implementation will require reorganisation of the internal practices of the bank, especially with regard to risk and data management. Some of these will be beneficial for the business: 'the ability to see the consolidated high-level picture and at the same time drill down into the detail will allow business managers to make timely and informed decisions, based on stronger insight' (Moody's 2011: 9)

Private sector resistance to elements of Basel III has been varied. The extension of the deadline for the completion of key elements of Basel III to as late as 2019 was a response to bank arguments that a faster pace would harm them and restrict their ability to lend. Following some of the more alarming warnings issued by the banking industry, the FSB and the BCBS produced studies concluding that 'the transition to stronger capital and liquidity standards is likely to have a modest impact on aggregate output' (Bank for International Settlements 2010). Nevertheless, the deadlines were extended. The Global Financial Markets Association (GFMA), the key representative of capital market actors, in its February 2011 remarks to the BCBS on Basel III noted that 'we acknowledge that the new standards will help protect financial stability and promote market confidence'. Its major emphasis was on requests for clarity and consistency, rather than demands to roll back or abandon Basel III (GFMA 2011). The IIF Managing Director, Charles H. Dallara, has indicated that banks can live with Basel III as long as there is enough time for them to adjust, but that he is concerned that some countries are raising the bar above the Basel standards (Ewing 2010).

Overall, it is clear that Basel III significantly increases the accountability of private financial actors for their risk management activities, imposing significant costs on them, with a strong but not certain probability that the implementation will be carried through in practice. Basel III does not displace private financial actors from their central role in global finance, as would other proposals, such as nationalising the banks. Instead, it seeks to alter the internal governance mechanisms of banks. In doing so, it is clear that it shifts the public–private balance incrementally towards the public side by reconfiguring the rules, incentives and accountabilities governing banks and other private financial actors. This does not mean that even stronger action would not be wise. Some observers have argued that Basel III is too weak. For instance, Lord Adair Turner, chair of the United Kingdom's Financial Services Authority, argued in early 2011 that Basel III should have set the core capital at a ratio of 15–20 per cent, rather than the 7 per cent that was agreed (Kumar 2011). Stefan Walter, Secretary General of the BCBS, also warned in April 2011 that, 'despite the severity of the crisis, we are already seeing signs that its lessons are beginning to fade' and that the risk of a banking crisis emerging in one of the BCBS members was roughly one in 20, 'unacceptably high' (Wilson 2011). However, Basel III, in strengthening the accountability of private financial actors, particularly the powerful G-SIFIs, challenges the picture of unmitigated runaway private irresponsibility continuing after the crisis, as was presented in the first paragraph of this chapter.

Other Cases: Derivatives and Credit Rating

While Basel III's provisions are central to banking and the activities that were at the centre of the 2008 crisis, it is important to provide a fuller picture by also commenting on other aspects of the transnational reform effort. Derivatives and credit rating are two other areas that not only played a key role in the crisis, but that are more reliant on collective private governance mechanisms than are the Basel standards. Accordingly, they may be more likely to exhibit a post-crisis continuation of private power and irresponsibility. While space constraints preclude extensive consideration of these two areas, it is possible to assess the overall state of reform in them.

As noted above, derivatives played a significant role in the crisis. Credit default swaps were used to insure the structured financial products that were created out of subprime mortgages, generating large profits for their sellers, but creating a false sense of security in a market which would subsequently collapse. The opacity and complexity of the linkages created by these CDS, and the way that they concentrated rather than dispersed risk, as evident in the AIG case mentioned above, but also in the collapse of confidence in other firms such as Lehman Brothers thought to hold large volumes of CDS, contributed to the severity and pace of the crisis.

Prior to the crisis the governance of derivatives had been left almost entirely to the market, and to private associations such as the Group of Thirty and the International Swaps and Derivatives Association (Tsingou 2007). In an episode that has become notorious, Clinton administration officials and Federal Reserve Chairman Alan Greenspan attacked Brooksley Born, the head of the Commodities Futures Trading Commission, which had the primary responsibility for derivatives regulation, when she warned about their risks, and the 2000 Commodity Futures Modernization Act subsequently decisively prohibited their regulation (Johnson and Kwak 2010: 8–9).

Yet, as carefully analysed by Helleiner (2011a, 2011b), demands and initiatives for stepping up public regulation and accountability in derivatives markets increased significantly after the crisis. Like Basel III, these initiatives retained a key role for private financial actors in governance, but increased their accountabilities. In the case of derivatives, the reform endorsed by the G20 governments especially sought to channel derivatives trading through central counterparties and organised exchanges, with increased collection and accessibility of data on those trades through private trade repositories. Banks would be given an incentive to do this by the imposition of higher capital charges for exposure to derivatives not using these mechanisms. The initiatives include greater standardisation of derivatives and the development of metrics to assess this standardisation. Moving towards these mechanisms, away from opaque, bilateral, over-the-counter transactions, aimed to increase transparency and accountability, thereby reducing the ability of the banks that have lately dominated over-the-counter trading to enhance their profits by keeping the process opaque. This change is further enhanced by specific mechanisms of accountability, such as making the private governance mechanisms in the market more representative and freer of conflicts of interest, and pressuring trade repositories to make their data more freely available to regulators and market participants.

The implementation of changes in derivatives regulation has nevertheless been slow, and there is remaining uncertainty about its effectiveness, once fully implemented. Helleiner (2011b) shows that the mechanism of accountability tends to focus on accountabilities to participants in markets, rather than to a larger public. Some market participants have self-interested reasons to favour these moves, such as the exchanges which hope to grab a larger share of derivatives trading from the banks that have recently generated such large profits from it, in part due to the banks' tight control of information. As well, in its October 2011 report the Financial Stability Board (2011a: 1), which was monitoring the progress towards the end-2012 deadline set by the G20, stated that 'few FSB members have the legislation or regulations in place to provide the framework for operationalising the commitments'. This included the US, where most of the rules needed to implement the Dodd–Frank provisions on derivatives had not been implemented, or even proposed, a full year after its adoption, even if the outlines of the intended regime were becoming clearer with the rules that had been initiated (Skadden 2011). However, it is most likely that the heightened post-crisis accountabilities, even if inadequate or delayed, will significantly increase the constraints on financial actors whose irresponsi-bility had seriously exacerbated the crisis. This, then, reveals a reform outcome that is very similar to the Basel III case.

The reform of the governance of credit rating agencies displays a similar pattern. During the crisis the CRAs received large fees from issuers of toxic subprime mortgage products for certifying their creditworthiness. For instance, Moody's net income grew from US\$159 million in 2000 to US\$705 million in 2006, at which point 44 per cent of its income was coming from the type of structured finance products that were central to the crisis (Mathis et al. 2009: 658). CRAs often received fees for advising those issuers how to structure the products in order to obtain favourable ratings – a relationship seen by many as involving conflicts of interest. The International Organization of Securities Commissions (IOSCO) has described the CRA role during the crisis as 'critical' since participants in markets for structured mortgage products had 'effectively outsourced their own valuations and risk analyses' to CRAs (IOSCO 2008). By 2010 more than three-quarters of the structured mortgage products at the heart of the crisis that were rated AAA by Standard & Poor's from 2005 to 2007 had fallen below investment grade.[6] This and other evidence suggests that reputational factors were not working as a form of accountability.[7] An initial regulatory response to the crisis was simply to strengthen the IOSCO Code of Conduct Fundamentals for Credit Rating Agencies (IOSCO Code) that had been developed to push individual CRAs to publish their own codes, and to step up monitoring of compliance of those individual voluntary codes with the IOSCO Code. An important aspect of the IOSCO Code was the principle that the ratings process and the fee generation process should be organisationally separate within the CRA. By 2009 an IOSCO (2009) report found substantial, but not full, compliance with these relatively modest and voluntary requirements. In April 2009 the G20 then agreed to supplement these requirements with stronger regulatory oversight by national authorities.

A 2010 IOSCO assessment of the state of this oversight, focusing especially on the US, the EU, Japan, Australia and Mexico, found that the main principles of CRAs that had been developed and agreed at IOSCO and were being implemented in national regulation were, namely, that the CRAs should be able to demonstrate their competence; manage their conflicts of interest properly; ensure that their methodology and the meaning of their ratings were transparent and disclosed in a consistent manner; and preserve the confidentiality of data where appropriate. Generally, the national regulations did not provide specific detailed requirements on how these principles should be implemented by CRAs, but instead mostly relied on a threat to restrict or terminate the legal authorisa-tion of CRAs to operate if they could not show they were in compliance; a threat that had become more credible with the increased adoption of mandatory CRA registration (IOSCO 2011). The call by the FSB and the G20 to remove references to credit ratings in public regulation (to push investors to use other forms of credit assessment) was, by 2012, still receiving a slow response (FSB 2012b). The EU has been particularly aggres-sive on CRA regulation, in part because of the perceived negative role played by CRAs in the EU's sovereign debt problems (Brummer and Loko, forthcoming). On 16 January 2013 the European Parliament approved rules previously provisionally agreed with the Council, requiring CRAs to make their methodologies more transparent, not seek to influence state policies, restrict the dates and time of day they can issue ratings on sovereign debt, and comply with restrictions on shareholdings linking CRAs and rated firms. Moves to expose CRAs to legal liability are also proceeding in the US and the EU, although a 'no-action' letter issued by the Securities and Exchange Commission to counteract the CRA liability provisions in the Dodd–Frank Act, following a market disruption from a CRA refusal to let their ratings be included in the issuance of some securities, had slowed the process in the US (Carbone 2010; Morgenson 2011).

Overall, then, the CRA case displays a similar pattern to the other Basel III and derivatives regulation reforms. The G20 has agreed that the role of CRAs needs to be altered, primarily by reducing reliance on their ratings, and IOSCO has agreed some general principles and revisions to its 2004 voluntary code of conduct that address the problems with CRAs that were most evident in the 2008 crisis. Especially, significant strengthening of CRA regulation is moving forward in the European Union. However, there has been no initiative to prohibit the operation of CRAs, and instead the emphasis has been on increasing the public accountability of these private actors.

CONCLUSION

This chapter has argued that the transnational regulatory response to the 2008 financial crisis represents an incremental increase in the public accountability of private actors. While there are a great many ways in which private financial actors have sought, often successfully, to block or reverse reform, these have not been enough to restore the levels of power and lack of accountability that private sector actors enjoyed before the crisis. While the measures that have been taken have fallen short of the type of far-reaching reform that many called for during and indeed since the crisis, and which are probably needed to prevent another crisis, there has nevertheless been a strengthening of transnational regulation in the Basel III, derivatives and credit rating cases. This strengthening has generally not eliminated private sector involvement in governance, but instead has reconfigured it through sets of incentives and legal conditions, such as the capital adequacy and liquidity provisions of Basel III; the requirements that derivatives begin to work through central counterparties, exchanges and trade repositories; and the registration requirements for CRAs. In all three cases the goal is to alter risk management and accountabilities within private institutions, so that private financial actors do not reap the rewards of risk while imposing the costs on other actors. In all three cases there are shortcomings and deficiencies of the reforms. Some of these reflect the lobbying efforts of financial firms, and some the complexity of the changes that are needed. However, there is nothing in the concept of using and constraining private sector governance mechanisms that inherently condemns this approach to fail. Capital adequacy requirements could be ratcheted up. Regulations could close loopholes that allow derivatives traders to avoid central counterparties, exchanges and trade repositories. Once registered, CRAs could be subject to yet more requirements. Thus, in the final analysis, it is not the state or business character of the rules and actors that are involved that in itself determines the quality of public and private accountabilities in regulation.

While not the focus of this chapter, there are a great many other ways that public accountability could be further enhanced and thus better complement private accountability mechanisms. Like private actors and institutions, state institutions do not inevitably work in the public interest, but can at times operate to advance the private interests of regulators, policy-makers or firms. Enhancing the public accountability of public sector institutions can not only hold public sector actors accountable, but also increase the probability that they, in turn, ensure that private sector actors are held accountable (Helleiner and Porter 2009).

Since these mechanisms of accountability are more complex than older, more exclusively national regulatory arrangements, they are easily overlooked. However, if we do not fully consider their potentials and deficiencies, we will not understand key aspects of the regulatory response that are consistent with broader changes in the international political economy, including the identified four themes of this book. We will also miss important practical opportunities for changing the governance of global finance in a way that makes a recurrence of the 2008 crisis less likely.

ACKNOWLEDGEMENT

Comments by Eric Helleiner on a previous version of this chapter, the research assistance of Falin Zhang and the financial support of the Social Sciences and Humanities Research Council of Canada are all gratefully acknowledged.

NOTES

1. The International Social and Environmental Accreditation and Labelling Alliance was created in 2002 by several non-governmental organisations which wished to coordinate their certification activities. It has subsequently been known by its acronym, the ISEAL Alliance. Accreditations are mechanisms to enhance the credibility of a firm's social or environmental policies. See http://www.isealalliance.org/.
2. These issues are the focus of a project initiated by Jacqueline Best and Alexandra Gheciu. See http://cips.uottawa.ca/projects/publicprivate-interaction-and-the-transformation-of-global-governance-2/
3. For a treatment of the BCBS similar to that developed here, see Tsingou (2008, 2009, 2010). For background on the BCBS, see Porter (2005) and the BCBS website.
4. The average was calculated by the author of this chapter. Some jurisdictions received more than one score to reflect variation in the implementation of different aspects of the rules. An average score for each jurisdiction was calculated and these averages were then averaged.
5. See James and Forde (2011) and Baran and Eckhardt (2011), on which this paragraph is based.
6. The figure refers to all private-label residential mortgage-backed securities issued in the United States during this time period (IMF 2010: 86–8).
7. There is a theoretical and empirical literature on the effects of CRA reputation. See, for instance, Mathis et al. (2009), which questions the effectiveness of reputational factors. See also IMF (2010, Chapter 3).

REFERENCES

Abbott, Kenneth W. and Duncan Snidal (2009), 'Strengthening international regulation through transnational new governance: overcoming the orchestration deficit', *Vanderbilt Journal of Transnational Law*, **42**, 501–78.
Adler, Emanuel and Vincent Pouliot (eds) (2011), *International Practices*, Cambridge: Cambridge University Press.
Alter, Karen J. and Sophie Meunier (2009), 'The politics of international regime complexity', *Perspectives on Politics*, **7** (1), 13–24.
Baker, Andrew (2010), 'Restraining regulatory capture? Anglo-America, crisis politics, and trajectories of change in global financial governance', *International Affairs*, **86** (3), 647–63.
Baker, Andrew (2012), 'The new political economy of the macroprudential ideational shift', *New Political Economy*, DOI: 10.1080/13563467.2012.662952, 23 April.

Bank for International Settlements (2010), 'Assessment of the macroeconomic impact of stronger capital and liquidity requirements', press release, 18 August, at http://www.bis.org/press/p100818.htm, accessed 8 May 2011.

Baran, Anne-Kathrin and Philipp Eckhardt (2011), 'Capital Requirements Directive (Basel III)', Centrum für Europäische Politik, 14 November, at http://www.cep.eu/fileadmin/user_upload/Kurzanalysen/ Eigenkapital_Basel_III/PB_Capital_Requirements_Directive.pdf, accessed 14 December 2011.

Barth, James R. and Gerard Caprio, Jr (2006), *Rethinking Bank Regulation: Till Angels Govern*, Cambridge: Cambridge University Press.

Basel Committee on Banking Supervision (BCBS) (2011), 'Progress report on Basel III implementation', October, at http://www.bis.org/publ/bcbs203.pdf, accessed 21 October 2013.

Brummer, Chris and Rachel Loko (forthcoming), 'The new politics of transatlantic credit rating agency regulation', in Tony Porter (ed.), *Transnational Financial Regulation after the Crisis*, London: Routledge.

Carbone, Danielle (2010), 'The impact of the Dodd–Frank Act's credit rating agency reform on public companies', *Insights: The Corporate and Securities Law Advisor*, **24** (9), 1–7.

Cashore, Benjamin (2002), 'Legitimacy and the privatization of environmental governance: how non state market-driven (NSMD) governance systems gain rule making authority', *Governance*, **15** (4), 503–29.

Claessens, Stijn and Geoffrey R.D. Underhill (2010), 'The political economy of Basel II in the international financial architecture', in Geoffrey R.D. Underhill, Jasper Blom and Daniel Mügge (eds), *Global Financial Integration Thirty Years On: From Reform to Crisis*, Cambridge: Cambridge University Press, pp. 113–33.

Cutler, A. Claire, Virginia Haufler, and Tony Porter (eds) (1999), *Private Authority in International Affairs*, Albany, NY: SUNY Press.

Davies, Howard (2010), 'Is regulation really for sale?', 20 December, Project Syndicate, at http://www.project-syndicate.org/commentary/davies11/English, accessed 22 December 2011.

Easton, Nina (2008), 'Main Street turns against Wall Street', *Fortune*, September 28, at http://money.cnn.com/2008/09/26/news/economy/easton_backlash.fortune/index.htm, accessed 6 December 2011.

Egenter, Sven (2011), 'IMF criticizes EU proposals for Basel III implementation', Reuters, 1 August, at http://uk.reuters.com/article/2011/08/01/uk-banks-baseliii-imf-idUKTRE7704QQ20110801, accessed 20 December 2011.

Epstein, G. (ed.) (2005), *Financialization and the World Economy*, Cheltenham, UK and Northampton, MA, USA: Edward Elgar.

Ewing, Jack (2010), 'Backing expected for bank rules: G-20 nations dismiss fears of damage from capital requirements', *International Herald Tribune*, 11 November, p. 4.

Financial Stability Board (FSB) (2011a), 'OTC derivatives market reforms', 11 October, at http://www.financialstabilityboard.org/publications/r_111011b.pdf, accessed 29 November 2011.

Financial Stability Board (FSB) (2011b), 'Policy measures to address systemically important financial institutions', 4 November, at http://www.financialstabilityboard.org/publications/r_111104bb.pdf, accessed 19 December 2011.

Financial Stability Board (FSB) (2012a), 'Strengthening oversight and regulation of shadow banking: an integrated overview of policy recommendations', Consultative Document, 18 November, at http://www.financialstabilityboard.org/, accessed 5 February 2013.

Financial Stability Board (FSB) (2012b), 'Roadmap and workshop for reducing reliance on CRA ratings: FSB report to G20 finance ministers and central bank governors', November 5, at http://www.financialstabilityboard.org/publications/r_121105b.pdf, accessed 5 February 2013.

Finnemore, Martha and Kathryn Sikkink (1998), 'International norm dynamics and political change', *International Organization*, **52** (4), 888–917.

Froud, Julie, Sukhdev Johal, Adam Leaver and Karel Williams (2006), *Financialization and Strategy: Narrative and Numbers*, London and New York: Routledge.

Gill, Stephen (2003), *Power and Resistance in the New World Order*, Basingstoke: Palgrave.

Global Financial Markets Association (GFMA) (2011), 'Basel 3 framework: outstanding issues on Basel III standards and processes', letter to Nout Wellink, Chair of the BCBS, 4 February.

Hacker, Jacob S. and Paul Pierson (2010), *Winner-Take-All Politics: How Washington Made the Rich Richer and Turned its Back on the Middle Class*, New York: Simon & Schuster.

Hansen, Hans Krause and Dorte Salskov-Iversen (eds) (2008), *Critical Perspectives on Private Authority in Global Politics*, Basingstoke: Palgrave.

Helleiner, Eric (2011a), 'Reining in the market: global governance and the regulation of derivatives', in Dag Harald Claes and Carl Henrik Knutsen (eds), *Governing the Global Economy*, London: Routledge, pp. 131–50.

Helleiner, Eric (2011b), 'Out from the shadows: governing of OTC Derivatives after the 2007–08 financial crisis', paper prepared for the annual conference of the Canadian Political Science Association, Waterloo, Ontario, 16–18 May.

Helleiner, Eric and Stefano Pagliari (2011), 'The end of an era in international financial regulation? A post-crisis research agenda', *International Organization*, **65**, 169–200.

Helleiner, Eric and Tony Porter (2009), 'Making transnational networks more accountable', in Sara Burke (ed.), 'Redefining the global economy', Dialogue on Globalization Occasional Paper No. 42, April, New York: Friedrich Ebert Stiftung, pp. 14–24, at http://library.fes.de/pdf-files/iez/global/06293.pdf, accessed 5 February 2013.

International Monetary Fund (IMF) (2010), 'Global financial stability report: sovereigns, funding and systemic liquidity', October, at http://www.imf.org/external/pubs/ft/gfsr/2010/02/index.htm, accessed 22 December 2011.

International Organization of Securities Commissions (IOSCO) (2008), 'The role of credit rating agencies in structured finance markets', Consultation Report, Technical Committee, March, at http://www.iosco.org/library/pubdocs/pdf/IOSCOPD263.pdf, accessed 11 November 2011.

International Organization of Securities Commissions (IOSCO) (2009), 'A review of the implementation of the IOSCO Code of Conduct Fundamentals for Credit Rating Agencies', Technical Committee, March.

International Organization of Securities Commissions (IOSCO) (2011), 'Regulatory implementation of the Statement of Principles Regarding the Activities of Credit Rating Agencies', Final Report, Technical Committee, February, at http://www.iosco.org/library/pubdocs/pdf/IOSCOPD346.pdf, accessed 11 November 2011.

James, Benedict and Andrew Forde (2011), 'Comparison between Capital Requirements Directive IV and Basel III' Linklaters, 12 August, at http://www.linklaters.com/pdfs/mkt/london/Comparison_between_Capital_Requirements_Directive_IV_and_Basel_I.pdf, accessed 14 December 2011.

Johnson, Simon and James Kwak (2010), *13 Bankers: The Wall Street Takeover and the Next Financial Meltdown*, New York: Pantheon.

Kumar, Nikhil (2011), 'Banking rules are not strong enough, warns FSA's chairman', *The Independent*, at http://www.independent.co.uk/news/business/news/banking-rules-are-not-strong-enough-warns-fsas-chairman-2244033.html, accessed 8 May 2011.

Lall, Ranjit (2010), 'Reforming global banking rules: back to the future?', ISS Working Paper 2010: 6, Danish Institute for International Studies.

Larner, Wendy and William Walters (eds) (2004), *Global Governmentality: Governing International Spaces*, London: Routledge, pp. 1–20.

Levi-Faur, David (2005), 'The global diffusion of regulatory capitalism', *Annals of the American Academy of Political and Social Science*, **598**, 12–32.

Lessig, Lawrence (2011), *Republic, Lost: How Money Corrupts Congress – And a Plan to Stop It*, New York: Twelve.

Mathis, Jérome, James McAndrews, Jean-Charles Rochet (2009), 'Rating the raters: are reputation concerns powerful enough to discipline ratings agencies?', *Journal of Monetary Economics*, 56, 657–74.

Mattli, Walter and Ngaire Woods (2009), 'In whose benefit? Explaining regulatory change in world politics', in Walter Mattli and Ngaire Woods (eds), *The Politics of Global Regulation*, Princeton, NJ: Princeton University Press, pp. 1–43.

McKinsey & Company (2010), 'Basel III and European banking: its impact, how banks might respond, and the challenges of implementation', Philipp Härle, Erik Lüders, Theo Pepanides, Sonja Pfetsch, Thomas Poppensieker, Uwe Stegemann (authors), November, at http://www.mckinsey.com/clientservice/Financial_Services/Knowledge_Highlights/~/media/Reports/Financial_Services/Basel%20III%20and%20European%20banking%20FINAL.ashx, accessed 13 December 2011.

Moody's (2011), 'Implementing Basel III: challenges, options and opportunities', *Moody's Analytics*, September, at http://www.moodysanalytics.com/basel3implementation2011, accessed 20 December 2011.

Morgenson, Gretchen (2011), 'Hey, SEC, that escape hatch is still open', *New York Times*, 5 March.

Ong, Aihwa and Stephen J. Collier (2005), *Global Assemblages: Technology, Politics and Ethics as Anthropological Problems*, Malden: Blackwell.

Pagliari, Stefano (ed.) (2012), *Making Good Financial Regulation: Towards a Policy Response to Regulatory Capture*, London: International Centre for Financial Regulation.

Porter, Tony (2005), *Globalization and Finance*, Cambridge: Polity Press.

Porter, Tony (2011), 'Public and private authority in the transnational response to the 2008 financial crisis', *Policy and Society*, **30** (3), 175–84.

Protess, Ben (2011), 'Wall Street lobbyists aim to "reform the reform"', *New York Times. Dealb%k*, 14 July.

Sassen, Saskia (2006), *Territory, Authority, Rights: From Medieval to Global Assemblages*, Princeton, NJ: Princeton University Press.

Skadden, Arps, Slate, Meager & Flom LLP & Affiliates (2011), 'Title VII of the Dodd–Frank Act one year later: piecing together the Dodd–Frank "mosaic" for derivatives regulation', 21 July, at http://www.skadden.com/newsletters/Title_VII_of_the_Dodd-Frank_Act_One_Year_Later.pdf, accessed 21 December 2011.

Slaughter, Anne-Marie (2004), *A New World Order*, Princeton, NJ: Princeton University Press.

Tsingou, E. (2007), 'The role of policy communities in global financial governance: a critical examination of the Group of Thirty', in T. Strulik and H. Willke (eds), *Towards a Cognitive Mode in Global Finance: The Governance of a Knowledge-Based Financial System*, Frankfurt: Campus Verlag, pp. 213–38.

Tsingou, Eleni (2008), 'Transnational private governance and the Basel process: banking regulation, private interests and Basel II', in Andreas Nölke and Jean-Christophe Graz (eds), *Transnational Private Governance and its Limits*, ECPR/Routledge series, London: Routledge, pp. 58–68.

Tsingou, Eleni (2009), 'Regulatory reactions to the credit crisis: analysing a policy community under stress', in Eric Helleiner, Stefano Pagliari and Hubert Zimmermann (eds), *Global Finance in Crisis: The Politics of International Regulatory Change*, London: Routledge, pp. 21–36.

Tsingou, Eleni (2010), 'Transnational governance networks in the regulation of finance – the making of global regulation and supervision standards in the banking industry', in Morten Ougaard and Anna Leander (eds), *Business and Global Governance*, London: Routledge, pp. 138–55.

Wilson, Harry (2011), 'Banking crisis risk "unacceptably high"', *Daily Telegraph*, 7 April, Business, p. 4.

Young, Kevin L. (2012), 'Transnational regulatory capture? An empirical examination of the transnational lobbying of the Basel Committee on Banking Supervision', *Review of International Political Economy*, iFirst, pp. 1–26, DOI:10.1080/09692290.2011.624976.

8 The governance of the global financial crisis in the Eurozone

Geoffrey R.D. Underhill

This chapter focuses on the governance of global financial crises in a rapidly changing context. The ongoing nature of the current financial turmoil and great recession, most marked in the developed economies, renders any conclusive analysis difficult. The chapter will use the latest Eurozone phase of the contemporary global financial crisis as a case to illustrate the problems of the current system of crisis management and work-out, with implications for the reform process that is under way.

One may begin by distinguishing nominally between two sorts of crises: (1) financial market and/or banking sector crises that (may) remain largely a private financial sector phenomenon but, if systemic in nature, can eventually threaten the general stability of the macroeconomy; and (2) currency-cum-sovereign debt crises that may arise from macroeconomic imbalances or exchange rate misalignment and/or government debt problems and that severely constrain the access of entire national economies to financial flows for governments and the private sector alike. In reality, the two are highly likely to be interlinked and the one may give rise to the other via spillover and market contagion. Recognising this linkage has often seen the combination dubbed a 'twin crisis' (Kaminsky and Reinhart 1999; Bordo et al. 2001). For an example of these interlinkages, one need look no further than the crisis that broke out in 2007 and was far from being resolved at the time of writing in 2013. The policy domains involved are those of financial supervision and the lender-of-last-resort facility for the banking sector; macroeconomic adjustment, exchange rate and monetary policy; and (sovereign) debt work-out processes. Once again, the interlinkages among these policy domains in crisis and good times alike should be emphasised. However, it is not the case that these policy domains are necessarily formally linked in terms of decision-making processes, and this is definitely part of the problem with how crises are dealt with.

The chapter begins by developing the themes that run through this volume, outlining the features and policy dilemmas of global financial governance. The argument here is that there is considerable power asymmetry between those who have input into system design and benefit the most from the opportunities presented by cross-border markets, and those who pay for what goes wrong, while accountability for bad outcomes is weak even at the national level. The chapter goes on to provide an account of the emergence and nature of the contemporary market-based financial architecture and its manifestation in the governance of crises. The argument here is that the system has tended to strengthen the benefits available to those who designed it, while failing to provide an adequate degree of financial stability for the real economy or the broader public. Although debtors and creditors together produce the outcomes, the contemporary financial architecture as it operates during financial crises and debt work-outs tends to favour (private) creditors. The third section focuses on the nature of the Eurozone as the most developed regionally based version of market-based governance and crisis work-out. The contention here is that the Eurozone exaggerates most of the weaknesses of the contemporary global financial architecture: it expects market disciplines under conditions of capital mobility to produce stable outcomes, yet it produced imbalances and instability instead. Although ostensibly an irrevocable currency union wherein the outcomes are collectively generated, it has little in the way of genuinely 'federal' institutional machinery or policy capacity. So great was the confidence in market-generated stability and the 'rules' of macroeconomic adjustment that there was no crisis work-out mechanism built into the system at all, and in sovereign debt crises the expectation is that debtors (read: states, though states are hardly responsible for the bulk of transactions in either the financial or tradable sectors) will resolve the problems for themselves despite systematically skewed benefits for the creditors (most of whom are private but are often backed by their governments). The 'federal' European Central Bank (ECB) was specifically forbidden from behaving like a proper central bank and thus monetising sovereign debt, although there are notionally ways around this. Even though the Commission has a substantial budget approved by a democratically elected parliament of the Union, there was no provision for a 'federal' resource base or treasury, or debt issuance function, beyond the ECB's own balance sheet. However, the ECB was permitted under its mandate to provide lender-of-last-resort facilities to financial institutions in distress, and has done so with great success. In practice, the Eurozone has turned out to be rather efficient at saving banks, but has shown only limited commitment to saving the citizen guarantors of the system. The burden of adjustment falls on the weaker, developing and debtor economies that already benefit less from the system of capital mobility than the more advanced economies, and had less say in setting the rules. The fourth section of the chapter examines the overall dynamics of the 'Eurocrisis', and the chapter ends with a summary and conclusion addressing the issues of political legitimacy and sustainability under the current policy mix and proposed reforms.

THE NATURE OF GLOBAL FINANCIAL GOVERNANCE

There are four features of the political economy of (global) governance that run through this volume and serve as a metaphor for this analysis of the governance of financial crises, to which this chapter adds a fifth that is highly relevant to financial markets and with which we begin. This first point notes that patterns of governance are unstable and are observably in constant flux. Markets require governance in order to function and this is simply axiomatic. Cross-border financial integration diminishes the efficacy of national mechanisms and policies, driving the need for adaptation in terms of regional or global instances. However, markets often integrate faster than cooperative or properly transnational institutions can be created or adapted. The economic volatility and asymmetric costs of adjustment to capital market integration challenge the functionality and legitimacy of national and international institutions alike, while democratic processes operate largely at the national level and thus feed a tendency for electorates to demand purely national solutions. This political dynamic may exacerbate the latent coordination problems of global financial governance, especially in a crisis. Furthermore, the crisis has accelerated the rise of the emerging market economies relative to the United States,

Europe and Japan, placing further pressures on the system that evolved under the aegis of the Group of 7 (G7) economies. Ideational, institutional and policy change are actively being discussed and in some cases implemented. Meanwhile, the outbreak of financial crisis and its spillover into sovereign debt markets has challenged the underlying premise of the past 30 years that financial openness and liberal markets play a necessarily positive role in the governance of the global economy. In short, the dynamics of cross-border integration challenge – across levels – the institutions without which the system cannot function, generating the flux that we observe. The tendency is to drag issues down to the national level, with a latent risk that financial openness becomes impossible, driving systemic collapse and a further round of flux.

Secondly, like theory all patterns of governance are '*for* something and *for* some purpose' and like theory they cannot be 'divorced from a standpoint in time and space' (Cox 1986: 207). This implies that the norms that underpin the system of governance typically manifest important material interest and ideational or ideological characteristics. Systems of governance have underlying norms that typically reflect the preferences of those constituencies with privileged access to decision-making. The governance of contemporary global finance certainly highlights the central role of private actors and authority, as well as the normative premises of market-based processes as mechanisms of governance. This reflects the input into the policy process of a highly restricted range of stakeholders, consisting largely of semi-autonomous or highly autonomous elite state agencies working in close historical association and interacting on a daily basis with private sector financial institutions (Underhill 1995; Claessens et al. 2008). In the past 30 years, a revolving door in terms of careers has seen many officials move from public to private sector appointments and back again, reinforcing the normative consensus and the sense of shared interests. Back to the issue of flux, the question is: where might it be going post-crisis?

Thirdly, governance operates at a variety of levels from the local via the national to the sometimes properly global. The way it cuts across levels is far more important than each discrete level taken on its own. This is certainly true of global finance: global standards and agreements interact with national and regional agreements (e.g. European Union, Asian), and also with private sector systems of governance and market authority that likewise cut across levels. How these public–private and multilevel interactions produce (or fail to produce) authoritative and hopefully legitimate mechanisms aimed at the provision of financial stability is crucial to understanding the global financial order. Coherence and coordination difficulties across levels are a serious challenge to the effectiveness of the system, and there are ongoing tensions across levels and agent constituencies about the distribution of the costs of both crisis prevention and work-out. Without sufficient coherence and cooperation across levels, including among states with frequently divergent interests, a global system cannot work.

Fourthly, as the third point implies, governance involves a dispersion of agency and authority across a range of actors: agency is not limited to the state. The crucial role played by private actors and authority referred to above emphasises the point. It is clear how the system works in good times: financial institutions and end-users benefit mutually from the opportunities offered by global financial market integration. Yet a central issue remains: who should pay when private markets prove dysfunctional and public resources are required to prevent collapse and restore systemic stability?

Fifthly and finally, this dispersion of agency and authority raises persistent and difficult issues of legitimacy and accountability for outcomes, and once again normative issues concerning input voice in the policy process, the effectiveness of governance, and *'cui bono?'* As global level processes emerged, policy was made by a range of highly autonomous, specialised, often transnational, agencies with systematically close relationships to the private sector in the major financial centres (Underhill and Zhang 2008). Stakeholder input to policy outcomes was limited, to say the least. The crisis showed national and global systems of financial governance to be singularly ineffective at crisis prevention, but not bad in at least the initial phases of the rescue, and eventually largely powerless to end the ongoing recession and sovereign debt problems. The *'cui bono?'* question concerns, in particular, the distributional impact of financial instability and crisis on the real economy, and the cost of financial rescue for the general public versus private agents and/or other, interdependent national economies. In short, defining the 'public good' and establishing lines of responsibility for the outbreak of crisis in a system characterised by private market transactions is inherently problematic, and the dispersion of authority across levels and to powerful private actors exacerbates the difficulty. In the face of systemic breakdown and painful post-crisis adjustment, what is politically legitimate and sustainable will prove to be the bottom line, and this for the most part will be played out at the national level in functioning democracies.

THE EMERGENCE OF MARKET-BASED FINANCIAL ARCHITECTURE

This section outlines the emergence of the contemporary financial architecture. Financial openness and market liberalisation, as a policy stance adopted by a broad range of national economies over the past 30 years, initiated nearly all the most important developments. The policy led to the cross-border integration of national financial markets; brought about the de-segmentation of securities and banking markets and the rapid securitisation of finance; generated powerful incentives towards financial innovation; and set in train the emergence of major transnational financial conglomerates of systemically important dimensions. This trend brought with it substantial benefits: those who could access global markets found the cost of capital much reduced and the variety of products greatly enhanced. Creditworthy governments and corporate treasuries alike gained access to larger pools of finance that released them from the constraints of their national markets and of sometimes arbitrary regulation. Developing countries were able to improve access to admittedly volatile capital flows. As wealth in the global economy increased, private savers and their pension and insurance funds could diversify investments and improve returns, and access to housing finance moved ever closer (tantalisingly, it turned out) to lower-income groups.

To these undoubted benefits delivered to a range of agents and constituencies one should add the dangers and policy dilemmas of capital mobility. Financial liberalisation has historically proved far from stable and the tendency towards crisis has been well documented in the literature (Bordo et al. 2001; Reinhart and Rogoff 2009). The interaction of open capital markets with the global monetary system and national macroeconomic policies is notoriously difficult, especially for debtor economies. Developing countries and sometimes wealthier economies were subject to impressive tides of capital inflows, but also to sudden droughts and withdrawals. The system of adjustment to global imbalances was no longer driven by the dynamics of international trade, but by capital mobility. Floating exchange rates suffered from chronic high–low overshooting, and the relationship between economic 'fundamentals' and patterns of capital flows was murky at best. So, for the political economist, the questions are, as always, 'Who benefits?' and 'Who sets the rules?'

So how did the system emerge and why? There are three points to develop in this section: (1) there were noble and not-so-noble motivations for the turn towards financial openness, but all were arguably in the cause of economic renewal and growth; (2) financial openness generated instability and a demand for governance; and (3) who set the rules and whom did they benefit?

Why Financial Liberalisation?[1]

An acceptable starting point is the introduction of floating exchange rates in the early 1970s. Governments perceptibly could no longer agree to manage exchange rates and the adjustment burdens' management implied by the Bretton Woods accords. Floating introduced market-based macroeconomic adjustment and thus boosted international capital markets enormously in the conspicuous absence of commensurate domestic or international institutions to ensure their governance. Firstly, the rapid growth of the eurocurrency markets had provided the functional equivalent of capital mobility on an offshore basis (Strange 1976). The US at the end of the 1960s had dissolved capital controls, an admission of defeat. London, Paris, the broader European Union (EU), Japan and parts of Asia would all follow in their own ways in the 1980s and 1990s. Exchange rate uncertainty generated by floating forced firms involved in cross-border trade and investment into the arms of bankers who helped firms adjust to the new volatility. Secondly, while states likewise confronted volatile swings in exchange rates, International Monetary Fund (IMF) resources were not increased and the private market became the alternative source of funding relatively free of IMF discipline. This was an effective 'privatisation' of balance-of-payments lending and it was not long before the bulk of balance-of-payments financing came from private, not official, sources. The theory was that the capital markets would discipline state and private behaviour alike. On the contrary, for creditworthy sovereigns, access to markets in the absence of conditionality *freed* them from the shackles of official policy (Cohen 1982).

A third reason for the expansion of the demand and supply sides of global finance was, perversely, the recession of the mid-1970s and 1980s. Economic downturn and market saturation at home meant that many, especially US banks, were in search of new clients overseas. Coincidentally, the fourfold rise in the oil price generated by the Organization of Petroleum Exporting Countries (OPEC) was recycled via Western banks and the eurocurrency markets grew commensurately. State borrowing needs expanded due to the greater level of international monetary volatility and rising payments imbalances linked to higher oil prices. In turn, economic stagnation and unemployment combined with rising inflation implied both lower tax revenues and higher welfare and social policy expenditure. A final reason for the emergence of an open financial system was that official policy began to dismantle post-Great Depression regulation. New York became the first of many financial centres to implement measures stimulating cross-border liberalisation. The efficacy of national policy instruments was deteriorating as fast as opportunities for jurisdiction-hopping and regulatory arbitrage by private financial institutions expanded.

The general policy argument from both state treasuries or central banks and the private sector was that market forces would discipline state and corporate behaviour better than had the government intervention of fixed exchange rates or regulation, while handing states more policy space via floating at the same time. While justified by the renewed popularity of neoclassical economics emphasising the benefits and stability of market solutions, this was of course a self-serving idea. While capital mobility would constrain macroeconomic policy-making autonomy in numerous ways, in the short term it did a great deal to ease access of (sovereign) debtors to international capital while increasing market access for the most competitive banks. The jamboree would continue until either the banks would lend no more, the cost of credit rose, the weaker links encountered difficulties with repayment, or some or all of the above. Then states and banks would be thrown back into the arms of the (chronically under-resourced) IMF and a debt crisis would ensue. As the 1980s began, this did of course happen, but only to developing countries (at least at first). The creditor economies of the developed world could escape policy constraints and gain better access to more global and innovative financial markets. Large financial institutions could and did serve the demand side with their enlarged pools of capital, using sovereign debt as ready collateral to expand their lending activities with no obligation to increase their capital reserves.

The liberal policy turn made considerable sense for developed national economies that had structurally matured. Socio-economic changes greatly altered the needs of these societies in terms of demand for products, supply-side considerations, finance, public services and government budgetary priorities. A 'wall of money' born of state and employer pension funds and a range of collective private investment vehicles from insurance policies to hedge funds began to seek new outlets and innovation. Capital mobility and more liberal trade led to the emergence of global production and corporate strategies. Emerging market economies were increasingly integrated into the strategies of private multinationals, especially once the Berlin Wall came down in 1989. Cross-border coalitions of state and market actors formed to press their own and foreign governments to engage in financial liberalisation. This proved an enduring alliance for the promotion of financial integration, even though increasing episodes of severe financial instability (Bordo et al. 2001) kept reminding even the optimists that the governance agenda required just as persistent attention.

Instability and the Demand for Governance

The first major crisis of the emerging new system of capital mobility was the Latin American debt crisis of the 1980s. Further serial instability followed, illustrating that, historically, highly liberal financial markets have tended to be characterised by inherent instability (Reinhardt and Rogoff 2009). At the risk of advancing a functionalist hypothesis, the emergence of this instability generated demands for new systems of governance aimed at future crisis prevention and also crisis management and resolution. With the establishment of the Basel Committee on Banking Supervision in 1974 (Wood 2005) and the reactivation of the IMF in debt work-out processes, efforts to develop these new and hybrid forms of global financial governance began in earnest.

Yet these new cooperative forums and institutions had a dual function. They did of course strengthen regulation and supervision, providing global codes and standards and levelling the regulatory playing field somewhat, seeking to reduce the risks to states and firms of operating in global markets. But, by apparently reducing risk, they also served to facilitate further market integration and functioned as a conduit for inserting private policy preferences at the heart of the very public task of financial supervision and regulation (Underhill 1995). It should not escape attention that allowing parties with a pecuniary and competitive market interest unduly to influence the nature of financial supervision, and therefore to affect the very terms of competition in emerging global markets, was fraught with danger. Without a firm assertion of public authority, policy would reflect a rising appetite for risk and profit while increasing the likelihood that the public would bear the costs of eventual failure. Intellectual arguments that justified the market approach to governance advocated by this transnational political alliance, which included state authorities in the key financial centres, generated claims that financial markets tend towards stability,[2] despite the accumulated real-world evidence to the contrary. The 1990s consequently had more liberalisation and of course more crisis in store, but some slightly more serious attempts at the development of cross-border governance as well.

The Crisis–Reform–Crisis Bicycle Race: *Cui Bono?*

There was little in the way of pre-emptive or proactive reform of the system of governance. Episodes of financial crisis interacted with attempts at improving the framework of global financial governance as private and public players were frightened into new efforts at collaboration. The approach was singularly oriented towards promoting market-based processes of adjustment, and that frequently meant that the weaker links in the chain of interdependence had to adapt to market forces, not the other way around. The approach adopted at Bretton Woods had now been precisely reversed: instead of adjustment being subordinated to national priorities, states and their citizens were now increasingly accountable to markets, and public authorities and policy priorities had been deliberately replaced by private actor preferences.

There emerged a constant bicycle race to keep up with the latest outbreak of financial instability, yet stay on wheels: 1992 in Europe; 1994 in Mexico and beyond; 1997–98 in Asia with contagion in Russia, Brazil, and even Wall Street's LTCM[3] collapse; plus 2000–01 in Argentina and Turkey, as well as Ukraine. This resulted in the 'new financial architecture' that mostly followed in the wake of the Asian financial crisis. The emphasis came to be on facilitating market processes and ensuring that firms were more responsible for and better at risk management in an increasingly complex market environment. The importance to the wider set of economic constituencies of developing a system of governance that produced a greater degree of financial stability was clear. Yet, apart from episodes of public indignation that typically followed the most recent crisis, the stakeholders in the policy dialogue remained restricted to the closed community of autonomous state agencies and major firms that had pushed for and organised financial globalisation in the first place. Not surprisingly, the major international banks that were permitted to apply the new approaches to bank supervision that were developed in Basel were also those that gained competitive advantage from the new system over their rivals (Claessens et al. 2008).

It is also important to observe that financial crisis management remained largely the preserve of national central banks and treasuries that intervened as they saw fit to the limits of their resources. Debt work-out problems, however, often born of financial crisis and spillover into currency instability, typically required assistance from the international community. The governance of external debt and 'twin crises' came to involve a combination of IMF loans based on an increasingly intrusive conditionality that involved not only budget and balance-of-payments targets, but also extensive structural and other economic reforms, the better to adapt the national economy to the market-driven pressures of capital mobility. The worst feature of this system of governance is that there was very little evidence that these assistance programmes, mostly implemented by the IMF, had ever contributed to improving the growth and development prospects of the economies on which they were practised.[4]

To summarise this section, the crises of the 1990s and early 2000s induced a wave of enhancements to the governance of the global financial system. New departures were rare (e.g. the Financial Stability Forum, FSF; now the Financial Stability Board, FSB – role unclear) and the market-based approach and financial openness were cemented in place, but there was at least an impression of considerable activity. A hybrid form of public–private governance spanning the national and regional and global levels emerged amid a persistent dash from crisis to reform and back to crisis again with no fundamental rethink. Nor was there any radical shift towards including those who paid the price of the system in the decision-making process. Furthermore, there was a clear conviction that the new architecture was working post-Argentina. The period from 2001 to 2007 was one of relative calm that induced the public–private sector cyclists to retire to the bar, tired after the latest race. They drank deeply with little regard for what was going on around them, and least regard of all for who would pay. Public authorities notably failed to take the punch bowl and other intoxicating beverages away, let alone before the party reached its peak.[5]

EU FINANCIAL INTEGRATION AND ECONOMIC AND MONETARY UNION (EMU): MARKET-BASED GOVERNANCE ON STEROIDS

The European Union is the most advanced example in the global economy of combined financial market and monetary integration among sovereign states. It also carries the norms and practices of market-based governance further than the global financial architecture. It should therefore not be surprising that the problems of market-based governance and macroeconomic adjustment, both on steroids, have turned out to be greater than in other regions of the global economy. This section will examine what a monetary union, in generic terms, implies, and will go on to reveal how EMU as a system of crisis governance was structured – with particular attention to the mandate of the European Central Bank.

What does a Monetary Union Imply?

EU monetary cooperation became relevant after the global post-war fixed exchange rate system collapsed during the period 1971–75. Experience with two versions of European exchange rate management in the 1970s and 1980s, not to mention the major exchange rate crisis of 1992, showed that capital mobility reduced state policy capacities considerably on several fronts. Monetary, exchange rate, fiscal and regulatory policy capacities were all affected. Financial and currency market instability also disturbed the operation of the single market and could endanger economic growth and development in general.

The principal aim of monetary cooperation and eventual currency union was thus to provide 'a zone of monetary stability in Europe' (CEC 1978a, 1978b) that would both allow the single market to function without exchange-rate driven competitive distortions and enhance the capacity of national states to manage their economies in a global monetary system characterised by capital mobility. The experience of the European Monetary System (EMS) of 1978 was that interim measures (such as a fixed exchange rate system) failed to end the problem of speculation and panics associated with the combination of financial market integration, plus exchange rate and internal EU and/or external payments imbalances. The firm commitment to capital account openness that was linked to both the single market and EMU precluded a range of other possible solutions at the same time as full capital mobility made the problem of managing internal payments imbalances more acute, not to mention the difficulty of achieving national monetary policy goals in a time of inflation (and, eventually, crisis). Something more radical was required. Over time a range of countries (Tsoukalis 1977: 172) had meanwhile realised that under conditions of capital mobility devaluations failed to restore competitiveness or correct external imbalances anyway. They were increasingly looking for external discipline on which to anchor their economic policies and bring inflation rates down to the level of the best performers in the EU (Tsoukalis 1997: 150). These countries, most importantly France, had therefore undergone an important shift in economic policy stance that permitted a broad consensus to emerge upon which monetary integration could reasonably be built (McNamara 1998: 122–58).

So the goals were clear. Monetary integration would increase the efficiency gains of the EU project. It would help the EU and its member-states to master the vagaries of financial and currency markets and deal with the dilemmas of capital mobility and imbalances under conditions of cross-border integration. The new currency zone would have a strong external balance, thus shielding the weaker members. Resources could be pooled to deal with financial and currency market volatility. EMU would also facilitate the implementation of the single market programme and the Common Agricultural Policy, removing the competitive distortions of exchange rate fluctuations. There was a clear implicit trade-off that harnessed the collective effort to the diverse interests of the different economies in the system: a commitment to adjustment under more stable conditions for the weaker economies, pooled resources in a crisis for everybody, and the end of persistent devaluations was a benefit to the more competitive export economies. EMU thus provided a potential and very particular set of solutions to domestic policy problems that member-states had experienced (McNamara 1998: Ch. 1), while precluding others – but that was part of the point.

But of course the creation of a monetary union also implied giving up national policy instruments and replacing them with collective policy 'machinery'. States no longer have their own currencies, and cannot therefore autonomously print money, manage interest rates and credit conditions, nor monetise debt in a crisis. These functions need to be carried out collectively. While all national economies have regional and other disparities that mean that setting a central interest rate is more beneficial for some than for others, in a monetary union monetary policy is typically made for a more diverse set of 'economies' than at the national level. Whatever the potential gains, national instances certainly lose the capacity to manipulate monetary flows to the advantage of their national economy.

EMU also implied the end of internal balance of payments within the Eurozone.[6] Conceptually, monetary union means that national economic borders no longer exist as a measurement of imbalances,[7] but this does not mean an end to de facto imbalances inside the currency zone as such. There is indeed nothing sacred about drawing attention to the imbalances among national entities.[8] The post-EMU focus is in principle no longer on what the states as units in the union do, but on how economic agents (firms, investors, consumers, workers, financial institutions) interact across the newly created economic space: 'it is necessary to dispense with the fiction that countries trade and to focus on firms and individuals' (Jones 2011: 331).

The outcomes of monetary union, imbalances and all, costs and benefits, are therefore by definition collectively generated by the whole through the interaction of these economic agents, and outcomes cannot be identified as the responsibility of single member-states.[9] If a new single currency zone is to function, then it is important that this conceptual leap is taken on board by policy-makers and that it is built into the institutional fabric of governance. The monetary and macroeconomic policies generated by the new monetary union, not to mention crisis management, should regard agents without discrimination in terms of national identity and take place regardless of the interests of the individual 'state' units. This does not mean that the units make no difference or that national identities and differences need disappear, on the contrary, but EMU was by clear implication a union of citizens and firms as in federal countries. As we shall see, the institutional and normative policy framework eventually chosen did not at all reflect such a conceptual leap in practice – far from it.

All economies, however defined, will respond somewhat differently to the removal of trade and other barriers, or to a change in the external economic climate. In other words, external events or 'shocks' have asymmetric effects on members of an economic club. Optimum Currency Area (OCA) theory tells us much about what is likely to happen when we put divergent economic entities together in a currency union. The process will be easier, in particular on the weaker economic 'units', if certain conditions are satisfied. No federal state or large economic entity properly fulfils the criteria in an ideal way, but some fit better than others; there are certainly important disparities in the Eurozone.[10] Firstly, partner countries should be sufficiently diversified in terms of trade and production; and, secondly, they should be economically open and integrated. The Eurozone satisfies these criteria, but less so the third: labour market mobility.[11] If labour can move, the costs of adjustment in terms of unemployment should be lower. Fourthly, it greatly helps if a currency area has a sufficient level of fiscal transfers to ease adjustment problems. The EU does have regionally based structural funds, but these are proportionately small and automatic stabilisers remain nationally based and may therefore worsen asymmetries. Fifthly, adjustment problems are eased if the units share policy preferences.[12] As

McNamara (1998) among others has argued, much convergence has taken place on this score over time. Yet the asymmetric impact of the current Eurozone crisis currently is pushing apart those that prefer a renewal of growth versus those favouring a strategy of retrenchment. But these preferences are relative to the conjunctural context, and ongoing recession may yet see them realign. Finally, a currency union will likely function better to the extent that the units involved are willing to develop a sense of collective interest and actively overcome their differences, or put in place institutional mechanisms that override or develop a voice that speaks for the whole, and deal with distributional costs of adjustment in an integrated fashion. This implies that 'federal' instances have sufficient capacity and legitimacy to do so, and that the units retain sufficient policy space, for example fiscal room and policy differentiation (Tsoukalis 1977: 103; De Grauwe 1997: 193), to absorb adjustment pressures in their own way.

In short, the move to monetary union was highly significant and represented a major step on the way to a more integrated political entity, and that was, as we shall see, the declared purpose. The economic and indeed policy benefits could be considerable, but would be achieved at a cost in terms of national policy autonomy. The institutional design and policy framework would be required to emphasise a sense of collective interest, putting its determination out of the reach of any one or small group of member-states. It would require the capacity to deal decisively with the vagaries of a world of currency and financial market volatility, and crisis–stability was, after all, its original motivation. It would need to cope with well-known asymmetries in the adjustment process in a way that would enhance the legitimacy of both national and EMU levels of governance. And, in doing so, it would need to deliver sufficient and in particular fiscal policy space to national governments so as to cope with structural economic variation and differences in national policy preferences and cultures. This would be the more necessary in the absence of a larger EU budget capable of realising automatic transfers.

EMU in Practice

This section will assess how well the actual design and real-time governance of EMU fit these conditions and might realise the longstanding objectives of European monetary cooperation. EMU was in fact established with a range of both institutional and policy lacunae. Policy responsibilities were therefore distributed unevenly and not always coherently in the new institutional framework. This was understood and it was assumed that these would be filled in as integration and practical problems emerged. We do not yet know if the gamble will pay off, or if crisis will destroy the edifice of monetary union.

Perhaps more importantly, the system was very much a product of the policy norms of the early 1990s, and could have been done differently. If the original purpose of European monetary cooperation had been to assist member-states to deal with the vagaries of global capital mobility, then the present form of EMU must be seen as a seriously missed opportunity. The system was based on the rather problematic assumptions of market-based governance analysed above: an adherence to some basic rules of the game plus, once again, market disciplines, would deliver a strong currency and stable monetary and financial conditions, underpinned by an emergent Eurozone 'stability culture' (Underhill 2002). Yet we have seen that it is precisely these market disciplines that in a context of capital mobility lead to instability and crisis. Furthermore, the primary impact of the macroeconomic policy framework that has accompanied EMU has been to restrict fiscal and other policy space for national governments. Yet above it has been observed that monetary integration required that fiscal policy space be preserved or enhanced to compensate governments for the loss of monetary and exchange-rate policy tools and provide them with the means for absorbing adjustment pressures in accordance with national political imperatives.[13]

This notion of 'stability culture' lay behind a number of the lacunae in Eurozone monetary and financial governance. The first problem was the truncated and skewed mandate of the most powerful of the new institutions: the European Central Bank. The ECB was created with a greater degree of independence from governments or national member banks than any national central bank of the time (EU 1992: article 107), including the Bundesbank. Its mandate placed unusual emphasis on price stability as the primary goal of policy: the ECB may only support the 'general economic policies in the Community with a view to contributing to the achievement of the objectives of the Community' without prejudice to that primary goal (EU 1992. article 105). Even the Bundesbank is obliged to support the 'general economic policies of the federal government' and must weigh responsibility for both the internal and external value of the currency (Kennedy 1991: 13, 21–8).[14] Unlike other central banks, the accountability of the ECB to the political process is unclear and the ECB's mandate is supremely difficult to change.

The narrowness of the mandate fits a particular understanding as to how a 'zone of monetary stability' was to be achieved, and what that meant in practice. Stability actually meant price stability, and if that were maintained 'in accordance with the principle of an open market economy with free competition' (EU 1992: article 105) there would be favourable conditions for growth and adjustment. Sound monetary policy and prudent member-state macroeconomic policies (such as the Growth and Stability Pact, GSP) would lead to financial market and currency stability and an adjustment process that dealt with imbalances.

This was a worrisome formula for the management of capital mobility because, as researchers at the ECB (Moutot and Vitale 2001) pointed out at the time, the pursuit of this peculiar policy mix under conditions of integrated goods, services and particularly capital markets would not necessarily produce (and indeed at the time had not produced) stability and payments equilibrium in the global economy. Debt and financial stability issues, as well as active coordination, had become more important. Cross-border financial integration and capital mobility could hardly be associated with stability (Bordo et al. 2001), so why would the Eurozone be different?

Monetary union would in fact accelerate internal financial market integration and therefore capital mobility by removing internal exchange-rate barriers as market distortions. It would do so without in any way reducing the vulnerability of member-states to external shocks born of global imbalances or for that matter financial and currency instability. Furthermore, this intensified capital mobility would exacerbate, not correct, internal Eurozone current account imbalances and make them easier to finance (Jones 2003). So adjustment might in fact be impaired without the requisite active policy instruments at the level of the Eurozone.

In more technical terms, there were no institutional or policy mechanisms developed to deal with the 'macroprudential' aspects of integration. Prudential supervision of financial markets remained largely a national preoccupation, though governments and national central banks would no longer have the instruments they required. The obvious linkages between the policy domains of monetary policy, exchange rate policy, prudential supervision, imbalances and fiscal policy debt management were ignored in the project. The central thrust was the 'marketisation' of the adjustment process, deliberately denuding the system of policy tools to deal with contingencies that did not fit the 'model'. Stability would flow from the stability culture, which meant price stability and constraints on excessive deficits.

Perhaps the greatest of the institutional and policy lacunae inherent in the peculiar design of EMU was that there was no crisis management mechanism in the event of the familiar 'twin crises' that under conditions of financial globalisation had so frequently combined financial market and banking crisis with acute sovereign debt problems in the emerging markets (Kaminsky and Reinhart 1999). These 'twin crises' result precisely from the linkages among policy domains: ultimately it is all the same money and financial flows are affected by the range of policy instruments, which under EMU could not properly be coordinated. As Hyman Minsky (1982) long ago pointed out, the interaction of monetary policy, leverage in the banking system, and financial market forces would produce an underlying instability even while they appeared to be functioning efficiently under stable conditions. The macroprudential interactions of the Eurozone were potentially dangerous, certainly without the requisite policy instruments. As this author (Underhill 2002: 50–51) wrote at the outset, 'the joker in the pack may well be some form of global monetary or financial turmoil from which the stability culture can provide scant protection . . . [implying] that Europe's long experiment with monetary cooperation is of questionable merit and may be prone to failure'.

In other words, although the Eurozone and ECB created the functional equivalent of a new national currency, the statutes of the ECB and the Treaty on Monetary Union lacked features that are critical to the successful functioning of national monetary systems, federal or otherwise. Firstly, notwithstanding the fact that the ECB was required to 'contribute to the smooth conduct of policies by the competent authorities relating to the prudential supervision of credit institutions and the stability of the financial system' (EU 2008: article 127.5), neither the ECB nor any other EU-level body had responsibility either for active supervision of the financial system or its (macro-)prudential oversight. The ECB might acquire such a mandate only upon unanimous agreement of the Council and if the Bank agreed (EU 2008: article 127.6[15]).

In addition to its monetary policy and note issuance role, the ECB was mandated to interact with the banking system (EU 2010: articles 17–24). The ECB could hold accounts for and accept collateral from private credit institutions, deal in any marketable instruments and make loans, require minimum reserve holdings from credit institutions, and have foreign exchange and other dealings with foreign central banks, credit institutions, or international organisations (e.g. the International Monetary Fund or Bank for International Settlements). So the ECB clearly had sufficient powers and policy instruments to support with liquidity private sector financial institutions in the event of market instability. In this sense it looked much like a typical central bank.

Nevertheless, there was a big 'however' that concerned its relations with governments. While the ECB could act as a fiscal agent to public authorities (EU 2010: article 21.2), other relations with governments were strictly curtailed. It was of course highly independent and, unlike typical central banks, was specifically disbarred from providing any form of credit facility for either EU or member-state institutions of government, whether national or local (EU 2010: article 21.1). The ECB could not, then, either monetise or mutualise Eurozone debt as could other 'national' central banks. Furthermore, there was a specific 'no bailout clause' for Eurozone and EU members:

> The Union shall not be liable for or assume the commitments of central governments, regional, local or other public authorities, other bodies governed by public law, or public undertakings of any Member State, without prejudice to mutual financial guarantees for the joint execution of a specific project. A Member State shall not be liable for or assume the commitments of central governments, regional, local or other public authorities, other bodies governed by public law, or public undertakings of another Member State, without prejudice to mutual financial guarantees for the joint execution of a specific project. (EU 2008: article 125.1[16])

Problems of sovereign or local authority debt, of whatever cause or origin, would be the responsibility of the individual member-states. The clause was strengthened by the 'Growth and Stability Pact' agreed in 1997 at the Amsterdam Council. The pact specified deficit limits and provided for a system of monitoring and an 'excessive deficit procedure' in case of member-state violation. The measures aimed at providing monetary and financial stability were essentially preventative: there was a total reliance on the market-based governance of the stability culture.

It is worth exploring briefly the political economy of the policy norms and assumptions that were in play here. This clause was inserted to placate the surplus countries (particularly Germany) and to circumvent any moral hazard problem: competitive (surplus) members did not want to be responsible for the debt problems of others, and wished above all to avoid any implication that EMU might involve new resource transfers in good times or bad. However collectively generated the outcomes of EMU might actually be, the costs and the benefits of what was known to be a highly asymmetrical affair would be appropriated by the members on their own. The norms of the 'stability culture' specified that the difficulties of debtors would anyway be self-inflicted by a failure to follow the rules. Other potential causes that might arise were unavailable to the policy discourse. Furthermore, there would be no genuine pooling of resources the better to deal with the vagaries of capital mobility. Thus one of the crucial strong–weak economy trade-offs and objectives of European monetary cooperation was specifically excluded, and therefore there was no comprehensive collective crisis management mechanism outside what the Council members might agree ad hoc.

The euro was therefore a real federal currency with underdeveloped institutions of governance, and no real federal machinery in the event of the emergence of the sort of serious trouble which verifiably afflicted the global monetary and financial system with increasing frequency and severity. In other words, EMU was not really to be conceived of as a collectively functioning entity: there was no genuine conceptual leap. The GSP reduced fiscal policy space, rather than providing members with the tools they would need to facilitate adjustment. There was no mechanism for dealing with the downside risks of the collective outcome monetary union was likely to generate as debtor and creditor zones interacted over time.

THE EUROCRISIS

This section will examine how EMU has operated as a system of financial crisis govern-ance in the period of acute financial turmoil and Great Recession since 2007. The aim is to link outcomes – what went wrong – to the peculiar policy mix and system of govern-ance adopted by the member-states in the context of a monetary union.

As established above, the stability culture implies that, while market discipline will function if price stability is provided, governments must pledge to respect specific macroeconomic policy guidelines to deal with fiscal and payments adjustment problems. Policy norms stipulate that facilitating market processes is the most important part of the solution, but also that governments are potentially the principal source of the problem despite their complex responsibilities to their societies in a democratic context. Furthermore, the country-by-country approach adopted in debt work-out mirrors that of the IMF system developed in the context of the global financial architecture, but on steroids. The intrusiveness of conditionality was redoubled, and little attention was paid to the well-aired inherent failures of the approach itself (see note 4). In other words, EMU market-based governance was essentially at variance with the likely realities of a world of accelerating capital mobility and economic imbalances.

Alternative policy responses would not be possible, and crucial tools of intervention available to modern central banks would be likewise unavailable to members of the Eurozone. At the same time the problems were unlikely to go away. What became the 'standard' explanation was essentially a self-fulfilling prophecy: trouble was the fault of those that experienced it. This involved a tale of fiscal incontinence, a lack of respect for the rules of fiscal discipline and a failure to adjust to Eurozone competitive pressures. As the sovereign debt elements of what has come to be called the Eurozone crisis began to take shape in late 2009, the creditor countries did indeed point the finger at those that found their sovereign debt markets under pressure. This policy discourse did little to explain properly either the problem at hand or the minimum conditions for either the successful operation of a currency union or the resolution of the crisis. Creditor and deficit countries alike were guilty of sins of commission in policy terms, and the outcome was collectively generated anyway; not by states as such, but by the interaction of eco-nomic agents.

Data reveal the essential inaccuracy of the story (see Table 8.1). Those countries with relatively high debt loads had improved their situation in the lead-up to and implemen-tation of EMU. Some of the countries suddenly in deepest trouble were among the best performers on both debt loads and annual deficits (Spain, Ireland). At any rate, observ-able debt problems had long been evident well before the crisis emerged, as were Greek 'transparency problems' (well predicted in IMF 2009), so these could not explain the problem, although they might make it worse. Furthermore, some of the countries pat-ently not (yet) directly affected by the crisis had a rather heavy debt load, and Dutch or German banks were neither particularly well supervised nor unaffected by the financial turmoil – on the contrary. If any country currently has a property bubble still to burst, it is The Netherlands. Not long ago, Germany was the country that had the apparently fatal combination of a current account deficit and heavy fiscal deficits. Germany con-sistently broke and indeed altered the GSP rules in its own favour. So government debt problems and property bubbles in themselves are unlikely to be the cause, even if they

Table 8.1 Gross consolidated debt and annual fiscal deficits, Eurozone and UK (% of GDP)

General government gross consolidated debt as a percentage of GDP for Eurozone and UK

	1999	2000	2001	2002	2003	2004	2005	2006	2007	2008	2009	2010	2011
Belgium	113.6	107.8	106.5	103.4	98.4	94.0	92.0	88.0	84.1	89.2	95.7	95.5	97.8
Germany	61.3	60.2	59.1	60.7	64.4	66.3	68.6	68.1	65.2	66.8	74.5	82.5	80.5
Estonia	6.5	5.1	4.8	5.7	5.6	5.0	4.6	4.4	3.7	4.5	7.2	6.7	6.1
Ireland	46.6	35.1	35.1	31.9	30.7	29.4	27.2	24.5	24.8	44.5	64.9	92.2	106.4
Greece	94.0	103.4	103.7	101.7	97.4	98.6	100.0	106.1	107.4	112.9	129.7	148.3	170.6
Spain	62.4	59.4	55.6	52.6	48.8	46.3	43.2	39.7	36.3	40.2	53.9	61.5	69.3
France	58.9	57.3	56.9	58.8	62.9	64.9	66.4	63.7	64.2	68.2	79.2	82.3	86.0
Italy	113.0	108.5	108.2	105.1	103.9	103.4	105.4	106.1	103.1	106.1	116.4	119.2	120.7
Cyprus	59.3	59.6	61.2	65.1	69.7	70.9	69.4	64.7	58.8	48.9	58.5	61.3	71.1
Luxembourg	6.4	6.2	6.3	6.3	6.1	6.3	6.1	6.7	6.7	14.4	15.3	19.2	18.3
Malta	57.1	54.9	60.9	59.1	67.6	71.7	69.7	64.4	62.3	62.0	67.6	68.3	70.9
Netherlands	61.1	53.8	50.7	50.5	52.0	52.4	51.8	47.4	45.3	58.5	60.8	63.1	65.5
Austria	66.8	66.2	66.8	66.2	65.3	64.7	64.2	62.3	60.2	63.8	69.2	72.0	72.4
Portugal	51.4	50.4	53.5	56.6	59.2	61.9	67.7	69.3	68.3	71.7	83.2	93.5	108.1
Slovenia	24.1	26.3	26.5	27.8	27.2	27.3	26.7	26.4	23.1	22.0	35.0	38.6	46.9
Slovakia	47.8	50.3	48.9	43.4	42.4	41.5	34.2	30.5	29.6	27.9	35.6	41.0	43.3
Finland	45.7	43.8	42.5	41.5	44.5	44.4	41.7	39.6	35.2	33.9	43.5	48.6	49.0
United Kingdom	43.7	41.0	37.7	37.5	39.0	40.9	42.5	43.4	44.4	52.3	67.8	79.4	85.0

	General government net lending or net borrowing as a percentage of GDP for Eurozone and UK												
	1999	2000	2001	2002	2003	2004	2005	2006	2007	2008	2009	2010	2011
Belgium	−0.6	0.0	0.4	−0.1	−0.1	−0.1	−2.5	0.4	−0.1	−1.0	−5.5	−3.8	−3.7
Germany	−1.6	1.1	−3.1	−3.8	−4.2	−3.8	−3.3	−1.6	0.2	−0.1	−3.1	−4.1	−0.8
Estonia	−3.5	−0.2	−0.1	0.3	1.7	1.6	1.6	2.5	2.4	−2.9	−2.0	0.2	1.1
Ireland	2.7	4.7	0.9	−0.4	0.4	1.4	1.7	2.9	0.1	−7.4	−13.9	−30.9	−13.4
Greece	:	−3.7	−4.5	−4.8	−5.6	−7.5	−5.2	−5.7	−6.5	−9.8	−15.6	−10.7	−9.4
Spain	−1.2	−0.9	−0.5	−0.2	−0.3	−0.1	1.3	2.4	1.9	−4.5	−11.2	−9.7	−9.4
France	−1.8	−1.5	−1.5	−3.1	−4.1	−3.6	−2.9	−2.3	−2.7	−3.3	−7.5	−7.1	−5.2
Italy	−1.9	−0.8	−3.1	−3.1	−3.6	−3.5	−4.4	−3.4	−1.6	−2.7	−5.4	−4.5	−3.9
Cyprus	−4.3	−2.3	−2.2	−4.4	−6.6	−4.1	−2.4	−1.2	3.5	0.9	−6.1	−5.3	−6.3
Luxembourg	3.4	6.0	6.1	2.1	0.5	−1.1	0.0	1.4	3.7	3.2	−0.8	−0.8	−0.3
Malta	−7.7	−5.8	−6.4	−5.8	−9.2	−4.7	−2.9	−2.8	−2.4	−4.6	−3.9	−3.6	−2.7
Netherlands	0.4	2.0	−0.2	−0.7	−3.1	−1.7	−0.3	0.5	0.2	0.5	−5.6	−5.1	−4.5
Austria	−2.3	−1.7	0.0	−0.7	−1.5	−4.4	−1.7	−1.5	−0.9	−0.9	−4.1	−4.5	−2.5
Portugal	−3.1	−3.3	−4.8	−3.4	−3.7	−4.0	−6.5	−4.6	−3.1	−3.6	−10.2	−9.8	−4.4
Slovenia	−3.0	−3.7	−4.0	−2.4	−2.7	−2.3	−1.5	−1.4	0.0	−1.9	−6.0	−5.7	−6.4
Slovakia	−7.4	−12.3	−6.5	−8.2	−2.8	−2.4	−2.8	−3.2	−1.8	−2.1	−8.0	−7.7	−4.9
Finland	1.7	6.9	5.1	4.1	2.6	2.5	2.8	4.1	5.3	4.4	−2.5	−2.5	−0.6
United Kingdom	0.9	3.6	0.5	−2.1	−3.4	−3.5	−3.4	−2.7	−2.7	−5.1	−11.5	−10.2	−7.8

Source: Eurostat.

are now the focus of attention. The pre-crisis policy stance probably has relatively little to do with the situation, though heavy debt loads are hardly likely to help in the resolution phase.

In explanatory terms, the financial crash is the more likely crisis trigger because countries with greater or lesser structural and budgetary problems alike have seen a worsening of their fiscal balance and debt loads as a result of the crisis. Across the advanced economies, bank rescues transferred trillions of private debt to public sector balance sheets (see Figure 8.1), whilst the long recession has eaten away at tax revenues and pushed up welfare expenditures alongside unemployment.[17] Recession and property market downturns (whether related to a genuine bubble or not) certainly worsened the situation of banks, even in countries not initially affected by the crisis, which include most of those receiving bailouts or in line for the same. In the end, while a sound policy stance by domestic governments seems intuitively helpful, a good or bad fiscal policy stance does not properly explain whether a country was caught in the crisis or not.

A more fruitful explanation focuses less on state policies and more on the effects of capital mobility. If capital mobility is greatly accelerated by a monetary union while exchange rate risk is absent, the different member economies benefit from this in different ways and run different sorts of risks. As one would expect, eliminating the risk of devaluation means that the benefits become heavily skewed towards the most competitive exporters. Evidence for this is that, under EMU, their current account surpluses have grown commensurately (see Figure 8.2). Meanwhile, the excess savings accumulated by the surplus countries flow through their banks to where returns are higher, often to the faster growing periphery with its well-known structural weaknesses. We can see from Figure 8.3 that, prior to the crisis, EMU led to a dramatic interest rate convergence between core and peripheral EMU economies. These economies gain cheaper capital through lower interest rate spreads for public and private borrowers alike, and experience fewer constraints in financing their ongoing current account deficits (Jones 2003). Capital inflows spur growth and investment, but also inflation, not to mention, in particular, property and other asset price inflation driven by tourism and foreign investment. These effects potentially exacerbate competitiveness problems and may set up future bank problems in a downturn.

In the upward part of the cycle, the situation looks positive and sustainable from both sides – a sign of investor confidence. However, in Minsky fashion, good times mask the underlying unsustainability and growing fragility of the phenomenon until the outbreak of crisis. In a downturn, the weaker economies fare worse because, well, they are weaker and less developed. The poorest regions of the weakest economies do the worst, no big surprise. This outcome is indeed inherent in the nature of a monetary union, as federal polities with domestic economies that are highly differentiated across regions know too well (Germany with its five eastern provinces or *länder* from the former German Democratic Republic being a prime example).

The institutional lacunae and policy failures of Eurozone governance were also important explanatory factors in the sovereign debt crisis. Following the rules of the Growth and Stability Pact would have been fatal in the financial crisis, so no one did.[18] Market forces, supposedly a discipline, had led in fact to imbalances, bank sector financial fragility and growing competitiveness problems during the good times. Then the crisis struck, followed by the costly rescue of the banks, recession and more debt for governments.

The ECB and national governments did a good job of rescuing the financial system in 2008–09, but at a huge cost to public sector balance sheets (Table 8.1, Figure 8.1). There was all along considerable ambiguity about what would happen if a country found itself in the rather broad margins between liquidity problems and insolvency. Would the no-bailout clause be respected no matter what? The former German finance minister, Peer Steinbrück, had once intimated: probably not.[19] New EU members hit by the crisis had been helped (somewhat) in 2008–09. Would the ECB intervene as it had in rescuing the banks, like a 'normal' central bank? After all, the emerging sovereign crisis was the flip-side of bank fragility and everyone knew this, especially the 'markets'. Would sovereign defaults be an option? Would economies under severe adjustment pressures leave the euro and devalue?

As we know, the ECB mandate specifically prevented an active crisis resolution approach in the case of sovereign debt, and creditor member-states that had sponsored the no-bailout clause and GSP came to be predictably against the idea, especially the new German coalition led by Angela Merkel and her Finance Minister, Wolfgang Schäuble. As the crisis gathered pace around the problems of Greece in early 2010, there were no clear answers to these questions, but there was plenty of ambiguity and open dissent among Eurozone member countries. When the markets began to panic, there was a loan-based bailout for Greece that clearly made the country's predicament worse, and the markets could see that. So bond spreads rapidly widened (Figure 8.3) and the price of rescue grew geometrically as doubts over sovereign debt repayments worsened the predicament of the banks that held it, and vice versa. Ireland, Portugal and Spain followed and contagion was off and running, eventually engulfing Italy as well by 2011. On the other hand, in a world of essentially zero and sometimes negative interest rates, the growing returns on distressed sovereign debt and high interest rates on rescue loans were a further transfer from debtor to creditor economies via the banks. The banks at least, it seemed, would consistently be bailed out by the ECB with the Eurozone taxpayer (rich or poor) as the ultimate guarantor. The longer the agony went on, the less clear were the signals from the Eurozone governments, and those measures that were proposed were long-term, not crisis solutions.

Debtor or creditor governments respectively settled on self-interested blame-game discourses while promising underspecified reforms domestically and at the EU level, in particular 'Banking Union'. Market volatility and occasionally panic continued apace and debt loads grew alarmingly despite stupefying austerity measures aimed at producing 'expansionary fiscal contractions' that were supposed to correct fiscal imbalances while restoring competitiveness and growth. Domestic electorates lined up behind their respective vituperative governments, undermining what might have been popular support for further cooperation and institution-building. A monumental distributional conflict over the present state and future of both monetary union and macroeconomic adjustment had been ignited. Meanwhile, the benefits of EMU continued to accrue to surplus countries, but in lesser measure as economic growth began to falter and renewed recession tightened its grip in the crisis countries, eventually hitting almost all Eurozone members. Contagion made the problem immeasurably greater than if there had been prompt central intervention.

By the summer of 2012, the situation was acute and the ECB once again took action. The Outright Monetary Transactions (OMT) programme announced by ECB President

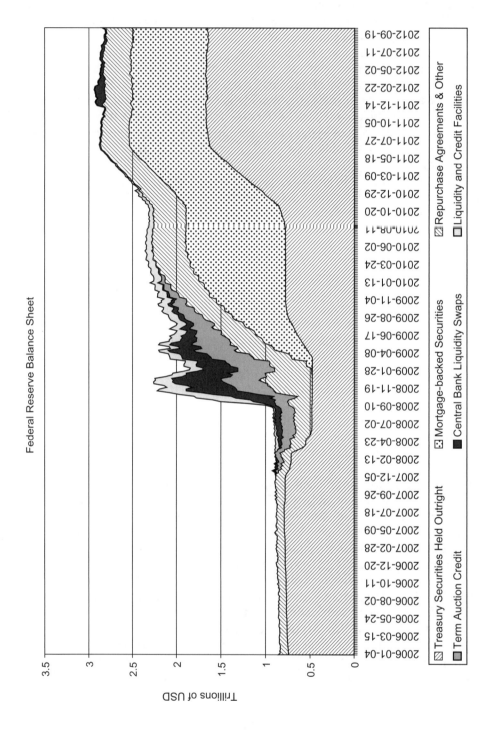

Federal Reserve Balance Sheet

Trillions of USD

Treasury Securities Held Outright   Mortgage-backed Securities   Repurchase Agreements & Other

Term Auction Credit   Central Bank Liquidity Swaps   Liquidity and Credit Facilities

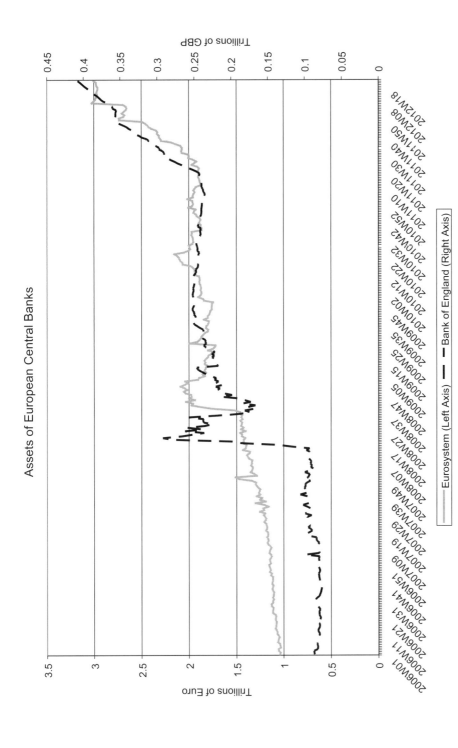

Sources: Federal Reserve, Bank of England, ECB.

Figure 8.1 Central bank balance sheets before and after the crisis

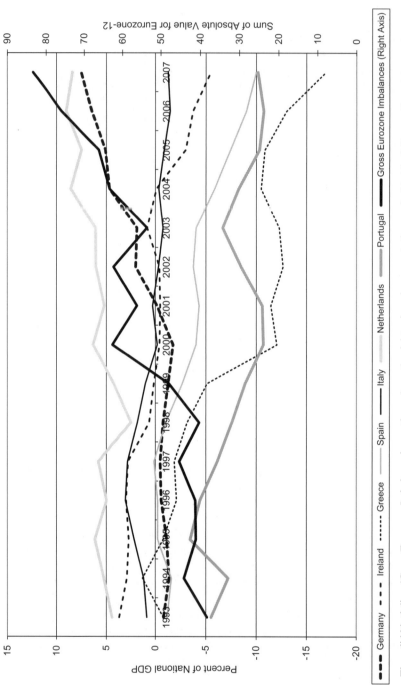

Note: The solid black line, 'Gross Eurozone Imbalances', uses the scale on the right axis and represents the nominal total of all gross Eurozone country imbalances, deficits and surpluses. The line shows us that around the time of monetary union in 1999 the growth of creditor and debtor imbalances alike accelerates considerably, signalling that EMU has had an important effect on the balances of payments of member countries. The other lines in the graph use the left-hand scale and illustrate the separate development of imbalances for the principal debtor and creditor economies. We can see the change that accelerates from 1999 on, and that the costs and benefits of EMU are highly asymmetrically distributed: creditors do better, while debtors do worse, and that the trend accelerates. Unfortunately, there is no data available that would allow an equivalent assessment of intra-Eurozone imbalances for each of the surplus and deficit countries respectively.

Source: AMECO.

Figure 8.2   Accelerating benefits: surplus and deficit economy current account balances prior to and after monetary union

162

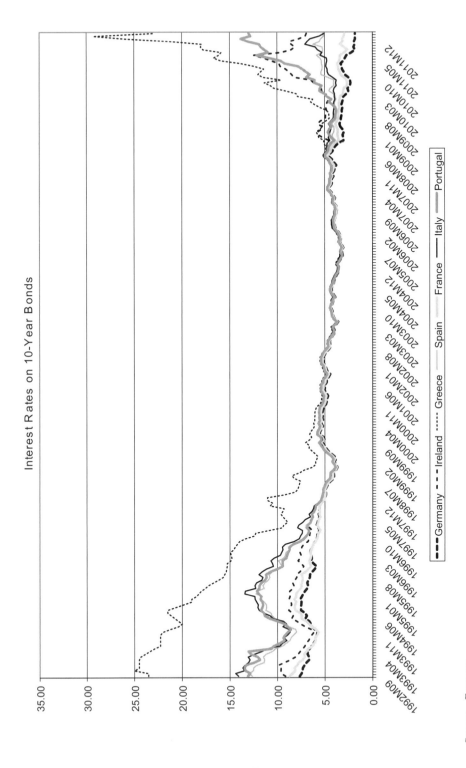

Source: Eurostat.

Figure 8.3   Interest rate convergence and divergence under monetary union

Mario Draghi for the first time offered the necessary unlimited financing to keep sovereign bond interest rates at sustainable levels. However, this would only be done if the troubled country formally applied for a bailout, so conditionality is far from absent. So far no member-state has applied for the programme, although some calm has returned to a range of troubled sovereign bond markets and spreads have indeed narrowed. Perhaps the threat of unlimited intervention was enough. But even OMT has not meant an end to contagion: Cyprus was next, and in addition to citizens, local and international bank deposit-holders were forced to contribute substantially to the rescue (although 'insured' depositors below €100 000 were eventually let off the hook) in exchange for a bailout. Slovenia and Malta may be next on the list, with Italy and France hovering near the danger zone. There were even fewer signs of recovery and growth in 2013 than in 2012.

At the time of writing in 2013, longer-run reforms such as the Fiscal Compact and a 'Banking Union' had been long debated. The Fiscal Compact was accepted by the member-states but is based on the same principle as the GSP, but on steroids. Meanwhile, it appears that the common deposit insurance and EU-level bank resolution aspects of 'Banking Union' proposals might never see the light of day in any meaningful form. But beyond the as-yet unused OMT, no immediate crisis resolution mechanism had been touted. The ECB mandate would remain the same, as would the lending-based approach to bailouts, and so the crisis could be expected to continue. In short, decisive action of the sort a national central bank would take was missing.

CONCLUSION

This chapter has demonstrated that Council decisions by responsible governments produced a European Central Bank that could fill a range of the functions normally attributed to national equivalents in federal economies. Its functions in relation to the problems of the Eurozone economy as a whole and its potential adjustment problems remained seriously underdeveloped. It was based on a normative preference for market-based governance and adjustment that was known to generate instability and asymmetries, and a debt work-out mechanism that was demonstrably dysfunctional. The longstanding central trade-off of efforts at monetary cooperation between surplus and deficit economies was deliberately set aside and the system was devoid of functional crisis-resolution mechanisms. Surplus countries would gain the benefits of irrevocably fixed exchange rates, but would not be required to pool their resources *ex ante* or *ex post* to pay for the costs of asymmetries that their societies helped generate. The central institution of EMU, the ECB, was provided with a plethora of powers and instruments to save banks. Meanwhile, there was a deliberate neglect of instruments to save erstwhile citizens in a crisis despite the explicit longstanding goals of the Union and its system of monetary cooperation. We now know that, in a crisis, EMU serially imposes the costs of rescuing banks on the very citizens who serve as the ultimate guarantors. The poorer countries and their poorest citizens fare the worst. Under the pressure of crisis the democratic process is likely eventually to reject this, even if one might say 'so far so good'. The EU governance of crises is merely the most acute example of a global problem. It is time, surely, to take a proper conceptual leap in the governance of both EU and global financial crises.

ACKNOWLEDGEMENTS

The research for this chapter was undertaken with the generous financial support of the research consortium 'Politics, Economics, and Global Governance: The European Dimensions' (PEGGED, research contract no. SSH7-CT-2008-217559), funded by the EU Commission's Framework 7 programme for the Social Sciences and Humanities.

NOTES

1. The following points are developed and argued at length in Underhill (2013). See also Helleiner (1994).
2. Known as the 'Efficient Market Hypothesis' (a subset of general equilibrium theory), as supplemented by modern portfolio theory, it has dominated theory and practice of contemporary financial markets; see discussion in Taylor (2004), esp. pp. 241–64.
3. Long-Term Capital Management (LTCM) was a hedge fund that collapsed spectacularly in 1998 and was founded by Meriwether, Scholes and Merton – the latter two sharing the 1997 Nobel Prize for economics for their work – you guessed it – on valuing derivatives.
4. On the contrary, Vreeland (2003) demonstrates this point comprehensively and robustly in relation to developing country debt work-out regimes sponsored by the IMF. He shows that these programmes had a clearly negative impact on growth and skewed distribution by hitting labour and the poor hardest (p. 8; Ch. 5; pp. 154–60). Klagsbrunn (2010) argues that default left Argentina no better or worse off than Brazil, which followed IMF medicine through the same series of crises. De Jong and van der Veer (2010) demonstrate that a crucial element of IMF programmes – that they act as a catalyst for private sector investment and involvement – has long been dysfunctional.
5. Reference to the dictum attributed to former Federal Reserve Chairman William McChesney Martin (in 1970) that it was the role of the central bank to '[take] away the punch bowl just when the party is getting good'.
6. According to the original plan for staged monetary union or Werner report (Council-Commission 1970: 11), 'only the global balance of payments of the Community [EU] vis-à-vis the outside world is of any importance. Equilibrium within the Community would be realized at this stage in the same way as within a nation's frontiers, thanks to the mobility of the factors of production and financial transfers by the public and private sectors.'
7. Although even in a properly federal entity, provinces retain some capacity to 'distort' economic flows in particular policy domains, for example taxation or labour market regulation.
8. The pattern of imbalances depends entirely on how the geographic 'accounting lines' are drawn. There are naturally imbalances among national economies, but also among the units of federal economies or corresponding to regional disparities within centralised political entities, even across cities.
9. Wherein the 'provincial' governments may continue to play an important role, and their policies may well affect outcomes positively or negatively, as in any federal country.
10. See the systematic and common sense discussion of OCA criteria in a European context in Baldwin and Wyplosz (2009: 322–44).
11. To which language, social security and educational systems, and national cultures remain important intra-EU barriers.
12. OCA theory is by no means the only way of thinking about the issue of monetary union. It may be argued (De Grauwe 1997: Ch. 2) that the differences among countries are not important enough to worry about; that the exchange rate instrument is less than effective under conditions of capital mobility (which EMS members, see above, had discovered of their own accord); and, finally, that politicians may frequently misuse or misjudge the utility of the exchange rate instrument as a tool of policy.
13. This might be done by enhancing resources at the level of the Union, or by preserving national capacities, or preferably a combination of both.
14. The statutes of the Federal Reserve of the United States at the time of Maastricht did not specify price stability at all (Henning 1994: 106–7).
15. Recent moves to establish an EU 'Banking Union' fall under this clause.
16. This was originally article 104b of the Maastricht Treaty (EU 1992).
17. In Table 8.1 one can see the dramatic rise in public debt from 2008 that is common to crisis and non-crisis countries.

18. And some, including creditors, had long played fast and loose in the first place (see Table 8.1).
19. Bertrant Benoit and Tony Barber, 'Germany ready to help Eurozone members', *Financial Times*, 18 February 2009.

REFERENCES

Baldwin, Richard and Charles Wyplosz (2009), *The Economics of European Integration*, 3rd edition, Maidenhead: McGraw-Hill.
Bank for International Settlements (BIS) (2012), *82nd Annual Report*, 24 June, Basle: Bank for International Settlements.
Bordo, M., B. Eichengreen, D. Klingebiel and M.S. Martínez-Peria (2001), 'Is the crisis problem growing more severe?', *Economic Policy*, **16** (32), 51–82.
Claessens, S., G. Underhill and X. Zhang (2008), 'The political economy of Basle II: the costs for poor countries', *World Economy*, **31** (3), 313–44.
Cohen, B.J. (1982), 'Balance of payments financing', *International Organization*, **36** (2), 457–78.
Council of the European Communities (1978a), 'Conclusions of the Presidency of the European Council on 6–7 July 1978 (Bremen)', *Bulletin of the European Communities* no. 6/1978, 17–21.
Council of the European Communities (1978b), 'Resolution of the European Council of 5 December 1978 on the establishment of the European Monetary System (EMS) and related matters (Brussels 5 December)', *Bulletin of the European Communities* no. 12/1978, 10–13.
Council-Commission of the European Communities (1970), *Report to the Council and the Commission of the European Communities on the realisation by stages of Economic and Monetary Union*, Supplement to *Bulletin of the European Communities* 11-1970, November.
Cox, Robert W. (1986), 'Social forces, states, and world orders: beyond international relations theory', in R.O. Keohane (ed.), *Neorealism and its Critics*, New York: Columbia University Press, pp. 204–54.
De Grauwe, Paul (1997), *The Economics of Monetary Integration*, 3rd edition, Oxford: Oxford University Press.
de Jong, E. and K. van der Veer (2010), 'The catalytic approach to debt workout in practice: co-ordination failure between IMF, Paris Club, and official creditors', in Geoffrey R.D. Underhill, J. Blom and D. Mügge (eds), *Global Financial Integration Thirty Years On: From Reform to Crisis*, Cambridge: Cambridge University Press, pp. 134–49.
European Union (EU) (1992), Treaty on European Union. *Official Journal of the European Union*, C191, 29 July.
European Union (EU) (2008), Consolidated version of the Treaty on the Functioning of the European Union. *Official Journal of the European Union*, C115/09 May, pp. 47–199.
European Union (EU) (2010), Protocol (no. 4) on the Statute of the European System of Central Banks and of the European Central Bank. *Official Journal of the European Union*, C83, 30 March, pp. 230–50.
Helleiner, Eric (1994), *States and the Re-emergence of Global Finance: From Bretton Woods to the 1990s*, Ithaca, NY: Cornell University Press.
Henning, C. Randall (1994), *Currencies and Politics in the United States, Germany, and Japan*, Washington, DC: Institute for International Economics.
International Monetary Fund (IMF) (2009), 'Greece: IMF Country Report for the 2009 Article IV Consultation', IMF Country Report 09/244, 30 June, Washington, DC: IMF.
Jones, Erik (2003), 'Liberalized capital markets, state autonomy, and European Monetary Union', *European Journal of Political Research*, **42** (2), 197–222.
Jones, Erik (2011), 'Europe and the global economic crisis', in R. Tiersky and E. Jones (eds), *Europe Today*, 4th edition, Lanham, MA: Rowman & Littlefield, pp. 327–50.
Kaminsky, G.L. and C.M. Reinhart (1999), 'The Twin Crises: the causes of banking and balance of payments problems', *American Economic Review*, **89** (3), 473–500.
Kennedy, E. (1991), *The Bundesbank: Germany's Central Bank in the International Monetary System*, London: Royal Institute of International Affairs/Pinter.
Klagsbrunn, Victor (2010), 'Brazil and Argentina in the Global Financial System: contrasting approaches to development and foreign debt', in Geoffrey R.D. Underhill, J. Blom and D. Mügge (eds), *Global Financial Integration Thirty Years On: From Reform to Crisis*, Cambridge: Cambridge University Press, pp. 187–203.
McNamara, Kathleen (1998), *The Currency of Ideas: Monetary Politics in the European Union*, Ithaca, NY: Cornell University Press.
Minsky, H. (1982), 'The financial-instability hypothesis: capitalist processes and the behaviour of the

economy', in C. Kindleberger and J.-P. Laffargue (eds), *Financial Crises: Theory, History, and Policy*, New York: Cambridge University Press, pp. 13–38.

Moutot, P. and G. Vitale (2001), 'Monetary policy and co-ordination in a globalized world', *Revue Économique*, **52**, 337–51.

Reinhart, C.M. and K.S. Rogoff (2009), *This Time is Different: Eight Centuries of Financial Folly*, Princeton, NJ: Princeton University Press.

Strange, Susan (1976), *International Monetary Relations*, Vol. 2 of A. Shonfield (ed.), *International Economic Relations of the Western World 1959–76*, Oxford: Oxford University Press.

Taylor, M.C. (2004), *Confidence Games: Money and Markets in a World without Redemption*, Chicago, IL: University of Chicago Press.

Tsoukalis, Loukas (1977), *The Politics and Economics of European Monetary Integration*, London: Allen & Unwin.

Tsoukalis, Loukas (1997), *The New European Economy Revisited*, Oxford: Oxford University Press.

Underhill, Geoffrey R.D. (1995), 'Keeping governments out of politics: transnational securities markets, regulatory co-operation, and political legitimacy', *Review of International Studies*, **21** (3), 251–78.

Underhill, Geoffrey R.D. (2002), 'Global integration, EMU, and monetary governance in the European Union: the political economy of the "stability culture"', in K. Dyson (ed.), *European States and the Euro: Europeanization, Convergence, and the Single Currency*, Oxford: Oxford University Press, pp. 31–52.

Underhill, Geoffrey R.D. (2013), 'Market based approach to financial governance', in G. Caprio (ed.), *The Evidence and Impact of Financial Globalization*, London: Elsevier, pp. 577–87.

Underhill, Geoffrey R.D. and Xiaoke Zhang (2008), 'Setting the rules: private power, political underpinnings, and legitimacy in global monetary and financial governance', *International Affairs*, **84** (3), 535–54.

Vreeland, James R. (2003), *The IMF and Economic Development*, Cambridge: Cambridge University Press.

Wood, D. (2005), *Governing Global Banking: The Basel Committee and the Politics of Financial Globalisation*, Aldershot: Ashgate.

9 The governance of money laundering
Eleni Tsingou

What are the drivers behind the anti-money laundering (AML) governance framework? Who are the actors and institutions, and what is the policy content? This chapter provides an overview of the processes and mechanisms of AML policy-making. AML is often presented as a financial problem, and something, moreover, that is key to debates about international political economy (IPE) since it goes to the heart of the integrity of the financial system and also, at least in principle, aims to impose controls on the movement of money. Yet, as a policy concern, thinking about money laundering was developed away from traditional settings for the regulation of global finance. Instead, AML policies were driven by and linked to the public policy objectives of law and order. As a result, the governance of money laundering encompasses a broad set of goals, techniques and professional knowledge. It brings together different types of official bodies and private institutions, more or less international in their orientation. Reconciling their aims and building a global regime that can translate into effective and tailored policies on the ground is thus a major challenge for the governors of money laundering. This challenge is made more acute by the lack of appropriate success criteria. By its very nature, AML is an issue area where defining and assessing the size of the problem is difficult enough: there is no reliable methodology for estimating the amounts laundered and much criminal activity behind money laundering remains undetected.

To analyse and explain this AML governance framework, the chapter deploys a political economy approach in two ways. Firstly, it unpacks the professional competition between the regulatory and law enforcement spheres that makes up the AML regime and is the source of some of its enduring tensions and contradictions. Secondly, it fully accounts for the role of the private sector, which has assumed quasi-public policy functions, thus blurring public–private distinctions in this area of the international political economy.

The chapter is organised in four further sections. The next section defines the policy problem in governance terms and outlines the institutional framework at the regional and global levels. The following section proceeds with a discussion of the main IPE debates in analysing the AML regime and elaborates the political economy approach to explaining the governance of money laundering, unpacking the actors and their motivations, including the tensions between (regulatory) prevention and (law) enforcement. The third section focuses on the role of the private sector, both in terms of the public policy role it has come to assume in the regime but also in relation to the way in which private financial institutions, banks and other financial firms have been adjusting their practices through the development and professionalisation of an AML compliance industry. The chapter closes by offering some conclusions on the frustrations and opportunities revealed in the governance of money laundering.

The underlying point throughout is that the governance structures in place fail to target seriously the processes that enable money laundering, but that actors and institutions with differing incentives and motivations are nevertheless using AML tools and processes to address a broad range of policy concerns. In this context, the chapter explains that the actors most commonly examined in the IPE literature, notably private financial institutions and their regulators in advanced economies, find themselves in an unfamiliar position of being rule-takers in relation to AML. Yet, whether public or private, their size, institutional capacity and geographical location affect their potential for shaping AML practices in ways that best suit their needs.

THE GOVERNANCE OF MONEY LAUNDERING: WHAT IS BEING GOVERNED AND WHO ARE THE GOVERNORS?

Money laundering is the process of disguising the illegal origin of the financial proceeds of crime. By its nature secretive and clandestine, it is widely understood as a policy problem but remains difficult to define explicitly. A general, content-driven definition of money laundering may be broadly accepted, but international harmonisation about which crimes are relevant has only developed slowly and is still evolving. Traditionally, rules and laws originated in the domain of narcotics, but a wide range of crimes has since been added to the list of so-called predicate offences for money laundering, ranging from illegal trafficking to, most recently, tax evasion. Attempts at measuring money laundering add another layer of difficulty in determining its significance as a governance challenge. The secretive and illegal nature of money-laundering processes results in scarce, incomplete and generally unreliable data. Although several attempts at calculating the scale of money laundering have been made, the methodology is challenged or the figures are limited to a few select jurisdictions (Unger 2007, 2009). The most often quoted figure comes from research by the International Monetary Fund (IMF), which estimates the total as a figure equal to between 2 and 5 per cent of the world's gross domestic product. However, considering that official efforts by specialist bodies to calculate estimates have failed (Reuter and Truman 2004), even such a broad approximation of the policy problem is seen to lack applicability.

These limitations are important, as it is difficult to know the significance of the money-laundering problem. The lack of methodological coherence and reliability (Naylor 1999) makes any pretence at an objective assessment of the effectiveness of AML policies particularly difficult to maintain. There can be no comprehensive cost–benefit analysis of the regime, either at the national or the global level. This lack of clarity matters to those internalising the costs of these policies as those costs are more easily quantifiable; even in the absence of reliable figures, AML costs can seem arbitrary and disproportionate, especially to developing countries (Sharman 2011). Furthermore, there is no clear benchmark of what would constitute success in the governance of money laundering or what (if any) figure for global laundered funds might be seen as acceptable. As such, much policy rhetoric and official assessments of success focus on detected money-laundering cases and the subsequently available legal and financial stories. Most of these are based on reported enforcement actions against individuals or financial institutions. More recently, however, we can observe increasing emphasis on procedure too, and pronouncements on the importance of money laundering based on failed compliance processes in large internationally active banks. The example of HSBC is particularly noteworthy: following a year-long investigation by the United States Senate Permanent Sub-committee on Investigations, it was found in 2012 to have a severely lax compliance structure which had permitted and enabled business relations with drug traffickers in Mexico, as well as suspected criminal and terrorist groups in Iran, Cuba, Sudan and North Korea and linked to the Taliban and Hamas.[1] As powerful as those cases can be in highlighting the links between finance and crime, they do not add substance to the key challenges of definition and measurement.

Against this background, the question of whether money laundering is a genuine threat to the financial system also remains open. The inclusion in the system of some dirty money may arguably be an acceptable price to pay for efficient and adaptable financial markets; in effect, for the type of system of financial governance which has been promoted by regulators and the private sector alike over the past 30 years of financial integration. As such, tackling money laundering goes to the heart of long-established principles and practices regarding what is appropriate in global financial governance. While 'money laundering, financial crime and terrorist financing have shattered the myth of capital neutrality' (Unger 2007: 184), the elimination of money laundering would require an extensive reworking of the system and affect how we understand the concept of free movement of money in general and the practice of capital mobility in particular. Yet the AML regime is not promoted along these lines: instead of focusing on explicit questions of IPE, official explanations and justifications of the importance of the governance of money laundering have focused on policy issues that reflect other public-policy concerns. Public officials have consistently presented the AML regime as a tool to tackle a wide variety of disparate policy goals (McDowell and Novis 2001). Starting with an AML framework aimed at addressing the drugs trade, the regime expanded to incorporate broader organised crime concerns, including the arms trade, people trafficking and related criminal activities. The regime has been further used to target the financing of terrorism and the proliferation of weapons of mass destruction (WMD). But it is also presented as an integral part of efforts to combat corruption and its economic and political consequences, especially in the developing world, and to promote economic development by ensuring that funds are channelled to appropriate economic endeavours and that economic activities contribute adequately to the public purse. Finally, AML policies have been also been advocated in relation to the integrity of the financial system, including the support of good governance and transparency. Of those, only the latter set of concerns is consistent with questions traditionally located in the sphere of IPE and financial governance. On the whole, AML has been defined in terms of crime, although a foreign-policy element is also in evidence, with AML measures fast becoming a potent foreign-policy tool via the introduction of an officially sanctioned focus on problem countries and politically exposed persons. Terrorist financing and the recent inclusion of the financing of proliferation of weapons of mass destruction in the AML framework can also be understood in this light.

There are also some less openly talked about IPE concerns in the governance of money laundering. AML policies are to some extent employed to strengthen the governance of related issue areas or to internationalise particular economic policies. An example of the first type of IPE concern can be observed when studying the links between money laundering on the one hand, and policies regarding tax havens or banking secrecy on the other. While formally distinct, an important part of the global strategy against money laundering has revolved around improving practices and promoting transparency in offshore financial centres. The drive towards building an AML governance framework has thus been connected with questions of competitive pressure from offshore centres and establishing a regulatory level playing field (Sharman 2006; Vlcek 2009; Palan et al. 2010). As will also be outlined below, the links between the core sponsors of the AML regime and members of the Organisation for Economic Co-operation and Development (OECD) are significant. As for the internationalisation of domestic policies and concerns, this is most apparent in the drive to tackle falling tax revenues in advanced economies, accentuated by the global financial and economic crisis. A prominent development in this sphere is the US Foreign Account Compliance Act, which targets banks outside the United States suspected of conspiring with wealthy US citizens to hide their bank accounts from the US tax authorities. While not explicitly part of the AML governance framework, many of the tools to be employed in complying with this policy are directly linked to AML provisions.[2]

Nevertheless, however loosely defined, money laundering as a governance issue is now well established and accepted. But who are the governors in this issue area, especially at the global level (Avant et al. 2010)? The remainder of this section describes the institutional setting, namely, a global framework of norm- and rule-makers and takers led by the Financial Action Task Force (FATF) and its network of regional bodies. FATF, a specialist organisation with an explicit AML mandate, was established by the Group of Seven (G7) in 1989. Its creation followed the criminalisation of money laundering in the 1980s in several OECD countries. Based in Paris and hosted by the OECD, the role of FATF is to issue regularly updated recommendations which aim to set global legislative and regulatory AML standards. FATF counts 36 members, including OECD countries, but also major economies and financial centres outside the OECD. It is a small organisation, operating with only 12 full-time professional staff members, with most of its work being done in conjunction with relevant experts in the ministries of member countries.[3]

FATF recommendations aim to provide a comprehensive framework for tackling money laundering across the financial and business sectors, offering guidance for the appropriate AML governance structure at the national level and for international cooperation, as well as specifying the detail in the content of AML rules. Specifically, FATF recommendations address national AML concerns by advocating a risk-based approach and offering guidance with respect to agency coordination. More broadly, they extend to defining money-laundering predicate offences and discuss confiscation provisions, as well as adopting preventive measures with respect to due diligence, reporting and correspondent banking. There are also recommendations covering transparency and beneficial ownership of legal persons and arrangements, measures specifically addressing financing of terrorist activities and WMD proliferation. As such, the recommendations help to harmonise definitions and AML rules and offer guidance in general on appropriate private sector practices and model official institutional set-ups. Furthermore, the work of FATF focuses on the regulatory and legislative framework that shapes the behaviour of banks and other financial institutions and non-financial corporate actors susceptible to money-laundering activity (in other words, regulation and prevention), but also outlines legal provisions that actually enable criminal prosecutions and confiscations (enforcement and punishment).

FATF issued its first set of 40 recommendations in 1990. In the early years they were fairly flexible in their guidance; however, as FATF evolved and was able to draw on a deeper pool of expertise, the recommendations became more precise and prescriptive and it started issuing Special Interpretative Notes in support of its work. Following the terrorist attacks of 11 September 2001, the recommendations were revised and a further nine were eventually added, focusing on the combating of terrorist financing. The recommendations were again amended in 2012. FATF moved to regroup and consolidate its recommendations which are now 40 once more. According to the official statement accompanying the adoption of the new recommendations:

> Money laundering, terrorist financing, and the financing of the proliferation of weapons of mass destruction are serious threats to security and the integrity of the financial system. The FATF Standards have been revised to strengthen global safeguards and further protect the integrity of the financial system by providing governments with stronger tools to take action against financial crime. At the same time, these new standards will address new priority areas such as corruption and tax crimes. (FATF 2012)

In other words, the eclectic mix of policy considerations at the origins of the governance of money laundering endures.

FATF recommendations are not formally binding, but are being widely adopted by member countries and form the basis for the European Commission's AML directives. As such, comprehensive monitoring activity of the implementation of the recommendations takes place and follows two forms. All member countries carry out self-assessment exercises and, in addition, FATF has put in place a mutual evaluation procedure, whereby on-site visits by legal, financial and law enforcement experts from other member governments are conducted. In 1999 FATF took a further step, engaging in a 'naming and shaming' campaign beyond the scope of its membership and identifying countries and territories considered guilty of non-cooperation. The first so-called 'Non-Cooperative Countries and Territories' (NCCTs) report was made public in 2000 and was subsequently regularly reviewed, although the programme was slowly wound down. FATF moved instead towards a softer approach: identifying High Risk and Non-Cooperative Jurisdictions, calling for counter-measures from its member countries or pushing for enhanced compliance.[4]

FATF is unlike other international organisations; it promotes global technical standards, yet is an explicitly political organisation in its membership and practices. While its scope is global, its membership, deliberately, is not: there are a number of technical criteria for membership, but, as part of the 'fundamental' criteria for membership, a jurisdiction has to be 'strategically important' or significantly enhance FATF's geographical balance. The inclusion of the Russian Federation is one example of the membership policy, with Russia joining FATF soon after being delisted from the NCCT list. This is widely acknowledged as symptomatic of the political character of FATF, as well as illustrating the organisation's emphasis on form (or paper compliance), rather than practice. Following Russia, China and India joined FATF in 2007 and 2009 respectively. This emphasis on size and significance is not unjustified, since work on the 'scale and impacts of money laundering' confirms that 'giants wash more' (Unger 2007). At the same time, however, the inclusion of these countries has not altered the ideational and expert core of the regime, which remains OECD-centred. The 2012 recommendations revision reflected

OECD priorities more than those of the large emerging countries. This is especially the case in the inclusion of proliferation financing (a US concern), but it can also be seen in the content of the recommendations, which now focus overwhelmingly on the activities (especially cross-border activities) of financial institutions. The recommendations have done less to help develop a methodology for banking activities in subnational settings or for expanding expert guidance on real estate, AML problems of greater significance in non-OECD countries.

In short, as viewed through the main specialist AML organisation, the governance of money laundering is one where there is a core of norm- (and rule-)makers and a periphery of norm- (and rule-)takers. According to Drezner (2007: 145), using a so-called 'club IGO' (international governmental organisation) allowed Group of Seven states to 'cajole, coerce, and enforce a global anti-money-laundering standard into existence', while Sharman (2008) explains how the diffusion of AML standards should not be understood as the result of a process of policy learning, but rather as exercises of power through direct coercion, mimicry and competition. Indeed, broadening participation in the AML regime has been deliberately restricted to the proliferation of regional task forces and agencies that mirror FATF practice and evaluation processes and whose structures replicate FATF's core-and-periphery approach, with some member countries being central in regional terms and better linked with FATF and others more marginal (Jakobi 2013: Chapter 5).[5] This is also reflected in the funding structure of these bodies which rely on financial size-related membership fees and donations from the largest member countries. Donations, in particular, can be earmarked for particular activities in line with donor wishes.

The AML activities of FATF and its regional networks are supplemented by the work of the Egmont Group, which brings together national AML officials on an annual basis. These officials are affiliated with and represent a country's Financial Intelligence Unit (FIU), a special office with assembled AML expertise, often housed within a law enforcement agency. FIUs are the recipients of suspicious transaction reports filed by financial institutions. Through the Egmont Group they have built a learning network, sharing experiences and best practice and strengthening cross-border ties for information exchange and cooperation. Importantly, the IMF, as part of its work on financial integrity, has also been examining AML standards in its financial sector reviews and, where appropriate, it offers technical assistance (Johnson and Abbott 2005). FATF, the IMF and indeed the World Bank all use similar assessment processes, documentation and procedures in their AML evaluations.

Against this ambitious and institutionalised AML governance framework, international coordination among law enforcement agencies more broadly remains a relatively underdeveloped and slow process. Limited interstate cooperation has been taking place in the context of Interpol (and Europol), and FATF is involved in some of those activities. It is still unclear, however, whether actual changes in the practices of law enforcement agencies have occurred as a result of the AML regime or whether it is merely that effective communication channels are being established. There are several challenges at the heart of cooperation in law enforcement, many of them legal and emanating from the confidential nature of the types of cases being examined and/or investigated. Moreover, AML provisions relate to both financial crime and the financing of crime, but international cooperation methods and processes differ in those two cases.

EXPLAINING THE GOVERNANCE OF MONEY LAUNDERING: REGULATORY PREVENTION AND LAW ENFORCEMENT

As the brief overview in the previous section shows, the governance of money launder-ing is at first glance a state-driven, state-focused affair, framed on the basis of interstate cooperation and institutions. Moreover, the emphasis on states and the role of state agencies has only intensified since the inclusion of attempts to combat terrorist financing in the AML governance framework after 2001 and the addition of concerns about the proliferation of weapons of mass destruction in 2012.

This is replicated in much of the IPE literature on money laundering. Realist work, such as that of Drezner (2007), focuses on the intergovernmental and club-like charac-ter of FATF, which is seen as an organisation that brings together like-minded states; according to this reading, these core states have used FATF to coordinate their standards but mostly to impose them on jurisdictions outside the club in a manner that would have been difficult to achieve by an organisation with universal membership such as the IMF. Neoliberal institutionalist approaches, such as the analysis provided by Simmons (2001), emphasise the role of the hegemon in ensuring compliance with non-binding standards and sustaining momentum through different phases of AML policies. A similar focus on hegemons exists in the literature on global prohibition regimes, including with respect to the role of the United States in the development of such regimes, as in the area of money laundering (Andreas and Nadelmann 2006). This literature is particularly useful in explaining the role of powerful states in the development, adoption and implementa-tion of particular prohibition norms and the global acceptance and compliance processes that make them into a regime. A focus on the interstate characteristics of the regime and FATF is also at the heart of much constructivist work, which explores the legitimacy, or lack thereof, of the global scope of standards and of policies of blacklisting beyond the standard-setting membership (see, for example, Hüllse 2008). Some work on 'gov-ernmentality' also takes FATF as the starting point, showing how the organisation's demands can lead to practices of 'self-discipline' when states are keen to assert compli-ance (for an example pertaining to the Philippines, see Vlcek 2011).

The most comprehensive of these state-centred approaches is the analysis developed by Sharman (2008, 2011), who looks beyond the work of FATF to examine how global diffusion of AML policies has taken place. He shows that, with little consideration for local conditions, AML standards have been adopted by countries large and small and investigates how this diffusion has been experienced (and with what consequences) by these countries. While much of his emphasis is on adoption by developing countries, especially small ones, Sharman shows that the governance of money laundering is not a simple core-and-periphery story, for, as he argues (Sharman 2011), AML policies fail to be of much benefit to core and periphery alike.

Yet, even though much of the governance of money laundering is indeed about FATF and interstate cooperation and coordination, what is generally missing in the IPE literature is a discussion of state–actor dynamics at both the national and the global levels. Specifically, state interests, preferences and policies are not monolithic. In the governance of money laundering, they are derived from the goals of different types of public actors. These public actors are regulators on the one hand, and law enforcers on the other, and they have different motivations and success criteria. So the relationship between these goals, and in turn understanding how regulation and law enforcement priorities are reconciled, is important. Shedding some light on this relationship is the task of the remainder of this section.

As is apparent from the overview of the institutional framework, the governance of money laundering encompasses two elements: prevention and enforcement. Prevention principles lead to regulatory tools and the development of regulatory and supervisory rules and standards, standardisation, harmonisation and consistency of reporting practices, and the adoption of customer due diligence measures and techniques. Enforcement principles, on the other hand, focus on legal tools, concentrating on investigation, confiscation, prosecution and punishment. So, while regulation is about procedure, enforcement emphasises results. Inevitably, the AML regime looks lopsided, with procedural standards universally applied to financial institutions large and small and results only visible when something actually happens. In this context, despite the criminalisation of money laundering and the increasingly prominent and public role of enforcement agencies in the AML governance framework, the process is most institutionalised, the policies clearest and the actors most transparent on the preventative regulatory side. Enforcement is usually discussed only once an investigation is complete, has led to a conviction and when the intelligence guiding that conviction is not compromised by disclosure. This makes AML methodology on the legal side particularly opaque. The addition of the combating of terrorist financing and, most recently, the financing of proliferation of weapons of mass destruction in the AML governance framework brings additional confidentiality and intelligence issues to the mix. In turn, this affects perceptions about the functions of regulation and enforcement as the roles of respective participants in the AML governance framework are necessarily blurred: are regulators and banks being turned into law enforcers, how can law enforcement best be integrated in the institutional framework, and at which level does policing best work? AML 'experts' in the previously purer financial realm of regulation may now be finance professionals, lawyers or specialists in police work. Regulatory and enforcement goals have come to be fused in definitions of regulatory compliance, and while regulators are in charge of monitoring the rules, they do so without having created the rules and, at times, with fewer resources than their law enforcement AML counterparts.

Technically, law enforcement should not play a role in regulation, but a consistent discussion on the nature and practice of these public functions has not taken place and the relevant distinctions remain blurred. Guidance, feedback and cooperation are to be encouraged, but the differing objectives of regulators and law enforcers are yet to be reconciled or, at the very least, openly acknowledged. The process of coordination and cooperation between regulators and supervisors on the one hand, and law enforcement agencies on the other, remains unbalanced at both the national and the regional and global levels. The relationship between them is also patchy and can be adversarial. Tensions can arise from different interpretations of the results of AML efforts. Regulators aim to address potential problems and thus assess success in terms not easily quantifiable: in essence, success equals the absence of problems. In contrast, law enforcement bodies concentrate on quantifiable confiscated sums and convictions. The strategies of regulators and law enforcement agents are thus markedly different. The first group focuses on the process, including persuasion, cooperation, self-regulation and risk-based discretion; while the second stresses prosecution, external regulation, and public justice and punishment (Croall 2003). Publicity in relation to these respective efforts is more or less welcome depending on the strategy. For regulatory agencies, no publicity is good publicity and the aim is lack of exposure. Where an institution deviates from the rules, regulators wish to appear firm and set the 'correct' precedents, but are embarrassed and constrained by the public scrutiny accompanying the resulting fines. On the other hand, law enforcers welcome public convictions and often seek the media hype associated with concrete results in the fight against money laundering.

The development of professional knowledge and expertise in the configuration of the respective regulatory and law enforcement policy networks is thus relevant, as is the potential for competition between professional financial regulatory knowledge and professional legal enforcement knowledge. The AML governance framework is shaped by the professional knowledge of two distinct groups with differing training, expertise, policy goals and professional aspirations. The dual goals of prevention and compliance have differing implications with regard to what is considered appropriate in regime governance, which means that what constitutes acceptable results is the result of ongoing coordination, socialisation and competition among the relevant professional networks. Where these two groups meet, questions of system and framework design arise. These relate to policy learning, peer reviews and feedback and also affect how the two groups view crime, and organised crime in particular. Following other facets of financial activity, regulators interested in prevention and standards-compliance adopt risk-based approaches which are understood to tailor compliance demands to the activities of a particular financial institution. If adopted, the principle would entail that a small bank with local customers and few international activities will be less exposed to the risk of money laundering than a bank in a border area or a high-crime area, or a sophisticated global conglomerate with sizeable international transactions. Professional knowledge associated with law enforcement, on the other hand, is about theorising organised crime; through the 'Theorem of Mismatch' (harmonising living standards between the better and worse off, for example) or the 'Theorem of Stream' (when you have a lot of trade, you have a little illicit trade as well), professional knowledge seeks to eliminate all such crime.[6]

This dichotomy is at the heart of public policy as it relates to the governance of money laundering, but is also reflected in the role of the private sector. As part of AML efforts, the private sector has assumed policy functions in the developing regime, has internalised many of its costs and has engaged in a series of compromises and opportunistic activity to compensate and/or benefit. So it is important and necessary to move beyond state-centric accounts. The private financial sector is much more familiar with the game of leading or pre-empting regulatory initiatives, but in this instance financial institutions have been followers, outwardly stuck with many of the costs and an unfamiliar incentive system. On the other hand, AML policies, especially since preoccupations relating to terrorism and proliferation have been added to the mix, have enabled the growth of a private intelligence industry, including intelligence-led policing. Such private actors have the flexibility to work with a variety of relevant actors (journalists, insolvency experts and others), whereas public prosecutors have to maintain higher standards of neutrality. In the same vein, the regime has led to the development of data-mining and other techniques which have given private sector actors a key public-security role in the context of terrorist financing (De Goede 2012).

WHAT ROLE FOR THE PRIVATE SECTOR? THE DEVELOPMENT OF A COMPLIANCE INDUSTRY[7]

In the history of AML efforts, the role of the private sector, and in particular internationally engaged banks, implies two sets of compromises. In the first place, following the criminalisation of money laundering in the 1980s and the introduction of initial controls, the relatively limited measures adopted can be understood as an acceptable 'price to pay' for the promotion of liberal capital mobility (Helleiner 1999). For financial institutions, these early measures were a mere extension of existing regulations on bank secrecy and did not threaten the content and form of, or indeed the rewards to be obtained from, international financial transactions. In the aftermath of the terrorist attacks of 2001, however, and following the somewhat arbitrary addition of efforts to combat terrorist financing to AML activities and the AML framework, measures became more constraining and costly. The private sector became accordingly a less willing participant, although in time it found market opportunities in the new regulatory framework by bridging regulatory and legal professional knowledge.

Financial institutions have certain straightforward incentives to take AML measures seriously, primarily as they relate to reputational and legal issues (Simonova 2011). As such, it is no surprise that private sector actors have been willing participants in the adoption of a number of procedures to combat money laundering and comply with regulatory requirements. These have included special identification measures, the 'know-your-customer' mantra applied to all financial services; monitoring processes based on internal systems and a comprehensive system of dealing with suspicious activity; the implementation of auditing procedures and accountability measures, such as signed attestations of knowledge of anti-money laundering measures, and periodic evaluations of AML systems; and the full participation and commitment of senior management (Vitale 2001). These activities have over time necessitated the establishment of dedicated AML units (at both the unit and group-wide levels), continuous AML training, and significant investment in compliance software. Yet, from the early stages of the development of the global AML governance framework, and especially since the intensification of AML activity in the aftermath of 11 September 2001, the predominant (and predictable) view in the private sector is that 'when the total costs to the banking system of the myriad anti-money laundering reporting requirements are correctly measured, few anti-money laundering efforts are cost effective' (Rahn 2003). This assessment is regularly confirmed by surveys undertaken by relevant banking associations and consultancies (see, e.g., *ABA Banking Journal* 2003; KPMG 2007). Even with attention to AML temporarily waning with the onset of the global financial crisis (especially as a cost priority within financial institutions), compliance procedures were maintained and reinforced for fear of official reprimand. In addition, in order to reduce uncertainty and avoid harmful attention to their reputation, large and smaller banks have over time engaged in pre-emptive money-laundering prevention moves, thus inadvertently contributing to a regulatory creep and making the regime more cumbersome and costly. All the while, it remains uncertain whether clear standards for monitoring are in place and private sector officials express doubt as to how well equipped (and funded) public agencies are to oversee these compliance developments effectively. Despite periodic high-profile cases of compliance failures being exposed (such as HSBC in

2012), this unavoidably adds further uncertainty to the current system of private sector incentives.

These private sector concerns emphasise the 'private costs of a public policy' (Serrano and Kenny 2003); they also exemplify how regulatory measures can be technical and difficult to implement, as well as highlighting the growing trend towards passing compliance responsibility to the private sector. Significantly, they also draw attention to the less tangible costs associated with assigning the legal role of 'capable guardian' to private sector officials (Levi and Maguire 2004: 417). For those managing large financial institutions, especially at the top level of management and with no experience of compliance work, this is an anomaly. Indeed, it should be noted that, as a development, the position of the private sector appears at odds with trends observed in other areas of financial governance, especially in relation to different aspects of banking regulation. In the shaping of the AML regime, public–private sector dynamics seem to be working to the financial detriment of the latter, with limited noticeable private access to policy debates and decision-making. Financial institutions adapt to the rules and are in no position to shape or challenge them. Cooperation and learning take place over time, but there are no formal or informal networks where these discussions take place on a regular basis and no suggestion that this is anything other than a top-down process.

That said, the costs associated with assuming public-policy functions in this way are borne differently across different actors in the private financial sector. Despite the adoption of risk-based principles in the AML regulatory approach, and even the formalisation of risk-based thinking in the 2012 revision of the FATF recommendations, costs affect small and large institutions disproportionately. Indeed, major actors in the financial industry unquestionably have the resources and organisational capacity to adjust; they also have sufficient common interests in the governance of money laundering that they have been able to take the initiative and create appropriate standards by establishing the Wolfsberg Group of Banks. This consists of banking leaders Banco Santander, Bank of Tokyo-Mitsubishi UFJ, Barclays, Citigroup, Credit Suisse, Deutsche Bank, Goldman Sachs, HSBC, J.P. Morgan Chase, Société Générale and UBS. The group was created in 2000 and issues global AML guidelines for international private banks, focusing at first on correspondent banking relationships but lately expanding its work to include guidelines on matters such as screening and monitoring of clients and transactions. The reasoning behind such a voluntary code of conduct is the harmonisation of principles and the strengthening of private sector reputation and credibility (Pieth and Aiolfi 2003). While membership of the group is practically closed to new members, the initiative has evolved to include an annual 'Wolfsberg Forum' which brings together a wider spectrum of financial institutions (some of the world's largest banks), as well as representatives from regulatory and supervisory agencies at the national and global level (for example, the Basel Committee on Banking Supervision) and from FATF (Pieth 2006). The group updates its guidance regularly, most recently in 2012 following the announcement of the revised FATF 40 recommendations.

Where the private and public, financial and legal elements of the regime most obviously come together, however, is in the development, in parallel to the AML framework, of a compliance industry. In the first place, this has led to an important by-product in the practices of financial institutions with their development of global compliance programmes. Aside from meeting AML compliance needs, these programmes can also serve as sophisticated database and marketing tools for the largest financial institutions. Indeed, at the high end of the market, banks and securities firms are working with complex compliance programmes that streamline performance by producing consistent standards for their global business and allow for the identification of clients, the monitoring of their transactions, the reporting of suspicious activities and the regular updating of global regulatory and legal requirements. The programmes are developed following a risk-based approach, where customers are categorised as high, medium or low risk at various stages in their dealings with the financial institution according to a variety of parameters including, importantly, country of birth and residence (although, increasingly, more sophisticated indicators are used in determining risk, geography is still the key factor). While the initial cost of starting such programmes is high, financial institutions admit that they have several valuable uses, including getting to know more about clients' needs and being able to customise products accordingly, offer global consistency for corporate and individual clients in global financial relationships across business lines, and create sophisticated 'valuable customer' profiles. Big institutions are also in a better position to have in place confidentiality arrangements which facilitate business-wide programmes, thus overcoming restrictions imposed by banking secrecy and data protection provisions. These methods have been further endorsed by the Wolfsberg Group which promotes a risk-based approach focusing on country, customer and services variables. Dealing with AML requirements in terms of risk management also leads the compliance departments of financial institutions to conceptualise reputational risk, including due diligence, brand protection and marketing. Finally, large financial institutions are trained to understand better the demands of law enforcement; they are in a position to recruit compliance officers from law enforcement bodies and to build informal channels of communication with judicial authorities. This has been especially documented in work by sociologists and criminologists who have followed the interaction of (public) law enforcement agents and (private) compliance officers (Favarel-Garrigues et al. 2011; Verhage 2009). In this sense, while banking practices have changed in terms of the collection and storing of data, they have been adapted to traditional marketing principles.

Smaller, local institutions, where 'know your customer' and reporting requirements are less automated, feel the burden of compliance more strongly. While risk-based approaches are also in operation (for the private institutions and their expected assessment by regulators alike), it is unclear whether in cases of irregularity such considerations carry much weight with respect to fines or criminal investigations. The reactive role of the private sector in the AML governance framework thus has a greater effect on small institutions, highlighting a justified concern in this part of the financial industry about policies that reflect their relative role in the financial system and are more appropriately proportionate to the effectiveness of the regime. Often, many of the smaller institutions do little more than document due diligence; they are also in a less privileged position when it comes to interpreting intelligence and establishing productive working relationships with examiners and law enforcement agents. This is the case across OECD countries, where small financial institutions often see fit to eliminate certain services altogether, rather than risk fines for failed compliance; this arguably restricts sections of the population from having full access to banking services, especially in areas of high immigration and undocumented work. But it also matters in non-OECD countries where authorities do not have the same expertise to apply a risk-based approach or fear that any compliance deficits, however small, may have repercussions for the reputation of a country's financial system as a whole.

But who operates these programmes? The role of the compliance officer and the broader development and professionalisation of the compliance industry to meet the needs of large financial institutions in particular are of great importance for understanding the evolving AML governance framework. As has been documented in studies of compliance officers in specific jurisdictions, compliance staff in banks are involved in the co-production of economic intelligence. These employees can closely follow the rules, but may also sabotage the system by overloading it, straddling as they do law enforcement and profit-making (Favarel-Garrigues et al. 2008). Following the inclusion of terrorist financing in the AML framework, compliance became an essential part of a bank's organisation and compliance officers carved a long-term role for themselves by professionalising their work through continuous training, software investment and the establishment of professional associations (with specialised accreditation functions). Having benefited from years of sustained financial support in these activities in the 2000s, the compliance industry sought to consolidate its place and maintain its share of available funding in the midst of the financial crisis. Compliance officers are forging important links with law enforcement agencies and officials and, at the most senior level, are often recruited from the highest echelons of the official sector. There are indeed important instances of revolving doors at that level; in the aftermath of the damning HSBC report in 2012, the bank enlisted as its new chief legal officer a former undersecretary for counter-terrorist financing and sanctions of the US Treasury. But the compliance industry is also actively seeking work for itself; aside from continuing to engage in 'regulatory creep', it is also pursuing important synergies. One such instance is the US Foreign Account Tax Compliance Act (FATCA), mentioned earlier, which is seen as an opportunity to strengthen the relative role of compliance departments. FATCA has led compliance officers and their professional associations to find ways to put forward their skills and expertise as essential in this new area of compliance. Compliance departments have started investing in software, programmes and staff to rationalise the links between these new requirements and AML. However, as telling as these trends are, it is important not to overestimate the importance of compliance within financial institutions. Compliance officers remain the far less glamorous cousins of those whose activities make banks profitable.

CONCLUSIONS

This chapter has shown that, although the AML governance framework is largely state-centric and reflects the interests of OECD countries, we need to provide a fuller account of the relationship between the prevention and enforcement sides of AML policies in order to grasp fully what it does and how it does it. Additionally, we require a better understanding of the evolving role of the private sector, especially growing segments within it such as the compliance industry. At the same time, the chapter has outlined several of the limitations of the AML governance framework and noted the difficulty of assessing its effectiveness. In this context, it can be argued that AML policies do not need to eradicate money laundering; the level of control measures required for such a task would affect the very nature of the global financial system. The question therefore becomes not so much whether money laundering can or cannot be effectively governed, but rather the extent to which fully effective AML policies are compatible with global financial activities and the movement of capital. Even in the midst of a global financial crisis, eliminating money laundering has been politically untenable, as it would have called for actions which would severely restrict the movement of money. Instead, the AML governance framework meets the more modest goal of providing the appearance of public action whilst enabling the big and strong players to set the rules, be they states or financial institutions. Yet whether these actors actually benefit from the regime is another matter, as we have seen.

It would be tempting to conclude that the governance of money laundering is more noise than substance. But there are two related areas that give cause for caution and offer AML provisions the possibility for greater impact in meeting their aspirations. As the latest FATF recommendations also indicate, there is a new interest in linking questions of money laundering and tax evasion at the global level. Governments looking to strengthen the health of their public finances are now beginning to move beyond mere rhetoric and thus the tools developed for AML may yet find a broader purpose. The professionalisation of compliance officers, on the other hand, and the attempts of this group to claim an important and essential role in bridging regulatory and law enforcement concerns, may also provide the skills and expertise needed for AML and tax evasion to be addressed more comprehensively.

NOTES

1. The full report and related hearing can be found at http://www.hsgac.senate.gov/subcommittees/investiga tions/hearings/us-vulnerabilities-to-money-laundering-drugs-and-terrorist-financing-hsbc-case-history.
2. More information on the US Foreign Account Tax Compliance Act can be found at http://www.irs.gov/ businesses/corporations/article/0,,id=236667,00.html. Implementation is phased in from 2013.
3. The full list of FATF member countries is as follows: Argentina, Australia, Austria, Belgium, Brazil, Canada, China, Denmark, Finland, France, Germany, Greece, Hong Kong – China, Iceland, India, Ireland, Italy, Japan, Korea, Luxembourg, Mexico, the Netherlands, New Zealand, Norway, Portugal, Russia, Singapore, South Africa, Spain, Sweden, Switzerland, Turkey, the United Kingdom and the United States. Additionally, the European Commission and the Gulf Cooperation Council are counted as members.
4. The countries facing counter-measures in 2012 were Iran and North Korea. Several countries are on the list of jurisdictions needing to strengthen their AML systems, varying in size, commitment and position in global governance institutional settings. They include Bolivia, Cuba, Ecuador, Ethiopia, Ghana, Indonesia, Kenya, Myanmar, Nigeria, Pakistan, São Tomé and Principe, Sri Lanka, Syria, Tanzania, Thailand, Turkey, Vietnam and Yemen. Of those, only Turkey is a FATF member.
5. There are several regional specialised organisations following the FATF institutional pattern and modus operandi. These include FATF associate members: the Asia/Pacific Group on Money Laundering, the Caribbean Financial Action Task Force, the Council of Europe Committee of Experts on the Evaluation of Anti-Money Laundering Measures and the Financing of Terrorism, the Financial Action Task Force on Money Laundering in South America, and the Middle East and North Africa Financial Action Task Force; as well as FATF observer bodies: the Eurasian Group, the Eastern and Southern Africa Anti-Money Laundering Group, and the Intergovernmental Action Group against Money Laundering in Africa.
6. AML law enforcement practitioners discussing the fundamentals of their work commonly make reference to these theorems in AML compliance training events.
7. This section is primarily based on extensive research interviews with public and private sector practitioners in Europe (Luxembourg, the Netherlands, Switzerland and the United Kingdom) and the United States in the period 2004–08 and 2012 and, outside the OECD, in China and Hong Kong in 2012.

REFERENCES

ABA Banking Journal (2003), 'Being good is just the beginning', June, 35–57.

Andreas, P. and E. Nadelmann (2006), *Policing the Globe – Criminalization and Crime Control in International Relations*, New York: Oxford University Press.

Avant, D., M. Finnemore and S.K. Sell (eds) (2010), *Who Governs the Globe?*, Cambridge: Cambridge University Press.

Croall, H. (2003), 'Combating financial crime: regulatory versus crime control approaches', *Journal of Financial Crime*, **11** (1), 45–55.

De Goede, M. (2012), *Speculative Security: The Politics of Pursuing Terrorist Monies*, Minneapolis, MN: University of Minnesota Press.

Drezner, D.W. (2007), *All Politics is Global – Explaining International Regulatory Regimes*, Princeton, NJ: Princeton University Press.

Favarel-Garrigues, G., T. Godefroy and P. Lascoumes (2008), 'Sentinels in the banking industry: private actors and the fight against money laundering in France', *British Journal of Criminology*, **48** (1), 1–19.

Favarel-Garrigues, G., T. Godefroy and P. Lascoumes (2011), 'Reluctant partners? Banks in the fight against money laundering and terrorism financing in France', *Security Dialogue*, **42** (2), 179–96.

Financial Action Task Force (FATF) (2012), 'International Standards on Combating Money Laundering and the Financing of Terrorism and Proliferation – the FATF Recommendations', February, available at: http://www.fatf-gafi.org/topics/fatfrecommendations/documents/internationalstandardsoncombating-moneylaunderingandthefinancingofterrorismproliferation-thefatfrecommendations.html.

Helleiner, E. (1999), 'State power and the regulation of illicit activity in global finance', in R.H. Friman and P. Andreas (eds), *The Illicit Global Economy and State Power*, Lanham, Boulder, New York, USA and Oxford, UK: Rowman & Littlefield, pp. 53–90.

Hüllse, R. (2008), 'Even clubs can't do without legitimacy: why the anti-money laundering blacklist was suspended', *Regulation and Governance*, **2**, 459–79.

Jakobi, A.P. (2013), *Common Goods and Evils? The Formation of Global Crime Governance*, Oxford: Oxford University Press.

Johnson, R.B. and J. Abbott (2005), 'Placing bankers in the front line', *Journal of Money Laundering Control*, **8** (3), 215–19.

KPMG (2007), 'Global anti-money laundering survey'.

Levi, M. and M. Maguire (2004), 'Reducing and preventing organised crime: an evidence-based critique', *Crime, Law and Social Change*, **41**, 397–469.

McDowell, J. and G. Novis (2001), 'The consequences of money laundering and financial crime', *Economic Perspectives*, May, 6–8.

Naylor, R.T. (1999), 'Wash-out: a critique of follow-the-money methods in crime control policy', *Crime, Law and Social Change*, **32**, 1–57.

Palan, R., R. Murphy and C. Chavagneux (2010), *Tax Havens: How Globalization Really Works*, Ithaca, NY: Cornell University Press.

Pieth, M. (2006), 'Multistakeholder initiatives to combat money laundering and bribery', Basel Institute on Governance, Working Paper No. 02.

Pieth, M. and G. Aiolfi (2003), 'The private sector becomes active: the Wolfsberg process', *Journal of Financial Crime*, **10** (4), 359–65.

Reuter, P. and E. Truman (2004), *Chasing Dirty Money: The Fight Against Money Laundering*, Washington, DC: Institute for International Economics.

Serrano, M. and P. Kenny (2003), 'The international regulation of money laundering', *Global Governance*, **9**, 433–39.

Sharman, J.C. (2006), *Havens in a Storm – The Struggle for Global Tax Regulation*, Ithaca, NY: Cornell University Press.

Sharman, J.C. (2008), 'Power and discourse in policy diffusion: anti-money laundering in developing states', *International Studies Quarterly*, **52**, 635–56.

Sharman, J.C. (2011), *The Money Laundry: Regulating Criminal Finance in the Global Economy*, Ithaca, NY: Cornell University Press.

Simmons, B. (2001), 'The international politics of harmonisation: the case of capital market regulation', *International Organization*, **55** (3), 589–620.

Simonova, A. (2011), 'The risk-based approach to anti-money laundering: problems and solutions', *Journal of Money Laundering Control*, **14** (4), 346–58.

Unger, B. (2007), *The Scale and Impacts of Money Laundering*, Cheltenham, UK and Northampton, MA, USA: Edward Elgar.

Unger, B. (2009), 'Money laundering – a newly emerging topic on the international agenda', *Review of Law and Economics*, **5** (2), 807–19.

Verhage, A. (2009), 'Between the hammer and the anvil? The anti-money laundering complex and its interactions with the compliance industry', *Crime, Law and Social Change*, **52** (1), 9–32.

Vitale, A. (2001), 'US banking: an industry's view on money laundering', *Economic Perspectives*, May.

Vlcek, W. (2009), 'A level playing field and the space for small states', *Journal of International Relations and Development*, **12** (2), 115–36.

Vlcek, W. (2011), 'Power and the practice of security to govern global finance', *Review of International Political Economy*, **19** (4), 639–62.

10 'Emerging' powers and the governance of global trade

Rorden Wilkinson

Conventional wisdom suggests that Western, and particularly United States, dominance of global economic regimes is being challenged by the rise of a group of 'emerging' powers known as the BRICS,[1] supported by a loose collection of second-tier states referred to rather colloquially as the 'next 11',[2] and followed by at least two dozen more that have rapidly moved from low- to middle-income status since the early 2000s (Kenny and Sumner 2011). Not only have the largest of these states experienced dramatic and enviable growth rates in recent years, but their control of energy supplies, importance in global food markets, dominance of production and consumption patterns, and resource acquisition strategies (Moyo 2012), among other things, have also singled them out as new forces to be reckoned with. Moreover, the attention devoted to the rise of these powers has been accentuated by the economic misfortunes of the Western powers following the 2007–09 financial crisis and the economic stagnation and recession it has engendered.

Perceptions of the relative demise of the industrial states and the rise of their non-Western counterparts have been driven by a scholarly, practitioner and media commentary that has sometimes been quite alarmist in tone. The most high-profile and newsworthy examples of this genre have tended to be realist analyses that link accelerations in economic performance with rising defence spending to proclaim the inevitability of a new conflictual phase in global politics (see Kaplan 2005 and Mearsheimer 2006 for two of the more hyperbolic accounts; see Huiyun 2009 and Nathan and Scobell 2012 for alternative views). While these accounts have tended to be confined to broad-brush discussions of the global political situation, tensions between industrial and developing countries in the World Trade Organization's (WTO) Doha round have lent credibility to the view that the WTO is in a period of long-term institutional stasis and decline and that the dominance previously enjoyed by the United States and the European Union (EU) in the governance of global trade is on the wane. Needless to say, the portrayal of pitched battles being fought between developed and developing countries in the WTO – so often the lifeblood of commentary on the Doha round (Wilkinson 2012) – has itself fed back into wider debates about changing global power relations, with many pointing to these tensions as firm evidence that the end of Pax Americana is nigh.

My purpose here is to look beyond speculation about the intentions of emerging powers, the raw economic data generated by their rise and the hyperbole that has accompanied their rapid economic development, to ask what actual impact these changes in the economic fortunes of some of the world's largest and poorest states have had, and are likely to have, on global trade governance. I start from a position of greater scepticism than many other commentators and hold a view shaped by a longer-run perspective than is normally associated with studies of global trade governance. My scepticism begins from the starting point that shifting relations of power have been a feature of the multi-lateral trade regime since the General Agreement on Tariffs and Trade (GATT) was first negotiated in 1947. These shifting relations of power have, in turn, underpinned previous episodes of heightened political contestation and generated speculation about the future shape of both the regime and the wider global political system. The rise of Japan and of Europe in the post-war era constitute cases in point, to which I return below. Yet it is also the case that shifts in relative power relations have not resulted in substantive changes in the overall design, functioning or governance of the GATT/WTO. Quite the contrary: they have served to consolidate its character, role and purpose. Likewise, it is also the case that multilateral trade negotiations have been replete with tensions, crises and moments of heightened political contestation from the very outset (see Wilkinson 2006). These events have almost always fuelled worries about the health of the multilateral trade regime, which have seldom been realised. It is no surprise, then, that contemporary commentary about the health of the global trading system should be so negative and dramatic, given that we are at a moment when the rise of emerging powers and a hiatus in a trade round coincide – the conclusion of a modest package of measures at the December 2013 Bali Ministerial Conference notwithstanding. My view is that we should resist the impulse to jump to conclusions drawn either from changing economic data or the existence of a deadlock in the round, and hold back from developing causal narratives about the consequences they might have for global and multilateral power structures.

Three factors are at play here. First, heightened political contestation is an inevitable result of competitive negotiating between states, particularly states differing dramatically in size as well as technical and political capability. Second, state capacities do fluctuate over time and significant long-lasting (but not system-altering) changes tend to manifest themselves in some way in the manner in which an institution functions, but not necessarily in its general character, role and purpose. Third, the way institutions are designed and function exerts an influence on, but does not strictly determine, the type of governance produced and the behaviour in which states engage. Hence my argument is that, much like the World Bank and International Monetary Fund (IMF) (see Momani 2010; Weaver 2010), the GATT/WTO has played and continues to play a key role in shaping the behaviour of member-states in a way that has helped preserve an existing set of power relations. The institution's primary purpose has been to aid economic growth, expansion and innovation in core countries (the United States and the industrial states), while at the same time offering non-core countries (their developing and least-developed counterparts) the prospect of real, but relatively smaller, gain. Inevitably, throughout the life cycle of the trade regime, non-core countries have risen and have appeared to offer a challenge to the existing set of underlying power relations. At the same time, it has always been the case that the rules, norms, practices and decision-making procedures embodied in the trade regime have helped socialise these countries into ways of operating that have ultimately assisted in reinforcing the status quo.

This leads me to a second position that is pertinent to the contemporary as well as prior and future eras. Rather than fundamentally altering how trade is governed, the rise of new powers and their socialisation into existing ways of operating suggests that we have yet to get a handle properly on how and why the institutional pillars of Pax Americana have proved to be so resilient and able to absorb challenges to the status quo. Indeed, given the length of time that scholars have been speculating over the coming demise of the United States (Keohane 1984), and the sloth with which it has happened (Strange 1987), we probably should have been engaged in questions such as these much earlier. In this way, the chapter responds to the call made in the opening chapter of this book to reconsider how we understand the core structural, ideological and political forces at play in the governance of the global political economy. My contribution is to draw attention to the deficiencies in our understanding of the resilience of established systems of governance by raising a question mark over the extent to which the rise of the BRICS countries and others has altered the way things are done in the WTO. We may be witnessing changes in the current system of global trade governance – accommodations made to account for movements in relative power capabilities – but we are not seeing a transformation in the core power relations that underpin the system. In so doing, I also seek to add to a growing body of literature that raises a note of caution about the extent to which the rise of new economic powers has been translated into substantive political influence (Wade 2011; Pei 2012) and to underscore the utility of a more established body of work on the role international institutions play in stabilising global configurations of power (Murphy 1994; Gill 1995; Cox with Sinclair 1996).

In pursuit of these aims, the chapter unfolds in three sections. In the next section I explore those elements of the relationship between international institutions and global configurations of power pertinent to my argument. I then explore how the multilateral trade regime has accommodated previous instances wherein states have risen as well as reflect on the coalition activities of emerging states in order to raise a note of caution over contemporary debate. Thereafter, I consider the challenges to global trade governance presented by the rise of new powers. Throughout I do not discount the fact that real changes have occurred in global power relations; nor do I deny that not-inconsiderable adjustments will be made globally, as well as in the governance of trade. Nevertheless, I remain sceptical of assertions that a fundamental change in the relations of power that underpin global trade governance has occurred, that the WTO has ceased to be of use to the leading industrial powers, and/or that a new world order is in the offing. Put succinctly, we may be witnessing changes in a system, but we are certainly not seeing a change of that system. Moreover, I proceed mindful of the fact that the terms 'rising' and 'emerging' are problematic ways of referring to states whose significance has come increasingly to the collective attention of Western scholars and commentators precisely because their economic performance of late has been perceived as rivalling that of the industrial states as well as representing significant economic opportunities to them, and not because they have somehow appeared out of nowhere (Turner 2009).

GLOBAL INSTITUTIONS AND THE CHALLENGE OF RISING POWERS

Much of the commentary about rising powers sees a move away from the unipolarity of the post-Cold War moment when the United States held economic and military preponderance, to a situation in which other regional powers – more often than not rising developing countries – have come to the fore. Hence, the rapid growth of China, India and Brazil, in particular, in terms of shares of global income and growing gross domestic product, has been seen as proof of a movement towards greater economic and, in extension, political multipolarity. The problems with this argument are that: (1) it is rather binary, tending to assume that it is either Pax Americana or another system that will hold sway; (2) it pays relatively little attention to the institutions put in place after the Second World War by the United States and its allies (what might be understood as the super-structural elements of Pax Americana), the ideological underpinnings of these bodies and their supporting discourses, and the effects that this institutional and ideological complex have had on maintaining particular patterns of behaviour and thus relations of power; and (3) it omits an understanding of the co-option of key states into existing systems of governance in ways that appear substantive but which seldom challenge US, and to a lesser extent European, pre-eminence.

The lack of such an appreciation causes analysts to interpret crude measures, such as economic growth rates, as evidence of shifting global power relations. Most certainly, the growth achieved by China, India and Brazil has been spectacular. However, what these economic data do not tell us is the capacity of rising powers to translate growing economic significance into sustained political power and influence. Moreover, they do not tell us about the capacity of a particular country to challenge directly a dominant state (and its inner circle) in such a way that the former forces the latter to agree to, or do, something it would otherwise not have done. This, of course, is not to mention the very good questions that have been raised – including by Jim O'Neill, the architect of the term 'BRIC' (Bloomberg 2012) – about the sustainability of the rates of growth recorded by these rising states, the long-term viability of their models of development, or the uses to which discourses about changing global power relations are put domestically in both established and emerging powers (Ismail 2012; Breslin 2003).

Research into the role and functioning of global institutions since they first became an established feature of international politics in the mid-nineteenth century shows that, when founded upon secure relations of power, and especially where one or a small number of states are dominant, they tend to encourage patterns of behaviour that, over time, have proven to be remarkably consistent with their founding aims and objectives (Murphy 1994; Cox with Sinclair 1996). When global institutions are not founded upon stable hierarchies of power, they tend to falter (with the League of Nations being the most obvious example). The IMF, World Bank and WTO (as the successor institution to the GATT) still form the mainstay of governance institutions for the global economy and dominate a supporting cast of regional organisations (development banks as well as trade institutions) and other bodies that deal with specialised tasks (such as intellectual property protection and financial transactions among other things); and they remain the principal means by which Group of 7 (G7) and Organisation for Economic Co-operation and Development (OECD) orchestrated policies are implemented.

It is also important to note that in the post-war era rising states have tended to be co-opted into existing systems of governance, rather than stand outside as challengers to those systems. The creation of the G7, and later G8, put in place a decision-making forum that reflected changes in the distribution of global power relations (Dobson 2007). Equally, it brought new countries into an existing mode of operation and form of governance based upon an established and unchanged power structure. The same can be said for the evolution and subsequent expansion of the OECD (Woodward 2009). Likewise, the Group of 20 (G20) can be seen to have given rising powers a more formal say at the global decision-making table (Germain 2002; Cooper and Thakur 2013), but also to have co-opted them into a modus operandi that has not fundamentally altered decision-making in the global political economy.

As this institutional creation and expansion suggests, a necessary cost of the maintenance of the integrity of the overall system has been the granting to non-dominant states of a measure of benefit in exchange for their participation (Cox with Sinclair 1996: 137–40). This form of concession-giving occurs via systems of rules developed specifically to offer concessions to non-dominant states while maintaining the advantages of core states. As a range of authors have noted, this is in part made possible by ensuring that an institution's architects maintain a measure of control over which states accede to an institution or regime and how they participate (Wade 2003; Keohane 2002; Tan 2011; Gill 1995). Thus key global institutions accommodate changes in relative power capabilities among participating states by offering the prospect of institutional benefit while preserving the status of the leading powers. We see this most clearly in the cases of the World Bank and IMF where recent reforms have given the BRICS countries a relatively greater share of voting rights. While this has not quenched their thirst for further reform (BRICS 2012; Wade 2011: 359–65), it has also not altered substantively the preponderance of the United States and Europe therein. Moreover, while it is clearly the case that institutions such as the WTO, the IMF and the World Bank – as well as their security counterparts, such as the North Atlantic Treaty Organization (NATO) and the United Nations Security Council (UNSC) – cannot stop a fundamental change in global power relations (at which point an entirely new set of global institutions or some other superstructural framework would presumably be established), they nonetheless mitigate aspects of the challenges presented by powers in the ascendancy, preserving the opportunities and advantages accrued from institutional membership and acting to pacify challenges by socialising rising states into non-system-challenging ways of operating (Jawara and Kwa 2003; Bayliss et al. 2011; Peet 2009).

These features are much in evidence in the way global trade has been, and is, governed. The entry of states into the trade regime has been heavily policed since the GATT was first agreed. New entrants were either (1) 'grandfathered' into the system (if they were deemed to be of little economic and political significance and threat, and/or were the former colonies of the European powers) during the institution's early years; (2) faced with a barrage of exception actions that nullified most of the benefits of membership (as was Japan's experience after its 1955 accession); and/or (3) required to agree to significant and overly burdensome protocols that went far beyond what was required of existing members (as in the case of China's accession, but also that of the least-developed small island state of Vanuatu – see Hayashi 2003; WTO 2012). Indeed, what is quite clear is that the accession requirements have become steadily more, rather than less, demanding over the institution's life cycle (Copelovitch and Ohls 2012; also UNCTAD 2001).

Other mechanisms have also been at play. The conduct of trade liberalisation in periodic rounds among small groups of economically significant states has enabled the leading industrial states to open markets in areas of economic benefit, while protecting and/or forestalling the liberalisation of those that were, and are, politically and economically sensitive to them. Moreover, precisely because the mechanism for accruing trade advantages is a system of barter wherein benefits are received for concessions given away, any rectification of the asymmetries that have resulted from prior trade negotiations has only been able to take place by non-core states agreeing to further concessions. This, in turn, has actually widened rather than attenuated the gap between the advantages accrued to dominant and non-dominant states alike, creating a highly imbalanced layer-cake effect and producing what Sylvia Ostry (2007: 18) called in its latest incarnation – the Uruguay round – a 'bum deal'. It is also why even meaningful 'early harvest' measures designed to assist the poorest, such as cotton farmers in Benin, Burkina Faso, Chad and Mali (collectively, the 'Cotton 4' or C4), have not been forth-coming in the Doha negotiations (Lee 2012).

Likewise, and despite a significant overhaul during the Uruguay round, the global trade regime is underwritten by a system of dispute settlement that favours those with the technical knowledge, expertise and resources to challenge 'unfair' trade practices (Lee 2004). Further, trade governance operates without transparent and steadfast rules of organisation, operation or method, relying instead on norm and practice – as well as knowledge of how those norms and practices work – for its functioning. This extends from the selection of the head of the WTO's Secretariat, the Director-General, to the composition of decision-making groups (which shift from one collective to another but which always comprise the United States and the EU). Moreover, the codification that has occurred has tended to entrench, rather than reform, norms and practices that con-tinue to favour the leading industrial states.

It is with these factors in mind – that, at a general level, there is an intimate relation-ship between established relations of power and the creation and continued functioning of institutions and that, at a more specific level, tendencies towards behavioural patterns consistent with status quo preservation are shaped in part by the detailed requirements of participation in a system of governance – that any enquiry into the impact that emerg-ing powers have on established systems must proceed. The next section stands back from most of the contemporary debate and explores how previous rising powers have fared in the GATT/WTO.

RISING POWERS AND THE GATT/WTO

Worries about rapidly rising powers and the threats that they might pose to established patterns of global trade and its governance have existed since at least the early 1950s, although this is seldom acknowledged in contemporary debate. In only one case (the European Union) have these powers risen to established positions of influence in the GATT/WTO. More usually, the rise of these powers has stopped some way short of accession to the decision-making core, stalled at an earlier stage, and/or fallen back. Not one example exists (even the EU) of a country or set of countries that has risen, directly challenged and succeeded in supplanting US preponderance, politically as well as eco-nomically. It is worth recovering some examples of where powers have risen in the past to highlight how their challenge was subsequently absorbed into business-as-usual in the trade regime in order to see more clearly how institutions like the WTO operate in ways that tend to co-opt rising powers and promote system-maintaining behaviour. We can then better understand the current era.

From the very outset the trade regime has functioned in such a way that the interests of the dominant states, and the United States in particular, have been preserved; while those of non-dominant states have been accommodated (sometimes significantly), albeit never to the same extent. During the wartime and post-war negotiations for what was originally intended to be the trade counterpart to the IMF and World Bank, a charter for an International Trade Organization (ITO) proposed by the United States and supported by the UK encountered strong criticism from developing countries (Viner 1947; Wilcox 1949). The extent of the criticism was such that the United States decided not to pursue its ratification of the ITO Charter. Instead, it negotiated a much lither agreement among a subset of 23 countries to circumscribe the blockages that the ITO negotiations had generated and ensure that a trade institution was put in place – the GATT – which met US industrial needs as well as those of its leading European allies. It also ensured that a system of trade governance was put in place that would remain largely incongruous with the needs of developing countries – a fact that has great resonance today.

The installation of the GATT was also significant because it established the terrain on which debate about the future of global trade governance would take place. The exclusivity of membership, particularly in the earlier years, further added to the organisation's legitimacy as the principal site of trade governance. This, in turn, helped expunge from memory other ideas about the form and substance of a post-war trade institution – such as the Brazilian proposal for an international trade body – and ensured that any talk of the codification of what had originally been intended to be a provisional agreement took place on the basis of what existed, rather that what ought to be in place. Moreover, it helped shroud the fact that, with the exception of China (whose signatory status was nullified by the 1949 revolution), the emerging powers had been trying to change aspects of the trade regime since it was first negotiated. As early commentators on the GATT noted, India, Brazil and Australia (then considered a developing country and previously held to be a rising power) all aspired at different times to lead the interests of their fellow developing countries (Gardner 1956: 365; Patterson 1966: 329–32).

The failure of the ITO negotiations and the establishment of the GATT set the tone of trade negotiations to come. For the most part, developing countries spent their time in the GATT/WTO attempting to change aspects of the trade institution so that it better suited their needs (Wilkinson and Scott 2008). This behaviour, in turn, helped socialise developing countries into modes of operating in the GATT/WTO that were and remain entirely orientated to the preservation of existing relations of power. Australia, for instance, although signing the GATT willingly, did so more out of strategic considerations than because of the substance of the Agreement; and while it certainly benefited from liberalisation under the GATT, as a major agricultural producing economy Australia also spent a significant proportion of its time attempting to correct the exclusion of agriculture from the GATT's purview.

The 'Rise' of Japan

Japan's experience of the GATT was more extreme than Australia's and gives a better example of an encounter between a previous rising power and the trade regime. Indeed, it is worth bearing in mind that most of the hyperbole that exists today about China's rise and its relations with the United States mirrors that which existed 30 years ago in relation to Japan. Japan's rapid industrialisation in the late 1940s and early 1950s, coupled with the cheap price of labour, generated fears of market disruption (essentially dramatically cheaper imports outcompeting Western goods), particularly in textile and clothing production (Patterson 1966: 272–300). These fears, in turn, generated a great deal of hostility to Japan's application to accede to the GATT, despite the existence of strong support from the United States (which had overseen much of Japan's economic recovery and post-war reconstruction). Much of the hostility was led by the UK, the country that stood to lose the most from the removal of trade barriers in areas of key economic interest to Japan. Given that the GATT had in part been designed as a crude instrument to help stave off post-war recession in the United States by stimulating European demand for capital goods, manufactures and semi-manufactures (which, in turn, would aid Europe's reconstruction), and not as an arrangement designed to offer all comers the prospect of liberalisation-led demand stimulation, it is unsurprising that, when Japan finally acceded, 40 per cent of the contracting parties invoked a non-application clause enabling them to withhold all institutional benefits. The result was to nullify the value of most-favoured-nation access into key European and other markets. Japan's response was to try to reverse this situation by developing a legal expertise to combat what it saw as unfair discrimination. The decision to respond in this way played a significant role in subsequently shaping Japanese commercial diplomacy around what Araki Ichirō (2007) has termed an 'aggressive legalism'. What is important here is that Japan's experience in the GATT generated a response that sought to redress the circumstances in which the country found itself, but did not challenge the system.

Japan's economic significance, combined with the economic opportunities its growth presented for Western companies, nonetheless saw its delegation brought into the inner circle of GATT decision-making during the Uruguay round. Entry into the quadrilateral group (more commonly known as the 'Quad'), along with the United States, the EU and Canada, was not however a reflection of the translation of economic power into political influence. It was a strategy on the part of the United States and the EU to force Japan to begin to open up closed aspects of its domestic markets in return for a measure of political influence in the Uruguay round. Moreover, this elevated position lasted only as long as Japan's markets (and the gains promised therein) were attractive to the United States and the EU. It was inevitable, then, that Japan's relative decline after a decade of stagnation and amid the rise of other markets, particularly China, would bring an end to its tenure in the core of GATT/WTO decision-making. It is nonetheless worth underlining the point that Japan's rise generated the very same worries about systemic changes in the balance of economic power that prevail today. Most notable was Lester Thurow's (1992) assertion that Japan's economic might would form the core of an Asian regionalism, which in conjunction with a consolidation of 'fortress Europe' and the emergence of a North American regionalism would fragment the global economy into three distinct spheres that would form the basis for a new global conflict (Wilkinson 1998).

Europe as a 'Rising' Power

The countries that have risen and come closest to challenging US dominance in the trade regime are ironically those that we seldom consider as rising powers.[3] Yet this is precisely what the European countries were, especially as a collective, after the Second World War. The difference, of course, was that they shared an ideology, a broad form of government and a set of established alliances with the United States. Despite these common factors, their rise nevertheless generated significant hostility in the United States during the post-war years, reaching a peak in the late 1960s and early 1970s, whereupon the crises generated by the Organization for Petroleum Exporting Countries (OPEC) helped shift attention away from the rise of Europe, solidified the transatlantic alliance and focused attention on the threats posed by undemocratic Third World regimes.

In many ways, for the United States and Europe the GATT reflected a classic 'double coincidence of wants' (Jevons 1875: Chapter 1).[4] The end of the Second World War, and of high levels of government demand (and finance) for goods and services, threatened to usher in economic recession in the United States. Wartime demand for US goods and services was unlikely to be replaced by post-war orders for US products from its principal market, Europe. Equally, the European governments had neither the financial wherewithal nor access to enough credit to pay for basic goods and services or the capital equipment required to reconstruct. The answer to both problems was provided in a plan hatched to lend (and to a lesser degree give) the West European countries money to buy US goods and services and to do so at cheaper rates through reductions in tariffs and other barriers to trade. The trade-off was that the European powers had to remain ideologically liberal. The financial component of this plan was Marshall Aid and the key, although not the sole, tariff-reducing mechanism was the GATT. These and other measures helped fuel an economic boom in the United States and the reconstruction of Europe.

Rapid European reconstruction, particularly in areas wherein European goods quickly grew to rival their US counterparts, generated resentment in the United States, as well as fears that US hegemony would be challenged. Paralleling aspects of the politics surrounding the rise of Japan and, more recently China, these fears centred on issues of unfair working practices, discrimination, unfair government interventions, ungratefulness and military security, among others. By the time of the Kennedy round (1964–1967), Europe had grown to be a considerable force in the global trade regime and was successfully installed at the core of global trade governance. This position has been continually refreshed by subsequent expansions of the European Union, as well as the economic performance and continuing development of the European economies. Yet, while the EU comprises one half of the Group of 2 (G2) in the WTO, it does not predominate over the United States, nor is it able to push through decisions without US support. It remains the case that the United States holds the balance of power in global trade, despite the combined size of the European economies, their share of global income and their political power. Moreover, for all of their differences, they share a common set of economic values that ensures their commitment to a broadly similar programme of global economic governance in which the WTO plays a central role (even if, at times, both the EU and the United States can appear to be distinctly unengaged in WTO negotiations).

Historically, the EU, Japan and Australia are perhaps the most important countries to have risen during the GATT years and to have attracted commentary akin to the game-changing accounts that now accompany the emergence of the BRICS. A series of other notable states have also risen, though their rise has not attracted the same kind of debate and speculation. For example, Canada rose to become a member of the Quad, though like Japan it no longer has the influence it once did; and the rapid growth of the so-called Asian Tigers of Singapore, Taiwan, Hong Kong and South Korea (O'Neill 1984) saw them elevated to important but not core WTO decision-making groups. We might also point to historic moments wherein the rise of Nigeria, Mexico, Argentina and

Egypt, among others, have been considered important. Yet more often than not these countries were considered important coalition players but not stand out power brokers in their own right.

It is also worth noting that rapid market growth, particularly in terms of export performance, and the trade imbalances that this generates (particularly with the United States), has often been at the root of fears of a changing global balance of economic power. Yet it is also often the case these trade imbalances are more complex than is appreciated. They can, for example, have a domestic political function, both in rising powers and in the United States as well as elsewhere. James Scott, for instance, argues that the US trade deficit with China is a consequence of a disparity between savings and investment rates and a large fiscal deficit. It is nonetheless presented as a consequence of unfair Chinese trading practices and plays into concerns about the state of the US economy. The result, however, is that this trade-deficit politics is used as a platform to pursue greater trade concessions from China in bilateral and multilateral fora (Scott 2007). Similar impulses marked both Japan's and Europe's rise. Of course, trade deficits – or at least the fears that they mobilise – have another important function: they are useful platforms upon which domestic economic restructuring can be pursued. In these instances, the perceived need to enhance national competitiveness and efficiency inevitably underpins drives to improve productivity. This method is particularly useful during times when there exists significant domestic opposition to restructuring and often takes the form of appeals to the economic nationalism of 'buy American' slogans.

Acting Together: Coalitions in Global Trade Governance

Yet it is not just the emergence of a set of new powers that many commentators have found troubling. It has been the emergence of coalitions of developing countries woven together by a desire to push against dominant power relations in the multilateral trading system that has ignited much speculation. For many, the first flexing of collective emerging world muscle took place at the WTO's September 2003 Cancún Ministerial Conference (Narlikar and Wilkinson 2004) – though for some a new act in the 'North–South' drama had already begun and was visible at the four previous WTO ministerial conferences (Singapore 1996, Geneva 1998, Seattle 1999 and Doha 2001). What is notable about the Cancún ministerial, however, is that it saw the emergence of a series of new developing-country coalitions coalescing around the major BRICS powers and their next-11 counterparts – perhaps most notably the Group of 20 (G20; but not to be confused with the Group of 20 finance ministers referred to at the outset of this chapter), the Group of 33 (G33) and the smaller single-issue C4 – that had some success in shaping agendas and formulating compromises. It is also worth noting, though, that some of the grander coalitions forged in Cancún have continued only to have a symbolic presence in the Doha Development Agenda (such as the Informal Group of Developing Countries, a group of 120 developing countries) (Scott and Wilkinson 2012).

Of these coalitions, the G20 is perhaps the most significant. It has at its core the leading emerging powers and has benefited from weekly meetings of BRICS ambassadors held in Geneva designed to, among other things, maintain a consistent line in opposition to aspects of the Doha negotiations. Yet the G20 has been far from a vehicle for displacing US and European preponderance in the WTO. It does not have the broad-based support among WTO members, reluctant or otherwise, required to assume a leadership role. Indeed, many non-G20 members have been concerned that this group might prove to be influential and have actively tried to undermine its authority. Moreover, it is clear that the G20 is effective only because it brings a group of economically significant countries together (none of which are able to act on their own); and the G20 is still only in the business of opposing, rather than determining, agendas. This is in marked contrast with the United States and the EU. Both have continued to dominate the negotiation process and each has been able singlehandedly to block the conclusion of the round and/or change the contours of the package by virtue of its economic and political power. It is inconceivable that any one of the BRICS could manage something similar, and unlikely that they could achieve it by acting in concert.

It is also the case that the G20's capacity to work together has not been properly tested. The differences between key members are such that serious questions have to be raised about the capacity of the group to work together in the longer term. Brazil has consistently raised concerns about the undervaluation of particular countries' currencies that undermine its competitiveness and artificially raise the price of its exports. While Brazil was pressed to distance these concerns from discussions of the value of China's currency at the April 2012 BRICS summit in New Delhi and to focus instead on the value of the dollar and euro, a perception that the level of the renminbi allows Chinese goods to outcompete their Brazilian counterparts has been an enduring complaint. Similarly, Indian and Chinese cooperation in the WTO, which is not extensive, papers over other significant economic and political tensions between the two powers which push against their capacity to work together. The same can be said when South Africa is thrown into the mix. Although South Africa's delegation in Geneva has been one of the most consistent and cooperative in pushing forward a collective solidarist developing-country position (Ismail and Vickers 2012), it is also the case that South Africa has strategic interests in the Indian Ocean region that bring it into conflict with India and China. Russian accession to the WTO (agreed in December 2011 and formalised in August 2012) adds another complication, with few commentators believing that Russia will cooperate substantively with its emerging-power counterparts anytime soon.

We should not perhaps be surprised that countries that are able to work together in opposing a third party or parties find it difficult to work together when negotiating among themselves, particularly when their interests bring them into competition with one another as those of the BRICS countries do. Again, the history of the GATT is replete with examples of countries that find it difficult to work together in coalition situations. Despite their membership of the influential Cairns group of agricultural exporters, tensions blighted Canada's relationship with Australia, particularly over the former's leadership role and membership of the Quad. Their relationship has waxed and waned since, especially during periods when Australia again found itself a member of a core decision-making group as it did in the mid-2000s when, along with the United States, the EU, India and Brazil, it became a member of the 'Five Interested Parties' (FIPs). It is also worth bearing in mind that particular behavioural dispositions tend to persist and that changes in these patterns are necessary if rising powers are to overcome some of the institutional obstacles they face in converting economic power into political influence. Japan's aggressive legalism, noted above, is one example that has persisted. China has yet to move beyond a responsive form of engagement (Scott and Wilkinson 2013) and

India, although undergoing some change (Narlikar 2010: 29–68), continues to operate as a perennial naysayer.

It is also worth bearing in mind that, while the BRICS and developing-country coalitions have been successful in resisting aspects of the Doha round, the current impasse is as much, if not more, the result of US ambivalence. From the outset, the United States has been at best lukewarm to the negotiations. Indeed, the George W. Bush administration only began to put effort behind the negotiations after the 11 September 2001 attacks on the World Trade Center and the Pentagon and only really did so then as part of a wider effort to build alliances. Prior to this, Europe had been the driving force in trying to get a 'millennium' round launched. Thereafter US engagement was fairly consistent until the round collapsed in July 2006 and only recovered in the run-up to the 2013 Bali Ministerial Conference. In the face of continued opposition and dwindling domestic support, the United States has since chosen to pursue its trade objectives regionally and bilaterally.[5] The United States, the EU and Australia, among others, have also sought to move forward in the WTO plurilaterally (that is, in smaller groups), engaging in exploratory talks on, for instance, services liberalisation (in the 'Real Good Friends' of services group).[6]

The point here is that over the course of almost 70 years the basic set of power relations that underpinned the creation of the GATT has continued to hold sway. Clearly exogenous factors have played a role; but the way trade has been governed has also mediated the extent to which economic growth has been translated into political influence in the international trade regime. This is not to say that non-core states – largely developing countries – have not played a role in shaping how trade is governed: they clearly have. Rather, the point is that other than the rare examples where groups of countries have acted as coherent blocs, or where the sum of uncoordinated efforts has combined to resist a form or an aspect of trade governance, the global trade regime has evolved in a way that speaks to core interests while at the same time offering non-core states concessions to ensure their acquiescence. And while it is the case that the changes in economic significance among WTO members are undoubtedly real, until the round has been concluded and the final details of any package are clear, caution must be exercised when considering claims that US and EU preponderance has waned.

CONCLUSION

George Orwell (1946) famously quipped: 'political predictions are usually wrong . . . we are all capable of believing things which we *know* to be untrue, and then, when we are finally proved wrong, impudently twisting the facts so as to show that we were right'. He continued: 'To see what is in front of one's nose needs a constant struggle . . . In general, one is only right when either wish or fear coincides with reality'. It is worth bearing these remarks in mind when thinking about shifting power relations and their impact on the governance of global trade: to look in front of one's nose and see what is going on. China's rise is the most spectacular of the emerging powers and the one whose development trajectory has seen it replace Europe and Japan in popular US trade discourse. It is equally the case that China's economic growth over the last three decades has been spectacular and its position as the second-largest national economy in the world requires attention. However, it is equally true that China's development trajectory is unsustainable in its current form. Not only has its growth rate tailed off significantly since the late 2000s, but its reliance on export markets makes it vulnerable to the kind of demand slowdown that is now evident in many of the world's industrial economies. The Chinese are themselves well aware that dependence on an export model is problematic in the long run and have begun moving towards a domestic consumption model – indeed, this is a key guiding principle of the latest (that is, the twelfth) Five-Year Plan.

It is also worth bearing in mind that Chinese development has been marked by rapidly growing inequalities, particularly between rural and urban areas. China's Gini coefficient has risen at a staggering rate over the last 30 years, from a relatively egalitarian 0.2 to a highly unequal 0.5 (Li 2011: 137–8). China has also faced increasing illiteracy, rising from 85 million to 114 million between 2000 and 2005 (Huang 2008: 244–5). Job creation has slowed significantly and has increasingly favoured the better-educated and the young (that is, those that are best placed to take advantage of China's entry to the global economy), while disadvantaging rural areas, the old and the less skilled (Sollinger 2003; Wang 2000). And growth in personal incomes has also moved from exceeding gross domestic product (GDP) growth to lagging significantly behind (Huang 2008: 238).

Equally, although some projections suggest India's economy will be the third-largest behind the United States and China by 2030, it too suffers from structural problems (rising inequalities, enduring poverty, poor infrastructure in large parts of the country) that will inevitably slow its rate of growth and force it to concentrate on domestic, rather than international, issues. Meanwhile, Brazil and South Africa, though clearly gaining in influence, look to be no more than significant regional powers. The point is that much of the commentary about rising powers and their impact on the governance of global trade is generated by fears of relative Western decline, or else it comes from overly celebratory accounts by non-Western authors or those sympathetic to their cause. Certainly, these powers have grown economically at spectacular rates, but questions remain as to the extent to which that growth will continue and about the capacity of that growth to be translated into political power.

It is also worth noting that a significant number of countries that have successfully managed the process of development have become 'stuck' at some point in their rise. This is particularly true of previous emerging powers: Australia, Canada, Japan and South Korea. Robert Wade (2010: 152–3) argues that there are fewer contenders to rich-country status now than there were 40 years ago. Middle-income countries today, he argues, have become caught in the middle: 'their firms [are] stuck in the relatively low value-added segments of global production chains, unable to break into innovation-intensive activities or into the market for branded products, where the high profits are to be made'. China in particular faces these challenges, albeit that it has so far been remarkably successful at handling the challenges thrown up by its rapid economic emergence (Huang 2008; Hutton 2007).

In looking in front of one's nose we should better appreciate the mediating effect of participation in regimes governed by institutions such as the WTO. The impact of the socialisation of previous 'rising' powers into the trade and other global regimes is instructive. It is also the case that none of the current crop of rising powers has proven to be system-challenging in their approach to the WTO. China has invested a great deal in the construction of the largest trade delegation in Geneva, but it has proven so far to be a rule-taker and has been entirely status quo orientated in its trade diplomacy (Lim and Wang 2010). For all of the bluster of the Indian delegation and of former trade ministers such as Kamal Nath, India has also not sought to challenge the system fundamentally. Brazil and South Africa have acted likewise. Russia's role in the WTO has yet to be determined, but there are few reasons to suppose it will be anything other than status quo maintaining in its behaviour.

We should not underestimate the dynamic qualities of global economic institutions to adjust to the challenges they face, or the importance that developing and industrial countries alike attach to bodies such as the WTO. Global institutions have shown remarkable qualities of adaptation and have generally done so without disrupting stable relations of power. We should ask more questions about why this is so, as well as why, despite repeated warnings, we are obsessed with what Susan Strange (1987) called 'the persistent myth of lost [US] hegemony'. I have argued in this chapter that we too often fail to acknowledge the capacity of global institutions to mediate challenges to dominant power relations, and that we underestimate this capacity at our peril. If we look in front of our nose, we see that core power relations have not changed in the global trade regime. A new supporting cast appears to be in the ascendancy, but these countries remain a long way from being able to challenge the dominance of the old order.

ACKNOWLEDGEMENT

I am grateful to James Scott, Oliver Turner, Nicola Phillips and Tony Payne for their comments on a draft version of this chapter.

NOTES

1. The term BRIC was first coined by Jim O'Neill, Chair of Goldman Sachs Asset Management, as shorthand for Brazil, Russia, India and China (O'Neill 2001). BRIC become BRICS with the accession of South Africa to the group (Cooper and Thakur 2013).
2. O'Neill is also credited with coining the term 'next 11' to refer to Bangladesh, Egypt, Indonesia, Iran, South Korea, Mexico, Nigeria, Pakistan, Philippines, Turkey and Vietnam. See http://www.goldmansachs.com/our-thinking/brics/brics-reports-pdfs/how-solid.pdf.
3. Particularly the original European Economic Community (EEC) 'six' of France, Germany, Italy, the Netherlands, Belgium and Luxembourg, along with those countries that acceded to the EEC in 1973: the UK, Denmark and Ireland.
4. Jevons's conception of a coincidence of wants is normally associated with problems of barter and not institution-building. The analogy nonetheless holds.
5. This should not, however, be confused with a preference for bilateral and regional solutions. On the contrary, a multilateral outcome remains the preferred option for the United States. See Former United States Trade Representative (2006–2009) Ambassador Susan Schwab, 'Reflections on Trade Policy', speech given at the University of Manchester, 20 May 2009.
6. The RGF group includes the United States, the EU, Japan, Canada, Australia, New Zealand, Norway, Switzerland, Singapore, South Korea, Hong Kong, Taiwan, Mexico, Chile, Colombia and Pakistan.

REFERENCES

Bayliss, Kate, Ben Fine and Elisa van Waeyenberge (eds) (2011), *The Political Economy of Development: The World Bank, Neoliberalism and Development Research*, London: Pluto.
Bloomberg (2012), 'O'Neill's BRICs risk hitting wall threatening G-20 growth', 14 June, available at: http://www.bloomberg.com/news/2012-06-14/o-neill-s-brics-risk-hitting-wall-threatening-g-20-growth.html.
Breslin, Shaun (2003), 'Reforming China's embedded socialist compromise: China and the WTO', *Global Change, Peace and Security*, **15** (3), 213–29.
BRICS (2012), Fourth BRICS Summit: Delhi Declaration, 29 March, available at: http://www.brics.utoronto.ca/docs/120329-delhi-declaration.html.
Cooper, Andrew F. and Ramesh Thukur (2013), *The Group of 20*, London: Routledge.
Copelovitch, Mark S. and David Ohls (2012), 'Trade, institutions and the timing of GATT/WTO accession in post-colonial states', *Review of International Organizations*, **7** (1), 81–107.
Cox, Robert W. with Timothy J. Sinclair (1996), *Approaches to World Order*, Cambridge: Cambridge University Press.
Dobson, Hugo (2007), *The Group of 7/8*, London: Routledge.
Gardner, Richard N. (1956), *Sterling–Dollar Diplomacy: Anglo-American Diplomacy in the Reconstruction of Multilateral Trade*, Oxford: Clarendon.
Germain, Randall (2002), 'Reforming the international financial architecture: the new political agenda', in Rorden Wilkinson and Steve Hughes (eds), *Global Governance: Critical Perspectives*, London: Routledge, pp. 17–35.
Gill, Stephen (1995), 'Globalisation, market civilisation and disciplinary neoliberalism', *Millennium*, **24** (3), 399–423.
Hayashi, Michiko (2003), 'Arrested development: Vanuatu's suspended accession to the World Trade Organization', case study prepared for the International Commercial Diplomacy Project, February, available at: http://www.vanuatu.usp.ac.fj/library/Online/Vanuatu/Hayashi.pdf.
Huang, Yasheng (2008), *Capitalism with Chinese Characteristics: Entrepreneurship and the State*, Cambridge: Cambridge University Press.
Huiyun, Feng (2009), 'Is China a revisionist power?', *Chinese Journal of International Politics*, **2** (3), 313–34.
Hutton, Will (2007), *The Writing on the Wall: China and the West in the 21st Century*, London: Little, Brown.
Ichirō, Araki (2007), 'Global governance, Japan and the World Trade Organization', in Glenn D. Hook and Hugo Dobson (eds), *Global Governance and Japan: The Institutional Architecture*, London: Routledge, pp. 179–93.
Ismail, Faizel (2012), 'Narratives and myths in the WTO Doha round: the way forward?', *Economic and Political Weekly*, **57** (31), 55–60.
Ismail, Faizel and Brendan Vickers (2012), 'Mandela's way: reflections on South Africa's role in the multilateral trading system', in Rorden Wilkinson and James Scott (eds), *Trade, Poverty, Development: Getting Beyond the WTO's Doha Deadlock*, London: Routledge, pp. 103–20.
Jawara, Fatoumata and Aileen Kwa (2003), *Behind the Scenes at the WTO*, London: Zed Books.
Jevons, William Stanley (1875), *Money and the Mechanism of Exchange*, New York: D. Appleton & Company.
Kaplan, Robert D. (2005), 'How we would fight China', *Atlantic*, June, pp. 1–12.
Kenny, Charles and Andy Sumner (2011), 'How 28 poor countries escaped the poverty trap', *Guardian PovertyMatters Blog*, 12 July, available at: http://www.guardian.co.uk/global-development/poverty-matters/2011/jul/12/world-bank-reclassifies-28-poor-countries.
Keohane, Robert O. (1984), *After Hegemony: Cooperation and Discord in the World Political Economy*, Princeton, NJ: Princeton University Press.
Keohane, Robert O. (2002), *Power and Governance in a Partially Globalized World*, London: Routledge.
Lee, Donna (2004), 'Understanding the WTO dispute settlement system', in Brian Hocking and Steven McGuire (eds), *Trade Politics*, 2nd edition, London: Routledge, pp. 120–32.
Lee, Donna (2012), 'Cotton and poverty in the Doha development agenda', in Rorden Wilkinson and James Scott (eds), *Trade, Poverty, Development: Getting Beyond the WTO's Doha Deadlock*, London: Routledge, pp. 72–90.
Li, Peilin (2011), 'China's new stage of development', *China: An International Journal*, **9** (1), 133–43.
Lim, C.L. and JiangYu Wang (2010), 'China and the Doha development agenda', *Journal of World Trade*, **44** (6), 1309–31.
Mearsheimer, John J. (2006), 'China's unpeaceful rise', *Current History*, **105** (690), 160–62.
Momani, Bessma (2010), 'IMF rhetoric on reducing poverty and inequality', in Jennifer Clapp and Rorden Wilkinson (eds), *Global Governance, Poverty and Inequality*, London: Routledge, pp. 71–89.

Moyo, Dambisa (2012), *Winner Take All: China's Race for Resources and What It Means for Us*, London: Allen Lane.

Murphy, Craig N. (1994), *International Organization and Industrial Change: Global Governance since 1850*, Cambridge: Polity Press.

Nathan, Andrew J. and Andrew Scobell (2012), 'How China sees America: the sum of Beijing's fears', *Foreign Affairs*, **91** (2), 32–47.

Narlikar, Amrita (2010), *New Powers: How to Become One and How to Manage Them*, London, UK and New York, USA: Columbia University Press.

Narlikar, Amrita and Rorden Wilkinson (2004), 'Collapse at the WTO: a Cancun post-mortem', *Third World Quarterly*, **25** (3), 447–60.

O'Neill, Helen (1984), 'HICs, MICs, NICs and LICs: some elements in the political economy of graduation and differentiation', *World Development*, **12** (7), 693–712.

O'Neill, Jim (2001), 'Building better global economic BRICs', Goldman Sachs Global Economics Papers, No. 66, 30 November, available at: http://www.goldmansachs.com/our-thinking/topics/brics/brics-reports-pdfs/build-better-brics.pdf.

Orwell, George (1946), 'In front of your nose', *Tribune*, 22 March.

Ostry, Sylvia (2007), 'Trade, development and the Doha development agenda', in Donna Lee and Rorden Wilkinson (eds), *The WTO after Hong Kong: Progress In, and Prospects For, the Doha Development Agenda*, London: Routledge, pp. 26–34.

Patterson, Gardner (1966), *Discrimination in International Trade: The Policy Issues 1945–1965*, Princeton, NJ: Princeton University Press.

Peet, Richard (2009), *Unholy Trinity: The IMF, World Bank and WTO*, 2nd edition, London: Zed Books.

Pei, Minxin (2012), 'Superpower denied? Why China's "rise" may have already peaked', *Diplomat*, 9 August, available at: http://thediplomat.com/2012/08/09/superpower-denied-why-chinas-rise-may-have-already-peaked/.

Scott, James (2007), 'How the poor pay for the US trade deficit: and why it matters for the Doha Development Agenda', in Donna Lee and Rorden Wilkinson (eds), *The WTO after Hong Kong: Progress In, and Prospects For, the Doha Development Agenda*, London: Routledge, pp. 97–118.

Scott, James and Rorden Wilkinson (2012), 'The promise of "development" and the Doha Development Agenda', in Rorden Wilkinson and James Scott (eds), *Trade, Poverty, Development: Getting Beyond the WTO's Doha Deadlock*, London: Routledge, pp. 1–14.

Scott, James and Rorden Wilkinson (2013), 'China threat? Evidence from the WTO', *Journal of World Trade*, **47** (4), 761–82.

Solinger, Dorothy J. (2003), 'Chinese urban jobs and the WTO', *China Journal*, 49, 61–87.

Strange, Susan (1987), 'The persistent myth of lost hegomony', *International Organization*, **41** (4), 551–74.

Tan, Celine (2011), *Governance through Development: Poverty Reduction Strategies, International Law and the Disciplining of Third World States*, Abingdon: GlassHouse/Routledge.

Thurow, Lester C. (1992), *Head to Head: The Coming Battle Among Japan, Europe, and America*, New York: William Morrow & Company.

Turner, Oliver (2009), 'China's recovery: why the writing was always on the wall', *Political Quarterly*, **80** (1), 111–18.

UNCTAD (2001), *WTO Accessions and Development Policies*, New York, USA and Geneva, Switzerland: UNCTAD.

Viner, Jacob (1947), 'Conflicts of principle in drafting a trade charter', *Foreign Affairs*, **25** (4), 612–28.

Wade, Robert Hunter (2003), 'What strategies are viable for developing countries today?', *Review of International Political Economy*, **10** (4), 621–44.

Wade, Robert (2010), 'After the crisis: industrial policy and the developmental state in low-income countries'. *Global Policy*, **1** (2), 150–61.

Wade, Robert H. (2011), 'Emerging world order? From multipolarity to multilateralism in the G20, the World Bank and the IMF', *Politics and Society*, **39** (3), 347–78.

Wang, Shaoguang (2000), 'The social and political implications of China's WTO membership', *Journal of Contemporary China*, **9** (25), 373–405.

Weaver, Catherine (2010), 'Reforming the World Bank', in Jennifer Clapp and Rorden Wilkinson (eds), *Global Governance, Poverty and Inequality*, London: Routledge, pp. 112–32.

Wilcox, Clair (1949), *A Charter for World Trade*, London: Macmillan.

Wilkinson, Rorden (1998), 'Reconciling regionalism and multilateralism in the international trading system', in Stephen Chan and Jarrod Wiener (eds), *Twentieth Century International History*, London: I.B. Tauris, pp. 126–39.

Wilkinson, Rorden (2006), *The WTO: Crisis and the Governance of Global Trade*, London: Routledge.

Wilkinson, Rorden (2012), 'Of butchery and bicycles: the WTO and the "death" of the Doha Development Agenda', *Political Quarterly*, **83** (2), 395–401.

Wilkinson, Rorden and James Scott (2008), 'Developing countries' participation in the GATT: a reassessment', *World Trade Review*, **7** (3), 473–510.

Woodward, Richard (2009), *The Organisation for Economic Co-operation and Development*, London: Routledge.

WTO (2012), 'WTO membership rises to 157 with entry of Russia and Vanuatu', Press Release, No. 671, 22 August.

11 The governance of primary commodities: biofuel certification in the European Union
Ben Richardson

Biofuels are transport fuels made largely from farm products such as maize, palm oil, rapeseed, sugarcane and soybean. Despite being promoted as a green alternative to fossil fuels they quickly became contentious among environmental campaigners, linked to deforestation, biodiversity loss and even increased greenhouse gas emissions. Responding to these concerns, the European Commission passed legislation in 2009 which required biofuels sold in the European Union (EU), including those imported from developing countries, to meet new, more demanding, sustainability standards. In its own words, this became 'the most comprehensive and advanced binding sustainability scheme of its kind anywhere in the world' (CEC 2010a: 1).

In two important ways, this legislation represented a watershed moment in the governance of primary commodities. First, the standards were applied not to the product itself but to the way it was produced, known in trade jargon as a 'process and production method'. This was significant given previous trade rulings under the General Agreement on Tariffs and Trade (GATT) and the World Trade Organization (WTO) which had made clear that discrimination in favour of 'dolphin-friendly' tuna and 'turtle-friendly' shrimp would be difficult to uphold. For some observers, discrimination in favour of 'eco-friendly' biofuels was simply the latest manifestation of green protectionism (Erixon 2012). Yet, to the extent that the EU has avoided legal challenge to its market access arrangement, it has suggested that an expanded remit for environmental stewardship within the multilateral trading system may be possible.

Second, accordance with the production standards would be monitored in a wholly novel way. Rather than relying on government legislation in third countries or inspections carried out by public agencies abroad (as the United States has), the EU chose to use certification systems. These are membership organisations typically composed of corporations and/or non-governmental organisation (NGOs) which devise their own standards against which producers are certified and then monitor compliance through site visits by impartial third-party auditors. Their use in this case thus led one scholar to label the EU's approach as 'regulatory outsourcing' to the private sector (Lin 2011).

At first glance, it might appear that these non-state certification systems have helped bridge the 'governance gap' between the supranational nature of ecological challenges such as biodiversity loss and the frequently ineffective attempts by international institutions to tackle them. Certainly, this has been the opinion of one of the leading NGO proponents of certification, the World Wide Fund for Nature (WWF). It has argued that, in the context of weak multilateral agreements on the environment, certification systems 'fill an important gap in the governance of natural resource use' and have 'raised the bar and contributed to strengthen and improve the regulatory and policy context for natural resource management' (WWF 2010a: 5). For others, the emergence of certification also suggested that a more consensual and scientific means of doing regulation was possible: one where attention could be focused on harmonisation of the various biofuel production standards and the methods of carbon foot-printing they relied on, rather than hard-nosed bargaining between states (IUCN 2010; UNCTAD 2008).

This chapter contests the benign view of governance underpinning this account. To begin, it establishes the role played by the European Union and its member-states in actively encouraging the formation of certification systems which they could then out-source functions to. State power remains crucial even for forms of non-state governance. Furthermore, rather than placating political opposition, this process has bifurcated it. While some NGOs such as the WWF have supported certification, others have claimed that the notion of sustainability on which it rests legitimises plantation production in the Global South whilst simultaneously denying the role of energy-intensive lifestyles in the Global North as a source of ecological crisis. Supporting this view, we argue that, while EU biofuel governance has partially tamed the production of primary commodities in developing countries, in so doing, it has also helped extend it.

The chapter proceeds by drawing on the existing literature on private governance to show how the twin concerns around the 'non-state' and 'market-driven' character of cer-tification systems have been discussed in relation to other primary commodity sectors. It then shows how the nascent biofuels market in the EU was undermined as these products became linked to rising food prices and environmental degradation, leading policy-makers to search for a more ambitious mode of governance to restore public faith in the project. Taking the insights from the literature review, the next two sections show how national governments helped 'ratchet up' the standards of certification systems which were then 'levelled down' by the EU, and how oppositional NGOs have since depicted them as 'smokescreens' which mask the bigger problems associated with biofuel produc-tion. A short conclusion then draws out the lessons of this case-study for our understand-ing of the contemporary international political economy of governance.

THE POLITICS OF PRIVATE CERTIFICATION AND NON-STATE GOVERNANCE

For scholars interested in the shift from government to governance, activity in the primary commodity sector has provided much food for thought. A variety of institu-tions have emerged over the last two decades that in one way or another have attempted to regulate corporate activity from 'beyond the state'. Examples include the Extractive Industries Transparency Initiative, which has encouraged oil, gas and mining companies to disclose their payments to governments; the UN Global Compact, which has aimed to instil values of good corporate citizenship among its multi-stakeholder membership; and the Kimberley Process, which has sought to identify 'blood diamonds' linked to armed conflict and put industry-led sanctions upon their trade (Haufler 2010; Woods 2002; Shaw 2003).

Despite the involvement of non-state actors and the use of 'soft law' compliance mech-anisms, these arrangements still included representatives of the state and/or were situ-ated in traditional intergovernmental forums. In contrast, other governance initiatives have had a purely private constitution, including, most notably, certification systems dealing with fair-trade, organic and food management standards. These self-regulating organisations have pulled businesses into their system of rule by relying on the desire of corporations to avoid reputational scandal and on the force of consumer demand for safe, sustainable and ethical products. This in turn provided the credible threat on which compliance with their respective standards has depended: expulsion from the scheme, accompanied by negative press and a loss of market share. Based on this particular make-up and mechanism of rule, these systems have been dubbed 'non-state market-driven' governance (Cashore 2002).

There were, of course, important differences identified between the individual systems. One of these was the mix of corporate and charitable actors that managed them. For instance, Fairtrade Labelling Organizations International (FLO) has traditionally been led by development NGOs, while the GlobalGAP farm management scheme has been led by Dutch and UK supermarkets. Another difference was the scope of retail sales they intended to cover. While the FLO targeted a middle-class niche with products from small-scale cooperatives, GlobalGAP effectively became a minimum requirement for any developing-country producer wishing to sell through multiple European retailers.

It is in this context that the Forest Stewardship Council (FSC) certification system must be understood, for it is one of the most ubiquitous case-studies in this field (see Auld and Gulbrandsen 2010; Bernstein and Cashore 2007). Bringing together a membership of major corporations and NGOs, subsequently known as a 'roundtable', the FSC seemed to encompass the best of both worlds. That is to say, it moved beyond the comfort-zone of business in tackling contentious practices such as illegal logging and deforestation, yet by virtue of its commercial orientation also targeted mainstream markets and now sees over US$20 billion of FSC-certified products sold per year (WWF 2010a: 31). Based on the success of this experiment, one of the founder members of the FSC, the WWF, came to launch roundtable certification systems for other commodities, including palm oil, sugarcane, soybeans and biofuels – each of which would later enter the world of EU biofuel governance.

In thinking about the politics of certification systems, many scholars have used the conceptual prism of legitimacy. As Ruggie (1982: 380) argued in the context of intergovernmental regimes, authority rests on a form of legitimacy that could only be derived from a 'community of interests'. Applied to the particular community relevant for certified products, it thus suggested that, unless NGOs and consumer-citizens saw the standards of production and rules of enforcement as justified, they were unlikely to function effectively. This led the FSC and its emulators to set themselves higher requirements for inclusiveness, transparency and accountability vis-à-vis existing forms of primary commodity governance (Bernstein and Cashore 2007). In practice, this meant the adoption of a member-based organisational form designed to facilitate input from groups in developing countries and/or with smaller budgets, the open publication of audit reports carried out on producers, and the tacit acceptance that NGO members would withdraw support should egregious environmental degradation and human rights violations not be prevented.

The conceptual focus on legitimacy has also been prominent within the literature on biofuels. For instance, Upham et al. (2011) have argued that, given the limited knowledge about the impacts of biofuels and the complexity of the policy arena, regulatory co-production between scientists and academics and the policy-making community was needed to provide the requisite cognitive legitimacy upon which a mandate for sustainability governance could be based. Looking at the certification systems themselves, Partzsch (2011) also noted that more developing-country producers and oppositional civil society groups needed to be drafted into the membership to make them representative, and that accountability processes beyond internal complaints procedures and the threat of NGO withdrawal had to be fostered.

While governments are not considered unimportant within this perspective, they have been cast as somewhat passive actors. As Hall (2010) has noted, states have often been written into the private governance story only in the context of trade liberalisation and deregulation, framed as a retreat from active economic management and another signal of the shift from public to private forms of standardisation, third-party monitoring and self-regulation. Again, this is reflected in the literature on biofuels, where authority has been depicted as a zero-sum contest which the state is losing, or at least conceding, due to globalisation and the de-territorialisation of the biofuels production network (Mol 2010).

Uneasy at this characterisation of 'the state in retreat', a number of scholars have questioned the 'non-state' credentials of certification systems. As Vandergeest (2007: 1154) put it, 'the idea that regulation is private, non-state and market driven assumes a clear separation between state and market, or public and private – a distinction that is difficult to sustain when examining specific examples of certification'. Exploring this theme, Hall (2010: 828) outlined three ways in which governments have purposefully advanced privatised forms of primary commodity governance. These were: (1) choosing to withdraw from particular markets and shift responsibility for expensive, difficult and controversial regulatory tasks onto others; (2) introducing new regulatory measures which, intentionally or not, stimulated the uptake of private standards and 'eco-labels'; and (3) providing direct support for the development of private governance through financial subsidies, network infrastructure, public research and discursive support.

Relevant to our study of roundtable certifications systems, Bell and Hindmoor (2011) have shown how important mechanism (2) above has been in the expansion of the FSC label in the UK and USA. In the former, the UK government's Forestry Commission helped negotiate the Woodland Assurance Scheme with environmentalists and landowners. Though this did not explicitly require FSC certification, since the scheme drew upon the FSC's own sustainability criteria, it meant that the FSC was in prime position to offer the auditing and traceability services to forestry companies once they were obliged to meet the UK's new standard. In the US, a similar but unintentional outcome followed the country's trade ban on illegally harvested wood. Not only did this prevent competition with the US timber industry from disreputable loggers, but it also required importing firms to undertake time-consuming and costly exercises in demonstrating the legality of their more reputable suppliers. Again, this created an opportunity for the FSC to provide buyers with a credible means of proving that the wood they had sourced was sustainably produced.

Such insights are useful for understanding how non-state governance has emerged through 'positive-sum' forms of public–private interaction. I return to this theme later in relation to the role of the state in shaping biofuel certification systems and their adoption by industry. However, this particular critique has had less to say about the purpose to which 'hybrid' governance is put and the mode of accumulation it underpins. As Payne

(2005: 78) has noted, within governance scholarship the notion that a clear separation exists between the public and the private is a classic feature of liberal thinking, and it has been the very liberalism of 'non-state market-driven' governance that others have sought to interrogate.

While some analysts have depicted certification systems as a means of re-embedding the economy in the Polanyian sense (Raynolds 2000; Watson 2006), others have been more wary of the compromises made in order to effect change through the market. For example, Ponte (2008) has noted how the Marine Stewardship Council, modelled on the FSC, has not attempted to redistribute wealth within the commodity chain. Rather, the requirement to provide large volumes of sustainably caught fish at no extra cost has acted as a barrier to entry to developing-country fisheries, especially the smallest among these, effectively putting 'certified sustainability at the service of dominant firms in the industry' (Ponte 2008: 171). Djama and Daviron (2010) suggest that this corporate orientation stems from the managerial perspective taken by professional NGOs involved in the schemes; the very same actors supposed to protect certification from capture by business interests.

Placing certification in the context of neoliberalism, Loconto and Busch (2010) offered the timely reminder that the ultimate objective of neoliberal policy, whether public- or private-led, is not to dispense with rules and laws, but rather to reorient them from a regulation of the market toward a regulation for the market. In this respect, Paterson's work on standards and certification in carbon markets is especially useful. In it he has made the case that this form of governance emerged precisely to deflect broader criticism that the marketisation of the environment had resulted in 'climate fraud' and 'carbon colonialism', whereby inaccurate emissions savings were claimed and the burden of adjustment forced upon developing countries. Thus, rather than constituting the second half of a Polanyian 'double movement', certification served as the very basis on which the carbon-trading industry was able to sustain support for the commodification of greenhouse gas emissions and their attendant profit-making opportunities (Paterson 2010: 362). This is particularly apposite to the case of biofuels, which like carbon was also a newly established and politically dependent EU commodity market. I later show how some NGOs have made the same criticism of certification in this industry too – that is, that non-state governance has been used to legitimise the expansion of harmful market activity, rather than rein it in – but first turn to the creation of the EU biofuel market to demonstrate its contingent and contested nature.

BUILDING A BIOFUEL MARKET IN THE EUROPEAN UNION

Biofuels were introduced to the EU policy debate in the late 1990s, framed very much as a measure to help meet the emission-reduction goals of the Kyoto Protocol. In a White Paper on energy, the European Commission noted how the transport sector contributed around a fifth of all greenhouse gas emissions in the EU and suggested that renewable fuel consumption should be doubled to try and reduce this (CEC 1997). With support from a coalition of farmers and crop processors, biotech and oil companies, and initially Green parties and NGOs as well, a range of EU-wide policies followed in the early 2000s. These included €3 billion of research funding for green technologies, tax breaks for companies that sold renewable fuels, and an indicative target for biofuel consumption set at 5.75 per cent of total transport fuel usage. Tariffs were also maintained to help European-based producers meet at least some of this demand, though it was considered by the Commission both 'likely and desirable' that imports would play a big part too (Oosterveer and Mol 2010: 68).

Writing the consumption target into national statute, some member-states introduced laws which obliged fuel suppliers to blend a minimum amount of biofuel into their petrol and diesel. The UK's 2005 Renewable Transport Fuel Obligation (RTFO), for example, required fuel providers to blend an increasing amount every year and gave them official credits for doing so. If these companies failed to meet the annual targets, they would either have to purchase surplus credits off other suppliers or else buy themselves out of their obligation by effectively paying a government fine.

Despite these various measures, it was clear by the mid-2000s that the EU as a whole would not reach its 5.75 per cent target. This led the Commission to promote mandatory rather than indicative targets, with the change ultimately brought into being as part of the EU Renewable Energy Directive in 2009. This also increased the target itself, from 5.75 per cent to 10 per cent biofuel usage by 2020. This political commitment sent a clearer message to investors that a European biofuel market would become a commercial reality, and indeed consumption increased from 1 per cent in 2005 to 4 per cent by 2009 – a market worth some €8 billion, of which roughly €3 billion came via public subsidies (CEC 2010b; Jung et al. 2010).

Several concerns were raised from the outset, including whether there would be enough land available to grow the extra crops needed (Monbiot 2004), and the Commission admitted that the negative effects of biofuels did need 'specific investigation and quantification and, if necessary, should be addressed through strong regulatory frameworks' (CEC 2006: 7). However, corporations opposed this virulently. Examining industry responses to the Commission's consultation on potential safeguards, the NGO Biofuelwatch (2006: 6) found that, while there was near unanimous support that biofuels were a good way to tackle climate change, so too was there near total rejection of any mandatory safeguards to ensure they made good on this promise. Reflecting this resistance to immediate, binding and publicly negotiated rules, the Commission's Biofuels Progress Report only mentioned sustainability standards in passing, as something 'that requires further study' (CEC 2007: 11).

This position became untenable as biofuels encountered a series of stinging attacks. Along with contributing to the reduction of greenhouse gas emissions, they had also been advanced as a way to boost agricultural demand and thereby support farmers. And indeed, after two decades of dwindling world market prices, the cost of agricultural commodities spiked in 2007, providing an opportunity for producers, especially the largest among them, to increase output and redirect it to the highest bidder. However, the flip-side to this was the effects on consumers, especially those dependent on cheap cereal imports from developing countries. The Food and Agriculture Organization (FAO 2008: 6) calculated that, in that year alone, an additional 75 million people were unable to afford basic staples as a result of this sudden inflation, pushing the total number of malnourished people globally toward 1 billion. As food riots from Mexico to Mozambique heightened tensions, fingers were pointed at biofuels for diverting crops into non-food markets. Most controversially, Jean Ziegler, the United Nations Special

Rapporteur on the Right to Food, called them a 'crime against humanity' and requested an immediate moratorium on their production (Ferrett 2007). The UN was followed by other international organisations such as the World Bank, which despite political pressure from the US to withhold its findings, published a damning report suggesting that biofuels had been responsible for 75 per cent of the rise in food prices (Chakrabortty 2008). Despite the defence offered by politicians in biofuel-exporting countries – George Bush in the US and Lula in Brazil among them – the debate quickly crystallised into one of 'food versus fuel', with critics pointing out that the same amount of maize needed to fill a sports utility vehicle with biofuel could otherwise feed a person for an entire year (Grunwald 2008).

The second attack on biofuels concerned their environmental credentials. It had already been established that different crops produced different greenhouse gas emissions savings, with US-grown maize faring particularly badly given the large amounts of fossil fuel that went into its cultivation. However, what was raised in a pair of widely cited scientific papers was the additional impact of land-use change (Fargione et al. 2008; Searchinger et al. 2008). This had two elements. Direct land-use change involved the clearance of land with high carbon stocks for new 'greenfield' biofuel production sites, resulting in a massive release of CO_2 into the atmosphere. It was claimed that if the palm oil industry in Southeast Asia expanded into peatland tropical forest, as was alleged to have been happening, it would create a carbon deficit that would take over 400 years to pay back through the use of the resultant biofuel (Fargione et al. 2008). Indirect land-use change involved the expansion of cropland to fill the supply gaps created by other farmers selling into the biofuel market. Crucially, this could happen anywhere in the world, so the decision by a farmer in Germany to divert rapeseed oil into the biofuel market, for example, could lead another in Guatemala to expand into forested land to grow vegetable oil for the food market. Initial attempts to factor the effects of land displacement into the life-cycle assessment of biofuel greenhouse gas emissions again suggested that their environmental benefits had been grossly exaggerated.

The mounting criticisms around these knock-on effects on food prices and land-use change were addressed in the high-profile Gallagher Review, undertaken by the UK government's Renewable Fuels Agency (RFA). This concluded that:

> There is a future for a sustainable biofuels industry but feedstock production must avoid agricultural land that would otherwise be used for food production. This is because the displacement of existing agricultural production, due to biofuel demand, is accelerating land-use change, and, if left unchecked, will reduce biodiversity and may even cause greenhouse gas emissions rather than savings. (RFA 2008: 8)

The UK's Renewable Transport Fuel Obligation was amended in light of this, pushing back the date by which the 5 per cent national target had to be met from 2010 to 2013. In order to mitigate the worst excesses of biofuel production, the Review also recommended the promotion of 'second-generation' biofuels made from non-food crops such as straw and grasses, that 'idle and marginal land' be targeted for cultivation, and that sustainability reporting be made mandatory and its criteria strengthened.

Politically, the Gallagher Review helped stake out some common ground on which the industry and NGOs began to interact. The UK biofuel association, for example, acknowledged that there were 'good and bad biofuels', with bad ones being those produced with grossly exploited labour, on deforested land, and with low greenhouse gas emissions savings (Renewable Energy Association 2008). This can be read as an admission that the biofuels project as a whole was facing a legitimacy crisis, and an attempt to 'decontaminate' British-grown biofuels by blaming those producers working under lax national regulation for the problems. For their part, some of the large NGOs began to encourage importing countries to build 'international sustainability standards' and also saw an opportunity to engage with biofuel producers (Oxfam 2008: 37). One appeal came from the recently inaugurated Roundtable for Sustainable Biofuels (RSB), which brought together over 300 experts from academic organisations, civil society groups and corporations, including multinationals such as BP and Shell, the oil companies which would ultimately have to source and sell the biofuel. In language directly mirroring that from industry, the Chair of the RSB, former Director-General of WWF International Claude Martin, declared:

> With all of the mixed messages we hear about biofuels, there is a clear need for a standard that can differentiate the good from the bad ... For an issue of such seminal importance, it was necessary to bring many different stakeholder groups together to agree on how to define and measure sustainable biofuels. (WWF 2008)

Just a few years later, those standards devised and administered by private certification systems would become the pre-eminent means of monitoring EU-bound biofuels.

THE MISNOMER OF NON-STATE GOVERNANCE: THE PLANNED ADOPTION OF PRIVATE CERTIFICATION SYSTEMS

Many accounts hold the driving force behind the rise of non-state governance in biofuels to have been consumer demand for environmentally and socially responsible products in the absence of strong domestic and international regulation (Kaphengst et al. 2009; Mol 2010). The previous section made the case that it was advocacy groups and environmental scientists that instigated the demand for governance; this section now shows how public authorities were instrumental in the provision of private certification systems which would ultimately deliver this. Two stages are discerned: the development phase (2005–09) and the adoption phase (2009 onward). Different state policies and mechanisms were at work in each. In the development phase, it was the use of government 'meta-standards' and benchmarking which established not just comparability of certification systems but also their credibility. In the adoption phase, it was EU legislation which mandated a form of due diligence on biofuel production processes, akin to the UK experience of the Forest Stewardship Council outlined earlier.

Development Phase (2005–09)

Meta-standards have been central to biofuel governance in the EU. They work by defining acceptable production processes according to a set of criteria against which existing certification systems and their respective standards are benchmarked. To become a 'qualifying standard', therefore, a minimum number of these meta-standard criteria must be met. They were used to provide an objective means by which the community of interests, to use Ruggie's term, could compare different standards. Moreover, they also allowed states to step back from endorsing one particular scheme or model of production; a useful way of steering clear of WTO rules which prohibit the use of state-defined technical regulations to discriminate against imports. Once benchmarked, public scrutiny could be harnessed to put weaker schemes under pressure to try and justify their lower standards. In this way, they could be ratcheted up to equivalence with the 'best in show', as happened in the forestry sector (Overdevest 2010). By the same token, fuel suppliers could also be 'named and shamed' for using low or non-qualifying standards, or even worse, for failing to report on the sustainability of their biofuel altogether.

Biofuel meta-standards were developed by public agencies in Germany, the Netherlands and the United Kingdom, with the latter the first to introduce benchmarking. As shown in Table 11.1, the UK's meta-standard had five environmental principles and two social principles, with a range of more specific criteria against which each principle could be measured. The carbon criteria covered minimum greenhouse gas emissions savings. The Roundtable for Sustainable Biofuels, as well as the crop-specific roundtables covering biofuels made from palm oil, sugarcane and soybean, were all benchmarked against these principles, along with industry-led certification systems designed essentially for domestic producers.

This process did not simply provide a common framework for assessment, but also actively involved UK state departments, especially the Renewable Fuels Agency, in shaping the content of the private certification systems. This happened through: (1) selecting the meta-standard criteria against which certification systems would later adjust themselves; (2) establishing and participating in the policy networks that provided evidence for this decision; (3) building methodological norms around supply-chain

Table 11.1   Meta-standard of the UK's Renewable Transport Fuel Obligation (RTFO)

Carbon criteria	Environmental principles	Social principles
1. Biofuel production should save 40 per cent greenhouse gas emissions compared to fossil fuels by 2008–09, rising to 50 per cent by 2010–11	1. Biofuel production does not destroy or damage large above- or below-ground carbon stocks 2. Biofuel production does not lead to the destruction of or damage to high biodiversity areas 3. Biofuel production does not lead to soil degradation 4. Biofuel production does not lead to the contamination or depletion of water sources 5. Biofuel production does not lead to air pollution	1. Biofuel production does not adversely affect workers' rights and working relationships 2. Biofuel production does not adversely affect existing land rights or community relations

Source: RFA (2011: 64).

auditing and carbon footprinting that were incorporated into many of the standards; and (4) liaising with the certification systems directly to provide recommendations on what they would need to do to become compliant with meta-standards in the UK and, later, the EU.

This facilitative approach spread beyond the UK to other EU member-states. The development of the UK principles for the RTFO meta-standard was the subject of regular discussion with the Dutch government, with the aim of aligning carbon calculation methodology and environmental criteria (Wallis and Chalmers 2007). This alliance was important, given that the two countries were the biggest importers of biofuel into the EU, and also home to the bloc's biggest oil companies, BP and Shell. The two governments, together with the FSC and WWF, had already commissioned studies on biofuel sustainability, one of which concluded that 'a situation in which each country has its own national scheme in place is likely to be inefficient, less effective, and will constrain the international development of the bioenergy sector' (Dehue et al. 2007: 61). Following the Cramer Commission – a Dutch enquiry into biofuel sustainability standards – it became apparent that the Netherlands had shifted toward the British approach, asking fuel suppliers to report on an almost identical set of criteria.

The UK approach was intended to utilise and further encourage the development of certification systems with ambitious sustainability standards and robust auditing procedures (interview, UK Department for Transport, 2011). This it did successfully. Where it was more limited was in getting these certification systems to be adopted within the various biofuel supply chains. To receive an RTFO credit a fuel supplier had to report monthly on their performance, referring to the extent to which they met criteria on greenhouse gas intensity and land-use, the level of data accuracy, and whether they were compliant with a qualifying standard. However, to encourage their uptake the UK relied on disclosure and disapproval, rather than any formal sanctions. Thus, despite naming and shaming certain suppliers, at the end of the second year of the RTFO, 63 per cent of biofuel sold in the UK did not meet any sustainability standard and 14 per cent was not even traceable to a particular country (RFA 2011: 17). Since palm oil biofuel was especially contentious, effort was made to encourage use of the Roundtable on Sustainable Palm Oil (RSPO) system in particular, with the UK government asking companies to reveal the proportion sourced from RSPO-compliant plantations and the Dutch government even going as far as to make this a national requirement. But, ultimately, the voluntary benchmarking approach taken could only really cajole biofuel exporters into agreeing to apply sustainability standards. The key to their widespread adoption was the imminent introduction of mandatory EU regulation.

Adoption Phase (2009 Onward)

Biofuel standards had faded from the Commission's agenda during the mid-2000s, but the combination of recommendations from EU heads of state that sustainability issues be addressed and pressure from the European Parliament that binding regulation on their social and environmental impacts was needed put the issue back on centre stage (Gilbertson et al. 2007). Although the European Parliament pushed for this to be included in the EU's Fuel Quality Directive, a legislative act setting common standards for petrol and diesel, it was addressed in the Renewable Energy Directive (RED) instead.

Table 11.2 Meta-standard of the EU's Renewable Energy Directive (RED)

Carbon criteria	Environmental criteria	Social criteria
1. Biofuel production must save 35 per cent greenhouse gas emissions compared to fossil fuels, rising to 50 per cent by 2017, and for those installations built after this date, 60 per cent	1. Biofuel shall not be made from raw material obtained from land with high biodiversity value – including primary forest, protected areas and highly biodiverse grassland 2. Biofuel shall not be made from raw material obtained from land with high carbon stock – including wetlands and continuously forested areas 3. Biofuel shall not be made from raw material obtained from land that was peatland	No compulsory criteria

Source: European Parliament and the Council of the European Union (2009: Article 17).

This was led by the Directorate-General (DG) Energy rather than DG Environment, and soon enough principles relating to excessive water use, soil degradation, rising food prices and the displacement of indigenous people were all swept off the policy table.

As this broader notion of sustainability attenuated, the carbon balance of biofuels and protection of pristine land emerged as the main issues to be managed. Passed by the Commission in April 2009, the Renewable Energy Directive thus required biofuels to provide at least 35 per cent greenhouse gas emission savings compared to fossil fuels and insisted that they did not come from crops cultivated on land with a high biodiversity value or high carbon stock. As shown in Table 11.2, this essentially replicated the carbon criteria and environmental principles 1 and 2 from the RTFO, which along with the Dutch initiative had provided the Commission with a practical example to follow (interview, UK Department for Transport, 2011; Oosterveer and Mol 2010: 74).

Two crucial differences with the approach taken by member-states were that all the criteria in the EU meta-standard had to be met (although there were less of them) and that these were now mandatory requirements. A failure to meet this new standard did not mean that biofuel could not be sold in the EU, only that it would not count against the binding energy targets of member-states nor qualify for tax relief. Nevertheless, since these incentives were so important within the biofuel market (recall the €3 billion subsidy supporting the industry), the Renewable Energy Directive effectively constituted a de facto market-access requirement.

To provide assurance that its meta-standard was being met, the EU chose to rely on the same certification systems that had been cultivated over the past few years. As noted in the introductory section of the chapter, this was a hugely significant public policy development. Just a few years before this official delegation of powers, the European Commission had abandoned an initiative to devise a guideline simply to help consumers select between various eco-labels, deciding that it was an inappropriate activity to undertake and unduly discriminatory (Bernstein and Hannah 2008). Now these certification systems had been made the watchdogs of the biofuels trade, with the coverage of certain schemes blossoming as a result. The sugarcane roundtable, Bonsucro, for example, had 12 of Brazil's biggest sugarcane mills certify their output in 2011 alone, all of which undertook this process essentially to rubber-stamp the entry of their biofuel into the EU.

So, in sum, to suggest that non-state governance usurped authority from state actors in this case would be quite misleading. Rather, encouraged by opportunistic NGOs and accepted by an industry under fire, certification systems were deployed by European state authorities as a means of tacking a route through domestic pressure for environmental safeguards on the one hand, and their commitments to the letter of WTO law on the other. Moreover, in so doing, they discharged the cost of applying sustainability standards onto the certification systems themselves, which would in turn pass this on to the farmers and agro-industrialists that became certified suppliers.

CONTESTING BIOFUEL CERTIFICATION: THE CARBONISATION OF SUSTAINABILITY AND THE SMOKESCREEN OF GOVERNANCE

As discussed above, state policy-makers were acutely aware of the potential illegality of discriminating against 'unsustainable' biofuels. Warnings continually circulated through international organisations such as the Organisation for Economic Co-operation and Development (OECD) on the 'question of if, and under what design criteria, trade rules should be allowed to exclude fuels that fail to meet minimum performance levels from mandatory schemes or preferential tax treatments' (Doornbusch and Steenblik 2007; see also UNCTAD 2008; WTO 2010). Indeed, when the discussion of standards first began in Europe, the Commission made clear that 'any system of certificates would need to apply in a non-discriminatory way to both domestically produced and imported biofuels and comply with WTO provisions' (CEC 2006: 8). For these reasons, the Commission never entertained the prospect of banning outright biofuel that did not meet the required criteria (interview, UK Department for Energy and Climate Change, 2011). Nor did it place any social principles in the meta-standard, which it felt would 'overstep some countries' red lines' and thereby lead to an action being brought against the EU at the WTO (Ackrill and Kay 2011: 560).

It has generally been assumed in the biofuels literature that avoiding WTO disputes is a good thing, since it creates scope to marry stronger regulation with a commitment to free trade. However, concern has been raised in practice that the process of ensuring WTO compatibility has led the European Commission to undercut existing standards. While the roundtable certification systems included social principles related to human rights and labour standards, the EU rejected any such requirements in its own meta-standard. This led to watered-down standards being developed which simply met the bare minimum. Indeed, two of the seven systems initially approved by the Commission lacked any social component at all: those industry-led ones developed for the French and Spanish markets respectively. Since these systems could in principle be used by biofuel exporters in all crop sectors and geographical regions, it was suggested that producers might adopt or switch to these less stringent options to gain easier access to the EU market (German and Schoneveld 2011). As the UK's own Renewable Fuels Agency recognised, the EU's 'requirements are primarily focused on avoiding the worst practices rather than promoting the best' (RFA 2011: 7). In other words, this would level down the gains that had just been made through ratcheting up.

Reaction to this problem varied. As a founder member of the roundtables, the WWF called for a framework to assess the credibility of certification schemes, implying that the familiar mechanisms of comparison and disclosure could push biofuel suppliers and producers into more stringent certification systems, preferably its own. Other NGOs called for social sustainability criteria to be added to the RED, particularly given the emerging scandal of 'land grabbing', the term used to describe the large-scale and unjust forms of land acquisition taking place in the Global South for the purposes of plantation production (Oxfam 2011). Finally, NGOs with a more antagonistic relationship to the biofuels industry – including ClientEarth, Friends of the Earth Europe and the Corporate Europe Observatory – actually took the Commission to court for failing to provide information on why particular certification systems had managed to gain approval (BusinessGreen 2011).

Underlying disappointment in the Commission's approach was discontent over the continued deference to WTO law. For some oppositional NGOs, this was considered a cynical move that allowed policy-makers to claim that they were unable to introduce measures regulating the social impacts of biofuels, despite the fact that the EU was a key player in writing these rules in the first place (Gilbertson et al. 2007: 46). Support for this scepticism over the limited availability of policy-space could be found in the reactions of developing countries to the EU RED. Brazil, an active user of the WTO dispute-settlement mechanism in other primary commodity sectors, has not threatened such action in relation to biofuels, most probably because the trade association of its sugarcane industry was a founder member of the Bonsucro certification system and, in that respect, was already signed up to more ambitious sustainability standards. This could also apply to Malaysia, which fired a warning shot across the bows of the EU but has yet to take remedial action, possibly pacified by the later acceptance of the RSPO as a qualifying certification system in 2012; an organisation co-founded by the Malaysian Palm Oil Association. Finally, while Argentina has initiated a WTO dispute against the EU, this was targeted specifically at the Spanish interpretation of the directive and its blanket discrimination against non-EU biofuels, rather than the EU RED itself for introducing minimum standards. In short, the criticism was that the EU's meta-standard unnecessarily focused on a narrow band of criteria that resulted in the 'carbonisation' of sustainability, reducing the notion of sustainability largely to the question of greenhouse gas emissions to the detriment of other social and environmental goals.

Another, more radical line of critique stemmed from the suggestion that, even if the standards of roundtable certification systems had not been undercut, they would still be ineffective as tools of governance. As noted previously, many NGOs had used the indirect effects of increasing food prices and land-use change as a means of challenging the biofuels project. To this end they argued that certification would be:

> Unable to solve indirect issues such as rising commodity prices or displacement effects [i.e. indirect land-use change] . . . The new plantation could be certified as 'sustainable' but if it has simply pushed other farming activities into sensitive areas then this makes a mockery of any certification scheme. This is a major failing that is unlikely to ever be solved by certification schemes. (Bebb, cited in ICTSD 2008)

Oppositional NGOs therefore rounded on this approach as a 'smokescreen' of the industry (Friends of the Earth 2008). Whereas 'greenwash' involves the deceptive use of marketing to make a product or company appear environmentally friendly, 'smokescreens' act to conceal from view the harmful activities in which they are engaged. Thus, the argument was made that debates over what should be included in a sustainability standard distracted from the bigger point: the fact that the most egregious impacts of biofuels could not be governed in this manner at all (World Rainforest Movement 2008).

As the spatial mismatch between 'farm-level' certification systems and the 'off-farm' effects of biofuel became apparent, two evolutions took place. The first was an attempt by some of the roundtables and their advocates, given that they could not outright prevent these negative trends from happening, to ameliorate or mitigate them instead. The RSB, for instance, included a principle in its standard which required biofuel producers to 'ensure the human right to adequate food and improve food security in food insecure regions' (RSB 2010). This placed a responsibility on companies to support the rural communities around their production site to feed themselves, say, through the sponsorship of agricultural support programmes. With regards to land-use change, the WWF argued that, if biofuel production took place on 'unused land' or used high-yielding crops, it would displace less land elsewhere. To this end it put forward a set of criteria that could be incorporated into certification systems to help distinguish biofuel that had a 'minimum risk' of indirect effects on food prices and conversion of pristine land to farming (WWF 2010b).

The second evolution was the re-entry of the state into the biofuels debate, despite previous efforts to delegate governance to non-state actors. The European Commission came under increasing pressure from civil society to reassess the green credentials of biofuels in light of the effects of indirect land-use change. However, facing complexities in accurately calculating these effects, as well as complaints from biofuel producers that they would be unduly punished for outcomes beyond their control, the Commission declined to count indirect effects against the official greenhouse gas emissions savings of biofuels. In its 2012 proposal to amend the RED, it recommended instead a cap on the use of biofuels made from food crops (limited to 5 per cent of the 10 per cent target) and more incentives for biofuels made from non-food crops such as grasses and algae (CEC 2012: 3). This fudging left few satisfied. The European biofuels industry complained that the proposals constituted 'a wholesale withdrawal of political support from the Commission' and would deter investment in the sector; NGOs countered that conventional biofuels produced within the 5 per cent limit would continue to cause upward pressure on food prices and land conversion (Nelson 2012).

With the Commission caught between a rock and a hard place, the UK for its part again slowed down its trajectory toward the EU requirement of 10 per cent biofuel consumption by 2020, leaving its national requirement of 5 per cent in place until at least 2014. With not some little irritation, the Under-Secretary of State for Transport, Norman Baker, said that:

> I listened when environmental pressure groups said that biofuels were the best thing since sliced bread; and I listen to them now when they express significant concerns about their sustainability . . . [UK policy] is about making biofuels more sustainable; it is not about supplying more biofuel. (Hansard 2011)

Yet, for some, this did not go far enough: without accounting for indirect land-use change, the sustainability and significant carbon savings of biofuels could not be guaranteed. From this position, the priority was to abandon biofuels targets wholesale and tackle climate change imperatives through the electrification of the transport system, promotion of effective renewable energy sources, and reductions in fuel demand (Friends of the Earth et al. 2011).

In this sense, these oppositional NGOs drew little distinction between the sources of governance in biofuels (state or non-state), but instead condemned the very essence of the project, which they saw as an attempt to incorporate ever-more land into monoculture production for the benefit of the Global North, including the urban middle classes in countries such as Brazil. In this view, not only were the indirect effects of biofuels virtually ungovernable, but the labour-expelling production systems adopted by the majority of agricultural exporters meant that the rural poor gained little from the conversion of traditional farming systems into capital-intensive plantations anyway, even if (technocratic) sustainability standards were adhered to. It was precisely the commodification of land and labour in this way that was deemed problematic, regardless of whether the cash crops grown ended up as biofuel, food or animal feed. The certification of biofuels, to the extent that it made this endeavour publically palatable, was seen merely to aid the expansion of agro-industry in the Global South.

CONCLUSION

Speaking at a symposium on Trade, Sustainability and Global Governance, Ruggie identified two kinds of governance gaps that had to be bridged:

> One consists of the gaps between the scope and complexity of the challenges we face, including environmental threats, and the institutional means through which we strive to deal with them. The other concerns a growing imbalance in global rulemaking. Those rules that favour global market expansion have become more robust and enforceable in the last decade or two . . . But rules intended to promote equally valid social objectives, be they poverty reduction, labour standards, human rights or environmental quality, lag behind and in some instances have actually been weakened. (Ruggie 2002: 2297–8)

This chapter has argued that, in relation to biofuels, private certification systems have helped span the first gap, but failed to bridge the second. With respect to the responsiveness of governance, I have argued that certification systems, in tandem with EU legislation, have proven a timely and institutionally innovative way of applying minimum standards to biofuel production. Certainly, they have offered a more robust alternative to the major intergovernmental initiative in this area, led by the Group of 8+5 countries, which has so far only offered a best-practice guide to national policy-makers. The main analytical point I stressed was that this innovation should not be equated with a swing away from the public sphere and toward the private. Rather, states have acted as advocates for private standards and been involved in shaping the way in which they have governed by providing techniques of calculation and undertaking benchmarking exercises. Most importantly for certification systems, the EU has underpinned their usage by outsourcing regulatory capacities to them, making their auditing services mandatory for all biofuel suppliers. However, with respect to the rule-making imbalance identified by Ruggie, while the type of governance adopted by the EU has attended to some environmental issues, it has marginalised land and labour issues and gone hand-in-hand with the growth of biofuel imports from developing countries. For this reason, sustainability standards have been criticised for facilitating the transformation of nature into primary commodities in the first place; that is, tradeable products subject to the price mechanism and put beyond the purchasing power of the world's poor. Recalling Paterson's findings in relation to carbon markets, in this view certification has served not so much to re-embed market exchange as to legitimise its extension.

Stepping back, two broader findings can be drawn out for the study of primary commodity governance more generally. The first relates to the scope for national protection of societal goods under international trade law. While many observers have suggested that the WTO has negated this goal in the name of free trade, this study suggests that it is possible to carve out policy space within the WTO's tightly written rulebook through the introduction of novel instruments. Yet, by the same token, this also happened within set parameters (i.e. no labour standards, no import bans) that were held up as a fixed reality, even in the absence of clear case law suggesting that more ambitious measures would not be permissible. The fact that this 'political reality' was also acknowledged by some NGOs such as the WWF indicates that the disciplinary power of the WTO has now spread beyond state bureaucracies and into the wider civil society arena.

The second finding relates to the delegation of power by the state to non-state actors. As used in the literature so far, the concept of regulatory outsourcing pertains to the initial transfer of defined duties and implies a likely de-politicisation of the issue as it becomes subject to technical deliberations away from the public eye. However, this chapter has shown that the process does not end there. While certification and 'eco-labelling' was adopted with much success in the forestry industry, those same instruments and policies were heavily contested when transplanted into the biofuels industry. A major reason was that, unlike the timber and paper market, the biofuel market was acutely dependent on government mandates and tax breaks; the implication being that if policy-makers really wanted to prevent deforestation, biodiversity loss and land grabbing, they should just pull the plug on their production incentives. Importantly, this meant that civil-society criticism was directed primarily at the EU and national governments, rather than the private certification systems these states had licensed. Any attempt by politicians to defuse debate by devolving responsibility had demonstrably failed. Looking forward, as these same European states consider applying certification governance to other primary commodities, such as palm oil used in food and woodchips used in power stations, we can anticipate that the perceived contingency of these markets will again shape its reception.

ACKNOWLEDGEMENTS

This chapter has benefited from conversations with Robert Ackrill and Adrian Kay as well as feedback from colleagues at the British International Studies Association panel at which it was presented in April 2011. It is part of a project on 'Social Justice in the Sugarcane Industry' funded by a Leverhulme Trust Early Career Fellowship.

REFERENCES

Ackrill, Robert and Adrian Kay (2011), 'EU Biofuels sustainability standards and certification systems – how to seek WTO-compatibility', *Journal of Agricultural Economics*, **62** (3), 551–64.

Auld, Graeme and Lars Gulbrandsen (2010), 'Transparency in nonstate certification: consequences for accountability and legitimacy', *Global Environmental Politics*, **10** (3), 97–119.

Bell, Stephen and Andrew Hindmoor (2011), 'Governance without government? The case of the Forest Stewardship Council', *Public Administration*, **90** (1), 144–59.

Bernstein, Steven and Benjamin Cashore (2007), 'Can non-state global governance be legitimate? An analytical framework', *Regulation and Governance*, **1** (4), 1–25.

Bernstein, Steven and Erin Hannah (2008), 'Non-state global standard setting and the WTO: legitimacy and the need for regulatory space', *Journal of International Economic Law*, **11** (3), 575–608.

Biofuelwatch (2006), 'How biofuel companies are lobbying against basic environmental safeguards: an analysis of industry responses to the EU Biofuel Directive Consultation 2006', report prepared for Biofuelwatch, 18 September, available at: http://www.biofuelwatch.org.uk/wp-content/uploads/biofuelindustryresponses.pdf (accessed 10 January 2012).

BusinessGreen (2011), 'Green groups take EU to court over biofuels – again', *Guardian*, 26 May, available at: http://www.guardian.co.uk/environment/2011/may/26/biofuels-energy (accessed 5 February 2012).

Cashore, Benjamin (2002), 'Legitimacy and the privatization of environmental governance: how non-state market-driven (NSMD) governance systems gain rule-making authority', *Governance: An International Journal of Policy, Administration, and Institutions*, **15** (4), 503–29.

Chakrabortty, Aditya (2008), 'Secret report: biofuel caused food crisis', *Guardian*, 3 July.

Commission of the European Communities (CEC) (1997), 'Energy for the future: renewable sources of energy', *White Paper for a Community Strategy and Action Plan*, COM(97)599, 26 November.

Commission of the European Communities (CEC) (2006), 'An EU strategy for biofuels', *Communication from the Commission*, COM(2006)34, 8 February.

Commission of the European Communities (CEC) (2007), 'Biofuels progress report', *Communication from the Commission to the Council and the European Union*, COM(2006) 845, 10 January.

Commission of the European Communities (CEC) (2010a), 'Communication from the European Commission on Voluntary Schemes and Default Values in the EU Biofuels and Bioliquids Sustainability Scheme', *Official Journal of the European Union*, 160/01, 19 June.

Commission of the European Communities (CEC) (2010b), 'Commission sets up system for certifying sustainable biofuels', Press Release, Memo/10/247, 10 June.

Commission of the European Communities (CEC) (2012), 'Proposal amending Directive 98/70/EC relating to the Quality of Petrol and Diesel Fuels and Directive 2009/28/EC on the Promotion of the Use of Energy from Renewable Sources', *Proposal from the Commission to the European Parliament and Council*, COM(2012) 595, 17 October.

Dehue, Bart, Sebastian Meyer and Carlo Hamelinck (2007), 'Towards a harmonised sustainable biomass certification scheme', Ecofys report commissioned by WWF, June, available at: http://www.ecofys.com/files/files/harmonisedsustainablebiomassscheme_final.pdf (accessed 5 October 2011).

Djama, Marcel and Benoît Daviron (2010), 'Managerial rationality and power reconfiguration in the multistakeholder initiatives for agricultural commodities: the case of the Roundtable for Sustainable Palm Oil', paper presented at the European Group for Organizational Studies summer workshop, Margaux, France, 26–28 May, available at: http://www.egosnet.org/jart/prj3/egosnet/data/uploads/OS%202010/W-031.pdf (accessed 12 January 2012).

Doornbosch, Richard and Ronald Steenblik (2007), 'Biofuels: is the cure worse than the disease?', report on the OECD Round Table on Sustainable Development, Paris, France, 11–12 September, available at: http://media.ft.com/cms/fb8b5078-5fdb-11dc-b0fe-0000779fd2ac.pdf (accessed 7 March 2012).

Erixon, Fredrik (2012), 'The rising trend of green protectionism: biofuels and the European Union', European Centre for International Political Economy (ECIPE) Occasional Paper, 2, available at: http://www.ecipe.org/media/publication_pdfs/OCC22012.pdf (accessed 1 November 2011).

European Parliament and the Council of the European Union (2009), 'Directive 2009/28/EC on the promotion of the use of energy from renewable sources', *Official Journal of the European Union*, **140** (16), 5 June, 16–62.

Fargione, Joseph, Jason Hill, David Tilman, Stephen Polasky and Peter Hawthorne (2008), 'Land clearing and the biofuel carbon debt', *Science*, 319 (5867), 1235–8.

Ferrett, Grant (2007), 'Biofuels a "crime against humanity"', *BBC News Online*, 27 October, available at: http://news.bbc.co.uk/1/hi/7065061.stm (accessed 8 October 2011).

Food and Agricultural Organization (FAO) (2008), *The State of Food Insecurity in the World 2008*, Rome: FAO.

Friends of the Earth (2008), *Sustainability as a Smokescreen: The Inadequacy of Certifying Fuels and Feeds*, Brussels: FoE.

Friends of the Earth, Royal Society for the Protection of Birds and ActionAid (2011), 'Biofuels in 2011: a briefing on the current state of biofuel policy in the UK and ways forward', FoE, RSPB and ActionAid Joint Policy Brief, available at: http://www.foe.co.uk/resource/briefing_notes/biofuels_in_2011_gathering.pdf (accessed 30 October 2011).

German, Laura and George Schoneveld (2010), 'Social sustainability of EU-approved voluntary schemes for biofuels: implications for rural livelihoods', Center for International Forestry Research (CIFOR) Working Paper, 75, available at: http://www.cifor.org/publications/pdf_files/WPapers/WP75German.pdf (accessed 13 November 2011).

Gilbertson, Tamra, Nina Holland, Stella Semino and Kevin Smith (2007), 'Paving the way for agrofuels: EU policy, sustainability criteria and climate calculations', Transnational Institute Discussion Paper, September, available at: http://www.tni.org/sites/www.tni.org/archives/agrofuels/pavingagrofuels.pdf (accessed 2 October 2011).

Grunwald, Michael (2008), 'The clean energy scam', *Time Magazine*, 27 March.

Hall, Derek (2010), 'Food with a visible face: traceability and the public promotion of private governance in the Japanese food system', *Geoforum*, **41** (5), 826–35.

Hansard (2011), House of Commons Debate, First Delegated Legislation Committee, Draft Renewable Transport Fuel Obligations (Amendment) Order 2011, 5 December, available at: http://www.publications.parliament.uk/pa/cm/cmtoday/cmstand/output/deleg/dg01111205-01.htm (accessed 3 March 2012).

Haufler, Virginia (2010), 'Disclosure as governance: the extractive industries transparency initiative and resource management in the developing world', *Global Environmental Politics*, **10** (3), 53–73.

International Centre for Trade and Sustainable Development (ICTSD) (2008), 'Biofuels and sustainability: is certification the answer?', *Bridges Trade BioRes Review*, **2** (2), available at: http://ictsd.org/i/news/bioresreview/12094/ (accessed 26 October 2011).

International Union for Conservation of Nature (IUCN) (2010), 'IUCN, Shell and Packard Foundation Host Workshop "Towards Harmonization for Biofuel Sustainability Standards"', *IUCN News*, 5 March, available at: http://www.iucn.org/what/tpas/energy/key/biofuels/?4856/harmonisationworkshop (accessed 4 February 2012).

Jung, Anna, Philipp Dörrenberg, Anna Rauch and Michael Thöne (2010), 'Biofuels – at what cost?', *Global Subsidies Initiative*, July, available at: http://www.iisd.org/gsi/sites/default/files/bf_eunion_2010update.pdf (accessed 3 March 2012).

Kaphengst, Timo, Mandy Ma and Stephanie Schlegel (2009), 'At a tipping point? How the debate on biofuel standards sparks innovative ideas for the general future of standardisation and certification schemes', *Journal of Cleaner Production*, **17**, S99–S101.

Lin, Jolene (2011), 'Governing biofuels: a principal–agent analysis of the European Union biofuels certification regime and the Clean Development Mechanism', *Journal of Environmental Law*, **24** (1), 43–73.

Loconto, Allison and Lawrence Busch (2010), 'Standards, techno-economic networks, and playing fields: performing the global market economy', *Review of International Political Economy*, **17** (3), 507–36.

Mol, Arthur (2010), 'Environmental authorities and biofuel controversies', *Environmental Politics*, **19** (1), 61–79.

Monbiot, George (2004), 'Fuel for nought', *Guardian*, 23 November, available at: http://www.guardian.co.uk/politics/2004/nov/23/greenpolitics.uk?INTCMP=SRCH (accessed 7 September 2011).

Nelson, Arthur (2012), 'EU calls time on first-generation biofuels', EurActiv, *News*, 18 October, available at: http://www.euractiv.com/climate-environment/eu-signals-generation-biofuels-news-515496 (accessed 3 January 2013).

Oosterveer, Peter and Arthur Mol (2010), 'Biofuels, trade and sustainability: a review of perspectives for developing countries', *Biofuels, Bioproducts and Biorefining*, **4**, 66–76.

Overdevest, Christine (2010), 'Comparing forest certification schemes: the case of ratcheting standards in the forest sector', *Socio-Economic Review*, **8** (1), 47–76.

Oxfam (2008), 'Another inconvenient truth: how biofuel policies are deepening poverty and accelerating climate change', Briefing Paper, 114, June, available at: http://www.oxfam.org.uk/resources/policy/climate_change/downloads/bp114_inconvenient_truth.pdf (accessed 5 November 2011).

Oxfam (2011), 'The EU must urgently fix biofuels policy driving scramble for land in poor countries', *Press Release*, 29 September 2011, available at: http://oxfameu.blogactiv.eu/2011/09/29/the-eu-must-urgently-fix-biofuels-policy-driving-scramble-for-land-in-poor-countries/ (accessed 10 January 2012).

Partzsch, Lena (2011), 'The legitimacy of biofuel certification', *Agriculture and Human Values*, **28** (3), 413–25.

Paterson, Matthew (2010), 'Legitimation and accumulation in climate change governance', *New Political Economy*, **15** (3), 345–68.

Payne, Anthony (2005), 'The study of governance in a global political economy', in Nicola Phillips (ed.) *Globalizing International Political Economy*, Basingstoke: Palgrave Macmillan, pp. 55–81.

Ponte, Stefano (2008), 'Greener than thou: the political economy of fish ecolabelling and its local manifestations in South Africa', *World Development*, **36** (1), 159–75.

Raynolds, Laura (2000), 'Re-embedding global agriculture: the international organic and fair trade movements', *Agriculture and Human Values*, **17** (3), 297–309.

Renewable Energy Association (2008), 'Government must not use Gallagher review as an excuse for inaction on climate change', REA Press Release, 2 July, available at: http://www.biofuelsnow.co.uk/press/pdf/18.pdf (accessed 10 September 2011).

Renewable Fuels Agency (RFA) (2008), *Gallagher Review of the Indirect Effects of Biofuels Production*, St Leonards-on-Sea, UK: RFA.

Renewable Fuels Agency (RFA) (2011), *Renewable Fuels Agency 2009/10 Annual Report to Parliament on the Renewable Fuel Transport Obligation*, London: Stationary Office Limited.

Roundtable on Sustainable Biofuels (2010), *RSB Principles and Criteria for Sustainable Biofuel Production*, Lausanne: RSB, available at: http://rsb.epfl.ch/files/content/sites/rsb2/files/Biofuels/Version%202/PCs%20V2/11-03-08%20RSB%20PCs%20Version%202.pdf (accessed 2 March 2012).

Ruggie, John Gerard (1982), 'International regimes, transactions, and change: embedded liberalism in the postwar economic order', *International Organization*, **36** (2), 379–415.

Ruggie, John Gerard (2002), 'Trade, sustainability and global governance', *Columbia Journal of Environmental Law*, **27** (2), 297–307.

Searchinger, Timothy, Ralph Heimlich, R. Houghton, Fengxia Dong, Amani Elobeid, Jacinto Fabiosa, Simla Tokgoz, Dermot Hayes and Tun-Hsiang Yu (2008), 'Use of US croplands for biofuels increases greenhouse gases through emissions from land-use change', *Science*, **319** (5867), 1238–40.

Shaw, Tim (2003), 'Regional dimensions of conflict and peace-building in contemporary Africa', *Journal of International Development*, **15**, 487–98.

United Nations Conference on Trade and Development (UNCTAD) (2008), *Making Certification Work for Sustainable Development: The Case of Biofuels*, Geneva: UNCTAD.

Upham, Paul, Julia Tomei and Leonie Dendler (2011), 'Governance and legitimacy aspects of the UK biofuel carbon and sustainability reporting system', *Energy Policy*, **39** (5), 2669–78.

Vandergeest, Peter (2007), 'Certification and communities: alternatives for regulating the environmental and social impacts of shrimp farming', *World Development*, **35** (7), 1152–71.

Wallis, Neil and Jessica Chalmers (2007), 'Environmental accreditation and carbon certification of biofuels for road transport – the UK experience', paper presented at the European Council for an Energy Efficient Economy conference, La Colle sur Loup, France, June, available at: http://www.lowcvp.org.uk/assets/reports/Eceee%20Biofuels%20%28Wallis%20&%20Chalmers%29%20Final%20%28May%2007%29.pdf (accessed 20 November 2011).

Watson, Matthew (2006), 'Towards a Polanyian perspective on fair trade: market-based relationships and the act of ethical consumption', *Global Society*, **20** (4), 435–51.

Woods, Ngaire (2002), 'Global governance and the role of institutions', in David Held and Anthony McGrew (eds), *Governing Globalization*, Cambridge: Polity Press, pp. 25–45.

World Rainforest Movement (2008), 'Why certification of agrofuels won't work', *WRM Bulletin*, 135, available at: http://www.wrm.org.uy/bulletin/135/viewpoint.html.

World Trade Organization (WTO) (2010), 'Biofuel subsidies and standards: WTO considerations', report on Session 35, Sub-Theme 2, of the WTO Public Forum on New Forces Shaping World Trade, Geneva, Switzerland, 17 February, available at: www.wto.org/english/forums_e/public_forum10_e/session35_summ_e.doc-2010-11-05 (accessed 17 February 2012).

World Wide Fund for Nature (WWF) (2008), 'Towards a biofuel standard to sort the green from the ungreen', Press Release, 13 August, available at: http://wwf.panda.org/index.cfm?uNewsID=143461 (accessed 12 March 2012).

World Wide Fund for Nature (WWF) (2010a), 'Certification and roundtables: do they work?' Gland, Switzerland: WWF, available at: http://awsassets.panda.org/downloads/wwf_msireview_sept_2010_lowres.pdf (accessed 10 October 2011).

World Wide Fund for Nature (WWF) (2010b), 'New method emerges to deter "indirect" land grab for biofuel production', Press Release, 8 October, available at: http://wwf.panda.org/who_we_are/wwf_offices/brazil/news/?uNewsID=195535 (accessed 28 March 2012).

Interviews

Interview, UK Department for Transport, 24 May 2011.
Interview, UK Department for Energy and Climate Change, 20 June 2011.

12 Food price volatility and global economic governance
Jennifer Clapp

The food crisis of 2007–08 ushered in an era of extreme food price volatility in world markets. Price volatility has a serious impact on access to food among the world's poorest people, who typically spend 50–80 per cent of their income on food. The number of people experiencing chronic hunger in sub-Saharan Africa, for example, rose sharply after 2007 (FAO 2012: 10). Sharp rises and falls in food prices are also devastating for farmers in the world's poorest countries. When prices rise, incomes may also rise. But, when prices are unpredictable, incomes also become more viable and the resulting uncertainty can easily stifle investment in future productivity increases. It is now widely predicted that volatility in food prices will be an ongoing feature of the world food economy, rather than just a temporary situation. There has been much discussion in international policy circles as to how best to reform global governance mechanisms to promote food security in this new era of unpredictable food prices.

This chapter examines the interface between the governance of the global political economy and food security. Specifically, it looks at food price volatility and frameworks for global economic governance; both the way in which those frameworks have contributed to bringing about a situation of food price volatility and the food crisis associated with it, as well as the ways in which global economic governance frameworks, shaped by the interests of various actors, are seeking to respond to those problems. In examining this interface, the chapter advances two key arguments. The first is that a complex set of governance arrangements must be taken into account in the promotion of food security in an era of highly volatile food prices. In a globalised world economy in which food price changes in one part of the world are easily transmitted to other parts of the world, food access becomes as tightly linked to global economic conditions as it is to levels of food production and distribution. Global governance arrangements that affect food security include those that govern global trade, investment and finance, as well as those that promote food production. The various global governance arrangements that affect food security, however, are not particularly well coordinated with one another. The result is a fragmented and highly complex governance landscape where some governance arrangements are tied to global economic issues broadly, and others are focused specifically on food security. None of these arrangements was able to prevent the onset of food price volatility in 2007–08, and in some cases the particular rules governing global economic relationships may even have encouraged it. They have also been slow in responding to that volatility.

The second argument made here is that the slow pace of reforms in global food security governance in the wake of food price volatility is a product of tensions among different actors and agencies; tensions which are shaped by ideological differences and interests. There have been debates in particular over whether the state should take a strong managerial role over food stocks or whether market mechanisms are the most appropriate means by which to smooth price volatility. At the same time, other debates that have erupted concerning food production have slowed progress, including discussion of the appropriate roles of agricultural biotechnology and agro-ecological farming methods, the extent to which farmers should be integrated into large-scale global agricultural value-chains as opposed to producing for local markets, and the degree to which funding for agriculture should come principally from public or private sources. In these various debates, civil society actors have tended to take positions at odds with those of the powerful states that dominate the structures of global economic governance.

The first part of the chapter looks at the ways in which international financial, trade and investment arrangements in the global economy have contributed to both the volatility of food prices and the vulnerability of developing countries to uncertain and rapidly changing food prices. 'Financialisation' of agricultural commodities, food export restrictions, uncertain stock levels and the adoption of trade-distorting biofuel policies have been the leading contributors to food price volatility. At the same time, declining investment and uneven agricultural trade rules have fostered vulnerability to erratic food prices on global markets, especially in the world's poorest countries. The chapter then maps out recent global governance responses to food price volatility and the political debates that have surrounded them. These include the implementation of a range of global initiatives for cooperation aimed at making agricultural markets function more smoothly, and a scaling-up of investment for agriculture, especially in developing countries, in order to improve productivity. In these contexts heated debates have erupted over the respective roles of the state and the market, and over technology, the scale of production and sources of funding. The chapter concludes by making the case that policy actions in these arenas have become increasingly fragmented from one another, risking a failure in the capacity of global economic governance to respond to food price volatility in a way that effectively promotes global food security.

GLOBAL ECONOMIC GOVERNANCE AND THE FOOD CRISIS

Although it was widely assumed that food supply was not keeping up with food demand when prices shot up in 2007–08, this was not actually the case. Food production per capita has in fact seen steady upward growth since the 1990s and overall cereals production was at a record high in 2008 (FAO data, cited in Rosset 2011: 473). The crisis was instead the product of a sudden drop in the ability of the world's poorest people to access food on markets, due to sharply rising food prices. In the years since the start of the crisis, a growing body of research has shown that the principal problem affecting food security was extreme volatility in prices, combined with high levels of vulnerability to that volatility in the world's poorest countries. It was these factors coming together that led to the dramatic rise in hunger and food insecurity that, in turn, resulted in widespread food riots in many poor countries in late 2007 and early 2008.

The volatility in food prices in the years since 2007 is the product of complex interactions between both short-term and longer-term international market forces. The short-term factors include a sharp rise in speculative investment in agricultural commodity markets, a rapid increase in investment in biofuel production, trade restrictions and the imposition of export bans. In addition, low and uncertain stocks of cereals inventory, combined with slowing yield increases, contributed to the sense of panic on world food markets. The combined result of these various forces was a sharp rise in food prices in a very short period of time. The combination of these factors was, as many have come to describe it, a 'perfect storm' (Headey and Fan 2008: 377).

The volatility that emerged at this time occurred in a context of high levels of vulnerability in the world's poorest countries to changes in food prices. Longer-term economic trends affecting these countries, including an unbalanced international agricultural trade regime and a long and steady decline in inward and domestic agricultural investment, served to weaken severely their agricultural sectors. In this context many countries had become dependent on imported food for a significant percentage of their food consumption, with the least-developed countries (LDCs), for example, importing approximately 20 per cent of the food they consume. The food import bill of these countries as a percentage of gross domestic product (GDP) thus doubled even before the food crisis erupted in 2007 (De Schutter 2011). When prices rose sharply, their ability to command food on world markets was severely compromised.

Economic governance arrangements in place at the international level shaped how these broader economic forces behind the global food crisis played out. As the following discussion shows, there was a lack of appropriate economic governance both to prevent the food crisis and to respond to it.

Food Price Volatility

The rise in speculative financial investment in agricultural commodity markets since the mid-2000s has been widely associated with the increase in the volatility of food prices. Although there is still disagreement on whether speculation on these markets was a leading cause of volatility or simply a consequence of it, most official analyses of the crisis consider it to be at least a contributing and exacerbating factor (IATP 2009; BIS 2011).[1] These markets were in fact previously regulated, with strict limits on how much exposure financial investors could have in commodity futures markets. These rules were relaxed with a series of deregulatory measures over the course of the 1980s and 1990s, which effectively increased the ability of financial investors to hold large amounts of commodity futures contracts (Clapp and Helleiner 2012). As such, the economic governance of these markets became quite 'loose'.

With less stringent rules on investment in agricultural derivatives, large investors – such as pension funds, hedge funds, sovereign wealth funds and other institutional investors – greatly increased their exposure to commodity market investments through instruments known as commodity index funds (CIFs) sold by large banks. CIFs track the prices of a bundle of commodities on futures markets, and food and agriculture items typically make up around one-third of the commodities tracked by these funds. Investment in CIFs offered by financial institutions increased from approximately US$15 billion to US$200 billion over the 2003–08 period (US Senate 2009: 5). In order to offset their own risks from sales of CIFs, banks increased their investment in commodity futures contracts purchased on futures exchanges, which they were able to do because of the relaxed regulations noted above. The exact extent to which this massive influx of financial investment in commodity futures was responsible for food price volatility is difficult to discern with precision, but it is widely seen to have been a major factor in the wild food price swings that have been experienced since 2007.

Export bans and other trade restrictions have also been identified as shorter-term factors that contributed to these price swings. A number of states prohibited exports of food, which in turn led to serious disruptions in global food trade and a subsequent spike in prices due to regional shortages (Headey 2011). In this context, countries that depended on food imports were forced to seek alternative sources of supply. The shutting down of exports from some countries also contributed to panic on markets, which fuelled further financial speculation in agricultural commodity markets. It was not clear whether the export bans themselves were a primary or even an initial cause of food price volatility, as they tend to be imposed in contexts where food prices are already high and volatile (Sharma 2011). However, they did unquestionably contribute to the volatile price situation.

The World Trade Organization (WTO) lacks specific rules on export restrictions, which meant that there was nothing preventing countries from imposing them as food prices began to rise sharply. As written, the WTO agreement specifies that countries must follow strict rules regarding restrictions on imports, but it does not prevent them from imposing a ban on exports. In this context, many states, including India, Vietnam, Egypt, China and Cambodia, implemented food export restrictions in the hope of keeping domestic food prices from rising (Sharma 2011). Such actions hampered some emergency operations of the World Food Programme (WFP), which procures its food in a variety of countries around the world.

In addition to its lack of strict rules on food export restrictions, the WTO also lacks rules regarding the use of policies that encourage biofuel production in ways that affect trade. The use of subsidies and blending mandates, for example, is highly distorting to trade. Their use to encourage domestic biofuel production – particularly the production of corn-based ethanol in the United States – has been widely seen as a key driver of higher and more volatile food prices since 2007 (UNCTAD 2011; Elliott 2009). The diversion of grain from the food supply by the United States, the world's largest producer of maize, as well as heightened speculative investment in commodity futures markets resulting from the biofuel boom, were significant forces influencing prices in this way.

Other economic governance arrangements were unable to prevent food price volatility from worsening. Differences between various countries' systems of grain stockholding have made it difficult to know with certainty what the level of available supply is at any given time. Grain stockholding was largely privatised in the late 1970s and early 1980s in most industrialised countries. In the United States, for example, the government got out of the grain stockholding business, with important changes implemented under the 1977 US Farm Bill (Clapp 2012a). Under the new rules, grain stocks were to be held by farmers and private actors (such as grain trading firms). Such changes saved the government the high costs of grain storage, but also put the knowledge of stock holdings in the hands of private actors. In other countries, governments have continued to hold stocks. The Chinese government, for example, holds significant public grain stocks, but due to a lack of transparent reporting it is unclear what amount it actually keeps in reserve. Under such circumstances, the reported level of global grain stocks is largely a guess. Nonetheless, the low levels that were reported in 2008 contributed to a sense of panic on world grain markets, although the high levels of uncertainty no doubt also contributed to the market disruptions.

These economic governance frameworks that touch on food prices were thus not only unable to stem food price volatility, but in fact appear to have contributed to its emergence.

Food Price Vulnerability

Volatile food prices in and of themselves might not have caused such a severe food crisis had it not been for the high level of vulnerability of developing countries to this volatility, created by their underlying dependence on food imports. Over the 2007–11 period around 80 countries were listed by the United Nations (UN) Food and Agricultural Organization (FAO) as being 'low-income food-deficit countries' (LIFDCs). Most of the 48 LDCs are also LIFDCs. As a group, the LDCs were net agricultural exporters in the 1960s, but starting in the mid-1980s they became net agricultural importers. These countries have been especially vulnerable to volatility in food prices, and it was primarily within these countries that hunger rose most dramatically when food prices rose in 2007–08 (FAO 2012: 10).

The forces contributing to weak agricultural performance in the LDCs after the mid-1980s are complex and varied, and the extent to which declining production is a result of internal or external forces is both unclear and debated. Despite these uncertainties and debates, there is clarity on certain points. One is that falling levels of investment in agriculture in these countries contributed to a decline in agricultural production and exports. Investment from international sources in particular has fallen sharply over the past 30 years. For example, some 30 per cent of the World Bank's lending was directed to agriculture in the 1980s, and this fell to just 12 per cent by 2007. Moreover, while 18 per cent of official development assistance (ODA) was agricultural aid in the 1980s, ODA for agriculture fell to just 3 per cent of all aid by 2007 (World Bank 2008; UN HLTF 2008). National investment in agriculture within the world's poorest countries also declined during this period. The low level of agricultural investment was further exacerbated by low prevailing world food prices over much of the 1980s and 1990s. Low world food prices at that time dampened interest in promoting food production in poor countries, particularly when cheap, subsidised food imports from industrialised countries were readily available on world markets.

Unbalanced trade policies over the course of these same decades have also been widely linked to weak agricultural performance in LDCs. Since the 1980s, many developing countries have liberalised their agricultural markets in return for World Bank-sponsored structural adjustment loans. Yet, even as the world's poorest countries liberalised in this way, industrialised countries continued to lavish heavy subsidies on their own domestic agricultural production and food exports. The latter also used mechanisms such as tariff peaks and tariff escalation to restrict imports of agricultural products from developing countries (Bello 2009). The 1994 Uruguay Round Agreement on Agriculture of the General Agreement on Tariffs and Trade (GATT) institutionalised this imbalance in trade practices. Agricultural tariffs were technically reduced by both rich and poor countries under the agreement, but in practice the relative depth of the tariff cuts in developing countries was much higher because it was on top of the already substantial tariff cuts they had made under structural adjustment programmes a decade earlier. At the same time, the high level of subsidies in the rich countries was allowed to continue (Clapp 2012a).

Uneven trade liberalisation has contributed to the dependence on food imports in the world's poorest countries (Clapp 2006; Khor 2009). Food 'import surges'– namely, an influx of imports over a short period of time – have been a particular concern of developing countries. The FAO found, for example, that for 23 food items in 102 developing countries, there were between approximately 7000 and 12000 import surges between the 1980s and 2003. Looking at data from 2004 to 2007 for a group of just 56 developing countries, the South Centre identified over 9000 import surges per year. These surges were experienced mainly in staple food items, typically those that are subsidised in industrialised countries, with cereals making up over 40 per cent of the surges in the poorest and most vulnerable developing countries. Senegal, for example, has seen its rice imports double and even triple over short periods of time since the 1990s (South Centre 2009). The impact of these surges is that imported food comes to 'outcompete' domestic production in agricultural markets in poor countries, in turn harming the livelihoods of farmers.

IN THE WAKE OF THE CRISIS: ECONOMIC GOVERNANCE REFORMS DEBATED

Discussions on reforms to global food security governance began almost immediately after food prices rose sharply in late 2007 and early 2008. The initial focus of responses at the level of international organisations was on increasing agricultural production. This early response reflected the lack of full understanding of the forces that were affecting food prices and a widely held assumption that, if prices were rising, it must mean that supply was short. But this was not the case, as noted above, since food production was at record levels in 2008. Because food prices moved sharply up and then down in the wake of the initial crisis, by 2010 policy-makers began to focus explicitly on the need to address the broad issue of volatility in food prices, which included but was not exclusively focused on the question of production.

The factors that contribute to food price volatility have much to do with global economic forces and weaknesses in existing economic governance arrangements, as noted above. Although global food governance agencies such as the FAO and the WFP have been actively involved in discussions on how the global community should respond to the crisis, these agencies on their own do not have the ability to address the broader economic forces that are contributing to the problem. The FAO specialises in analysis of hunger and food production and the WFP is the lead agency on emergency response and food aid. As such, these agencies must rely on other economic governance fora to implement governance reforms that address the ways in which international trade, finance and investment affect volatility in food prices.

These issues have indeed been discussed in international cooperation forums such as the WTO, the Group of Twenty leading economies (G20), the World Bank and the United Nations Committee on World Food Security (CFS). Yet progress has been both slow and uneven (Wise and Murphy 2012). The WTO Doha round of trade negotiations, which began in 2001, is nowhere near completion. These talks have been stalled since mid-2008 when food prices were especially high, due to the unwillingness of the rich countries to allow the developing countries to use a special safeguard mechanism to protect themselves from surges of cheap food imports from industrialised countries.

With the WTO talks paralysed, most action with respect to coordinating international economic governance responses to food price volatility has taken place in other fora. The G20 took up the issue under the leadership of France in late 2010, after French President Nicolas Sarkozy pledged to do something to curb financial speculation on food commodities. In early 2011 international organisations prepared a guidance document for the G20 agriculture ministers who met for the first time in June that year (FAO et al. 2011). This document was important in establishing the G20 agenda on food price volatility and made specific recommendations for how best to tackle the issue. But, at the autumn 2011 summit, the G20 governments failed to adopt most of the recommendations that were outlined in that report.

As the G20 discussed what might be done about food price volatility, other bodies were also working on coordinating economic governance responses to the crisis, including the World Bank which has taken a key role in coordinating investment funds for the sector. Also active has been the CFS, a body that is tasked with coordinating global action on food security. The CFS itself underwent reforms in 2009 to allow more non-state actor voices, including civil society and the private sector, to participate in its decision-making. The CFS also established a High Level Panel of Experts from which to draw the best of current technical advice (CFS 2009; McKeon 2011). These reforms were explicitly aimed at making the CFS the foremost international forum for coordinating efforts to address world food security issues. At its autumn 2011 meeting, however, the CFS found itself unable to make any recommendations that took it beyond what the G20 was likely to endorse, which, as noted above and as will be explained more fully below, was not much.

Although little has yet been accomplished in these forums, it is worth examining the types of reforms that have been proposed and the reasons why progress has been so slow. Two principal types of responses have emerged out of these various efforts to coordinate global governance responses in the wake of the food crisis. The first are efforts aimed primarily at improving the functioning of agrifood commodity markets, with the aim of smoothing prices by increasing the flow of goods, finance and information in the marketplace. The second are efforts aimed at improving agricultural productivity via increased investment, with the aim of smoothing price spikes by making more local production available in the world's most vulnerable countries.

There is broad agreement that there is a need for both market improvements and agricultural investment if volatility in food prices is to be effectively reduced. But, at the same time, there is a complex mix of clashing visions and misaligned interests among the key players in these governance fora that has slowed progress. There are contrasting views not only over the appropriate role of the state in market reforms and in agricultural investment, but also over the extent to which agricultural investment should support large-scale agricultural operations and agricultural biotechnologies as opposed to small-scale production and ecological forms of agriculture. At the same time, differing economic interests among key players with respect to both market improvements and agricultural investment have contributed to the lack of agreement on the best way forward.

Improving the Functioning of Agrifood Commodity Markets

A number of global economic governance initiatives have been proposed that seek to improve the functioning of agrifood commodity markets in ways that reduce volatility in food prices. Some efforts are explicitly aimed at reducing state intervention in international food markets, while others seek to strengthen the role of the state in managing or regulating the market. Although a number of initiatives have been put forward, not all have received equal support from global economic institutions. For example, as we have seen, the G20 took on food security as one of its key themes in 2011 and 2012. However, although it was well placed to reform some of the broader structural features of the global economy that have worked against food security, such as unbalanced trade rules, biofuel policies and financial speculation, it has chosen to put most of its effort behind the improvement of markets via information flows (Clapp and Murphy 2013).

Trade rules

The eruption of food prices in 2007–08 brought a heightened call for a rapid conclusion to the Doha round from most international economic organisations. The initial assumption was that food was not getting to where it was needed, and that the further liberalisation of agricultural trade, as called for in the Doha agenda, would bring relief on that front. For the WTO Director-General Pascal Lamy (2011), food prices would be smoothed out through a lubrication of international trade: 'Trade becomes the transmission belt through which supply adjusts to demand. It allows food to travel from the land of the plenty to the land of the few. When that transmission belt is disrupted through trade barriers, unexpected turbulence arises on the market.'

Because the Doha round has been stalled since mid-2008, little progress has been made on the broad goal of liberalising agricultural trade. Even as food prices reached record highs, key agricultural exporting countries – the United States, Canada and Australia – were unwilling to concede to the developing countries' request for a special safeguard mechanism that would enable them to protect themselves from import surges. At the same time, the subsidy reductions offered by the rich countries were only minimal (Clapp 2012b).

Export restrictions were not part of the original Doha agenda, but have been pinpointed as a key source of volatility since the food crisis erupted. However, attempts to include new mechanisms to address export restrictions in the current round have not been successful. In autumn 2011, the WTO members dropped the idea of incorporating rules to exempt the poorest countries and humanitarian aid from export bans, due to widespread lack of agreement on the issue. The fact that WTO members could not even support discussion of these specific measures does not bode well for the adoption of a broader and more comprehensive food security agenda at the WTO. Indeed, it is unclear what benefits a conclusion to the round would actually have for food security (De Schutter 2011; Clapp 2012b).

Financial market regulation

In addition to initiatives to liberalise trade, there have been calls from a number of quarters for tighter regulation on financial speculation on agricultural commodity markets. Such efforts have been bundled with broader financial sector reforms in both the United

States and in the European Union (EU) following the financial crisis of 2008. In the US the Dodd–Frank Wall Street Reform and Consumer Protection Act was passed into law in July 2010. This legislation includes tighter controls on agricultural commodities' trade and commodity index funds. It mandates regulators to impose tighter position limits on financial actors operating across all agricultural commodity markets, including foreign markets (Clapp and Helleiner 2012). In late 2008 the European Commission also began the process of financial market reform, including measures to reduce speculation through position limits and more detailed reporting. These measures included specific reforms to the European Market Infrastructure Regulation (EMIR) and the Markets in Financial Instruments Directive (MiFID) (van Tilberg and Vander Stitchele 2011). Given the existence of widespread disagreement over the extent to which financial speculation contributed to episodes of food price volatility, there was heated debate in both the US and the EU over whether such reforms were required. In both cases, reforms were eventually endorsed, although they were resisted by the financial sector and agricultural commodity trading firms. It is also the case that these reforms have not yet been fully put into place, and resistance to them by financial investors remains.

Following the lead of the US and the EU, there were also calls for global cooperation on the use of position limits in agricultural commodity futures markets. A growing number of food security non-governmental organisations (NGOs), as well as President Sarkozy in his leadership role for the 2011 G8 and G20 meetings, championed the idea as part of a broader set of initiatives to combat food price volatility (Clapp 2012a). Following much debate and discussion, the final communiqué from the Cannes G20 leaders summit in November 2011 did endorse the use of position limits. But this does not guarantee that they will be used, or that such measures will be coordinated, across all international commodity markets.

Biofuel policies

In the wake of the crisis there were also calls from a number of international organisations for coordinated action on biofuels (UN HLTF 2008; Sustainable Biofuel Consensus 2008). However, there has been very little uptake of this idea, despite widespread understanding that biofuel policies are deeply distorting and contributors to food price volatility. Among the recommendations made has been the removal of trade-distorting blending mandates and subsidies, or at the very least the imposition of a trigger for their reduction when food prices hit a certain level.

The G20 was an obvious place for reforms on biofuels to be endorsed. Member-countries are the major players in global biofuel production, and many directly subsidise production and/or have blending mandates which encourage investment in biofuels, including the EU, the US, Brazil, Canada, China and Australia. Yet the G20 Agricultural Ministers' Action Plan put forward in 2011 did not go any further than to recommend further analysis on the issue. This outcome is not surprising, given that the US and Brazil have been resistant to policy changes.

Food reserves

Another prominent proposal for market improvement in the wake of the food crisis was the establishment of food reserves (Murphy 2009; McCreary 2011). Because food price volatility tends to be more pronounced when food stocks are low, the idea here is to promote stockholding through publicly managed reserves. There are a number of possible models and uses. An international reserve could be used explicitly as a means by which to smooth volatility on world markets; national reserves could be used to manage prices within a country; and there could also be emergency reserves held for purposes of moving food aid more quickly to areas of need when food prices shoot up. All three kinds of reserves have been discussed in international fora following the initial spike in food prices in 2008. For instance, the International Food Policy Research Institute (IFPRI) put forward a proposal that included an emergency reserve, a globally coordinated reserve and a virtual reserve, the latter involving financing for intervention on agricultural commodity futures markets (Von Braun and Torero 2008).

The idea of implementing food reserves has not gained widespread traction in international economic policy circles. There has been discussion of reserves in international economic fora, although the most ambitious of the proposals – such as those involving a globally coordinated reserve, either real or virtual, to manage prices – have dropped away from the agenda. There is broad concern in the WTO and the rich industrialised countries, for example, about potential inefficiencies associated with enhancing the state's role in the management of food supplies. FAO (2011a: 4) comments on the report prepared for the G20 on food price volatility summarise this view: 'The international organizations concluded that buffer stocks, stocks constituted and management with the intention of influencing prices, have a poor record and that such schemes are particularly inappropriate and ineffective when the intention is to mitigate a price peak.'

Several larger developing countries do not share this concern. India and China, for example, already hold established domestic grain reserves for such purposes, while others in Africa and Asia are putting resources into establishing them (ActionAid 2011). Meanwhile, national reserves continue to be actively discouraged by the WTO and the G20. In 2011, however, the G20 did endorse the idea of a very small pilot project for an emergency food reserve, to be managed by the WFP (G20 2011). It is unclear whether this project will eventually be scaled up.

Information flows

Although concrete action on these various initiatives was only spotty in some areas and completely missing in others, the G20 did endorse a new initiative specifically aimed at improving the functioning of agrifood commodity markets in order to smooth out price volatility. This initiative was the Agricultural Market Information System (AMIS), set up in autumn 2011. Given the debates surrounding the other initiatives outlined above, one of the suggestions in the price volatility document prepared for the G20 contained a proposal for an information system for agricultural commodity markets (FAO et al. 2011). The attraction of this system for most G20 members was that it was market-based and relatively cost-free compared to the other options. There were also no real vested interests to object to it. AMIS is similar to another initiative on oil markets that came into place some ten years earlier, namely, the Joint Oil Data Initiative (JODI). The main idea behind it is to provide more and better information on grain stocks and prices to market actors in order to reduce the kind of panic and confusion that can contribute to price volatility (FAO 2011b).

AMIS will provide information on global food commodities and initially its work has focused on wheat, maize, rice and soybeans. It encourages all major producing, consuming and exporting countries to provide data on these markets. Although the initiative is government-based, it also seeks cooperation and inputs from the private sector, including the major grain companies controlling the bulk of the world's grain trade. The AMIS is based in the FAO, but includes active input from a number of international organisations that assist in the provision and analysis of agricultural market data (FAO 2011b). Under the AMIS umbrella are two groups: the Global Food Market Information Group and the Rapid Response Forum. The former provides information and analysis of global food markets, and the latter works to improve policy dialogue in situations of high food insecurity with a view to enhancing emergency response. The latter is to work closely with the CFS. This initiative has only just been established and, as such, its performance thus far is difficult to evaluate.

While support for other initiatives to improve the functioning of agrifood markets has been difficult to attract, the AMIS was approved relatively swiftly without much debate. This is not particularly surprising, given that support for an initiative to gather market information was politically much easier to garner among the G20 membership than that needed to tackle tougher issues such as trade liberalisation, commodity speculation, biofuels and reserves, each of which requires the confrontation of powerful vested interests.

Boosting Agricultural Investment

As noted above, levels of agricultural investment in developing countries declined sharply between the 1980s and the early 2000s. In the aftermath of the 2007–08 food price crisis, there was widespread recognition that the level of support for agriculture was at a critically low level and that the trend of falling investment needed to be reversed. Global institutions and rich-country governments made pledges substantially to increase investment in food and agriculture. While welcomed, the promised investments have also been subject to intense debate among different actors over how best to direct the new resources in order to promote most effectively the objective of enhanced food security. These debates – shaped by differences in ideas and interests among different actors – help to explain the slow and piecemeal global governance responses to the food crisis.

Investment promises

The G8 countries and others pledged at the L'Aquila summit in Italy in 2009 to mobilise US$22 billion over a three-year period for investments in sustainable agricultural development as part of the so-called L'Aquila Food Security Initiative (AFSI). This funding pledge was reiterated by the G20 leading economies at their Pittsburgh summit later that year. The G8 and G20 both endorsed the establishment of a new World Bank-managed multilateral fund, the Global Agriculture and Food Security Program (GAFSP), as a key channel for these funds. Not all of the pledged US$22 billion represented new funds that went beyond previous promises, but the initiative did nevertheless represent a political commitment to boost investment support for agriculture in the world's poorest countries.

Although US$22 billion is an impressive figure, it has been difficult to ascertain how much of it has actually reached developing countries. By the end of 2011 only US$1.1 billion had actually been pledged to the GAFSP by a handful of donors, and only just over half of that amount, US$612 million, was actually received into the fund (GAFSP

2011). The 2011 G8 Deauville Accountability Report noted that only 22 per cent of the total amount pledged been disbursed by mid-2011, indicating that much of the funding was being channelled bilaterally, rather than through the GAFSP. The report also noted that the scope, components and time periods of the pledges are different for each donor, making the process of tracking progress on this pledge 'challenging'. According to the report, an additional 26 per cent of the funds are on track to be disbursed and donors are expected to disburse all pledged funds by 2012 (G8 2011).

In terms of bilateral funding, the United States and the European Union have been among the larger donors and it is worth examining their progress briefly. In 2009 the US established a major initiative, called Feed the Future, which promised US$3.5 billion in agricultural investment for developing countries over a period of three years. In the first two years of the programme, less than US$2 billion had been disbursed (Wise and Murphy 2012).[2] The European Commission similarly launched a Food Security Thematic Programme in response to the food crisis which included a pledge to provide over €1.5 billion over the 2007–13 period. The EU established a Food Facility though which this funding would be channelled, largely in coordination with UN agencies (Murphy and Wise 2012; European Commission 2011).

The World Bank also ramped up its agricultural investment in the wake of the food price crisis. As noted above, the Global Agricultural and Food Security Program was launched in 2009 as a channel for G20 funds. The Bank also established a new Agricultural Action Plan in 2009 to increase its own lending to the sector. Set up in 2009, the aim is to increase the World Bank's agricultural funding to a level of between US$6.2 billion and US$8.3 billion per year, which would more than double the approximately US$2–4 billion annually it provided in the 2000–08 period (World Bank 2009).

Debates over how to direct agricultural investment
Overlaying concerns about whether the financial outlays for agricultural assistance will meet the amounts that have been pledged from these various quarters are debates over how precisely this money should be invested. There is a major clash of visions regarding this question. The World Bank has been perhaps the most forthcoming in its views on how this new investment should be spent. The World Bank's Agricultural Action Plan, for example, explicitly focuses on providing funding for agricultural productivity increases, market improvements, risk mitigation for farmers, facilitation of entry and exit in farm activities, and environmental services. Among the specific measures it promotes are the use of agricultural biotechnologies and better integration of developing-country agricultural production into global agricultural value chains. These goals mirror those mapped out in the GAFSP, as well as those articulated in the World Bank's 2008 World Development Report, *Agriculture for Development* (World Bank 2007).

The World Bank's vision for agricultural investment is not, of course, universally supported. Just as food prices were reaching record highs in early 2008, a key report articulating a different vision was released. The International Assessment of Agricultural Knowledge, Science and Technology for Development (IAASTD) report, titled *Agriculture at a Crossroads,* came out of a major multi-year, multi-stakeholder and multi-agency process (IAASTD 2009). The idea of this process was to create an assessment panel not dissimilar to the Intergovernmental Panel on Climate Change in order to try to articulate a global consensus on the way forward in agricultural development.

However, the assessment report came to conclusions that in some ways clashed with the World Bank's vision, despite the fact that the IAASTD process included the World Bank and the UN among its stakeholders. The IAASTD report concluded that 'business as usual' in the agricultural realm was not an option and emphasised as its priority environmental sustainability – and specifically support for agro-ecological farming methods – as well as a reversal of the inequities in global food markets that have disadvantaged smallholders in developing countries.

The differences in priorities of these two reports have largely shaped the way debates have unfolded with respect to agricultural investment since 2008, and they are likely to continue to do so into the future. Powerful states, especially those in the G20, have tended to promote the views outlined by the World Bank. Civil society groups and food import-dependent developing countries have tended to promote the ideas outlined in the IAASTD report. Already, we have seen some funding programmes lean more in one direction than the other, with the result that there is no consensus on how best to direct agricultural investment funds. Three issues in particular are likely to generate ongoing debate among the various agricultural investment funding initiatives mapped out above.

The first relates to the role of technology, in particular agricultural biotechnology. The World Bank (2009: 20) has been explicit in its support of the use of agricultural biotechnology, noting that these technologies hold the potential for increased crop yields. But many developing countries have been wary of adopting agricultural biotechnology for a variety of reasons, ranging from a lack of regulatory capacity, to concerns about biosafety and genetic erosion, to fears of loss of export markets in Europe where there are stringent controls on imports of genetically modified organisms (GMOs). They are also sceptical of the interests of the large agricultural biotechnology firms, and the countries in the West that host them, which will benefit from a more global spread of genetically modified seeds (Zerbe 2009).

While the World Bank has pursued investment in building capacity around questions of agricultural biotechnology in developing countries, others – civil society groups, in particular – have pushed instead for greater investment in agro-ecological farming methods that exclude the use of GMOs. The UN Special Rapporteur on the Right to Food, for example, has argued that the new agricultural investment funds that have been forthcoming in recent years should be focused on agro-ecological farming methods, a view that closely tracks that of major groups working on food security, such as La Via Campesina. The Special Rapporteur's recommendations were based on a growing body of research that shows that agro-ecological farming methods can both produce higher yields and contribute to more sustainable farming systems, including the protection of genetic diversity and the mitigation of climate change (De Schutter 2010).

The second key debate that has emerged is over the extent to which new funds for agriculture should be geared toward inserting developing-country farmers into large-scale production systems for more efficient integration into global agricultural value chains, rather than supporting them in smaller-scale production geared toward local and domestic markets. The World Bank, for example, is explicitly gearing its agricultural investment towards linking developing-country farmers into both domestic and international markets for high-value agricultural commodities. In many cases, this means encouraging farmers to move into production of new products, such as fruits, vegetables and livestock, which fetch higher prices than staple grains (World Bank 2009). This stronger integration of developing country farmers into global markets is seen by the World Bank to be the key to raising incomes, ending poverty and ultimately improving food security.

But, while the World Bank has pressed for integration of small farmers into global value chains, a growing movement of peasant farmers has resisted this strategy. Farmer and peasant groups in the developing world have instead endorsed the idea of food sovereignty, a concept that originated with the peasant movement, La Via Campesina. Food sovereignty calls for the right of communities to determine their own food security and emphasises production for local markets and ecological farming methods (Nyéléni Declaration 2007). The International Planning Committee for Food Sovereignty, an umbrella group claiming to represent hundreds of millions of peasant farmers around the world, has become active in global food governance fora, including the CFS, along-side grassroots groups like La Via Campesina (McKeon 2011: 5). There is strong support for the notion of food sovereignty in many developing countries, as it resonates with developing-country desires to enhance their own domestic food production in the face of uncertain global markets. Ecuador, for example, has officially incorporated the notion of food sovereignty into its constitution. The idea of food sovereignty has also gained traction in UN bodies such as the FAO and the CFS, and increasingly within food move-ments in the global North. In response to this increased attention to the concept, the WTO and the G20 have tried to convince developing countries to eschew any ambitions of self-sufficiency in food.

A third key debate over agricultural investment revolves around the role of private funding for agricultural development in developing countries. This issue had already emerged with the growing involvement of private actors such as the Bill and Melinda Gates Foundation in funding agricultural research and development, including through its participation in the Alliance for a Green Revolution for Africa (Holt-Jiminez 2008).[3] The World Bank and other donors have welcomed the growing role of private donors. Private investment can help to fill the gap after a general clawing back of public funding for agricultural development in recent decades. The Gates Foundation, for example, is one of the key donors to the GAFSP. Many are sceptical of the growing role of private investors in agricultural development. A number of NGOs, such as the Oakland Institute, are concerned that the Gates Foundation is interested in promoting agricul-tural biotechnology in countries that have to date resisted the adoption of that technol-ogy (Mittal and Moore 2009).

The debate over private investors in agriculture has sparked controversy around the rapid growth in investment in large-scale tracts of land in developing countries in the wake of the food crisis. A mix of both public and private actors has been engaged in this investment, with sovereign wealth funds and private hedge funds the most active. The World Bank has seen this renewed interest in agricultural land investment as positive, potentially leading to a 'win–win' outcome of private funding and improved agricultural productivity (Deininger et al. 2011). In order to ensure that it is positive, the World Bank has supported the development of guidelines for investors, the so-called Principles for Responsible Investment in Agriculture (PRAI) (FAO et al. 2010). Others, however, have been highly critical of the role of private investors in these land deals and have called on states to take a more active role in ensuring land rights. The CFS, for example, has sup-ported the process of developing Voluntary Guidelines on the Responsible Governance of Land Tenure.[4]

These debates over how agricultural investment funds should be directed will continue to shape global governance responses to the food crisis. In the meantime, the lack of widespread agreement in these key areas has contributed to a fragmented and piecemeal investment response to the food crisis.

CONCLUSION

This chapter has attempted to untangle the complexity of the interface between global economic governance, food price volatility and food security. It has shown that global trade, finance and investment governance arrangements have enormous implications for people's access to food. Indeed, in today's globalised world economy, international economic relationships have as much significance as food production in determining food security. As such, governance arrangements for food security are highly complex and span a range of institutions and frameworks that include both those directly concerned with food issues as well as those that set the rules and norms for broader economic relationships. Without a firm understanding of the way in which global economic governance frameworks are integral to food security, reforms to promote greater global food security cannot be effective. But, even as we gain a clearer picture of how global economic governance frameworks interface with problems such as food price volatility, moving forward with global economic governance reforms in support of greater food security has been both slow and highly uneven.

Most of the efforts to improve global food security governance in this era of increased food price volatility have thus far been directed to improving the functioning of global agrifood commodity markets and increasing investment in agriculture. Policy initiatives in both of these areas have nevertheless been rife with debate. Various disagreements – over the appropriate role of states and markets in shaping the global agrifood scene, over the merits of agricultural biotechnologies versus agro-ecological methods, over production in global market systems versus production for local markets, and over the relationship of public versus private investment in production systems – have slowed responses to worsening global food insecurity. These disagreements have been the product of a clash of ideas and actors. Private interests and industrialised states have largely pushed for a minimal state role in the agricultural sector, for more private sector investment and for an enhanced role for modern technologies in production systems that feed into global value chains. Civil society actors and a number of developing-country governments have taken opposing positions, pressing instead for more ecologically oriented, local-scale agriculture combined with a greater role for state regulation and management of the sector. Overall, the result is that policy reforms to address food price volatility have been piecemeal at best, limited by these competing visions of what constitutes a sustainable and abundant food system and the varying strengths of the different interests in pushing their ideas.

The case of food price volatility reveals broader lessons for economic governance. In a globalised world economy, the general rules that seek to govern international economic relationships also have important implications for a wide range of issues that affect people's basic needs, such as access to food. Yet, because global economic governance arrangements are wide-ranging and complex, and do not have these other goals as a central focus, coordination to tackle specific issues can be particularly difficult. It is in such cases, where broad global economic governance arrangements do not match up particularly well with those specifically geared toward other goals, that we see highly fragmented global governance responses to pressing global issues. In such fragmented governance situations, fissures can and often do open up where different actors and ideas compete for influence in the governance process, resulting in slow and uneven progress. But, at the same time, such fissures can also be spaces for creative dialogue that results in new kinds of governance initiatives that link global economic governance institutions more effectively with those that focus on specific issues. This is something that the actors involved in the food price volatility debate continue to work towards despite differing outlooks on the causes of and solutions to the problem.

NOTES

1. Some economists, such as Dwight Sanders and Scott Irwin, staunchly deny that there is any connection between commodity speculation and food prices. See Sanders and Irwin (2010).
2. See the Feed the Future website: http://www.feedthefuture.gov/.
3. See also the AGRA website: http://www.agra-alliance.org/.
4. See the FAO Land Tenure website: http://www.fao.org/nr/tenure/voluntary-guidelines/en/.

REFERENCES

ActionAid (2011), 'No more food crises: the indispensable role of food reserves', at: http://www.actionaid.org/sites/files/actionaid/policy_briefing_-_the_role_of_food_reserves.pdf.
Bank for International Settlements (2011), *81st Annual Report*, at: http://www.bis.org/publ/arpdf/ar2011e.pdf.
Bello, Walden (2009), *The Food Wars*, London: Verso.
Clapp, Jennifer (2006), 'WTO agriculture negotiations: implications for the Global South', *Third World Quarterly*, **27** (4), 563–77.
Clapp, Jennifer (2012a), *Food*, Cambridge: Polity Press.
Clapp, Jennifer (2012b), 'Food security and the WTO', in Rorden Wilkinson and James Scott (eds), *Trade, Poverty, Development: Getting Beyond the Doha Deadlock*, London: Routledge, pp. 57–71.
Clapp, Jennifer and Eric Helleiner (2012), 'Troubled futures? The global food crisis and the politics of agricultural derivatives regulation', *Review of International Political Economy*, DOI: 10.1080/09692290.2010.514528, 181–207.
Clapp, Jennifer and Sophia Murphy (2013), 'The G20 and food security: a mismatch in global governance?', *Global Policy*, **4** (2), 129–38.
Committee on World Food Security (CFS) (2009), 'Reform of the Committee on World Food Security', at: http://www.fao.org/fileadmin/templates/cfs/Docs0910/ReformDoc/CFS_2009_2_Rev_2_E_K7197.pdf.
De Schutter, Olivier (2010), 'Report Submitted by the Special Rapporteur on the Right to Food, Olivier De Schutter', UN General Assembly, A/HRC/16/49.
De Schutter, Olivier (2011), 'The World Trade Organization and the post-global food crisis agenda: putting food security first in the international trade system', Activity Report of the UN Special Rapporteur on the Right to Food, at: http://www.wto.org/english/news_e/news11_e/deschutter_2011_e.pdf.
Elliott, Kimberly Ann (2009), 'US biofuels policy and the global food price crisis', in Jennifer Clapp and Marc Cohen (eds), *The Global Food Crisis: Governance Challenges and Opportunities*, Waterloo: Wilfrid Laurier University Press, pp. 59–75.
European Commission (2011), 'Food security thematic programme', Thematic Strategy Paper (update) and Multiannual Indicative Programme 2011–2013, at: http://ec.europa.eu/development/icenter/repository/FSTP%202011-2013_Commission%20adoption.pdf
FAO (2011a), 'Improving global governance for food security – the role of the international organizations', *Food Outlook*, November (supplement), 2–10.
FAO (2011b), 'Agricultural Market Information System (AMIS)', *Food Outlook*, November (supplement), 11–17.
FAO (2012), *The State of Food Insecurity in the World 2012*, Rome: FAO.

FAO, IFAD, IMF, OECD, UNCTAD, WFP, World Bank, WTO, IFPRI and UN HLTF (2011), 'Price volatility in food and agricultural markets: policy responses', June, at: http://www.oecd.org/dataoecd/40/34/48152638.pdf.

FAO, IFAD, UNCTAD and World Bank (2010), 'Principles for responsible agricultural investment that respects rights, livelihoods and resources', at: http://siteresources.worldbank.org/INTARD/2145741111138388661/22453321/Principles_Extended.pdf.

G8 (2011), 'Deauville accountability report', at: http://www.g20-g8.com/g8-g20/root/bank_objects/Rapport_G8_GB.pdf.

G20 (2011), 'Emergency humanitarian food reserves', at: http://www.g20-g8.com/g8-g20/root/bank_objects/food_reserves.pdf.

GAFSP (2011), 'Funding', at: http://www.gafspfund.org/gafsp/content/funding.

Headey, Derek (2011), 'Rethinking the global food crisis: the role of trade shocks', *Food Policy*, **36** (2), 136-46.

Headey, Derek and Shenggen Fan (2008), 'Anatomy of a crisis: the causes and consequences of surging food prices', *Agricultural Economics*, **39** (supplement), 375–91.

Holt Jiminez, Eric (2008), 'Out of AGRA: the Green Revolution returns to Africa', *Development*, **51** (4), 464–71.

Institute for Agriculture and Trade Policy (IATP) (2009), 'Betting against food security: futures market speculation', Minneapolis: IATP, at: http://www.iatp.org/tradeobservatory/library.cfm?refID=105065.

International Assessment of Agricultural Knowledge, Science and Technology for Development (IAASTD) (2009), *Agriculture at a Crossroads*, Washington, DC: Island Press.

Khor, Martin (2009), 'Analysis of the Doha Negotiations and the functioning of the WTO', Geneva: The South Centre.

Lamy, Pascal (2011), 'Lamy on the rise in food prices; trade is part of the answer, not part of the problem', speech, 22 January, at: http://www.wto.org/english/news_e/sppl_e/sppl183_e.htm.

McCreary, Ian (2011), 'Protecting the food insecure in volatile international markets: food reserves and other policy options', Canadian Foodgrains Bank Occasional Paper, at: http://www.foodgrainsbank.ca/uploads/Food%20Security%20Price%20Volatility%20and%20Policy%20Responses-%20final%20-%2025%20March%2011.pdf.

McKeon, Nora (2011), 'Global governance for world food security: a scorecard four years after the eruption of the "food crisis"', Heinrich Böll Foundation, at: http://www.boell.de/downloads/Global-Governance-for-World-Food-Security.pdf.

Mittal, Anuradha and Melissa Moore (eds) (2009), *Voices from Africa: African Farmers & Environmentalists Speak Out Against a New Green Revolution in Africa*, Oakland Institute, at: http://oaklandinstitute.org/sites/oaklandinstitute.org/files/voicesfromafrica_full_0.pdf.

Murphy, Sophia (2009), 'Strategic grain reserves in an era of volatility', IATP, at: http://www.iatp.org/files/451_2_106857.pdf.

Nyéléni Declaration (2007), 'Forum for Food Sovereignty', at: http://viacampesina.org/en/index.php?option=com_content&task=view&id=282&Itemid=38.

Rosset, Peter (2011), 'Preventing hunger: change economic policy', *Nature*, 24 November, 479.

Sanders, Dwight and Scott Irwin (2010), 'A speculative bubble in commodity futures prices? Cross-sectional evidence', *Agricultural Economics*, **41** (1), 25–32.

Sharma, Ramesh (2011), 'Food export restrictions: review of the 2007–2010 experience and considerations for disciplining restrictive measures', FAO Commodity and Trade Policy Research Working Paper No. 32, at: ictsd.org/downloads/2011/05/sharma-export-restrictions.pdf.

South Centre (2009), *The Extent of Agriculture Import Surges in Developing Countries: What are the Trends?* Geneva: The South Centre.

Sustainable Biofuel Consensus (2008), 'Bellagio', at: http://www.renewableenergyworld.com/assets/documents/2008/FINAL%20SBC_April_16_2008.pdf.

UN High-Level Task Force on the Global Food Security Crisis (UN HLTF) (2008), 'Comprehensive framework for action', at: http://www.un.org/en/issues/food/taskforce/pdf/OutcomesAndActionsBooklet_v9.pdf.

UNCTAD (2011), 'Price formation in financialized commodity markets: the role of information', at: http://www.unctad.org/en/docs/gds2011_en.pdf.

United States Senate (2009), 'Excessive speculation in the wheat market', Majority and Minority Staff Report, Permanent Subcommittee on Investigations, Washington, DC: US Senate.

van Tilburg, Rens and Myriam Vander Stichele (2011), *Feeding the Financial Hype: How Excessive Financial Investments Impact Agricultural Derivatives Markets*, Amsterdam: SOMO, November, at: http://www.s2bnetwork.org/fileadmin/dateien/downloads/Feeding_the_Financial_Hype.pdf.

Von Braun, Joachim and Maximo Torero (2008), 'Physical and virtual global food reserves to protect the poor and prevent market failure', Washington, DC: IFPRI, at: http://www.ifpri.org/sites/default/files/publications/bp004.pdf.

Wise, Timothy and Sophia Murphy (2012), 'Resolving the food crisis: assessing global policy reforms since

2007', Institute for Agriculture and Trade Policy and Global Development and Environment Institute, at: http://www.ase.tufts.edu/gdae/Pubs/rp/ResolvingFoodCrisis.pdf.

World Bank (2007), *World Development Report 2008: Agriculture for Development*, Washington, DC: World Bank.

World Bank (2008), *Double Jeopardy: Responding to High Food and Fuel Prices*, Washington, DC: World Bank.

World Bank (2009), *Agriculture Action Plan 2010–2012*, Washington, DC: World Bank, at: http://siteresources.worldbank.org/INTARD/Resources/Agriculture_Action_Plan_web.pdf.

Zerbe, Noah (2009), 'Setting the global dinner table: exploring the limits of the marketization of food security', in Jennifer Clapp and Marc Cohen (eds), *The Global Food Crisis: Governance Challenges and Opportunities*, Waterloo: Wilfred Laurier University Press, pp. 161–75.

13 The global governance of development: development financing, good governance and the domestication of poverty

David Hudson and Niheer Dasandi

The realities of global poverty and inequalities between the haves and the have-nots are clear and well documented. Poverty is high, but – using a frugal measure – is falling; welfare outcomes are improving across the board, but international inequalities remain large. The latest figures from the World Bank report that in 2008 there were 801 million people living below US$1 a day, which is 14 per cent of the developing world's population, down from 31 per cent in 1990 and 42 per cent in 1981 (Chen and Ravallion 2012). Much has indeed improved. Charles Kenny (2011) has argued that on almost any quality of life indicator the world has seen rapid and universal improvements in life chances.

Nevertheless, the gaps between the world's richest and poorest countries have grown larger, despite the sustained growth of a subgroup of big industrialising countries. Inequalities between individuals, across countries, have grown larger with the richest 5 per cent of people receiving one-third of total global income, the same amount as the poorest 80 per cent (Milanovic 2005). The political economy of inequality matters. It works against all countries having a fair voice in global decision-making and allows rich countries systematically to distort trade rules (Pogge 2008; Wade 2003). Inequalities also work against the possibility of a long-term convergence in incomes – the great liberal hope. As Milanovic (2011: 103) has noted:

> If the US GDP [gross domestic product] per capita grows by 1 per cent, India's will need to grow by 17 per cent, an almost impossible rate, and China's by 8.6 per cent, just to keep absolute income differences from rising. As the saying goes, you have to run very, very fast just to stay in the same place. It is therefore not surprising that despite China's (and India's) remarkable success, the absolute income differences between the rich and poor countries have widened.

This is the 'Matthew effect' (Merton 1968; Wade 2004): 'For to all those who have, more will be given, and they will have an abundance; but from those who have nothing, even what they have will be taken away'.

In this chapter, with these issues firmly in mind, we examine the global governance of the development project: the modern effort to reduce world poverty that began after the end of the Second World War. We pay particular attention to the dominant ideas that have shaped the system and continue to shape its future. We agree with the editors of this volume that 'all forms and projects of governance are intrinsically ideological' and that these ideas serve to constitute the structures of the global political economy and act as a source of power. In the chapter we apply this to the global governance of development and, in doing so, identify three foundational ideas that explain the structure of the governance system: (1) the belief that poverty is predominantly caused by domestic factors, such as difficult geography, bad policies, corruption, weak institutions, lack of savings or culture; (2) the belief that underdevelopment is a function of a lack of resources – usually financial, but also technical or human – and that this can be tackled with a sufficient infusion of capital; and (3) the belief that the key to effective aid and long-term development is for countries to build strong and robust institutions, such as the rule of law, multi-party democracy, effective bureaucracy, private property and free markets – in short, to follow the rubric of 'good governance'.

Taken together, these three foundational ideas provide a powerful, and mutually reinforcing, ideological structure; one which reduces development to a technical focus on domestic poverty. In sum, we argue that the global governance of development is built around an effort to reduce poverty without significantly changing the unequal distribution of power between and within countries. This means that the system is governed in such a way that it ignores and systematically sidelines questions of power and politics. Crucially, this exclusion is reproduced at both the international and domestic level. This ideological structure shapes the power, authority, beliefs, strategies, decisions and behaviour of development actors, from rich donor countries and their development agencies, poor recipient or partner countries, international financial institutions (IFIs), international organisations (IOs), non-governmental organisations (NGOs), civil society and other new actors.

In the chapter we trace empirically the emergence of these foundational ideas, explore the exclusion of politics and power, and reflect on the ongoing shifts in and of the global governance of development. The chapter is structured as follows. First, we briefly recount the origins of the development project at the end of the Second World War and the roots of the three foundational ideas. In the second section, we discuss the current development landscape by mapping out the roles of the key actors in the global governance of development. We also consider the Millennium Development Goals (MDGs), which have both exemplified and institutionalised the ideological foundations of the governance of development. Third, we discuss in greater detail the three foundational beliefs of the governance of development, highlighting their ongoing reinforcement in public policy and academia. This is followed by an extended critique of these fundamental ideas. Finally, we consider what the future may hold for the governance of development, based on recent shifts.

GOING GLOBAL: THE EMERGENCE OF MODERN DEVELOPMENT

The emergence of the global governance of development, as we now know it, began following the end of the Second World War. Prior to this, the promotion of development was largely seen as the domain of the state or domestic authority (Rist 2002; Desai and Potter 2002). A number of important features of the post-war environment led to the rise of international development as an area of global public policy. The United Nations and the Bretton Woods institutions were set up with the principal objective of promoting peace and prosperity in the new global order. The process of decolonisation, which began at the end of the war, led to the creation of new independent states in Africa and Asia. These ex-colonial and largely poor states were marred by significant economic, social and political problems. Furthermore, they were almost immediately caught up in the struggle between the two rival superpowers in the Cold War (Payne and Phillips 2010). The combination of these factors led to the view that global action was required for the successful development of these newly independent states.

As Gilbert Rist (2002: 71) has described, this was articulated in Point Four of United States President Harry Truman's inauguration speech which marked the beginning of the 'development age', emphasising the need to 'embark on a bold new program for making the benefits of our scientific advances and industrial progress available for the improvement and growth of the underdeveloped areas'. There were three aspects to Point Four of Truman's speech that were fundamental in shaping the global governance of development. First, the 'problem of underdevelopment' was framed as a fixable problem, a technical problem pertaining to knowledge and expertise, and one that could be (and needed to be) fixed from the outside (Rosenstein-Rodan 1943; Nurske 1953; Rostow 1960). As Truman (1949) said, 'for the first time in history, humanity possesses the knowledge and skill to relieve the suffering of these people'. The development vision presented, and widely accepted, was that poverty was a domestic condition and that underdeveloped regions had always experienced poverty and misery (Dasandi 2009). Second, a major cause of underdevelopment was a shortage of technical and financial capital. This 'lack' needed to be filled by rich countries through the provision of aid to developing countries. As Truman put it, 'in cooperation with other nations, we should foster capital investment in areas needing development'. Third, Truman argued that 'democracy alone can supply the vitalizing force to stir the people of the world into triumphant action, not only against their human oppressor, but also against their ancient enemies – hunger, misery, and despair'.

These three aspects have become the underpinning ideological beliefs that have shaped the global governance of development. The first – the view that the causes of poverty are exclusively domestic, which we term the 'domestication' of poverty – has reinforced the view of development as an action that one agent performs upon another (Rist 2002: 73). It has led to the transfer of power away from domestic authorities – seen as the problem – to external agents, in particular rich nations and multilateral institutions. By framing poverty as a problem arising from factors within developing countries, the implication was that the developed nations, for which extreme poverty was no longer seen to be a major problem, clearly understood how to eradicate poverty around the world.

The second aspect, the view that the lack of financial resources is the key problem of development, has shaped both the modalities of development (based largely on aid financing) and the assessment of who the key agents of development are (namely, those with the ability to provide finance) (Hudson, forthcoming). Investment is of course necessary to bring about sustainable and autonomous development. But we suggest that the almost exclusive focus on financial resources serves to depoliticise development. It frames the responsibilities of rich countries in purely 'positive' terms – governments and individuals have a duty to provide more and better quality aid. This obfuscates the 'negative' duties that rich countries – governments, citizens and consumers – also have to address, namely, the harms caused by the existing institutional organisation of the world economy, such as trade rules, intellectual patents and financial market regulation (Pogge 2008).

The third, the emphasis on democracy, is part of a broader, evolving focus on governance and institutions in developing countries. This focus has been driven by the failings of aid and financing, and is about getting the policies 'right', the institutions in place, corruption down, and the governance capacity and bureaucratic competence of recipient countries up. Because of the focus on 'making aid work' and effective liberalisation of economies, the initiatives around political development have developed a distinctively economistic and technocratic view of governance. The consequence has been a systematic depoliticisation of development at the domestic level.

THE STRUCTURE, AGENTS AND GOALS OF THE DEVELOPMENT PROJECT

In this section we provide a map of the key actors in the current system of global governance of development, discussing their roles and fit within the ideological structure we describe here. We also introduce the MDGs as the institutional, and to some extent intellectual, glue that holds together (or at least coordinates) the system of actors.

The Structure of the Global Governance of Development

In Figure 13.1, we lay out the key actors in the governance of development. These actors are placed into five groups: bilateral donors, international organisations, international financial institutions, developing countries and private organisations. The arrows in the diagram principally represent the flow of development finance. However, as we discuss, these financial flows are closely linked to the flows of knowledge and influence. The ideological foundations influence development policies and who the key actors are in the governance of development and their relative influence.

In Figure 13.1 we place 'the' developing country at the heart of the diagram. The partner – or in older language, the recipient – country (and its population and institutions) is the object of development. It is the thing being developed. As noted, the development project originally shifted responsibility and capacity away from developing countries' domestic authorities. With the emergence of this project, developing countries were portrayed as being stuck in a trap, in order to escape from which they both required and could expect external assistance ('aid') (Rosenstein-Rodan 1943; Nurske 1953; Rostow 1960). This view persists (Sachs et al. 2004; Sachs 2005; UN Millennium Project 2005). As such, the partner country continues to be seen as the problem that needs to be fixed – by providing capital, but also increasingly helping to get the governance and institutions right. Over the 2000s there was greater attention on promoting 'country ownership' of development policies (OECD 2005, 2008). Yet the unequal balance of power ensures, as Paul Cammack (2004: 190) has highlighted, that 'country ownership and local participation are disciplinary rather than empowering in intent'. Developing-country governments know what they are expected to do and so are indirectly coerced into doing it (Lukes 1974; Larmour 2002).

Traditionally, and for the foreseeable future, rich countries have provided most of the aid to developing countries (OECD-DAC 2013). The 24 members of the Organisation for Economic Co-operation and Development (OECD)'s Development Assistance Committee (DAC) are the most high profile and established group of donors. The

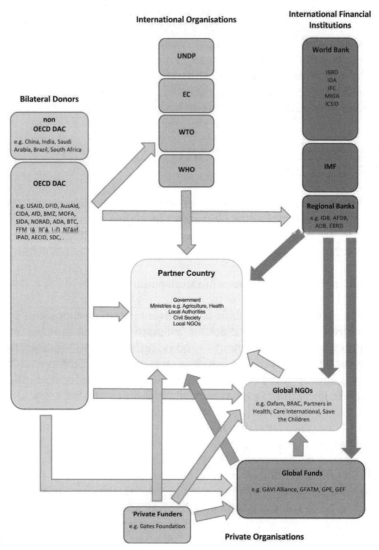

Figure 13.1   Key actors in the global governance of development

OECD acts as the traditional forum for coordination and cooperation with developing countries related to aid and aid effectiveness. Truman's vision was deployed by national governments, ostensibly in the name of solidarity and justice (Lumsdaine 1993), but also from self-interest (Morgenthau 1962). As Truman (1949) put it, 'their poverty' is a 'threat' to 'more prosperous areas'. In the political climate of the Cold War it was recognised that US security concerns relating to the spread of Communism were well served by channelling aid into the rest of the world. In the contemporary era, security concerns such as immigration and terrorism are used to justify foreign aid being in the national interest as well as bringing benefits from commercial and economic ties (van Heerde and

Hudson 2010). Nevertheless, recent econometric analysis of the drivers of aid concludes that donor self-interest has been somewhat overstated, explaining only about 16 per cent of the variation in aid allocation, whereas 'recipient need' accounts for about 36 per cent (Hoeffler and Outram 2011).

The multilateral institutions are the other key players. These are the IOs such as the United Nations (UN) agencies and the World Trade Organization (WTO), and the IFIs: the International Monetary Fund (IMF), the World Bank and the various regional development banks. The role of the IMF in the governance of development has become less prominent with the decline of the 'Washington Consensus' paradigm and the implementation of Structural Adjustment Programmes (SAPs). These SAPs demonstrate most clearly and uncompromisingly the emphasis on external finance, together with technical expertise, in governance reform. However, widespread criticism of the SAPs has led to a debate on whether the IMF should be in the 'development business' at all (Vreeland 2003: 1). The perception of the IMF as excessively austere, neoliberal and Washington-biased has reduced its relevance, at least in terms of loans. Following the East Asian financial crisis, many countries chose to self-insure against the cost of future financial crises by building up large reserves, rather than having to go cap in hand to the IMF (Hudson 2010). In the context of the global financial crisis the IMF has been seeking to re-establish itself through lending, but in a slightly more flexible fashion, such as allowing short-term capital controls (Broome 2010), as well as boosting its global surveillance activities.

In contrast to the IMF, the World Bank's identity has always been fundamentally that of a 'development organisation' (Payne 2005: 113). The World Bank Group is made up of five organisations, the two most important ones being the International Bank for Reconstruction and Development (IBRD) and the International Development Association (IDA). The former provides loans to middle-income countries, while the latter provides concessional loans and grants to the poorest nations. However, in addition to its role providing external finance to developing countries, the World Bank is the largest producer of research and evaluation, and disseminator of knowledge, claiming a 'monopoly of "development knowledge"' (Cammack 2004: 190; see also Payne 2005).

The IOs play a significant, but less immediately powerful, role than the World Bank or the IMF. For example, the United Nations Development Programme (UNDP) has consistently acted as a coordinator within the development system. This role has been cemented as the 'scorekeeper' of the MDG framework. Craig Murphy's (2006) historical account of the organisation portrays it as being much closer to developing countries (operationally and ideologically) than the IFIs. The UNDP is an organisation which prefers to work behind the scenes and has historically promoted a more social and human vision of development as 'freedom', in marked contrast to the view of development as 'efficiency' and 'growth'.

The OECD's role, as already noted, is as a convenor of the major bilateral donors. But it also acts as a forum for policy dialogue, identifying and leading on emerging issues – such as tied aid, aid effectiveness, international tax competition, capital account liberalisation – thereby setting international standards on issues such as corporate governance and providing support to other international organisations such as the WTO (Woodward 2004, 2009). Traditionally a 'rich countries' club', it was designed to manage the Marshall Plan in Europe and so is very much a creature of the international aid regime.

The WTO's aim (and, before it, that of the General Agreement on Tariffs and Trade, GATT) has always been to establish an open trading system on the assumption that this boosts growth, employment and incomes, and reduces costs for consumers. Indeed, in its foundational Agreement, the WTO (1995: 9) makes it clear that open markets themselves are not the goal; rather, sustainable development is the goal and open markets are the tool (see Rodrik 2001). The WTO's attempt to address the needs of developing countries was, in 2001, to launch the Doha Development Agenda (DDA). However, the DDA remains at a stalemate, with disagreements between the wealthy countries (the US, Japan and the European Union) and the emerging economies (Brazil, India, China and others) over agricultural market access, cotton, services, non-agricultural market access, and a package for less-developed countries (LDCs). It is clear that domestic politics in donor countries make granting aid easier than reducing protection for special interest groups.

In looking at the role of the IOs compared with the IFIs, two things become clear. First, because finance is central to the governance of development, it is the latter, with their ability to access and provide financial resources, that are the most influential international actors. Second, if IOs (and global NGOs) deviate from the dominant model of development, particularly by challenging prevailing ideas or power hierarchies, they are likely to see their role diminished. Evidence for this is provided in Murphy's account of the UNDP, but it is also illustrated by the case of the World Health Organization (WHO). Having sought to promote universal access to primary healthcare during the neoliberal 1980s, it found itself marginalised by the increasing influence of the World Bank in the area of public health in developing countries. By the early 1990s, the World Bank had become the dominant force in international health because of its 'ability to mobilize large financial resources' (Brown et al. 2006: 68). The WHO was only able to survive as a key actor in global health policy-making by refashioning itself as 'the coordinator, strategic planner, and leader of global health initiatives' (Brown et al. 2006: 62). Indeed, most IOs in the governance of development typically play the role of coordinator.

While for a long time the governance of development has been dominated by OECD donor nations, IOs, IFIs and recipient governments, in more recent times a number of additional development actors have emerged. The four key additional actors in the governance of development are shown in Figure 13.1: emerging donors, private funders, global funds and global NGOs. We offer a series of reflections at the end of the chapter on their future and how the system of global governance of development is being transformed, or not, by their emergence.

The Millennium Development Goals

Since the start of the 2000s, the entire development system has been organised around the MDGs, 'the most important promise ever made to the world's most vulnerable people' (UN 2010a: 5). The MDGs have shaped the current development context in terms of setting spending priorities and defining what counts as development. They have come to occupy the central position within development policy and practice, both within developing countries and in terms of the development policies of richer nations, NGOs and civil society organisations (Wilkinson and Hulme 2012). For example, the UK's Department for International Development (DfID) (2004) stated early in the new century that 'all of DfID's efforts are directed towards achieving the targets set by the world community in the Millennium Development Goals by 2015'. The MDGs have shaped the discourse and policies of development, providing a common language, a tool for advocacy, monitoring and evaluation, and a common series of expectations and demands, as well as identifying the hoops that organisations must jump through to access funding.

The main contribution of the MDGs has been to set time-bound and quantified goals based on improving economic and human development, with a view to focusing development efforts globally. However, beyond this, the MDG framework has also served to entrench both the structure of the governance of development – in terms of being centred on a top-down global governance approach driven by rich donor nations, IOs and the IFIs (Bond 2006) – and the ideological foundations of the global governance of development.

IDEOLOGICAL FOUNDATIONS OF THE GOVERNANCE OF DEVELOPMENT

We have argued that three core beliefs have shaped the governance of development: poverty is a domestic problem; problems can be fixed with money; but for development to be sustainable the governance of developing countries also needs to be reformed. These 'missing money' and 'missing institutions' views (Gibson et al. 2005) have sustained a predominantly economistic and technocratic approach to development.

The 'Domestication' of Poverty

The view that the causes of poverty and development are exclusively domestic is fundamental to the governance of development. As Thomas Pogge (2001) has pointed out, while there may be much debate among actors involved in development policy, the assumption that poverty arises from domestic factors is largely unquestioned. This belief can be seen in the major development approaches that have consistently informed development policy. For example, modernisation theory, which significantly influenced development policy in the 1960s, considered development to be a linear process in which countries began as impoverished 'traditional societies' and passed through different stages of economic growth before entering the 'age of mass consumption' (Rostow 1960). From this viewpoint, poverty is considered endogenous to a country and unrelated to external factors. Crucially, even if people rarely talk in terms of 'modernisation theory' these days, the underlying view that poverty is domestic remains. This belief informed the Washington Consensus, which, as Charles Gore (2000: 792) points out, used a 'methodologically nationalist form of explanation which attributed what was happening within countries mainly to national factors and policies'. Furthermore, this view has continued into the Post-Washington Consensus and the MDGs. Moreover, the World Bank's Poverty Reduction Strategy Papers (PRSPs) and Poverty Assessments (PAs) continue to ignore international factors in their analyses of poverty in developing countries. One analysis of the PRSPs and PAs of 20 countries finds that only 10 per cent of documents had any reference to global factors (Dasandi 2009).

The 'internalist' view of poverty is also demonstrated by the dominant views of the causes of poverty in academic debates. The explanations for differences in poverty levels around the world largely focus on unfavourable geography (Sachs 2001, 2005), bad governance and policies (Burnside and Dollar 2000; Dollar and Kraay 2002) and, in particular, the quality of countries' domestic institutions (Easterly and Levine 2003; Rodrik et al. 2004; Acemoglu and Robinson 2012). The broader international structure tends to be excluded in analysis of the root causes of poverty. The solution continues to be seen to be: provide more aid and improve the governance of developing countries.

'Missing Money': Financing for Development

In September 2010 world leaders convened for a three-day summit at the United Nations to address the MDGs. The outcomes of the summit were summarised in the document 'Keeping the promise: united to achieve the Millennium Development Goals', which was accompanied by a 'global action plan' (UN 2010b). One of the headline successes was a big push on women's and children's health, specifically the issuing of a pledge of over US$40 billion for the next five years. In a telling phrase, Ban Ki-moon, the UN Secretary General, was confident that 'we know what works to save women's and children's lives' (UN 2010b). The implicit message was that the solution to global poverty is financial resources alongside sufficient political will to help realise and apply expert knowledge. Tellingly, the press release that followed detailed the amounts of money pledged to agriculture, education, women's empowerment, environmental sustainability, health, and so forth.

This view that the solution to global poverty is external financing is central to the governance of development and has a long and well-established logic (Nurkse 1953; Nelson 1956; Leibenstein 1957). The injection of capital will allow poor countries to address the causes of economic backwardness and to develop. Jeffrey Sachs, a well-known proponent of a 'big push' for development aid, also argues that developing countries are caught in a 'poverty trap' (Sachs et al. 2004). The poverty trap consists of high levels of initial poverty, very low household savings rates (because money is more than taken up by necessities), low levels of infrastructure capital, and population growth. Together, these interact to make it almost impossible for countries or households to exit this self-reinforcing cycle. An external injection of capital, though, would break the cycle and allow a positive cycle of increased savings and investment. From this perspective the relationship between development and finance is framed as one of resources, and the subsequent debates are about the provision of these resources, the lack of these resources, the reasons for shortfalls, and to whom and how money should be given to maximise its effectiveness. Success is measured in dollars and failure to meet pledges or backsliding are the key problems.

The chief statement of this position is the Monterrey Consensus of the International Conference on Financing for Development, adopted by heads of states and governments in March 2002. This was a crucial moment for development financing as it provided an international framework for cooperation on these issues, hailed as a 'landmark' and a 'watershed' (UN Millennium Project 2005). In a report prepared to feed into the conference, the High-Level Panel on Financing for Development estimated that an extra US$50 billion per year in aid would be necessary to help reach the MDGs (Zedillo et al. 2001). More recently, the Millennium Development Project led by Sachs estimated that the total costs to support the low-income and middle-income countries, as well as the costs of capacity-building and debt relief, would start at US$121 billion per year in 2006 and reach US$189 billion by 2015. As such, overseas development assistance (ODA) should be US$135 billion in 2006 and rise to US$195 billion in 2015, which would be equivalent to 0.54 per cent of the gross national product (GNP) of donor countries. Of course, these kinds of exercises are inevitably rough and ready, and make a number of 'heroic assumptions' (Clemens et al. 2007: 737). But the lessons are clear.

First, the MDGs arc framcd as a gap needing to be filled by financial resources. Indeed, the UN has an annual report, prepared by its Millennium Development Goal Gap Task Force, which outlines how much aid donor countries have provided, how much they have fallen short of their commitments and what is necessary to reach the MDGs (UN MDG Gap Task Force 2011). Second, one of the key heroic assumptions is an improved policy environment within developing countries. Better domestic govern-ance of aid flows will mean less waste and greater effectiveness. Governance enters here as a technical solution to a financing problem. This fits with a series of more general arguments about the technocratic and apolitical notion of governance.

Missing Institutions: Governance in Development

While the issue of governance has long been a part of development studies and policy, the end of the Cold War saw the rise of the 'good governance' agenda. Since the 1990s, the study and practice of development has undergone a 'political turn' (Jones et al. 2012). It is in fact useful to think of not one political turn, but a series of connected turns as the development community tried to navigate back out of the neoliberal dead end.

The Washington Consensus marked the attempt to import or impose liberal policies and structural adjustment through strengthening property rights, deregulating and liber-alising domestic markets, privatising state-owned companies and, in particular, opening up economies to free trade and financial investment. The implementation of these poli-cies was largely justified on the basis that they would promote economic growth. The major criticism of the Washington Consensus is that during its period of dominance, when many developing countries were forced to implement neoliberal reform, growth rates in developing countries worsened (Easterly 2001; Chang 2003). The attempts to deal with this failing led to the rise of the so-called Post-Washington Consensus.

The failure of the Washington Consensus invited in 'governance' as the solution, at least within the mainstream. The early important statement of this was World Bank's 1989 report *Sub-Saharan Africa: From Crisis to Sustainable Growth*. The report argued that developmental failure was not simply a result of bad (read: non-liberal) economic policies, but could be attributed to 'a crisis of governance' (World Bank 1989: 60; see also Mosley and Toye 1988). The understanding of good governance which emerged, however, is strikingly technical, managerial and administrative, not political. For example, the World Bank's 1992 paper on *Governance and Development* (1992: 1) defined 'good' governance as 'synonymous with sound development management'. Similarly, governance failings were seen by many as an important reason for the failure of interna-tional aid to promote development. Improving bureaucratic competence and reducing corruption were proposed as the solution (UN Millennium Project 2005). Consequently, good governance became a central principle for donor agencies, and was incorporated into the requirements they set out for developing countries to receive development assistance (Doornbos 2001).

Most recently, there has been a move away from a focus on good governance and policies towards an emphasis on the role of institutions in shaping development. Following the seminal work of Douglas North (1981, 1990), a number of economists have argued that differences in countries' institutional quality is the key determinant of differences in levels of poverty and development (see Acemoglu et al. 2001; Easterly and Levine 2003; Rodrik et al. 2004). In examining institutional quality, the emphasis has largely been on the protection of property rights, and constraints on elites and politicians, which ensure that they cannot expropriate incomes or create a highly uneven playing field (Acemoglu et al. 2006). This perspective has proved enormously influential, both in academic circles and policy and practitioner worlds.

BEYOND THE DOMESTICATION AND DEPOLITICISATION OF POVERTY

In this section we develop critiques of the domestication and depoliticisation of poverty at the international and domestic levels. The assumption that poverty is caused exclusively by domestic factors means that the impact of the international system on development is largely ignored in the governance of development. The broader international system in which developing countries are embedded matters in two principal ways. The first relates to the unequal economic relations between states in the international system, whereby trade, investment and financial ties reflect and reproduce structural inequalities between states (Braithwaite et al. 2012; Dasandi, forthcoming). The effect of unequal trade relations between countries on development has long been noted, whereby the secular deterioration in the terms of trade between primary commodities, mainly produced in the developing world, and manufactured goods, produced in more developed countries, has led to a transfer of resources from poorer countries to richer countries (Prebisch 1950). Despite increasing industrialisation within many developing countries, primary products continue to form the largest share of exports for the majority of developing countries. Moreover, the terms of trade between labour-intensive, low-skill manufactures, such as textiles, and capital and knowledge-intensive manufactures, such as electronics, continue to deteriorate (UNCTAD 2005; Kaplinsky 2005; Harvey et al. 2010). Similar analyses of foreign direct investment (FDI) (Bornschier and Chase-Dunn 1985; Tsai 1995; Mihalache-O'Keef and Li 2011), aid (Hayter 1971; Easterly 2006) and portfolio capital (Rodrik 1997; Tornell et al. 2004; Crotty and Lee 2006; Reinhart and Rogoff 2009) tell a similar story: unequal economic ties serve to reproduce international inequalities and perpetuate poverty.

The second way in which the international system influences development is through the global decision-making structures and the increasing number of international laws, which govern the economic and political interactions between states and significantly hinder development opportunities in developing countries. These laws are shaped by the unequal power that exists between countries, resulting in rules that serve the economic and political interests of the most powerful nations (Hurrell and Woods 1999; Deaton 2004; Payne 2005). As such, these international laws – themselves the result of existing international inequalities – serve further to reinforce the structural inequalities between countries.

This, again, is particularly notable in the case of international trade laws, which have enabled richer nations to continue using tariff and non-tariff barriers to prevent developing nations from entering markets (Wade 2003; Bardhan 2006; Pogge 2008); allowed richer nations to subsidise agriculture, adversely impacting developing-country agricultural producers (Khor 2005; Charlton and Stiglitz 2005); pushed developing countries into rapid and comprehensive trade liberalisation, which, as Ha-Joon Chang (2003) has pointed out, runs counter to the historic experience of the richer nations (see also Rodrik 2001); and, in the area of intellectual property rights, restricted developing countries' access to technology (Wade 2003; Pogge 2008; Bardhan 2006; Gallagher 2008).

Beyond the direct influence of international politics on the availability of resources to developing countries, the international context also affects development by influencing institutions and policies in the developing world. Pogge (2001, 2008) has highlighted the manner in which the international system permits any group that comes to power in a national territory to borrow funds in the name of the country, regardless of the means through which the group came to power and exercises its power. Furthermore, the international system also provides such groups with the legal rights to sell the country's natural resources internationally, regardless of how repressive this group may be or how its governmental power was acquired. An example is Mobutu's ability to seize power in the Congo and sell minerals, such as cobalt and diamonds, to wealthy companies. These factors, combined with the power vacuum that emerged in many developing countries in the wake of colonial rule, have provided strong incentives for coups, civil wars, high levels of corruption, and authoritarianism, which have resulted in bad governance and weak institutions in these countries.

At the domestic level, the rise of new institutionalism has to a limited degree highlighted the importance of politics in development. The effect has been to open up space to start to talk and think about politics and development. However, despite the headline claims about the 'centrality of politics' in development, or that 'politics matters', it is manifestly the case that what is meant by 'politics', and how to deal with it, remains unclear and uncertain (Carothers and de Gramont 2013). Specifically, the focus on institutions has led to greater attention being given to the role and interests of elites in mainstream development analysis. However, the focus is on a narrow range of fixed political attributes at the state level, and how these political attributes relate to economic growth. In this deeply economistic approach, there is little consideration given to political processes, such as contestation, mobilisation and the role of social movements. So, if certain types of institutions work better, how are they brought about, and maintained and defended? Who does it? How do they achieve it? These are live questions of politics, requiring analysis of agency, contingency and ideas – the stuff of political analysis (Hay 2002).

A number of recent contributions on the role of politics and political leadership and coalition-building have begun to emerge, but they remain on the margins (Lyne de Ver 2009; Leftwich, forthcoming). For example, Melo et al. (2012) look at the cases of Museveni in Uganda, Digvijay Singh in India's Madhya Pradesh state, and Fernando Henrique Cardoso in Brazil. The authors show how, through building consensus, the three politicians worked through or around the binding political constraints they faced.

More analysis like this is needed, which weaves together agency and political dynamics with institutional accounts. After all, institutions are nothing but empty boxes without understanding the role of agents that inhabit them (Levi 2006). For example, both Pakistan and India inherited the same formal colonial institutions. However, their subsequent variation in government effectiveness arises in large part from the differences between Jinnah's and Nehru's approach to post-colonial state-building. Institutions do not determine outcomes. Likewise, in their discussion of Botswana's success story, Acemoglu et al. (2003) note that good institutions did play a significant role in Botswana's development. But they also note how the institution-building just would not have happened without 'a number of important and far-sighted decisions by the post-independence political leaders, in particular Seretse Khama and Quett Masire' (2003: 84) (see also Poteete 2009).

In turn, development agencies need to take such issues seriously, for they are essentially all about the 'enlightened Machiavellian management of politics' (Melo et al. 2012: 109). There is some evidence of this beginning to happen. For example, in one of the background papers to the World Bank's recent Commission on Growth and Development, David Brady and Michael Spence (2009) underline the centrality of leadership and successful coalition building to generate economic growth. Getting things done cannot be reduced to technical fixes, but rather is about politics and agency.

This is a criticism that can be applied to the governance of development more generally, where the concept of governance centres on a technical, economistic understanding of how societies should be governed, linking different components of governance to economic growth and greater aid effectiveness. From this perspective, the role of governments is simply to manage development, meaning that the politics of governance have been excluded from mainstream development approaches (Hickey 2008; Doornbos 2001). Consequently, issues such as historic struggles for power between different societal interests receive little attention in the analysis of governance in development.

THE FUTURE OF THE GLOBAL GOVERNANCE OF DEVELOPMENT

What does the future hold? Current trends point towards a number of exciting and interesting changes in the global governance of development, for example increasing aid transparency, and some deeper geopolitical shifts. Figure 13.1 notes the emergence of a new set of actors within the development landscape. Will they challenge the underlying ideology of the global governance of development? Prediction is always a dubious business, especially in politics. The outcomes will, of course, be contingent upon agents winning arguments, changing beliefs, wielding power and negotiating compromise. Nevertheless, we conclude with some tentative suggestions about the post-MDG agenda and the impact of new actors on the system.

First, private donors range from private individuals who are rich (such as Bill Gates or Warren Buffett), to people who are well off (such as most individuals in OECD countries who make donations to charity), to the poor (such as migrant workers who send their income home as remittances). In terms of our three core ideological beliefs we see little prospective change. The rise of private funders is seen by some as a rival to official development assistance (Kharas 2007; Bishop 2008; Brainard and LaFleur 2008). The most notable of these, such as the Bill and Melinda Gates Foundation, are now already established as major actors in the governance of development. These organisations have been spending around US$3–5 billion annually on international development activities in recent years (Marten and Witte 2008; see also Brainard and LaFleur 2008). The prevalent technocratic view of development has enabled these private funders to emerge as key players, and their rise to prominence in turn has reinforced this depoliticised and technocratic approach to development. As Marten and Witte (2008: 15) point out, private philanthropic funders 'claim their work is apolitical and "problem-oriented"'. Similarly, global funds, such as the GAVI Alliance and the Global Fund to Fight AIDS, Tuberculosis and Malaria (GFATM), demonstrate the continuing, fundamental belief that shortages of financing are the principal problem of development.

Charitable donations from the public to NGOs, through appeals, or through micro-lending sites such as Kiva, have a very clear logic: money is given by a powerful donor to a grateful receiver (Darnton and Kirk 2011). The notion is deeply entrenched that development is a problem to be solved by giving small sums of money, which collectively add up to large amounts (such as Comic Relief events), to provide for technical apolitical solutions such as mosquito nets or digging wells, which instantly save lives. There is, of course, a great deal of generosity at work here. Nonetheless, the understandings of development which circulate among the general public tend to see poverty as home-grown (generated by corruption, culture, conflict), with the resulting responsibility being largely charitable (rather than perceived as a question of justice or politics) (Henson et al. 2010).

Meanwhile, the emergence of remittances as a source of development financing has seen them brought into the existing governance of development. Remittances are the portion of migrant workers' earnings which they send home to their country of origin, often to their family. While the act of sending money home is not new, the size of the phenomenon and its recognition are. The World Bank estimates that in 1990 remittances to developing countries were around US$31 billion, whilst the latest estimates suggest that remittance flows to developing countries have reached US$351 billion in 2011 (Mohapatra et al. 2011). Remittances dwarf aid flows; they are almost two and a half times the volume of global ODA, which stood at US$128.5 billion in 2010. The World Bank has taken the lead in trying to harness the impact of remittances for poverty reduction through a series of initiatives designed to increase remittances volumes, leverage the impact of inflows, 'bank the unbanked' and spur financial development (Hudson, forthcoming). Harnessing remittances may help individual households, but these will not be the poorest. Some evidence suggests that remittances increase inequality at the global level (World Bank 2006). Furthermore, remittances do not challenge the assumption that development is a problem of missing money, nor the underlying structural causes of poverty, given that migration is not the solution to underdevelopment so much as an outcome of underdevelopment. Sceptics of the so-called remittance euphoria argue that, 'if migration brought development, Mexico would be Switzerland' (DeParle 2008).

Second, what role for NGOs? While we distinguish between global NGOs and local NGOs in developing countries in Figure 13.1, many of the challenges and debates around the two are similar. NGOs differ significantly from the other actors involved in the governance of development because many have provided an important challenge to the dominant ideological beliefs that shape the governance of development and, in doing so, have challenged some of the key actors in international development. For example, the NGOs Oxfam and Christian Aid have frequently emphasised in their campaigns how the policies and behaviour of rich nations have produced poverty and prevented the achievement of the MDGs in many developing countries (Oxfam 2010; Christian Aid 2012). However, the greater inclusion of NGOs within the governance of development has again come about in large part due to efforts to increase aid effectiveness and, as such, NGOs are largely seen by the more dominant actors as 'service deliverers'. In recent times, this has led to much attention being given to whether these NGOs do challenge the dominant approaches or rather conform to the existing power structures. Are NGOs 'transforming or conforming' (Bristow 2008)? Are they 'political entrepreneurs or development agents' (Chhotray 2008)?

The MDGs are particularly important in this regard. The broad appeal of the goals and the vast resources directed towards achieving them have left NGOs caught in the classic 'insider–outsider' dilemma: work within the existing power hierarchies and be part of the global effort to achieve these momentous goals, which could improve the lives of many; or try and effect change from the outside by challenging global inequalities, but face being marginalised in the process and having little impact on changing the situation of the global poor. Some of the larger NGOs have recently tried to move beyond this quandary by trying to get inequality into development policy and the post-2015 development agenda. For example, Oxfam has called for a 'global new deal' to address inequality, while Save the Children has sought to incorporate inequality into a proposal for a new set of global development goals to replace the current MDGs after 2015 (Oxfam 2013; Save the Children 2013). The extent to which these more radical ideas are realised in the post-2015 development agenda will be revealing. The UN has convened a High Level Panel to deliberate and develop a post-MDG vision. Our sense is that the foundational ideas run deep, and consequently the issue of inequality will be severely diluted or discarded altogether.

Third, and finally, what impact will the emerging donors such as China, Brazil and India have on the global governance of development? Some research has been done on this, but as yet not much (Manning 2006; Woods 2008). Here we think that the fate of NGOs over the past few decades provides an instructive lesson. There is a contingent dialectic process of incorporation and resistance to the existing structures and ideology of global governance. It is clear that a stronger China, for example, would bring with it its own way of doing things and could potentially remould the system of global governance around its norms and practices (Jacques 2009). The discomfort Western donors have felt with the emergence of China and its very different way of 'doing' aid has seen vocal criticism, such as in former US Secretary of State Hillary Clinton's comments about China plundering Africa and 'chequebook diplomacy' (as opposed to the putative US commitment to democracy and human rights). Yet this comes up against the US's own record in Africa and elsewhere, as well as China's presentation of its aid ideology as harmonious and in partnership (Brautigum 2009). It is also worth noting that aid sums from the emerging donors remain small compared with those provided by the traditional OECD donors.

On the other hand, there are significant signs of the attempted incorporation of new donors into the formal structures of the Western aid regime. For example, at the Busan High Level Forum on Aid Effectiveness in 2011, a new Partnership for Effective

Development Cooperation was signed. The declaration brings China, India, Brazil and South Africa into the fold as they signed up 'on a voluntary basis' to endorse the 'principles, commitments and actions agreed in the outcome document' which include transparency and accountability but also aid reporting standards (OECD 2011). However, Busan also saw the launch of the Global Partnership for Effective Development Cooperation, which will effectively relegate the OECD's DAC from its traditional role at the centre of the aid donor governance architecture. Notably, the new institution will have a joint OECD–UNDP secretariat, mirroring the shift from the Group of 7 (G7) to the Group of 20 (G20) in recognition of the emergence of a new multipolar world. In sum, the future is open, but is still a long way away.

CONCLUSION

In this chapter, we have examined the global governance of development from its emergence after the Second World War to its focus on the MDGs. In doing so, we have focused on three core ideological beliefs that have shaped the governance of development: the domestication of poverty, the view that missing money is the core problem of development, and the technocratic focus on governance. In arguing that these are the core ideological foundations, we do not claim that other ideological factors have not influenced the governance of development; they have. For example, the pendulum has swung back and forth between the state and the market in mainstream development thinking, which in turn has had important repercussions for development policies (Kanbur 2004). However, the ideological beliefs that we identify have remained constant and fundamental to the manner in which development is done, providing the foundations for the global governance of development. Significantly, the three elements have provided the ideological basis for the overarching objective of the governance of development which, we argue, is the effort to reduce poverty without changing existing power structures globally and domestically.

The 'domestication' of poverty, and the subsequent failure to consider the impact of international inequalities, can be seen in the MDG framework. In asking 'why the world is falling short of the Goals', the answers focus almost exclusively on domestic factors in developing countries, primarily on governance failures and countries being caught in a 'poverty trap' due to insufficient capital availability (UN Millennium Project 2005: 29). Consequently, the structural inequalities discussed above, which are bound up in the system of international governance, receive little attention in the MDGs. The eighth and final goal – to develop a global partnership between countries to achieve the other seven goals – highlights issues such as trade, debt and technological transfer. However, the targets included are vague and are not time-bound. Perhaps of greater significance is that these issues are framed as areas in which rich nations can assist poorer nations, rather than as harms that result from structural inequalities.

Hence, in general, the issue of harms resulting from the structure of the international system is missing from the MDG framework. Instead, the international sphere is seen only in terms of providing external technical assistance in the form of development finance to correct problems in developing countries that have arisen due to various domestic weaknesses. Consequently, Saith (2006: 1186) points out that, 'essentially, what is called a global partnership for development has little more in it than some additional, but conditional, ODA'. This approach can be seen in the UNDP's (2003: v) assertion that the 'global partnership' needed for the MDGs to be met is one 'requiring bold reforms from poor countries and obliging donor countries to step forward and support those efforts'. A further issue that arises when we consider the broader international context and the structural inequalities between countries is whether development finance can be seen simply as a form of technical assistance, as is the case in the MDG framework (Soederberg 2004; Hudson, forthcoming). When aid is considered in the context of the significant inequalities between donor and recipient countries, instead of being just a transfer of resources from the former to the latter, it 'performs the political function of maintaining the status quo' (Morgenthau 1962: 302). The transfer of aid enables developed countries to exert their power over developing countries in a less coercive and more consensual manner (Hattori 2003; Gronemeyer 2010; Mosse 2005). By accepting aid from the donor nations, developing countries provide consent to the unequal global system.

The goals, which focus on promoting different dimensions of human development, exclude any real focus on inequalities of wealth and power between and within countries (Saith 2006; Hickey 2008). In looking at the feasibility of achieving the MDGs and asking 'Can the rich afford to help the poor?', Sachs (2005: 289) argues that 'the goal is to end *extreme* poverty, not to end all poverty, and still less to equalize world incomes or to close the gap between the rich and the poor'. The implication is that the unequal distribution of wealth and power is largely unrelated to the poverty we see around the world, and that the MDGs can be achieved, as long as the necessary finance is provided, without addressing existing global and domestic inequalities.

Yet, as we have argued in this chapter, such an approach is highly questionable. Domestic politics, and issues of power and distribution, are central to explaining current poverty. As Andy Sumner (2012) has highlighted, most of the world's poor now live in middle-income countries. As such, issues of distribution need to be better incorporated into development policy. In addition, the broader international system has a significant effect on contemporary poverty. This too has been demonstrated in recent analyses that consider the impact of the unequal structure of trade relations on poverty (Braithwaite et al. 2012; Dasandi, forthcoming). In conclusion, we believe that it is important to identify and explore the three component ideas which form the bigger neoliberal ideology underpinning the global governance of development precisely because doing so demonstrates how individually plausible ideas such as increasing aid as the solution to global poverty, which are often championed in good faith, together serve to exclude politics and power from the domestic and international development agendas.

REFERENCES

Acemoglu, D., S. Johnson and J.A. Robinson (2001), 'The colonial origins of comparative development: an empirical investigation', *American Economic Review*, **91** (5), 1369–1401.
Acemoglu, D., S. Johnson and J.A. Robinson (2003), 'An African success: Botswana', in D. Rodrik (ed.), *In Search of Prosperity: Analytic Narratives on Economic Growth*, Princeton, NJ: Princeton University Press, pp. 80–122.
Acemoglu, D., S. Johnson and J.A. Robinson (2006), 'Understanding prosperity and poverty: geography,

institutions, and the reversal of fortune', in A.V. Banerjee, R. Bénabou and D. Mookherjee (eds), *Understanding Poverty*, Oxford: Oxford University Press, pp. 19–36.

Acemoglu, D. and J.A. Robinson (2012), *Why Nations Fail*, London: Profile Books.

Bardhan, P. (2006), 'Globalization and the limits to poverty alleviation', in P. Bardhan, S. Bowles and M. Wallerstein (eds), *Globalization and Egalitarian Redistribution*, Princeton, NJ: Princeton University Press, pp. 13–32.

Bishop, M. (2008), 'Fighting global poverty: who will be relevant in 2020?', in L. Brainard and D. Chollet (eds), *Global Development 2.0: Can Philanthropists, the Public, and the Poor Make Poverty History?*, Washington, DC: Brookings Institution, pp. 42–52.

Bornschier, V. and C. Chase-Dunn (1985), *Transnational Corporations and Underdevelopment*, New York: Praeger.

Bond, P. (2006), 'Global governance campaigning and MDGs: from top-down to bottom-up anti-poverty work', *Third World Quarterly*, **27** (2), 339–54.

Brady, D. and M. Spence (2009), 'Leadership and politics: a perspective from the Growth Commission', *Oxford Review of Economic Policy*, **25** (2), 205–18.

Brainard, L. and V. LaFleur (2008), 'Making poverty history? How activists, philanthropists, and the public are changing global development', in L. Brainard and D. Chollet (eds), *Global Development 2.0: Can Philanthropists, the Public, and the Poor Make Poverty History?*, Washington, DC: Brookings Institution, pp. 9 41.

Braithwaite, A., N. Dasandi and D. Hudson (2012), 'Does poverty cause conflict? Isolating the causal origins of the conflict trap', Working Paper, London: University College London.

Brautigum, D. (2009), *The Dragon's Gift: The Real Story of China in Africa*, Oxford: Oxford University Press.

Bristow, K.S. (2008), 'Transforming or conforming? NGOs training health promoters and the dominant paradigm of the development industry in Bolivia', in A.J. Bebbington, S. Hickey and D.C. Mitlin (eds), *Can NGOs Make a Difference? The Challenge of Development Alternatives*, London: Zed Books, pp. 240–60.

Broome, A. (2010), 'The International Monetary Fund, crisis management and the credit crunch', *Australian Journal of International Affairs*, **64** (1), 37–54.

Brown, T.M., M. Cueto and E. Free (2006), ' The World Health Organization and the transition from "international" to "global" public health', *American Journal of Public Health*, **96** (1), 62–72.

Burnside, C. and D. Dollar (2000), 'Aid, policies, and growth', *American Economic Review*, **90** (4), 847–68.

Cammack, P. (2004), 'What the World Bank means by poverty reduction and why it matters', *New Political Economy*, **9** (2), 189–211.

Carothers, T. and D. de Gramont (2013), *Development Aid Confronts Politics: The Almost Revolution*, Washington, DC: Carnegie Endowment for International Peace.

Chang, H.-J. (2003), *Kicking Away the Ladder: Development Strategy in Historical Perspective*, London: Anthem Press.

Charlton, A.H. and J.E. Stiglitz (2005), 'A development-friendly prioritisation of Doha Round proposals', *World Economy*, **28** (3), 293–312.

Chen, S. and M. Ravallion (2012), 'More relatively-poor people in a less absolutely-poor world', Policy Research Working Paper 6114, Washington, DC: World Bank.

Chhotray, V. (2008), 'Political entrepreneurs or development agents: an NGO's tale of resistance and acquiescence in Madhya Pradesh, India', in A.J. Bebbington, S. Hickey and D.C. Mitlin (eds), *Can NGOs Make a Difference? The Challenge of Development Alternatives*, London: Zed Books, pp. 261–78.

Christian Aid (2012), 'Shared future, shared responsibilities: rethinking global development goals post-2015', Christian Aid Policy Briefing, November, London: Christian Aid.

Clemens, M.A., C.J. Kenny and T.J. Moss (2007), 'The trouble with the MDGs: confronting expectations of aid and development success', *World Development*, **35** (5), 735–51.

Crotty, J. and K.K. Lee (2006), 'The effects of neoliberal "reforms" on the post-crisis Korean economy', *Review of Radical Political Economics*, **38** (4), 669–75.

Darnton, A. and M. Kirk (2011), 'Finding frames: new ways to engage the UK public in global poverty', London: BOND.

Dasandi, N. (2009), 'Poverty reductionism: the exclusion of history, politics, and global factors from mainstream poverty analysis', IPEG Papers in Global Political Economy, British International Studies Association (BISA), Paper No. 39.

Dasandi, N. (forthcoming), 'International inequality and world poverty: a quantitative structural analysis', *New Political Economy*.

Deaton, A. (2004), 'Health in an age of globalization', paper presented at Brookings Trade Forum, 13 May, Washington, DC: Brookings Institution.

DeParle, J. (2008), 'World banker and his cash return home', *New York Times*, 17 March, available at: http://www.nytimes.com/2008/03/17/world/asia/17remit.html?_r=1&ref=world_bank&pagewanted=all (accessed 3 September 2010).

Desai, V. and R.B. Potter (2002), *The Companion to Development Studies*, London: Arnold.

DfID (2004), 'Research Funding Framework: 2005–07', London: Department for International Development.

Dollar, D. and A. Kraay (2002), 'Growth is good for the poor', *Journal of Economic Growth*, 7 (3), 195–225.

Doornbos, M. (2001), '"Good governance": the rise and decline of a policy metaphor?', *Journal of Development Studies*, 37 (6), 93–108.

Easterly, W. (2001), 'The lost decades: developing countries' stagnation in spite of policy reform 1980–1999', *Journal of Economic Growth*, 6, 135–57.

Easterly, W. (2006), *The White Man's Burden: Why the West's Efforts to Aid the Rest Have Done So Much Ill and So Little Good*, Oxford: Oxford University Press.

Easterly, W. and R. Levine (2003), 'Tropics, germs, and crops: how endowments influence economic development', *Journal of Monetary Economics*, 50 (1), 3–39.

Gallagher, K.P. (2008), 'Understanding developing country resistance to the Doha Round', *Review of International Political Economy*, 15 (1), 62–85.

Gibson, C.C., K. Andersson, E. Ostrom and S. Shivakumar (2005), *The Samaritan's Dilemma: The Political Economy of Development Aid*, Oxford: Oxford University Press.

Gore, C. (2000), 'The rise and fall of the Washington Consensus as a paradigm for developing countries', *World Development*, 28 (5), 789–804.

Gronemeyer, M. (2010), 'Helping', in W. Sachs (ed.), *The Development Dictionary: A Guide to Knowledge as Power*, 2nd edition, London: Zed Books, pp. 55–73.

Harvey, D.I., N.M. Kellard, J.B. Madsen and M.E. Wohar (2010), 'The Prebisch–Singer hypothesis: four centuries of evidence', *Review of Economics and Statistics*, 92 (2), 367–77.

Hattori, T. (2003), 'Giving as a mechanism of consent: international aid organizations and the ethical hegemony of capitalism', *International Relations*, 17 (2), 153–73.

Hay, C. (2002), *Political Analysis*, Basingstoke: Palgrave.

Hayter, T. (1971), *Aid as Imperialism*, Harmondsworth: Penguin.

Henson, S., J. Lindstrom, L. Haddad and R. Mulmi (2010), 'Public perceptions of international development and support for aid in the UK: results of a qualitative enquiry', IDS Working Paper, Brighton: IDS.

Hickey, S. (2008), 'The return of politics in development studies I: Getting lost within the poverty agenda?', *Progress in Development Studies*, 8 (4), 348–58.

Hoeffler, A. and V. Outram (2011), 'Need, merit, or self-interest – what determines the allocation of aid?', *Review of Development Economics*, 15, 237–50.

Hudson, D. (2010), 'Financing for development and the post Keynesian case for a new global reserve currency', *Journal of International Development*, 22 (6), 772–87.

Hudson, D. (forthcoming), *Global Finance and Development*, London: Routledge.

Hurrell, A. and N. Woods (1999), *Inequality, Globalization and World Politics*, New York: Oxford University Press.

Jacques, M. (2009), *When China Rules the World: The End of the Western World and the Birth of a New Global Order*, London: Allen Lane.

Jones, H., N.A. Jones, L. Shaxson and D. Walker (2012), *Knowledge, Policy and Power in International Development: A Practical Guide*, Bristol: Policy Press.

Kanbur, R. (2004), 'The development of development thinking', *Journal of Social and Economic Development*, 6 (2), 147–58.

Kaplinsky, R. (2005), *Globalization, Poverty and Inequality*, Cambridge: Polity Press.

Kenny, C. (2011), *Getting Better: Why Global Development Is Succeeding – And How We Can Improve the World Even More*, New York: Basic Books.

Kharas, H. (2007), 'The new reality of aid', presented at Brookings Blum Roundtable 2007 in Brookings Institution, Washington, DC, 1 August.

Khor, M. (2005), 'The commodities crisis and the global trade in agriculture: present problems and some proposals', in F. Cheru and C. Bradford (eds), *The Millennium Development Goals: Raising the Resources to Tackle World Poverty*, London: Zed Books, pp. 97–117.

Larmour, P. (2002), 'Conditionality, coercion and other forms of "power": international financial institutions in the Pacific', *Public Administration and Development*, 22 (3), 249–60.

Leftwich, A. (forthcoming), 'Leadership and the politics of development', in N. van de Walle and C. Lancaster (eds), *Oxford Handbook on the Politics of Development*, Oxford: Oxford University Press.

Leibenstein, H. (1957), *Economic Backwardness and Economic Growth*, New York: Wiley.

Levi, M. (2006), 'Why we need a new theory of government', *Perspectives on Politics*, 4, 5–19.

Lukes, S. (1974), *Power: A Radical View*, London: Macmillan.

Lumsdaine, D. (1993), *Moral Vision in International Politics: The Foreign Aid Regime, 1949–1989*, Princeton, NJ: Princeton University Press.

Lyne de Ver, H. (2009), 'Conceptions of leadership', Developmental Leadership Program Background Paper 4, available at: http://www.dlprog.org.

Manning, R. (2006), 'Will "emerging donors" change the face of international co-operation?', *Development Policy Review*, **24** (4), 371–85.

Marten, R. and J.M. Witte (2008), 'Transforming development? The role of philanthropic foundations in international development cooperation', GPPi Research Paper Series No. 10, Berlin: Global Public Policy Institute.

Melo, M.A., N. Ng'ethe and J. Manor (2012), *Against the Odds: Politicians, Institutions, and the Struggle Against Poverty*, London: C. Hurst & Co.

Merton, Robert K. (1968), 'The Matthew effect in science', *Science*, **159**, 56–63.

Mihalache-O'Keef, A. and Q. Li (2011), 'Modernization vs. dependency revisited: effects of foreign direct investment on food security in less developed countries', *International Studies Quarterly*, **55**, 71–93.

Milanovic, B. (2005), *World Apart: Measuring International and Global Inequality*, Princeton, NJ: Princeton University Press.

Milanovic, B. (2011), *The Haves and the Have Nots*, New York: Basic Books.

Mohapatra, S., D. Ratha and A. Silwal (2011), 'Outlook for remittance flows 2012–14', *Migration and Development Brief 17*, Washington, DC: World Bank Migration and Remittances Unit.

Morgenthau, H. (1962), 'A political theory of foreign aid', *American Political Science Review*, **56** (2), 301–9.

Mosley, P. and J. Toye (1988), 'The design of structural adjustment programmes', *Development Policy Review*, **6**, 395–413.

Mosse, D. (2005), 'Global governance and the ethnography of international aid', in D. Mosse and D. Lewis (eds), *The Aid Effect: Giving and Governing in International Development*, London: Pluto Press, pp. 1–36.

Murphy, C.N. (2006), *The United Nations Development Programme: A Better Way?* Cambridge: Cambridge University Press.

Nelson, R.R. (1956), 'A theory of the low-level equilibrium trap in underdeveloped economies', *American Economic Review*, **46** (5), 894–908.

North, D.C. (1981), *Structure and Change in Economic History*, New York: Norton & Co.

North, D.C. (1990), *Institutions, Institutional Change and Economic Performance*, Cambridge: Cambridge University Press.

Nurske, R. (1953), *Problems of Capital-Formation in Underdeveloped Countries*, Oxford: Oxford University Press.

OECD (2005), 'The Paris Declaration on Aid Effectiveness', Paris: OECD, available at: http://www.oecd.org/development/effectiveness/34428351.pdf.

OECD (2008), 'The Accra Agenda for Action (2008)', Paris: OECD, available at: http://www.oecd.org/development/effectiveness/34428351.pdf.

OECD (2011), 'Busan Partnership for Effective Development Co-operation', available at: http://www.aideffectiveness.org/busanhlf4/images/stories/hlf4/OUTCOME_DOCUMENT_-_FINAL_EN.pdf (accessed 21 December 2011).

OECD-DAC (2013), *Geographical Distribution of Financial Flows to Developing Countries 2012: Disbursements, Commitments, Country Indicators*, Paris: OECD.

Oxfam (2010), 'Millennium Development Goals update: are we on target?', Oxford: Oxfam.

Oxfam (2013), 'Post-2015 Development Goals: Oxfam International position', 28 January, Oxford: Oxfam.

Payne, A. (2005), *The Global Politics of Unequal Development*, Basingstoke: Palgrave MacMillan.

Payne, A. and N. Phillips (2010), *Development*, Cambridge: Polity Press.

Pogge, T.W. (2001), 'The influence of the global order on the prospects for genuine democracy in the developing countries', *Ratio Juris*, **14** (3), 326–43.

Pogge, T. (2008), *World Poverty and Human Rights*, 2nd edition, Cambridge: Polity Press.

Poteete, A.R. (2009), 'Is development path dependent or political? A reinterpretation of mineral-dependent development in Botswana', *Journal of Development Studies*, **45** (4), 544–71.

Prebisch, R. (1950), *Change and Development – Latin America's Great Task: Report Submitted to the Inter-American Development Bank*, New York: Praeger Publishers.

Reinhart, C.M. and K.S. Rogoff (2009), *This Time is Different: Eight Centuries of Financial Folly*, Princeton, NJ: Princeton University Press.

Rist, G. (2002), *The History of Development: From Western Origins to Global Faith*, London: Zed Books.

Rodrik, D. (1997), *Has Globalization Gone Too Far?* Washington, DC: Institute for International Economics.

Rodrik, D. (2001), 'The global governance of trade as if development really mattered', UNDP Background Paper, New York: UNDP.

Rodrik, D., A. Subramanian and F. Trebbi (2004), 'Institutions rule: the primacy of institutions over geography and integration in economic development', *Journal of Economic Growth*, **9** (2), pp. 131–65.

Rosenstein-Rodan, P.N. (1943), 'Problems of industrialisation in Eastern and South-Eastern Europe', *Economic Journal*, **53** (210–11), 202–11.

Rostow, W.W. (1960), *The Stages of Economic Growth: A Non-Communist Manifesto*, Cambridge: Cambridge University Press.

Sachs, J.D. (2001), 'Tropical underdevelopment', NBER Working Paper 8119, Cambridge, MA: National Bureau of Economic Research.

Sachs, J.D. (2005), *The End of Poverty*, London: Penguin Books.

Sachs, J.D., J.W. McArthur, G. Schmidt-Traub, M. Kruk, C. Bahadur, M. Faye and G. McCord (2004), 'Ending Africa's poverty trap', *Brookings Papers on Economic Activity*, **35** (1), 117–240.

Saith, A. (2006), 'From universal values to millennium development goals: lost in translation', *Development and Change*, **37** (6), 1167–99.

Save the Children (2013), 'Ending poverty in our generation: Save the Children's vision for a post-2015 framework', London: Save the Children.

Soederberg, S. (2004), *The Politics of the New International Financial Architecture: Reimposing Neoliberal Dominance in the Global South*, London: Zed Books.

Sumner, A. (2012), 'Where do the poor live?', *World Development*, **40** (5), 865–77.

Tornell, A., F. Westermann and L. Martinez (2004), 'The positive link between financial liberalization, growth and crises', NBER Working Paper No. 10293, Washington, DC: National Bureau of Economic Research.

Truman, H.S. (1949), Inaugural address of Harry S. Truman, Speech, Presidential Inauguration Ceremony, Washington, DC, 20 January.

Tsai, P. L. (1995), 'Foreign direct investment and income inequality: further evidence', *World Development*, **23** (3), 469–83.

UN (2010a), 'The Millennium Development Goals report', New York: United Nations, available at: http://www.un.org/millenniumgoals/pdf/MDG%20Report%202010%20En%20r15%20-low%20res%202010 0615%20-.pdf.

UN (2010b), 'Keeping the promise: united to achieve the Millennium Development Goals', Resolution adopted by the General Assembly, A/RES/65/1, 19 October, available at: http://www.un.org/en/mdg/summit2010/pdf/outcome_documentN1051260.pdf.

UNCTAD (2005), *Trade and Development Report 2005*, Geneva: United Nations Conference on Trade and Development.

UNDP (2003), *Human Development Report 2003: Millennium Development Goals: A Compact among Nations to End Poverty*, Oxford: Oxford University Press.

UN MDG Gap Task Force (2011), 'The Global Partnership for Development: time to deliver', MDG Gap Task Force Report, available at: http://www.undp.org/content/undp/en/home/librarypage/mdg/the_mdg_gap_taskforcereport2011.html.

UN Millennium Project (2005), *Investing in Development*, London: Earthscan.

Van Heerde, J. and D. Hudson (2010), '"The righteous considereth the cause of the poor"? Public attitudes towards poverty in developing countries', *Political Studies*, **58**, 389–409.

Vreeland, J.R. (2003), *The IMF and Economic Development*, New York: Cambridge University Press.

Wade, R.H. (2003), 'What strategies are viable for developing countries today? The World Trade Organization and the shrinking of "development space"', *Review of International Political Economy*, **10** (4), 621–44.

Wade, R.H. (2004), 'On the causes of increasing world poverty and inequality, or why the Matthew effect prevails', *New Political Economy*, **9** (2), 163–88.

Wilkinson, R. and D. Hulme (eds) (2012), *The Millennium Development Goals and Beyond: Global Development after 2015*, Abingdon, UK: Routledge.

Woods, N. (2008), 'Whose aid? Whose influence? China, emerging donors and the silent revolution in development assistance', *International Affairs*, **84** (6), 1205–21.

Woodward, R. (2004), 'The Organisation for Economic Cooperation and Development', *New Political Economy*, **9** (1), 113–27.

Woodward, R. (2009), *The Organisation for Economic Co-operation and Development*, London: Routledge.

World Bank (1989), *Sub-Saharan Africa: From Crisis to Sustainable Growth; A Long-Term Perspective Study*, Washington, DC: World Bank.

World Bank (1992), *Governance and Development*, Washington, DC: World Bank.

World Bank (2006), *Global Economic Prospects 2006: Economic Implications of Remittances and Migration*, Washington, DC: World Bank.

World Trade Organization (WTO) (1995), 'Agreement establishing the World Trade Organization', Geneva: WTO Information and Media Relations Division, Geneva.

Zedillo, E., A.Y. Al-Hamed, D. Bryer, M. Chinery-Hesse, J. Delors, R. Grynspan, A.Y. Livshits, A.M. Osman, R. Rubin, M. Singh and M. Son (2001), 'Report of the High-Level Panel on Financing for Development', for the Monterrey Conference, available at: http://www.un.org/reports/financing/panel.htm.

14 The governance of the World Bank

Liam Clegg

The World Bank remains a high-profile and controversial arena of global economic governance.[1] Given the volume of resources circulating around the organisation, it is perhaps unsurprising that the organisation attracts such a degree of critical attention (e.g. Clegg 2013; Park 2010; Park and Vetterlein 2010; Griffin 2009; Phillips 2009; Weaver 2008; Stone and Wright 2007). In 2010 the Bank reached the peak of its post-Global Financial Crisis lending, with total new commitments amounting to over US$44 billion. While through 2011 new lending dropped back to around US$30 billion, this volume remains far above the organisation's recent historic average of around US$13.5 billion (World Bank 2011b: 2). Beyond the impressive scale of these figures, the precarious state of public finances in many of the middle- and low-income states with which the Bank does business further serves to enhance the structural power of the organisation. With this operational context, it is of first-order importance that analysts look inside the Bank, and enhance our understanding of the governance processes through which key actors attempt to shape and reshape how the organisation approaches its mission. By offering a review of broad contemporary trends with a detailed analysis of the dynamics surrounding the World Bank's shifting engagement with domestic institutional reform, this chapter sheds new light on the inner workings of this important governance institution.

The core insight of this exploration of the governance of the World Bank is that, while the organisation is undoubtedly a large and complex bureaucracy, member-states' control over rule-making processes and their ability to release supplementary finance constitute potent mechanisms through which to exercise influence over operational outcomes. This dynamic is evident in the provision of resources by the United Kingdom, Dutch and Norwegian governments to small groups of Bank staff with a commitment to extending the organisation's engagement with domestic institutional reform, which has helped to catalyse operational shifts across the wider organisation. Indeed, through their ongoing endowment of a range of Trust Funds with a focus on generating innovative approaches to reforming public institutions, these member-states continue to test where the boundaries of legitimate domestic intervention lie for Bank-supported projects. By examining the Bank's incursion into the realm of domestic institutional reform, this chapter captures the workings of these internal governance processes in action. Considering the Bank's initial *raison d'être* was the funding of infrastructure projects capable of generating a clear economic return, the organisation's expansion into issues surrounding the creation of appropriate legal and regulatory frameworks, citizen empowerment, and (most recently) the promotion of human rights marks a change of focus that is impressive in its scope. The provision of tied resources – finance that is released on the condition that it is used in accordance with closely specified aims – by key donor states continues to drive forward innovations in these areas.

The themes and dynamics that are reviewed in this chapter coalesce with each of the lines of analysis introduced by the editors of this volume, regarding actors, levels, ethics and ideology in the governance of the international political economy. First, and most significantly, I demonstrate that, despite the Bank's intricate 'matrix' structure, materially powerful state actors retain particular capacity to shape its operational practices. Second, in relation to levels of governance in the international political economy, this chapter demonstrates the necessity of integrating the international, national and subnational levels in international political economy (IPE) scholarship. With donor states' interventions working to further enhance the 'new intrusiveness' of the Bank's operations (Woods and Narlikar 2002), analytic frameworks must remain capable of capturing the complexity of contemporary governance networks. Finally, by examining the processes through which normative concerns have become increasingly incorporated into the World Bank's expanding 'post-Washington Consensus' world-view, the chapter highlights the linkages between ethics and ideology in contemporary global economic governance.

In developing these insights, the chapter proceeds according to the following structure. After this introductory overview, the first section serves to outline a brief history of the World Bank's lending activities. This overview introduces the International Bank for Reconstruction and Development (IBRD) and International Development Association (IDA), the lending arms of the World Bank that provide the empirical focus of the chapter. Through the second section, detailed information is provided regarding the mechanisms through which influence is exerted over processes of operational reform at the Bank. While the primary channel has shifted over time from IDA replenishment negotiations to Trust Fund endowments, state actors' periodic provision of large-scale finance continues to underpin Bank operations and provides a unique tool through which to shape the organisation's activities. The third section moves on to explore the scale and scope of the Bank's engagement with domestic institutional reform. Innovations in this field have been catalysed by creditor states' strategic deployment of Trust Fund resources, with the UK, Dutch and Norwegian governments leading the way in this regard. Finally, in the last section reflections are offered on the intersection between the exploration of the governance of the World Bank and the themes introduced by the editors of this volume in relation to actors, levels, and ethics and ideology in the governance of the international political economy.

THE WORLD BANK'S EVOLVING APPROACH TO LENDING

It is common for the Articles of Agreement laid out at the foundation of an international organisation to be underpinned by a high degree of ambiguity. Beneath the detailed 'legalese' setting out the formal status of an organisation, outlining the departments that together form its bureaucratic skeleton, and laying down the mechanisms through which member-states retain control and oversight of these new structures, core aspects of an organisation's mission often remain fixed to very loosely defined terms. In the case of the World Bank, understandings of how the organisation should operationalise its mission to 'assist in the reconstruction and development of members' territories' changed dramatically over time.[2] The following brief review of these developments outlines the breadth and complexity of the activities that have over time been layered into the Bank's operations, and serves to contextualise the contemporary dynamics that are examined.

When it was established, the Bank was endowed by signatory member-states with a lending base with which to pursue its reconstruction and development mission. This capital was provided either in the form of 'paid-in' subscriptions that were transferred to the Bank, or in the form of 'call-able' resources that national authorities pledged to release to the organisation as and when the need arose. However, in order to maximise the lending potential of the Bank, its founders agreed that the organisation should be permitted to leverage its capital base through access to private markets. With the Bank needing to mediate the flow of resources from financial markets to states that were struggling to borrow at sustainable rates, it became imperative for the organisation to establish a strong reputation with market actors (Woods 2006: 22–6). From the outset, senior management sought to address this issue proactively. Under the presidency of Eugene Black (1949–1962), attaining a triple-A rating on the New York market became a core organisational goal. Within the Bank, the Central Projects Staff (CPS) became a valuable tool with which to embed – and be seen to embed – a culture of fiduciary responsibility. By evaluating lending plans in order to ensure their economic viability, CPS served to maintain internal and external confidence that approved projects would generate stable revenue streams, thereby enabling borrowing country governments to repay the Bank, and the Bank in turn to service its bond holders. Under the watchful gaze of CPS, through its first decade the organisation's operations concentrated heavily on providing funds for large infrastructure projects with clear revenue-generating capability, in particular in the realms of energy and transportation. By the late 1950s, aided by these internal processes, the Bank had attained its sought-after triple-A rating. However, at the very point that this approach to catalysing development by funding revenue-generating projects was receiving its market-based seal of approval, the foundations of dramatic transformation were simultaneously being laid. The creation of IDA was at the core of this transformation.

By the late 1950s the World Bank had firmly established itself as a significant feature of global economic governance. Indeed, with the Bank having become accustomed to generating healthy annual surpluses by this time, pressure began to grow on the organisation to move beyond its conservative business model. The IDA was formed in 1960, with the aim of allowing the Bank to more effectively respond to the needs of its lower-income members. IDA has been described as having 'changed the whole history of the World Bank' (Kapur et al. 1997: 13–14), and there are two main reasons why this was the case. First, in order to allow low-income governments to access IDA resources, it was decided that the rate of interest charged on its lending was to be significantly below market rates. With IBRD profits only able to supply a modest volume of the necessary subsidy, IDA was from the outset structurally dependent on the regular injection of resources from a relatively small group of creditor states. Through regularised 'IDA replenishment' negotiations, these states gained a new mechanism through which to attempt to shape the Bank's operations (Woods 2006: 27–9), and over time their willingness to attach formal conditions to the provision of financial resources increased appreciably (Clegg 2010: 481–2). Second, when the guidelines were agreed for IDA operations, it was deemed that projects representing a high development priority would be supported by the Bank, even if these projects were not revenue-producing or directly productive (Marshall 2008: 36–8). This refocusing provided an opening for a dramatic expansion in the range of operations funded by the organisation over following decades.

It was under the presidency of Robert McNamara (1968–1981) that the transformation in the scale and scope of Bank lending was realised. When McNamara entered the Bank, each year around US$1 billion was released in support of new operations. By the time of his departure, the figure was US$12 billion. Accompanying this step change in the volume of lending, the type of operation within the Bank's portfolio shifted significantly through this period. In addition to its 'traditional' focus on transportation and power-generating infrastructure projects, the Bank expanded its support for projects aimed at raising agricultural productivity, modernising communications networks and improving the provision of water supplies to households and industry. Moreover, from a position of non-engagement with what were deemed 'social issues' in the early 1960s, lending to support education, family planning and health grew through the McNamara years to encompass a significant proportion of resource commitments (Mason and Asher 1973: 200). The Bank's contemporary operations remain characterised by this heterogeneous patchwork of focuses within project lending.

While the organisation's early engagement with large infrastructure projects has been maintained through to the contemporary period, it has been supplemented, such that the largest recipients of Bank resources by sector now runs: public administration (22 per cent), transport (20 per cent), health and social services (16 per cent), energy and mining (14 per cent), water and sanitation (11 per cent), and agriculture, fishing and forestry (6 per cent) (World Bank 2011b: 4). With around US$32 billion committed to new projects and US$11 billion committed in the form of new programme arrangements through the course of 2011,[3] the Bank's eclectic approach to fulfilling its development mandate continues. This panoply of activities is controlled by an equally complex set of institutional structures and processes. As is explored below, this matrix serves to empower particular (groups of) actors in the governance of the World Bank. In particular, the forging of links between providers of supplementary finance and internal advocates of a given agenda has become an increasingly significant means of achieving operational change across the Bank's governance matrix.

THE WORLD BANK'S GOVERNANCE MATRIX

Over recent years, there has been a renewed focus in IPE scholarship on the manner in which international organisations are able to shape global politics. Following Barnett and Finnemore's (2004) seminal contribution, a wide range of scholars have moved to open up the 'black box' of international organisations (e.g. Broome and Seabrooke 2012; Broome 2010; Chweiroth 2010; Moschella 2010; Park and Vetterlein 2010; Weaver 2008; Broome and Seabrooke 2007; Momani 2007; Nielson et al. 2006; Gutner 2005; Leiteritz 2005; Momani 2005). These analysts remind us that, while international organisations (IOs)' control over flows of finance constitutes a significant form of influence, their capacity to frame understandings of a policy issue provides an additional – and potentially even more potent – means of shaping behaviour in the international political economy. By working to reframe the way in which an IO 'sees' its mission, strategically located actors can alter the established hierarchies of operational means and ends, both inside the institution and amongst the satellite organisations that directly and indirectly orient their activities in relation to its practices. Within this literature, there is a shared appreciation that control over operational practice is contingent on the capacity to influence both formal rule-making procedures and the more informal processes that shape beliefs about what constitutes appropriate behaviour in a given policy context. Under the Bank's formal governance structure advanced industrialised members retain significant influence over rule-making processes. While the organisation's matrix structure was intended to empower staff to independently engage in innovation, these states have increasingly used the provision of tied trust funds to shape these more informal governance processes too.

The World Bank's Articles of Agreement serve to position representatives of member-states at the head of formal rule-making processes at the organisation. The Bank's Executive Board forms the primary location in which decisions are taken on reforms to operational policy. On the Board, voting power is divided between the 25 executive directors selected by member-states to represent their interests. All member-states are not created equal in the Bank, with voting shares distributed broadly according to a member's economic strength. The top five powers (United States, Japan, Germany, France, the United Kingdom) control around 40 per cent of total votes and each select an individual director, and the remaining 183 members are divided into an array of constituency groupings. The largest of these constituencies (the Francophone Africa Group) includes 21 members, but holds a combined voting bloc of just 1.9 per cent.[4] In addition to signing-off individual loans and grant distributions, the Board is ultimately responsible for approving the operational guidelines that staff are required to follow when designing, implementing and monitoring projects and programmes (World Bank 2011a: 61–3). With the organisation's Operations Policy and Country Services (OPCS) unit working assiduously to ensure that these guidelines are applied consistently by staff across the Bank, the ability to shape the outcomes of such decisions constitutes a valuable resource.

Alongside OPCS's monitoring of staff, an additional mechanism through which policy guidelines are communicated to staff is through the World Bank's *Operational Manual*.[5] The Manual contains procedures to be followed when, for example, carrying out lending operations that entail potentially negative impact on the natural environment (Operational Policy 4.01), indigenous populations (Operational Policy 4.10), or gender groups (Operational Policy 4.20). Beyond this manual, OPCS also takes the lead in drafting Strategy Papers and related framework documents to guide staff activities in a given sphere of operations. With the Board holding the formal power to request and sign off Operational Guidelines and Strategy Papers, executive directors – and particularly directors from advanced-industrialised members – have significant rule-making capacity in the Bank. In order to understand the dynamics that shape Bank staff's operational behaviour more fully, it is useful to explore the organisation's governance matrix.

As a consequence of reforms implemented during the presidency of James Wolfensohn (1995–2005), the World Bank entered the twenty-first century with a highly decentralised structure. Under the Bank's matrix, operational activities were made contingent on the forging of entrepreneurial links between the Bank's Regional Vice-Presidencies (Africa, East Asia, Latin America, Middle East, South Asia) and its Network Vice-Presidencies (Finance and Private Sector, Human Development, Poverty Reduction and Economic Management, Sustainable Development) on a loan-by-loan basis. It was hoped that Regions would work collaboratively with member-states to foster an increasingly 'client-focused' approach, with Network staff serving as repositories of specialised knowledge that could be efficiently plugged in to country-specific projects and programmes. This structure was further complicated by the existence of Sector Management Units within Regional Vice-Presidencies, whose function was to smooth the flow of expertise from the Networks to individual Country Management Units. The Bank's matrix structure was designed to function as an internal market, with Network staff facing particular pressure to supplement their core budget allocation by being 'contracted in' to supply analytic and advisory services to particular lending operations (IEG 2012a: 1–7).

The matrix system was formally established through reforms introduced in 1997 and rolled out across the institution through the course of the following years (IEG 2012a: xv). The introduction of the matrix system was guided by the aim of achieving operational improvement by fostering an environment of competitive innovation. Within the matrix, individual Units and Groups are required to proactively 'sell' their ideas and their services; 'policy entrepreneurship' is hard-wired into the Bank's contemporary structure (Coll 2005). The conventional wisdom is that the matrix allows World Bank staff significant new autonomy, with particular Units and Groups gaining reputations as particularly effective 'players' of the matrix game. The Poverty Reduction and Economic Management Unit (PREM)'s Poverty Group, for example, is identified as a 'powerhouse' in shaping key disputes between economists and non-economists in the Bank (Clegg 2010: 486–7; Bebbington et al. 2004: 49). However, a close analysis of contemporary dynamics reveals a nuanced image of this environment, one in which state actors can play a significant role. In particular, in the years since the launch of the matrix, creditor states have come to direct their ad hoc provision of tied financial resources increasingly towards the Trust Fund modality as a means of influencing staff behaviour.

Historically, IDA replenishment negotiations have provided the most significant mechanism through which creditor states have sought to leverage operational change in the Bank. Building on a long-established upward trend in the size of settlements (Marshall 2008: 38), the most recent agreements have seen record transfers being made to the Bank. Creditors continue to use these IDA negotiations to push for reform, and through negotiations concluded in 2010 were successful in pushing the Bank to establish institution-wide management processes to enhance its focus on gender-mainstreaming and its engagement with fragile and conflict-affected countries (IDA 2010: 25–36). However, IDA replenishments no longer constitute the main channel for creditor states' provision of financial resources to the Bank. As of the mid-2000s, Trust Fund resources have surpassed the volume of contributions provided through IDA replenishments. In 2003–05, the figures were US$12.5 billion and US$13.5 billion respectively; by 2006–08 the gap had widened with the Trust Fund total standing around US$3 billion above the US$17.5 billion IDA replenishment (IEG 2011: 12).

The World Bank's Management Framework for the Administration of Trust Funds was approved by the Executive Board in 2007 and sets the parameters surrounding the use of this increasing significant modality. According to this Framework (World Bank 2007a: 1):

> A typical Trust Fund is established with contributions from one or more donors to support development-related activities with clearly identified beneficiaries. The Bank channels Trust Fund resources . . . to the intended recipients in accordance with agreements with the donors. In some cases donors may request that the Bank itself utilise these funds to carry out activities that bring about desired outcomes in developing countries.

The first stage in establishing a Fund is for the donor organisation to collaborate with the proposed Programme Manager to set out its terms of reference in an Initiating Brief (IB). The IB is then screened for compliance with the Bank's operational guidelines by the Legal Department, OPCS, and other relevant Units and Groups; it is then either passed to the host Vice-Presidency for approval, or if deemed to present a 'significant or novel policy issue' is passed to the Board for an approval decision (World Bank 2007a: 23–6). Although the Bank currently manages Funds from over 200 donors (including member-states, international and regional organisations, and private actors), advanced-industrialised countries dominate the field. The top ten originators consist of nine members of the Organisation for Economic Co-operation and Development (OECD) and the European Commission (World Bank 2010: 7–9). While Trust Funds come in a range of forms, three general observations can be made regarding their intersection with the governance of the World Bank.

First, state actors consciously employ Trust Funds as a means of catalysing operational change at the Bank. A recent internal evaluation of the use of Trust Funds found that donors 'mainly use' Trust Funds to fill perceived gaps in multilateral aid provision, to increase the Bank's focus on their preferred target countries or issues, and to influence the way in which the organisation approaches its developmental mission (IEG 2011: 5–6). Second, different donors have divergent approaches to the use of the Trust Fund modality. Amongst the top ten donors, four (the US, Japan, Germany, France) mainly supply the Bank's small number of very large Financial Intermediary Funds (FIFs), over which the Bank acts as holding agent before transferring resources (and the power to take decisions on expenditure) to a third-party agent. In contrast, four 'activist' donors (the UK, European Commission, Netherlands, Norway) mainly utilise smaller entities over which they set the customised terms of reference and whose focus typically entails significant overlap with Bank operations (IEG 2011: 15–16). Third, while the majority of Trust Fund resources at the Bank come through FIFs that are passed directly to third-party agents, the Bank has nonetheless become heavily reliant on the modality as a means of financing its core budget. By 2008–10, Trust Funds covered almost one-quarter of the US$6.5 billion total administrative outlays made by the Bank (IEG 2011: 18). Within this trend, Network Vice-Presidencies have become particularly dependent on direct donor support. In the 2008–10 period, Trust Fund support made up 43 per cent of total Network budgets, with more than 50 per cent of the Social Development Network's base coming from this source (IEG 2011: 71–3). While the matrix structure was intended to push the Networks to cooperate with staff within Regional Vice-Presidencies to design innovative services that would flourish on the Bank's internal market of decentralised budgets, in recent years donor states' Trust Funds have increasingly stepped into the breach.

In spite of their growing visibility and quantitative importance, the evolving role of Trust Funds at the World Bank has yet to attract the attention of academic analysts. The following section, which explores the organisation's engagement with the issue of domestic institutional reform, serves to address this surprising lacuna. While the history of the Bank's increasing focus on public administration reform can be traced back several decades, the provision of Trust Funds in recent years by the Bank's leading activist donors has played a central role in shaping the evolution of this controversial area of operational practice. With the UK, Dutch and Norwegian governments hooking up with internal advocates of the agenda in PREM and elsewhere, areas of domestic reform once considered 'off-limits' by many Bank staff are becoming integrated into projects and programmes across the whole sweep of the organisation's operations.

THE MATRIX IN ACTION: ENGAGING WITH DOMESTIC INSTITUTIONAL REFORM

Staff inside the World Bank have long held the belief that domestic institutions matter in shaping a country's development prospects. The genesis of this view can be traced back to the 1970s and Michael Cernea's establishment of a Sociological Group in what at the time was an organisation dominated by economists and engineers. For Cernea and other advocates, the Bank's ultimate success was seen to be dependent on the creation of effective formal institutional structures, such as central and local government agencies and judicial systems, and more informal institutional reforms to enhance citizens' capacity to influence decision-making processes. The provision of projects to improve formal public administrative structures has become a centrepiece of the Bank's contemporary operations, particularly to member-states where strong support for such measures exists amongst governing authorities. However, there has been a reluctance either to target these areas when authorities' support has not been forthcoming, or to proactively enhance civil society organisations' capacity to support such reforms. Through their establishment of the Governance Partnership Facility and related Trust Funds, the UK, Dutch and Norwegian governments have sought to increase the Bank's support for these latter types of activities. By engaging with supportive Groups and Units inside the Bank, these mechanisms are fostering notable operational innovation across the organisation.

Since its inception, key clauses in the Bank's Articles of Agreement have served to render the organisation's engagement with domestic institutional reform problematic. Article IV Section 10 was long interpreted as positioning such matters outside of the organisation's legitimate sphere of operations. The clause notes that:

> Only economic considerations shall be relevant to their decisions . . . The Bank and its officers shall not interfere in the political affairs of any member; nor shall they be influenced in their decisions by the political character of the member or members concerned.

In addition, Article III Section 2 mandates that Bank staff will only deal with official government representatives, specifically in the form of personnel from a treasury, central bank or 'similar agency'. However, under the ebullient leadership of Wolfensohn, these lines in the sand began to be redrawn. In particular, Wolfensohn's work as a leading advocate of the Bank's focus on anti-corruption served to open the door onto a more proactive form of engagement with domestic institutional reform (Phillips 2009: 130–31; Marshall 2008: 49–52). At the close of the 1990s, the compatibility of these operations with the organisation's mandate was confirmed by the World Bank General Counsel's declaration that domestic institutional reform 'would be tackled . . . to the extent it helps the country in the efficient management of its resources . . . and does not entangle the Bank in the country's partisan politics' (Shihata 1999: 1048). With the Board's endorsement of this guideline, internal advocates were provided with the necessary base from which to continue their proselytising efforts.

Through the early to mid-2000s, support for strengthening its proactive stance on domestic institutional reform grew significantly inside the Bank. When Paul Wolfowitz assumed the presidency of the Bank in 2005, the anti-corruption inspired focus on institutional reform received a particular fillip. During his first year in office, Wolfowitz led boardroom actions to block a total of nine major loans or debt-relief packages on the basis of inadequate institutional processes for monitoring and managing expenditure and procurement, or for reasons of outright corruption (Weaver 2008: 131–3). With the strong support of the PREM Public Sector Governance Group (PREMPS), the profile of efforts to 'improve the performance and accountability of public institutions' began to rise in the Bank (PREMPS 2012: 1). While the strict interpretation of the Bank's Articles began to be diluted, during this time the organisation remained deeply divided. On the one side sat PREMPS and a cohort of supportive advanced-industrialised Executive Directorates advocating the prospect of the Bank proactively seeking to address institutional shortcomings in member-states and engage with non-traditional partners; on the other side sat a group of low- and middle-income members that were keen to protect their domestic autonomy, and country directors who were concerned to maintain close working relationships with these authorities (Ebrahim and Herz 2011). Events of 2006–07 served to clarify the shape of the Bank's engagement with these issues. These events demonstrate that, through their control over rule-making processes and the provision of supplementary finance, advanced-industrialised states can exert significant influence over the organisation's operational agenda.

It was at the Annual Meeting in September 2006 that government ministers from developed and developing countries met to discuss the Bank's engagement with domestic institutional reform.[6] The ministerial meeting focused on a Strategy Paper drawn up by OPCS. While the six hours of ensuing discussion demonstrate that the paper did not serve to resolve pre-existing disputes (Weaver 2008: 135), the ministers present did confirm that 'a principal objective of the Bank . . . should be to help develop capable and accountable states to deliver services to the poor, promote private sector development and tackle corruption effectively' (World Bank 2007b: Annex C). By approving the core premises of the Strategy Paper, these state actors enabled the paper to progress toward boardroom endorsement. This point was reached in September 2007, when the Board approved a revised Strategy Paper and Implementation Plan. Although continuing differences of opinion among developed- and developing-country Executive Directors resulted in a 'heated' boardroom discussion (Teskey 2012), the Plan served to endorse formally the expansion of the Bank's focus on domestic institutional reform. This outcome demonstrates the importance of state actors' control over the Bank's formal decision-making processes. However, by hooking up ad hoc funding to the Strategy Paper, a coalition of supportive member-states sought also to operationalise influence through a more informal mechanism.

Together, the UK, Dutch and Norwegian governments mobilised over US$60 million to boost the Bank's engagement with domestic institutional reform. The UK provided US$50 million of the resources behind the Governance Partnership Facility (GPF), with the Dutch and Norwegian governments contributing the remainder (GPF 2008: 3). The GPF follows the general pattern identified above of creditors using the Trust Fund modality to enhance the Bank's operational focus on favoured issues. In the case of the GPF, each of the contributors has a history of targeting domestic institutional reform to minimise corruption and enhance the poverty-reduction impact of its development aid (Harrison 2008; Hout 2007). The Fund was started when an entrepreneurial advocate of the agenda within the PREM Network contacted like-minded associates in the three national development agencies, who agreed to use the 2007 Strategy Paper to guide the GPF's terms of reference.[7] The GPF was subsequently housed within the PREM Network Vice-Presidency and, commensurate with the size and profile of the Fund, its Steering Committee was co-chaired by the Network Vice-President and the Permanent Secretary of the UK Department for International Development (DfID). Any member of World Bank staff was able to submit an application for GPF support, with successful plans being selected by a process integrating input from both PREM senior management and representatives of the three national development agencies (GPF 2010: 7–8).

GPF resources have been directed to three operational areas: country-level activities, sectoral innovation and building global leadership. These activities have sought in particular to further embed the Bank's proactive approach to institutional reform, and its engagement with civil society as a means of catalysing domestic change. Through the GPF, 18 Country Management Units have received a total of US$30 million to support the enhanced integration of such activities into their lending portfolios. Examples of such developments include funding an assessment of the current and potential future role of civil society participation to support Bank activities in Burkina Faso, and enabling an Accra-based consultant to integrate 'social accountability' mechanisms into natural resource tax administration reforms in Ghana. By aiming to influence the design of Country Assistance Strategies (CASs), the documents drawn up by Country Management Units outlining the priority areas for lending activities to be achieved over the medium term, the GPF architects intended to use their resources to leverage broad-based change in the Bank's lending operations (GPF 2011: 51–6). A second channel of GPF finance has been directed toward operations to catalyse operational change at the sector level of the Bank's matrix. In this regard, around US$25 million has been allocated to support initiatives including the employment of specialist staff to advise on mechanisms for deterring corruption in large-scale water and energy infrastructure projects, and the funding and dissemination of research into the 'political economy' of health and education reforms (GPF 2010: 17–18). Finally, in terms of promoting the profile of domestic institutional reform on the global development agenda, GPF resources have been used to support the establishment and dissemination of 'best-practice' guides (GPF 2010: 18–19). With their particular emphasis on harnessing the transformative power of civil society organisations (the 'demand side' of institutional reform, in Bank staff's language), these activities serve to stretch conventional understandings of the limits imposed by Article IV Section 10 and Article III Section 2.

In terms of its intersection with the World Bank's matrix structure, GPF resources followed the general trend amongst Trust Funds in gravitating towards the organisation's Network Vice-Presidencies. As the largest single recipient, PREM received over US$30 million of GPF awards (IEG 2012b). While it is difficult to gauge precisely the effectiveness with which PREM and other internal advocates were able to transform GPF resources into operational reform, the GPF has contributed to an increased level of engagement with domestic institutional reform at the Bank in a number of observable respects. A recent internal review found there to have been a threefold increase in the number of CAS documents including a focus on domestic institutional strengthening over the period of the GPF's operations (IEG 2012b: ix). Given the role of CAS as the primary mechanism for allocating lending resources, this development marks a significant refocusing at the Bank. The review also found evidence that the core aim of GPF creditors of sharing knowledge and expertise across the Bank was being achieved. In this regard, 70 per cent of staff reported a belief that the organisation's ability to identify the institutional impediments to effective poverty reduction had improved appreciably from 2007–12, and a similar proportion declared themselves to be familiar with the 2007 Strategy Paper, the implementation of which the GPF was established to support (IEG 2012b: 88, xix). By catalysing these developments, the GPF's founders have supported the Bank's turn toward domestic institutional reform.

In addition to the observed outcomes in relation to altered operational practices, the 'demonstration effect' of the GPF has contributed to a more general ideational shift amongst executive directors. Staff within the GPF Secretariat and the Executive Directorates of GPF donors believe that the Fund has not lived up to the fears of the members that had opposed the agenda in 2007,[8] and further evidence of this shift can be taken from the tenor of directors' most recent review of operational guidelines on domestic institutional reform. As is reported by Graham Teskey (2012), a PREMPS Senior Advisor:

> It is easy to forget just how contentious the [2007 boardroom discussion] was. At that time I was at DfID and it fell to me to follow what was going on, do the briefing, and draft the 'line to take'. We were all pretty aghast at the degree of – what seemed to us at least – outright hostility and ill-feeling in the debate . . . Board members this time were remarkably and genuinely supportive.

Mainstream understandings of the appropriate boundaries of the Bank's sphere of influence are, then, continuing to align with the goals laid out by the GPF's creditors in 2008. This is true in the case of both staff and senior management, as is represented by shifting operational practice and reported knowledge and beliefs. However, far from resting on their laurels, these states continue to employ the Trust Fund modality to further extend the range of domestic interventions undertaken by Bank staff.

Individually, the UK, Dutch and Norwegian governments come first, second and joint-fifth respectively in terms of volume of IBRD and IDA Trust Funds initiated (IEG 2011: 16). Within their portfolios, each of these donors exhibits a clear focus on expanding the focus on domestic institutional reform within the Bank's remit. Around two-thirds of the 77 Funds to which the UK contributes explicitly target domestic institutional reform and anti-corruption in their terms of reference,[9] including notably the Communication for Governance and Accountability Programme that works to establish independent media organisations as a means of facilitating civil society organisations' execution of their 'watchdog' function (Kalathil 2011). With the Netherlands, the Bank–Netherlands Partnership Programme continues to be used to promote the integration of institutional reform into country-level planning processes, and the Programme for Community Empowerment in Indonesia provides funds directly to community organisations to engage 'hard-to-reach' poverty groups in official decision-making processes (World Bank 2012: 21, 53). Finally, and most controversially, the Norwegian government is one of the backers of the Nordic Trust Fund (NTF), which was launched in 2010 to 'help the World Bank develop an informed view on how human rights relate to its core mission' (NTF 2010: 3). In the words of Ulrika Sundberg (2006: 1), former Swedish Development Minister and one of the leading figures behind the creation of the Fund, the NTF aimed to 'link the normative work of the UN . . . with the World Bank's "big bucks"' by convincing staff that 'human rights considerations constitute value added to the economic development process'. While NTF operations remain ongoing, the Fund's supporters have succeeded in securing a Legal Opinion from the World Bank General Counsel noting that human rights issues represented an 'integral' aspect of the organisation's work (Dañino 2007: 3; Palacio 2006: 1). With each of these cases we see donor states promoting activities that lie at the margins of conventional interpretations of its Articles of Agreement.

Within the World Bank's governance structure, the power to make the rules according to which staff orient their activities lies with its Executive Board. The ability of directors representing advanced-industrialised members to secure approval for their favoured reforms is demonstrated by the passing of the 2007 Strategy Paper on the Bank's engagement with domestic institutional reform. By backing the turn towards a more proactive approach to the issue and a greater engagement with non-traditional partners in support of these efforts, the paper served to legitimise activities that had historically been resisted by some developing-country constituencies. In addition, through the endowment of the GPF, key donor states have sought to advance the pace of operational change across the organisation. Under the Bank's matrix governance structure Network Vice-Presidencies are structurally dependent on supplementary income; with the GPF, actors within PREM in particular have received a significant material injection with which to operationalise their advocacy of the renewed focus on domestic institutional reform. Recent developments suggest that this intervention has filtered through into tangible operational change. With donors' continued support of this agenda through the Trust Fund modality, this direction of travel appears set to continue through the medium term at least. In the concluding section below, reflections are provided on the intersection of this examination of the governance of the World Bank with the broad themes that are introduced by the editors of this volume.

CONCLUSION

In the framing chapter, the editors noted that the story of the international political economy of governance is destined to remain one of flux and evolution. As with earlier decades, the 2010s can be characterised by shifting configurations of actors involved in governance projects, levels at which these governance projects are articulated, and intersections of ethical issues and dominant ideological frameworks. The foregoing analysis has demonstrated that what is true at the systemic level in relation to these dynamics is true also in relation to the governance of the World Bank.

Firstly, regarding actors, the picture at the Bank is one of broad stability in terms of the leading figures in the governance of the organisation, accompanied by change to the primary mechanisms of influence. There is broad stability in terms of both the privileged role of representatives of advanced-industrialised member-states within the Bank's formal decision-making processes, and their operationalisation of influence through the provision of supplementary finance. However, with their turn towards the use of Trust

Funds, these agents are more actively engaging with supportive internal groupings as a means of catalysing change across the Bank's complex matrix structure. Although driven by materially powerful state actors, attempts to influence the organisation's activities are increasingly operationalised through ad hoc Trust Fund arrangements rather than the rolling, multi-party IDA replenishment negotiations.

Though propelled by the 'usual suspects', these mechanisms of influence are in important respects serving to introduce a greater degree of complexity into the levels of governance across which the organisation's reach extends. Through the Governance Partnership Facility and other funds, the UK, Dutch and Norwegian governments have worked in particular to encourage staffs' proactive engagement of civil society organisations in support of projects to improve the performance and accountability of public sector institutions. Through these processes, conventionally held understandings of the limits of the Bank's legitimate sphere of operations are being recast. Where once the Bank's Articles of Agreement were seen to limit staff to interacting with official government partners and to steering clear of projects that impinged on domestic social and political issues, through Trust Fund interventions staff are being encouraged to focus on the demand side of domestic institutional reform. By promoting efforts to enhance domestic citizens' capacity to monitor the performance of government agencies and influence decision-making processes, these interventions challenge past reluctance within the organisation to test the limits of its apolitical boundaries.

Finally, through their contribution to the embedding of this more proactive engagement with issues of domestic institutional reform, donor states' deployment of Trust Funds has helped to secure the position of core ethical issues on the organisation's agenda. Where the question of the form taken by the relationship between the state and its domestic population was once held to exist within the reified boundaries of national sovereignty, Bank staff now increasingly utilise the organisation's lending resources to achieve reform in the direction of a liberal-democratic ideal. Indeed, lively discussion continues over the desirability of the state–society model being promoted through such activities (Scholte 2011; Long and Duvvury 2011; Thirkell-White 2004). The layering of a concern with issues of accountability, empowerment and human rights into the Bank's purview is broadly consistent with observations of the ongoing transition from a Washington Consensus to a 'post-Washington Consensus' ideology across leading arenas of global economic governance (Craig and Porter 2006; Öniş and Şenses 2005; Stiglitz 2004; Williamson 2000); where once the Bank and partner organisations aimed to roll back the frontiers of the state, the emerging post-Washington Consensus vision foregrounds the importance of enhancing (certain aspects of) state performance. With operations supported by a range of Trust Funds serving to embed the reformulated ideology across the Bank's activities, this normative engagement with state–society relationships could over coming years enjoy a significant advance.

The incorporation of issues that have conventionally been understood to be ethical in nature (and therefore outside of the Bank's area of legitimate operations) has been founded on two key developments. First, advocates of the agenda have succeeded in securing formal confirmations that such concerns constitute 'economic' issues (and so are in *de jure* compliance with the Bank's mandate); second, the provision of financial resources to entrepreneurial Units and Groups inside the organisation has been used to support the establishment of associated operational practices. Further incorporation of ethical issues into this evolving ideological framework will remain contingent on the effective management of these processes by shifting alliances of state actors and internal Bank advocates. Taken together, the dynamic trends surrounding ethics and ideology, actors, and levels of engagement remind us that the governance of the World Bank remains characterised by substantial reconfiguration, albeit shaped by existing structural boundaries.

It is now almost two decades since James Rosenau (1995) issued his call for scholars to focus their attention on exploring the shifting patterns of global governance in the twenty-first century. For Rosenau, the core challenge for analysts in this area was to learn to enhance their appreciation of nuance, to acknowledge that detailed investigation provides the foundations on which enhanced understandings can emerge. The injunction to explore contemporary governance networks by engaging in empirically driven research continues both to retain its pertinence and to offer fruitful guidelines for shedding light on both the governance of the World Bank and the wider governance of the international political economy.

NOTES

1. The World Bank Group comprises five subunits. This chapter focuses exclusively on the International Development Association and the International Bank for Reconstruction and Development, the Bank's two state-centred lending organisations. The other subunits under the Bank's umbrella are the International Centre for the Settlement of Investment Disputes, the International Finance Corporation (which lends to private enterprises engaged with developing countries), and the Multilateral Investment Guarantee Agency (which provides political risk insurance to 'developmentally sound' private sector lending and investment projects). For further information see the World Bank official website, available at: http://web.worldbank. org/WBSITE/EXTERNAL/EXTABOUTUS/0,,contentMDK:20046292~menuPK:1696892~pagePK:511 23644~piPK:329829~theSitePK:29708,00.html (accessed 7 December 2012).
2. See World Bank official website, available at: http://web.worldbank.org/WBSITE/EXTERNAL/EXT ABOUTUS/ORGANIZATION/BODEXT/0,,contentMDK:20049563~menuPK:64020045~pagePK:6402 0054~piPK:64020408~theSitePK:278036~isCURL:Y~isCURL:Y,00.html (accessed 22 October 2012).
3. Programme lending refers to operations designed to support broad-based policy packages. This modality tends to be directed towards middle-income members, and to constitute around a quarter of total lending. See World Bank (2009: 1–5); Ritzen (2007: 576); Kapur et al. (1997: 513–93); and Mason and Asher (1973: 260–94).
4. See World Bank official website, available at: http://siteresources.worldbank.org/BODINT/ Resources/278027-1215524804501/IBRDCountryVotingTable.pdf (accessed 1 November 2012).
5. Available at: http://web.worldbank.org/WBSITE/EXTERNAL/PROJECTS/EXTPOLICIES/EXTOPM ANUAL/0,,menuPK:64142516~pagePK:64141681~piPK:64141745~theSitePK:502184,00.html (accessed 1 November 2012).
6. This meeting took place in the Development Committee, which convenes every six months and is composed of 25 government ministers. Each World Bank Executive Directorate selects one representative to the Committee, and decisions taken are used to guide the Executive Board in relation to particularly contentious policy issues. For further information on the Development Committee, see World Bank official website, available at: http://web.worldbank.org/WBSITE/EXTERNAL/DEVCOMMEXT/0,,contentMD K:23158487~menuPK:7348076~pagePK:7347738~piPK:7347796~theSitePK:277473,00.html (accessed 7 November 2012).
7. Information provided by staff within the GPF Secretariat and the PREM Vice Presidency in interviews with the author, September 2011 and November 2008, Washington, DC.
8. Interviews with the author, September 2011, Washington, DC.
9. Author's analysis of World Bank (2012). Programmes were counted as targeting domestic institutional reform if synopses included the key terms 'public administration reform', 'public sector governance' and / or 'anti-corruption'.

REFERENCES

Barnett, M. and M. Finnemore (2004), *Rules for the World: International Organizations in Global Politics*, Ithaca, NY: Cornell University Press.

Bebbington, A., S. Guggenheim, E. Olson and M. Woolcock (2004), 'Exploring social capital debates at the World Bank', *Journal of Development Studies*, **40** (5), 33–64.

Broome, A. (2010), *The Currency of Power: The IMF and Monetary Reform in Central Asia*, Basingstoke: Palgrave Macmillan.

Broome, A. and L. Seabrooke (2007), 'Seeing like the IMF: institutional change in small open economies', *Review of International Political Economy*, **14** (3), 576–601.

Broome, A. and L. Seabrooke (2012), 'Seeing like an IO', *New Political Economy*, **17** (1), 1–16.

Chwieroth, J. (2010), *Capital Ideas: The IMF and the Rise of Financial Liberalization*, Princeton, NJ: Princeton University Press.

Clegg, L. (2010), 'Our dream is a world full of poverty indicators: the US, the World Bank, and the power of numbers', *New Political Economy*, **15** (4), 473–92.

Clegg, L. (2013), *Controlling the World Bank and IMF: Shareholders, Stakeholders, and the Politics of Concessional Lending*, Basingstoke: Palgrave Macmillan.

Coll, X. (2005), 'Changing the bank's culture', in R. Kagia (ed.), *Balancing the Development Agenda: The Transformation of the World Bank under James D. Wolfensohn*, Washington, DC: World Bank, pp. 120–25.

Craig, D. and D. Porter (2006), *Development Beyond Neo-Liberalism: Governance, Poverty Reduction and Political Economy*, London: Routledge.

Dañino, R. (2007), 'Legal aspects of the World Bank's work on human rights', *Yearbook of International Financial and Economic Law*, **8** (1), 3–9.

Ebrahim, A. and S. Herz (2011), 'The World Bank and democratic accountability: the role of civil society', in J. A. Scholte (ed.), *Building Global Democracy? Civil Society and Accountable Global Governance*, Cambridge: Cambridge University Press, pp. 58–77.

GPF (2008), *Governance Partnership Facility Program Document*, Washington, DC: World Bank.

GPF (2010), *Governance Partnership Facility Progress Report*, Washington, DC: World Bank.

GPF (2011), *Governance Partnership Facility: A Review of Window One Country Programs*, Washington, DC: World Bank.

Griffin, P. (2009), *Gendering the World Bank: Neoliberalism and the Gendered Foundations of Global Governance*, Basingstoke: Palgrave Macmillan.

Gutner, T. (2005), 'World Bank environmental reform: revisiting lessons from agency theory', *International Organization*, **59** (3), 773–83.

Harrison, E. (2008), 'Unpacking the anti-corruption agenda: dilemmas for anthropologists', *Oxford Development Studies*, **34** (1), 15–29.

Hout, W. (2007), *The Politics of Aid Selectivity*, London: Routledge.

IDA (2010), *IDA 16: Delivering Development Results*, Washington, DC: World Bank.

IEG (2011), *An Evaluation of the World Bank's Trust Fund Portfolio: Trust Fund Support for Development*, Washington, DC: World Bank.

IEG (2012a), *The Matrix System at Work: An Evaluation of the World Bank's Organizational Effectiveness*, Washington, DC: World Bank.

IEG (2012b), *World Bank Country-Level Engagement on Governance and Anti-Corruption*, Washington, DC: World Bank.

Kalathil, S. (2011), *Developing Independent Media as an Institution of Accountable Governance*, Washington, DC: World Bank.

Kapur, D., J. Lewis and R. Webb (1997), *The World Bank: Its First Half Century*, Washington, DC: Brookings Institution.

Leiteritz, R. (2005), 'Explaining organizational outcomes: the International Monetary Fund and capital account liberalization', *Journal of International Relations and Development*, **8** (1), 1–26.

Long, C. and N. Duvvury (2011), 'Civil society and accountability promotion in the Global Fund', in J.A. Scholte (ed.), *Building Global Democracy? Civil Society and Accountable Global Governance*, Cambridge: University Press, pp. 245–66.

Marshall, K. (2008), *The World Bank: From Reconstruction to Development to Equity*, London: Routledge.

Mason, E. and R. Asher (1973), *The World Bank Since Bretton Woods*, Washington, DC: Brookings Institution.

Momani, B. (2005), 'Recruiting and diversifying IMF technocrats', *Global Society*, **19** (2), 167–87.

Momani, B. (2007), 'IMF staff: missing link in Fund reform proposals', *Review of International Organizations*, **2** (1), 39–57.

Moschella, M. (2010), *Governing Risk: The IMF and Global Financial Crises*, Basingstoke: Palgrave Macmillan.

Nielson, D., M. Tierney and C. Weaver (2006), 'Bridging the rationalist–constructivist divide: re-engineering the culture of the World Bank', *Journal of International Relations and Development*, **9** (2), 107–39.

NTF (2010), *Knowledge and Learning for Human Rights and Development: Nordic Trust Fund Progress Report*. Washington, DC: World Bank.

Öniş, Z., and F. Şenses (2005), 'Rethinking the emerging Post-Washington Consensus', *Development and Change*, **36** (2), 263–90.

Palacio, A. (2006), 'The way forward: human rights and the World Bank', *Development Outreach*, World Bank online publication, available at:
http://web.worldbank.org/WBSITE/EXTERNAL/TOPICS/EXTLAWJUSTICE/0,,contentMDK:2110661 4~menuPK:445673~pagePK:64020865~piPK:149114~theSitePK:445634,00.html (accessed 12 November 2012).

Park, S. (2010), *The World Bank Group Interactions with Environmentalists: Changing International Organisation Identities*, London: Manchester University Press.

Park, S. and A. Vetterlein (2010), 'Owning development: creating policy norms in the IMF and World Bank', in S. Park and A. Vetterlein (eds), *Owning Development: Creating Policy Norms in the IMF and World Bank*, Cambridge: Cambridge University Press, pp. 3–26.

Phillips, D. (2009), *Reforming the World Bank: Twenty Years of Trial – and Error*, Cambridge: Cambridge University Press.

PREMPS (2012), *Poverty Reduction and Economic Management Governance and Public Sector Management: At A Glance*, Washington, DC: World Bank.

Ritzen, J. (2007), 'In search of world governance: books on the bank', *Global Governance*, **13** (4), 575–9.

Rosenau, J. (1995), 'Governance in the twenty-first century', *Global Governance*, **1** (1), 13–43.

Scholte, J.A. (2011), 'Global governance, accountability, and civil society', in J.A. Scholte (ed.), *Building Democracy? Civil Society and Accountable Global Governance*, Cambridge: Cambridge University Press, pp. 8–41.

Shihata, I. (1999), 'The creative role of the lawyer: the office of the World Bank's General Counsel', *Catholic University Law Review*, **48** (8), 1041–53.

Stiglitz, J. (2004), 'The Post-Washington Consensus Consensus', Initiative for Policy Dialogue Working Paper.

Stone, D. and C. Wright (2007), 'The currency of change: World Bank lending and learning in the Wolfensohn era', in D. Stone and C. Wright (eds), *The World Bank and Governance: A Decade of Reform and Reaction*, London: Routledge, pp. 1–26.

Sundberg, U. (2006), *The World Bank Takes on Human Rights Agenda*, Stockholm: Swedish Ministry for Foreign Affairs.

Teskey, G. (2012), 'Reflection on the Bank's updated governance and anti-corruption strategy', *World Bank Governance for Development Blog*, 29 March, available at: http://blogs.worldbank.org/governance/comment/reply/917 (accessed 7 November 2012).

Thirkell-White, B. (2004), 'The International Monetary Fund and civil society', *New Political Economy*, **9** (2), 251–70.

Weaver, C. (2008), *Hypocrisy Trap: The Poverty of Reform at the World Bank*, Princeton, NJ: Princeton University Press.

Williamson, J. (2000), 'What should the World Bank think about the Washington Consensus?', *World Bank Research Observer*, **15** (2), 251–64.

Woods, N. (2006), *The Globalizers: The IMF, the World Bank, and Their Borrowers*, Ithaca, NY: Cornell University Press.

Woods, N. and A. Narlikar (2002), 'Governance and the limits of accountability: the WTO, the IMF, and the World Bank', *International Social Science Journal*, **53** (1), 569–83.

World Bank (2007a), *A Management Framework for the Administration of World Bank-Administered Trust Funds*, Washington, DC: World Bank.

World Bank (2007b), *Implementation Plan for Strengthening World Bank Group Engagement on Governance and Anti-Corruption*, Washington, DC: World Bank.

World Bank (2009), *Development Policy Lending Retrospective: Flexibility, Customization, and Results*. Washington, DC: World Bank.

World Bank (2010), *Trust Fund Annual Report*, Washington, DC: World Bank.

World Bank (2011a), *A Guide to the World Bank*, Washington, DC: World Bank.

World Bank (2011b), *World Bank Annual Report*, Washington, DC: World Bank.

World Bank (2012), *Directory of Programs Supported by Trust Funds*, Washington, DC: World Bank.

15 The role of the United Nations in the governance of development

Jean-Philippe Thérien

This chapter analyses the role played by the United Nations (UN) in the global governance of development since the end of the Cold War. The topic is quite appropriate to a volume concerned with the international political economy of governance. For one thing, development has emerged since the 1950s as a major subject of debate within the sphere of global governance (Payne 2005; Rist 2008; Burnell et al. 2011). Furthermore, the legitimacy of the UN as a global 'governor' is well established, especially in the development field (Jolly et al. 2004; Toye and Toye 2004; Murphy 2006; Weiss and Daws 2007; Stokke 2009; Avant et al. 2010). The chapter sustains the argument that the international political economy of governance is always constructed on the basis of an ideology which expresses a comprehensive set of beliefs pertaining to the international political and economic order, and whose goal is the regulation of political practices. Governance can be described in terms of its ultimate purpose, that is, to be a problem-solving mechanism by which 'individuals and institutions . . . manage their common affairs' (Commission on Global Governance 1995: 2). Yet it must be kept in mind that, for this mechanism to function, a prior framing of issues must take place, based on an overall view of 'how society should be organised' (Schwarzmantel 2008: 27). As shall be seen, the UN's governance of development clearly indicates the pertinence of such an explanatory framework.

In greater detail, the chapter argues that over the past two decades the ideology of human development has been the driving normative force behind the governance practices advocated by the UN in the area of development. This is certainly not to deny that the UN's approach to development governance has been influenced by a host of material and structural factors. Nevertheless, the contention is that it is impossible to grasp the UN's positions on development unless they are properly located within their normative context. In order to unpack that context, the notion of human development is unequalled as an interpretive key. The UN's initial attraction to the human development approach derived from two complementary factors. First, this approach offered an alternative to the neoliberal orthodoxy promoted from the 1980s onwards by the Bretton Woods institutions. Second, it made possible the renewal, on the basis of a more market-friendly outlook, of the development paradigm traditionally upheld by the UN. Human development has thus served as an intellectual device that has helped the UN to achieve an innovative compromise in the governance of North–South relations. For the countries of the South the concept was useful because it provided a systematic critique of the international order; for those of the North it had the advantage of putting forward a vision of development largely grounded in liberal values.

The body of the chapter explains how the UN has systematically promoted the ideology of human development since the end of the Cold War. The first section examines the

UN's official discourse and shows how it has been influenced by the concept of human development. The following section focuses on a set of global policies that illustrate how the UN has sought to put the principles of human development into governance practices. The chapter thus contributes to two ongoing debates in the contemporary study of world politics: illustrating the increasingly active role played by international institutions such as the UN in 'the functions of governance' (Diehl and Frederking 2010: 5) and providing additional evidence to support the argument that 'ideas and concepts are arguably the most important legacy of the United Nations' (Jolly et al. 2009: 39).

THE UN DISCOURSE ON HUMAN DEVELOPMENT

Keeping in mind the work of the UN specialised agencies, Richard Jolly et al. (2004: 289) concluded that 'human development, in its widest sense, has been at the heart of UN efforts for economic and social progress over most of the past half-century'. This indisputable conclusion must not, however, obscure the fact that until the 1980s the UN conceived of development primarily as an economic process whose objective was that poor countries caught up with the rich. It was not until the end of the Cold War that the idea of human development truly came to the fore as the guiding principle of the UN approach towards the governance of development. As it happens, the notion holds no monopoly in UN rhetoric since it operates alongside various concepts, such as 'people-centred development', 'social development' and 'sustainable development'. What these various terms have in common far outweighs the differences between them. They all refer to a conception of development centred on individuals and inclusive of all facets of human activity. But, when compared to related terms, 'human development' has the clear advantage of a more solid theoretical framework and stronger institutional support.

The UN's turn toward human development can to a great extent be attributed to the United Nations Development Programme (UNDP), which in 1990 published its first Human Development Report (UNDP 1990; Payne and Phillips 2010: 123) and thus made human development its 'overriding priority' (Murphy 2006: 240). As Ban Ki-moon (2010a) asserted when the twentieth edition of the report was released in 2010, the UNDP document 'stunned the international community with the simple premise that people are the true measure of a nation's wealth'. Drafted by the Pakistani economist Mahbub ul Haq, with the assistance of Nobel Prize laureate Amartya Sen and several other renowned development economists, the initial 1990 Report was greeted with reservations, even inside the UN (McNeill 2007). At the time, there was nothing to suggest that it would not only become the UNDP's flagship publication, but also give rise to the framing of a new UN ideology for the governance of development.

The UNDP's Big Push

The emergence of the human development concept and the publication of the first Human Development Report resulted from the concurrence of highly favourable circumstances. 'The idea of human development won', Amartya Sen (2000: 21) has observed, 'because the world was ready for it'. On the economic level, the hegemony of the Washington Consensus had been undermined by the criticisms voiced by the UN Children's (Emergency) Fund (UNICEF) and non-governmental organisations (NGOs) pressing for adjustment with a human face. On the political level, the end of the Cold War and the collapse of socialism had discredited state planning and revalorised individual freedoms. Against this backdrop, ul Haq and his team were able to put forward a conception of development less centred on the state and less concerned with economic growth. Their report opened with the statement, 'People are the real wealth of a nation', and defined human development as 'a process of enlarging people's choices' (UNDP 1990: 9–10). While declaring that the essential choices of individuals had to do with health, education and income, the document furthermore specified that 'additional choices, highly valued by many people, range from political, economic and social freedom to opportunities for being creative and productive, and enjoying personal self-respect and guaranteed human rights' (UNDP 1990: 10). In short, viewing individuals as both beneficiaries and agents of development, the Human Development Reports have consistently underscored two objectives: the increase of well-being and the empowerment of people.

Twenty years on, the core of the UNDP's approach has remained remarkably stable. Yet this stability has not kept the human development concept from undergoing some significant adjustments (Fukuda-Parr 2003; Alkire 2010). In this regard, four trends can be discerned in the UNDP's thinking. First, the human development approach has placed more and more emphasis on empowerment and the political dimension of development. Second, this approach has been increasingly inspired by the language of human rights and its legal foundations. Third, the human development framework has become ever more attuned to the economic and political aspects of gender disparities. Finally, human development has attributed growing importance to sustainability and the rights and needs of future generations. That none of these changes has entailed a disavowal of the basic principles of human development clearly points to one of the concept's strengths: flexibility.

The success of the Human Development Report can be ascribed to its being at once 'policy-relevant' and 'academically respectable' (McNeill 2007: 12). That success is perhaps best illustrated by the 600 global, regional and national reports on human development sponsored to date by the UNDP. These reports have not only given the concept exceptional visibility but have also showed that it could serve as an analytical framework for studying almost every facet of development governance. Furthermore, the Human Development Index (HDI) created by the UNDP in 1990 has stimulated public debate in both developed and developing countries. Although it has been criticised for being overly simplistic, the HDI has become a methodological tour de force by establishing itself as an international ranking indicator that currently rivals per capita gross domestic product (GDP). The series of Human Development Reports has also acted as a catalyst for getting a number of development agencies to devote more resources to poverty reduction. Even international financial institutions have come to incorporate human development in their programmes. Lastly, the notion of human development has encouraged the entire UN system to take 'a more holistic approach to development' (Jolly et al. 2009: 194).

A New Vision of Development Governance

The UN system has never advocated the concept of human development with the same enthusiasm as the UNDP. One reason is that UN agencies are not mandated to promote sophisticated development paradigms. What is more, UN leaders have had to deal with the fact that many governments are troubled by the political implications of the UNDP's theses. But, even though the UNDP approach has visibly been watered down, the UN as a whole has nevertheless held to the core norms of human development as guidelines for behaviour regarding the governance of development. As a result, since the early 1990s, no other concept has had a greater impact on the organisation's development ideology. For example, from that time the UN has consistently and actively defended the idea that the referent of development should be the individual, rather than the state. Viewing development as a 'fundamental human right', Boutros Boutros-Ghali, in his *Agenda for Development*, adopted the UNDP's line of argument: 'People are a country's principal asset. Their well-being defines development' (United Nations 1994: paras 3, 96). A few years later, Kofi Annan (1997) also defined development as the 'furthering [of] the well-being of people', a stance that he justified on the grounds that 'no shift in the way we think or act can be more critical than this: we must put people at the centre of everything we do' (Annan 2000: 7). For his part, Ban Ki-moon (2007), maintaining the orientation of his two predecessors, has stressed that the 'human dimension' was the unifying theme of his work. 'Ultimately', Ban (2010b) has stated, 'everything we do is tested by one criterion: has it improved peoples' lives?' As these various official positions suggest, the UN's post-Cold War discourse on development governance has replaced the old idea of national development with a new focus on individuals (Gore 2010).

The UN has also made clear that, far from being limited to the economy, development is a multidimensional undertaking that must take into account 'the full range of human endeavour'. 'Each dimension of development', Boutros-Ghali explained, 'is vital to the success of all others, as well as to the core concept of human-centred progress' (United Nations 1994: paras 211, 235). Annan (2005: 6) subsequently defended in no uncertain terms the need for an integrated approach to development governance: 'We will not enjoy development without security, we will not enjoy security without development, and we will not enjoy either without respect for human rights'. In the same perspective, Ban (2011) has frequently noted the need to 'connect the dots' among global challenges, 'so that solutions to one can become solutions to all'. The UN quest for an integrated approach to the governance of development was also the main motivation behind the holding of a series of global conferences from the early 1990s onwards. These meetings made it possible to articulate a development agenda reflecting the UN's comprehensive outlook. While that agenda has been dominated since 2000 by the pursuit of the Millennium Development Goals (MDGs), the broader set of international objectives that were adopted by the UN conferences aim in fact at achieving improvements 'in total human well-being' (United Nations 2007: 5).

In sum, human development ideology has widened the traditional notion of development by circumscribing the economy as only one of the numerous facets of social activity. Within this process of reconceptualisation, the most innovative aspects have surely been those bearing on the environmental and political dimensions of development governance. In light of the greening of politics everywhere, it is not surprising that human development ideology has focused more and more on the environment. In 1994, Boutros-Ghali declared that 'preserving and protecting the ecological equilibrium of our environment is a vital component not only of human development, but also of human survival' (United Nations 1994: para. 77). His successors have similarly argued that vigorous action in environmental governance was needed because 'our efforts to defeat poverty and pursue sustainable development will be in vain if environmental degradation and natural resource depletion continue unabated' (Annan 2005: 23). Ban Ki-moon has added a distinctive note to this warning, saying more than once that the achievement of the MDGs depends on firm international action in the face of climate change.

The UN has innovated as well through its ever-greater emphasis on the political aspect of the governance of development. UN leaders have thus stressed the need to foster social integration and create 'a society for all' (United Nations 2003a: 31). The goal of social integration goes a long way to explaining why the UN has devoted so much effort since 2000 to poverty reduction. With the recent economic crisis, the question of social integration has generated a particularly strong defence of the most vulnerable, 'those least responsible for the crisis and those least able to respond' (Ban 2009a). The *Report on the World Social Situation 2010* argued that 'it is time to open up a discourse on poverty reduction that centres on inclusive development and the ending of social exclusion' (United Nations 2009a: 156), whilst Ban Ki-moon has contended that 'one of the most important roles that the United Nations can play is that of champion of the powerless, the forgotten and the marginalized' (United Nations 2008: 3). For the UN, reducing global inequalities is the key to the reinforcement of social integration. In fact, the concern 'for equity and for equality of all persons' (United Nations 2007: iii) is today identified as the basic feature of the UN development agenda. As mentioned by certain observers, it is true that the UN's current concern with poverty has drawn attention away from inequality (Fukuda-Parr 2010; Gore 2010). Yet it is just as true that, from the mid-2000s, the question of inequality has gained increasing prominence in UN deliberations on development governance (United Nations 2005a, 2006a).

From the UN's perspective, human maldevelopment is mainly the result of inadequate national policies, particularly on the part of rich countries. Since the end of the Cold War the leaders of the institution have noted repeatedly that states' focus on short-term interests has made globalisation and global governance systemic sources of tension for human development. Kofi Annan (2000: 10), for instance, vigorously denounced the fact that the benefits of globalisation were 'highly concentrated among a relatively small number of countries' and Ban Ki-moon (2008a) has often observed that 'the rising economic tide has not lifted all boats'. Moreover, the recent economic crisis prompted the UN to criticise the principles underpinning globalisation in a discursive tone that the organisation had abandoned since the 1970s. The *Report on the World Social Situation 2010*, which urged 'a strategic shift away from the market fundamentalist thinking, policies and practices of recent decades towards more sustainable development' (United Nations 2009a: iv), came hard on the heels of Ban Ki-moon's interrogation of the 'magic' of the markets: 'We live in the real world', Ban (2008b) stated, 'not the world of economic theory'.

With respect to global governance, the UN has deplored the imbalance between the sophistication of the rules that facilitated market expansion and the weakness of international norms regarding labour standards, the environment, human rights and poverty reduction (Annan 2000: 10). In this connection, Ban Ki-moon has spoken of the need for a 'new global social contract' in support of 'a fairer and sustainable process of globalization' (United Nations 2009b: 36). In Ban's view, such a global contract ought to include a fundamental reform of the Bretton Woods institutions that would 'significantly enhance the voice and participation of developing countries' (Ban 2010c). Although the recently established Group of 20 is widely seen as a sign of progress, it certainly does not fulfil UN expectations, because 'more than one-third of the world's population, and more than 85% of the world's countries are not represented' (Ban 2009b).

The preceding analysis shows that over the past two decades the UN has consistently defended a new vision of international development governance focused on individuals and grounded in a holistic approach. Indeed, the magnitude of the transformations envisioned by the UN became most starkly apparent in 2012 when Ban Ki-moon (2012) made this candid comment on the global development situation: 'Let us face the facts: the old model is broken'. While the UN's desire for change is both explicit and firm, it remains constrained by the fact that the human development approach is the product of a political arrangement resting on global power relations. It is telling, for example, that the UN criticises capitalism's excesses, but not the validity of the market economy or the objective of economic growth. In this sense human development ideology is ultimately more reformist than revolutionary. Pervaded by complex constitutive tensions, it continues to face resistance from the right and the left, although the soft law of development has on many occasions confirmed its political legitimacy. Beyond the symbolic support provided by a variety of UN resolutions and declarations, it must be acknowledged as well that the values and principles of human development have found expression in a whole series of global governance practices.

HUMAN DEVELOPMENT PRACTICE

It is widely recognised that a deep gap exists between the discourse and the reality of human development. Still, it would be fair to assume that the 'global convergence in human development' (UNDP 2011: ii) is due in part to the governance practices promoted by the UN. In this section, four such practices will be analysed. These practices are related to the MDGs, the promotion of democracy, the fight against climate change and the architecture of global development.

The Millennium Development Goals

Human development ideology was undeniably an intellectual catalyst for the MDGs, a set of eight socio-economic objectives adopted by the member-states of the UN at the 2000 Millennium Summit. These objectives constituted a global strategy intended to guide international development governance until 2015. Revolving around the 'super-norm' of poverty eradication (Hulme and Fukuda-Parr 2009: 5), the MDGs are often deemed 'the single most important focus of international efforts to promote human development' (Alston 2005: 755). The eight goals are as follows: (1) eradicate extreme poverty and hunger; (2) achieve universal primary education; (3) promote gender equality and empower women; (4) reduce child mortality; (5) improve maternal health; (6) combat HIV/AIDS, malaria and other diseases; (7) ensure environmental sustainability; and (8) develop a global partnership for development (United Nations 2001a).

The MDG process is the most significant development initiative ever taken, and its innovativeness in the governance of development must not be underestimated. First, having been approved by the leaders of 189 countries, including 147 heads of state and government, the MDGs have been invested with unprecedented political legitimacy. This explains why they were immediately adopted as a key conceptual reference for the development policies of most state and non-state actors (Jolly et al. 2004: 305). Second, the MDGs established an action plan with measurable results, thanks to the inclusion of 21 targets and 60 indicators. Many experts thus argue that the goals can be subjected to systematic accountability procedures (Alston 2005: 756). Third, the MDGs constitute a historic North–South compact. By introducing the notion of a 'global partnership for development' (Goal 8), they sanction the idea that the rich countries have to increase their aid and change the rules of international trade and finance in order better to address development needs (Hulme 2010: 19). Fourth, the MDGs are grounded in an approach to development that is less focused on economic growth and is more people-centred than the traditional approach. As Sakiko Fukuda-Parr (2004: 395) has argued, 'the MDGs speak directly to improving human lives'.

The UN played so central a role in the MDG process that these objectives have been described as a 'UN creation' (Jolly et al. 2009: 195). In fact, it is difficult to see how the MDGs could have come into being without the UN's leadership. Most of the MDGs were first articulated in the world conferences organised by the UN during the 1990s. Once the Organisation for Economic Co-operation and Development (OECD), the World Bank and the International Monetary Fund had endorsed the idea of mobilising the international community around a limited number of development targets, this approach was endowed with universal moral authority by the UN General Assembly and the Millennium Declaration (Fukuda-Parr 2010: 27; Hulme 2010: 16–18). Lastly, it was the UN General Secretary who, in the *Road Map towards the Implementation of the United Nations Millennium Declaration*, framed the definitive list of MDGs in 2001 (United Nations 2001a).

The MDGs quickly became the priority of the entire UN system for the governance of development. In addition to reorienting programmes on the ground, the organisation's commitment took a variety of forms. In 2002, for example, Kofi Annan set up the UN Millennium Project, under the direction of the United States economist Jeffrey Sachs, with the purpose of determining 'a concrete action plan for the world to achieve the MDGs' (UN Millennium Project 2006). Based on the work of ten task-forces assembling 250 government and non-government experts, the Millennium Project's report, published in 2005, recommended a set of measures geared to the implementation and funding of the MDGs (Stokke 2009: 461–8). The Millennium Campaign, launched by the UN Secretariat in 2002, was designed to raise public support for the MDGs. As Eveline Herfkens (n.d.), the campaign's founder, recalled, this was 'the first time ever the UN initiated an effort to build awareness of internationally agreed objectives and to inspire and mobilize citizens to hold their governments accountable for their achievement'. Finally, the UN instituted a sophisticated system of global monitoring to assess the progress of the MDGs. National governments have been expected to produce Millennium Reports on the performance of each country, while the UN specialised agencies have been charged with reporting each year on the situation worldwide (Fukuda-Parr 2004: 397).

To date, the MDG strategy has yielded mixed results. The Secretary General's 2010 report noted that 'collective efforts towards achievement of the MDGs have made inroads in many areas', but that progress has remained 'uneven'. 'Without a major push forward', the UN has warned, 'many of the MDG targets are likely to be missed in most regions' (United Nations 2010: 4). The World Bank (2010a: 97) has confirmed this conclusion, asserting that 'several of the MDGs will not be attained, globally or by a majority of countries'. In fact the situation varies widely from one region to another. In Asia and Latin America, many countries have achieved or are on their way to achieving most of the MDGs, whereas sub-Saharan Africa and the least advanced countries are lagging behind. Almost everywhere, however, the economic crisis of 2008–09 has slowed progress on poverty reduction, a negative trend that is unlikely to be reversed before the end of the 2010s (Hulme and Fukuda-Par 2009: 28; World Bank 2010b: 6; United Nations 2012).

Within this disparate picture, the pivotal success of the MDGs relates to the probable achievement of the symbolic objective of Goal 1: the reduction of global poverty by half. Thanks largely to the performances of China and India, the extreme poverty rate plummeted from 46 per cent in 1990 to 27 per cent in 2005, and is expected to drop to 15 per cent by 2015 (United Nations 2010: 6–7). Optimists can furthermore boast that 'most countries are making progress on most of the key MDG indicators' (Overseas Development Institute and UN Millennium Campaign 2010: 2). At the same time, the greatest disappointment no doubt concerns Goal 8, the accomplishment of which depends on the leadership of the developed countries. Development aid, which has fallen in 2011 and 2012, remains far from the United Nations target of 0.7 per cent of donors' gross national income (GNI), the conclusion of a pro-development Doha Round looks highly unlikely, and a large number of developing countries are facing the risk of debt distress (MDG Gap Task Force 2012; OECD 2013).

The jury is still out with regard to the impact of the MDG strategy on the governance of development. Some critics contend that for many poor countries the proposed targets are quite simply unrealistic (Clemens et al. 2007: 747). Others hold that, by placing the accent on poverty reduction, the MDGs have marginalised the more political issues of inequality and empowerment (Watkins 2008; Jolly et al. 2009: 224–5; Fukuda-Parr 2010). And still others maintain that, 'despite their grand claims of mutual accountability, [the MDGs] actually hold no one accountable at all' (Moss 2010: 219). Yet such failings must not obscure the fact that the MDGs constitute 'the most comprehensive and most detailed set of human development goals ever adopted' (UNDP 2005: 39). Not only have they introduced an innovative 'meta-goal' in the global governance of development (Hulme and Fukuda-Parr 2009: 20), but they have also helped to refocus North–South cooperation on basic human needs. Although it is certainly true that the MDGs' discursive impact has thus far exceeded their practical impact, and that their full meaning will ultimately depend on the UN's capacity to establish an ambitious consensus on a post-2015 global development agenda, the MDGs have nonetheless represented a decisive turn in the history of development governance (Manning 2010; UN System Task Team 2012).

Democracy Promotion

The promotion of democracy provides another illustration of how the principles of human development have shaped global governance practices. It is noteworthy in this connection that democracy and human development have always been intertwined. Indeed, the UN presents democratic governance as the third pillar of human development, alongside health and education, and equitable economic growth (UNDP 2002: 53). Democracy, regarded as a universal right and a source of empowerment, is generally described as 'a critical end of human development' as well as 'a means of achieving it' (UNDP 2002: v). Built on the principle that 'there is no single model of democracy' (United Nations 2005b: 30), the UN approach towards democratic governance has remained wide open – and some would say vague. However, the lack of specificity has not stopped the UN from making the promotion of democracy one of its global governance priorities, particularly in post-conflict situations (Santiso 2002: 559). In 2011, democracy-related programmes accounted for 26 per cent of the UNDP's budget and represented the second-largest area of investment of that agency, just behind poverty reduction and the MDGs (at 28 per cent) (UNDP 2012: 6).

Originally concentrated on electoral processes, UN policies concerning the promotion of democracy go back to the 1960s and 1970s. During those two decades the Trusteeship Council backed the holding of some 30 elections and referenda worldwide, and the UNDP began to elaborate its first electoral assistance programmes (Ponzio 2004: 210–13). By widening the UN's latitude in the field of human rights and conflict resolution, the end of the Cold War cleared the way for a major expansion of those first initiatives relating to democracy. A decisive step was taken in 1991 when the UN General Assembly adopted a resolution that underscored the importance of better coordination of UN electoral assistance activities and led to the creation of the Electoral Assistance Division within the Secretariat (Ludwig 2004: 171). Over the years UN electoral assistance programmes – whose priorities have been election monitoring, technical assistance and the exchange of good practices – have steadily grown (Ludwig 2004: 173–6). In 2010, the UNDP estimated that it provided some form of electoral support to 30–40 countries each year (UNDP 2010b: 34).

Although it may be the most noticeable aspect of UN activities pertaining to democracy, electoral assistance is only one dimension of a much broader policy. The democracy promotion agenda was considerably enlarged in the 1990s when the UNDP adopted its Governance for Sustainable Human Development policy and resolved to make governance one of its primary fields of intervention (UNDP 1997; Santiso 2002: 574). The process of enlarging the agenda, still under way, has drawn much of its legitimacy from the more and more holistic conception of democracy that the UN started advocating after the Cold War, which in its most recent version encompasses 'the procedural and the substantive; formal institutions and informal processes; majorities and minorities; men and women; governments and civil society; the political and the economic; at the national and the local levels' (United Nations 2009c: 2). UN activities in the area of democracy promotion have been diversified in accordance with this wide-ranging vision of democracy. In addition to its work on elections and electoral institutions, the UNDP is active in a whole range of areas, including access to justice, human rights strengthening, parliamentary development, anti-corruption and governance assessments (UNDP

2010b: 7). A distinctive feature of the UNDP approach is that it openly acknowledges the need to finance initiatives 'in politically sensitive areas' (UNDP 2010b: 110). Since 2005, the UNDP's work has been supplemented by the UN Democracy Fund (UNDEF), whose resources are earmarked essentially for civil society organisations. In 2010 the UNDEF had received voluntary contributions of US$110 million from 39 countries and financed over 300 projects, especially in the spheres of community development and women's empowerment (UNDEF 2010).

The policy of democratic governance promoted by the UN has received active support from the aid community (Stokke 2009: 325–6). Donors' support was institutionalised in 1995 when the governments of the OECD adopted the Orientations on Participatory Development and Good Governance, wherein it was recognised that 'assisting democratisation should be viewed as a long-term process' (OECD 1995: 13). This priority was confirmed in the Paris Declaration on aid effectiveness (2005) and in the Accra Agenda for Action (2008), which stated that the purpose of aid was to 'strengthen governance' (OECD 2005) and that democracy was one of 'the prime engines of development in all countries' (OECD 2008). To better coordinate their policies, the OECD countries established a Network on Governance, whose work concentrates on aid and domestic accountability, human rights, anti-corruption, taxation, governance assessments and capacity development (OECD 2010a). Moreover, since 2007, the OECD has been home to the Partnership for Democratic Governance (PDG), a multilateral forum bringing together governments of the North and South, the UN and regional organisations. The objective of the PDG is to help fragile democracies 'to build their governance capacity and improve service delivery to their citizens' (OECD 2010b: 3). Concentrating their aid on economic and development policy and the strengthening of civil society, the OECD countries devoted 12.5 per cent of their aid to governance issues in 2009 (OECD 2010c: 89; 2011: Table 19).

Given the polysemy of the term 'democracy', the global policy of democracy promotion is condemned to ongoing controversy. Indeed, it is not always easy to see the common rationale for practices as diverse as election monitoring, the financing of tax reforms and the improvement of access to justice for marginalised minorities. But it is beyond dispute that the post-Cold War period has witnessed a considerable expansion of multilateral and bilateral programmes related to democracy. Democratic governance has thus gradually become a standard component in the global governance of development. To date, democracy promotion initiatives have clearly favoured a procedural approach and, as evidenced by the contrasting assessments of such initiatives in Afghanistan and Iraq, their social impact has at times been highly ambiguous (Whitehead 2009; Kalilzad 2010; Worden 2010). Yet many projects conducted on behalf of democratic governance have incontrovertibly helped to strengthen the rule of law and empower ordinary citizens. In addition, democracy promotion activities are systematically legitimised on the grounds that democracy is based 'on the freely expressed will of people to determine their own political, economic, social and cultural systems and their full participation in all aspects of their lives' (United Nations 2005b: 30). For these reasons, it can certainly be argued that the human development ideology put forward by the UN has provided a sturdy normative framework in support of democracy promotion policies. At the same time, however, such policies reveal the degree to which human development ideology is the product of a delicate political compromise. Thus, while the human development approach does indeed propose social changes tending toward a more emancipatory model of democracy, it is striking that the extent of those changes remains largely confined to the parameters determined by the dominant values underpinning the contemporary liberal order.

Climate Change

In recent years, the issue of climate change has dominated international discussions on environmental governance. Out of these discussions a growing consensus has emerged around the idea that global warming could have a serious negative impact on water supplies, agricultural production, human settlements and human health. Closely echoing Ban Ki-moon's appraisal of climate change as 'the defining challenge of our time' (UNCEB 2008: 5), the UNDP (2008: 1) has stated that it is the 'defining human development issue of our generation'. The 2010 Human Development Report argued, still more explicitly, that 'climate change may be the single factor that makes the future very different from the past, impeding the continuing progress in human development that history would lead us to expect' (UNDP 2010a: 102). Hence, efforts in the struggle against climate change are arguably one of the best illustrations of a global governance practice favouring human development. Always in the vanguard of this policy, the UN has distinguished itself through its leadership on various fronts: scientific, legal, political and economic.

The UN's interest in climate change became apparent at the first World Climate Conference, organised by the World Meteorological Organization (WMO) in Geneva in 1979. From that point on, the WMO and the United Nations Environment Programme (UNEP) were deeply involved in a series of scientific meetings devoted to the climate. The meeting held in Toronto in 1988 was particularly decisive and marked a turning point in the world's attitude toward global warming (Betsill 2005: 105–6). A few months later, the WMO and the UNEP created the International Panel on Climate Change (IPCC) to provide the international community with 'a clear scientific view on the current state of knowledge in climate change' (IPCC 2011). The IPCC's mandate covers the science of climate change, both the impacts and possible response strategies (Bulkeley and Newell 2010: 26–7). Although its analyses have been met with criticism, the IPCC is still considered to be by far the most authoritative international source on climate change issues. The assessment it released in 2007, and for which the IPCC won the Nobel Peace Prize, received a great deal of media attention because for the first time the IPCC concluded, with 'very high confidence', that climate change was due to human activity (IPCC 2007: 37).

The Toronto conference also prompted the UN to initiate international negotiations, which in 1992 led to the adoption of the United Nations Framework Convention on Climate Change (UNFCCC). Ratified by 195 countries as of 2013, the UNFCCC has been referred to as the 'constitution' of the climate change regime (Danish 2007: 10). Its main objective has been to stabilise greenhouse gas emissions 'at a level that would prevent dangerous anthropogenic interference with the climate system'. Founded on a North–South approach, the UNFCCC upholds the principle that in the struggle against climate change developed countries (including economies in transition) and developing countries have 'common but differentiated responsibilities' (UNFCCC 1992). The countries of the North are not only committed – like those of the South – to making regular reports on their greenhouse gas emissions and their climate change mitigation programmes, but they have also agreed to reduce their emissions to 1990 levels and provide technological and financial assistance to the developing countries (Betsill 2005: 111). To this end, the UNFCCC has set up the Global Environment Facility (GEF), a financial mechanism based on an innovative collaboration involving the World Bank, UN agencies and regional development banks (GEF 2010).

In 1995 the first conference of the parties to the UNFCCC concluded that the greenhouse gas reduction commitments stipulated in the convention were insufficient and set in motion a new negotiation process aimed at establishing 'binding targets and timetables' (Betsill 2005: 113). In 1997 those negotiations produced the Kyoto Protocol, where the developed countries agreed to take additional measures to fight global warming and undertook to reduce their aggregate greenhouse gas emissions by 5.2 per cent, compared to the 1990 level, before 2012. The agreement offered the developed countries three market-based mechanisms to help meet their obligations: emissions trading, joint implementation and the so-called Clean Development Mechanism (Bulkeley and Newell 2010: 24–5). As Elizabeth DeSombre (2006: 121) has noted, the Kyoto commitments were based 'on what individual states were willing to agree to, rather than any specific environmental or economic logic'. For all its weaknesses, the Kyoto Protocol nonetheless represents 'the current apogee of international efforts to address global climate change' (Danish 2007: 11).

Although the UN process on climate change has been pursued without pause, no international accord has thus far taken over from the Kyoto Protocol in order to establish new binding greenhouse gas reduction targets. International negotiations have stumbled on the sharing of responsibilities between developed and developing countries and on the funding of poor countries' policies. But the legal impasse has not prevented all progress on the political front. One significant step forward has been the emergence of a new consensus on the role that countries of the South have necessarily to play in the global governance of climate change. In 2007 they broke with their traditional positions and agreed to take 'measurable, reportable and verifiable' mitigation actions (UNFCCC 2008). Moreover, in Cancún in 2010, the so-called 'emerging countries' committed themselves to reducing their greenhouse gases within the framework of the UNFCCC. Another advance has stemmed from the strengthening of the funding mechanisms for the fight against climate change. The most ambitious accord was reached in Cancún, where the developed countries promised to provide the developing countries with US$30 billion for the 2010–12 period and US$100 billion per year by 2020 (Pew Center on Global Climate Change 2010). Even though the slowness of international negotiations is out of step with the magnitude of the climate change problem, the UN still appears to be 'the only forum in which agreement can be crafted on the objectives and scope of international action' (UNCEB 2008: 7).

Parallel to its work concerning scientific knowledge-sharing and the supervision of intergovernmental negotiations, the UN takes part in climate change governance through the assistance it provides to developing countries with respect to mitigation, adaptation, technology transfer and financing. Several UN agencies contribute to these aid programmes, including the UNDP, the Food and Agriculture Organization, the United Nations Industrial Development Organization and the UNEP. Oriented toward capacity-building, UN actions are intended to help developing countries improve their national institutions and human resources in order to confront climate change (UNCEB 2008). This multilateral aid complements the programmes of bilateral donors, who are the financial mainstays of global climate change policy. In 2010, OECD countries devoted 15 per cent of their aid (US$22.6 billion) to climate change-related activities (OECD 2012).

The global governance of climate change has often been depreciated for being 'toothless' and because the accords on which it is based are 'hardly abiding' (Huang 2009: 438). One of the crucial failures of the contemporary governance framework has clearly been its inability to halt the continuous increase in greenhouse gas emissions (IEA 2010: 11). Global warming seems to provide one of the strongest demonstrations that governments always think in terms of national interests and are unable to adopt a long-term perspective. With this in mind, the UN's leadership on climate change must not be overrated. Nevertheless, one can assume that, without the UN, even the limited progress that has been made until now would not have been achieved. Indeed, this progress is due in great measure to the UN's action in favour of new rules and structures of international cooperation.

From a normative perspective, it is also clear that the UN's involvement in strengthening climate change governance took shape in anything but an ideological void. Rather, it was determined by two key principles of the human development approach. First, the UN was one of the primary international forces fighting to broaden the traditional definition of development and pushing for development policies that factor in global warming. Second, it is largely thanks to UN efforts that the human rights implications of climate change have been increasingly acknowledged (Jodoin 2011). In sum, the slow progress thus far of climate change governance must not obscure either the UN's leadership role or the importance of the values on which it has based its actions.

The Architecture of Development Governance

Anchored in the belief that 'global forces also create and constrain opportunities for human development' (UNDP 2010a: 109), human development ideology has also found expression in a variety of initiatives designed to reform the architecture of development governance. These initiatives, centred on issues of process rather than substance, generally do not attract much attention from scholars or the media. Yet, even when they pertain to technical matters, such as institutional structures or administrative procedures, it should be emphasised that governance mechanisms always involve a political dimension and have a practical impact. Since the end of the Cold War, the UN has helped transform the architecture of development governance by stressing three objectives: to strengthen multilateral cooperation, improve the cohesion of the UN system and develop public–private partnerships. The changes implemented in these areas have, in fact, been so numerous that the recent history of the UN could justifiably be characterised as one of permanent reforms (Stokke 2009: 490).

On the multilateral level, the UN has undertaken an unprecedented collaboration with the Bretton Woods institutions. This collaboration, based on a narrowing of the gap between the UN's social-democratic approach and the liberal approach of the major international economic organisations, has opened a new phase in the UN's long struggle to be recognised as the multilateral institution with the greatest legitimacy to govern the world economic order (Noël and Thérien 2008: 181–2). Starting in 1998 with a series of historical meetings between the Economic and Social Council (ECOSOC) and representatives of the International Monetary Fund (IMF) and the World Bank, the new cooperation between the UN and the Bretton Woods institutions gained momentum following the 2002 'Financing for Development' Summit held in Monterrey. Today, it has become routine, thanks to annual high-level meetings bringing together ECOSOC, IMF, World Bank and World Trade Organization (WTO) officials.

The periodic meetings between the ECOSOC and the major international economic bodies have given rise to wide-ranging discussions on several global governance issues, including implementation of the MDGs, the place of development in multilateral trade negotiations, debt alleviation, IMF decision-making rules, and innovative sources of development finance. The head of the ECOSOC, Lazourous Kapambwe, summed up the usefulness of this new consultation mechanism by noting that it enabled the participants to 'speak with each other', rather than 'talk at each other' (United Nations 2011). While it is difficult to measure the effect of institutionalising dialogue between the ECOSOC and the Bretton Woods institutions, it has arguably contributed to enhancing the governance of development by facilitating the identification of successful practices and the sharing of information.

In addition to its efforts on the systemic level, the UN has taken a series of measures aimed at improving its own institutional efficiency in the development field. It is true that since the 1960s UN development agencies have constantly sought to get more value for money. But reforms initiated since the end of the Cold War have been unparalleled in scope and motivated more by a concern for results. Two of these reforms deserve special attention. The first relates to the bureaucratic restructuring that led to the creation of the UN Development Group (UNDG) in 1997. The UNDG brings together the 32 UN funds, programmes and agencies that 'play a role in development' (UNDG 2009). Chaired by the UNDP Administrator, the UNDG is one of the three pillars of the United Nations Chief Executives Board, which is the UN's top governing structure. Focused on country-level work, the mandate of the UNDG is to provide 'system-wide guidance to coordinate, harmonize and align UN development activities' (UNDG 2009). Its goal, in other words, is to improve the ways in which UN country teams work together in each of the 135 countries where they are based. The UNDG has responsibility, in particular, for elaborating the United Nations Development Assistance Frameworks (UNDAF), a strategic planning instrument intended to describe 'the collective response of the UN system to national development priorities' (UNDG 2010: 3). The work of the UNDG also includes support to UN country offices and the Resident Coordinator System, which is responsible for coordinating UN field operations. One of the UNDG's other achievements is to have expanded the network of UN houses: these bring the various UN activities in a country under one administrative roof and have grown since 1997 from four to 60 worldwide.

The UN's new concern for results also prompted the establishment of the 'Delivering as One' policy. The policy stems from the work of the High-Level Panel on UN System-Wide Coherence in the areas of development, humanitarian assistance and the environment, established by the Secretary-General in 2006 under the chairmanship of the prime ministers of Mozambique, Norway and Pakistan. The High-Level Panel's report put forward an integrated approach to reinforcing inter-agency governance on the basis of four principles: one leader, one budget, one programme and one office (United Nations 2006b). In 2007 eight pilot countries (Albania, Cape Verde, Mozambique, Pakistan, Rwanda, Tanzania, Uruguay and Vietnam) were selected to implement the 'Delivering as One' concept. It remains to be seen to what extent this approach can effectively bring about a reduction in administrative costs, for both the UN system and national governments. That said, the political pressures to enhance the cohesion of UN activities and bring UN priorities closer into line with those of the countries where it intervenes will certainly be maintained over the long term. It would therefore be reasonable to suggest that 'Delivering as One is the future for UN development activities' (Clark 2011).

The other major reform of significance has been the UN's attempt to reshape the architecture of development governance by promoting local and global partnerships with non-state actors. Conceived as collaborative initiatives in which 'participants agree to work together to achieve a common purpose or undertake a specific task' (United Nations 2003b: para. 9), partnerships have of course existed since the UN's early days. However, their number exploded in the wake of the global conferences held in the 1990s, particularly in the areas of development and the environment. Aside from the increased number of such initiatives, two qualitative changes were also introduced. First, NGOs are increasingly involved in the actual design of partnerships; second, private sector participation in UN partnerships is more frequently solicited.

Global partnerships are politically more significant than local ones, chiefly because they are more visible. In recent years two have come to dominate the UN agenda: one is related to the MDGs and the other is the Global Compact. While states retain the prime responsibility for meeting the MDGs, it has been widely recognised that mobilising non-state actors is crucial for their achievement. Indeed, the MDG framework established a 'clear mandate to develop partnerships with the private sector, non-governmental organizations and civil society in general' (United Nations 2001b: para. 106). Civil society groups thus contribute to the achievement of the MDGs through activities related to advocacy, policy design, implementation and monitoring. For its part, the Global Compact is the world's largest corporate social responsibility programme (Thérien and Pouliot 2006). Along with its 6000 corporate members and the UN Secretariat, the Compact includes six UN agencies, as well as NGOs, labour associations, think-tanks and government representatives. Focused on giving support to four international agreements in the areas of human rights, labour standards, the environment and the fight against corruption, the Global Compact has now become a key instrument in the UN's strategy to give a 'human face to the global market' (UN Global Compact 2011: 7).

The policies promoted by the UN to strengthen the architecture of development governance have clearly not fulfilled all the expectations initially aroused. Management of the international economy continues to be dominated by the Bretton Woods institutions; the 'Delivering as One' policy is still in its breaking-in period; and the added value of UN partnerships remains a subject of debate. Nevertheless, following the institutional reforms promoted by the UN over the past 20 years, the international governance of development has been significantly transformed. By attributing greater importance to poverty reduction, while at the same time moving closer to partner governments and ordinary citizens, the development architecture is more human-centred today than it was in the days of the Cold War.

CONCLUSION

The UN has consistently played a leadership role in the governance of global development since its creation, and since the early 1990s the UN's leadership has been exercised largely on the basis of orientations underpinned by the ideology of human development. This ideology has not only allowed the UN to articulate a world-view encompassing all aspects of social life, but has also provided the UN with a conceptual toolbox for framing a broad range of global governance practices. While the human development ideology may not have upset the dominance of the Washington Consensus, it has represented for 20 years the most credible critique of mainstream development policies.

As noted in the introduction to the chapter, this analysis provides grist to the mill of two current debates in the study of global governance. The first relates to the general contribution of international institutions to this process, wherein the argument mounted here shores up the position that international organisations do affect the patterns of global governance because they 'help to realize common interests in world politics' (Keohane 2005: 245). The UN's sustained efforts in the development arena also indicate the degree to which international governance is increasingly institutionalised through multilateral arrangements. Of course, the ability of international organisations generally, and the UN in particular, to take action is restricted by power structures whereby political authority continues to reside in states. The rigidity of these power structures is what explains, for example, the persistent gap between the discourse and the reality of human development. Yet, even though the UN scarcely holds a hegemonic position on the development scene, it remains a pivotal 'global governor'. It is indisputable in this connection that the UN actively promotes 'new structures and rules . . . to solve problems, change outcomes, and transform international life' (Avant et al. 2010: 1). In addition, the UN represents the most tangible expression of what is often referred to as the 'international community' and thus enjoys greater legitimacy than any government or any competing international institution.

The second debate relates to the intellectual role of the UN, wherein once more this chapter lends weight to the view that one of the UN's central contributions to the governance of international relations is the production of ideas. Actually, this statement simply reasserts one of the core findings of the United Nations Intellectual History Project (UNIHP), which from 2001 to 2010 oversaw the publication of 15 monographs on UN activities. Kofi Annan encapsulated the UNIHP's originality, noting that it had revealed one of the most under-researched facets of the UN's role, namely, 'the quality and diversity of its intellectual leadership and its values-based framework for dealing with the major challenges of our times' (Jolly et al. 2009: xiii). The directors of the UNIHP were modest enough to recognise that their project was just the beginning of a discussion on the role of UN ideas. Based on a literal interpretation of that remark, this chapter has sought to demonstrate that the notion of ideology helps to understand how the values and policies associated with human development are articulated in a cohesive and structured manner. A key insight of this demonstration has been that the UN is fully involved in the 'great ideological struggle of the 21st century' between the different visions of globalisation (Steger 2009). Not surprisingly, the issue of governance is ever present within that struggle because a major point of contention between the rival political ideologies concerns the process of collective decision-making. The UN's preferred line of action, in keeping with the social-democratic tradition, is ultimately to promote a development model that encourages economic growth but does a better job of factoring in social equity (Noël and Thérien 2008).

The UN's exact impact on development governance can be debated indefinitely, but there are two points where consensus seems possible. First, even though the UN is subordinated to more powerful political actors, it is still a key player, thanks not only to the considerable political and economic resources it devotes to transforming the international order, but also to the unmatched legitimacy it enjoys. While the power wielded by the UN is no doubt more soft than hard, it is nonetheless real power. Second, it is remarkable that the UN's contribution to development governance is tied to a political project explicitly grounded in values of democracy and global justice. Although it is hard to imagine the day when the UN will become the dominant force in world politics, the interests and ideas that it defends will most certainly endure within the global public sphere.

REFERENCES

Alkire, S. (2010), 'Human development: definitions, critiques, and related concepts', Human Development Research Paper 2010/01, New York: UNDP, available at: http://hdr.undp.org/en/reports/global/hdr2010/papers/HDRP_2010_01.pdf.

Alston, P. (2005), 'Ships passing in the night: the current state of the human rights and development debate seen through the lens of the Millennium Development Goals', *Human Rights Quarterly*, **27** (3), 755–829.

Annan, K.A. (1997), 'Foreword', *Agenda for Development*, UN General Assembly Resolution 51/240 (A/RES/51/240), New York, 15 October, available at: http://www.un.org/Docs/SG/ag_index.htm.

Annan, K.A. (2000), *We the Peoples: The Role of the United Nations in the 21st Century*, New York: United Nations Department of Public Information.

Annan, K.A. (2005), *In Larger Freedom: Towards Development, Security and Human Rights for All*, New York: United Nations Department of Public Information.

Avant, D.D., M. Finnemore and S.K. Sell (2010), 'Who governs the globe?', in D.D. Avant, M. Finnemore and S.K. Sell (eds), *Who Governs the Globe?*, Cambridge: Cambridge University Press, pp. 1–31.

Ban, K. (2007), 'Why the world has changed in the UN's favor', *Newsweek International*, 4 June, available at: http://www.newsweek.com/2007/06/03/this-i-pledge-to-do.html.

Ban, K. (2008a), 'Remarks to the 12th United Nations Conference on Trade and Development – "We Can Do This"', Accra, Ghana, 20 April, available at: http://www.un.org/apps/news/infocus/sgspeeches/search_full.asp?statID=222.

Ban, K. (2008b), 'World food crisis: through Africa with hope', *International Herald Tribune*, 1 May, available at: http://www.un.org/sg/articleFull.asp?TID=78&Type=Op-Ed.

Ban, K. (2009a), 'Come together, right away', *International Herald Tribune*, 2 July, available at: http://www.nytimes.com/2009/07/03/opinion/03iht-edmoon.html?scp=1&sq=come+together&st=nyt.

Ban, K. (2009b), 'Remarks to the G-20 Summit, by the UN Secretary-General Ban Ki-moon', Pittsburgh, 25 September, available at: http://www.un.org/apps/news/infocus/sgspeeches/search_full.asp?statID=598.

Ban, K. (2010a), 'Remarks at Launch of 20th *Human Development Report*', New York, 4 November, available at: http://www.un.org/apps/news/infocus/sgspeeches/search_full.asp?statID=1002.

Ban, K. (2010b), 'Remarks at concluding session of the 18th Session of the Commission on Sustainable Development', New York, 14 May, available at: http://www.un.org/apps/news/infocus/sgspeeches/search_full.asp?statID=816.

Ban, K. (2010c), 'Remarks to Climate Change Conference (UNFCCC COP16 High-Level Segment)', Cancún (Mexico), 7 December, available at: http://www.un.org/apps/news/infocus/sgspeeches/statments_full.asp?statID=1028.

Ban, K. (2011), 'Secretary-General's statement to ECOSOC to launch the 2011 Millennium Development Goals Report', Geneva, 7 July, available at: http://www.un.org/apps/sg/sgstats.asp?nid=5401.

Ban, K. (2012), 'Remarks to high-level thematic debate on "The State of the World Economy and Finance and its Impact on Development"', New York, 17 May, available at: http://www.un.org/apps/news/infocus/sgspeeches/search_full.asp?statID=1538.

Betsill, M.M. (2005), 'Global climate change policy: making progress or spinning wheels?', in R.S. Axelrod, D. Leonard Downie and N.J. Vig (eds), *The Global Environment: Institutions, Law and Policy*, Washington, DC: CQ Press, pp. 103–24.

Bulkeley, H. and P. Newell (2010), *Governing Climate Change*, London, UK and New York, USA: Routledge.

Burnell, P., V. Randall and L. Rakner (eds) (2011), *Politics in the Developing World*, 3rd edition, Oxford: Oxford University Press.

Clark, H. (2011), 'Remarks on "Delivering as one: follow-up to Hanoi"', 7 February, available at: http://www.dev.undp.org/undp/en/home/presscenter/speeches/2011/02/07/helen-clark-remarks-on-delivering-as-one-follow-up-to-hanoi.html.

Clemens, M.A., C.J. Kelly and T.J. Moss (2007), 'The trouble with the MDGs: confronting expectations of aid and development success', *World Development*, **35** (5), 735–51.

Commission on Global Governance (1995), *Our Global Neighbourhood: The Report of the Commission on Global Governance*, Oxford: Oxford University Press.

Danish, K.W. (2007), 'An overview of the international regime addressing climate change', *Sustainable Development Law and Policy*, **7** (2), 10–15.

DeSombre, E.R. (2006), *Global Environmental Institutions*, London, UK and New York, USA: Routledge.

Diehl, P.F. and B. Frederking (eds) (2010), *The Politics of Global Governance: International Organizations in an Interdependent World*, 4th edition, Boulder, CO: Lynne Rienner Publishers.

Fukuda-Parr, S. (2003), 'The human development paradigm: operationalizing Sen's ideas on capabilities', *Feminist Economics*, **9** (2–3), 301–17.

Fukuda-Parr, S. (2004), 'Millennium Development Goals: why they matter', *Global Governance*, **10** (4), 395–402.

Fukuda-Parr, S. (2010), 'Reducing inequality – the missing MDG: a content review of PRSPs and bilateral donor policy statements', *IDS Bulletin*, **41** (1), 26–35.

GEF (2010), 'What is the GEF?', available at: http://www.thegef.org/gef/whatisgef.

Gore, C. (2010), 'The MDG paradigm, productive capacities and the future of poverty reduction', *IDS Bulletin*, **41** (1), 70–79.

Herfkens, E. (n.d.), 'Looking back, looking forward: the successes and challenges of the Millennium campaign', available at: http://www.endpoverty2015.org/en/global-partnership/news/millennium-campaign-successes-challenges.

Huang, J. (2009), 'A Leadership of Twenty (L-20) within the UNFCCC: establishing a legitimate and effective regime to improve our climate system', *Global Governance*, **15** (4), 435–41.

Hulme, D. (2010), 'Lessons from the making of the MDGs: human development meets results-based management in an unfair world', *IDS Bulletin*, **41** (1), 15–25.

Hulme, D. and S. Fukuda-Parr (2009), 'International norm dynamics and the "end of poverty": understanding the Millennium Development Goals (MDGs)', Working Paper 96, Brooks World Poverty Institute (BWPI), Manchester, available at: http://www.eadi.org/fileadmin/MDG_2015_Publications/fukudaparr_and_hulme_2009_international_norm_dynamics.pdf.

IEA (2010), *World Energy Outlook 2010 Executive Summary*. Paris: OECD and IEA, available at: http://www.worldenergyoutlook.org/docs/weo2010/WEO2010_ES_English.pdf.

IPCC (2007), *Climate Change 2007: Synthesis Report*, Geneva: IPCC, available at: http://www.ipcc.ch/pdf/assessment-report/ar4/syr/ar4_syr.pdf.

IPCC (2011), 'Organization', available at: http://www.ipcc.ch/organization/organization.shtml.

Jodoin, S. (2011), 'From Copenhagen to Cancún: a changing climate for human rights in the UNFCCC?', CISDL Legal Brief, Centre for International Sustainable Development Law (CISDL), Montreal, available at: http://www.preventionweb.net/files/17552_fromcopenhagentocancun20110110.pdf.

Jolly, R., L. Emmerij, D. Ghai and F. Lapeyre (2004), *UN Contributions to Development Thinking and Practice*, Bloomington, IN: Indiana University Press.

Jolly, R., L. Emmerij and T.G. Weiss (2009), *UN Ideas that Changed the World*, Bloomington, IN: Indiana University Press.

Kalilzad, Z. (2010), 'Lessons from Afghanistan and Iraq', *Journal of Democracy*, **21** (3), 41–9.

Keohane, R.O. (2005), *After Hegemony: Cooperation and Discord in the World Political Economy*, 2nd edition, Princeton, NJ: Princeton University Press.

Ludwig, R. (2004), 'The UN's electoral assistance: challenges, accomplishments, prospects', in E. Newman and R. Rich (eds), *The UN Role in Promoting Democracy: Between Ideals and Reality*, Tokyo and New York: United Nations University Press, pp. 169–87.

Manning, R. (2010), 'The impact and design of the MDGs: some reflections', *IDS Bulletin*, **41** (1), 7–14.

McNeill, D. (2007), '"Human development": the power of the idea', *Journal of Human Development and Capabilities*, **8** (1), 5–22.

MDG Gap Task Force (2012), *MDG Gap Task Force Report 2012: The Global Partnership for Development: Making Rhetoric a Reality*, New York: United Nations.

Moss, T. (2010), 'What next for the Millennium Development Goals?', *Global Policy*, **1** (2), 218–20.

Murphy, C.N. (2006), *The United Nations Development Programme: A Better Way?* Cambridge: Cambridge University Press.

Noël, A. and J.-P. Thérien (2008), *Left and Right in Global Politics*, Cambridge: Cambridge University Press.

OECD (1995), *Participatory Development and Good Governance*, Paris: OECD, available at: http://www.oecd.org/dataoecd/27/13/31857685.pdf.

OECD (2005), *Paris Declaration on Aid Effectiveness*, available at: http://www.oecd.org/dataoecd/11/41/34428351.pdf.

OECD (2008), *Accra Agenda for Action*, available at: http://www.oecd.org/dataoecd/11/41/34428351.pdf.

OECD (2010a), 'The OECD-DAC Governance Network (GOVNET)', available at: http://www.oecd.org/dataoecd/33/62/44637282.pdf.

OECD (2010b), *Partnership for Democratic Governance 2010 Activity Report*, Paris: OECD.

OECD (2010c), *Development Co-operation Report 2010*, Paris: OECD.

OECD (2011), *Statistics on Resource Flows to Developing Countries*, Paris: OECD, available at: http://www.oecd.org/dataoecd/53/43/47137659.pdf.

OECD (2012), *OECD DAC Statistics on Climate-related Aid*, Paris: OECD, available at: http://www.oecd.org/dac/stats/FactsheetRio.pdf.

OECD (2013), *Aid to Poor Countries Slips Further as Governments Tighten Budgets*, Paris: OECD, available at: http://www.oecd.org/dac/stats/aidtopoorcountriesslipsfurtherasgovernmentstightenbudgets.htm.

Overseas Development Institute and UN Millennium Campaign (2010), *Millennium Development Goals Report Card: Learning from Progress*, London: Overseas Development Institute, available at: http://www.odi.org.uk/resources/download/4908.pdf.

Payne, A. (2005), *The Global Politics of Unequal Development*, New York: Palgrave Macmillan.

Payne, A. and N. Phillips (2010), *Development*, Cambridge, UK and Malden, MA, USA: Polity Press.

Pew Center on Global Climate Change (2010), 'Summary of COP 16 and CMP 6', available at: http://www.pewclimate.org/docUploads/cancun-climate-conference-cop16-summary.pdf.

Ponzio, R. (2004), 'UNDP experience in long-term democracy assistance', in E. Newman and R. Rich (eds), *The UN Role in Promoting Democracy: Between Ideals and Reality*, Tokyo, Japan and New York, USA: United Nations University Press, pp. 208–29.

Rist, G. (2008), *The History of Development: From Western Origins to Global Faith*, 3rd edition, London: Zed Books.

Santiso, C. (2002), 'Promoting democratic governance and preventing the recurrence of conflict: the role of the United Nations Development Programme in post-conflict peace-building', *Journal of Latin American Studies*, **34** (3), 555–86.

Schwarzmantel, J. (2008), *Ideology and Politics*, London: Sage.

Sen, A. (2000), 'A decade of human development', *Journal of Human Development*, **1** (1), 17–23.

Steger, M.B. (2009), *Globalisms: The Great Ideological Struggle of the Twenty-first Century*, 3rd edition, Lanham, MD: Rowman & Littlefield.

Stokke, O. (2009), *The UN and Development: From Aid to Cooperation*, Bloomington, IN: Indiana University Press.

Thérien, J.-P. and V. Pouliot (2006), 'The Global Compact: shifting the politics of international development?', *Global Governance*, **12** (1), 55–75.

Toye, J. and R. Toye (2004), *The UN and Global Political Economy: Trade, Finance, and Development*, Bloomington, IN: Indiana University Press.

UN Global Compact (2011), *United Nations Global Compact Annual Review 2010*, New York: UN Global Compact Office, available at: http://www.unglobalcompact.org/docs/news_events/8.1/UN_Global_Compact_Annual_Review_2010.pdf.

UN Millennium Project (2006), 'UN Millennium Project – Home', available at: http://www.unmillenniumproject.org.

UN System Task Team on the Post-2015 UN Development Agenda (2012), *Realizing the Future We Want for All: Report to the Secretary-General*, New York: United Nations.

UNCEB (2008), *Acting on Climate Change: The UN System Delivering as One*, New York: UNCEB, available at: http://www.un.org/climatechange/pdfs/Acting%20on%20Climate%20Change.pdf.

UNDEF (2010), 'About UNDEF', available at: http://www.un.org/democracyfund/About_Us/about_us_index.html.

UNDG (2009), *UNDG Fact Sheet*, available at: http://www.undg.org/docs/10350/UNDGFactSheet_August2009.pdf.

UNDG (2010), *How to Prepare an UNDAF. Part I: Guidelines for UN Country Teams*, available at: http://www.undg.org/docs/11096/How-to-Prepare-an-UNDAF-%28Part-I%29.pdf.

UNDP (1990), *Human Development Report 1990: Concept and Measurement of Human Development*, New York, USA and Oxford, UK: Oxford University Press.

UNDP (1997), *Governance for Sustainable Human Development: A UNDP Policy Document*, available at: http://mirror.undp.org/magnet/policy/.

UNDP (2002), *Human Development Report 2002: Deepening Democracy in a Fragmented World*, New York, USA and Oxford, UK: Oxford University Press.

UNDP (2005), *Human Development Report 2005. International Cooperation at a Crossroads: Aid, Trade and Security in an Unequal World*, New York: UNDP.

UNDP (2008), *Human Development Report 2007/2008. Fighting Climate Change: Human Solidarity in a Divided World*, New York: UNDP.

UNDP (2010a), *Human Development Report 2010. The Real Wealth of Nations: Pathways to Human Development*, Basingstoke, UK and New York, USA: Palgrave Macmillan.

UNDP (2010b), *A Guide to UNDP Democratic Governance Practice*, New York: UNDP.

UNDP (2011), *Human Development Report 2011. Sustainability and Equity: A Better Future for All*, New York: UNDP.

UNDP (2012), *Annual Report 2011/2012: The Sustainable Future We Want*, New York: UNDP.

UNFCCC (1992), *United Nations Framework Convention on Climate Change*, available at: http://unfccc.int/resource/docs/convkp/conveng.pdf.

UNFCCC (2008), 'Bali Action Plan', *Report of the Conference of the Parties on its Thirteenth Session, Held in Bali from 3 to 15 December 2007*, available at: http://unfccc.int/resource/docs/2007/cop13/eng/06a01.pdf#page=1.

United Nations (1994), *An Agenda for Development: Report of the Secretary-General*, New York: United Nations, available at: http://www.un.org/Docs/SG/agdev.html.

United Nations (2001a), *Road Map towards the Implementation of the United Nations Millennium Declaration: Report of the Secretary-General*, New York: United Nations, available at: http://www.un.org/documents/ga/docs/56/a56326.pdf.

United Nations (2001b), *Cooperation Between the United Nations and All Relevant Partners, in Particular the Private Sector: Report of the Secretary-General*, New York: United Nations, available at: http://www.un.org/partnerships/Docs/partnershipreport_a-56-323.pdf.

United Nations (2003a), *Report of the Secretary-General on the Work of the Organization*, New York: United Nations, available at: http://www.un.org/Docs/journal/asp/ws.asp?m=%20A/58/1%28SUPP%29.

United Nations (2003b), *Enhanced Cooperation Between the United Nations and All Relevant Partners, in Particular the Private Sector: Report of the Secretary-General*, New York: United Nations, available at: http://www.unglobalcompact.org/docs/issues_doc/un_business_partnerships/A_58_227.pdf.

United Nations (2005a), *The Inequality Predicament: Report on the World Social Situation 2005*, New York: United Nations.

United Nations (2005b), *2005 World Summit Outcome*, UN General Assembly Resolution 60/1 (A/RES/60/1), New York, 24 October, available at: http://www.un.org/Docs/journal/asp/ws.asp?m=A/RES/60/1.

United Nations (2006a), *World Economic and Social Survey 2006: Diverging Growth and Development*, New York: United Nations.

United Nations (2006b), *Delivering as One: Report of the High-level Panel on United Nations System-wide Coherence in the Areas of Development, Humanitarian Assistance and the Environment*, New York: United Nations, available at: http://www.un.org/Docs/journal/asp/ws.asp?m=A/61/583.

United Nations (2007), *The United Nations Development Agenda: Development for All*, New York: United Nations.

United Nations (2008), *Report of the Secretary-General on the Work of the Organization*, New York: United Nations, available at: http://www.un.org/Docs/journal/asp/ws.asp?m=%20A/63/1%28SUPP%29.

United Nations (2009a), *Rethinking Poverty: Report on the World Social Situation 2010*, New York: United Nations.

United Nations (2009b), *The World Financial and Economic Crisis and its Impact on Development: Report of the Secretary-General*, New York: United Nations, available at:http://www.un.org/esa/desa/financialcrisis/document/s-g_fin_crisis_final_advance.pdf.

United Nations (2009c), 'Guidance Note of the Secretary-General on Democracy', New York, 11 September, available at: http://www.un.org/democracyfund/Docs/UNSG%20Guidance%20Note%20on%20Democracy.pdf.

United Nations (2010), *The Millennium Development Goals Report 2010*, New York: United Nations.

United Nations (2011), 'Economic and Social Council concludes special high-level meeting with Bretton Woods institutions, other bodies', New York, 11 March, available at: http://www.un.org/News/Press/docs/2011/ecosoc6472.doc.htm.

United Nations (2012), *The Millennium Development Goals Report 2012*, New York: United Nations.

Watkins, K. (2008), *The Millennium Development Goals: Three Proposals for Renewing the Vision and Reshaping the Future*, Paris: UNESCO.

Weiss, T.G. and S. Daws (eds) (2007), *The Oxford Handbook on the United Nations*, Oxford: Oxford University Press.

Whitehead, L. (2009), 'Losing "the Force"? The "dark side" of democratization after Iraq', *Democratization*, **16** (2), 215–42.

Worden, S. (2010), 'Afghanistan: an election gone awry', *Journal of Democracy*, **21** (3), 11–25.

World Bank (2010a), *Global Monitoring Report 2010: The MDGs after the Crisis*, Washington, DC: World Bank.

World Bank (2010b), *The Millennium Development Goals and the Road to 2015: Building on Progress and Responding to Crisis*, Washington, DC: World Bank.

16 Governing intellectual property rights and development
Valbona Muzaka

Compared to trade, production and finance, intellectual property rights (IPRs) have not been central to the study of international political economy. Nevertheless, their importance can hardly be overstated. Because they ultimately determine how knowledge – which some see as the 'new capital' – is generated, owned, controlled, protected and distributed, the mechanisms by which IPRs are governed have direct and profound consequences not only on the economy, but also on how societies create, learn, live and develop. IPRs are highly political, which is why their governance has been contested ever since its rudimentary beginnings in the sixteenth century. Today, contests over intellectual property (IP) have become ever more intense, especially since the negotiation and coming into force of the 1994 WTO TRIPS (Trade-Related Aspects of Intellectual Property Rights) Agreement. Although it launched a far-reaching and globally enforceable IPRs regime, TRIPS failed to reconcile the many tensions inherent in IPRs, and indeed made them more problematic, obvious and acute. Moreover, because the way IPRs are governed has direct consequences for many issue-areas (e.g. healthcare, education, creativity, agriculture, human rights, culture and biodiversity), contests over IPRs involve a number of state and non-state actors with diverse normative positions, interests and capabilities and are currently unfolding in a number of global governance fora, including the World Intellectual Property Organization (WIPO), regional or bilateral trade agreements, the World Trade Organization (WTO), the World Health Organization (WHO), the UN Food and Agriculture Organization (FAO), the Convention on Biodiversity (CBD), the United Nations Educational, Social and Cultural Organization (UNESCO), various human rights bodies, and even the Group of Eight (G8) and the Group of Twenty (G20) (Muzaka 2010).

Current IP contests stem partly from the profound significance of IPRs for economies and societies, and partly from the fact that the current arrangement, set in place through TRIPS, governs IPRs primarily as a trade matter to the exclusion of other – often public – concerns. Indeed, what characterises most of the political conflicts unfolding in various global governance fora since the conclusion of the TRIPS agreement is a persistent concern that the current maximalist, 'one-size-fits-all' approach to IP undermines the achievement of a number of other public goals, such as access to affordable medicines, protection of human rights, promotion of education, biodiversity, development and so on. Despite their complex nature, it can be argued that these contests are ultimately symptomatic of state and non-state actors disagreeing over how to govern IPRs globally, for what purposes and with what consequences. It is in this contested post-TRIPS terrain that a group of developing countries led by Argentina and Brazil, and supported by a number of civil society actors, proposed a Development Agenda for WIPO in September 2004, opening up a 'new' set of disputes over how to govern IP for development. Their proposal was made on the grounds that developmental concerns needed to be brought into the core of WIPO and of the entire IP governance edifice. In the view of these actors, IPRs are currently governed in ways that fall short of their potential to contribute to development because TRIPS, and the global IP regime it set in motion, imposes strict and binding standards from 'above', thus diminishing the flexibility of designing IP systems which correspond to these countries' domestic socio-economic context and exigencies, especially developmental ones. In light of these concerns, the 2004 call for a Development Agenda proposed a balanced approach to IP that would both provide the necessary incentives for innovative and creative processes to take place and, importantly, ensure their greater dissemination to the benefit and development of the society as a whole (WO/GA/31/15).

While the call for a Development Agenda was underpinned by these specific concerns and is embedded in the post-TRIPS context, it did not represent the first time that developing and developed countries have entered into conflict over the issue of IP and development. Led by India and Brazil, some developing countries sought to reform the international IP regime during the 1960s and 1970s, especially patent and copyright rules, so as to facilitate and accelerate their development. These efforts were not only unsuccessful, but they were also succeeded by the negotiation of the WTO TRIPS Agreement (1986–93) that incorporated a stricter and ultra-binding version of the very IP rules developing countries had sought to reform. Among other ongoing IP contests, the WIPO Development Agenda brought the issue of IP and development to the fore again in 2004. Yet, at the time of writing in 2013, nine years after its emergence, it does not appear that the governance of intellectual property is likely to be transformed in ways envisaged by its original proponents. By focusing on a widely supported, politically important and seemingly ambitious initiative such as the WIPO Development Agenda, the aim of this chapter is to uncover why, despite continued mobilisation, key developing countries and civil society actors have been unable, so far, to transform the way IPRs are governed in order to serve their developmental needs and steer the IP regime in directions that better match their requirements. In other words, the aim is not necessarily to show empirically how to govern IPRs for development, but rather to uncover how efforts to change IP rules in the name of development have been absorbed and neutralised in the course of political contestations at WIPO. The ongoing ability of dominant regime members to neutralise challenges like the Development Agenda has important implications for how IPRs are governed, and with what consequences. Furthermore, understanding how challenges are made, and then absorbed, in this particular area of IP governance brings into clear view not only its essentially political and ideological nature, but also the enormous difficulty of effecting transformative change in the absence of explicit challenges to the status quo.

More specifically, the main argument of the chapter suggests that part of the reason why the Agenda is unlikely to bring about the changes it seeks is to be found in its failure to challenge in a fundamental way the normative and ideological underpinnings of the current IP governance regime. As will be discussed shortly, despite appearing daring and comprehensive, developing countries' demands are in fact organised around the very assumptions about IP and development that they nominally seek to change. Such internalisation and re-enactment of dominant assumptions and categories in effect strengthens them, enabling the key developed countries (e.g. the United States and key European states) that have historically created them to absorb challenges more effectively in the present. The Agenda is not an exception in this respect, for most current IP contests initiated by developing countries and civil society groups shy away from fundamental challenges to the dominant common sense and in the process actually strengthen it, even as they try to challenge it. As will be shown in more detail in the second section, both proponents and opponents of the Development Agenda came to occupy ample areas of overlapping consensus in the process of 'talk and talk back' in relation to political contests over IP and development, thus limiting the possibility of transformative changes at WIPO and in IP governance more broadly. I have relied extensively on the various submissions made to WIPO between 2004 and 2006[1] and on minutes of meetings and General Assembly sessions until 2007 for this part of the analysis. This material is voluminous and, for this reason, I have focused only on the most important areas of overlapping consensus between actors who seemingly hold opposed stances on how to govern IP for development. Before turning to the call for a Development Agenda, the following section seeks to expose the commonsense assumptions and categories that continue to underpin contests over IP and development.

'COMMONSENSE' ASSUMPTIONS IN THE IP AND DEVELOPMENT DEBATE

As several studies have shown convincingly, TRIPS was driven not by concerns over development but by the commercial interests of a limited group of business actors, namely, large entertainment and high-tech business actors in Europe and the US with an interest in high and globally enforceable IP standards (Ryan 1998; Drahos and Braithwaite 2002; Matthews 2002; Sell 2003). The TRIPS agreement represents not only the most transformative moment in the governance of intellectual property during the twentieth century, but also one of the most successful cases of political action undertaken by private business actors at the global level. For it was undoubtedly a major feat to persuade and compel all WTO members, the vast majority of whom are net IP-importers, to commit to the extensive and binding obligations demanded by TRIPS on behalf of private (often foreign) IPR-holders (Braithwaite and Drahos 2000). Certainly, this was not how business actors and WTO members with stakes in high IP standards sought to legitimise TRIPS. Rather, their arguments were that 'better' IP protection and enforcement would stimulate domestic research and development (R&D) and increase inward foreign direct investment (FDI) flows, transfers of technology and, ultimately, economic growth and development (Matthews 2002; Watal 2001). These 'commonsense' assumptions about the positive and indispensable role IPRs play in development were particularly important in legitimising TRIPS and the global IP arrangement it set in place, just as they were fundamental to the incorporation of Western IP laws into the laws of developing countries after decolonisation.

   IP laws had been introduced to most of what are referred today as developing and less-developed countries during the era of colonisation, especially as it consolidated through the nineteenth century. This was also the period during which an international IP regime of sorts began to emerge among the developed countries of the time. IPRs then were governed through a series of bilateral treaties that later were formalised into the Berne and Paris Conventions of the 1880s (on copyright and industrial property respectively). Initially the extension of IP laws to the colonies had nothing to do with these societies per se but rather had everything to do with securing the coloniser's economic interests against other European countries in the colonial territories (Okediji 2003). In short, being part and parcel of empire-building strategies, the IP laws that found their way into colonial territories were completely alien to the socio-economic realities over which they exerted their power. Despite their violent introduction, these IP laws were generally retained after decolonisation. Indeed, the incorporation and internalisation of European IP laws in the newly independent states was a central part of their transformation into sovereign states, which in turn was mediated by the very international institutions and treaties that had facilitated their earlier subjugation. Hence, most newly independent states continued to adhere to IP obligations present in their inherited statutes as a 'privilege' and 'duty' of statehood, either by virtue of customary international law, or through specially developed declarations that stated their intention to honour them (Drahos 2002; Okediji 2003).

Nevertheless, the continued commitment to (foreign) IP protection by developing countries required more than an initial promise at the moment of their independence. It could only be fully secured by socialising them into the view that the 'proper' protection of IPRs was not only the duty of a sovereign state, but also in fact crucial to its continued development. This socialisation was achieved in great part through the dominant development discourse of the immediate post-colonisation period, as espoused by nearly all the major international organisations. This continued to define development as the unilinear process of socio-economic realities being transformed in the image of the West, achieved *inter alia* via investment flows, technology transfer and economic growth. This discourse, in part legitimised by Western scholars, continued to justify the enactment of Western IP laws as a necessary prerequisite for the evolution from 'primitive' to 'developed' and 'civilised' (Ricketson 1987). The view that a 'proper' IP system was central to development was reinforced often without any evidence, with very few dissenting voices raising doubts about the adequacy of such a system for the particular needs of developing countries (see, for examples, Kronstein and Till 1947; Anderfelt 1971; Vaitsos 1972; Penrose 1973). As a result, the developing countries' representatives themselves appeared early on to have largely internalised the view that IPRs were important to economic growth, technology transfer and domestic creativity. Indeed, it appears to be largely the case that this view continues to shape and underpin the participation of developing countries in IP governance even today (Oddi 1987; Gana 1996; Okediji 2009).

This claim can be supported by a number of examples. Some developing countries (e.g. Kenya, Brazil, Mexico and India) did in fact make some changes to their IP laws during the 1970s, but no real or substantial changes to the structure of the inherited IP models took place (Okediji 2003). Even the most comprehensive challenge to the IP regime of the day, which was mounted during the 1960s and 1970s by a group of developing countries, led by Brazil and India amongst others, reflected how comprehensively views and assumptions about IP and development had been internalised, notwithstanding the fact that, in this earlier kind of 'development agenda', developing countries' proposals to reform the copyright and patent rules so as to facilitate their development strategies appeared genuinely threatening to key developed countries (see Drahos and Braithwaite 2002; Menescal 2005; Yu 2009). For instance, the Brazilian delegation that proposed a draft resolution to the UN General Assembly in 1961 noted the 'conditioned reflexes, biased . . . narrow, and sclerotic views' held by dominant actors (i.e. the US and key European states) in resisting calls to reform the patent system in order to respond to 'the needs and requirements of under-developed countries'.[2] It was not, however, as self-aware of the manner in which, by calling for there to be a balance between 'the legitimate claims of patentees' with the needs of developing countries, and of the need not to abolish the patent system but rather to 'cure it of its imperfections', it further secured the legitimacy of the existing international IP regime and the role that IPRs presumably played in meeting the needs of developing countries (Okediji 2008).

It is important to understand this previous experience, because, just as in this earlier challenge, commonsense assumptions about the generally positive role IPRs play in development were incorporated without much reflection in the 2004 call for a Development Agenda. But, as Bourdieu (1992) has argued, political challenges are likely to be successful only when they fundamentally question the legitimacy of, and sever adherence to, the dominant categories of perception of the social order. No more than in the 1960s and 1970s do the current contests at WIPO explicitly question the dominant views of IP and development; indeed, it is well known that these earlier efforts to reform the international IP rules ultimately failed. Contests over copyright reform precipitated a crisis in international copyright in the late 1960s when a rather watered-down version of developing countries' demands (in the form of the 1967 Stockholm Protocol to the Berne Convention) was adopted, although it never actually came into force (Drahos and Braithwaite 2002). Those over patent reform and technology transfer continued well into the 1970s and early 1980s, when they were subsumed under the 'New International Economic Order' (NIEO) agenda and the plans to establish an International Code of Conduct on the Transfer of Technology at the United Nations Conference on Trade and Development (UNCTAD) (Yu 2009). Not only did they fail to achieve their aim, but, as noted earlier, these efforts were succeeded by the negotiation (1986–93) of the WTO TRIPS Agreement which incorporated a stricter and ultra-binding version of the very IP rules developing countries had sought to reform (and much more). Unsurprisingly, during the TRIPS negotiations, the US, the European Union (EU), Switzerland and IP-reliant business actors continued to reassure other regime members that 'better' IP protection and enforcement was a boon to development, since it would stimulate more R&D, thus generating innovation and creativity, increase FDI flows, effect more transfers of technology and bring about economic growth (Watal 2001; Matthews 2002). It was difficult to counter these arguments successfully, given that developing countries' attempts to reform the IP system during the 1960s and 1970s had not seriously challenged the presumed relation between IP protection and these other categories.

Furthermore, dominant actors presented these assumptions as neutral and scientific 'truths', having recourse to a number of studies that supported the positive role of IPRs on development, especially economic growth (e.g. Llal 1976; Beier 1980; Rapp and Rozek 1990; Gould and Gruben 1996; Ginarte and Park 1997; Vandoren and Martins 2006). However, the provision of this evidence, and its acceptance as 'true', conceals the fact that, despite the deployment of sophisticated analytical tools, we have as yet attained a very limited understanding of even the most basic relationships in this sphere of knowledge, such as, for instance, what the grant of IPRs accomplishes, or what is the relation between IPRs and innovation, even in countries with a relatively long IP history

(Nogués 1990; World Bank 1998, 2005; Abbott et al. 1999; Duran and Michalopoulos 1999; Simon 2005; Reichman 2009). Given the difficulties of establishing the direction and nature of causality in these somewhat more basic relations, it is almost impossible to prove convincingly that IPRs are a boon to development. As it happens, the current of dissenting views that question the veracity of 'commonsense' assumptions about IP and the IP–development link is now stronger than it had been earlier (Oddi 1987; Deardorff 1990; Stiglitz 1999; Drahos and Braithwaite 2002; Blakeney 2006; Beattie 2006; Reichman 2009). Nonetheless, as the case of the 2004 Proposal for the Development Agenda demonstrates, developing countries' representatives have by and large failed once again to challenge fundamentally the veracity of commonsense assumptions in their recent demands at WIPO.

Moreover, not only is this still the case, but also the definition of development itself, a category central to the Development Agenda, is also incorporated wholesale from the mainstream. This is not a minor omission: in fact, it has fundamental repercussions on the ability of the Agenda to bring about transformative changes to the governance of IPRs. By accepting, or at least not challenging, the commonsense assumptions under-pinning 'development' as a category, the entire mainstream development discourse and practice is legitimised, as is the authority of the dominant actors that have historically produced and maintained it. Development is without doubt central to the 2004 Proposal at WIPO (WO/GA/31/11); for example, the Proposal makes it quite explicit that it is an Agenda for Development, authored by a group of developing countries, the Group of Friends of Development.[3] The 'development' category is not, however, a neutral one. As Bourdieu (1987: 23) has argued, the ability to impose one's own classifications as legitimate and natural lies at the core of political power, defined as 'the power to impose and to inculcate a vision of divisions . . . to make groups, to manipulate the structure of society'. The category of 'developing countries' was not produced by the group of peoples who are now subsumed into it, although it seems to have been internalised and accepted by them, or by the actors who speak on their behalf at WIPO and elsewhere. To my knowledge, developing countries' representatives have not seriously – if at all – challenged this categorisation or classification in international fora, even as the devel-opment discourse and practice based on it has had incalculable effects on the material reality of the people they represent. On the contrary, this categorisation has often been used to legitimise their varied demands for special and differential treatment, thus vali-dating the existence of 'developing countries' as a group, insofar as a group exists only where there are agents who can speak publically, legitimately and officially in its name (Bourdieu 1987). However, by virtue of reproducing the category of developing coun-tries, the properties imposed on it are also reinforced, as well as the authority of those who produced it in the first place.

As some critics have pointed out, despite its universalistic claims, development is a world-view with a specific historical and political genealogy (Escobar 1995; Perry 1996; Pieterse 1998; Tucker 2001). Here, the division between the 'inferior', 'undeveloped' world, with its attendant properties (e.g. 'backward', 'primitive', 'traditional', 'stag-nant'), and the 'superior', 'advanced', 'modern' and 'civilised' West is seen as one of the founding acts of the imagination of the latter. A well-known element of this critique is uncovering the way in which European Enlightenment ideals of rationality, science and progress produced, in time, a view of human history as a necessary, inevitable and even obligatory destiny towards the standards of European or Western civilisation, providing in the process not only the rationale for colonising the realities and social imaginaries of other peoples, but also the moral justification for it. As part of a broader modernity discourse, development was what happened – indeed, ought to happen – to other peoples in the process of acquiring the properties and standards of Western civilisation. This development or modernity discourse came to be seen as natural and even progressive, permeating international institutions and laws, as well as the practices of the powerful states that created and sustained them. Importantly, just like the dependency theory from which it partly drew its inspiration, the major effort by the developing countries to reconfigure the world order in which they found themselves – the NIEO movement of the 1970s – only challenged dependent development, not 'development' itself or their categorisation as 'developing countries' per se. These classifications and their attendant properties, ultimately symbolising the power of one group to dominate and transform others according to its world-view, continue to remain unchallenged currently, even as 'developing countries' as a group have become more resistant in various regimes and international fora, including those related to IPRs. As will become clear in the next section, the incorporation of dominant assumptions into current demands for changing the way IPRs are governed has the effect of strengthening such assumptions and thus enabling key developed countries that have historically created them to absorb such demands for change more effectively in the present. In other words, understanding how an issue-area (such as IPRs and development) is currently governed not only requires understanding how the preferences of the dominant actors have historically been and continue to be expressed within it, but also how weaker actors help reproduce such governance arrangements, even when they seek to challenge and change them. As has been argued, the main reasons for this seemingly strange state of affairs are to be found in the manner in which weaker actors choose to formulate their challenges and engage in political conflicts within that specific area of governance.

PROPOSING AND CONTESTING THE WIPO DEVELOPMENT AGENDA (2004–07)

Exploring the way in which the proposal for the Development Agenda was made and contested at WIPO helps illustrate how challenging actors may reinforce the very arrangement they set out to challenge, and specifically the continued difficulty they encounter in bringing about transformative changes in how IPRs are governed. The first point to be made is that the 2004 Proposal was a widely supported and politically ambitious initiative. Indeed, when the Proposal for a Development Agenda was presented at the WIPO General Assembly in September 2004 (WO/GA/31/11), it was seen by many of its supporters not only as a call to reform WIPO's mandate and activities, but also as a historical step towards restructuring the traditional IP paradigm (Khor and Shashikant 2009; Muzaka 2012). The ambition of the original drafters, most notably the Argentine and Brazilian delegates in Geneva, was vindicated by the wide support lent to the Proposal by many developing countries, some of whom were to become known as the Group of Friends of Development, as well as by a large number of civil-society actors.[4] According to the many supportive delegates, the main purpose of a Development

Agenda was to return WIPO to its core mission of promoting creativity and the transfer of technology for developmental purposes, as befitted its UN agency status (WO/GA/31/15). Moreover, a transformed WIPO needed to be embedded in a rebalanced IP regime that promoted both innovation and creativity, and dissemination, a regime ultimately designed with development and public interests in mind. In line with common-sense views, as well as arguments already iterated before and during TRIPS negotiations, leading developed countries, especially the US, argued that IP governance was already geared towards such goals and that the Agenda was unnecessary (WO/GA/31/15). These views were indicative of what was to come, for although the WIPO General Assembly officially welcomed the initiative for a Development Agenda with much fanfare, its decision was not to adopt, but merely to examine the Proposal in the course of intergovernmental meetings until it met again one year later. As it turned out, it was only after three difficult years that a watered-down list of recommendations for a Development Agenda was adopted by the General Assembly in September 2007, ushering in another period of disagreements over how such recommendations were to be implemented and monitored.

Although the nature and extent of the changes demanded by the supporters of the Agenda did evolve throughout the several years of contestations that followed the 2004 Proposal, their essence can be clearly traced back to it. Having recognised from the outset the 'persistent challenge of development', the Proposal continued with a call to view IP protection not simply as a right, but as a policy instrument whose role in development should be assessed on a case-by-case basis, ensuring that the costs and benefits of IP protection are balanced. This issue of balance – not the purpose and necessity of IP protection itself – is central to the Proposal and appears in a number of guises, whether in the call for balancing the interests of IP-users with those of IP-owners, balancing the societal interests and social costs of IP protection, ensuring that IP laws are balanced with competition laws, balancing incentives for creativity and innovation with the dissemination and transfer of technology, and so on (WO/GA/31/11). Its key demand, incorporating development concerns fully into all WIPO activities, is thus thoroughly permeated by this particular understanding of balance. Yet the Proposal's plea for balance in the name of development has important consequences for the way the Agenda has unfolded so far and on its chances of success. It may be too early to tell conclusively, but the 45 recommendations that were eventually adopted in 2007 appeared to hold no great promise for transformative changes at WIPO. Some of the bolder demands made by developing countries during the preceding three years, such as an amendment of the WIPO Convention, the signing of a multilateral agreement for access to publicly funded knowledge, a continuous assessment of the social costs of existing and new treaty proposals through a new WIPO Evaluation and Research Office and, perhaps most importantly of all, the construction of alternative systems of creativity and innovation not based on IP, had been completely sidelined by then. The 45 recommendations certainly retained the language of balance, but, as will be seen, because all the actors held similar beliefs and effectively spoke the same language during the contests, the 2007 recommendation merely encouraged WIPO to 'promote', 'discuss', 'explore', 'consider', 'undertake', 'conduct studies', 'exchange experiences', and so on (WIPO 2007).

This said, the Proposal for a Development Agenda certainly disturbed the order of activities at WIPO, whose rule-making bodies[5] had their hands tied up with a number of initiatives pertaining to WIPO's Digital and Patent Agendas. The main purpose of these other agendas had been to harmonise upwards existing IP standards and/or introduce new ones on behalf of IP-owners, trends often referred to as 'TRIPS plus'. Indeed, it was against this flurry of activities designed primarily with the interests of IP-owners in mind that a group of developing countries, all of which are net IP-importers, proposed a Development Agenda for WIPO. As a matter of fact, many of them saw it in large part as a direct response to WIPO's 'TRIPs-plus' activities in the 1990s and early 2000s (Muzaka 2012). Nevertheless, the Proposal was not solely concerned with such activities; it made the rather more comprehensive and ambitious – if vague – demand of balancing the IP regime to meet the 'daunting challenge' of development (WO/GA/31/11 section I). This said, the demand for a Development Agenda was not of itself necessarily far-reaching, notwithstanding its seemingly comprehensive nature. Although it started by noting the wide recognition that the development challenge enjoys within the international community, the Proposal did not explicitly clarify, let alone challenge, the meaning and premises of 'development', or the category of a 'developing country' as such. This omission was surely serious for a call whose aim was to bring 'development' to the heart of the IP regime. To be sure, appeals to 'development' legitimised the Agenda within and without WIPO, for a development initiative has never been deemed non-legitimate. As will be seen, through re-enacting commonsense views, the very category that gives the supporters of the Development Agenda a sense of legitimacy and identity – namely, 'development' – may in fact have hindered their success in achieving the changes they sought.

This is so because, as mentioned earlier, the more that commonsense assumptions remain unrecognised and unchallenged, the smaller is the likelihood of transformative changes in dominant practices (Bourdieu 1992). Because it implicitly accepts the dominant categories of development and IP, and of the relation between them, the Proposal for a WIPO Development Agenda re-enacted the particular ways in which IP and development have been linked historically. This does not mean, of course, that the Development Agenda is indistinguishable from earlier challenges, but merely that, as long as new challenges continue to be organised according to dominant assumptions, the dominant actors are likely to continue to absorb them successfully. Although it is still in the implementation phase and work on a number of its recommendations is yet to start, it is possible to probe further into why this may turn out to be the case for the WIPO Development Agenda.

To do so, it is worth returning to the main category that remains unrecognised and unchallenged in the Agenda: development. As indicated, this category is at the very core of the Agenda and successfully brings seemingly opposing groups together into an ample area of consensus. Neither the original Proposal (WO/GA/31/11), nor an additional and lengthier document submitted on behalf of the Group of Friends of Development during the first intergovernmental meeting in April 2005 (IIM/1/4), questioned the meaning and substance of development. To the extent that development was discussed, it was only in the context of it being an enormous challenge that underpinned a number of development agendas and initiatives undertaken by the international community (e.g. the Millennium Development Goals, the Monterrey Consensus, the WTO Doha Development Agenda, and so on). This move may have helped to make the Agenda legitimate, but it can hardly be said that the development initiatives to which it likens itself constitute themselves meaningful challenges to the dominant view of development. By way of an example, the 2005 submission by the Group of Friends of Development (GFD) betrayed the extent to which development (viewed essentially still as a unilinear, catch-up process) had been internalised, as it sought to legitimise its demands on account of the challenges developing countries faced 'in the[ir] path towards development' (IIM/1/4, para. 10). Not surprisingly, the US submission to that 2005 meeting reiterated the important role of IP and appealed to the same deterministic vision of development as a 'journey from developing to developed' (IIM/1/2, para. 3).

Another manifestation of this internalisation of views of development on the part of supporters of the Agenda is to be found in their arguments about the 'knowledge gap' and 'the digital divide' that separates the developing and developed world (e.g. WO/GA/31/11, section II). The existence of this gap underpins some of the most important demands for changes to WIPO and the IP regime, namely, improved access to knowledge and real transfer of technology to developing countries (WO/GA/31/11, section V; IIM/1/4, paras 21, 38; IIM/3/2, para. D(ii); PCDA/1/5, section III 4, 5). However, it is precisely in demanding that WIPO and the IP regime contribute to the closure of this so-called gap in this manner that 'knowledges' and experiences residing in these countries are unwittingly devalued, and their status as 'traditional' cemented. This is problematic, not least because, as anthropologists tell us, there is no such thing as a 'traditional society'; members of any society are always engaged in the active elaboration, appropriation and modification of knowledge and technology as a means of sustaining their lives (Fores 1982; Pfaffenberger 1992). In other words, the call to close the gap that divides developing and developed countries through the transfer of knowledge and technology from the latter once again reinforces the categorisation of Western knowledge as 'valid' and that produced elsewhere as 'useless' for developmental purposes. In doing so, these demands fail not only to expose and question dominant assumptions, but they also do not properly recognise and incorporate marginalised 'knowledges'. These failures, in turn, entrench further the authority of the dominant regime members to prescribe what development is and what role IPRs can play in it. On this front it is clear that neither the IP regime of the nineteenth century, nor its twentieth-century version, was established to aid developing countries in their 'path to development'. This is no less the case with TRIPS and the global IP regime it set in train from the late 1990s onwards. As May (2000) has argued, TRIPS was enacted precisely with the aim of safeguarding the competitive advantage of key developed countries in IPRs by means of establishing and maintaining – not narrowing – the technological and knowledge gap.

Furthermore, the language of a technological and knowledge gap fits well within the mainstream view of development as a unilinear, catch-up process that is technologically deterministic (i.e. underpinned by assumptions that development challenges can be met through access to the knowledge and technology that developed countries possess). This reductionist view lies at the core of developing countries' demands for a real transfer of technology through, for instance, the establishment of a WIPO body dedicated to such transfer and the negotiation of an Access to Knowledge Treaty that would allow developing countries to access publicly funded knowledge produced in the developed countries (e.g. WO/GA/31/11, section V; IIM/1/4, section V; PCDA/1/5, III 4, 5). In the end, neither of these two new proposals made it to the 2007 recommendations, although a number of suggestions to facilitate the IP-related aspects of information and communication technologies (ICTs) did (WIPO 2007: section IV). While the 2004 Proposal problematised the 'digital divide' and called for balance and flexibility, the relative eagerness with which ICTs were included in the 2007 recommendations is not necessarily a sign of success on the part of the Agenda supporters. Rather, it reflected in part the interests of key developed countries with a comparative advantage in this area, and in part the optimism that the supposed ability of ICTs to 'leapfrog' (another 'journey' metaphor) developmental stages has engendered in more recent development debates (Heeks 2002; Schech 2002). One of the main pitfalls of this reliance on technology as a solution to development – present both in the mainstream discourse and in the developing countries' proposals in the Agenda – rests not only in its unproblematic acceptance of the familiar commonsense view of development, but also in a conceptualisation of technology that is wholly detached from the political, social, economic, cultural and institutional context in which it is developed, used and transformed.

The argument so far has been that neither the 2004 Proposal nor subsequent submissions on the part of developing countries managed to challenge or problematise inherited commonsense assumptions regarding the relationship between IPRs and development. Above all, as was argued, the Proposal was in fact a call for balance, which in essence means that IP governance, as far as developmental needs are concerned, is seen as being merely off-kilter but not inappropriate or illegitimate. This already closes off the necessary space for transformative changes to occur and enables dominant actors to absorb more effectively the challenge at hand. Indeed, given the extent to which the 2004 Proposal itself reflected commonsense assumptions, it is not surprising that the US submission in 2005, the first formal response to the 2004 Proposal, was non-polemical in nature. It is also the case that the use of apolitical language is generally an effective tool for negating political struggle as struggle (Bourdieu 1992). As the Proposal had done earlier, the US submission confirmed the apparently obvious but as yet unproven role IPRs play in development, highlighting in particular their positive role in promoting innovation and creativity and the transfer of technology (IIM/1/2, para. 3). The underlying argument in the US submission was that, if developing countries had not yet seen the full benefits of IP protection on development, this constituted a technical rather than a political issue. WIPO certainly needed to undergo some changes, but only so as to enhance its capacity to assist developing countries make better use of existing IPRs. This position effectively removed the possibility of questioning the ability of the current IP arrangement to serve the different economic and social realities prevailing in developing countries in the first place. This is yet another area of overlapping consensus, insofar as the latter countries, too, are primarily concerned with balancing the existing IP regime, and not with questioning its purpose and validity. Such consensus is clear in the following submissions by developed countries (Group B), the Group of Friends of Development (GFD) (e.g. IIM/1/4, para. 10) and other developing countries; in fact, it is difficult to find a submission that fails to mention the important role that IPRs supposedly play in creativity and innovation, and development.

The technical solution proposed by the US amounted to another attempt to depoliticise and absorb the call for a Development Agenda. In line with dominant views on IP and development, the solution involved the establishment of a WIPO Partnership Office and Database that would channel existing knowledge on how to use IP to accelerate development by the simple means of bringing together the expertise of various actors (e.g. patent offices, WIPO experts, business groups and other international organisations) (IIM/1/2, para. 9-19). The GFD sought to counter attempts to reduce the Agenda to an improved technical assistance plan by referring to 'a misconception' that the development dimension of IP was the same thing as technical assistance (e.g. IIM/1/4 para. 19, II.1(b)). Nonetheless, receiving technical assistance remained a key element of developing countries' demands, especially those put forward by the so-called less-developed countries, with the caveat that it needed to be balanced and tailored to specific developmental needs. The paradox of this demand rested not only in the fact that it further entrenches the role that the current IP regime and WIPO can play in these countries, but also in the (unfounded) optimism that increasingly global and restrictive IP rules can still be tailored to serve the domestic exigencies of developing countries, even when these countries have by and large not taken any serious steps to design such domestically tailored IP rules for themselves. This paradox in fact becomes more visible in the context of other substantial demands made in the Agenda, especially those related to 'policy space' (e.g. IIM/1/4, II, III/36; PCDA/1/5, III/6; PCDA/2/2, 7(f)). In this respect, it is striking that developing countries' submissions during 2004–06 envisaged an expanded role for WIPO (coordinating technical assistance, sharing information, managing transfer of technology, negotiating new IP treaties, conducting IP studies and so on), precisely as they demanded that their policy space in IP policy be safeguarded. Unsurprisingly, the 2007 recommendations (WIPO 2007) and the plan of implementation that started in 2008 (see CDIP/1/3), incidentally with the Technical Assistance cluster, appear largely as a licence for WIPO to penetrate even more deeply into the socio-political realities of developing countries.

It was, then, because the 2004 Proposal and subsequent submissions did not challenge in any fundamental way the assumptions that underpin the way IPRs are currently governed that both opponents and proponents of the Agenda found themselves coming to occupy rather large areas of consensus during the 'talk and talk back' of political contestation at WIPO. In other words, it was very much the way the challenge in the form of the Proposal was made that allowed more dominant actors to absorb it and, in so doing, thwart the likelihood of radical changes taking place within the IP regime. Other, more visible means of rebuttal were also used, such as, for instance, shifting the focus of the debate away from the substance of developing countries' demands towards procedural issues regarding the arena where discussions should take place. For observers of international negotiations, this is a classical move through which dominant actors seek to neutralise the political nature of the challenges they face at a moment in time. Regarding the Development Agenda, much energy was exhausted over this issue during 2005, with developed countries suggesting the existing WIPO Permanent Committee on Cooperation for Development Related to Intellectual Property, and developing countries opposing it on account of the Committee's narrow focus on technical assistance (see minutes of 2005 meetings, IIM/1/6; IIM/2/10; IIM/3/3; WO/GA/32/13). Moreover, after the 45 recommendations were adopted in 2007, long debates followed over which body would be responsible for overseeing their implementation. As had been the case with the 2004 Proposal itself, the adoption of the recommendations was greeted with much apparent optimism on all sides. But, soon enough, another period of disagreement about how to finance, implement and monitor the recommendations set in. Unsurprisingly, despite efforts on the part of developing countries to approach all the recommendations in a holistic manner, a cluster-by-cluster approach prevailed, with the technical assistance cluster being amongst the first to be implemented. An IP Development Database coordinating technical assistance along the lines proposed by the US in 2005 was already up and running in 2009. Meanwhile, in the Committee on Development and Intellectual Property[6] meeting in 2011, some developing countries were complaining that the most important element of the Committee's mandate, that discussing the relation between IP and development, was still being neglected (CDIP/7/8 PROV, para.18-20). By the end of 2012, developed countries' representatives were still resisting calls by their developing counterparts to make 'IP and Development' a stand-alone issue of debate within the Committee.

CONCLUDING THOUGHTS

The purpose of undertaking the analysis provided here was to show why, despite continued mobilisation on the part of some developing countries and civil society actors, IP governance has not lately been transformed in significant ways. Focusing on one of the main contests currently unfolding in the IP regime complex – that over IP and development at WIPO – the aim was to uncover how recent efforts to change IP rules in the name of development have been absorbed in the course of political contestations at WIPO. This is not to say that WIPO is the same post-Development Agenda as it ever was. On the contrary, many committee debates and studies are now conducted on themes related to development, most of which is new for WIPO as an organisation. Rather, the aim was to show why, despite repeated mobilisation on the part of key developing countries' representatives, IPRs' governance has not been transformed to meet their demands in significant ways. As for the Development Agenda, it was argued that one of the main reasons is to be found in the fact that it did not fundamentally question the dominant 'commonsense' assumptions about development and IP that underpin WIPO's activities and the current IP regime. It was mainly framed around a call for balance in the current system, thereby legitimising its existence and the role it plays in development, as well as the entire mainstream 'development' discourse and practice. In so doing, the authority of the dominant actors that have historically produced and maintained such 'common sense' is strengthened and, with it, their authority to prescribe what is the best way of governing IP for development. In the process, their ability to absorb any challenges they face is also enhanced, especially if, as has been the case with the Development Agenda, such challenges are constructed upon dominant assumptions and classifications.

Actors seeking to pose a political challenge undoubtedly face enormous difficulties in their efforts to fashion an alternative 'common sense' that is not captive to the dominant categories and assumptions. Challengers and observers alike are all socialised, to different degrees, to the dominant 'common sense'. Nevertheless, imagining challenges that undermine the contingent ideological underpinnings of the current IP arrangement is not beyond the realm of the possible. What we observe in practice is not lack of reflexivity on the part of challengers, but rather a decision to play within the 'rules of the game' and within what appears to be politically feasible; in effect, to raise a challenge at the margins. Most IP contests that developing countries and civil society actors have initiated post-TRIPS are challenges of this nature; they are primarily aimed at bringing more balance to the existing arrangements, rather than truly questioning and challenging their validity and legitimacy. This is the case even with the most noticeable IP 'victory' won by the coalition of some developing countries and (health) non-governmental organisation (NGOs), the 2001 Doha Declaration on the TRIPS Agreement and Public Health agreed amongst all WTO members at the height of contests over the impact of pharmaceutical patents on access to affordable medicines. Despite the enthusiasm with which it was greeted, the 2001 Declaration did not change the way pharmaceutical IPRs are governed globally; rather, it merely confirmed TRIPS provisions and flexibilities which, as noted at the start of this chapter, can hardly be classified as a balanced agreement, or one geared towards improving the provision of public goods.

Another reason for observing how challenges are made and absorbed in the case of IP and development rests on the way it brings into focus the political and ideological nature of IP governance. As I have argued throughout, the 'commonsense' assumptions that underpin the governance of development and intellectual property are not based on scientific truths; rather, they are contingent ways of 'seeing and knowing' that are produced and maintained by, and thus serve, specific interests at the expense of marginalising others. The main argument in this chapter has been to suggest that, unless marginalised actors make these ideological assumptions the explicit object of their challenges, transformative changes in the way IPRs – or any other issue-area for that matter – are governed are not likely to be forthcoming. As we saw, the Proposal for a WIPO Development Agenda, despite appearing daring and comprehensive, was in fact organised upon the very assumptions about IP and development that it nominally sought to change, thus further legitimising them. This means that, when studying particular areas of global governance, attention must be paid not only to the political and contingent nature of the 'commonsense' assumptions upon which the governance of an issue-area is organised, but also to the way in which weaker actors themselves help reproduce and legitimise it through their political action (and, obviously, inaction).

NOTES

1. A total of 111 proposals were made under the Development Agenda by 2006. During 2007 these proposals were reduced to the 45 recommendations that were eventually adopted by the General Assembly.
2. All quotes are extracted from the statement of the Brazilian delegate in that session, as quoted in Menescal (2005: 769–70).
3. Friends of Development included co-signatories of the Proposal: Argentina, Bolivia, Cuba, Dominican Republic, Ecuador, Egypt, Iran, Kenya, Peru, Sierra Leone, South Africa, Tanzania and Venezuela, as well as other supporters, such as Sri Lanka, India, Pakistan, the Philippines, Colombia, Senegal and Nicaragua.
4. A list of the civil society groups and their Future of WIPO Declaration can be found at: http://www.future-ofwipo.org/ (last accessed 10 February 2012).
5. Rule-making in WIPO takes place in three bodies: the Standing Committee on the Law of Patents, the Standing Committee on the Law of Trademarks, Industrial Designs and Geographical Indicators and the Standing Committee on Copyright and Related Rights.
6. The Committee on Development and Intellectual Property (CDIP) replaced the Provisional Committee on Proposals Related to a WIPO Development Agenda (PCDA) in 2007.

REFERENCES

Abbott, Fredrick, Thomas Cottier and Francis Gurry (1999), *The International Intellectual Property System: Commentary and Materials*, Part I and II, London: Kluwer Law International.

Anderfelt, Ulf (1971), *International Patent-Legislation and Developing Countries*, The Hague: Martinus Nijhoff.

Beattie, Peter (2006), 'The (intellectual property law &) economics of innocent fraud: the IP & development debate', Bepress Legal Series, Paper 1415, available at: http://works.bepress.com/peterbeattie/1/.

Beier, Friedrich-Karl (1980), 'The significance of the patent system for technical, economic and social progress', *International Review of Industrial Property*, **11**, 563–84.

Blakeney, Michael (2006), 'A critical analysis of the TRIPs Agreement', in Meir Pugatch (ed.), *The Intellectual Property Debate: Perspectives from Law, Economics and Political Economy*, Cheltenham, UK and Northampton, MA, USA: Edward Elgar, pp. 17–32.

Bourdieu, Pierre (1987), 'Social space and symbolic power', *Sociological Theory*, **7** (1), 14–25.

Bourdieu, Pierre (1992), *Language and Symbolic Power*, Cambridge: Polity Press.

Braithwaite, John and Peter Drahos (2000), *Global Business Regulation*, Cambridge: Cambridge University Press.

Deardorff, Alan (1990), 'Should patent protection be extended to all developing countries?', *World Economy*, **13**, 497–508.

Drahos, Peter (2002), 'Developing countries and international intellectual property standard-setting', *Journal of World Intellectual Property*, **5**, 765–89.

Drahos, Peter and John Braithwaite (2002), *Informational Feudalism: Who Owns the Knowledge Economy?* London: Earthscan.

Duran, Esperanza and Constantine Michalopoulos (1999), 'Intellectual property rights and developing countries in the WTO Millennium Round', *Journal of World Intellectual Property*, **2**, 853–74.

Escobar, Arturo (1995), *Encountering Development: The Making and Unmaking of the Third World*, Princeton, NJ: Princeton University Press.

Fores, Michael (1982), 'Technical change and the "technology" myth', *Scandinavian Economic History Review*, **30** (3), 167–88.

Gana, Ruth (1996), 'The myth of development, the progress of rights: human rights to intellectual property and development', *Law and Policy*, **18**, 315–54.

Ginarte, Juan and Walter Park (1997), 'Determinants of patent rights: a cross-national study', *Research Policy*, **26**, 283–301.

Gould, David and William Gruben (1996), 'The role of intellectual property rights in economic growth', *Journal of Development Economics*, **48**, 323–50.

Heeks, Richard (2002), 'i-Development not e-Development', *Journal of International Development*, **14**, 1–12.

Khor, Martin and Sangeeta Shashikant (2009), *Negotiating a Development Agenda for the World Intellectual Property Organisation*, Penang: Third World Network.

Kronstein, Heinrich and Irene Till (1947), 'A re-evaluation of the International Patent Convention', *Law and Contemporary Problems*, **12** (4), 765–81.

Llal, Sanjaya (1976), 'The patent system and the transfer of technology to less-developed countries', *Journal of World Trade Law*, **10**, 1–16.

Matthews, Duncan (2002), *Globalising Intellectual Property Rights: The TRIPs Agreement*, London and New York: Routledge.

May, Chris (2000), *A Global Political Economy of Intellectual Property Rights: The New Enclosures?*, London and New York: Routledge.

Menescal, Andrea (2005), 'Changing WIPO's ways? The 2004 Development Agenda in historical perspective', *Journal of World Intellectual Property*, **86**, 761–96.

Muzaka, Valbona (2010), 'Linkages, contests and overlaps in the global intellectual property rights regime', *European Journal of International Relations*, OnlineFirst, 1–22.

Muzaka, Valbona (2012), 'Contradictions, frames and reconstructions: the emergence of the WIPO Development Agenda', *Review of International Political Economy*, iFirst, 1–25.

Nogues, Julio (1990), 'Patents and pharmaceutical drugs – understanding the pressures on developing countries', Policy Research Working Paper Series, No. 502, Washington, DC: World Bank.

Oddi, Samuel (1987), 'The international patent system and Third World development: reality or myth', *Duke Law Journal*, November, 831–77.

Okediji, Ruth (2003), 'The international relations of intellectual property: narratives of developing country participation in the global intellectual property system', *Singapore Journal of International and Comparative Law*, **7**, 315–85.

Okediji, Ruth (2008), 'History lessons for the WIPO Development Agenda', in Neil Weinstock (ed.), *The Development Agenda*, Oxford: Oxford University Press, pp. 137–61.

Okediji, Ruth (2009), 'The regulation of creative under the WIPO internet treaties', *Fordham Law Review*, **77**, 2379–410.

Penrose, Edith (1973), 'The economics of the international patent system', *Economic Journal*, **83** (331), 768–86.

Perry, Richard (1996), 'Rethinking the right to development: after the critique of development, after the critique of rights', *Law and Policy*, **18** (3–4), 225–49.

Pfaffenberger, Bryan (1992), 'Social anthropology of technology', *Annual Review of Anthropology*, **21**, 491–516.

Pieterse, Jan Nederveen (1998), 'My paradigm or yours? Alternative development, post development, reflexive development', *Development and Change*, **29**, 343–73.

Rapp, Richard and Richard Rozek (1990), 'Benefits and costs of intellectual property protection in developing countries', *Journal of World Trade*, **24**, 75–102.

Reichman, Jerome (2009), 'Intellectual property in the twenty-first century: will the developing countries lead or follow?', *Houston Law Review*, **46**, 1115–85.

Ricketson, Sam (1987), *The Berne Convention for the Protection of Literary and Artistic Works 1886–1986*, London: Centre for Commercial Law Studies, Queen Mary College.

Ryan, Michael (1998), *Knowledge Diplomacy: Global Competition and the Politics of Intellectual Property*, Washington, DC: Brookings Institution Press.

Schech, Susanne (2002), 'Wired for change: the links between ICTs and development discourses', *Journal of International Development*, **14**, 13–23.

Sell, Susan (2003), *Private Power, Public Law: The Globalization of Intellectual Property Rights*, Cambridge: Cambridge University Press.

Simon, Bradford (2005), 'Intellectual property and traditional knowledge: a psychological approach to conflicting claims of creativity in international law', *Berkley Technology Law Journal*, **20**, 1613–84.

Stiglitz, Joseph (1999), 'Knowledge as a global public good', in I. Kaul, I. Grunberg and M. Stern (eds), *Global Public Goods: International Cooperation in the 21st Century*, New York: Oxford University Press, pp. 308–25.

Tucker, Vincent (2001), 'The myth of development: a critique of a Eurocentric discourse', in R. Munck and D. O'Hearn (eds), *Critical Development Theory: Contributions to a New Paradigm*, London: Zed Books, pp. 1–26.

Vaitsos, Constantine (1972), 'Patents revisited: their function in developing economies', *Journal of Development Studies*, **9** (1), 71–97.

Vandoren, Paul and Pedro Martins (2006), 'The enforcement of intellectual property rights: an EU perspective of a global question', in Meier Pugatch (ed.), *The Intellectual Property Debate: Perspectives from Law, Economics and Political Economy*, Cheltenham, UK and Northampton, MA, USA: Edward Elgar, pp. 62–80.

Watal, Jayashree (2001), *Intellectual Property Rights in the WTO and Developing Countries*, The Hague: Kluwer Law International.

WIPO (2007), 'The 45 Adopted Recommendations under the WIPO Development Agenda, General Assembly, September 2007', available at: http://www.wipo.int/ip-development/en/agenda/recommendations.html (accessed on 22 February 2012).

World Bank (1998), *World Development Report: Knowledge for Development*, Washington, DC: World Bank.

World Bank (2005), *Global Economic Prospects Report*, Washington, DC: World Bank.

Yu, Peter (2009), 'A tale of two development agendas', *Ohio Northern University Law Review*, **35**, 465–573.

17 Innovation and the limits of rebranded privatisation in global health
Sophie Harman

Innovation has become a buzz-word in the political economy of governance. Whether used in the context of higher education reforms, investment in domestic manufacturing, beauty products for ageing populations, or solutions to climate change, this buzz-word is meant to reflect the emphasis on new ideas, new structures, new solutions and new forms of financing for contemporary global political issues. The use of innovation has been particularly popular in describing new forms of governance, funding, projects and approaches for tackling global health problems. New public–private partnerships, such as the Global Alliance for Vaccines and Immunisation (GAVI Alliance), describe themselves as innovative; Bill Gates has advocated the need for more innovation to solve global health problems; and philanthropic donors continue to set aside funds for researchers to innovate. Yet in these different contexts the meaning of the word 'innovation' remains slightly dubious: all that is certain is that people working in global health like to use it, and describing something as innovative is generally seen as positive. Conventionally, the word 'innovation' refers to the introduction of new ideas, methods or change, and is applied to describe research outcomes, new findings or something that the world needs more of. In this sense, the word 'innovation' can be seen to rest on a specific set of assumptions: that it is in itself a public good; is something that contributes to the advancement and sustenance of social life; shows the efficacy of applied knowledge; and is something that should not be curtailed or limited by excessive regulation or state control. However, its application to global health is often confusing and makes it hard to pin down what is actually the purpose of innovation in global health governance. This chapter argues that the application of the word 'innovation' to describe and advocate new global health structures and projects is deliberately vague and designed to conceal privatised reform of global health. Innovation has come to represent little more than privatisation. Instead of presenting a new approach to tackling the problems of global health, innovation refers to a rebranded form of privatisation that reasserts and reloads a specific type of market-oriented neoliberalism through results-oriented policy planning, deliverable returns, diversification in sources of income, and accountability to investors as opposed to users. The word 'innovation' is thus used as a rhetorical cover for a wider project of privatised reform of global health governance.

The chapter makes this argument in the following manner. First, it outlines how the word 'innovation' has been used by global health actors such as the World Bank and World Health Organization (WHO) to describe new changes to global health institutions and financing over the last ten years. In so doing, it highlights how innovation is applied to describing new funding mechanisms such as cash transfers, new forms of governance such as multisectoral inclusion, new institutions such as the Global Fund to Fight AIDS, Tuberculosis and Malaria (the Global Fund), the GAVI Alliance and UNITAID, and new ways of health financing developed by bodies such as the Bill & Melinda Gates Foundation (hereafter the Gates Foundation). It shows that innovation is used by these new actors and their partners both to describe themselves and their work and as an advocacy tool and justification for more of the same. Second, the chapter examines the shortcomings and limitations of these new processes of global health governance to unpack the problems inherent in arguing for more of the same and to demonstrate how innovation has come to represent little more than privatisation. It draws out some of the complexity and limitations to these new initiatives, revealing what is left out in partnerships and multilevel governance, how inclusion can be distorted in relation to accountability, and what role exactly the state and civil society organisations play in enhancing or curtailing the classical understanding of innovation with regard to alternatives and new ideas. Third, the chapter concludes with an exploration of what the use of innovation in global health means to practical and conceptual understandings of the political economy of governance, the promotion of better health for all and the privatisation of governance.

INNOVATION IN GLOBAL HEALTH

The use of the word 'innovation' in global health has traditionally come from the private sector, specifically pharmaceutical and biotechnology companies, to stimulate entrepreneurship and creativity. Both the state and non-state sectors advocate the need for innovation, by which they mean investment in new research to advance knowledge; generate profit and returns on investment; develop esteem and prestige within an individual, company or state; promote investment in a state's economy; or provide solutions to complex social issues. In this sense, the word 'innovation' in global health has traditionally been used in support of core Enlightenment principles relating to the pursuit of knowledge and discovery, but it also goes beyond the idea of knowledge for knowledge's sake to include applied knowledge that seeks a return, either through financial reward or the application of a social policy or a political idea. The last ten years have seen a great deal of emphasis placed on the need for innovation in global health. The WHO has put innovation at the centre of access to medicines and debates on intellectual property rights and technology transfer to developing countries (WHO 2011). The WHO does not define innovation within its *Global Strategy and Plan of Action on Public Health, Innovation and Intellectual Property* (WHO 2006); yet it situates it within the broader context of needs-driven, rather than market-driven, research through capacity-building in developing countries and better management of intellectual property (WHO 2006). The World Bank has discussed innovation in regards to new ideas from local communities in China, nutrition financing and health-system strengthening (World Bank 2007). The Center for Global Development refers to innovative advances in global health as 'one of the greatest human accomplishments', citing rising life expectancy, technology and specific case-studies as evidence of this (Levine and Kinder 2004). The United Kingdom's 2011 Health and Social Care Bill incorporates a 'Duty to promote innovation' as part of the mandate of the National Health Service Commissioning Board (Department of Health 2011: 15). Innovation is a priority for the Gates Foundation's work on global health and agriculture, with Bill Gates noting in his 2012 annual letter that 'throughout my careers in software and philanthropy . . . a recurring theme has been that innovation is the key to improving the world' (Gates 2012).

Yet what innovation is, means or entails remains dubious. It is used both to describe new ideas and solutions to problems for global health governance and to advocate more such ideas and solutions. Actors such as the WHO and government health systems have used the word 'innovation' as a call to explore alternative means of addressing pressing health concerns beyond the health service. The relationship between the determinants of poor health, socio-economic status, individual behaviour and self-esteem, and state provision requires governments and international actors to consider ways of expanding health delivery beyond biomedical and public health interventions. The result is the introduction of new policy ideas such as 'nudges' (Thaler and Sunstein 2009) and conditional cash transfers. Nudges that rest on social or economic incentives or choice ordering have lately become popular with governments in Europe and North America as a means of changing behaviour in regards to smoking, eating and exercise. Forms of social protection such as insurance and child allowance schemes have always been prominent features of welfare states in the West since the end of the Second World War (Marmor 1971). However, these types of social protection have grown in their application to poverty alleviation strategies in Latin America and Asia and are increasingly being used as a means of incentivising behaviour change in sub-Saharan Africa (Hanlon et al. 2010). Key conditions of these cash transfers have been associated with better health outcomes, whether child nutrition or HIV status (Harman 2011). Whilst they resemble the old idea of targeted welfare interventions, these policies are labelled innovative because of their global application as non-state-based interventions by institutions such as the World Bank. Whereas global health projects have tended to be more systematic in reforming country health systems or providing treatment to specific diseases, these policies target the individual and take a so-called innovative approach to individual change and personalised outcomes. These interventions are not necessarily new, but are branded as innovative solutions to old governance problems of behaviour change and service uptake because they borrow ideas from other fields and apply them to health.

One of the main uses of the word 'innovation' in global health has been to describe new forms of multisectoral health governance and partnerships. In the context of global health, multisectoral governance is based on the inclusion of government agencies (health-specific and non-health-specific), non-governmental organisations (NGOs), community groups, the private sector, intergovernmental institutions and non-health-specific agencies at the local, regional, national and global level in decision-making and implementation of policies. This type of multisectoral governance has been applied to multiple health topics, from neglected diseases and HIV/AIDS, to maternal and child health and, most recently, new strategies for combating non-communicable diseases such as diabetes (UNGA 2011). The governance arrangements surrounding this form of multisectoralism involve the formation of agencies for specific health issues at the national, subregional and community levels in a country. The role of these decentralised bodies is both to highlight the need for effort over a specific issue and to coordinate the different actors involved in response (Harman 2010). Rhetoric on the need for multisectoral health interventions was evident in United Nations Development Programme (UNDP) and WHO directives in the early 1990s, but did not come into practice until the World Bank's large-scale AIDS programme in Africa, the Multi-Country AIDS Program

(MAP) (Harman 2010). Since the early 2000s and the creation of the MAP, multisectoralism has become the main paradigm of governance in which health is framed; the clearest evidence for which has been the institutionalisation of multisectoral aspects of governance through the creation of new bodies such as the Global Fund and the emergence of 'the era of partnerships' (Walt et al. 2009) within global health.

The Global Fund, new forms of public–private partnership such as GAVI and UNITAID, and new models of philanthropy by actors such as the Gates Foundation are also labelled as innovative by the institutions themselves and their global health partners. The word 'innovative' is used by these actors to describe their institutional make-up. The priority within such bodies is not the state as the primary site of activity, but rather civil society actors, the private sector and institutions. Such priority is reflected in the decision-making boards, implementation and service-delivery functions of these bodies. The Global Fund is the clearest example of this. Established in 2002, it is a funding mechanism to support country-based interventions into the 'big three' diseases: HIV/AIDS, malaria and tuberculosis. The Fund has representatives from civil society and the private sector on its board of directors, with voting rights equal to those of member-states. Moreover, the mandate of the Fund is to generate resources direct to both state and non-state-based actors, with an emphasis on civil society organisations as both principal and sub-recipients of Global Fund money (Global Fund 2011a, 2011b; Harman 2012). It is this inclusion of non-state actors in the agenda-setting, decision-making and implementation capacity of the Global Fund that has led to its identification as a new and somewhat more advanced model of inclusive, deliberative democracy within global governance (Brown 2009). Perhaps less advanced, but no less relevant here, are the institutional arrangements of UNITAID. The purpose of UNITAID is to improve access to medicines and treatment for people affected by HIV/AIDS, malaria and tuberculosis, particularly in low- and middle-income countries, through what it calls 'innovative financing' (UNITAID 2011b; Harman 2012). Based at the WHO offices in Geneva, UNITAID takes a standard partnership form, being governed by an Executive Board made up of state and civil-society representatives, Chair and WHO representative, serviced by a secretariat chaired by an Executive Secretary and consisting of the secretary's office and operations, and operating through three working groups. Actors familiar to new partnerships, such as the World Bank, United Nations Children's (Emergency) Fund (UNICEF), and UNAIDS, as well as the Global Fund, 'Stop TB, Roll Back Malaria', the Clinton HIV/AIDS Initiative and the Foundation for Innovation New Diagnosis (FIND), are the main partners of the organisation.

The proclaimed benefits of these kinds of multisectoral partnerships are that they tend to be results-oriented and generate clearly defined and regulated outputs built on a business model of project development (Grimsey and Lewis 2004) that sees a clear relationship between supply and demand (Chataway and Smith 2006). Objectives tend to be defined by the institutions and states involved on the public side of the partnership, with risk and responsibility falling more to the private aspect in terms of service delivery and support for clearly identified outcomes (Grimsey and Lewis 2004). With regard to health, partnerships have concentrated on product development, new vaccines and medicines, information systems and incentives for industry (Chataway et al. 2007; Harman 2012). As such, the focus of such partnerships has been towards vertical interventions for disease eradication, from issues such as HIV/AIDS to forms of neglected tropical disease. One of their central roles, however, has been to generate, sustain and offer alternatives in the all-important matter of funding for health issues. These funding mechanisms often sit in stark contrast to those of other underfunded UN bodies and thus offer them an alternative source of resource mobilisation (Buse and Walt 2000). Underpinning such partnerships are the key fundamentals of privatisation: market models of supply and demand; private sector inclusion in the planning and delivery of services; and results-oriented funding. These elements are all evident in the mechanisms and style of project financing of GAVI, the Global Fund, UNITAID and the Gates Foundation.

Innovation has also often been claimed as a means to describe the financial ability of partnerships to enact new approaches to how global health is funded. With the exception of large-scale philanthropy in scientific endeavour and the promotion of global health by organisations such as the Rockefeller Foundation and the Ford Foundation at the turn of the twentieth century (Berridge et al. 2009), historically global health has principally been funded and organised by states, through direct state provision in the context of domestic socialised medical systems, or bilateral aid, or support for intergovernmental bodies such as the WHO and the World Bank. In many cases such state support has been subsidised by private investment in research innovation and complex insurance schemes, but the site in which this has happened has been located within the wider discourse of the responsibility of the state for the rights of its citizens. The last ten years have seen a change in this regard: total development assistance for health has increasingly been sourced from non-state private actors, particularly the Gates Foundation. Bilateral funding has also continued to increase, but not at the same rate as non-state and non-intergovernmental institutions during this period. Importantly, the aid money of these new actors is not tied to the political concerns of domestic populations and objectives, thereby allowing donors and partnerships greater freedom to be flexible in where, to what, to whom and how their money is targeted. The relevance and utility of this funding rests on the ability to deliver sufficient and efficient results to the financial backers of these partnerships. Financial commitments only go towards those initiatives that have measurable outcomes. Bill Gates refers to such performance-based funding as 'creative capitalism', in which market forces are applied to making a gain or profit that benefits the worse-off or addresses inequities (Gates, in Bishop and Green 2010: 177). These outcomes still have to be framed in ways that are reasonable to the states in which they operate and key bilateral donors; yet there is more flexibility in approach offered by having a budget not only independent of state funding but in some cases greater than the budget of specific states and institutions.

A key part of such flexibility is sustainable and new forms of global health financing. New forms of financing are described by actors such as the Global Fund (that have developed these mechanisms) and the Gates Foundation (that invest in and promote the mechanisms) as innovative, and are then used as evidence for more innovation. Since its creation the Global Fund has looked to multiple sources of public and private finance. These finance innovations as defined by the Global Fund are sourced from three areas. The first is the Dow Jones Global Fund 50 Index which tracks those companies supporting the Fund. The Global Fund Supporters exchange-traded fund (ETF) is seen by the Fund as a means of providing 'the financial community with incentives to participate in financing health development' (Global Fund 2011c). The second, Debt2Health, is a debt exchange where the debt of a country is dropped on condition that this money is then invested in public health through the Global Fund. The Fund's third type of innovative financing is sourced from its partnership with UNITAID, whose slogan is 'making markets work for people' (UNITAID 2011b). It does this by generating health finance through taxes on air travel, either through tickets for air travel or from broader taxes on carbon dioxide emissions. Twenty-nine countries have agreed to tax flights leaving their countries according to destination, ticket class and budgetary contributions, nine of which have begun to implement this (UNITAID 2011a). UNITAID also operates its patent pool facility which encourages pharmaceutical companies to make their patents available before their 20-year expiry, thus making them more affordable for developing countries (UNITAID 2011a).

The GAVI Alliance has similarly taken steps to become less dependent on donor support by also looking to ways in which it can sustain funding levels and speed up price reductions. GAVI has begun to implement such measures through the International Finance Facility for Immunisation (IFFIm) and the Advance Market Commitment (AMC). The purpose of the IFFIm is to elicit 10–20-year donor commitments, which are then leveraged in capital markets. The leveraged money is then transferred to support the immunisation of 500 million children against measles, tetanus and yellow fever. The AMC works with donors and the pharmaceutical industry to set a price for vaccines before they have been developed. The logic here is that, if the prices of vaccines are set, donors will buy such products, thereby ensuring a suitable return and, crucially, making these products more affordable to low- and middle-income countries (see Harman 2012). It should of course be noted that such innovative financing is always underpinned by the safety net of public financing – which in all three cases makes up the majority of core budgetary support – and thus creates the supposed stable basis on which flexibility and risk-taking in the playing of financial markets to benefit global health can rest.

Beyond these alternative sources of finance, where such finance goes and how it is delivered to real health outcomes is another allegedly innovative feature of these governance initiatives. The one actor that has fundamentally shifted how global health is viewed and delivered in the last ten years has been the Gates Foundation. Like the Global Fund, the Gates Foundation is a grant-making body with an annual budget larger than the WHO (Ravishankar et al. 2009; McCoy et al. 2009; Harman 2012). The main focus of the Foundation's Global Health Program is 'research, science and innovation' as mechanisms of providing solutions to some of the world's biggest health concerns. This emphasis comes from a personal commitment on the part of Bill and Melinda Gates to put right the lack of investment in research and find innovative ways to tackle longstanding problems of global health such as polio via a US$36.4 billion endowment. In this sense, the Gates Foundation emphasises a more traditional view of innovation: investment in science and technology as a means of generating new tools to address complex issues that follows old models of private philanthropy for global health established by previous wealthy Americans (Berridge et al. 2009). However, the Gates Foundation differs in ambition and scope from previous philanthropic efforts towards health. The focus of the Foundation is very much global and is evident in its wide grant-making portfolio and country presence through offices in Seattle, Washington, London, New Delhi and Beijing (Bill & Melinda Gates Foundation 2011). It is its desire and ability to fund large research projects and invest in ideas in ways that public bodies with limited funds are unable to do (on such a grand scale) that has led the Gates Foundation both to describe itself, but also to be seen by others, as innovative. The perceived success of the Foundation's Global Health Program – for example, in accelerating the decline of polio to the point of near eradication – perpetuates the use of the word 'innovation' as meaning something that there needs to be more of.

In summary, despite having different mandates and roles within global health, these actors exhibit similar tendencies: they did not exist in their current form prior to 2000; they engage in vertical interventions in global health whilst stressing the benefits of more horizontal approaches; they have increased the amount of funding given to and the importance attributed to global health; they have broad inclusion of public and private bodies on their boards; and they all prioritise private sector investment and market principles in global health policy-making. Each of these characteristics feeds into the claim to be innovative in healthcare delivery. As we have seen, they are described as innovative in respect of how they are funded, the projects they pursue and the multilevel governance structures around which they are organised. These actors also deliberately use the label of innovation as a tool to develop and promote further innovation. The type of innovation they represent and promote rests on certain key assumptions: knowledge for reward; the private sector as the primary site of innovation; the need for new ideas, new actors and new processes; and the notion of innovation as a public good. However, beyond the deployment of such assumptions there has been little attempt to define innovation precisely, and so it remains hard to define what it really means in regard to global health governance beyond a broad need for the new. It is thus important to move on to consider how the practical applications of such innovative structures and financing mechanisms actually work, whereupon we shall see that innovation is used in good part as a cover for referring to private sources of finance and privatised structures of governance.

THE PROBLEM WITH INNOVATION

The new forms of financing and governance arrangements for global health delivery that have come to be labelled as innovative introduce a range of actors and alternatives with different approaches to and understandings of health. This should in principle provide plurality in decision-making and implementation and decentralised forms of governance that are accessible and transparent. However, these notions are simply assumptions of what innovation can or should do or be, and of the outcomes such new structures and processes will generate: in practice, how these so-labelled innovative systems of governance are expressed in global health suggests something else. It suggests that the word 'innovation' has become little more than a rhetorical cover for processes of privatisation that are not about change and newness, but rather the familiar embedding of neoliberal forms of governance that articulate the need for market-based reform, private-sector delivery of services and, crucially, the inclusion of the private sector in decision-making and project and programme planning for a variety of global health initiatives. This is evident in how those governance arrangements described as innovative are applied in practice, how funding is sourced and arranged, and how the role of the state adds legitimacy within this system.

Politics of Inclusion and Accountability

One of the main reasons why global health governance is described as innovative by policy-makers and those interested in governance and organisation is the inclusion of non-state actors and a shifting of decision-making and service delivery away from the state. However, the degree to which such actors are included is somewhat skewed between the balance of state and non-state interests. This is evident in the decision-making structures of multisectoral bodies and programmes such as the World Bank's HIV/AIDS programmes. In practice, this form of governance has not included multiple actors in decision-making and agenda-setting, but has also led to hierarchy and mar-ketised forms of implementation. The Bank's HIV/AIDS projects showed that agenda-setting rested with the Bank and the donors which were paying for the projects, with government agencies making decisions that were micro-managed from the Bank. Despite the rhetoric of civil society and private sector inclusion in such processes, this only referred in practice to such actors implementing the strategies designed at the national and global level (Harman 2010). What is more, the motivation for such implementation was financial gain (Harman 2010). The stated purpose of including non-state actors on the Board of the Global Fund was to overcome such a disaggregation in hierarchy and decision-making and to create the space for innovation through new ideas and actors in global health (Brown 2009). However, the inclusion of such bodies did not lead to the inclusion of alternative voices and ideas, but at best only a more consensual form of decision-making in which those alternative voices adhered to the norm. Civil-society representatives on the Global Fund's Board have tended to be drawn from a narrow pool of the 'usual suspects' (Harman 2010) drawn from organisations familiar to institutions and actors in Geneva. These organisations, such as national associations of people living with HIV, are well versed in the language of global health, understand the delicate balance of negotiation and diplomacy within these institutions, and engage in a form of institutional 'paradigm maintenance' (Wade 1996) in which opinions and innovations regress to the norm. In other words, those that are included within these structures tend to be organisations sympathetic to the mandate and approach of the partnerships or institutions within which they act. Whilst they acquire a degree of leverage, this exists within a pre-established framework and the longevity of such non-state actors in decision-making depends on their ability to act as appropriate partners. Moreover, despite having equal voting systems within these partnerships, as evidence from the Global Fund suggests (Brown 2009), voting cleavages within the Board of Directors reflect a hierarchy among partnerships. This all suggests that the inclusion of civil society organisations is about consensual participation rather than innovative deliberative democracy. Decision-making with the Global Fund is directed by its largest donors, its executive and key members of its board of directors, and reveals only the familiar pattern of hierarchy through budgetary commitment.

The issue of lack of plurality and hierarchy in decision-making through budgetary commitment is not unique to the Global Fund and older institutions of global health such as the World Bank. This is a central problem too within the Gates Foundation and the Foundation's relationship with GAVI and UNITAID through which most of its investment in health is channelled (McCoy and McGoey 2011). The Gates Foundation contributes 3.3 per cent of the Global Fund's total pledges and 22.9 per cent of GAVI's

(Global Fund 2011d; GAVI 2011). Such budgetary support allows the Foundation to have disproportionate influence on the types of research conducted by GAVI and its supporting university research centres, and has meant that the influence of the Gates Foundation on distorting research priorities has been one of the central criticisms levied against it (McCoy and McGoey 2011; Global Health Watch 2008). The Foundation has attempted to combat such criticism by suggesting it frees up money for the public sector then to invest elsewhere. This is a fair point, but it does not address the crux of the problem: whether such considerable influence is met with a similar level of accountability. The Gates Foundation is run by the Gates family – Melinda, Bill and Bill Senior – and ex-Microsoft employees in its Seattle headquarters, with a huge presence around the world through its Washington, London, New Delhi and Beijing offices. It takes the majority of its considerable endowment from the Gates family, Warren Buffet and private donations. Project design and strategy takes place in Seattle, with Bill, Bill and Melinda all taking an active role in the direction of the Foundation and the types of programmes it funds (Lee 2010). For the Foundation, accountability is a struggle, 'partly just being a scale issue' (Lee 2010) and partly because accountability is dependent on partner states and non-governmental organisations feeding back information.

Accountability is in fact a wider problem within new forms of innovative governance in terms of responsibility. The diffuse nature of decision-making makes responsibility for projects, and more importantly blame for when they go wrong, hard to trace. In funding as opposed to implementing programmes, new partnerships and mechanisms can apportion blame to partner organisations in-country, most often state-based institutions or non-governmental organisations, and take responsibility or credit themselves when a project goes well. A key example has been the recent accusations of corruption within the Global Fund, where allegations of misappropriation of money at the in-country level have led to the withdrawal of bilateral aid from Ireland, Sweden and Germany (Boseley 2011). The Global Fund's response has been to stress its rigorous monitoring and accountability mechanisms, assert its successes in global health and, crucially, assign the blame to recipient states (Kazatchkine 2011), particularly in the cases of Zambia and Mauritania. In practice, those actors responsible for decision-making within new forms of global health governance are accountable to the boards of the organisation, their donors, public opinion and the states that give and borrow money from them; not to the people whose lives they effect. Accountability is problematic with regard to who these actors represent, what interests they have, and where responsibility is placed. This stands in stark contrast to the positive potential for inclusion and transparency that these models of multisectoral governance are seen by themselves and donors to possess and promote. The reality is that hierarchy in decision-making remains, with the only innovative change being that it is private actors such as the Gates Foundation which dominate the agenda, not states and intergovernmental organisations.

In many ways the assertion that the state has come under increased threat as a result of multisectoral governance, new actors and the permeation of large grant-making bodies such as the Gates Foundation is somewhat overstated. Actors such as the Gates Foundation, World Bank and Global Fund are consistently keen to assert that the state remains the primary focus in multiple levels of global health governance. This is to a certain extent true. Public money makes up 37.8 per cent of GAVI's total budget, 94.9 per cent of the Global Fund's and 96.6 per cent of UNITAID's (GAVI 2011; Global

Fund 2011d; UNITAID 2011c). It is mainly the lack of state-based financing that led to the Global Fund's suspension of Round 11 funding and the subsequent crisis in which the Global Fund now finds itself. Protests over the lack of Global Fund money in Nairobi, Kenya have focused on the responsibility of states in fulfilling their pledges and maintaining the treatment services that Fund money provides (Klein 2012). State representatives not only sit on the boards of these partnerships, but also set the sovereign laws within which projects and politics are implemented and practised. New models of global health governance still work with states and rest on working agreements, concessions and financial support from states. However, the state's role as the main provider, distributor and measure of global health is changing, with privatised models of both service delivery and decision-making coming to the fore. One of the key factors that has led to such change is the greater financial clout and flexibility of private investors within new institutions in comparison to that of intergovernmental and bilateral funding initiatives. The state, whether a site to which blame is allocated or a key actor in the delivery of new innovative outcomes, is still a key source of legitimacy and accountability. Partnerships that do not engage with the state – those states either receiving funds or giving funds in support of partnerships – lack legitimacy and full systems of accountability, and programme longevity is poor. States and state-based intergovernmental organisations set the context within which these new, innovative programmes take place. Indeed, partnerships have to have agreements with governments to operate within a territory. They require the knowledge, research and institutional legitimacy of intergovernmental organisations, such as the WHO, to be seen as viable and relevant actors within the global health sector. Finally, decision-making within partnerships still has to be framed within the interests of both donor and borrower states. However, the degree to which the state remains relevant to these partnerships and innovative forms of privatisation depends on the type of state.

Donor states have greater leverage on the mandate of partnerships and in some cases a vested interest in the types of privatised technological and scientific innovations that such partnerships promote. This tends to be because of their financial and political investment in the partnerships (for example, France with UNITAID), their membership in core structures of decision-making in other multilateral bodies, and the associated influence of key companies and research based in these countries. For example, while the production of key drugs may take place in countries such as Brazil, their research and development takes place in North America and Western Europe. Borrower states, or states in which these technologies and systems are trialled, have less leverage. Despite high-profile concessions to countries such as South Africa in the public health amendment to the World Trade Organization's (WTO) Trade-Related Intellectual Property rights (TRIPs) agreement and the introduction of the WHO's Pandemic Influenza Preparedness Framework (PIPF) after Indonesia withdrew from sharing virus samples of H5N1 over the inequitable system of drug access (Kamradt-Scott and Lee 2011), many developing countries remain cautious over the kind of critical leverage they have over donors that support their health systems. Developing countries require funds to support expensive drug treatment programmes, improvements to infrastructure and evolving responses to changing diseases. This places them in a bind where they require the funds and thus have less space for negotiation as to the type of finance they receive. The governments of developing countries thereby often find themselves caught in the same form of consensual decision-making as civil-society organisations where they give legitimacy to privatised systems of healthcare as a means of receiving the benefits of such innovation and enjoy little public input as to how such funds are spent.

The lack of developing-country input into health strategies is not new to global health governance. What is new is the shift from global intergovernmental decision-making that prioritises rights-based public interventions to new partnership models (described as innovative) that emphasise privatised forms of delivery and governance. The health agenda for millions of people and the governments that represent them is made by wealthy philanthropists, Western-educated Geneva bureaucrats and well-paid academic consultants. Agendas are set through personal interest and reflect swings in global trends from the public to the private, and shifts between vertical and horizontal planning and investment. In this sense, these new models of global health do not represent a source of innovation in terms of newness, but only a slight adjustment of the status quo. However, it is the imperceptible changes to the state arising from such innovative governance structures that are of interest here. Emphasis on multisectoral governance and the need to form partnerships with the private sector has advanced processes of privatisation in multiple different countries and contexts. This is the case in developed countries such as the United States and the United Kingdom where the private sector is seen as the only option for reform of health systems, but is acutely felt in middle-income countries such as South Africa and low-income countries such as Tanzania where donor conditionalities are more tied these days to multisectoral forms of governance and private partnership in-country than they are to health outcomes (Harman 2010). These new innovations rely on state support as security for risky ventures: yet this requires governments to enter into partnership with a host of non-state, private actors such as Deutsche Bank and Pilipinas Shell. In other words, the state has not gone away as a central actor of global health, but the public governmental nature of the state is shifting to include non-state actors and to rely more and more on principles of private sector delivery and privatisation. This is most clearly the case when considering the role of innovation in the types of health projects and reform financed.

Wanting Results: Hindering Innovation

The last ten years have seen not only changes in the types of actors and governance arrangements for global health, but also a new form of financing and grant-making that stresses the need for results-based financing and vertical interventions into specific diseases. The emphasis placed on these two areas by institutions such as the World Bank, the Gates Foundation and the Global Fund is underpinned by the assumption that new, innovative projects and finance mechanisms must have a clear and measurable return that is of either financial or social benefit. The benefits of results-oriented approaches are clear to see: global health money should go to successful projects where progress and results can be clearly seen and monitored; moreover, these projects can also provide models for other interventions. Crucially, results-based financing provides solutions to questions of accountability and provides a response to the oft-cited problem within global health and development assistance of deciding where the money should go. In this sense, measurable success is a seductive mechanism within global health, development policy and global governance more broadly. However, results-based strategies run the risk of sidelining those health issues that do not demonstrate an adequate return on a donor's investment. This form of financing ignores issues that cannot be measured, does not address the socio-economic determinants of ill health and has the perverse effect of undermining innovation in the classical sense of the word (referring to new ideas, research and Enlightenment values). Issues such as gender equality, the right to health, individual choice and behaviour patterns are all integral components of the promotion of better health for all, but are either hard or impossible to measure. Where they are measured, they tend to focus on inclusionary practices, paid initiatives and the nature of government policies and legislation in regard to the promotion of human rights. Gender difference is only measured by disaggregated data about the prevalence of specific health concerns, not the gender component of policies or projects or the different impact they have on men and women. Such measurement ignores wider issues of how men and women experience health and health delivery differently, the degree to which rights-based approaches to health are put into practice, the whole question of inequalities in access to health. The promotion of measurement means issues such as gender equality – which is not the same as women's equality – tend to be excluded from global health strategies, as they are seen as too broad to fit under specific health initiatives, do not show a deliverable return, or are otherwise included anyway under the heading of 'women's health' issues, such as maternal and child health.

Addressing the socio-economic determinants of ill health has proved perilously difficult to achieve through global health initiatives alone, and efforts to do so offer little immediate return or evidence of success for the actors engaging in this activity. The structural and behavioural determinants of ill health cannot be overcome by a privatised framework that quantifies people's health through measurable outcomes and efficiency savings. Where efforts to address the structural and behavioural determinants of ill health exist, they do so in a way that uses market incentives to promote change. This is evident in the increased use of social protection or cash transfer programmes to change behaviour: sexual behaviour, eating and exercise habits, tobacco use or alcohol abuse. Yet these reward-based interventions ignore wider issues that contribute to individual behaviour choice, such as self-esteem, inequality, options and force, and use the market and financial incentive as a short-term mechanism for changing behaviour in the immediate term (Harman 2011).

The predominance of measurement and reward-based interventions has heightened and further complicated the debate between vertical and horizontal health interventions. Institutions and initiatives such as GAVI have prioritised vertical interventions into vaccine research, treatment acceleration and prevention campaigns for key diseases, primarily HIV/AIDS, tuberculosis and malaria, but increasingly maternal health, non-communicable diseases and the eradication of polio. Institutions such as the Global Fund and the Gates Foundation are keen to stress their health system strengthening role as a by-product of their vertical investment (Leloup 2010; Bains 2010), but overall less attention, and crucially less funding, has been given to the support systems and health services that underpin the delivery of vertical interventions. Part of the explanation is that results-oriented funding is more easily measured when invested in vertical interventions. Broader health system strengthening or horizontal interventions often require multiple actors, funding streams and both state and non-state participation, which makes the proof of success harder to attribute to a specific actor, and thus harder also to justify to donors and/or taxpayers. An alternative explanation suggests that, when privatised reforms have been applied to health systems in the past, health provision in developing countries has suffered. Privatised approaches to health systems and infrastructure have historically emphasised the need for subcontracting, user fees and privatised forms of procurement that, taken alone without additional public support, have seen minimal investment in healthcare as the private sector in developing countries fails to grow and private investment from new health partnerships stops (Sparke 2009). Privatisation rests on a thriving private sector, global growth and a state's ability to produce checks and balances on the system; factors that are difficult to achieve in countries where health indicators are low, leverage within global trade and financial regimes restricted and susceptibility to fluctuations within the global economy are high. The private sector does not lead to efficiency in this respect, but generates greater confusion and complication. Whether because of measurement, justification or inability to make clear returns in channelling finance towards horizontal strategies, the result of this distortion towards vertical priorities has led to significant underfunding in the development of health systems, health staff and practitioners, and technologies, specifically within developing countries. Lack of funding for transportation, road-building, hospitals, training of healthcare professionals and medical equipment reverses any long-term health gains and limits the sustainability of innovative vertical strategies. It is the case that new vertical funding mechanisms such as the Global Fund have led to benefits in some aspects of healthcare, whilst neglect of infrastructure is not the responsibility of new actors and funding mechanisms alone. However, the amount of funding that these actors generate and the private sector principles that they promote further reinforces the preoccupation of vertical interventions within global health governance.

The final problem with how innovation is used to describe the political economy of global health is that the structures and mechanisms to which the term is generally applied have the perverse effect of restricting innovation in the classical sense of the term. As this chapter highlighted at the start, innovation has traditionally meant new ideas, new research and new solutions in line with Enlightenment principles of discovery and knowledge. New partnerships and new funding mechanisms are meant to be flexible in approach with adaptable strategic aims; yet the practical application of funding streams results in narrow strategies, goals and objectives that inhibit the space for ideas and alternatives. Hence initiatives that require financial support to maintain operations or develop new strategies for global health are restricted to the underlying assumptions of what innovation is, how it is applied and what it is for. This restricts ideas to those that can be framed within the priorities of new partnerships, show measurable deliverables and produce evidence that the ideas can work. A core component in creating conditions for innovation, in the full 'discovery' sense of the word, to flourish is greater space for the development of alternative knowledge, seed-funding for ideas and more flexibility in what constitutes a measurable outcome. The new form of innovation as privatisation reduces space, which means that governance can only be understood in classic market terms. The hierarchical nature of these innovative organisations, the predominance of performance-based funding, the sidelining of complex social issues and the scale of the available budgets all reduce the space for alternatives that go beyond the market-based, privatised innovation that these new actors and programmes promote. As a result, the principles on which the structures and processes most widely seen as innovative in global health rest – namely, applied research for measurable return, whether social or financial

– undermine the very purpose of classical understandings of the word 'innovation'. As we have seen, this has significant implications not only for global health but also for the wider political economy of governance.

CONCLUSION: INNOVATION, PRIVATISATION AND THE POLITICAL ECONOMY OF GOVERNANCE

The new strategies, actors and partnerships that have come to characterise global health governance over the last ten years have identified themselves and been described as innovative or as sources of innovation. Innovation has traditionally been used to refer to the research and development of new medicines and vaccines, but over the last ten years has been increasingly used to describe and advocate new forms of governance that promote a merging of the public and private sector; as such, a new approach to how health is delivered. The word has not only been used to describe new actors, but has been used as a measure of success and as justification for more of the same. The problem here is that the word 'innovation' is not just a handy method of describing new actors and funding streams; instead it underpins a wider ideological commitment to privatised reform of how global health is organised, seen and delivered. As the preceding exploration of these forms of governance actors and strategies has shown, the so-called innovative approach rests on several core assumptions: that innovation comes from a private sector that is more flexible, specialised and adaptive than the public sector; that governments and intergovernmental bodies are still key to governance but, to be effective, need to adopt innovation principles of research investment, performance-based funding and return, and private sector partnership; and that innovation must be applied knowledge for a specific reward, either financial or social, that must also be measurable. Fundamentally, these assumptions are not new, nor do they have any relation to classical definitions of the word 'innovation'. But they do provide a unique ideological cover for the old idea of the supremacy of the market in delivering better health outcomes and the need for privatisation.

What the Gates Foundation, the Global Fund, GAVI and UNITAID have in common is that they all adopt private sector principles to address global health problems. This is not in itself a bad thing. Using the word 'innovation' to mask private reform of global health has been intrinsic to the formulation and sustenance of political will. However, this general push towards the privatisation of global health has made some states, non-governmental organisations and public health experts uneasy that the traditional public good of health is being transmuted before our eyes into a private good. Hence, the notion of innovation has come to be used as a more palatable way of presenting and legitimising privatisation, stressing the benefits of the private sector – technological advancement, investment in scientific research – and downplaying its more controversial dimensions, such as user-fees for health services and preferential access. Whilst older institutions such as the WHO are deemed to suffer from the institutional inertia, lethargy and constraints of state interests, new models of partnership present themselves as alternatives free of such constraints. Key has been the presentation of global health and the promotion of better health for all as something straightforward and measurable with clear outcomes and deliverables. This is a positive tool of international diplomacy in support of global health initiatives as it keeps health on a crowded international agenda, sustains much-needed funding, avoids donor fatigue and positions health at the centre of development policy and global governance more broadly. It provides a model for inclusion that overcomes multiple questions of democratic deficits within institutions. It brings in alternative views and perspectives from civil society and the private sector to balance the long-dominated state-based realm of doing international politics. As such, it frames the future of global public health in terms of hope and opportunity. However, presenting innovation in a way that stresses this new, results-oriented approach to health inevitably ignores other, arguably fundamental, parts of global health – individual rights, behaviour, choice and the need for state intervention – that have in the past made its governance so problematic. It also sidelines the very concerns about privatisation, and more specifically neoliberal forms of privatisation, that has led to its rebranding as innovation.

The stratification of governance through multisectoral actors, private philanthropists, finance initiatives and public–private partnerships has helped to embed the notion that private sector principles of reduced state involvement, results-based funding and corporate social responsibility are less about new ideas and inclusivity and more about the extension of neoliberal forms of governance within the health sector. Innovation has replaced privatisation in discussions of global health reform and how healthcare can be better delivered; yet at its core innovation has come to constitute little more than an advanced form of neoliberalism. The word 'innovation' has come to rest on privatised, medicalised solutions to global health problems without consideration as to how we understand behaviour and decision-making within certain socio-economic contexts outside of the neoliberal paradigm of health delivery. This has long been the case with targeted investment in innovation by pharmaceutical companies and private health bodies, but has now been extended to models of health governance. It is difficult to argue against innovation in the traditional sense of the term because of the impact it has long had on advances in medical treatment; yet it is important not to accept innovation as a good in itself without questioning the application of the term and the merits of the private sector principles that underpin so-called innovative institutions, projects and funding mechanisms. These principles are more about the provision of investment return than the development of knowledge and expertise. This has the perverse effect of limiting the space for knowledge and ideas that cannot be measured or do not necessarily present a clear return.

In sum, global health provides one of the most advanced forms of the application of the word 'innovation' as a means of both describing and advocating greater privatised governance with growing partnerships between business, finance and the public sector at multiple levels. At the same time global health has seen a growth in public attention and financing. Combined, these two factors – new structures and increased financing – have led global health to be recognised by policy-makers as a model of governance for other initiatives and policy areas to follow. Innovation is thus increasingly used as a core feature of governance, whether in regard to education reform, climate change, energy or business. Yet in each of these areas the new or the innovative stems from market-based principles of how to enact social policy. In this sense, as we have argued, innovation as applied to multiple domains of governance within the global political economy is little more than the rhetoric of extension of the neoliberal paradigm. Something valuable that was once about the Enlightenment, progress and alternative ways of thinking about problems and solutions is now more about the old idea of the triumph of the market.

REFERENCES

Bains, Anurita (2010), Senior Advisor, Global Fund to Fight AIDS, Tuberculosis and Malaria, Interview 3 September, Geneva.
Berridge, Virginia, Kelly Loughlin and Rachel Herring (2009), 'Historical dimensions of global health governance', in Kent Buse, Wolfgang Hein and Nick Drager (eds), *Making Sense of Global Health Governance: A Policy Perspective*, Basingstoke: Palgrave Macmillan, pp. 28–46.
Bill & Melinda Gates Foundation (2011), 'About the Foundation', http://www.gatesfoundation.org/about/Pages/overview.aspx (accessed March 2011).
Bishop, Matthew and Michael Green (2010), *Philanthrocapitalism: How Giving Can Save the World*, 2nd edition, London: A&C Black Publishers.
Boseley, Sarah (2011), 'Can the Global Fund weather the corruption storm?', *Guardian*, http://www.guardian.co.uk/society/sarah-boseley-global-health/2011/jan/28/aids-infectiousdiseases (accessed March 2011).
Brown, Garrett Wallace (2009), 'Multisectoralism, participation and stakeholder effectiveness: increasing the role of non-state actors in the Global Fund to Fight AIDS, Tuberculosis and Malaria', *Global Governance*, **15** (2), 169–77.
Buse, Kent and Gill Walt (2000), 'Global public–private partnerships: part I – a new development in health?', *Bulletin of the World Health Organization*, **78** (4), 549–61.
Chataway, Joanna, Stefano Brusoni, Eugenia Cacciatori, Rebecca Hanlin and Luigi Orsenigo (2007), 'The International AIDS Vaccine Initiative (IAVI) in a changing landscape of vaccine development: a public/private partnership as knowledge broker and integrator', *European Journal of Development Research*, **19**, 100–117.
Chataway, Joanna and James Smith (2006), 'The International AIDS Vaccine Initiative (IAVI): is it getting new science and technology to the world's neglected majority?', *World Development*, **34** (1), 16–30.
Department of Health (2011), *Health and Social Care Bill*, Department of Health: London, http://www.dh.gov.uk/en/Publicationsandstatistics/Legislation/Actsandbills/HealthandSocialCareBill2011/index.htm (accessed May 2011).
Gates, Bill (2012), 'Annual letter from Bill Gates', Bill & Melinda Gates Foundation, http://www.gatesfoundation.org/annual-letter/2012/Documents/2012-annual-letter-english.pdf (accessed January 2012).
GAVI (2011), 'Cash received by GAVI 2000-2011 as of June 2011', http://www.gavialliance.org/funding/donor-contributions-pledges/ (accessed September 2011).
Global Fund (to Fight AIDS, Tuberculosis and Malaria) (2011a), 'Grant portfolio', http://portfolio.theglobalfund.org/?lang=en (accessed September 2011).
Global Fund (to Fight AIDS, Tuberculosis and Malaria) (2011b), 'About the Global Fund', http://www.theglobalfund.org/en/about/?lang=en (accessed September 2011).
Global Fund (to Fight AIDS, Tuberculosis and Malaria) (2011c), 'Innovative financing', http://www.theglobalfund.org/en/about/donors/innovativefinancing/ (accessed September 2011).
Global Fund (to Fight AIDS, Tuberculosis and Malaria) (2011d), 'Pledges and contributions', http://www.theglobalfund.org/en/ (accessed October 2011).
Global Health Watch (2008), 'The Gates Foundation', *Global Health Watch 2: An Alternative World Health Report*, London: Zed Books.
Grimsey, Darrin and Mervyn Lewis (2004), 'The governance of contractual relationships in public–private partnerships', *Journal of Corporate Citizenship*, **15**, 91–109.
Hanlon, Joseph, Armando Barrientos and David Hulme (2010), *Just Give Money to the Poor*, Sterling, VA: Kumarian Press.
Harman, Sophie (2010), *The World Bank and HIV/AIDS: Setting a Global Agenda*, Abingdon: Routledge.
Harman, Sophie (2011), 'Governing health risk by buying behaviour', *Political Studies*, **59** (4), 867–83.
Harman, Sophie (2012), *Global Health Governance*, Abingdon: Routledge.
Kamradt-Scott, Adam and Kelley Lee (2011), 'The 2011 pandemic influenza preparedness framework: global health secured or a missed opportunity?', *Political Studies*, **59** (4), 831–47.
Kazatchkine, Michel (2011), 'How the Global Fund protects its grant money', Global Fund to Fight AIDS, Tuberculosis and Malaria, http://www.theglobalfund.org/en/howprotect/ (accessed March 2011).
Klein, Alice (2012), 'Kenyan AIDS activists demonstrate in support of Global Fund', *Guardian*, 2 February, http://www.guardian.co.uk/global-development/2012/feb/02/kenya-activists-march-support-global-fund?INTCMP=SRCH (accessed February 2012).

Lee, Laurie (2010), The Bill & Melinda Gates Foundation, Interview 12 November, London.

Leloup, Madeleine (2010), Senior Advisor, Global Fund to Fight AIDS, Tuberculosis and Malaria, Interview 31 August, Geneva.

Levine, Ruth and Molly Kinder (2004), *Millions Saved: Proven Success in Global Health*, Washington, DC: Center for Global Development.

Marmor, Theodore (1971), *Poverty Policy: A Compendium of Cash Transfer Policies*, Chicago, IL: Transaction Publishers.

McCoy, David, Gayatri Kembhavi, Jinesh Patel and Akish Luintel (2009), 'The Bill & Melinda Gates Foundation's grant-making program for global health', *Lancet*, **373**, 1645–53.

McCoy, David and Linsey McGoey (2011), 'Global Health and the Gates Foundation – in perspective', in Owain Williams and Simon Rushton (eds), *Health Partnerships and Private Foundations: New Frontiers in Health and Health Governance*, Basingstoke: Palgrave, pp. 143–63.

Ravishankar, Nirmala, Paul Gubbins, Rebecca Cooley, Katherine Leach-Kemon, Catherine Michaud, Dean Jamison and Christopher Murray (2009), 'Financing of global health: tracking development assistance for health from 1990 to 2007', *Lancet*, **373**, 2113–24.

Sparke, Matthew (2009), 'Unpacking economism and remapping the terrain of global health', in Adrian Kay and Owain David Williams (eds), *Global Health Governance: Crisis, Institutions, and Political Economy*, Basingstoke: Palgrave Macmillan, pp. 131–59.

Thaler, Richard and Carl Sunstein (2009), *Nudge*, London: Penguin.

UN General Assembly (UNGA) (2011), 'Political declaration of the High-Level Meeting of the General Assembly on the prevention and control of non-communicable diseases', United Nations: New York, http://www.un.org/ga/search/view_doc.asp?symbol=A%2F66%2FL.1&Lang=E (accessed October 2011).

UNITAID (2011a), 'Innovative financing', http://www.unitaid.eu/en/about/innovative-financing-main-menu-105/163.html (accessed September 2011).

UNITAID (2011b), http://www.unitaid.eu/ (accessed September 2011).

UNITAID (2011c), 'Budget revenue 2011', http://www.unitaid.eu/en/about/budget-mainmenu-130.html (accessed October 2011).

Wade, Robert (1996), 'Japan, the World Bank, and the art of paradigm maintenance: the East Asian miracle in political perspective', *New Left Review*, **1** (217), 3–36.

Walt, Gill, Neil Spicer and Kent Buse (2009), 'Mapping the global health architecture', in Kent Buse, Wolfgang Hein and Nick Drager (eds), *Making Sense of Global Health Governance: A Policy Perspective*, Basingstoke: Palgrave Macmillan, pp. 47–71.

WHO (2006), *The Global Strategy and Plan of Action on Public Health, Innovation and Intellectual Property*, Geneva: WHO, http://www.who.int/phi/implementation/phi_globstat_action/en/index.html (accessed September 2011).

WHO (2011), 'Public health, innovation and intellectual property', http://www.who.int/phi/en/ (accessed March 2011).

World Bank (2007), *China and the World Bank: A Partnership for Innovation*, Washington, DC: World Bank.

18 The global governance of gender

Jacqui True

Gender has moved from the margins to the centre of the governance of the global political economy. Divisions of labour by gender are – and have always been – a key dimension of the global political economy. Recently, though, gender equality has been touted as a solution to a range of global governance problems, including sustainable economic development, financial stability and the eradication of poverty (World Bank 2012; United Nations Development Programme 2012; Clinton 2010). Despite this, gender has yet to become a central category in the study of the global political economy. This chapter examines the emerging global governance of gender equality and, to a lesser extent, the gendered governance of the global political economy by subjects and processes that reflect hegemonic masculine ways of knowing and acting. These are distinct but related subjects of increasing concern to many scholars and policy-makers.

In the wake of the global financial crisis, gender equality in economic participation and gender balance in economic decision-making institutions are increasingly on the policy-making agendas of governments and international organisations. Ideas about gender are reconstituting both the ideologies and agents of governance – how the global political economy is governed and by whom. Deep gender divisions and inequalities persist, shaping the material structures of production and reproduction that sustain and trouble the dominant paradigms of economic growth and sustainable development and their global governance. From a critical feminist perspective that views gender relations as socially and historically constructed, 'gender' is a characteristic of individuals and individual behaviour (masculine, competitive, rational and autonomous versus feminine, caring, emotional and relational) as it appears in prevailing 'gender balance' discourses about the need for women as well as men leaders of the global political economy. But 'gender' is also a social structure that organises the allocation of productive and reproductive labour within and across 'public' institutions such as governments and markets, and 'private' institutions such as family households. Moreover, 'gender' is a symbolic feature of all collective institutions, including corporations and the state, and their style of doing business, especially the business of governing (Harding 1986).

These myriad ways in which gender affects the governance of the global political economy are not fully appreciated within the field of international political economy (IPE). For instance, liberal commentators now tout the gender make-up of individual decision-makers involved in governance as a key factor in achieving a more balanced approach to economic management and growth. They frequently cite evidence by the US think-tank Catalyst, the Harvard Business School and, lately, a report by the Credit Suisse Research Institute which revealed that those firms dominated by men have recovered more slowly after the 2008 financial downturn than those with a more balanced male–female ratio (Credit Suisse 2012). However, such commentators rarely mention the gendered structural inequalities in the global economy or the gendered organisational logics of business corporations, which represent significant institutional barriers to that desired gender diversity in corporate governance or other forms of institutional economic decision-making (Prügl and True 2014; Prügl 2012; Elias 2013).

There are four main sections to this chapter. In the first section, I examine how notions of 'gender equality' and 'gender balance' are woven into contemporary ideologies of liberal, market-based governance. In the second section, I consider how the focus on changing gender relations in the global political economy has relied on new forms of governance, especially informal types of governance that involve partnerships and coordination, rather than the dispersion and disaggregation of authority per se (cf. the Introduction to this volume; Rosenau 1995: 39). Rather than asking how or at what level gender is governed, I explore what new types of power are being created to govern gender in the global political economy (cf. Prügl 2011b). In the third section, I consider how the governance of gender has reconfigured state and global governing by involving a wider 'nébulese' of actors than has been the case before with economic management, even in the context of recent globalisation (Cox and Sinclair 1996). In the fourth section of the chapter, I reflect on the normative and ethical implications of the governance of gender and the gender of governance. Here I highlight how the governance of the international political economy attends to gender equality and gender balance in the formal, market economy, but fails to recognise the gendered nature of the informal economy, especially the unremunerated economic activity related to social reproduction and provisioning that is crucial for markets to operate efficiently. This neglect of the reproductive economy means that even innovative forms of global governance may reinscribe, rather than redress, gender inequalities and barriers to women's participation in the market economy, let alone in economic governance and decision-making.

The chapter concludes by considering what the governance of gender reveals about the emergent patterns and transformation of governance in the global political economy. The coordination of authority and diffusion of knowledge about patterns of gender inequality within and across countries has the potential to progress women's status in the global political economy, but only insofar as it also addresses the structural underpinnings of women's economic disadvantage in informal and household economies.

GENDER BALANCE IN GLOBAL GOVERNANCE

'Gender balance' in economic participation and decision-making is the new mantra for good governance and competitiveness in the global political economy. Liberal, market approaches single out two dimensions of gender relations as crucial to governance of the global political economy: first, equalising women's and men's labour market participation and productivity in national economies; and second, increasing women's leadership presence in the boardrooms and institutions where economic decisions are made.

The first dimension of the liberal governance approach is summed up by *The Economist*'s (2006) 'womenomics' view, which argues that women's increased participation in labour markets has added more to global growth than the growth of China, India and the internet combined. Thus, women are conceived as an important resource to be governed in the quest continually to grow and develop the global economy. The approach is exemplified by the World Economic Forum's sophisticated Global Gender Gap Index (GGGI), introduced in 2006 and updated annually (WEF 2012). The index ranks 135 countries (93 per cent of the world's population) according to gender equality in economic, political, education and health spheres. It provides powerful benchmarking evidence intended to prompt state policy-makers to address gender inequalities and facilitate greater female participation in the labour market. The GGGI has consistently revealed a strong correlation between the economic competitiveness of a country (another ranking based on 12 enabling pillars; WEF 2012) and the relative gender equality between women and men in that country. For instance, six of the top ten most competitive nations in 2012 were also among the top 20 most gender-equal countries (WEF 2012). For all countries, however, the economic gender gap is the largest and the slowest to close. In 2012 the global gap between women and men, as calculated by reference to three indicators of labour force participation, remuneration and advancement by gender,[1] was 40 per cent. Just nine countries have seen more than a 10 per cent improvement in closing the economic gender gap over the past seven years, with 75 countries experiencing less than a 5 per cent improvement.[2]

The World Economic Forum argues that, 'because women account for one-half of a country's potential talent base, a nation's competitiveness in the long term depends significantly on whether and how it educates and utilizes its women'.[3] It is not alone in this view. The World Bank's (2008) *Doing Business 2008* report finds that the benefits of reforming business regulations and levelling the playing field are especially significant for women. Countries with higher rankings for the ease of doing business have both more women entrepreneurs and more women in the workforce. Reform is good for women and fuels development. Moreover, Goldman Sachs, the global investment bank, has also produced analysis of several economies pointing to the significant gains to national gross domestic product (GDP) that could result from increasing women's labour market participation rates. For example, its economists have estimated that closing the male and female employment gap alone would increase GDP by 11 per cent in Australia, 10 per cent in the USA, 14 per cent in the Eurozone economies and 21 per cent in Japan. Further, devising policies to increase the productivity of women's labour to the same historical levels as men's labour, they argue, could boost economic activity even more. Closing the 'gender productivity gap' would mean not merely increasing women's participation, but also redirecting women's labour into the more productive sectors of the economy, away from non-cyclical sectors such as education, health and retail, and away from part-time, low-skilled work (Goldman Sachs 2009, 2011).

Economic analysis by Goldman Sachs and the World Economic Forum presents a strong case globally for governing gender to increase economic growth and prosperity. States are encouraged to harmonize their institutional and policy settings to achieve greater gender equality in the economy, society and polity. Countries such as Sweden have become 'policy entrepreneurs' in this arena. The 'Swedish model' of gender equality is promoted to its non-European Union (EU) eastern neighbours, for instance, at a recent conference on 'Gender equality for economic growth' hosted by the Swedish Institute with European Union funding. The model combines high rates of economic participation for both women and men, with strong state and institutional support for children and families, resulting in both fertility rates consistently above replacement levels and the creation of a 'good stock of human capital' for continued economic growth and enhanced competitiveness in global markets.

The second dimension of the liberal governance of gender is the idea that gender balance in economic decision-making is preferable because it generates greater market efficiency. Men overwhelmingly dominate economic decision-making positions as corporate board members, business executives, government financial regulators, trade negotiators and central bankers around the world (Young 2013). Rational argument supported by powerful quantitative analysis reveals strong associations between greater gender balance on corporate boards and other governance bodies and higher investment returns, as well as between high economic participation of women and national competitiveness (McKinsey 2007; Daly 2007).[4] Research by Catalyst attributed increased financial returns to the magical number of 'three' women present on the board of a firm (Joy et al. 2007). Recent evidence has also linked the paucity of women on corporate boards and management executives across countries to suboptimal decision-making against the backdrop of the global financial crisis (True 2013). Credit Suisse Research Institute (2012) found that shares of 2400 companies with a market capitalisation of more than US$10 billion listed on the MSCI ACWI World Index[5] and with women board members outperformed comparable businesses with all-male boards by 26 per cent worldwide over a period of six years (2005–11), with most of the outperformance in global markets between 2008 and 2011. This is taken to indicate that more diverse corporate governance boards were better at being defensive and limiting debt exposure in a market downturn (Credit Suisse 2012). Yet women make up just 11 per cent of the board membership of the 5000 companies with greater than US$1 billion free float market capitalisation in 45 countries (Gladman and Lamb 2013). Moreover, with respect to the UK's boardrooms, the UK's Equalities and Human Rights Commission (2011) estimates it will take another 70 years to achieve gender balance.

Many governments, international organisations and corporations are persuaded by these empirical studies associating greater gender balance in decision-making with enhanced competitiveness and growth and increased returns on sales, investment and equity (World Economic Forum 2011a; McKinsey 2007; Joy et al. 2007; Daly 2007; Goldman Sachs 2009). Calls to rebalance the economic sphere – by, for example, promoting 'balanced, inclusive, sustainable and knowledge-based growth', 'to strengthen the social resilience of individuals, particularly the most vulnerable' – are thus often associated with calls to achieve greater gender balance in decision-making (Prügl 2012; Bouchet and Isaak 2011).[6]

Gender quotas first adopted in electoral politics (see Krook 2010) are now being designed to bolster greater gender balance in economic decision-making, primarily at corporate board level and in national stock exchanges and regulatory authorities, and to a lesser degree in global economic governance bodies. More equal representation of women at the top is expected to deliver better results for citizens, states, employees and shareholders alike. The World Economic Forum first researched the gender gap in the governance of corporations only in 2011; as compared with its analysis of gender equality within the governance of states beginning in 2006 (World Economic Forum 2011b). Scrutinising who makes decisions in corporations, and how they do so, is more important than ever, because, as IPE scholars have underlined, power has increasingly shifted away from the legislatures of the state toward a range of private actors, including corporations, since the beginning of the most recent era of globalisation (Cutler et al. 1999; Cutler 2003; Porter and Ronit 2010). States under pressure to attract (foreign) investment by ensuring good returns are adopting various types of affirmative actions to regulate business performance on gender equality because it makes a difference to the bottom line. Gender is now an essential part of rational economic governance. It is no longer a social policy add-on, but 'smart economics', to use the World Bank lingua franca (World Bank 2006; Prügl and True 2014).

GOVERNING THE GLOBAL ECONOMY THROUGH GENDER

The turn to governing gender equality as a means to achieving sustained global economic development and growth is largely taking place through mechanisms of informal governance. By contrast with formal global governance mechanisms such as delegated state authority in international organisations, international agreements and treaties, and regulatory legal rules, governing gender in the global economy largely involves transgovernmental elite policy and advocacy networks (Slaughter 1997) and the policy coordination, diffusion and learning that they make possible. Informal governance is not equivalent to mere dispersion and disaggregation of authority. Rather, the authority of hegemonic discourse is in many ways more universal and global than ever before. It is the recourse to the force of the rational economic argument and related international benchmarking practices, rather than any directive from an international organisation or powerful state, which prompts states to compare and rank themselves on gender indicators (cf. Towns 2010).

With new benchmarks such as the Global Gender Gap, Women's Economic Opportunity Indexes (*The Economist* 2010), gender analysis of country gross national product (GNP) and productivity, and the International Finance Corporation's (IFC) women's 'ease of doing business' ranking of countries (World Bank 2008, 2012b), to mention just a few, there is now compelling global evidence for setting and harmonising policy agendas. The World Economic Forum, *The Economist*, Goldman Sachs and the World Bank – a think-tank, international magazine, investment bank and intergovernmental organisation respectively – all aim to create awareness about the collective economic benefits to be gained from gender equality by providing an evidence base that enables benchmarking. Agenda-setting initiatives and policy changes to address gendered inequalities and institutional barriers by governments, corporations and other economic actors too are intended to follow from global ranking exercises.

One area where we can clearly see informal governance mechanisms at work with demonstrable outcomes is the growth of transnational research, networking, benchmarking and measurement around gender balance on corporate boards. Knowledge generation by think-tanks, business and academic experts has played a major role in promoting policy learning and experimentation by governments, regulatory bodies and corporations on how to increase both the supply and visibility of qualified women in corporate governance and the demand for gender equity in the world of private business. The proportion of women on corporate boards is now being globally monitored as a gender equality indicator, alongside more traditional such indicators in political representation, health and education (see True 2013).

Much of the academic and public media discussion has focused on Norway's adoption of mandatory 'gender quotas' for public boards in 2004, which was extended to private boards in 2008. Certainly, Norway's success in increasing women's presence on boards from 6 per cent in 2002 to over 36 per cent in 2011 is breathtaking (although falling slightly short of the 40 per cent quota). Those six countries that followed suit with mandatory quotas by 2010 were the only ones to have a statistically significant representation of women on boards which exceeded 10 per cent, with an average proportion of 22 per cent.[7] (In the 39 countries without quotas, the average proportion of women on boards was 8 per cent.[8])

While legal requirements have been effective, informal 'nudge' approaches, which force reflection on the extent of gender diversity but allow for different approaches to improving this diversity, are also increasingly driving change within corporations and at the country level (Thaler and Sunstein 2008). In the United Kingdom and the United States a lobby group, which has become known as the '30% Club', has emerged to drive voluntary efforts to increase the numbers of women in economic management and boardroom positions. This focus on the 30 per cent threshold was inspired by research by Catalyst, which as mentioned shows increased financial returns when just three women are present on the board of a firm (Joy et al. 2007). In Australia the 'nudge' approach to increasing gender balance in private sector economic management is having an impact. Since 2010 the Australian Securities Exchange (ASX) under its corporate governance guidelines has required listed companies to adopt and disclose their diversity policy, including the number of women on their executive boards and in senior management, and to report annually on these gender breakdowns and diversity policies to the federal government. As a result of the reporting requirement, the average proportion of women on boards for all ASX companies rose from 8.7 per cent to 13.8 per cent in one year, with one in three new appointees to boards being women compared to one in 20 in 2009 (*The Australian*, 8 March 2012).

In the economic decision-making realm, the competitive pressures of market integration and shareholder activism make it almost certain that institutional isomorphism will expeditiously occur between proximate countries and states pursuing regional free trade agreements together. This is precisely the policy diffusion process that has taken place in Scandinavia and Europe with respect to mandatory corporate board gender quotas after Norway's first-mover law reform, but also in the New Zealand stock exchange two years after the ASX changed its corporate governance guidelines. Mirroring the reluctance to consider quotas in the political realm, quotas or even 'nudge' reporting mechanisms are unlikely to be adopted by US corporations until the gender balance of the executive board becomes a competitive advantage in global markets. This could happen, given Catalyst's research, and especially if new research shows that increases in the number of female board directors in Europe significantly improves the performance of companies (Joy et al. 2007).

The microcosm example of the movement for gender balance on boards reveals the multi-scalar policy diffusion, learning and institutional isomorphism that characterise global governance today. These governance dynamics are a response to new knowledge about women's productive capacities and about how diversity and collective gendered behaviour shapes economic decision-making and the workings of competitive markets. Governance of gender in the economy is occurring simultaneously in multiple, mutually reinforcing settings. In some contexts, it is affecting changes in gender relations not previously thought possible, including breaking down legal and social barriers to women's equality with men. For instance, the Women, Business and the Law Group

(WBL) (Women, Business and the Law 2012) objectively measures legal differentiations based on gender in 141 economies around the world, covering six areas: accessing institutions, using property, getting a job, providing incentives to work, building credit and going to court. Within these six areas, there were a total of 45 gender differences, covering issues such as being able to get a job, sign a contract, register a business, open a bank account, own property, work at night or in all industries, and retire at the same age as men. A total of 103 countries have at least one legal form of gender differentiation in economic access, and 24 countries have more than ten. From 2009 to 2011 the WBL recorded 46 legal and regulatory changes occurring in 39 economies relating to these areas; 41 of these changes were toward more gender parity. The highest number of changes was in the sphere of 'getting a job', in which there were 19 reforms. Gender equality is now one of the goals of neoliberal governance of the macroeconomy; it is no longer represented as costly, 'a social aspiration to be achieved in good economic times'. Rather, it is now inequality that is considered costly.

As in other areas of the global political economy, gender equality is the focus of new private forms of governance, especially private–public partnerships (Bexell 2012; Pattberg et al. 2012). These partnerships are transnational, involving business, government and philanthropic actors. They often overlap and are closely tied by a shared 'rational' consensus that maximising gender equality is the key to increasing global economic growth and competitiveness. States are open to this new mode of governing because they are increasingly constrained by a politics of austerity that mandates public funding only for goods and activities that support business and market expansion. Elisabeth Prügl and I (Prügl and True 2014) define them as 'business partnerships' which are reshaping gender relations across political economies through norm creation, diffusion and processes of learning. We argue that this attention to gender equality in the business world is inextricable from the neoliberal transformation of politics and policy-making, where we see the progressive merging of the prerogatives of profit and efficiency with the provision of public goods and values such as equity and justice. The question of how gender in the global political economy is being governed leads us logically and programmatically to ask: by whom? (What actors are involved in transnational business partnerships for gender equality?) And for what purpose? (Whose interests are being constructed and advanced through them?) These matters are the focus of the next section.

GOVERNANCE ACTORS

The global governance of gender has reconfigured state and global power, involving a wide *nébulese* of actors (Cox with Sinclair 1996). Feminist analysis is concerned not just with the masculinity or femininity of governance actors, be they institutions, organisations or elites, but also, importantly, with the way gender divisions and ideologies structure the governance of political economies, including those actors who are authorised to govern (Harding 1986; Locher and Prügl 2001). In a globalised context we are witnessing new roles for business and the state. As power has shifted away from legislatures toward a range of technocratic, private actors, corporations behave more like states, building corporate patriotism, emphasising so-called 'soft issues', such as their value to society, poverty eradication, environmental sustainability and gender equality, and delivering community well-being. By contrast, states are coming to behave more like traditional corporations, branding themselves, using business-speak, downsizing and privatising. The new focus on gender equality and economic competitiveness is part of this transformation in the identities of the state and transnational business.

Whereas government action on behalf of gender equality is well institutionalised, private business has only more recently become an actor and advocate of this cause. Governments and international organisations are partnering with businesses and corporate actors to advance gender equality. The novelty of public–private partnerships lies precisely in the fact that actors driven largely by private and economic motives have entered the realm of public policy-making and are participating in making rules and implementing policies about the appropriate gender divisions of labour within and across states. In an article on these 'business partnerships' for gender equality and women's empowerment, Elisabeth Prügl and I (Prügl and True 2014) examine four governance initiatives involving public and private actors. They are instructive for illuminating these changing actors and relationships. All four share a transnational, networked approach to governing and authorise for-profit business actors as participants in public policy and governance.

Private business actors with public involvement ostensibly delivering public goods lead two of the four initiatives that we studied: the World Economic Forum's Gender Parity and Women's Leaders Programme and the Goldman Sachs 10000 Women Programme. The other two initiatives – the EU's Gender Balance in Economic Decision-Making Programme and the United Nations Global Compact Women's Empowerment Principles – are led by public government actors involving business as a partner in making commitments to promote gender equality and join a network for that purpose.

The World Economic Forum is a non-profit institution that invites key stakeholders and leaders from both the public and private sectors to collaborate on a range of global governance issues, including enacting changes towards more gender equity both in public policy and within corporations. However, the first Corporate Gender Gap report (World Economic Forum 2012), revealing the gap between the aspiration of gender equality in an organisation and the reality, was initiated only in 2011, while the Global Gender Gap report (Hausmann et al. 2010), which ranked states in this respect, was launched in 2006. Goldman Sachs is a private investment firm and its 10000 Women Programme involves an US$100 million investment over five years. The programme offers practical business and management education to potential women entrepreneurs in 20 developing countries. The firm partners with business schools and other private and non-profit organisations in delivering this programme, intending to influence further investments in women entrepreneurs by business and government. The Women's Empowerment Principles amount to a global corporate code of conduct with regard to enhancing gender equality. They were developed through an international process of multi-stakeholder consultation beginning in 2010. The EU's programme pursues a narrower goal of bringing more women from government, unions and private sectors into positions of decision-making, including gender balance in business leadership.

The four business partnerships operate through multiple stakeholder networks with considerable overlapping membership among them. They differ in their emphasis on agenda-setting, networking, formulation of new standards and benchmarks, versus the implementation of programmes; however, they all share an interest in leveraging social and policy change. As well as delivering governance tools and outcomes for states, corporations and individuals, the business partnerships for gender equality and women's empowerment have spawned a new network of global elite actors. This network includes think-tanks such as Catalyst and the World Economic Forum; the business schools of prestigious US and European universities; advocacy groups such as the 30% Club in the US and the UK; policy entrepreneurs in government, such as Melanne Verveer, former head of the Global Women's Issues office in the US State Department; and global media magnates, such as Facebook's Sheryl Sandberg, whose 'TED women' talks and autobiographical book, *Lean In* (Sandberg and Scovell 2013), have further helped to popularise the movement supporting women's leadership. Together, these actors are forging a new policy consensus, problematising gender inequalities and providing business-friendly solutions.

The strong presence of US and European elites within the network of actors suggests a Eurocentric bias to the policy consensus about global gender equality. *The Economist* (2011) reported that 'women are storming emerging world boardrooms globally'. This is not quite the case yet, but the situation could rapidly change. Currently, 32 per cent of senior managers in Chinese corporations are women, compared with 23 per cent in US corporations; 11 per cent of chief executive officers (CEOs) in large Indian companies are female, compared with 3 per cent of Fortune 500 CEOs in the US. However, just 8.5 per cent of board directors in Chinese corporations and 5.3 per cent in Indian corporations are female, compared with the 12.6 per cent women directors in US corporations (World Economic Forum 2011b). Taking emerging market corporations as a group, only 7.4 per cent of directors are women, compared with 11.8 per cent in the corporations of industrialised countries (Gladman and Lamb 2013). Global competition may yet accelerate the progress toward gender-balanced leadership, especially when set against the familiar journalistic slogan that 'men made the global financial crisis and it is up to women to clean it up' (Prügl 2011a; O'Connor 2008). Financial crises and scandals create an opportunity for contesting the normal, masculinist ways of governing the global economy, an opportunity that is often lost when attention is diverted to blameworthy individuals, rather than structures of governance.

One of the challenges of initiatives to change the gender balance within the institutions of economic governance is to create more opportunities for more women in an area where there are inherently very few opportunities. Generally, it is only women and men who are highly educated with MBAs, PhDs and the like, possessed of technical expertise in an area and already having access to elite business and government networks through their careers, who will be considered for positions on global regulatory, corporate or statutory public boards. Given that power is increasingly wielded by private economic actors, including corporations, the men currently filling those boardroom seats are likely to be reluctant to give them up since that involves relinquishing an important site of power. Although easy to count the gains, increasing the number of women at economic decision-making tables may be very difficult to achieve, precisely because it is most threatening to existing power structures. During an evaluation of a gender mainstreaming programme in the Asia Pacific Economic Cooperation (APEC), the most hotly contested recommendation was the one to establish a voluntary register of qualified women candidates from which member economies could select in order to increase the number of women appointed to the APEC Business Advisory Council (ABAC) from the then figure of only three out of 64 members (True 2008b). Achieving a critical mass of women on boards, as the 30% Club movement suggests, may indeed be the strategy most likely to put a chink in the armour of corporate and male power.

TRANSFORMING ECONOMIC POWER? IMPLICATIONS OF GOVERNING GENDER

The governance of gender and the gender of governance are underpinned by normative arguments and linked to economic and ethical recovery after the recession. Global governance is often seen as a politically and ideologically neutral terrain, but this is far from the case. One of the key purposes of feminist perspectives is to lay clear the gendered assumptions and material structures underpinning governance projects. Like other IPE scholars, feminists are concerned about the extent to which democratic principles of inclusion, representation, transparency, accountability and public debate are potentially undermined by rationalist and informalised modes of global governance (True 2008a). Democratic deficits are problematic from feminist perspectives, not least because the expansion of political participation en masse has brought major gains in social and economic equality over the past century.

From this concern with democratic legitimacy, the normative assumptions and the processes of change set in motion by recent global gender governance initiatives need to be scrutinised. The initiatives of the World Bank/IFC, World Economic Forum and Goldman Sachs all make the assumption that business leads social change and that states should support rather than regulate their role in structuring the economy. They perceive gender equality to be always 'good for business', rather than potentially challenging or forcing the rethinking of business norms and values. Moreover, there is hardly any admission of the potential trade-offs between economic growth and human well-being outcomes, not least because women's labour is seen to be an 'elastic' factor of production, able to sustain reproductive economies and expand further into market economies without any apparent 'externalities' or 'adjustment costs' in gendered social relations (Elson 2002). For instance, an issue of epidemic proportions – namely, that of violence against women and girls – is rarely addressed at all within economic governance agendas or by multilateral economic institutions. The issue is now being taken up by the World Bank because gender-based violence has been identified as a major 'constraint' on gender equality and women's agency, which are both seen as crucial drivers of economic development (Women, Business and the Law, forthcoming 2014). Yet the evidence is growing that economic policies can exacerbate and fuel gender-based violence, especially in the context of globalisation and the stress, illness and survival strategies enforced by financial recession, government austerity, and situations of transition and post-conflict economic recovery (True 2012).

However, gender equality agendas are potentially constructing new norms of governance. Corporations and states are engaged in changing gender norms and removing institutional barriers to help markets function more effectively and legitimately. They are empowering many individual women and achieving this empowerment by breaking down traditional oppressive social relations codified in laws and customs to free up market activity. Such approaches, however, do not completely address the roots of women's oppression in social and political structures, as well as economic relations. The governance of the global political economy increasingly attends to gender equality and gender balance in the formal, market economy, but lacks recognition of the often unremunerated economic activity related to social reproduction and provisioning, which is crucial for markets to operate efficiently. This neglect of the reproductive economy means that even innovative forms of global governance that advance women's status and opportunities in some dimensions may reinscribe, rather than redress, gender inequalities overall and have limited impact on women's equal participation. The issue of who takes care of the children, the elderly and the household economy, which has been a central focus of analysis for feminist political economists, is not adequately addressed within any of the global governance frameworks discussed in this chapter.

The new gender-sensitive governance largely fails to address the unequal distributional consequences of globalisation and the post-crisis politics of austerity which have negatively affected women's and men's employment and access to services, often in an 'equalizing-down' fashion (Fawcett Society 2011; True 2012). The problem is that global governance initiatives seek to diffuse knowledge and policy models based on comparative evidence, but they do not closely study the national and local implementation or impacts of high-level agenda-setting, benchmarking, ranking and other strategic activities. What if equality is not good for business in all cases? Is there still a case to be made for promoting equality as a societal and global priority? There is no question that the global governance of gender is advancing women's economic opportunities and strengthening feminist calls for gender-equal global economic development. However, governance at the global or transnational level is also severely limited with respect to acknowledging women's household economic activity and the construction of gender inequality in and through the market. We need only think of local and global market prices for care-giving, social and educational services, compared with professional services such as law, finance and accounting, and reflect on the gendered hierarchies that have contributed to that differential valuation and indeed, by some accounts, the global financial crisis.

In this respect, the focus of the governance of gender on targeting women on boards and in economic decision-making is ethically questionable. These initiatives represent opportunities for a qualified, privileged few and are dependent on elite men giving up some power. While attention to women's participation in governance marks significant progress in the acceptance of gender equality as a societal – even global – value, global governance, with the exception of the UN Women's Empowerment Principles, has not been concerned with the conduct of businesses towards women employees outside the leadership ranks. The idea that principled business is necessary to uphold state commitments to human rights, and indeed to realise women's rights to decent employment in particular (not to mention other economic and social rights), is not the orthodoxy (Montreal Principles 2004; Balakrishnan 2005). Human rights perspectives increasingly come up against purely economic rationales for development and gender equality (True 2009). They cause us to reflect critically on the impact of actions to increase the number of women in positions of economic power. Will more gender balance in governance improve outcomes for citizens, including for women employees and female-headed households, as well as generate returns for investors and support macro indicators of growth?

Scholars of gender and governance do not assume that there is a one-to-one relationship between 'who governs' and 'for whom'; that is, between progress in the economic, political and social dimensions of equality. Current scholarship on 'critical mass' in the field of gender and politics is sceptical of the theory that women-friendly policies can only be achieved through coalitions of women representatives. Indeed, this research suggests that the backlash against women and women-friendly policies may increase as the number of women rises, and that a skewed gender balance or a few outstanding women leaders as role models may achieve similar or better results for women than any 'critical mass' (Childs and Krook 2007; Beckwith and Cowell-Meyers 2007).

CONCLUSION

The global governance of gender is highly salient and visible in the post-global financial crisis environment (Prügl 2011b; Elias 2013; Roberts 2012; Hozic and True 2013). Compelling analysis reveals that gendered political, economic and social inequalities across political economies are a major constraint on the growth and competitiveness of economies. Gender equality in economic participation and gender balance in economic governance are increasingly seen as significant drivers of new and more sustainable forms of economic growth. As such, they are key issues on policy agendas within and across states and at the global level. New transnational actors and networks have arisen to promote the integration of gender into economic policy-making and governance, largely drawing on these rational, economic arguments.

At the same time as gender equality has become part of the 'core business' of economic management, the skewed gender profile of economic decision-makers has been made visible. Thanks to the availability of a growing body of empirical evidence, governments and firms are also becoming aware of the potentially negative performance implications of their largely male-dominated governance structures. Women's leadership in economic governance is seen as a panacea, restoring confidence in markets and embodying hope that socio-economic disadvantage, created by gender, sexuality, race, nationality and migrant status, and so on, might be redressed and thus globalisation might begin to work for everyone.

Feminist perspectives on global governance have shaped and been shaped by these debates. They are centrally concerned with who governs, how they govern, and with what social, political and economic outcomes, especially for groups historically marginalised in the global economy. Feminists view gender balance in governance as a necessary, but not sufficient condition for enabling increased access to economic resources and making the goal of living a dignified life more achievable for more people. How we govern is as crucial for this outcome. Without accountability to publics concerned with human development outcomes, it is possible that decision-makers, regardless of gender, may advance economic agendas that make equal access to resources, let alone decision-making power, more unrealisable for many women and men. Thus, increasing women's participation in economic governance is only one dimension of a feminist perspective on governance. It must be supplemented by other approaches to global governance that address the devaluation of feminised sectors of economies, promote rights and resources to support workers, particularly migrant care workers, and expand the spaces for women to contribute to political debates about economic policies and priorities, as well as governance arrangements.

NOTES

1. The indicators consist of data on: (a) gender differences in labour force participation rates; (b) gender ratios of estimated female-to-male earned income; (c) a qualitative variable calculated through the World Economic Forum's Executive Opinion Survey (wage equality for similar work); (d) the ratio of women to men among legislators, senior officials and managers; and (e) among technical and professional workers (WEF 2012a: 4).
2. World Economic Forum Press Release, 'Slow progress in closing global economic gender gap, new major study finds', 24 October 2012, Davos, Switzerland.
3. Stated on the World Economic Forum website, http://www.weforum.org/issues/global-gender-gap, accessed 1 May 2012.
4. Interestingly, new research based on a data set of 22 countries and corporations constituting 70 per cent market capitalisation shows a strong correlation between the level of women's full-time labour market participation and the proportion of women on corporate boards in a country. Renee Adams, 'To reach the board women need support to stay in the workforce', *Conversation*, 8 March 2013. See http://theconversation.com/to-reach-the-board-women-need-support-to-stay-in-the-workforce-12685, accessed 6 June 2013.
5. A free float-adjusted market capitalisation weighted index designed to measure the equity market performance of developed and emerging markets (see http://www.msci.com/products/indices/tools/index.html#ACWI, accessed 9 June 2013).
6. See for example, the APEC Leaders Statement, 'Sustaining growth, connecting the region', 17th APEC Economic Leaders' Meeting, Singapore 14–15 November 2009; also Joint Statement, 21st APEC Ministerial Meeting, Singapore, 11–12 November 2009.
7. These descriptive statistics are based on the author's analysis of the Governance Metrics International data set 2000–12 (Gladman and Lamb 2013).
8. The difference in the mean proportions of women's representation between the countries with quotas and those without quotas is highly statistically significant.

REFERENCES

Balakrishnan, Radhika (2005), 'Why MES with human rights? Integrating macroeconomic strategies with human rights', Working Paper, Marymount Manhattan College, USA.
Beckwith, Karen and Kimberley Cowell-Meyers (2007), 'Sheer numbers: critical representation thresholds and women's political representation', *Perspectives on Politics*, **5** (3), 553–65.
Bexell, Magdalena (2012), 'UN–business partnerships for women's empowerment', *International Feminist Journal of Politics*, **14** (3), 389–407.
Bouchet, Michel-Henry and Robert Isaak (2011),'Is the financial crisis a male syndrome?', *Businessweek*, 29 November, http://www.businessweek.com/authors/3298-michel-henry-bouchet-and-robert-isaak.
Childs, Sarah and Mona Lena Krook (2007), 'Critical mass theory and women's political representation', *Political Studies*, **56**, 725–36.
Clinton, Hillary (2010),'Development in the 21st century', *Foreign Policy*, January, http://www.foreign-policy.com/articles/2010/01/06/hillary_clinton_on_development_in_the_21st_century?page=full, accessed 21 October 2013.
Credit Suisse Research Institute (2012), *Gender Diversity and the Impact on Corporate Performance 2005–2011*, Zurich: Credit Suisse.
Cox, Robert W. with Timothy J. Sinclair (1996), *Approaches to World Order*, Cambridge: Cambridge University Press.
Cutler, Claire (2003), *Private Power and Global Authority: Transnational Merchant Law in the Global Political Economy*, Cambridge: Cambridge University Press.
Cutler, Claire, Virginia Haufler and Tony Porter (eds) (1999), *Private Authority and International Affairs*, New York: State University of New York Press.
Daly, Kevin (2007), 'Gender equality, growth and global ageing', Goldman Sachs Global Economics Paper No. 154, 3 April.

The Economist (2006), 'A guide to womenomics: forget China, India and the internet, economic growth is driven by women', 12 April.

The Economist (2011), 'Women are storming boardrooms', 27 April.

Elias, Juanita (2013), 'Davos woman to the rescue of global capitalism: postfeminist politics and competitiveness promotion at the World Economic Forum', *International Political Sociology*, 7 (2), 152–69.

Elson, Diane (2002), 'Gender justice, human rights, and neoliberal economic policies', in Maxine Molyneux and Shahra Razavi (eds), *Gender Justice, Development, and Rights*, New York: Oxford University Press, pp. 79–115.

Fawcett Society (2011), *A Life Raft for Women's Equality*, London: Fawcett Society.

Gladman, Kimberly and Michelle Lamb (2013), 'Governance Metrics International Ratings, 2013 Women on Boards Survey', April, http://www.gmi3D.com.

Goldman Sachs (2009), 'Australia's hidden resource: the economic case for increasing female participation', December.

Goldman Sachs (2011), 'Closing the gender gap: plenty of potential economic upside', Auckland, August.

Harding, Sandra (1986), *The Science Question in Feminism*, Ithaca, NY: Cornell University Press.

Hausmann, Richard, Laura Tyson and Saadia Zahidi (2010), 'Global Gender Gap Report', December, Geneva: World Economic Forum.

Hozic, Aida and Jacqui True (2013), 'The spectre of gender, crisis and haute finance: theorizing IPE in the new millennium', paper presented at the Annual Convention of the International Studies Association, San Francisco, CA, 1–5 April.

Joy, Nancy M. Carter, Harvey M. Wagner and Sriram Narayanan (2007), 'The bottom line: corporate performance and women's representation on boards', Catalyst.

Krook, Mona Lena (2010), *Quotas for Women in Politics: Gender and Candidate Selection Reform Worldwide*, New York: Oxford University Press.

Locher, Birgit and Elisabeth Prügl (2001), 'Feminism and constructivism: worlds apart or sharing the middle ground?', *International Studies Quarterly*, 45 (1), 111–29.

McKinsey & Company (2007), *Women Matter, Gender Diversity: A Corporate Performance Driver*, New York.

'Montreal Principles on Women's Economic, Social and Cultural Rights' (2004), *Human Rights Quarterly*, 26 (3), 3–7.

O'Connor, Sarah (2008), 'Icelandic women to clean up "male mess"', *Financial Times*, 13 October.

Pattberg, Philipp, Frank Biermann, Sander Chan and Aysem Merg (eds) (2012), *Public–Private Partnerships for Sustainable Development: Emergence, Impacts, and Legitimacy*, Cheltenham, UK and Northampton, MA, USA: Edward Elgar.

Porter, Tony and Karsten Ronit (2010), *The Challenges of Global Business Authority: Democratic Renewal, Stalemate or Decay?* Albany, NY: State University of New York Press.

Prügl, Elisabeth (2011a), *Transforming Masculine Rule: Agriculture and Rural Development in the European Union*, Ann Arbor, MI: University of Michigan Press.

Prügl, Elisabeth (2011b), 'Diversity management and gender mainstreaming as technologies of government', *Politics and Gender*, 7 (1), 71–89.

Prügl, Elisabeth (2012), '"If Lehman Brothers had been Lehman Sisters . . .": gender and myth in the aftermath of the financial crisis', *International Political Sociology*, 6 (March), 21–35.

Prügl, Elisabeth and Jacqui True (2014), 'Equality means business? Governing gender through public–private partnerships', *Review of International Political Economy*, DOI: 10.1080/09692290.2013.849277.

Roberts, Adrienne (2012), 'Financial crisis, financial firms . . . and financial feminism? The rise of transnational business feminism and the necessity of Marxist-Feminist IPE', *Socialist Studies/Études socialistes*, 8 (2), 85–108.

Rosenau, James N. (1995), 'Governance in the twenty-first century', *Global Governance*, 1 (1), 13–43.

Sandberg, Sheryl and Nell Scovell (2013), *Lean In: Women, Work and the Will to Lead*, New York: Alfred P. Knopf.

Slaughter, Anne-Marie (1997), 'The real New World Order', *Foreign Affairs*, 76, 183–97.

Thaler, Richard H. and Cass R. Sunstein (2008), *Nudge: Improving Decisions about Health, Wealth, and Happiness*, New Haven, CT: Yale University Press.

Towns, Ann. E. (2010), *Women and States: Norms and Hierarchies in International Society*, Cambridge: Cambridge University Press.

True, Jacqui (2008a), 'Global accountability and transnational networks: the Women Leaders' Network and Asia Pacific Economic Cooperation', *Pacific Review*, 21 (1), 1–26.

True, Jacqui (2008b), 'Independent assessment of the ECOTECH implementation of APEC working groups and SOM taskforces: Gender Focal Point Network', APEC Secretariat, Singapore, May.

True, Jacqui (2009), 'Trading-off gender equality for Global Europe: the European Union and free trade agreements', *European Foreign Affairs Review*, 14 (4), 723–42.

True, Jacqui (2012), *The Political Economy of Violence Against Women*, New York: Oxford University Press.

True, Jacqui (2013), 'Counting women, balancing gender: increasing women's participation in governance', *Politics and Gender*, **9** (3), 351–9.

United Kingdom Equalities and Human Rights Commission (2011), *Women on Boards*, February.

United Nations Development Programme (2012), *Powerful Synergies: Gender Equality, Economic Development and Environmental Sustainability*, New York: United Nations.

Women, Business and the Law (2012), *Removing Barriers to Economic Inclusion: Measuring Gender Parity in 141 Countries*, Washington, DC: IFC/World Bank.

Women, Business and the Law (forthcoming 2014), *Removing Restrictions to Enhance Gender Equality*, Washington, DC: IFC/World Bank.

World Bank (2006), 'Gender equality as smart economics: a World Bank Group gender action plan (fiscal years 2007–2010)', Washington, DC, September.

World Bank (2008), *Doing Business*, Washington, DC: World Bank Group.

World Bank (2012), *World Development Report: Gender Equality and Development*, Washington, DC: World Bank.

World Economic Forum (WEF) (2011a), *Global Gender Gap Report*, Geneva.

World Economic Forum (WEF) (2011b), *Corporate Gender Gap Report 2010*, Geneva.

World Economic Forum (WEF) (2012), *Global Gender Gap Report*, Geneva.

Young, Brigitte (2013), 'Structural power and the gender biases of technocratic network governance in finance', in Gülay Caglar, Elisabeth Prügl and Susanne Zwingel (eds), *Feminist Strategies in International Governance*, London: Routledge, pp. 267–82.

19 Leveraging private governance for public purpose: business, civil society and the state in labour regulation
Frederick W. Mayer

For years Apple, perhaps the world's most iconic brand, appeared largely unresponsive to pressures to improve pay and working conditions of the Chinese labourers who assembled its wildly profitable iPod, iPhone and iPad products. Despite several exposés about treatment of workers in its supplier's Chinese factories, including extensive publicity of an apparent epidemic of suicides in 2010 at the plant producing the iPhone, Apple suffered no apparent commercial harm. In fairness, Apple, like virtually all modern corporations, had long stated its commitment to corporate social responsibility (CSR) and had conducted internal audits of many of its suppliers, but Apple resisted calls for disclosure of its audits or for third-party monitoring of its factories. As of August 2011, according to a long-time Beijing-based observer of business in China, Apple remained 'completely unfazed' by the pressures, including the negative publicity about the suicides.[1]

In the first three months of 2012, however, Foxconn, the Taiwanese-based electronics manufacturer that operates Apple's major assembly operations in China, announced significant wage increases, opened its factories to a camera crew from ABC's *Nightline* and brought in the Fair Labor Association (FLA) to conduct an audit of working conditions. At the end of March, when the FLA released its report, Apple and Foxconn openly admitted to non-compliance with China's labour laws and jointly announced their commitment to respond with major changes in working conditions and wages. Whether the steps Apple and Foxconn have announced will be taken in fact, and whether, if taken, they will change much for workers, remains unclear. Critics of the deal were certainly sceptical. Yet, Apple's stance was clearly a break from the past.

What happened? One interpretation is that the Apple–Foxconn story is a recapitulation of the first wave of CSR in which non-governmental organizations (NGOs) in the United States and Europe used the threat of negative publicity to compel lead firms to discipline the behaviour of their suppliers in developing countries (Gereffi et al. 2001). In this telling, Apple finally recognized a threat to its brand and used its clout to pressure Foxconn. It is likely that this dynamic played a part in the story. But there is good reason to believe that private governance, alone, would not have been sufficient to move Foxconn. Rather, it seems, the change at Foxconn also reflected two other dynamics. One was an increasingly restive and assertive Chinese workforce capable of pressuring Foxconn directly. The other was a growing determination of China's national and provincial governments to regulate labour conditions.

In this chapter, I argue that the Apple–Foxconn case illustrates a more general development in the evolution of the international political economy of governance. It is an argument about the co-evolution of the global economy and institutions of governance: private, social and public. I begin by characterizing the form of economic globalization and the governance challenge it poses, arguing, as I have elsewhere (Gereffi and Mayer 2006), that a consequence of globalization was a deficit of governance in the global economy. I then turn to a consideration of the rise of private governance in the form of CSR, codes of conduct for suppliers, auditing and monitoring capacities, and social labelling, among others. I consider, in particular, the circumstances under which there might be a sufficiently strong business case for corporate responsibility that purely private governance could provide strong labour self-regulation, and those in which it will likely be inadequate.

As many have documented, private governance has had some notable successes in promoting better labour practices (Vogel 2005). Nevertheless, private governance, alone, appears insufficient to meet the demand of society (Mayer and Gereffi 2010; Vogel 2009). Now the still unmet demand for governance, particularly in the emerging economies of China, India and Brazil, is driving a strengthening of the state. We should not expect, however, a reprise of the history of the creation of the welfare state, with its strong regulatory and social protection capacities and its minimal role for private governance. For the foreseeable future, private governance is here to stay. What seems to be emerging instead is a new form of tripartite governance in which still-limited public and societal institutions seek to leverage private governance for public purposes.

GLOBALIZATION AND THE GOVERNANCE DEFICIT

As Gereffi and I have argued, economic globalization created something of a global 'governance deficit' (Gereffi and Mayer 2006). When production shifted from developed nations with thick governance regimes to countries with both weak worker organizations and limited governmental regulatory and social protection capacities, business practices, including labour practices, increasingly lay beyond the effective reach of governance. We argued, further, following the logic of Polanyi (1944), that the widespread social protests against globalization were a predicable consequence of the governance deficit and constituted something of a global demand to regovern the market.

As the industrializing nations of the nineteenth and early twentieth centuries learned the hard way, an economy dominated by large industrial concerns required new forms of governance. In one form or another, the industrialized nations of Europe, North America, Japan and Australia established an array of regulatory and redistributional governance institutions. (Of course, other nations, notably the Soviet Union and China, rejected capitalism altogether.) By the second half of the twentieth century, these roughly comparable systems of governance had enabled the club of developed countries to establish a high degree of economic commerce with each other, a system Ruggie (1982) referred to as 'embedded liberalism'.

Then, economic globalization began to undermine that system. What followed marked a break from the past in two distinctive ways. The first was a 'global shift' (Dicken 2007) in the geography of global production. Manufacturing, particularly assembly operations, began to be outsourced from developed to developing countries with lower labour costs, most dramatically to China, but also to other locations in Asia and Latin America. Gereffi (2006: 9) summarized three drivers of the shift:

First, following the breakup of the former Soviet Union in 1989 and the end of the Cold War, about 3 billion workers from China, India, Russia, and Eastern Europe – half of the world's labour force – joined the capitalist world economy, creating a labour supply shock on a scale unlike anything experienced before. Second, technological changes associated with the Internet allowed a dramatic expansion of outsourcing and offshoring options in services as well as manufacturing, and this real-time connectivity has converted what were once segmented national labour markets into an integrated, global production system. Third, TNC [transnational corporation] business strategies have been unrelenting in their search for new efficiencies, especially on the labour side where substantial cost gains can be found.

The second break from the past was a change in the structure of industrial organization away from vertically integrated production to a new pattern of segmented production in which less profitable elements of the production process were outsourced to suppliers and coordinated through global value chains (GVCs) (Gereffi et al. 2005). Increasingly, final products sold in one market might have raw material inputs from several locations, include components manufactured in still others, and be assembled in yet another, all coordinated through a series of formal and informal contractual relationships. An implication of this new form of industrial organization and the nature of power relationships in GVCs was that a relatively small share of the profits was captured by suppliers and workers in developing countries, despite their growing share of production and exports.

Taken together, the two trends mean that developing countries account for an ever larger share of globally traded production and that a growing portion of that production is integrated into GVCs. One measure of these trends is the share of global value-added trade (which nets out imported inputs when calculating the value of exports), which has rocketed from 20 per cent in 1990, to 30 per cent in 2000, to over 40 per cent in 2010 (UNCTAD 2013: 13). The extent to which developing countries are integrated into GVCs as well as their location in the chain – whether they tend to be 'upstream' producers of relatively unprocessed commodities or somewhat more 'downstream' producers engaged in a mix of lower- and higher-value-added activities – varies considerably. The large Asian economies, most notably China, increasingly operate in the middle of GVCs, whereas countries such as Brazil and South Africa, more reliant on commodity exports, tend to be located more 'upstream'.

The changed global economic landscape had profound implications for governance related to labour. First, a growing share of work took place beyond the reach of effective governance. The shift of production from developed to developing countries partially disembedded the market from those institutions of the welfare state that had evolved to govern labour issues in the developed nations (Gereffi and Mayer 2006). Globally traded production increasingly shifted to developing countries with limited state regulatory capacity and minimum social protection. Worker organizations and other civil-society institutions in those countries were also often lacking or ineffective. And, at the global level, international institutions had little bite.

Second, the organization of production into global value chains compounded the governance problem. Chains are commonly organized around very large 'lead' firms who contract with a number of suppliers, who in turn contract with even more sub-suppliers, and so forth (Gereffi et al. 2005). Lead firms typically have considerable market power in their supply chains, and are therefore able to capture most of the rents produced by the whole chain (Mayer and Millberg 2013). Suppliers, often in competition with each other and under considerable pressure to keep costs down, have incentives to pay their workers as little as possible and to cut corners on work rules. And workers, particularly those employed by small suppliers at the extremity of the chain, have very little ability to demand better pay or working conditions. The concentration of market power in the hands of large lead firms, therefore, meant that developing-country governments found themselves at a severe bargaining disadvantage as they competed with each other to attract foreign investment, further limiting their ability to provide meaningful regulation, a new wrinkle on Vernon's old prediction of 'sovereignty at bay' (Vernon 1971).

Taken together, the incongruence between the landscape of industrial organization and the geography of production on the one hand, and the asymmetry of power between lead firms and production workers on the other, greatly limited the effectiveness of traditional institutions of labour governance. Given the absence of strong international institutions, the weakness of organized labour and other civil-society organizations in the new locations of production, and the limited capacities of state regulatory and distributive capacities in most developing countries, the result was a global deficit of governance.

THE RISE OF PRIVATE GOVERNANCE

The rise of private governance, in the form of codes of conduct and monitoring of suppliers, can be viewed as a partial remedy to the deficit. As Polanyi (1944) had observed about the tumultuous era of rapid industrialization a century earlier, disembedding the market from systems of governance triggered a societal response. Worker organizations and other NGOs in the developed world, reeling from the loss of jobs in manufacturing and shocked by exposés of labour and environmental exploitation, began to push back at the system. In the United States, the negotiations for the North American Free Trade Agreement (NAFTA) provided a particular catalyst for social mobilization (Mayer 1998). Globally, the 1990s were marked by the rapid rise of what could, by the end of the decade, be described as a global social movement (Bandy and Smith 2005). By the end of the 1990s, as the 'Battle in Seattle' dramatically demonstrated, resistance had become much broader and more international (Thomas 2000).

Initially, discontent with globalization had only limited success in pressuring national governments and international organizations to adopt more effective policies. In the context of NAFTA, discontent translated into supplemental agreements on labour and environment, but the labour agreement, in particular, was not strong (Mayer 1998). Similar efforts to link social issues to the World Trade Organization (WTO) met with even less success (Cho 2005). But in the new structures of global production, social activists discovered a new point of leverage for pushing back at the system: the same bargaining power used by lead firms to demand price, quality and reliable delivery from their suppliers could be harnessed to demand better treatment of workers and other social goals in the supply chain.

Thus was born the phenomenon of private governance. The campaigns to force Nike and other high-visibility brands to improve labour practices in their supply chains has been well documented (Gereffi et al. 2001; Locke 2007). Under the banner of corporate social responsibility, major corporations began to adopt codes of conduct for their suppliers, conduct or commission audits of their suppliers, and in some cases enforce compliance. In the last two decades, regimes of private governance have matured, to the point that virtually every corporation's annual report trumpets its commitment to corporate responsibility and highlights some measures the firm is taking in this regard. There remain significant questions, however, about the extent, effectiveness and sustainability of private governance.

Although the initial wave of private governance clearly came in response to pressures from civil society, enthusiasts for private governance argue that businesses have learned that they can do 'well' by doing 'good', that there is a business case for CSR (Carroll and Shabana 2010; Tonello 2011). Certainly, a more satisfied, better-trained and stable workforce can be a source of efficiency. Just as new technologies of production that improve efficiency constantly enter business practice, treating workers better might be such an innovation. For example, the British retailer Marks & Spencer is reported to have:

> worked in partnership with factories to improve process efficiency as a means to increase wages, reduce working hours and protect the quality of products. Productivity in the Bangladeshi Ethical Model Factories increased by 42%, while staff turnover reduced from 10% to 2.5%, and absenteeism reduced from 10% to 1.5%. (Doughty Centre for Corporate Responsibility 2011)

Similarly, Esquel, maker of cotton apparel, has discovered that investments in communities where its long-staple cotton is grown and ginned provide it with a more reliable and better-quality supply of cotton fibre.[2] The British confectioner Cadbury has come to believe that the sustainability of its supply of high-quality cocoa makes investments in rural communities a good business practice (Cadbury 2012).

Alternatively, a reputation for responsibility can provide a competitive advantage in some markets. The most familiar example of product differentiation is the case of Fair Trade Coffee and other fair trade products, for which labour practices are part of what the consumer buys when they purchase the good. Demand for fair trade products has grown rapidly, particularly in Europe, and continues to expand. In 2012, for example, sales of fair trade products boomed in Britain, jumping 18 per cent from the previous year according to one report (Smithers 2013). In addition, it should be noted, when businesses occupy relatively protected market niches and can, therefore, capture substantial economic rents, there may be enough 'slack' in the system to enable managers to express their own preferences by engaging in CSR beyond what would be strictly justified by the business case (Reinhardt et al. 2008).

But the self-interest of businesses, or of business executives, is unlikely to solve the problems to which various corporate responsibility initiatives are a response. To cite instances in which there appears to be a business case for progressive labour practices only gets us so far. Having demonstrated the possibility of a business case, the question becomes under what circumstances it is most likely that there will really be one. Two assumptions are implicit in the logic for a business case. The first is that there are real cost savings and/or possibilities for competitive advantage from better labour practices by suppliers. The second is that the lead firm enjoys sufficient power in its supply chain to compel their adoption. Let us consider each in turn.

Higher wages, better work conditions and greater investments in the workforce can lower the costs of production when production requires more-skilled labour inputs and when workforce stability improves efficiency. When, on the other hand, less-skilled labour is sufficient and high turnover rates present little problem, it is likely that greater investments in workers will simply translate into higher production costs. In the apparel sector, for example, a maker of lower-end apparel sold under several brand names reported that it will move production out of China rather than pay higher wages, a move it claims is necessitated by the demands of the market:

> When wages are US$100 per month, you can produce for Walmart; if $200 per month, for JC Penney; if $300 per month, for Macy's and Dillard; and if $400 or more, only for Nieman Marcus or Saks Fifth Avenue. Wage increases in China and the efficiency of workers are now reaching equilibrium.[3]

Similarly, although more progressive CSR policies with respect to workers can be a way to differentiate oneself and create competitive advantage, it is not clear how far consumer sympathy for workers in distant lands extends. If, for example, low wages are the norm in other countries, even a very low-paying job in a global supply chain may seem better than the alternative (and, indeed, may be) and therefore elicit little willingness to alter buying habits. Consumer sensitivity to social conditions in the workplace likely varies depending on the product. Brands whose market share depends less on product performance than on intangible attributes are likely to be more vulnerable (Mayer and Gereffi 2010). Even the most successful example, that of Fair Trade Coffee, still accounted for only 1 per cent of world coffee consumption in 2008, according to the United Nations (UN) Food and Agriculture Organization (Pay 2009). Interestingly, some of the most progressive corporations seem not to view their progressive labour practices as a source of competitive advantage. GAP, for example, a clothing retailer that has some of the most well-developed codes of conduct for its suppliers and most aggressive monitoring of them, makes virtually no effort to use its CSR practices to differentiate its brand.

Finally, even assuming a desire on the part of lead firms to press their suppliers to adopt better labour practices, whether because of cost or competitive advantage, the ability of firms to alter the behaviour of their suppliers will depend in large part on power relationships in the value chain. This in turn hinges on the alternatives available to actors at different locations in the chain. If a supplier has no choice but to supply to a particular lead firm, while the lead firm has many actual (or possible) suppliers, the lead firm will have leverage to dictate contractual terms, power it could also use to insist on progressive labour practices if it so chose. On the other hand, if a lead firm is in a relatively competitive market and is reliant on a few large suppliers which themselves have multiple actual or potential customers, the lead firm will have less leverage over its supplier, and therefore less ability to dictate labour practices.

With these considerations in mind, we can now turn back to the question of why a business case, alone, might have failed to achieve substantial improvements in working conditions in Apple's Chinese assembly operations. On the face of things, Apple would appear a good candidate for a strong corporate responsibility regime: a powerful firm heavily dependent on its brand identity. Moreover, Apple's assembly labour costs were dwarfed by its profit margins. According to one study, 'only $10 or less in direct labour wages that go into an iPhone or iPad is paid to China workers' (Kraemer et al. 2011: 7), an estimate consistent with other studies. Given the enormous profit margins with the iPad and iPhone (by one estimate, Apple made US$270 per iPhone; Ganeshon

2010), Apple obviously could easily have afforded to double or triple wages if it were so inclined.

Yet, on closer inspection, Apple i-product supply chains did not fit well the profile of businesses most likely to adopt strong labour measures. First, although dependent on its brand identity, Apple buyers appeared to constitute a kind of 'brand community' whose loyalty was so strong that news about treatment of workers was unlikely to shake it (Muniz and O'Guinn 2001). Second, because Apple's assembly operations in China involved largely unskilled labour, there were few costs to high turnover and therefore few productivity gains to better labour practices. For both reasons, the business case for significant investments by Apple in its assembly workers in China was actually fairly weak.

Moreover, even if Apple had a desire to see its suppliers improve their labour practices, its leverage in its supply chain might be somewhat less than meets the eye. Apple's iPhone and iPad products are both assembled by only one supplier, Hon Hai Precision Industry Company, Ltd, generally known by its trade name, Foxconn. Foxconn is now the world's largest electronics manufacturer and China's largest exporter. It is, therefore, perhaps unique in its ability to manufacture new products on the scale and with the speed that Apple's business plan demands. In addition, Apple is not Foxconn's only customer: Foxconn sells to most of Apple's competitors. For these reasons, Apple may be at least as dependent on Foxconn as Foxconn is on Apple. As the *New York Times* reported in early 2012, 'some former Apple executives say there is an unresolved tension within the company: executives want to improve conditions within factories, but that dedication falters when it conflicts with crucial supplier relationships or the fast delivery of new products' (Duhigg and Barboza 2012).

In sum, in the absence of other considerations, Apple had little incentive to push Foxconn to improve its labour practices because there was no strong business case for doing so.

THE NEW PUSH FROM CIVIL SOCIETY

Societal institutions have long played an important role in governing economic activity, including the treatment of workers. In the industrialized world, collective bargaining by labour unions was historically perhaps the most significant means for workers to improve their wages, working conditions and benefits (Freeman 1981; Freeman and Medoff 1979; Nickell and Andrews 1983). The trade unions and other worker organizations of the nineteenth century enabled collective action by workers to push back at the excesses of early capitalism (and to secure labour regulation). By the mid-twentieth century, relatively stable patterns of production rooted to place, a generally sympathetic public and supportive labour legislation made labour unions an established feature of European and American society. Globalization, however, profoundly disrupted this arrangement by shifting production to locations that lacked strong unions or other societal institutions capable of restraining business practices.

The first wave of modern 'private governance' was also largely driven by civil society, as activists in the United States and Europe engaged in pressure campaigns against the labour practices of suppliers to high-profile Northern brands. The genius of the tactic lay in its use of the power of lead firms in their supply chains. By threatening a backlash by consumers in developed countries, these campaigns sought to compel firms to take responsibility for supplier labour practices in the developing world. But campaigns of this kind are ultimately extremely difficult to sustain, in part because they demand collective action by activists with little direct stake in the outcome, and in part because, as discussed above, their ultimate efficacy depends on the willingness of consumers to alter their buying patterns in response to information about the labour practices of producers.

Now, increasingly, civil-society pressure is coming from the strengthening of societal institutions in the developing countries where production for global supply chains takes place. Populist pushbacks at foreign corporations have a long history in developing countries, of course, but social organizing has gained considerable momentum in recent years, as partly evidenced by the rapid growth in the number of NGOs in the developing world. In part, this may represent a kind of social Kuznets Curve: as incomes have risen, worker expectations have risen as well, along with their ability to organize. Accelerating this trend, social media have lowered the cost of coordination and facilitated both new organizing and the ability of existing organizations to share information. And the new media have made it easier for civil-society organizations to share information with a wider public (and harder for corporations and governments to restrict such information-sharing). Taken together, these developments amount to a greater capacity of civil society in developing countries to bring pressure to bear on businesses.

Returning to the case of labour conditions in Apple's Foxconn assembly operations in China, pressures from civil society have been growing over the years. To be sure, the pressure came in part from increased attention in the Northern media. A 2006 *Daily Mail* report of working conditions in Shenzhen sparked a flurry of attention (Frost and Burnett 2007). A steady stream of media reports on factory conditions continued to trickle out in the following years, culminating in 2010 with a spike in media interest in an apparent epidemic of suicides at the Shenzhen plant. In 2011, an explosion in Foxconn's new Chengdu facility garnered further media attention.

Yet an exclusive focus on the Western media misses developments in Chinese civil society and the steady rise of local social pressures. For example, the Hong Kong-based Students and Scholars Against Corporate Misbehaviour (SACOM), organized in 2005 to investigate and publicize labour abuses Chinese manufacturing, was largely responsible for bringing the suicide issue to the attention of the Northern media. In 2010, it issued a series of reports on work conditions in Foxconn's Shenzhen plant, including documenting the large number of suicides (Chan and Pun 2010). That report also circulated in the large and growing transnational network of NGOs attending to the issue.

Accompanying this has been a rising assertiveness on the part of workers in China. As many observers of Chinese society have noted, workers today are less willing than their predecessors to accept the low wages and long hours that once characterized the export sector, and expect considerably more from their employers. One indication is an increase in the number of labour protests. In January 2012, 150 workers at Foxconn's Wuhan plant were reported to have protested against work conditions; some apparently threatened to jump off the roof if their demands were not met (Ong and Lee 2010). In February, the *China Labour Bulletin* identified 27 reports of strikes and protests in a variety of industries across China (Cheung 2012).

The confluence of media attention, NGO activism and worker unrest reached a crescendo in early 2012. One catalyst was a front-page story in the *New York Times* entitled:

'In China, human costs are built into the iPad' (Duhigg and Barboza 2012). Although the story appeared to have done little to dampen demand for the new iPad (Mosher 2012), the juxtaposition of the story with Apple's astonishing record profits seemed to strike a chord. The claim by a 'former Apple executive' that '[w]e've known about labour abuses in some factories for four years, and they're still going on' became grist to the mill for advocates pressuring for change (Duhigg and Barboza 2012).

By March 2012, SACOM and 48 other NGOs could author an open letter to Tim Cook, the new chief execeutive officer (CEO) of Apple, that called for an end to 'poverty wages', 'excessive and forced overtime', use of involuntary student labour, and exposure to hazardous conditions (SACOM 2012). Separately, two international unions – the International Metalworkers Federation and the International Trade Union Confederation – issued a joint statement with four NGOs – SumOfUs, makeITfair, GoodElectronics and SACOM – calling on Apple to hold fair union elections and to improve pay and working conditions (International Metal Workers Federation et al. 2012).

All of these pressures likely contributed to a change of direction by Apple and Foxconn. In January 2012, Apple and Foxconn announced that the Fair Labor Association (FLA), an international NGO, would be brought in to conduct an independent audit of work conditions. Shortly after that announcement, Foxconn announced a major raise in pay (Barboza 2012). In March 2012, Apple CEO Tim Cook travelled to China, touring the Foxconn factories and meeting with government officials.

Then, on 29 March, the FLA issued a strongly worded audit report, which documented 'excessive overtime and problems with overtime compensation; several health and safety risks; and crucial communication gaps that have led to a widespread sense of unsafe working conditions among workers' (Fair Labor Association 2012). In response, Foxconn 'pledged to sharply curtail working hours and significantly increase wages inside Chinese plants making electronic products for Apple and others' (Duhigg and Greenhouse 2012) Simultaneously, Apple issued a statement of full support for the FLA's recommendations (Franzen 2012).

THE RETURN OF THE STATE

Missing from the story so far, and conspicuous by its absence in the case of Apple–Foxconn's China operations, is the role of government. Yet, along with the private sector and societal response to the global governance deficit, governments have been responding too. What we are also seeing throughout the developing world, particularly in the larger emerging economies of China, Brazil, India and other middle-income countries, is a partial return of the state.

In the early years of globalization, when the rush was on to connect to the global economy, many countries were more interested in competing for foreign capital than in regulating its behaviour. As economies in the developing world have matured, though, and production has become less footloose, states have begun to reassert control. Stronger regulation has taken the form of increases in minimum wages, limits on overtime, restrictions on informal work, and stronger workplace safety rules, as well as greater willingness to enforce these policies. The trend is perhaps clearest in the large emerging economies such as Brazil and China, but it also appears to be under way in next-tier economies (Mayer and Pickles 2014). In Latin America, Piore and Schrank (2006: 2) report that 'Brazil, Chile, Costa Rica and the Dominican Republic have rededicated themselves to labour law enforcement in recent years. And potentially more fundamental reforms are under way from Argentina, where they are motivated by domestic party politics, to Central America, where they are a product of transnational pressure emanating from the campaign for a US–Central America Free Trade Agreement (FTA).'

Governments have also moved to raise and enforce minimum wage requirements. Part of the strategy in China involves substantial increases in the minimum wage. Although minimum wages are set at the provincial or city level, the central government set a national goal of a 13 per cent annual increase (Reuters 2012). From 2008 to 2012, minimum wages are reported to have increased by 12.6 per cent a year (China News Service 2013). Local governments in both Shenzhen and Sichuan, the province in which Foxconn's Chengdu facilities are located, both announced significant minimum wage increases in 2012. In Bangladesh, the government increased the minimum wage in the apparel sector by 80 per cent in response to a coalition of private actors, notably many of the major apparel buyers and labour advocates (Pickles 2012).

In China, the 2008 Labour Contract Law marked a reassertion of the state in protecting labour, specifically to deal with some of the ways enterprises were circumventing existing labour laws. Increasingly, employers had avoided offering permanent contracts by employing workers on a series of short-term contracts. Under the new law, employees must be given an open-ended permanent contract after a maximum of two short-term contracts (Lan and Pickles 2011). The law also made it much easier for workers to challenge labour practices. During the first quarter of 2008 alone, the labour courts in Dongguan, Shenzhen and Guangzhou accepted more than 10 000 cases, double the number over the same period the year before (Wang et al. 2009: 492).

In other formerly planned economies, notably those of Central and Eastern Europe, massive deregulation and privatization after 1989 weakened state institutions. Nevertheless, in most post-socialist states labour and health inspectorates, working hours laws, overtime regulations, and insurance and pensions requirements remained in place, and by the late 1990s and early 2000s some governments (such as Bulgaria and Slovakia) were providing those institutions with additional funding to ensure that basic working conditions were better regulated (Mayer and Pickles 2014; Pickles et al. 2006; Smith et al. 2008).

Similarly, as globalization proceeded, many developing countries lacked anything like the public pensions, unemployment insurance, public health care and other forms of social protection prevalent in the welfare states of developed countries, and relied more on traditional family and community institutions to provide these functions. As developing countries have become wealthier, though, they have also begun to provide more of these services. As Barrientos reports:

> In the last 15 years, there has been a great deal of innovation in social assistance programmes, and a step increase in their reach. Regular and reliable social assistance programmes based around income transfers, but increasingly combining access to basic services and investment in human development, now reach a significant proportion of those in poverty in the South. (Barrientos 2010: 21)

It is notable, however, that the growth of social assistance has not been in traditional social insurance programmes. Rather, the growth has been in many other forms of social assistance: the introduction and extension of pure income transfers, such as non-contributory pensions or child-based transfers; income transfers conditional on work, such as public works or employment guarantee schemes; income transfers combined with services, such as conditional cash transfers or integrated social assistance schemes; and, more recently, the development of integrated poverty reduction programmes (Barrientos 2010).

The emerging regulatory and social protection capacities of governments are part of a general swing back from the minimalist role envisioned by the neoliberal orthodoxy of the 1980s and 1990s. Increasingly, in the developing world, states are challenging strict adherence to free trade and recognizing a role for the state in industrial and other economic development policies (Rodrik 1999).

SYNERGISTIC GOVERNANCE

The re-emergence of the state does not, however, prefigure the rise in the developing world of the traditional welfare state. Rather, what seems to be happening might be called synergistic governance. Alongside the strengthening of public governance is a trend towards greater state coordination, with civil society and collaboration with institutions of private governance. Rather than replacing social and private governance, governments appear to be finding ways to leverage those institutions for public purposes.

For years, developing countries appeared more interested in attracting foreign investment than in supporting workers' rights. More recently, however, despite occasionally fierce opposition from business interests, some states have begun to adopt (or to enforce) measures that protect workers, including the right to organize and bargain collectively. One measure of this is that, despite a continuing decline of membership among Organisation for Economic Co-operation and Development (OECD) countries, union membership in China, India and Brazil grew during the first decade of the twenty-first century.[4] In part, this trend represents a concession to societal forces that are demanding a greater voice. In part, too, it likely represents the sober realization on the part of governments in these countries that most of the gains from global production are captured by foreign lead firms rather than sticking in the local economy. In Latin America, for example, Murillo and Schrank found that 13 of the 18 collective labour reforms approved between 1985 and 1998 'enhanced rather than undercut labor's ability to organize and bargain collectively' (Murillo and Schrank 2005: 972). They explain the trend as a consequence of the intersection of interest between labour-backed domestic parties and international human rights activists. In China, the government appears to be gradually accepting a different role for unions, one in which unions promote workers' interests in addition to their traditional role in harmonizing employee relations (Lu et al. 2010). The move towards worker empowerment is far from universal, however, and should not be overstated. In South Africa, union membership has been stable; in the Philippines and other middle-tier countries it has dropped.[5]

To focus exclusively on the interaction between governments and trade unions, however, is to miss the extent to which states are increasingly relying on other elements of civil society. Although there is no comprehensive list of NGOs, it is clear that there has been an explosion in the number of NGOs throughout the developing world, in part reflecting a growing tolerance of them on the part of governments. In China, the number of officially registered NGOs reached nearly half a million in 2012, according to Chinese minister of civil affairs (*China Daily* 2012), and there is a much larger number of unregistered organizations tolerated by the state to one degree or another (Xu and Zhou 2010). In India, there are a stunning 3.3 million NGOs according to a government estimate (Shukla 2010). In Brazil, according to the Brazilian Institute of Geography and Statistics, the number of NGOs has reached more than 350 000 organizations (Ferriera 2011). The number of NGOs with official consultative status to the UN (or more specifically to the Economic and Social Council), for example, grew by more than 50 per cent from 2001 to 2010.[6]

Although only a small fraction of these NGOs focus on labour issues, they appear to play important roles in providing welfare functions traditionally reserved for the state. In China, although the state remains wary of civil society, there is also growing collaboration between them. Spires finds that the state tolerates NGOs, even non-registered ones, 'as long as particular state agents can claim credit for any good works while avoiding blame for any problems' (Spires 2011: 1). He describes the arrangement as one of coexistence in a 'contingent symbiosis' that allows ostensibly illegal groups to operate openly while relieving the state of some of its social welfare obligations. (It does not, however, in his analysis, ultimately challenge the authority of the authoritarian state.) Some provinces appear to be experimenting with cooperation with labour NGOs. In Guangdong, for example, a Federation of Social Service Organization for workers was created in May 2012 under the aegis of the Guaongdong All-China Federation of Trade Unions, which may be a step towards labour NGOs gaining legal status (International Center for Not-For-Profit Law 2013). In India, collaboration between NGOs and governments appears more firmly established and less contentious. There is extensive coordination between the ministries in government and NGOs in many social policy areas through the government's 'NGO Partnership System'.[7] Increasingly, too, the international donor community is emphasizing the need for such government–NGO partnerships in developing countries (Brinkerhoff 2003).

Second, and even more promising, states are using mechanisms of private governance to accomplish public goals with lower cost. By aligning with the interests of lead firms in regulating labour practices in their value chains, for example, states can lower the costs of monitoring and enforcement of labour law. Collaboration between governments and CSR is well advanced in Europe and the United States. Governments in the European Union have increasingly turned to private actors to advance policy objectives such as sustainable development, environmental protection and human development, in part because they have found it more politically expedient than traditional governmental approaches (Steurer 2010). In the United States, CSR and other forms of public–private partnerships figure prominently on the website of the US Agency for International Development.[8] Increasingly, CSR is not so much an alternative to government but a complement. As Steurer (2010: i) puts it, 'CSR started out as a neo-liberal concept that helped to downscale government regulations, but . . . it has in turn matured into a more progressive approach of societal co-regulation in recent years.'

A similar delegation of governmental functions to the private sector is now at work in many developing countries. As Büthe (2010) notes, 'one of the most interesting developments in global governance has been the increase in the explicit delegation of regulatory authority by states to private actors'. In India, legislation passed in 2013 now requires that every company earmark 2 per cent of its average net profits to CSR initiatives (Singh 2013). In China, after a slow start, CSR has taken off with governmental blessing (Kolk et al. 2010). Since 2006, when China's 11th Five-Year Plan first made CSR part of its national strategy, the central government has required CSR reporting for large firms (APCOWorldwide 2010). Although not mandates for CSR, the reporting requirements have spurred CSR by signalling their importance (Marquis and Qian 2010). Marc Parich, senior associate director at the Beijing office of APCO, a government relations consultancy, noted: 'While wary of CSR in the past, the Chinese government has in recent years promoted the practice as a means to fill developmental gaps and meet social objectives' (Wharton 2010).

A further example of government-business synergy on labour issues is the Better Work programme of the International Finance Corporation (IFC) and the International Labour Organization (ILO), which seeks to reinforce private governance by monitoring compliance of apparel factories with national labour laws, providing that information to international buyers, and providing technical assistance and training to enable firms to comply. The programme began as Better Factories Cambodia, where participation was linked to trade benefits in the US–Cambodia free trade agreement. It now operates in seven countries. In Cambodia, the programme led to an increase in national labour law compliance, particularly in those factories selling to reputation-sensitive buyers (Robertson et al. 2011).

In the case of Apple–Foxconn, notwithstanding the value of Apple's own CSR initiatives and the clear impetus given to them by pressures from international NGOs, the media, workers and groups in Chinese civil society, the Chinese government was almost certainly a major driver in the dramatic changes announced in March 2012. As is made clear in its most recent Five-Year Plan, the Chinese government has embarked on a strategy of moving away from the labour-intensive export production model exemplified by Foxconn's operations in Shenzhen. As summarized in an APCOWorldwide report, 'the financial crisis, in particular, has made Chinese officials aware of the importance of creating a growth model that moves away from the country's overreliance on investments and exports and toward consumption-led growth' (APCOWorldwide 2010: 3). Whereas once China was so eager to attract foreign investment that it was quite willing to countenance the low wages and poor working conditions typified by Foxconn, now it seems to view that model as a source of social unrest and potential political instability.

What seems to be emerging is a different implicit social contract between foreign corporations and the Chinese government. Remarkably, in 2012 Chinese government officials were among those publically criticizing Foxconn, aligning themselves with their own (and international) civil society against the foreign manufacturer. And it would seem no coincidence that Apple CEO Tim Cook and Chinese government officials met on the eve of the announcement of the FLA findings and of Apple and Foxconn's response.

The Apple–Foxconn story, then, is not only a story of traditional private governance, in which pressure on Apple led it to use its clout with its supplier; nor only a story of Chinese civil society flexing its muscle with Foxconn; nor only a story of the Chinese government's new policies – it is all of these at once. And the governance regime that has emerged involves both international and Chinese civil society, Apple and Foxconn, and the Chinese government. In essence, Apple has agreed that, as part of the terms of doing business it will pay a third-party NGO, the FLA, to monitor compliance of Foxconn with Chinese labour law.

CONCLUSION

The scope and pace of economic globalization created a crisis of governance, including of practices related to the condition of labour. In response to the crisis, new institutions of governance have arisen. Private governance, whether based on a pure business case or induced by pressures from civil society, was always at best a partial solution, for the reasons I have explored. And, at the end of the day, societal demands for governance are hard to sustain unless institutionalized in governmental policy. Effective governance still requires the state.

It is for this reason, in part, that we are seeing the development of greater state regulatory and social insurance capacity, particularly in the larger emerging economies. But the return of the state is not simply a recapitulation of the history of the welfare state. In a world characterized by an ongoing disjuncture between the national scale of the state and the global scale on which economic activity is organized, states will never be in a position to assert the kind of authority they enjoyed when markets were, to a much greater extent, contained within their jurisdiction. What the Apple–Foxconn case seems to exemplify, therefore, is the possibility of partnership between public and private, in which states are discovering that they can leverage the new institutions of private governance to accomplish public purposes.

We should not be too sanguine about how effective or benign greater collaboration between states and corporations will be. Along with the potential for greater efficacy comes a danger that alliances between states and corporations will devolve into capture of the state by corporations. Governance is always endogenous: it is produced by political power refracted through political processes. In a world in which large multinationals dominate, corporate power, unless countervailed by other forces in society, could well result in public–private governance that largely reflects corporate interests.

How the balance between effective cooperation and corporate capture plays out will surely differ in different countries and different sectors. The Apple–Foxconn case illustrates one possibility. But the balance will depend, among other things, on national size (what is possible for the Chinese government to do in partnership with Apple might not be possible for smaller nations) and the nature of the political system (what is possible for the Chinese government may be less possible for the Indian, for example). Nations also differ in the extent to which their civil societies have the capacity to mobilize political pressure. Chinese civil society, although potent to some extent, may lack the clout that Indian or Brazilian civil society enjoys. And the balance may well play out differently in different sectors, depending on the degree of concentration within the sector and the geographic location of lead firms.

Whether the emerging architecture of governance will result in a leveraging of private governance for public purposes, or a leveraging of public governance for private purposes, is far from a settled matter. Indeed, it is unlikely to be ever fully settled. With some form of private governance here to stay, states will likely find ways to coordinate their efforts with those of the private sector. But, because the interests of national publics will always diverge from those of corporations, no matter how enlightened, the balance between public and private will likely always be contested.

NOTES

1. Interview with the author.
2. Interview with the author.
3. Interview with the author.
4. Data from International Labour Organization, Laborsta Internet database: http://www.laborsta.ilo.org.
5. Data from International Labour Organization, Laborsta Internet database: http://www.laborsta.ilo.org.
6. Data from Statista: 'Changes in the number of non-governmental organizations (NGOs) with consultative status with ECOSOC * 1948 to 2010', http://www.statista.com/statistics/158268/changes-in-the-number-of-ngos-worldwide-since-1948/.
7. See http://ngo.india.gov.in/auth/default.php.
8. See http://www.usaid.gov.

REFERENCES

APCOWorldwide (2010), 'China's 12th Five-Year Plan: how it actually works and what's in store for the next five years', APCOWorldwide.
Bandy, Joe, and Jackie Smith (2005), *Coalitions across Borders: Transnational Protest and the Neoliberal Order*, Lanham, MD: Rowman & Littlefield.
Barboza, David (2012), 'Foxconn plans to lift pay sharply at factories in China', *New York Times*, 18 February.
Barrientos, Armando (2010), 'Social protection and poverty', Social Policy and Development Papers, Geneva: United Nations Research Institute for Social Development.
Brinkerhoff, Jennifer M. (2003), 'Donor-funded government–NGO partnership for public service improvement: cases from India and Pakistan', *Voluntas: International Journal of Voluntary and Nonprofit Organizations*, **14** (1), 105–22.
Büthe, Tim (2010), 'Private regulation in the global economy: a (P) review', *Business and Politics*, **12** (3), 2.
Cadbury (2012), 'Cadbury Cocao Partnership', http://www.innovation.cadbury.com/ourresponsibilities/cadburycocoapartnership/Pages/cadburycocoapartnership.aspx
Carroll, A.B. and Kareem M. Shabana (2010), 'The business case for corporate social responsibility: a review of concepts, research, and practice', *International Journal of Management Reviews*, **12** (1), 85–105.
Chan, Jenny, and Ngai Pun (2010), 'Suicide as protest for the new generation of Chinese migrant workers: Foxconn, global capital, and the state', *Asia-Pacific Journal*, **37** (2), 2–10.
Cheung, Jennifer (2012), 'Strikes and worker protests continue throughout February', *China Labour Bulletin*, http://www.clb.org.hk/en/node/101257.
China Daily (2012), 'Number of NGOs in China grows to nearly 500 000', 20 March, http://www.chinadaily.com.cn/china/2012-03/20/content_14875389.htm
China News Service (2013), 'China initiates new round of minimum wage increases', *China News Briefing*, 4 January.
Cho, Sungjoon (2005), 'Linkage of free trade and social regulation: moving beyond the entropic dilemma', *Chicago Journal of International Law*, **5**, 625–74.
Dicken, Peter (2007), *Global Shift: Mapping the Changing Contours of the World Economy*, 5th edition, New York: Guilford.
Doughty Centre for Corporate Responsibility (2011), 'The business case for being a responsible business'.
Duhigg, Charles and David Barboza (2012), 'In China, human costs are built into an iPad', *New York Times*, 25 January.
Duhigg, Charles and Steven Greenhouse (2012), 'Electronic giant vowing reforms in China plants', *New York Times*, 29 March.

Fair Labor Association (2012), 'Foxconn investigation report', http://www.fairlabor.org/report/foxconn-investigation-report.

Ferriera, Gustavo (2011), 'Brazil – the role of NGOs in Brazilian politics', http://publicaffairslatinamerica.com/2011/10/the-role-of-ngos-in-brazilian-politics/

Franzen, Carl (2012), 'Apple supplier Foxconn violate numerous worker rights audit finds', 30 March, http://idealab.talkingpointsmemo.com/2012/03/apple-supplier-foxconn-violated-numerous-worker-rights-audit-finds.php.

Freeman, Richard B. (1981), 'The effect of unionism on fringe benefits', *Industrial and Labor Relations Review*, **34** (4), 489–509.

Freeman, Richard B. and James L. Medoff (1979), 'The two faces of unionism', NBER Working Paper, Cambridge: NBER.

Frost, Stephen and Margaret Burnett (2007), 'Case study: the Apple iPod in China', *Corporate Social Responsibility and Environmental Management*, **14**, 103–13.

Ganeshon, Ram (2010), 'The iPhone supply chain', http://operationsbuzz.com/2010/11/the-iphone-4-supply-chain/, accessed 2 April 2012.

Gereffi, Gary (2006), 'The new offshoring of jobs and international development', Geneva: ILO.

Gereffi, Gary, Ronie Garcia-Johnson and Erika Sasser (2001), 'The NGO–industrial complex', *Foreign Policy*, **125**, 56–65.

Gereffi, Gary, John Humphrey and Timothy Sturgeon (2005), 'The governance of global value chains', *Review of International Political Economy*, **12** (1), 78–104.

Gereffi, Gary and Frederick W. Mayer (2006), 'Globalization and the demand for governance', in Gary Gereffi (ed.), *The New Offshoring of Jobs and Global Development*, Geneva: International Labor Organization, pp. 39–58.

International Center for Not-For-Profit Law (2013), 'NGO Law Monitor: China', http://www.icnl.org/research/monitor/china.html.

International Metal Workers Federation Students, Scholars Against Corporate Misbehaviour (SACOM), International Trade Union Confederation (ITUC), GoodElectronics and MakeITfair, SumOfUs (2012), 'Give Apple workers a voice in their future', 23 March, http://www.imfmetal.org/files/12032217085966/Give_Apple_workers_a_voice.pdf.

Kolk, Ans, Hong, Pan and Willemijn van Dolan (2010), 'Corporate social responsibility in China: an analysis of domestic and foreign retailers' sustainability dimensions', *Business Strategy and the Environment*, **19**, 289–303.

Kraemer, Kenneth L., Greg Linden and Jason Dedrick (2011), 'Capturing value in global networks: Apple's iPad and iPhone', http://pcic.merage.uci.edu/papers/2011/Value_iPad_iPhone.pdf.

Lan, Tu and John Pickles (2011), 'China's new labour contract law: state regulation and worker rights in global production networks', Capturing the Gains Working Paper, http://www.capturingthegains.org/pdf/ctg-wp-2011-05.pdf.

Locke, Richard M. (2007), 'Does monitoring improve labor standards? Lessons from Nike', *Industrial and Labor Relations Review*, **61**, 3–31.

Lu, Yi, Zhigang Tao and Jijiang Wang (2010), 'Union effects on performance and employment relations: evidence from China', *China Economic Review*, **21**, 202–10.

Marquis, C. and C. Qian (2010), 'Stakeholder legitimacy and corporate social responsibility reporting in China', paper presented at the Academy of Management Annual Meeting, Montreal.

Mayer, Frederick W. (1998), *Interpreting NAFTA*, New York: Columbia University Press.

Mayer, Frederick W. and Gary Gereffi (2010), 'Regulation and economic globalization: prospects and limits of private governance', *Business and Politics*, **12** (3), 1–25.

Mayer, Frederick and William Millberg (2013), 'Aid for Trade in a world of global value chains: chain power, the distribution of rents and implications for the form of aid', Working Paper, Manchester.

Mayer, F. and J. Pickles (2014), 'Re-embedding the market: global apparel value chains, governance, and decent work', in Arianna Rossi, Amy Luinstra and John Pickles (eds), *Toward Better Work – Understanding Labour in Global Value Chains*, London: Palgrave Macmillan/ILO.

Mosher, David (2012), 'iPad goes on sale; launch barely bruised by anti-Apple protest', *Wired*.

Muniz, Albert M. and Thomas C. O'Guinn (2001), 'Brand community', *Journal of Consumer Research*, **27** (4), 412–32.

Murillo, M. Victoria and Andrew Schrank (2005), 'With a little help from my friends: partisan politics, transnational alliances, and labor rights in Latin America', *Comparative Political Studies*, **38**, 971–99.

Nickell, S.J. and M. Andrews (1983), 'Unions, real wages and employment in Britain 1951–79', *Oxford Economic Papers*, **35**, 183–206.

Ong, Janet and Mark Lee (2012), 'Apple supplier Foxconn says 150 workers at South China factory in protest', *New York Times*, 12 January, http://www.bloomberg.com/news/2012-01-12/foxconn-says-150-workers-at-china-plant-protest-redeployment.html.

Pay, Ellen (2009), 'The market for organic and fair trade coffee', Rome: Food and Agriculture Organization of the United Nations, http://www.fao.org/fileadmin/templates/organicexports/docs/Market_Organic_FT_Coffee.pdf.

Pickles, J. (2012), 'Economic and social upgrading in apparel global value chains: public governance and trade policy', Capturing the Gains Working Paper, Brooks World Poverty Institute, University of Manchester, http://www.capturingthegains.org/publications/workingpapers/wp_201213.htm.

Piore, M.J. and A. Schrank (2006), 'Trading up: an embryonic model for easing the human costs of free markets', *Boston Review*, **31** (5), 11–14.

Pickles, J., A. Smith, P. Roukova, R. Begg and M. Bucek (2006), 'Upgrading and diversification in the East European industry: competitive pressure and production networks in the clothing industry', *Environment and Planning*, **38** (12), 2305–24.

Polanyi, Karl (1944), *The Great Transformation*, Boston, MA: Beacon Press.

Reinhardt, Forest L., Robert N. Stavins and Richard H.K. Vietor (2008), 'Corporate social responsibility through an economic lens', *Review of Environmental Economics and Policy*, **2** (2), 219–39, doi: 10.1093/reep/ren008.

Reuters (2012), 'China sets target of average 13 percent annual minimum wage rise', 8 February.

Robertson, Raymond, Rajeev Dehejia, Drusilla Brown and Debra Ang (2011), 'Labour law compliance and human resource management innovation: better factories Cambodia', Better Work Discussion Paper Series (Vol. 1), Geneva, Switzerland and Washington, DC, USA: ILO and IFC.

Rodrik, Dani (1999), *The New Global Economy and Developing Countries: Making Openness Work*, Washington, DC/Baltimore, MD: Overseas Development Council /Johns Hopkins University Press.

Ruggie, John (1982), 'International regimes, transactions and change: embedded liberalism in the postwar economic order', *International Organization*, **36**, 379–415.

SACOM (2012), 'An open letter to Apple CEO Tim Cook: stop using student workers and ensure decent working conditions at Apple suppliers!', http://sacom.hk/archives/925.

Shukla, Archna (2010), 'First official estimate: an NGO for every 400 people in India', *Indian Express*, 7 July, http://www.indianexpress.com/news/first-official-estimate-an-ngo-for-every-400-people-in-india/643302.

Singh, Mahendra Kumar (2013), 'Govt sees Rs 10000 crore flow a year from CSR spend', *Times of India*, 9 February, http://articles.timesofindia.indiatimes.com/2013-02-09/india/37007084_1_csr-initiatives-csr-activities-corporate-social-responsibility.

Smith, A., J. Pickles, M. Bucek, R. Begg and P. Roukova (2008), 'Reconfiguring "post-socialist" regions: cross-border networks and regional competition in the Slovak and Ukrainian clothing industry', *Global Networks*, **8** (3), 281–301.

Smithers, Rebecca (2013), 'Growing taste for Fair-Trade shows its Britain's cup of tea', *Guardian*, 1 March, http://www.guardian.co.uk/money/2013/mar/02/fairtrade-taste-growing-britain.

Spires, Anthony J. (2011), 'Contingent symbiosis and civil society in an authoritarian state: understanding the survival of China's grassroots NGOs', *American Journal of Sociology*, **117** (1), 1–45.

Steurer, Reinhard (2010), 'The role of governments in corporate social responsibility: characterising public policies on CSR in Europe', Discussion Paper, InFER.

Thomas, Janet (2000), *The Battle in Seattle: The Story Behind the WTO Demonstrations*, Golden, CO: Fulcrum Publishing.

Tonello, Matteo (2011), 'The business case for corporate social responsibility', Harvard Law School Forum on Corporate Governance and Financial Regulation, blogs.law.harvard.edu/corpgov/2011/06/26/the-business-case-for-corporate-social-responsibility/.

UNCTAD (2013), *Global Value Chains and Development: Investment and Value Added in the Global Economy*, Geneva: UNCTAD.

Vernon, Raymond (1971), *Sovereignty at Bay: The Multinational Spread of US Enterprises*, New York: Basic Books.

Vogel, David (2005), *The Market for Virtue*, Washington, DC: Brookings Institution.

Vogel, David J. (2009), 'The private regulation of global corporate conduct', in Walter Mattli and Ngaire Woods (eds), *The Politics of Global Regulation*, Princeton, NJ: Princeton University Press, pp. 151–88.

Wang, Haiyan, Richard Appelbaum, Francesca Degiuli and Nelson Lichtenstein (2009), 'China's new labour contract law: is China moving towards increased power for workers?', *Third World Quarterly*, **30** (3), 485–501.

Wharton (2010), 'Corporate social responsibility in China: one great leap forward, many more still ahead', *Knowledge @ Wharton*.

Xu, Ying and Litao Zhou (2010), 'China's rapidly growing non-governmental organizations', EAI Background Brief EIA, http://www.eai.nus.edu.sg/BB514.pdf.

20 Private governance and social legitimacy in production

Peter Knorringa

Private governance is defined as the 'non-governmental institutions that govern – that is they enable and constrain – a broad range of economic activities in the world economy', and 'serve functions that have historically been the task of governments, most notably that of regulating the negative externalities of economic activity' (Mayer and Gereffi 2010: 1). In its early stages before much empirical research was done on private governance, it was often either glorified or demonised. At mainstream corporate social responsibility (CSR) conferences or in executive Master of Business Administration (MBA) programmes one might encounter triumphant corporate presentations about businesses' inherently positive societal impacts through creating win–win situations that addressed major societal challenges. Alternatively, critical thinkers often quite dismissively labelled private governance as the latest trick in the capitalists' box of tricks to hide their real exploitative intentions. While both camps could easily produce cases to support their claims, the underlying ideas that private governance is either a silver bullet or still-born were not based on any systematic examination of the actual impacts of private governance (Knorringa and Helmsing 2008).

Fortunately, more empirically grounded research on private governance has boomed in recent years, looking at, for example, the 'privatisation of regulation' by global and national standard-setters (Büthe and Mattli 2011), the impacts of private governance initiatives (Reed et al. 2012) and the 'drivers and limitations' of private governance through standards (Ponte et al. 2011). This chapter aims to contribute to this emerging more empirical and analytical literature on private governance. My focus is on where and when entrepreneurs are more likely to be incentivised to (be seen to) improve labour conditions and enable the rights of workers. This might be operationalised through standards and codes of conduct, but not necessarily. After all, the largest part of the global production system – the informal sector and formal firms that operate out of the limelight of brand sensitive consumer goods – are routinely neglected in the private governance literature (Knorringa 2010). This broader focus also helps to further integrate private governance research with public governance or regulation on labour issues (Amengual 2010; Kim 2013).

This chapter is structured as follows. In the next section I explain the popularity of private governance as part of a neoliberal ascendency and argue that we primarily need to judge private governance on its impacts, not its ideological roots. Moreover, the concept of social legitimacy is introduced as a tool to assess where and when entrepreneurs are more likely to be incentivised to improve labour conditions and enable the rights of workers. The following section proposes a typology of four distinct layers in a pyramid of global production, which possess different social legitimacy profiles. I then move on to discuss two main processes that interconnect these layers. The next section critically assesses the flagship of private governance, private labour standards and codes. The penultimate section brings in a potential game-changer: the influence of states, firms and consumers from China, India and Brazil on the future of private governance. In the conclusion I summarise some main points and suggest a research agenda in which private governance is analysed more systematically in interaction with public and civic governance.

THE RISE OF PRIVATE GOVERNANCE AND THE USE OF SOCIAL LEGITIMACY

Private governance became very fashionable in recent decades as part of a more general belief in market-oriented solutions for societal issues (Vogel 2010). Three interrelated processes can explain this popularity. First, in the post-colonial period after the Second World War many development scholars and donor agencies became disappointed with the achievements of public agencies in delivering development, not least because of unrealistic expectations of what governments were supposed to deliver (Englebert 2002; Chesterman et al. 2005). We are less naive now about what states can achieve, even though there is still no real substitute for the state in terms of its legislative responsibilities (Milliken and Krause 2002). Still, reduced legitimacy and severe budget cuts have meant that in many domains the state has withdrawn. In the 1990s, enthusiasm in the development discourse about civil society in general, and non-governmental organisations (NGOs) in particular, led to a wave of interventions in which NGOs were hailed as the new heroes delivering development, as they were perceived as embodying the interests of the poor and marginalised (Rugendyke 2007; or, for a more critical perspective, Fowler 2000). Civil society would essentially fill the vacuum left by government withdrawal, such as in providing the poor with access to finance as a way to 'elevate them out of poverty' (Matin et al. 2002; and, for a critical assessment, Rogaly 1996). Not surprisingly, NGOs could not live up to this expectation (Zaidi 1999). The second process that explains the increased attention for private governance is that civil society organisations have in recent decades increasingly discovered that lobbying businesses can, for certain objectives, be more effective and visible than their traditional arena of lobbying the state. Civil-society organisations have, at times, become real experts in influencing firms and 'punching above their weight' (Gereffi et al. 2001; Spar and La Mure 2003), notwithstanding their own legitimacy challenges (Hudson 2001).

The third process is less tangible and more ideological, and relates to perceptions of how a more market-oriented economy would be better able to address societal challenges. In what Ronen Shamir (2008: 3) calls the 'age of responsibilization', he claims that 'the . . . discourse and practice of business and morality is grounded in a (neo-liberal) epistemology that dissolves the distinction between economy and society', and enables moralisation processes that 'amount to an epistemological breakthrough in that they ground and reframe socio-moral concerns from *within* the instrumental rationality of capitalist markets'. Shamir is very critical about such attempts to marketise socio-moral concerns and fears a society dominated by neoliberal market-driven logics. In contrast, one of the more nuanced ideologues of 'advanced capitalism', Simon Zadek (2008), claims that advanced capitalism will, inevitably, embrace collaborative hybrid forms of governance in which private (for-profit), public and civic (private non-profit) actors will work 'together'. Such collaborative hybrid forms of governance, with pragmatic leadership by for-profit private actors, would internalise incentives to deliver longer-term win–win societal outcomes. However, such a depoliticised view that simply expects an evolutionary process towards inherently benign and responsible forms of capitalism denies major tensions and contradictions in capitalist development (Schumpeter 1962; Gray 2007).

My position in this debate is to recognise the inevitability of conflicting interests and contradictions, while at the same time trying to identify where and when private governance is more likely to improve labour conditions and the rights of workers. So, while it remains important to be aware that the popularity of private governance can at least partly be traced back to a broader neoliberal agenda, it is also important to judge private governance primarily on its achievements and not only on its ideological roots (see also, for example, Newell and Frynas 2007; Mayer and Gereffi 2010).

Social Legitimacy

In this chapter I focus on private governance of social and labour issues, and not on environmental issues, for two reasons. First, most attention in the literature so far has gone to environmental issues, and environmental standards are also more widespread (Henson and Humphrey 2010). Second, the environmental sustainability domain has a higher potential for achieving so-called win–win situations, where investments in more sustainable production processes also serve core business interests, at least in the longer run. Such 'business cases' are much less widespread and less likely to emerge in the social responsibility domain, which makes it a useful 'least-likely case' scenario to explore the potential impacts of private governance. In most of production the attention paid to social responsibility is confined to maintaining one's social licence to operate, combined with the individual norms and values of entrepreneurs. I propose social legitimacy as a concept that helps to operationalise the extent to which specific actions are seen as legitimate by entrepreneurs and by their external stakeholders.

A widely used definition of legitimacy is: 'a generalized perception or assumption that the actions of an entity are desirable, proper, or appropriate within some socially constructed system of norms, values, beliefs and definitions' (Suchman 1995). As a further specification, I will focus on social legitimacy in production, for which the Decent Work indicators by the International Labour Organization provide a useful point of departure (ILO 2002). These Decent Work indicators distinguish between relatively easier-to-measure indicators on minimum wages and health and safety conditions on the one hand, and less tangible indicators of enabling rights in relation to freedom of association and the right to collective bargaining on the other (Barrientos and Smith 2006). Both dimensions are crucial elements to assess the impacts of private governance on labour. As we will see below, private labour standards tend to prioritise easier-to-measure, more tangible indicators such as health and safety conditions. Notwithstanding the importance of such outcome indicators, at a more structural level it is at least as important to assess whether private labour standards enable workers to develop more effective countervailing power, for example through representative unions (Merk 2009; Taylor 2008).

While the role of unions and other civil-society actors is crucial for effective collective action by formal employees in global value chains, most non-agricultural workers in the global economy are situated in the (semi-)informal economy in which clear-cut and legally enshrined employer–employee relationships are not the norm.[1] In the informal economy, power differences between workers and employers are often embedded in tacit patron–client relationships, often intertwined with (extended) family relationships, in which access to income opportunities and accepting dependence go hand in hand (Holmstrom 1984; Platteau 1995). Often, the weaker actor can only strive for better 'terms of surrender' at the micro and household level (Putterman 1987: 429). In such situations where owners and workers are less clearly distinguishable, upscaled collective action by workers versus employers is less likely. This is also where the debate on the role of the state in providing generalised social protection comes in, as well as the role of civil-society organisations in pushing both states and firms to take their responsibility to maintain or enhance the minimum level of social legitimacy that has been agreed upon in a given society (Saith 2006; Sen 2009).

I propose social legitimacy as a broader concept that encompasses both more formal labour standards and more informal attempts by various actors to push for improved labour conditions and enabling rights of workers. With a social legitimacy perspective, we can see formal labour standards for export-oriented industries as the tip of the iceberg in terms of analysing social legitimacy concerns in production. States, trade unions and civil society organisations, but also entrepreneurs, are part of societal processes in which norms defining what is seen as socially legitimate are set and evolve over time. In private governance we focus in particular on how entrepreneurs handle such social legitimacy issues.

From the entrepreneurial or managerial perspective, one can identify three dimensions of legitimacy – pragmatic, moral, cognitive – each with an internal propriety and external validity dimension (Thomas and Lamm 2012). Pragmatic motivations have to do with whether investments in social legitimacy are expected also to benefit the company; the so-called business case or win–win situation. Moral motivations are about the belief that this is the 'right thing to do'. Cognitive considerations deal with the issue of whether investing in social legitimacy will make one's life easier or more complicated. All three dimensions have an internal dimension (do I believe it will?) and an external dimension about the extent to which peers and authorities are likely to support the individual preferences (do your peers or the authorities believe it will?).

The remainder of this chapter aims to provide a nuanced and empirically driven attempt to show where and when private governance is more likely to offer leverage points for enhancing social legitimacy.

A PYRAMID WITH DIFFERENT SOCIAL LEGITIMACY PROFILES

This section introduces a pyramid of four layers in production with different social legitimacy profiles (Knorringa 2010, 2011). The idea is to move beyond the case-study approach towards showing the relative importance of private governance in specific layers and identifying patterns in social legitimacy profiles.

Moral Win–Win, Value Creation

The top of the pyramid is formed by a small but significant set of firms for which achieving and maintaining social legitimacy is a key element in their value creation strategy. Examples that are often mentioned are the Body Shop, Ben & Jerry's ice cream and Triodos Bank. In this top layer all dimensions of legitimacy push in the same direction. Entrepreneurs leading such organisations have internalised that this is the 'right thing to do', and their employees, customers and shareholders expect a continued superior social legitimacy profile. Moreover, both the entrepreneurs and their stakeholders are convinced of the pragmatic win–win business case of this value creation model and see possible cognitive hurdles as challenges to be addressed, not as reasons to shy away from investing in social legitimacy. Next to rather straightforward for-profit firms like the ones mentioned above, this layer also contains a broad variety of more hybrid private–civic organisations. Examples are fair trade organisations that operate in the commercial mainstream (Taylor 2005) and social entrepreneurs who aim for blended value creation (to focus on economic as well as social outcomes) (Emerson 2006). Such hybridisation comes with inherent tensions and contradictions, but nevertheless seems to be feasible in specific market niches targeting committed and relatively wealthy consumers. In this small but significant layer of the pyramid, private–civic interactions and hybrids play a lead role in setting and periodically refreshing the expected levels of social legitimacy. Public sector actors are less visible in this top layer, as the norm-setting here usually moves (far) beyond the legislative and political discourse in a specific place at a particular time. In other words, the top layer is where one finds those who not only (say they) dream of a better world, but are also trying to develop and implement business models that revolve around or at least incorporate social legitimacy ambitions which are 'ahead of the pack'.

Pragmatic Win–Win, Risk Minimisation, Brand Protection

The next and larger layer is formed by (groups of) often larger companies that aim to protect their brands and see investing in, for example, multi-stakeholder initiatives as a sensible strategy to boost their social legitimacy reputation and strengthen continuity in their supply base. Many examples exist, such as the round-tables for soy and palm oil, the Forest Stewardship Council for responsibly produced wood, 'Made By' and 'Fair Wear' for clothing, the Ethical Trade Initiative in the United Kingdom and the Sustainable Trade Initiative in the Netherlands. While these initiatives display significant differences between them (as will be discussed below), they can all be positioned in the second layer of the pyramid as firms that in one way or another follow a pragmatic social legitimacy strategy. Entrepreneurs are convinced (in different degrees) of the business case for investing in social legitimacy to protect their brands. Also, their external stakeholders appreciate – 'within reason, of course' – the business logic of investing in social legitimacy to minimise the risk of losing reputational brand value. In some sectors, such as cocoa, this logic has in recent years been propped up strongly by a fear among brand companies that quantity and quality of supply of the raw material is threatened by the miserable conditions under which small farmers grow these highly profitable commodities. Local young farmers increasingly abandon agriculture, and this has sent shockwaves through the industry (Ton et al. 2008; Potts et al. 2010).

Civil society organisations (almost always), trade unions (sometimes) and public authorities (often) play a role in broader 'private sector voluntary initiatives on labour standards' (Newitt 2012). In these mainstreaming initiatives the pragmatic 'business case' is the dominant driver, which in some cases is complemented with the moral belief of 'doing the right thing' (van Tulder et al. 2009). A key observation on these larger initiatives is that the private, civic and public actors usually have different incentives and objectives. Most of these companies would not have started these social legitimacy initiatives without initial societal pressures, which come from different directions. It typically starts with consumer activists or other civil-society organisations, who claim to lobby on behalf of 'concerned consumers'. Firms with valuable brand names prefer to play it safe and respond at least partially, without actually knowing whether these civic actors would be able to mobilise latent social concerns among consumers.

Moreover, private companies cannot implement sustained social legitimacy improvements without support from civic and public organisations. Such coalitions or 'partnerships' do not assume a smooth and cosy cooperation. These configurations usually bring together people with inherently conflicting interests. Still, the first decade of the twenty-first century did show a significantly increased willingness by various groups in business, government and civil society to confront these conflicts of interest and try to find negotiated ways forward, as reflected in the rapidly increasing number of high-profile 'market transformation' initiatives such as the Ethical Trade Initiative in the UK or the Dutch Sustainable Trade Initiative, and the qualified successes of the round-tables for soy and palm oil (Schouten and Glasbergen 2011). Notwithstanding the increase in numbers and attention to such voluntary cross-sectoral partnerships to govern environmental and labour issues, challenges remain in terms of upscaling and inclusiveness (Knorringa et al. 2011; Kolk et al. 2008).

Nevertheless, there are serious concerns about the actual impacts on labour of many if not most of these initiatives in the top two layers of the pyramid. Most of these voluntary private initiatives use some kind of standard or code of conduct that periodically checks employment conditions in workplaces along the supply chain. Longer-term impacts are difficult to ascertain as few in-depth impact assessments exist (Newitt 2012). Still, most observers feel that these codes have had some limited positive impacts, in particular to improve the health and safety of workers (Barrientos and Smith 2006; Newitt 2012). However, fundamental challenges remain (Utting 2008), also because working conditions are generally co-determined by a host of political, legal, economic and cultural factors that are beyond the influence sphere of the firms involved in these voluntary private initiatives (Mayer and Gereffi 2010; Newitt 2012). Finally, all existing overview studies converge on concluding that private governance can only achieve modest results in isolation, and that the state needs to be brought back into the equation as a critical actor, given its legislative responsibilities (Mayer and Gereffi 2010; Vogel 2010; Newitt 2012).

I will look into these concerns in more detail later in the chapter. But first I want to make a very different point, which also emphasises the inherent limitations of being too much absorbed by these high-end initiatives. Most by far of the business school literature on CSR, and the more critical development studies literature, focuses on the two top layers in the pyramid that I have introduced so far. However, these two layers cover only a small percentage of all firms in the global economy. By far, most firms operate out of the limelight of global activist campaigns around media-sensitive brand images.

Abide by the Law, Active–Reactive Public Standard Compliance

The next and much larger layer in the pyramid consists of formal sector firms across the globe producing for domestic and export markets, but which do not produce highly visible branded final products. Many of these formally registered firms may actually abide by the law, which means they conform to national legislation on, for example, minimum wages and health and safety provisions. Entrepreneurs who wish to 'play by the rules' have incentives to abide by the labour and social laws, both because it is the right thing to do – and their peers and social networks are likely to hold similar views – and because abiding by the law, and being able to show that, is a way to attract and maintain customers. So, while there may not be incentives to go beyond legislative requirements, as in the top layers of the pyramid, entrepreneurs do face concrete and legally enshrined social legitimacy expectations from their external stakeholders. Entrepreneurs may well abide by the law because of their own morality, but the point here is that, in addition, they face pressures from other stakeholders to do so (Barkemeyer 2007). However, messy realities are even more complex. Towards the top end of this layer, firms may aspire to join the bandwagon of sectoral or regional responsibility initiatives led by brand-sensitive firms, and cautiously move beyond legislative requirements. Towards the low end of this layer in the pyramid, which contains many more firms and employees, entrepreneurs often dodge legislation or, for example, systematically bribe officials as a cheaper way to keep up social legitimacy appearances.

Any person who has been in factories around the world – perhaps especially but not exclusively in the Global South – knows that it is quite a leap of faith to claim that formally registered firms do indeed ensure conformity with all national and local legislation (Pearson et al. 2002). In China, for instance, managers sometimes say that firms that comply with all laws and regulations are already 'doing CSR', because there are so many loopholes to avoid having to comply with existing regulations.[2] In terms of the pyramid, in this third layer the main driver to enforce social legitimacy concerns is regulation; that is, public governance. Some limited room exists for more individual morality preferences by entrepreneurs, but structural factors, such as whether they own a brand name or whether they can afford a longer-term strategy, dominate the behavioural options of entrepreneurs. The distinction between those entrepreneurs that can and those that cannot afford a longer-term strategy is simple but crucial. Only firms which can look beyond the immediate present – which are not in a destructive race to the bottom in terms of always pushing for lower costs given their minimal margins – can afford to even consider the longer-term benefits of investing in a higher social legitimacy profile. In some cases this is driven by more individual moral considerations (Sachdeva and Panfil 2008). Nevertheless, by and large only firms in the top two layers can afford and benefit from such longer-term strategies. Some firms in the third layer may also be able to benefit from longer-term strategies, but in the fourth layer discussed below this becomes quite exceptional.

Informal Sector and Low-road Cost-cutting

Finally, the fourth and by far the largest group of firms, forming the base of the pyramid, is made up of informal sector firms that as a rule do not comply with existing minimum legal requirements. This large army of invisible firms may operate as subcontractors to formal firms, and most of them produce for local and domestic markets. Individual entrepreneurs might seek a relatively high social legitimacy profile because they feel 'it is the right thing to do'. But they are not likely to have additional incentives from external stakeholders to go 'against the tide' of informal sector production, which is cut-throat price competition in which one needs to assume that at least some of the many competitors will do anything to lower costs, and that most customers go for the lowest price and cannot afford to worry about the resulting rock-bottom social legitimacy profile. Not in all cases does this mean that working conditions are extremely bad, nor that they are always worse than at the low end of the formal sector (Perry 2007). The idiosyncratic labour relations in this layer often are not anonymous, but are characterised by intricate relations of obligation, debt and patronage, and also often intertwined with family or neighbourhood relationships (Bromley 1978; Berner et al. 2012). Notwithstanding these nuances, it is especially in this informal production layer that entrepreneurs do not generally feel any pressure from external stakeholders to boost their social legitimacy profile. Instead, most customers buy from them precisely because all incentives push them towards a rock-bottom social legitimacy profile, with only their own possible ethical concerns perhaps pushing the other way.

Public regulation has hardly any grip on this layer, in spite of an avalanche of development projects to 'formalise' the informal sector. Civil-society organisations also carry out many projects in informal production settings and can sometimes create higher social legitimacy examples through co-operatives or social enterprises, but these tend to remain small islands in an ocean of exploitative informality.

This initial pyramid typology is a useful starting point to segment the global production system along the lines of the likely relative importance of social legitimacy concerns. By presenting it in this way, I aim to highlight that the major challenges in enhancing social legitimacy do not lie with the relatively few firms operating in the top two layers of the pyramid. Instead, they lie in the two bottom layers, where the incentives for firms to enhance their social legitimacy profile are lower. Pragmatic motivations for enhancing social legitimacy profiles do not exist in the lowest informal layer, where perverse incentives may well dominate in many of the harsher cut-throat competitive segments. In the bottom layer, therefore, only moral motivations might push towards higher social legitimacy profiles, made more unlikely by the competitive pressures that push in the opposite direction, as products from this layer are judged on their price-setting, not on their social legitimacy profile.

On the whole, this means that, while incentives to invest in social legitimacy are stronger at the top of the pyramid, incentives are much lower at the lower layers where labour conditions are generally worse to start with. This gloomy picture is to some extent reinforced by the fact that most private governance research and policy interventions focus on the top two layers, which can be explained by the larger scope for achievable improvements in the top layer within the time-frame of a standard project intervention cycle. Nevertheless, how then might we start addressing these daunting challenges in the bottom layers of the pyramid? One way is to identify situations wherein processes in the top layers might be used to leverage improvements in the bottom layers.

CROSS-CUTTING PROCESSES TO ENHANCE SOCIAL LEGITIMACY AT LOWER LEVELS

The previous section may give the impression that these layers are rather fixed and sepa-rate. However, these layers reflect an analytical typology with permeable boundaries. This section discusses two important phenomena that in practice connect actors in these different layers and can influence social legitimacy profiles across the boundaries of specific layers.

Value Chains Cutting across Layers in the Pyramid

A key characteristic of private sector globalisation is the prominence of global value chains or global production networks, in which many producers are somewhere in a chain producing inputs to other firms, and this distribution of tasks is primarily based on differences in labour costs, productivity and efficiency differences across space (Kaplinsky 2000; Gereffi et al. 2005; Coe et al. 2008; Nadvi 2008). These value chains are usually presented as relatively clear-cut hierarchies with a strong lead firm at the top, the archetypical example being a US multinational with an A-brand to protect. The second level typically consists of a selected few first-tier suppliers from Asia which in turn manage much of the actual production and logistics, have long-term relationships with lead firms and contract out especially the more labour-intensive parts of the produc-tion process to a variety of lower-tier producers, some on longer-term contracts, most not (Barrientos et al. 2011; Hayter 2004). Moreover, these second-tier firms again often subcontract part of the production and processing work, depending on the complexity of the product and the differentiation of production phases in terms of knowledge, capital and labour requirements. Labour conditions tend to worsen in lower tiers (Barrientos et al. 2011; Knorringa and Pegler 2006). These fragmented chains systematically cut across the different layers in the pyramid discussed above, even though higher-tier firms rou-tinely try to hide this well-documented reality (Merk 2009; Mezzadri 2008). This means that lead firms and first-tier suppliers, themselves usually in the second layer of 'brand protection', do have a strong influence on lower-level 'sub-subcontractors'. But, since they often source from these lower-level subcontractors precisely because of their lower labour costs, they by and large do not exert their influence to push for higher social legiti-macy profiles of their subcontractors (Mezzadri 2008).

While this system was complicated enough, in recent years we have seen that at least some first-tier suppliers have become so powerful that they increasingly challenge the chain dominance of lead brand-name companies (Appelbaum 2008). Some of these first-tier suppliers from Asia are gearing up to become lead firms themselves, as discussed later in the chapter. The fact that global value chains connect the different layers of the pyramid offers a potential opportunity to leverage pressure for higher social legitimacy profiles. However, because firms in upper layers subcontract to lower layers precisely because of their lower costs, and because most firms in the bottom layers do not work as (indirect) subcontractors to brand-name companies, we should not get carried away by the leverage potential of these subcontracting relationships.

Evolving Social Legitimacy Expectations

The second process that cuts across layers in the pyramid is more long-term and less tangible, but potentially at least as important. To analyse the process of how new norms of what constitutes social legitimacy can become mainstreamed, I introduce another conceptual tool, the Norm Life Cycle model (Finnemore and Sikkink 1998: 898). This distinguishes three stages: norm emergence, norm cascading and norm internalisation, with a key role assigned to the 'norm tipping' that takes place between the first and second stage (Segerlund 2005: 5). Below I introduce how this may apply to new norm setting in the more formal sector of the economy. In the first stage of norm emergence, altruism, empathy, idealism and commitment are seen as the main motives for 'norm entrepreneurs' to push, for example, for better labour conditions. This refers to front-runners in responsible production such as fair trade initiatives. Moreover, it also includes those firms that use their high-end social legitimacy image to create value.

Once a certain critical mass of key companies has adopted such a norm, 'norm tipping' brings us to the second stage of norm cascading. In this stage more generalised legitimacy, reputation and esteem become the main motives of companies to join what is now seen as 'the right thing to do'. This is also where risk minimisation comes in. A-brand companies start seeing that they need to invest in boosting their social legitimacy image, in order not to 'fall behind' those firms who used to be seen as front-runners but are now increasingly setting the new level of expected social legitimacy behaviour. Many recent multi-stakeholder initiatives are at least partly driven by such brand-name companies which wish simultaneously to minimise risk and maximise social legitimacy exposure.

In the third stage of norm internalisation, the new norm has become a generally accepted minimal level of social legitimacy with which all participants need to conform. At this stage, new laws on specific labour issues, for instance, can further institutionalise the now generally accepted new norm. Those firms which do not wish to engage explicitly with social legitimacy also need to respond to the changed situation in that the law now requires them to operate at a higher level of social legitimacy. In an economy with a significant informal economy, this may also be the point at which some firms may decide to disappear from the regulatory radar screen. Simultaneously, it may well provide an additional incentive to informal firms to remain informal. In any case, adding this dynamic dimension shows that firms need to respond actively to changes in norms, even when they continue to follow the same strategy. Moreover, through this dynamic process of new norms becoming mainstreamed and subsequently internalised over time, the 'floor' of basic expectations related to the social legitimacy behaviour of firms can be raised over time. So, while such processes are likely to be initiated by firms in the top layer of the pyramid, such norms can be and in some cases have become mainstreamed in lower layers in the pyramid.

The danger with these types of models is that one might be tempted to think only in terms of inevitable improvements leading up to a steady state of utopia. Obviously, over time companies may move up and down through this model, and it is important not to be naive about ever reaching a state in which a majority of companies would use their social legitimacy profile to differentiate themselves from competitors. Nevertheless, I suggest that the Norm Life Cycle model provides a step towards a more analytical understanding of where and when different combinations of public, private and civic governance are more likely to engage with evolving social legitimacy expectations. This can address two of the main weaknesses in most of the existing literature on private governance: that it remains caught at the level of doing case-studies, and that it investigates private governance in isolation from public governance. As yet, strikingly few studies exist that systematically investigate how to dovetail state-driven legal regulation and voluntary self-regulation by corporations, with civil organisations as both watchdogs and catalysts in these processes (for notable exceptions, see Braithwaite 2006; O'Rourke 2006; Amengual 2010).

IMPACTS OF PRIVATE LABOUR STANDARDS

This section aims to assess the impacts of private labour standards and their relation to public labour standards.[3] Public labour standards are part of national legislation and are implemented by government agencies; at least in the formal sector and to the extent that legislation is actually implemented. Private labour standards, in contrast, are implemented by companies, NGOs or in-between hybrids and can be self-controlled or administered through (independent) third-party certification. The four layers of the pyramid showed how the bottom layer of informal production goes without any labour standards, and how the third layer of formal production in principle is governed through public labour standards. The two top layers of the pyramid take public labour legislation as their point of departure. On top of that, they set more ambitious targets, usually on specific issues such as wages or health and safety conditions, and/or they ensure more rigorous implementation as compared to locally existing practices by public labour inspectors. Private and public implementation bodies tend to downplay each other's roles, instead of trying to reap potential synergies between public and private implementation mechanisms (Amengual 2010). Moreover, lead firms are especially anxious to include those issues perceived to be prioritised by consumers in the countries of the Organisation for Economic Co-operation and Development (OECD), which may paradoxically marginalise poorer producers in developing countries from these supply chains, especially when implemented through a so-called zero-tolerance methodology (Knorringa 2011). Nevertheless, in many developing countries with lapsing implementation of labour legislation, private labour standards can often rightly claim a higher social legitimacy profile on specific labour conditions. However, due to prevalent subcontracting arrangements that cut across the pyramid, actual compliance strategies differ significantly. The remainder of this section will first look into the practice of compliance strategies, and how possibly to move beyond the present 'ticking the boxes' approach; and, second, will discuss the issue of certification fatigue among producers.

From 'Ticking the Boxes' to Commitment?

In general, it is important to not get carried away by the impacts of existing private labour standards, also in the upper layer of the pyramid. A significant gap exists between the spirit and the letter of standards. Standards tend to reduce complex intentions to superficial and easy-to-quantify proxy indicators, which actually say little about their impact. Firms in the value-creation layer of the pyramid can and do comply with often quite advanced standards, and many of them also genuinely try to avoid the subcontracting of their products to lower levels in the pyramid. Front-runner firms increasingly offer 'full' transparency of their supplier base and include civil-society organisations in their third-party certification mechanisms (Newitt 2012).

In the second layer of brand protection and risk minimisation, we see that firms can and do comply with private standards, but in many cases their longer-term strategy is to become more capital-intensive – substitute capital for labour – to enhance productivity and to steer clear of potential future difficulties with (public and private) labour standards (Taylor 2011; Mezzadri 2008). In other words, they more narrowly define the core shell of highly skilled, relatively scarce workers that possess significant tacit knowledge and offer those workers attractive labour conditions to keep such 'repositories of know-how'. Next to these core workers, they aim to minimise their direct labour involvement in order to minimise their risks. Paradoxically, this may well lead to higher risks further down the chain, with labour contractors hired to deliver the more labour-intensive and less skill-intensive services (Barrientos 2011).

The next compliance strategy is the partial compliance strategy, which is followed by some large first-tier suppliers and especially by the larger firms that supply to first-tier suppliers in the second layer of the pyramid. This partial compliance strategy focuses on the relatively easy-to-measure indicators on minimum wages and health and safety conditions, and implicitly or explicitly sidelines the – at least equally important – indicators of enabling rights relating to freedom of association and collective bargaining (Barrientos and Smith 2006). According to Taylor (2011: 458), this is not a coincidence, as 'provisions that empower workers to self-organise are commonly disrupted because such trends threaten the very political basis upon which the restructuring of the global division of labour over the past four decades has been predicated'.

A probably even larger group of producers – formal and semi-formal, medium- and small-scale suppliers to second- and first-tier suppliers – actually invest most of their time and effort in falsifying reports and influencing auditing visits. So they participate in the 'game' around private (and indeed public) labour standards, but they do not even try to conform to the letter of these standards, let alone their spirit. These firms can be positioned in the third and sometimes also in the fourth layer of the pyramid. However, by far the majority of firms, especially in the lowest informal layer, do not need to bother about such certifications at all.

These sobering certification practices have led some authors to argue that the superficiality and fraud currently in evidence are inherent to such a formalised accountability approach, and that developmental outcomes can only be achieved through a less tangible commitment approach (Locke et al. 2009). In this approach buyers try to work together with suppliers to address simultaneously supply-chain challenges and labour constraints through localised stepwise factory-level plans. The inherent limitation of this commitment approach is that it only works for buyers and producers that seek and can afford a longer-term approach: *ergo* firms in the upper layers of the pyramid.

Certification Fatigue and Harmonisation

Important recent initiatives are attempting to improve upon existing practices through harmonisation. The arresting proliferation of standards has become a major headache also for lead firms. They are now trying desperately to harmonise and streamline standards. The most important initiative from within the business community – founded and embraced by, among others, the largest global retail chains such as Walmart, Tesco and Carrefour, plus other leading global consumer brands – is the Global Social Compliance Programme (GSCP). In this 'engine room' of global capitalism, standards and certification experts from these globally operating companies sit together in working groups to sort out commonly agreed indicators and their required minimum scores. The idea is not to create yet another standard, but to harmonise existing standards in a way that they can serve as equivalent, so that a supplier with, say, a Walmart certificate can use that certificate also to supply Carrefour. This would significantly simplify purchasing practices for lead firms, as well as for suppliers, and reduce certification expenditures. For my focus on labour or social standards, three tendencies in these equivalence processes are worth mentioning. First, environmental issues, which are more technical and tangible, take precedence over social issues in attempts at harmonisation. Second, also within social standards, the more tangible rights on minimum wages or health and safety conditions take precedence over more intangible issues such as freedom of association and the right to collective bargaining. As discussed earlier in the chapter, this is problematic as these more intangible issues are a crucial element in inclusive development strategies. Third, such harmonisation negotiations tend to gravitate towards a lower common denominator. This has its advantages in terms of ensuring more critical mass and keeping 'laggards' on board. It has its disadvantages in setting a lower minimal standard than many companies would have settled for. Simultaneously, it may well offer top-end brands a new reason to again differentiate themselves from the 'pack' and venture into the top-end layer of the pyramid. Finally, and perhaps most importantly, such harmonisation attempts may set a new 'floor of social legitimacy expectations' in the second layer, which firms with less well-known brands may increasingly aspire to latch on to. The GSCP thus offers a powerful toolkit for companies to deal with evolving social legitimacy concerns. A main criticism of the GSCP is that it does not systematically involve public and civic actors, and therefore does not qualify as a multi-stakeholder initiative (Newitt 2012).

CHINA, INDIA AND BRAZIL: FROM 'STANDARDS TAKERS' TO 'STANDARD MAKERS'?

In the coming years the 'Rising Powers' – China, India, Brazil – may well change the rules of the global private governance game (Nadvi 2008). Here I wish to highlight three issues. First, these three large countries, and China in particular, possess quite different business models (Whitley 1999) or varieties of capitalism (Hall and Soskice 2001) compared to Europe and the USA. Among others, this is reflected in different divisions of tasks and interaction patterns between state, private and civic organisations. This may again influence the relative importance given to private governance, as compared to public governance, in the Rising Powers.

  Second, new middle-class consumers in the Rising Powers may have different ideas about social legitimacy, in terms of not only demanding 'higher' or lower' levels as compared to OECD consumers, but also how they will influence the meaning and content of what is considered to be socially legitimate in the first place. Moreover, the role of civil-society organisations in mobilising latent social legitimacy concerns among consumers is likely to play out differently in China as compared to, for example, India. Not knowing the preferences of new middle-class consumers from the Global South is a major gap in our know-how on private governance. After all, it can make a lot of difference whether most people in a society are desperately poor, or whether more and more people can afford to consider other attributes of products besides their price. Additionally, and at least partly irrespective of income levels, norms and values in societies regarding the minimal expected level of ethical behaviour change over time, as exemplified by how thinking on child labour has evolved over the last two centuries (Appiah 2010; Sen 2009). Unfortunately, almost all research thus far on ethical consumer preferences targets OECD consumers. At this point in time we do not have any convincing hypotheses on consumer preferences of these new middle-class consumers from the Global South (Guarin and Knorringa, forthcoming).

Third, firms from the Rising Powers are increasingly directly competing with OECD lead firms in consumer markets. One major question for all increasingly globally organised lead firms – retailers as well as branders – is whether to go for one standard in all their consumer markets, or to develop 'layers' of tailor-made standards for different segments of consumers. More sceptical observers even predict that private labour standards in particular may disappear altogether with the rise of Chinese lead firms in global supply chains (Kaplinsky and Farooki 2010). In my view this is essentially an empirical question. But, whether we are more likely to see increasingly one harmonised standard, or layers of standards, or no standards, it seems clear that states, firms and consumers from the Rising Powers will play an increasingly significant role in the reach and content of private labour standards as a tool for enhancing social legitimacy.

CONCLUSION

The debate around private governance is becoming more empirically grounded and analytical. This chapter has aimed to contribute to the debate by including the more invisible parts of global production. Standards and codes of conduct, a main manifestation of private governance for branded consumer goods, do not play a role in the informal sector and play a limited role among most small and medium-scale firms in the Global South. Therefore, we have used the broader concept of social legitimacy to examine differentiation in such profiles among four layers in the global economy.

I conclude that private governance can play a modest role in enhancing social legitimacy in production, especially in the higher layers of the pyramid, and especially when it more effectively participates in hybrid configurations with public and civic governance actors to achieve particular goals. Public regulation remains key to a broader development agenda (Barrientos 2000). A future research agenda could focus on two related issues. First, it could seek to identify and investigate public–private–civic configurations that deal more effectively with social legitimacy challenges in a particular layer of the pyramid and to see how such advances can be used to synergise social legitimacy progress in other layers. Second, it could strive to repoliticise an empirically more grounded debate on private governance as a potentially meaningful but inherently modest element of broader development strategies. The main challenge, though, is to combine a critical stance towards self-congratulatory private governance claims by corporates with a keen eye for where and when private governance might actually catalyse development processes that reach beyond their existing imagination. This chapter has tried to provide a more systematic and empirically grounded basis for such future studies.

NOTES

1. Recent statistics on the share of non-agricultural informal employment in most developing countries can be found at ILO, http://www.ilo.org/global/statistics-and-databases/WCMS_179795/lang--en/index.htm; or via the WIEGO website: 'Informal employment is particularly significant in developing countries, where it comprises one half to three quarters of non-agricultural employment: specifically, 48 per cent in North Africa; 51 per cent in Latin America; 65 per cent in Asia; and 72 per cent in sub-Saharan Africa. If South Africa is excluded, the share of informal employment in non-agricultural employment rises to 78 per cent in sub-Saharan Africa. If comparable data were available for other countries in South Asia in addition to India, the regional average for Asia would likely be much higher. If informal employment in agriculture is included, as is done in some countries, the proportion of informal employment greatly increases: from 83 per cent of non-agricultural employment to 93 per cent of total employment in India; from 55 to 62 per cent in Mexico; and from 28 to 34 per cent in South Africa', http://wiego.org/wiego/core-programmes/statistics.
2. Personal interviews in China (2010, 2011). See also van Dijk (2009).
3. I steer clear of discussing the more intricate details about different types and forms of private standards. For useful overviews, see Nadvi and Waltring (2004), Hensen and Humphrey (2010) and Newitt (2012).

REFERENCES

Amengual, M. (2010), 'Complementary labor regulation: the uncoordinated combination of state and private regulators in the Dominican Republic', *World Development*, **38** (3), 405–14.
Appelbaum, R. (2008), 'Giant transnational contractors in East Asia: emergent trends in global supply chains', *Competition and Change*, **12** (1), 69–87.
Appiah, Kwame Anthony (2010), *The Ethics of Identity*, Princeton, NJ: Princeton University Press.
Barkemeyer, R. (2007), 'Legitimacy as a key driver and determinant of CSR in developing countries', University of St Andrews and Sustainable Development Research Centre (SDRC) School of Management, Fife, http://www. 2007amsterdamconference.org/Downloads/07SummerSchool, 20.
Barrientos, S. (2000), 'Globalization and ethical trade: assessing the implications for development', *Journal of International Development*, **12**, 559–70.
Barrientos, S. (2011), '"Labour chains": analysing the role of labour contractors in global production networks', *Journal of Development Studies*, **49** (8), 1058–71.
Barrientos, S., G. Gereffi and A. Rossi (2011), 'Economic and social upgrading in global production networks: a new paradigm for a changing world', *International Labour Review*, **150** (3–4), 319–40.
Barrientos, S. and S. Smith (2006), *Evaluation of the Ethical Trading Initiative*, Brighton: IDS.
Berner, E., G. Gomez and P. Knorringa (2012), 'Helping a large number of people become a little less poor: the logic of survival entrepreneurs', *European Journal of Development Research*, **24** (3), 382–96.
Braithwaite, John (2006), 'Responsive regulation and developing economies', *World Development*, **34** (5), 884–98.
Bromley, R. (1978), 'Introduction: the urban informal sector: why is it worth discussing?', *World Development*, **6** (9), 1033–9.
Büthe, T. and W. Mattli (2011), *The New Global Rulers: The Privatization of Regulation in the World Economy*, Princeton, NJ: Princeton University Press.
Chesterman, S., M. Ignatieff and R. Chandra Thakur (2005), *Making States Work: State Failure and the Crisis of Governance*, Tokyo: United Nations University Press.
Coe, N.M., P. Dicken and M. Hess (2008), 'Global production networks: realizing the potential', *Journal of Economic Geography*, **8** (3), 271–95.
Emerson, J. (2006), 'Moving ahead together: implications of a blended value framework for the future of

social entrepreneurship', in A. Nicholls (ed.), *Social Entrepreneurship: New Paradigms of Sustainable Social Change*, Oxford and New York: Oxford University Press, pp. 391–406.

Englebert, P. (2002), *State Legitimacy and Development in Africa*, Boulder, CO: Lynne Rienner Publishers.

Finnemore, Martha and Kathryn Sikkink (1998), 'International norm dynamics and political change', *International Organization*, **52** (4), 887–917.

Fowler, A. (2000), 'NGDOs as a moment in history: beyond aid to social entrepreneurship or civic innovation?', *Third World Quarterly*, **21** (4), 637–54.

Gereffi, G., R. Garcia-Johnson and E. Sasser (2001), 'The NGO industrial complex', *Foreign Policy*, **125**, 56–65.

Gereffi, Gary, John Humphrey and Timothy Sturgeon (2005), 'The governance of global value chains', *Review of International Political Economy*, **12** (1), 78–104.

Gray, J. (2007), *Black Mass: Apocalyptic Religion and the Death of Utopia*, London: Penguin.

Guarin, A. and P. Knorringa (forthcoming), '"New" middle class consumers in rising powers: responsible consumption and private standards', available at SSRN 2198971, forthcoming in *Oxford Development Studies*.

Hall, P.A. and D.W. Soskice (eds) (2001), *Varieties of Capitalism: The Institutional Foundations of Comparative Advantage*, Vol. 8, Oxford: Oxford University Press.

Hayter, S. (2004), 'The social dimension of global production systems: a review of the issues', available at SSRN 908175, ILO Working Paper 25, Geneva: ILO.

Henson, S. and J. Humphrey (2010), 'Understanding the complexities of private standards in global agri-food chains as they impact developing countries', *Journal of Development Studies*, **46** (9), 1628-46.

Holmstrom, M. (1984), *Industry and Inequality: The Social Anthropology of Indian Labour*, Cambridge: Cambridge University Press.

Hudson, A. (2001), 'NGOs' transnational advocacy networks: from "legitimacy" to "political responsibility"?', *Global Networks*, **1** (4), 331–52.

ILO (2002), *Decent Work and the Informal Economy*, Geneva: ILO.

Kaplinsky, R. (2000), 'Globalisation and unequalisation: what can be learned from value chain analysis?', *Journal of Development Studies*, **37** (2), 117–46.

Kaplinsky, R. and M. Farooki (2010), 'What are the implications for global value chains when the market shifts from the North to the South?', World Bank Policy Research Working Paper 5205, February.

Kim, J.Y. (2013), 'The politics of code enforcement and implementation in Vietnam's apparel and footwear factories', http://dx.doi.org/10.1016/j.worlddev.2012.12.004.

Knorringa, P. (2010), 'A balancing act: private actors in development processes', Inaugural address, ISS, Erasmus University Rotterdam, The Netherlands, November.

Knorringa, P. (2011), 'Value chain responsibility in the global south', in S.M Murshed, P. Goulart and L.A. Serino (eds), *South–South Globalization: Challenges and Opportunities for Development*, London and New York: Routledge, pp. 194–208.

Knorringa, P. and A.H.J. (Bert) Helmsing (2008), 'Beyond an enemy perception: unpacking and engaging the private sector', *Development and Change*, **39** (6), 1053–62.

Knorringa, P., G. Meijerink and G. Schouten (2011), 'Voluntary governance initiatives and the challenges of inclusion and upscaling', in A.H.J. (Bert) Helmsing and S. Vellema (eds), *Value Chains, Social Inclusion and Economic Development: Contrasting Theories and Realities*, London and New York: Routledge, pp. 42–60.

Knorringa, P. and L. Pegler (2006), 'Globalisation, firm upgrading and impacts on labour', TESG *Tijdschrift voor Economische en Sociale Geografie*, **97** (5), 470–79.

Kolk, A., R. Van Tulder and E. Kostwinder (2008), 'Business and partnerships for development', *European Management Journal*, **26** (4), 262–73.

Locke, Richard, Matthew Amengual and Akshay Mangla (2009), 'Virtue out of necessity? Compliance, commitment, and the improvement of labor conditions in global supply chains', *Politics and Society*, **37** (3), 319–51.

Matin, I., D. Hulme and S. Rutherford (2002), 'Finance for the poor: from microcredit to microfinancial services', *Journal of International Development*, **14** (2), 273–94.

Mayer, F.W. and G. Gereffi (2010), 'Regulation and economic globalization: prospects and limits of private governance', *Business and Politics*, **12** (3), 1–25.

Merk, J. (2009), 'Jumping scale and bridging space in the era of corporate social responsibility: cross-border labour struggles in the global garment industry', *Third World Quarterly*, **30** (3), 599–615.

Mezzadri, A. (2008), 'The rise of neo-liberal globalisation and the "new old"social regulation of labour: the case of Delhi garment sector', *Indian Journal of Labour Economics*, **51** (4), 603–18.

Milliken, J. and K. Krause (2002), 'State failure, state collapse, and state reconstruction: concepts, lessons and strategies', *Development and Change*, **33**, 753–74.

Nadvi, Khalid (2008), 'Global standards, global governance and the organization of global value chains', *Journal of Economic Geography*, **8** (3), 323–43.

Newell, P. and J.G. Frynas (2007), 'Beyond CSR? Business, poverty and social justice: an introduction', *Third World Quarterly*, **28** (4), 669–81.

Newitt, Kirsten (2012), 'Private sector voluntary initiatives on labour standards', Background paper for the *World Development Report 2013*.

O'Rourke, Dara (2006), 'Multi-stakeholder regulation: privatizing or socializing global labor standards?', *World Development*, **34** (5), 899–918.

Pearson, R., G. Seyfang and R. Jenkins (eds) (2002), *Corporate Responsibility and Labour Rights: Codes of Conduct in the Global Economy*, London: Routledge.

Perry, G. (2007), *Informality: Exit and Exclusion*, Washington, DC: World Bank Publications.

Platteau, J.P. (1995), 'A framework for the analysis of evolving patron–client ties in agrarian economies', *World Development*, **23** (5), 767–86.

Ponte, S., P. Gibbon and J. Vestergaard (2011), *Governing through Standards: Origins, Drivers and Limitations*, International Political Economy Series, Basingstoke: Palgrave Macmillan.

Potts, J., J. Van Der Meer and J. Daitchman (2010), 'The State of Sustainability Initiatives Review 2010: sustainability and transparency', Winnipeg: International Institute for Sustainable Development.

Putterman, L. (1987), 'Corporate governance, risk-bearing and economic power: a comment on recent work by Oliver Williamson', *Journal of Institutional and Theoretical Economics*, **143**, 422–33.

Reed, A.M., P. Utting and D. Reed (2012), *Business Regulation and Non-state Actors: Whose Standards? Whose Development?*, London and New York: Routledge.

Rogaly, B. (1996), 'Micro-finance evangelism, "destitute women", and the hard selling of a new anti-poverty formula', *Development in Practice*, **6** (2), 100–112.

Rugendyke, B. (ed.) (2007), *NGOs as Advocates for Development in a Globalising World*, London and New York: Routledge.

Sachdeva, A. and O. Panfil (2008), 'CSR perceptions and activities of small and medium enterprises (SMEs) in seven geographical clusters – survey report', cooperation with the UNIDO Cluster Development Programme, India, Vienna: UNIDO.

Saith, A. (2006), 'Social protection, decent work and development', in D. Ghai (ed.), *Decent Work: Objectives and Strategies*, Geneva: ILO, pp. 127–74.

Schouten, G. and P. Glasbergen (2011), 'Creating legitimacy in global private governance: the case of the Roundtable on Sustainable Palm Oil', *Ecological Economics*, **70** (11), 1891–99.

Schumpeter, J.A. (1962), *Capitalism, Socialism and Democracy*, New York: Harper & Row.

Segerlund, Lisbeth (2005), 'Corporate social responsibility and the role of NGOs in the advocacy of new norms for transnational corporations', PhD dissertation, Stockholm University, Sweden.

Sen, A. (2009), *The Idea of Justice*, London: Allen Lane.

Shamir, R. (2008), 'The age of responsibilization: on market-embedded morality', *Economy and Society*, **37** (1), 1–19.

Spar, D.L. and L.T. La Mure (2003), 'The power of activism: assessing the impact of NGOs on global business', *California Management Review*, **35** (3), 78–101.

Suchman, Mark C. (1995), 'Managing legitimacy: strategic and institutional approaches', *Academy of Management Review*, **20** (3), 571–610.

Taylor, M. (ed.) (2008), *Global Economy Contested: Power and Conflict across the International Division of Labour*, Vol. 14, London and New York: Routledge.

Taylor, M. (2011), 'Race you to the bottom . . . and back again? The uneven development of labour codes of conduct', *New Political Economy*, **16** (4), 445–62.

Taylor, Peter Leigh (2005), 'In the market but not of it: Fair Trade Coffee and Forest Stewardship Council certification as market-based social change', *World Development*, **33** (1), 129–47.

Thomas, Tom E. and Eric Lamm (2012), 'Legitimacy and organizational sustainability', *Journal of Business Ethics*, **110** (2), 191–203.

Ton, G., G. Hagelaars, A. Laven and S. Vellema (2008), 'Chain governance, sector policies and economic sustainability in cocoa: a comparative analysis of Ghana, Côte d'Ivoire, and Ecuador', Markets, Chains and Sustainable Development Strategy and Policy Paper, 12.

Utting, P. (2008), 'The struggle for corporate accountability', *Development and Change*, **39** (6), 959–75.

Van Dijk, M.P. (2009), *The New Presence of China in Africa*, Amsterdam: Amsterdam University Press.

Van Tulder, R., J. van Wijk and A. Kolk (2009). 'From chain liability to chain responsibility', *Journal of Business Ethics*, **85** (2), 399–412.

Vogel, D. (2010), 'The private regulation of global corporate conduct achievements and limitations', *Business and Society*, **49** (1), 68–87.

Whitley, R. (1999), *Divergent Capitalisms: The Social Structuring and Change of Business Systems*, Oxford: Oxford University Press on Demand.

Zadek, S. (2008), 'Global collaborative governance: there is no alternative', *Corporate Governance*, **8** (4), 374–88.
Zaidi, S. Akbar (1999), 'NGO failure and the need to bring back the state', *Journal of International Development*, **11** (2), 259–71.

21 The governance of migration beyond the state
Georg Menz

International migration has attracted significant scholarly attention and inspired often vociferous public debates. Yet it is striking that in both academic and policy discussions the state is still commonly assumed to constitute the most appropriate level of analysis. Such a focus might appear intuitively plausible because regulating geographical access and citizenship are considered to be the primary prerogatives of the modern state. Generally speaking, the right to regulate migration flows is jealously guarded by states. In addition to enduring lock-in effects and significant path-dependency, there are significant political implications in abandoning control over a highly politicised and often controversial policy domain, or even in being perceived as doing so. Much of the existing scholarship in political science reflects this concentration on the state as the primary arena of migration policy.

An ontological and methodological bias towards focusing on idiosyncratic national models of immigration and integration also still lingers, often obscuring from view the commonalities in migration regulation between countries with similar levels of socio-economic development. These 'stamps, coins and flags' approaches, for all their empirical richness, may impede meta-level attempts at theorising migration regulation, inflating the importance of national idiosyncrasies. Furthermore, the state is commonly undertheorised and simply taken for granted. Interestingly, the neo-Marxist accounts of migration from the 1970s (Castles and Kosack 1973; Castells 1975) were much more advanced in this regard, critically reflecting on the role of the state and the motivations underlying its involvement in migration regulation. In much of the scholarship that has emerged since that time (*inter alia* Cornelius et al. 2004), the state is treated simply as a black box and its role is not critically examined, despite fundamental and transformational underlying changes in state–society relations since the late 1970s.

The focus of this chapter is the governance of migration beyond the state. Its main argument is that the functions of migration control have been passed on to alternative actors, notably private companies. In addition, governments on the periphery of Europe have been co-opted into acting as gatekeepers of migration flows. However, this 'outsourcing' to private actors has carried substantial unanticipated consequences, as the privatisation of control functions and the involvement of private sector actors becomes self-reinforcing and creates significant lock-in effects. The prism of the principal–agent relationship will be deployed to examine these developments, exploring multilateral and bilateral forms of governance alongside those associated with the increased involvement of private actors in migration control. In the anarchic low-trust environment of international politics, multilateral migration governance has remained extremely limited. The construction of institutions of international governance to aid coordination and overcome collective action problems remains restricted in scope and ambit. Such institutions as the intergovernmental International Organization for Migration (IOM) or the transnational United Nations High Commissioner for Refugees (UNHCR) can be regarded as examples of states pooling expertise, sharing policy approaches and insights, and collectively seeking to address migration matters.

The transnational governance of migration now also involves bilateral collaboration in border management. The empirical focus in the discussion here lies on Northern African countries which are co-opted into serving as 'deputy sheriffs' in guarding Europe's external migration control zone. Migration governance thus unfolds over a more complex and richer tapestry than prior to the commencement of such co-opting in the 1990s and is by no means limited to state actors. Similarly, the involvement of private actors creates lock-in effects and is self-perpetuating. Migration control is indeed being extended 'upwards . . . downward . . . and outward' (Guiraudon and Lahav 2000: 164). These processes do not unfold in a random fashion, but rather are intrinsically linked to the outsourcing to private actors of functions traditionally considered part of the core domain of state responsibility.

The chapter is organised as follows. First, I will briefly set out the principal–agent framework which informs my analysis of the changing governance of migration. I then explore multilateral efforts at enhancing migration governance, which, as indicated, have been limited but not non-existent. Next, I will turn to exploring principal–agent relationships in bilateral relationships with North African countries. Finally, I will explore the involvement of private sector companies in migration governance, which is especially common in the US, Australia and the UK. A conclusion will discuss the findings succinctly.

DELEGATION AND AGENCY IN INTERNATIONAL MIGRATION GOVERNANCE

Transnational governance and cooperation in managing (and, more often than not, attempting to arrest) migration movements is of relatively recent provenance. Western countries turned to new partners in migration governance, which included both private companies and governments in the geographic vicinity. The politics of delegating control in migration can be analysed fruitfully through the prism of the principal–agent framework (Kiewit and McCubbins 1991; Hawkins et al. 2006). In the international relations (IR) literature, it has long been recognised that designing an international institution helps to minimise transaction costs, monitor compliance and overcome collective action problems (Keohane 1984). Similarly, at the domestic level, the delegation of technocratic regulatory tasks to specific agencies might allow the achievement of greater efficiency, foster arm's-length relationships with the regulated sector involved, bolster credibility and avoid moral hazards, and afford relative insulation from political pressure. The partial privatisation of formerly state-provided services is generally also advocated on the grounds of efficiency gains that are assumed to stem from higher productivity, accumulated expertise and know-how, and greater exposure to disciplining market forces.

However, dilemmas associated with delegating powers from a principal to an agent are well documented in the literature, and relate to agents pursuing policy outputs that reflect their own interests and preferences rather than those of the principal – a problem known as 'agency slack'. There is both '*shirking*, when an agent minimises the effort it exerts on its principal's behalf, and *slippage*, when an agent shifts policy away from its principal's preferred outcome and toward its own preferences' (Hawkins et al. 2006: 8). This literature therefore addresses the question posed in contributions on the rise of regulatory agencies and the 'regulatory state' (Bernstein 1955; Peltzman 1989; Majone 1996, 1999) of how incentive structures for actors are affected by the principal–agent relationship and what strategies these actors pursue in taking advantage of the rules of the game that emerge in such a relationship. Interest groups, 'by creating structures to control or adapt to uncertainty . . . have contributed to the development of a more complex and rapidly changing policy environment' (Heinz et al. 1993: 371). Pollack's useful summary of the literature (1997: 103–4) stresses that agents might bring credibility to increasingly complex regulatory affairs and solve problems of incomplete contracting, that is, less than explicitly regulated aspects of regulation. In addition, they are able to monitor state compliance with given contracts and raise alarm in case of breach of contract. Of course, this last point also entails the possibility of principals monitoring agents and using them to shift (or even attempt to avoid) blame.

This framework illuminates the rationale behind attempts at outsourcing migration control functions to private actors, as opposed to other governments. The construction of global institutions of migration governance has generated only very limited outcomes. Earlier work in the vein of neoliberal institutionalism suggested that such efforts would unfold even in an anarchic world because of the benefits for all parties involved. Keohane (1984: 50) wrote: 'Cooperation is possible after hegemony not only because shared interests can lead to the creation of regimes, but also because the conditions for maintaining existing regimes are less demanding than those required for creating them.' Actors adapt their behaviour in light of expectations of others through mutual policy coordination. They do so even if one maintains essentially neorealist assumptions about the self-interested pursuit of often narrowly confined interests. Yet there is scant empirical evidence to sustain such claims in the domain of migration governance, as I shall argue in the next section. Transnational and intergovernmental forms of governance, whilst far from being non-existent, are ultimately neither very elaborate nor typically very intrusive, as states are reluctant to accept the concomitant constraints on their sovereignty.

Notwithstanding potentially serious problems with the delegation of power to agents, principal–agent relationships involving the governments in the geographic vicinity as well as private sector companies are well under way.

TRANSNATIONAL AND INTERGOVERNMENTAL FORMS OF GOVERNANCE

International institutions of migration governance are the outgrowth of the postwar foundation of international law concerning refugees, especially the 1951 Geneva Convention. International institutions offer reduced transaction costs, help disseminate know-how and expertise, and assist in developing transnational policy approaches to dilemmas that would be difficult or even impossible to address for individual countries acting alone. In that sense, they might be regarded through the prism of neoliberal institutionalism (Keohane 1984), as institutions such as the IOM and the UNHCR, initially created to address the chaotic postwar situation in Europe, replete with stateless and displaced persons, have persisted to create something akin to a global migration regulation regime. But beyond creating a common regulatory obligation, these two international institutions also foster and develop expertise, monitor policy developments on the ground and administer international responses.

Whether, in Keohane's terms, the consolidation of such an institutionalised 'regime' has generated norms and thus led to a certain degree of convergence of policy ideas and concepts, is debatable. It could be argued that the de facto undermining of the Geneva Convention's concept of non-refoulement – that is, the obligation to examine every refugee's individual case without *de facto* or *de jure* impeding geographical access to lodging an asylum application – by governments impeding the physical access to their territory does not support such a claim at all. Also, whilst these institutions provide useful fora for dialogue and exchange, it is debatable just how much impact their research, expertise and attempted policy input actually have in practice. In that sense, it is not clear whether the UNHCR, for example, can be truly considered a 'norm entrepreneur'. Alexander Betts (2009) claims that this is the case, suggesting in line with institutionalist predictions that the UNHCR framework has created not only issue-linkages, but also what he calls 'cross-issue persuasion'. Whilst there is no doubt that such institutions have thus spawned new multilateral initiatives by virtue of providing a policy platform, it is worth highlighting that ultimately there is no single institution of migration governance (Betts 2010). Instead, different aspects of migration are dealt with by sector-specific institutions, or become subject to international law developed by those institutions, such as the International Labour Organization (ILO) for labour migration and Interpol for trafficking in human beings.

The absence of a global forum for migration governance is thus striking. The conclusion that the Global Commission on International Migration reached in its 2005 report is broadly correct:

> The very nature of transnational migration demands international cooperation and shared responsibility. Yet the reality is that most states have been unwilling to commit fully to the principle of international cooperation in the area of international migration, because migration policy is still mainly formulated at the national level. (GCIM 2005: 67)

This Commission, established in 2003 by the then-Secretary General of the United Nations, Kofi Annan, has since spawned the annual Global Forum on Migration and Development. Another more extensive multilateral forum for global discussions about migration governance is the International Agenda for Migration Management, which can be traced back to the 2001 Berne Initiative (Lavenex 2011). Ultimately, however, these are fairly loosely organised multilateral policy forums that are as yet not producing legally binding outputs.

Substantial pooling of sovereignty in the regulation of migration is rare, as are instances of at least partial liberalisation of immigration controls. However, there are instances of countries liberalising or even waiving entry visa requirements. Examples include measures taken within economic partnerships such as the European Union, the Protocol for the Free Movement of Persons and the Right of Residence and Establishment adopted in 1979 by the Economic Community of West African States (ECOWAS), or the 2002 Free Movement and Residency Agreement of the Mercado Común del Sur (Mercosur) (Lavenex 2011: 13).

An additional channel for the global liberalisation of migration, primarily for economic purposes, has been the World Trade Organization (WTO). As part of the Uruguay Round of negotiations in 1993, 'essential personnel' may be seconded temporarily amongst signatory states within the framework of service provision. The so-called 'Mode 4' provisions of the General Agreement on Trade in Services (GATS) refer to short-term business visitors who enter a foreign country for up to 90 days, or senior managerial staff who are posted for periods of two to five years (WTO 2004). In practice, however, it is worth noting that member-states maintain the right to limit access through this channel very carefully, to set quotas and to prescribe wages and working conditions. It is also worth noting that, in legal terms, these seconded persons do not formally enter the labour market of the host country.

Despite the potential benefits of the use and development of institutions of transnational migration governance, the empirical evidence suggests limited endeavours in this vein. This finding is somewhat unsurprising because of the general persistence of a low-trust anarchic environment in international relations. There are a number of international institutions in migration governance, yet their impact is quite limited and they are perhaps better understood as fora for intellectual exchange. Exceptions to the generally limited pooling of sovereignty are the internal liberalisation of labour flows within economic cooperation institutions. However, a low-trust environment need not impede bilateral governance efforts, and it is to these that I turn next.

TRANSNATIONAL MIGRATION CONTROL: EUROPE'S DEPUTY SHERIFFS

European states involve other governments in their geographic periphery in the policing of borders, thus delegating responsibility to these 'agents'. Such bilateral efforts create a new buffer zone of control in Eastern Europe and Northern Africa. Increasingly, the European Union is creating an additional layer of such cooperation, supplementing bilateral cooperation schemes. The incentive to serve as an agent in this capacity is enhanced by considerable side-payments, and military, logistical and financial support. The existing scholarly literature documents such efforts in Eastern Europe, although not in Northern Africa (Grabbe 2005; Lavenex 1998, 2006).

The emerging policy pattern bears remarkable resemblance to the concentric buffer zone circles surrounding the geographic core of Europe, first suggested in a leaked draft paper by the Austrian Presidency in 1998, entitled 'Strategy paper on immigration and asylum policy' (Presidency to the K4 Committee, Doc 9809/98, CK 4, Brussels 1 July 1998). This paper suggested bringing countries in the geographic proximity 'into line with the first circle's standards'. The third circle, comprising North Africa, Turkey and the Commonwealth of Independent States (CIS), would concentrate on 'transit checks and combating facilitator networks'. From the introduction of visas for nationals of key sending countries via carrier sanctions, to the roll-out of safe third-country status and repatriation agreements, commencing with Central and Eastern Europe in the early 1990s and later extending to the Middle East, Central and even South and East Asia, the external dimensions of European Union (EU) migration policy closely correlate with the contours of policy developed in this draft paper. The Budapest Group is an important informal forum for discussions on migration control between the 'old' EU-15 member-states and Central and Eastern European (CEE) countries, originally growing out of a German unilateral initiative and from the early 2000s onwards extended to cover Russia, Ukraine, Moldova and all of the CIS (Lavenex 2006).

Bilateral and limited multilateral initiatives seek to prod and cajole North African governments into performing the roles of gatekeepers. In 2001, the 5+5 dialogue group for the western Mediterranean was established, comprising Algeria, France, Italy, Libya, Malta, Mauritania, Morocco, Portugal, Spain and Tunisia. The 'Wider Europe – neighbourhood: a new framework for relations with our Eastern and Southern neighbours' of March 2003 (Commission 2003) and the 'European neighbourhood policy strategy paper' of May 2004 (Commission 2004) aimed at creating a circle of 'friends' in the eastern and south-eastern periphery. Even before the establishment of the EU border police Frontex in 2005, joint naval patrols between Italian and Tunisian and Spanish and Moroccan officers patrolled the Mediterranean.

In relation to Libya, the EU lifted its eight-year embargo on weapons sales on 11 October 2004, a mere four days after a massive deportation measure saw 1153 migrants returned from the southernmost Italian island of Lampedusa to Libya. In August 2004, the Italian and Libyan governments had signed a bilateral migration cooperation agreement (Andrijasevic 2006: 11). 2003 saw the construction of a major Italian-funded detention camp in Gharyan in northern Libya, followed in 2004 by one in the south-east (Kufra) and one in the south-west (Sebha) (*Espressonline* 5 May 2005). Italy also provided tents and other material for the construction of the camps (AFP Rome 11 November 2004), while providing necessary equipment such as boats, jeeps, radar equipment and helicopters for sale to the Libyan armed forces. Maps provided by the non-governmental organisation (NGO) Migreurop (2007) provide the location of a total of 19 such camps in Libya alone, nine in Tunisia and Algeria, and seven informal camps in Morocco. The implications of serving as 'agents' of European governments are not altogether positive for the Maghreb countries and Libya in particular, as the booming oil industry in these countries has relied on economic migrants, especially from Egypt, but also temporary labour migrants from neighbouring Sudan, Chad and Niger. Under the terms of the Community of Sahel-Saharan states (CEN-SAD), freedom of labour mobility is assured amongst member-states, yet European pressure to impede transnational migrant movements directly jeopardises this commitment.

The German government has provided major military assistance to the border police forces and regular armed forces of North Africa. In 2005, six high-speed boats were provided to the Tunisian border police. Egyptian forces had received six such boats two years earlier, while in 2002 Algeria received surveillance equipment worth €10.5 million. In addition, Tunisia received communication and surveillance equipment between 2002 and 2004 worth €9.77 million, and Morocco received trucks worth €4.5 million (Bundesregierung 2002; BICC 2007). Also, in June 2010, the European Commission signed a Memorandum of Understanding with Libya, entailing technical assistance and cooperation for the period from 2011 to 2013. The Migration Cooperation Agenda agreed in October 2012 by the European Commission with Libya aims to address jointly the challenge of managing migration and protecting refugees by offering €50 million in aid to stop migrants and would-be refugees transiting through Libya on their way to Europe.

Meanwhile, the European Union has developed a more ambitious involvement of third countries, though the intellectual origins of such 'outsourcing' endeavours can be found in the former British Prime Minister Tony Blair's proposal to the Council meeting in Thessaloniki on 19–20 June 2003. A draft had been leaked to the British daily, *The Guardian*, in February. The idea of processing refugees and asylum seekers extraterritorially had been suggested informally by the Danish government in the later part of its EU presidency in late 2002 (*Politiken* 4 May 2003; Noll 2003). The so-called Pacific solution in Australia – that is, the processing of claimants on foreign territory (Christmas Island, Papua New Guinea and Nauru), which was introduced by the Howard government in the Border Protection Bill of 2001 – and possibly also the US response to the Haitian refugee crisis in 1994 and its processing of prisoners in the offshore zone of Guantánamo Bay may have served as sources of inspiration. The suggestion entailed the creation of regional protection areas (RPAs) and transit processing centres (TPCs). The EU Justice and Home Affairs Council considered the proposal on 5–6 June 2003 and most member-states, with the notable exception of France and Sweden, were broadly supportive.

In October 2004, EU-funded pilot schemes for regional detention centres were rolled out in Algeria, Libya, Mauritania, Morocco and Tunisia. In September 2005, the Commission set out the establishment of regional protection programmes (RPPs) in the western CIS and the Great Lakes region of Africa, with a view to taking future action in the Horn of Africa, North Africa and Afghanistan (COM (2005) 388 final; Amnesty International 2005). Following an incident off the Italian coast in July 2004, during which the vessel *Cap Anamur* owned by a German NGO rescued Sudanese refugees and Italian authorities at first refused to permit landing in Italy (*Berliner Zeitung* 12 July 2004), both the Italian and German governments expressed support for the Danish–British initiative. The European Commission made €2 million available from its budget for external migration management, known as AENEAS (COM (2005) 388 final, 1 September 2005). This funding was geared at pilot projects in the Western Newly Independent States and the Great Lakes region of Africa. RPPs were subsequently established in Ukraine and Tanzania (UNHCR 2006a), in the latter case as early as 2004 and with bilateral funding from the UK, Denmark and the Netherlands (UNHCR 2006b). Financial support from the Commission continues under the auspices of the 2007–13 AENEAS replacement, entitled the Thematic Cooperation Programme with Third Countries in the Development Aspects of Migration and Asylum, with €900 000 earmarked for the Tanzanian project alone.

Although the use of concentric circles of migration governance and the role of Northern African governments as 'deputy sheriffs' has widely been regarded as a success in terms of the decrease in numbers of sub-Saharan Africans crossing the Mediterranean, there are a number of unintended consequences that arise from the process. Following the principal–agent framework, these problems are to be anticipated. Paoletti and Pastore (2010: 16ff.) document in detail how the Libyan government was 'brought in from the cold', financially enticed and increasingly leaned upon to detain both cross-Saharan immigration and exits to southern Europe. Notwithstanding the colourful rhetoric of an increasingly desperate Gaddafi who threatened to facilitate sub-Saharan African migration towards Europe, the Libyan government had traditionally been highly reliant on migrant labour itself and used migration as a carrot in improving bilateral relations with the Arabic world and sub-Saharan Africa. The prospect of the illegalisation of such migrant networks and the emergence of a trafficking 'industry' (Andrijasevic 2010) was an unpalatable consequence of a more restrictive approach, especially vis-à-vis Sahelian and sub-Saharan Africa. In the terminology of principal–agent theory, the Libyan government thus attempted to 'slip', threatening to 'turn Europe black', but was somewhat torn internally on how to reconcile its own migration needs with the lucrative role of arresting transit migratory flows to Europe. Given the ultimately very small number of migrants moving to Italy from Libya, with the route accounting for only an estimated 3 per cent of total immigrants to Europe (de Haas 2008), the Libyan government was quite successful in extracting substantial financial concessions until the outbreak of civil unrest and Western bombardments led to the fall of Colonel Gaddafi's government (*BBC News* 2010).

Ultimately, however, the attempt to 'slip' and renege on the contract implied in the principal–agent relationship was unsuccessful. Despite the tumultuous events of the Arab Spring of 2011, the new incumbent governments in the region are unlikely to seek to exit from this relationship. The anxieties surrounding the mass exodus of nationals of these countries, notably Tunisians, were not reflected in a genuine mass exodus. From the European angle, the advantages of employing 'deputy sheriffs' are well worth the considerable financial expense, affording blame avoidance where necessary, substantial practical impact, deterrence effects by credible partners with a very loose attachment to human rights, and the ability to mutually monitor compliance.

DOMESTIC PRINCIPAL–AGENT RELATIONSHIPS IN MIGRATION MANAGEMENT

New forms of migration governance also involve principal–agent relationships with private sector companies. This is an often neglected aspect of new forms of migration control. Transportation companies are incorporated into the design of migration flow management and, in some cases, private security companies manage detention facilities. Zolberg (2000) helpfully referred to the geographical shift of control as constituting 'remote control' migration detention.

The involvement of private actors creates new policy dynamics in at least three different ways. Firstly, path-dependent lock-in effects are being created that shape – though do not determine – subsequent developments. The privatisation of detention facilities has proven in practice to be a self-perpetuating policy choice that seems difficult to limit or undo, even after a change in government. What is more puzzling is that the potential to sanction poorly performing companies involved in migration detention appears extremely limited. Shirking can thus be pursued without much fear of sanctions or even demands for real accountability. Monitoring seems largely perfunctory and the sanctions applied somewhat limited. Secondly, new actors in migration policy present a potential for regulatory capture in the sense of agents successfully influencing the principal's position. This is somewhat ironic, given that privatisation was often pursued to widen margins of manoeuvre by allowing speedy and flexible provision of detention space, unencumbered by lengthy public sector procedures. There is thus considerable potential for agency slippage: that is, the loss of control over agents. Thirdly, the involvement of private sector companies can also be seen as a way for governments to extract themselves from accountability and avoid the often unpleasant implementation of the most immediate and potentially aggressive forms of direct interaction with migrants. In many cases the use of multinational corporations, many of which enjoy oligopolistic market positions in key markets, does offer advantages of credibility, notwithstanding their often remarkably poor performance in practice.

The involvement of private sector companies has principally been associated with the involvement of transportation companies and private security companies in the management of migration detention centres. Let us take these in turn.

By the mid-1980s, European governments were gradually discovering a cost-effective way of outsourcing aspects of immigration controls to transportation companies, especially airlines. This coincided with the gradual privatisation of the airline industry (Staniland 2003). While airlines had always been required to check the documentation of passengers at point of embarkation under the terms of the 1944 Chicago Convention on International Civil Aviation (Annex 9), this document did not prescribe carrier sanctions and in fact expressly forbade them, with an important caveat: '[carriers] shall not be fined in the event that any control document in possession of a passenger are found by a Contracting State to be inadequate or if . . . the passenger is found to be inadmissible to the State' (Art. 3.36 Annex 9), unless 'there is evidence to suggest that the carrier was negligent in taking precautions' (Art. 3.37.1).

The rationale behind the introduction of carrier sanctions was to impede unauthorised physical entry to Europe. Similar considerations motivated Australian and US policymakers. In practice, most of the burden fell on airlines, since few migrants chose to enter Europe as stowaways (interviews DE-TRANS-1; UK-TRANS-1) and trucking played only a minor role, primarily in the early 2000s as a means to cross the English Channel and enter the United Kingdom clandestinely (interview DE-TRANS-2; UK-TRANS-2). Shipping today plays practically no role whatsoever as a route of transportation for undocumented or 'stowaway' migrants in northern Europe, although people 'trafficking' using sea transport is commonplace in the Mediterranean.

This shedding of traditional state responsibilities to private sector actors initially met with little enthusiasm among the airlines. Little by little, European governments developed legislation that imposed sizable fines and required airlines to repatriate undocumented travellers, and in some instances even to cover their secure lodging expenses whilst they were in the European country of destination illegally. Although the authorities in some cases offered training and education measures (notably in Australia, Germany and the Netherlands) (interview DE-TRANS-1; AUS-GOV-2), this new approach imposed significant financial burdens in terms of the obligation to repatriate and statutory fines. Even such training measures often involved a financial contribution by the airlines. In practice, it often proved difficult to enforce payment of fines levied, especially on foreign airlines. Annual expenditure for major European airlines on this aspect of migration management was around €50 million in 2010 (interview UK-TRANS-1), while in Australia in 2009, 0.12 per cent of all arriving airline passengers were refused entry and consequently repatriated at the airline's expense (interview AUS-GOV-2). On top of preventive measures, constant training measures for employees and even research into 'hotspots' for emigration and passport fraud, the airlines face the unpleasant spectre of being obliged to carry deportees who commonly resist repatriation, with the attendant negative implications for public relations, the hazardous impact on operational maintenance and the undesired attention of anti-deportation political activists (interviews

UK-TRANS-1; DE-TRANS-1; UK-SEC-1). For major European airlines which rely on revenues from transit passengers for the lucrative transatlantic routes, the control obligations imposed by North American governments also have important financial ramifications, as does the problem of passengers absconding whilst in transit in the airlines' European hubs (interviews UK-TRANS-1; DE-TRANS-1).

It is worth mentioning that airlines are also implicated in the deportation of failed migrants, although the legal framework is a very different one and the financial implications are more clearly positive, notwithstanding the potential negative fallout in relation to public perception and public relations more generally. Airlines also profit from ticket sales; one source suggests that British Airways received £4.3 million in 2006 alone for the transportation of returned migrants (Ginn 2008: 14). This appears a rather low estimate, given that throughout the 2000s in excess of 50000 individuals were deported from the UK annually. In 2007, UK carrier XL Airways withdrew from a £1.5 million contract with the Home Office entailing the removal of failed asylum seekers to the Democratic Republic of Congo. As the company could extract itself without legal repercussions, some doubt is cast on the allegedly legal obligation to partake in deportation. At any rate, deportation is big business in the UK: in 2009–10, 64750 individuals were forcibly removed, necessitating a total spend of £18073370 on scheduled flights and £10300000 on chartered flights by the UK Border Agency (Hansard 6 September 2010: 36W).

Involving transportation companies in the management of migration at a time when they were only just emerging as private sector actors was an ingenious tactic of developing a principal–agent relationship that would be based on monitoring, credibility and, in more practical terms, deterrence. Initially, this appeared to be a very one-sided affair, but, with time, governments offered some training and logistical assistance in the carrying out of such processes. Legislation effectively curtails either 'shirking' or 'slipping'.

While the outsourcing of physical control was proceeding apace, the management of the detention of 'undesirable' immigrants by private sector companies also commenced in the mid-1980s. In Europe, the UK was the first country to embrace the management of migration detention by private companies. The legislative foundation for detention was created in the shape of the 1971 Immigration Act. However, detention was intended as a tool for brief periods immediately prior to deportation. The UK Border Agency's *Enforcement Instructions and Guidance* states, 'Detention must be used sparingly, and for the shortest period necessary' (UKBA 2009: Ch. 55.1.3), although this appears to be frequently ignored in practice. As early as August 1970, the Conservative government contracted Securicor to manage a small detention facility in Harmondsworth near Heathrow airport, and a second one near Manchester airport. Thus, the privatisation of migration detention predates prison privatisation. In February 2013, ten detention centres in the UK focused exclusively on migration detention, seven of which were managed by private sector companies with a total capacity of 3408 places, representing a significant increase from a capacity of 250 in 1993 (Bacon 2005: 2; AVID 2013). Strikingly, the contracts all involve only three multinational conglomerates, with recent consolidation and a bewildering array of trading names obscuring the picture of what is an essentially oligopolistic market structure dominated by Geo Group Limited, G4S and Serco. The former two are active in the United States and Australia as well. The contracts are lucrative, with total costs charged to the Home Office per detainee per week reaching up to £1230, and £840 on average (Hansard 2 October 2006, 4 February 2010). G4S is also responsible for providing transportation services, including between detention centres and to deportation flights, for both the Home Office and HM Prison Services. Details of the contracts regarding transportation are not in the public domain.

In light of the high operating costs, perennially resurfacing problems with abusive treatment of inmates and an uncertain deterrence effect on would-be migrants, it seems surprising that the privatisation course was not seriously questioned. Reports of abusive treatment of inmates were frequent (Ginn 2008). A fire and major unrest at the Yarl's Wood Immigration Removal Centre in Bedfordshire in February 2002, that erupted over alleged mistreatment of inmates a mere three months after the opening of the site, highlighted the substandard quality of both service and infrastructure provision and, in the detailed enquiry that followed the riots, the extremely tight schedule imposed on private contractors to construct the site (Shaw 2004). Major disturbances have also been recorded at the Campsfield, Lindholme and Harmondsworth centres over the years. A number of these centres have been the subjects of highly critical reports by the Chief Inspector of Prisons (2008).

Yet, notwithstanding these serious problems, no attempt has been made to reverse the privatisation of migration detention and control. A number of scholars support the view that in the UK 'lock-in effects' have been created, rendering any kind of policy reversal extremely difficult (Harding 1998). In addition, continuous lobbying proceeded apace (interview UK-SEC-1). The profitability of immigration detention induces companies to play an 'originating role' (Newburn 2002: 180) and act as policy entrepreneurs. The predominant role that private contractors play in British migration detention management also, oddly, places the government in a relatively weak bargaining position and perhaps partially contributes to the feeble degree of oversight and accountability exercised. Key operational and financial details of the contracts between the Home Office and private contractors are treated as confidential and of a private contractual nature, which impedes oversight by parliament.

The privatisation of detention facilities proved more politically contentious in most other continental European countries. In the Netherlands, for instance, there are presently six detention centres and three 'application centres'. In 2005 a total of 12 485 people were detained; in 2006, 12 480; in 2007, 9595; and in 2008, 8585. G4S is involved in operating the Detentiecentrum Zeist with 540 inmates, which is located in Soesterberg near Schiphol airport. Public outcry over harsh conditions at detention sites, which was sparked in part by a 27 October 2005 fire at the Schiphol Airport detention facility that resulted in the deaths of 11 detainees due to poor fire safety procedures, has gradually led to some reforms, in particular with respect to safety regulations at detention facilities (interview NL-SEC-1). The Minister of Justice resigned over the ensuing protest and a subsequent study by this ministry confirmed poor health and safety practices (*Dutch News* 22 September 2006).

In the Dutch debate, the introduction of private sector companies has been relatively controversial. The main arguments used in favour were related to alleged efficiency and the potential for better value for money, yet the political backlash created by the incident at Schiphol has stalled any considerations of increased involvement of private sector companies. However, despite the Schiphol scandal, with earlier fires on the site reported in 2004 and 2003, the contract with G4S was extended in 2007 for another six years, suggesting a lock-in effect. In 2010, G4S also provided approximately 50 per cent of all security personnel for detention centres elsewhere, including in Zaandam, Rotterdam, and the Rotterdam-based detention boats (Ministerie van Justitie 2007, 2010; interview NL-SEC-1). Regular inspections are carried out by the Inspectorate for Sanction Implementation.

Outside Europe, privatisation of migration detention centre management was undertaken in Australia and the United States. Remarkably, the involvement of private actors has also been continued even after the election of centre-left governments. In Australia, privatisation of detention facilities commenced in 1997 under the conservative Howard government. The 1992 Migration Amendment Act modifying the original 1958 Migration Act has rendered mandatory the detention of 'unlawful immigrants', including all asylum seekers, which had previously been only permitted but not prescribed. The new legislation also removed the previous maximum time limit to detentions of 273 days. The responsible Department of Immigration and Australian Citizenship (DIAC) first cooperated with Australasian Correctional Services (ACC), a subsidiary of the US Wackenhut Corrections Corporation, entering a ten-year general contract on 27 February 1998. Considerations of economising, 'value for money', the US as a role model, a new public management preference towards private sector solutions and of capacity concerns in the public sector were all factors in the initial decision (interview AUS-GOV-1). The Financial Management and Accountability Act of 1997 obliges government procurement to be led by considerations of 'value for money'. By 2001 DIAC was no longer convinced that ACC was providing this, but, rather than rethinking privatisation altogether, DIAC simply retendered the job in August 2001, eventually deciding to replace ACC with Group 4 Falck on 27 August 2003 (ANAO 2006). After a change in government in 2007 there were expectations that the new Labour government of Kevin Rudd would modify immigration policy significantly (Evans 2008). Indeed, mandatory detention was modified somewhat and rendered no longer applicable to asylum seekers not deemed to constitute a security threat. However, surprisingly to many and despite Labour's promise in opposition, the tender under way in 2007 was continued.

A parliamentary enquiry into migration detention in August 2009 highlighted the persistent concerns of NGOs over the lack of scrutiny and accountability of private service provision, and reiterated earlier criticism regarding poor quality management, excessively high costs and ineffective performance management systems (Parliament of Australia 2009). Insisting that the standards of service provision had been raised in the new tender, in May 2009 GSL was selected as the provider of services at the more low-security immigration residential housing facilities and transit accommodation, while Serco was awarded the contract for the 11 more high-security detention centres and related transportation services.

In the United States, immigration detention itself is a relatively new phenomenon and the involvement of private companies spearheaded prison privatisation. As early as 1979 the then Immigration and Naturalization Service (INS) began involving private companies in the detainment of undocumented immigrants prior to hearings or deportation, whilst, by 1988, 800 of the 2700 foreigners in INS custody were held by private companies (Mcdonald 1994: 30). In 1983, the INS entered its first major contract with the newly founded Corrections Corporation of America (CCA), established in 1980 by the Corrections Commissioners of Tennessee and Virginia along with the Chairman of the Tennessee Republican Party. Shortly thereafter, the INS concluded a second contract with Wackenhut Services (since consolidated with Geo Group Limited), initially to build and operate a detention facility in Denver, Colorado (Mcdonald 1994: 30). The 1996 Illegal Immigration Reform and Immigration Responsibility Act proved a watershed, for it rendered even minor offences committed by legal residents grounds for mandatory detention and deportation and, in such cases, could also be applied retroactively. Consequently, the number of deportations doubled to nearly 60 000 between 1995 and 1997 (INS data in Ellermann 2009: 114).

The INS continued to own a few facilities itself and cooperated with state and local authorities for the detention of immigrants. In 2010, 67 per cent of all detainees were kept in state and county jails, 13 per cent in facilities owned by the rechristened Immigration and Customs Enforcement (ICE) and 17 per cent in privately owned facilities (ICE 2010; interview US-GOV-1). A recent study suggests that repeated cases of overcharging ICE for migrant detention by county governments and the spectacular growth in local prison facilities are the result of wrong incentives created by the outsourcing of migrant detention to local government (Greene and Patel 2007). Such federal funding has become a major source of revenue, amounting to US$55.2 million in 2008 alone (*San Diego Union-Tribune* 2008; *Los Angeles Times* 2009). The NGO American Civil Liberties Union reports that, in 2011, 429 000 immigrants were held in 250 facilities nationwide, costing US$2 billion annually (ACLU 2013).

The self-reinforcing nature of the involvement of private sector actors in migration governance suggests major slipping. Lock-in effects proved difficult to counteract. Few sanctions were applied, contracts were renewed even in light of poor performance, and the credibility of these actors might have also turned out to be somewhat exaggerated. The case thus highlights the considerable amount of power that agents can exercise if principals are weak or, for ideological reasons, so strongly committed to maintaining the principal–agent relationship that even poor delivery and clear slippage are not sanctioned.

CONCLUSION: MIGRATION GOVERNANCE BEYOND THE STATE

Much of the political science literature on migration remains heavily state-centric. Furthermore, although there are structures of governance that move beyond the confines of the state and in some instances might be conceptualised as regimes in the sense of neoliberal IR theory, arguably their impact remains somewhat feeble and has not truly challenged the state-centric nature of the control of migration management. Indeed, given the anarchic low-trust environment, the ultimately limited significance of institutions of international migration governance is unsurprising.

A more fruitful avenue of analytical enquiry lies in exploring the governance dynamics and implications of government principals employing agents. They do so either through bilateral agreements with third governments or through the privatisation of migration management, which is creating significant lock-in effects, securing lucrative oligopolistic markets for private sector companies managing detention centres. Outsourcing of control has also meant enlisting transportation companies in an effort to impede unsolicited and spontaneous migration movements. Such dissolution of the state monopoly over the legitimate use of violence is influenced by ideological tenets of new public management doctrine and a neoliberal faith in the superiority of private sector involvement of public service provision.

Principal–agent structures appeared perfect for the involvement of deputy sheriffs and, despite some misgivings, the lucrative nature of these roles has led North African governments to accept such contracts. As noted, however, there is some potential for slippage in these circumstances and the ramifications for domestic migration management in these countries are considerable. Similarly, the ingenious timing of legislative changes creating carrier sanctions brought airlines on the brink of privatisation into the functions of migration co-management. Lucrative contracts in deportation and some training assistance have rendered this agent relationship slightly more attractive over time.

However, it is noticeable how ideological zeal has left governments exposed to considerable shirking and slippage in the relationship with private security companies managing immigration detention centres. Despite an often spotty track record and poor delivery, governments struggle to extract themselves from contracts, to exercise oversight and monitoring, and to enforce meaningful sanctions. It is not clear whether this outsourcing truly provides better value for money and, revealingly, contracts are not in the public domain, making this claim impossible to verify.

Governance structures of migration thus remain somewhat loose and ultimately link back to what is still a highly state-centric architecture regarding migration control and management. By contrast, a number of Western states have extensively made recourse to private sector companies in the co-management of migration affairs, which has unleashed unanticipated and sometimes problematic side-effects that lead to a self-perpetuation of such approaches. While, externally, governance is thus fairly state-centric and international institutions offer only loose consultative venues, the nature of domestic migration governance has changed considerably since the 1980s.

REFERENCES

ACLU (2013), 'Immigration detention', available at: http://www.aclu.org/immigrants-rights/immigration-detention, accessed on 18 June 2013.
Andrijasevic, R. (2006), 'How to balance rights and responsibilities on asylum at the EU's southern border of Italy and Libya', Working Paper 27, Oxford: COMPAS.
Andrijasevic, R. (2010), 'Deported: the right to asylum at the EU's external border of Italy and Libya', *International Migration*, **48** (1), 148–74.
Association of Visitors to Immigration Detainees (AVID) (2013), 'Immigration detention in the UK: residential detention spaces', available at: http://www.aviddetention.org.uk/images/uk%20residential%20spaces%20feb%202013.pdf, accessed on 18 June 2013.
Australian National Accounting Office (ANAO) (2006), *Management of the Tender Process for the Detention Services Contract*, Canberra: ANAO.
Bacon, C. (2005), 'The evolution of immigration detention in the UK: the involvement of private prison companies', Working Paper 27/2005, RSC, Oxford: University of Oxford.
BBC News (2010), 'Gaddafi wants EU cash to stop African migrants', 31 August, available at: http://www.bbc.co.uk/news/world-europe-11139345, accessed on 26 April 2012.
Bernstein, M. (1955), *Regulating Business by Independent Commission*, Princeton, NJ: Princeton University Press.
Berliner Zeitung (2004), 'Der mutige Kapitän', 13 July.
Betts, A. (2009), *Protection by Persuasion: International Cooperation in the Refugee Regime*, Ithaca, NY: Cornell University Press.
Betts, A. (2010), 'Survival migration: a new protection framework', *Global Governance* (special edition on International Migration), **16** (3), 361–82.

Bonn International Center for Conversion (BICC) (2007), 'Informationsdienst Sicherheit, Rüstung und Entwicklung in Empfängerländern deutscher Rüstungsexporte: Tunesien', Bonn: BICC.

Bundesregierung (2002), 'Rüstungsexportbericht der Bundesregierung 2002', Berlin: Federal Government.

Castells, M. (1975), 'Immigrant workers and class structure in Western Europe', *Politics and Society*, **5** (1), 33–66.

Castles, S. and G. Kosack (1973), *Immigrant Workers and Class*, Oxford: Oxford University Press.

Chief Inspector of Prisons (2008), 'Report on an unannounced full follow-up inspection of Harmondsworth Immigration Removal Centre', London: HM Inspectorate of Prisons.

Commission of the European Communities (2003), 'Communication from the Commission to the Council and the European Parliament: Wider Europe – neighbourhood: a new framework for relations with our Eastern and Southern neighbours', Brussels, 11 March, COM(2003) 104 final.

Commission of the European Communities (2004), 'European neighbourhood policy strategy paper', Brussels, 12 May, COM(2004) 373 final.

Cornelius, W., T. Tsuda, P.L. Martin, J.F. Hollifield (eds) (2004), *Controlling Immigration: A Global Perspective*. Stanford, CA: Stanford University Press.

Ellermann, A. (2009), *States Against Migrants: Deportation in Germany and the United States*, New York: Cambridge University Press.

Espressonline (2005), 'Lampedusa', 5 May.

Ginn, E. (2008), 'Outsourcing abuse: the use and misuse of state sanctioned force during the detention and removal of asylum seekers', London: Medical Justice Network.

Global Commission on International Management (GCIM) (2005), *Final Report*, Geneva: GCIM

Grabbe, H. (2005), 'Regulating the flow of people across Europe', in F. Schimmelfennig and U. Sedelmaier (eds), *The Europeanization of Central and Eastern Europe*, Ithaca, NY: Cornell University Press, pp. 112–34.

Greene, J. and S. Patel (2007), 'The immigrant gold rush: the profit motive behind immigrant detention', Geneva: UN Special Rapporteur on the Rights of Migrants.

Guiraudon, V. and Lahav, G. (2000), 'A reappraisal of the state sovereignty debate: the case of migration control', *Comparative Political Studies*, **33** (2), 163–95.

De Haas, Hein (2008), 'The myth of invasion: the inconvenient realities of African migration to Europe', *Third World Quarterly*, **29** (7), 1305–22.

Evans, C. (2008), 'New directions in detention: restoring integrity to Australia's immigration system', speech at Australian National University, Canberra, 29 July.

Harding, R.W. (1998), 'Private prisons', in M. Tonry (ed.), *The Handbook on Crime and Punishment*, Oxford: Oxford University Press, pp. 19–56.

Hawkins, D.G., D.A. Lake, D. Nielson and M.J. Tierney (eds) (2006), *Delegation and Agency in International Organisations*, Cambridge: Cambridge University Press.

Heinz, J.P., E.O. Laumann, R.L. Nelson and R.H. Salisbury (1993), *The Hollow Core: Private Interests in National Policy-Making*, Cambridge: Cambridge University Press.

ICE (2010), 'US immigration and customs enforcement: detention management program', available at: www.ice.gov/partners/dro/dmp.htm, accessed on 18 June 2013.

Keohane, R. (1984), *After Hegemony*, Princeton, NJ: Princeton University Press.

Kiewit, D.R. and McCubbins, M.D. (1991), *The Logic of Delegation: Congressional Parties and the Appropriations Process*, Chicago, IL: University of Chicago Press.

Lavenex, S. (1998), 'Asylum, immigration and Central-Eastern Europe: challenges to EU enlargement', *European Foreign Affairs Review*, **3** (2), 275–94.

Lavenex, S. (2006), 'The competition state and the multilateral liberalization of skilled migration', in A. Favell (ed.), *The Human Face of Global Mobility: International Highly Skilled Migration in Europe, North America and the Asia-Pacific*, New Brunswick, NJ: Transaction Publishers, pp. 329–50.

Lavenex, S. (2011), 'Venue-shopping in global migration policy: multileveling EU external governance', paper presented at the Biannual Research Conference of the European Union Studies Association, Boston, MA, March.

Majone, G. (1996), *Regulating Europe*, London and New York: Routledge.

Majone, G. (1999), 'The regulatory state and its legitimacy problems', *West European Politics*, **22** (1), 1–24.

Mcdonald, D.C. (1994), 'Public imprisonment by private means', *British Journal of Criminology, Delinquency and Deviant Social Behaviour*, **34**, Special Issue, 29–48.

Migreurop (2007), 'Les camps d'étrangers en Europe et dans les pays méditerranéens', Brussels: Migreurop.

Ministerie van Justitie (2007), 'Detentibooten Zuid-Holland locatie Rotterdam Inspectiebericht Vervolgonderzoog', The Hague: Ministry of Justice.

Ministerie van Justitie (2010), 'Detentiecentrum Noord-Holland locatie Zaandam Inspectierapport Doorlichting', The Hague: Ministry of Justice.

Los Angeles Times (2009), 'Cities and counties rely on immigrant detention fees', 17 March.

Newburn, T. (2002), 'Atlantic crossings: "policy transfer" and crime control in the United States and Britain', *Punishment and Society*, **4** (2), 165–94.

Noll, G. (2003), 'Visions of the exceptional: legal and theoretical issues raised by transit processing centres and protection zones', *European Journal of Migration and Law*, **5**, 303–41.

Paoletti, E. and F. Pastore (2010), 'Sharing the dirty job on the southern front? Italian–Libyan relations on migration and their impact on the European Union', Working Paper 29, December, Oxford: IMI.

Parliament of Australia (2009), 'Immigration detention in Australia: facilities, services and transparency', Canberra: House of Representatives Printing and Publishing Office.

Peltzman, S. (1989), 'The economic theory of regulation after a decade of deregulation', *Brookings Papers Econ. Activity* (suppl.), 1–41.

Pollack, M. (1997), 'Delegation, agency, and agenda-setting in the European Community', *International Organization*, **51** (1), 99–134.

San Diego Union-Tribune (2008), 'Detention dollars: tougher immigration laws turn the ailing private prison sector into a revenue maker', 4 May.

Shaw, S. (2004), 'Investigation into allegations of racism, abuse and violence at Yarl's Wood Removal Centre: a report by the Prisons and Probation Ombudsman for England and Wales', March, London: Prisons and Probation Ombudsman.

Staniland, M. (2003), *Government Birds: Air Transport and the State in Western Europe*, Lanham, MD: Rowman & Littlefield

UK Border Agency (UKBA) (2009), *Enforcement Instructions and Guidance*, London: UKBA.

UNHCR (2006a), 'Global approach: Eastern Europe', Geneva: UNHCR.

UNHCR (2006b), 'SOPCP Tanzania update', Geneva: UNHCR.

WTO Secretariat (2004), *World Trade Report 2004: The Liberalization of Services Trade through the Temporary Movement of Natural Persons*, Geneva: WTO.

Zolberg, A. (2000), 'Matters of state: theorizing immigration policy', in Charles Hirschman, Philip Kasinitz and Josh DeWind (eds), *The Handbook of International Migration*, New York: Russell Sage, pp. 71–93.

Interviews

AUS-GOV-1 interview with Australian Ministry for Immigration and Citizenship.

AUS-GOV-2 interview with Australian Ministry for Immigration and Citizenship.

DE-TRANS-1 interview with representative of German airline.

DE-TRANS-2 interview with representative of German trucking sector interest association.

NL-SEC-1 interview with representative of Dutch security company.

UK-SEC-1 interview with representative of British security sector interest association.

UK-TRANS-1 interview with representative of British airline.

UK-TRANS-2 interview with representative of British trucking sector interest association.

US-GOV-1 interview with US Immigration and Customs Enforcement.

22 Migration in European governance: the constitution of a transgovernmental policy field
Andrew Geddes

This chapter analyses the relationship between the social, political and economic constitution of 'the European project' and the governance of migration. It does so in the context of what the European Union (EU) now calls its Global Approach to Migration and Mobility (GAMM) (see CEC 2011a). This has both an 'internal' governance dimension applied to the 28 member-states and an 'external' governance dimension as it affects non-member-states. The chapter seeks to account for the development of EU migration governance, its links to the broader political economy of European integration, and the particular policy focus within both its internal and its external dimensions. It thus asks why, how and with what effects the EU has developed common migration policies and a system of migration governance.

The EU's GAMM built on what was initially called a Global Approach to Migration, which emerged during the UK's presidency of the EU in 2005. The addition of the word 'mobility' may seem like a marginal difference, but is significant in the development of EU migration governance because of the distinction it creates between 'virtuous' mobility (involving the highly qualified and economically beneficial forms of migration) which, it is argued, should be encouraged, and more 'problematic' migration, which is to be controlled and restricted. Increased emphasis within this debate has been placed on temporary and circular forms of migration. In 2012, the European Commission (CEC 2012: 4) highlighted a continued demand for migrant workers even in the face of economic crisis, noting that 'member states tend to focus their approach to economic migration of TCNs [third-country nationals] more on (highly-) skilled workers, although several also require low skilled workers, albeit in most cases for a temporary period'. The mobility–migration distinction could be puzzling at a conceptual level because international migration is actually a form of human mobility: that part that involves the crossing of state borders. However, this discursive development is significant because it allows us to explore the ways in which the political economy of European integration and the notion of mobility therein play a key part in conditioning and constituting the governance of migration by imposing on it particular meanings that are linked to the constitution of the European project and, particularly, the pursuit of economic liberalisation.

There are two main strands to the argument developed in this chapter. The first focuses on the relationship between migration and the underlying political economy of European integration by addressing the relationship between migration and a series of economic, political, social, demographic and environmental factors that can drive it. International migration is shown to be closely linked to the effects of and interactions between these underlying drivers, and is shaped by – but can also help to shape – these drivers. International migration is thus linked to underlying inequalities in the global system that 'produces' it. An implication of this is that migration is not simply a challenge for governance, but also fundamentally a challenge of governance. Put another way, international migration is not something that simply happens to destination states in the EU as though migrants arrived from another planet; rather, it is inextricably bound to the structure of the international system and inequalities therein.

The second strand of the argument focuses on the governance of European migration, with a particular focus on the EU level. While migration is typically understood as an arena of 'high politics' in which it would be difficult to secure integration, it is shown that the development of transgovernmental networks involving ministers and officials from member-states, as well as EU officials and representatives of a range of other organisations, has helped to create a migration policy field at EU level that has both multi-level and transgovernmental aspects. There is a particular focus on the characteristic features of transgovernmentalism as a feature of European migration governance. In terms of the more specific features of migration governance the chapter shows that there has been movement away from pursuit of a comprehensive policy and towards a sectoral approach focused on particular forms of migration (such as a 'blue card' for highly qualified migrants plus proposals for rules governing seasonal workers and intra-corporate transferees), with a special interest in temporary and circular migration. There is no clear EU-wide definition of temporary migration, but underlying it is a migrant's intention to return to their country of origin. Similarly, there is no agreed definition of circular migration, but it takes the form of repeated temporary migration with possibilities of repeated movement between origin and destination countries (EMN 2011; see also CEC 2007). These EU migration measures do not as yet touch upon the authority of member-states to determine the numbers of migrants to be admitted, but could be seen as indicative of 'integration by stealth' as the EU moves into areas related to admissions policy (Carrera et al. 2011).

The chapter's next section presents a brief overview of mobility and migration in EU development. This is followed by a section that specifies at a conceptual level the relationship between migration and governance. The third section moves on to explore migration drivers and the effects of inequalities on both migration and, importantly, non-migration. The fourth assesses the development of migration governance beyond the state and the fifth section explores the specific forms this takes at EU level in terms of both 'internal' and 'external' governance. A final section draws conclusions.

THE EU GOVERNANCE OF MIGRATION AND MOBILITY

Just over 3 per cent of the world's population are international migrants, equivalent to around 214 million people. Around 20.2 million people, or around 4 per cent of the EU's total population, are not nationals of an EU member-state – so-called TCNs. The EU accounts for fewer than 10 per cent of the world's total number of international migrants. This contrasts with Canada where 21.3 per cent of its national population are TCNs, and the USA where the figure is 13.5 per cent. Fewer than 45 per cent of the world's international migrants reside in either the EU or North America. The three largest origin countries for migrants in Europe in 2011 were Turkey (around 2.4 million people), Morocco (around 1. 8 million) and Albania (circa 1 million). Using the UN's Human Development Index (HDI), 47 per cent of EU migrants come from high-HDI countries, 46 per cent from medium-HDI countries and around 7 per cent from low-HDI countries (CEC 2012: 3).

Migration in its various forms has been, is and will continue to be an important characteristic feature of European societies. Mobility in the form of free movement is a key component of the EU treaty framework, itself dating back to the 1950s, that seeks to guarantee free movement rights for certain categories of people holding the nationality of a member-state (and who, since the Maastricht Treaty came into force in 1993, hold the status of EU citizens). This right was initially extended to workers, but has since become a more generalised right of free movement with only certain provisos and limitations (such as public health and public order). Free movement is thus highly institutionalised at EU level in the sense of the establishment of clear competencies for supranational institutions. It is also constitutionalised in the sense that a body of law has developed at EU level that protects the right to free movement. Free movement is thus closely linked to the origins of the European project and the centrality of market-making as its core purpose. Free movement as a form of intra-EU mobility was largely uncontroversial until the 'big bang' enlargement of 2004 that saw 12 member-states (excepting Ireland, Sweden and the UK) impose restrictions on movement by nationals of the accession states for a transition period of up to seven years.

In contrast, migration policy as it relates to TCNs has been less institutionalised and constitutionalised. Formal cooperation between member-states on an intergovernmental basis began when the Maastricht Treaty came into force in 1993. Prior to this time there was cooperation outside the Treaty framework in the form of the Schengen Agreement (initially applying to only five countries), plus informal intergovernmental cooperation between member-states in the form of networks of national ministers and officials working together outside of the Treaty framework, mainly on internal security issues that included immigration. These networks were significant in that they provided the origins for the transgovernmental governance of migration at EU level, which is discussed more fully below. It was only when the Amsterdam Treaty came into force in 1999 that migration and asylum became 'communitarised' policy issues – that is, they were located within the main body of the Treaty and subject, albeit initially with significant limitations, to supranational decision rules. Since 1999, there has been a steady movement towards a greater role for supranational institutions, as well as agreement on directives and regulations on issues such as asylum, family reunion and rules governing entry by highly qualified migrants. These developments do not amount to a comprehensive EU migration and asylum policy. The EU-level governance of migration is fragmented and does not cover all aspects of policy. There is also 'variable geometry' in the migration governance system since Denmark, Ireland and the UK have opted out of the common migration and asylum policy as it has developed after 1999. Furthermore, a highly significant area of policy – the numbers of migrants to be admitted – remains firmly within the domain of member-state competencies, as affirmed by Article 79(5) of the Treaty of Lisbon, which came into force in 2009. The Lisbon Treaty was also significant because it applied what is known as the Ordinary Legislative Procedure (OLP) to migration policy. This implies qualified majority voting (QMV), a weighted voting system, in the Council of Ministers representing the member-states; the use of co-decision between the Council and the European Parliament (thus giving a co-legislative role to the Parliament); and full jurisdiction for the Court of Justice (CJEU) on migration policy.

These institutional developments affect conceptualisations of European migration governance. In the 1990s and early 2000s, EU migration governance was seen as a form of 'vertical policy-making' allowing the executive branches of member-state governments to seek new EU-level venues for policy cooperation that would allow them to circumvent national-level constraints, particularly judicial and legislative, on their capacity to pursue restrictive policies (Guiraudon 2000; see also Freeman 1998). The application since the Lisbon Treaty came into effect of the OLP with co-decision-making between the Council and the European Parliament, plus a full role for the CJEU in this area, serves to challenge this conceptualisation of vertical policy-making by the executive branches of national governments, as the Parliament and the CJEU have seen their powers grow in this policy area. This creates scope for a greater degree of institutionalisation and constitutionalisation. For example, it has been shown that CJEU decisions have begun to affect national policies on expulsion and family migration (Acosta and Geddes 2013).

For the purpose of the analysis that follows, three themes can be extracted from this overview of the development of competencies. The first is the link between market-making within the EU and a particular understanding of mobility linked to economic integration. This was applied to nationals of EU member-states (EU citizens), but a key argument underpinning arguments for application to TCNs is that similar economic efficiency arguments apply to non-EU nationals and that their greater mobility could also be virtuous in the context of economic liberalisation and other challenges, such as demographic change (CEC 2000, 2005). The European Commission has played a particularly important role in seeking to stimulate EU policy because of its agenda-setting and policy-proposing role within the EU system. The Commission faced objections to calls for a more comprehensive approach as outlined in its Communication in 2000 on a Community Immigration Policy (CEC 2000). Since then, the Commission has sought to link arguments about security, economic, welfare and demographic challenges to an agenda for the development of EU responsibility in the area of migration policy, but focused on particular types or forms of migration and with a growing interest in temporary and circular flows. Thus EU intervention in the field of migration policy is linked to the particular construction of the virtues of mobility in the context of economic liberalisation. It is also linked to a more general interest at international level in new approaches to migration that could focus on the stimulation of temporary flows and the pursuit of the so-called 'triple win', whereby new migration schemes could benefit both sending and receiving states and also the migrants themselves (GCIM 2005; Ruhs 2006; Vertovec 2007).

The second theme relates to the ways in which the antecedents of the governance of migration can be traced back to early cooperation on internal security from the 1980s onwards. Particular ways of working led to habits of cooperation developing between national-level actors. The effect has been to change the strategic context within which migration governance occurs and also to shape the perceptions of policy problems as being linked to EU interdependencies. This became particularly apparent after the end of the Cold War, when a 'geopolitical' widening of migration meant that migration governance could no longer be construed as an issue for a relatively small group of 'older' immigration countries in North-West Europe, such as France, Germany, the Netherlands and the UK. Instead, Southern, Central and Eastern European countries became new countries of migration, which significantly changed the dynamics of European migration governance and helped to generate a stronger sense of interdependence linked to EU widening. This geopolitical widening of migration also played a key role in impelling the 'external' governance of migration as EU member-states sought to influence migration policy development both in potential member-states and in non-member-states.

The third point is that the emergent governance of migration did not necessarily lead to some form of common migration and asylum policy. The Commission faced initial setbacks when seeking to develop a more comprehensive, common approach. EU-level law has emerged in the form of directives on asylum, family migration, the rights of TCNs who are long-term residents, return or expulsion and rules governing the entry of highly qualified migrants (the so-called 'blue card' directive). As already noted, proposals for seasonal migrants and intra-corporate transferees remain on the table (CEC 2012).

INTERNATIONAL MIGRATION AND THE CHALLENGES OF GOVERNANCE

This section accounts for the developments sketched in the previous section and links them to conceptualisations of governance. The focus is on the relationship between international migration and the borders and boundaries of governance systems in Europe, as well as on the ways in which these borders and boundaries constitute and condition international migration as a challenge of governance. It is in this context that the distinction between migration and mobility becomes particularly significant, with the latter connected in policy discourse to EU market-making. The section also seeks to specify the meaning of transgovernmentalism in the context of European migration governance as way of circumventing an 'intergovernmental versus supranational' dichotomy in analysis of European migration governance.

As Heisler (1992) noted, international migration is simultaneously a societal and an international issue and needs to be analysed across those levels. International migration as a distinct social and political process is made visible by the borders of states (Zolberg 1989). Without states and their borders there would be no such thing as international migration. Thus, international migration is constituted and conditioned by the borders and boundaries of governance systems which, within the EU, retain a strong state-centred focus. Indeed, it has been shown that a precondition for EU membership is the demonstration by a candidate country that it can control its borders (a condition for this power then to be 'pooled' at EU level) (Geddes and Taylor 2013).

European integration does challenge state-centred analyses, however, by creating new forms of social and political power and authority 'above' the state at supranational level and generating new forms of international migration relations between member-states and between member- and non-member-states (Boswell 2003; Geddes 2005; Lavenex 2006). This could then lead to a supranational versus intergovernmental dichotomy, where the question becomes whether it is member-states or supranational institutions that drive cooperation and integration. However, this dichotomy is mistaken and potentially misleading when applied to migration governance. The hybrid structures of the EU contain both intergovernmental and supranational elements that have become melded since the 1980s into forms of intensive transgovernmental cooperation with a strong sectoral focus involving key migration policy actors, such as interior ministry officials, EU institutions, international organisations, employers, trade unions, think-tanks and non-governmental organisations (NGOs), with varying degrees of power and influence. Circumventing an intergovernmental versus supranational dichotomy allows the analysis to connect with an important body of work in international relations and international political economy (IPE) that focuses on the dynamics of transgovernmentalism (Keohane and Nye 1977; Slaughter 1997; Wallace 2000).

For the purpose of the analysis that follows, governance is taken to possess a 'dual meaning' as both an empirical manifestation of state adaptation and the conceptual representation of social systems (Pierre 2000: 3). This understanding privileges no particular site or location of governance and leaves open the scope for 'multilevel' dynamics and for many political 'centres', as well as for migrant networks to challenge or reconfigure states. The dynamics of international migration question the ideal type of modern statehood resting on notions of both internal and external sovereignty (Risse 2011). This questioning has been particularly evident in areas of 'limited statehood' within which states experience constraints on both their external and their internal sovereignty. Transgovernmentalism in the area of migration governance can thus be understood as a response to constraints on sovereign authority, but also needs to be related to the underlying conditions – economic, social, political, demographic and environmental – that 'produce' it, which I now explore.

THE DRIVERS OF MIGRATION AND NON-MIGRATION

The previous section focused on the ways in which international migration is defined by border relationships within and between member-states and between member-states and non-member-states. It was also argued that these border relationships are shaped by underlying economic, political, social, demographic and environmental factors. This section seeks to specify the effects of these migration drivers in more detail in order to specify the inequalities that play a key role in constituting European migration governance. It emphasises the importance of linking sending and receiving states, as well as of accounting for both mobility and immobility linked to inequalities within the global system, which play a key part in affecting international migration.

Extensive research evidence demonstrates the centrality of economic inequalities as key drivers of international migration. These take the form of, for example, wage and income differentials. In addition, international migration can become embedded within social networks leading to 'cumulative causation' (Massey 1990) whereby earlier migration flows become the basis for further flows. This can help to explain the specificity of migration as people move from particular places in origin countries to specific places in receiving countries. Political factors, such as conflict and the breakdown of governance systems, can also cause people to migrate, although conflict can also reduce people's ability to migrate by making it less safe. The Arab Spring saw around 25 000 people move to the EU from countries such as Libya and Tunisia, although far more movement was to neighbouring states in the Middle East and North Africa notwithstanding the re-emergence of a familiar rhetoric about the potential for 'swamping' or 'invasion' by migrants fleeing civil war and repression (Fargues and Fandrich 2012). Demographic factors such as age, fertility, morbidity and mortality can also drive migration, but their effects are likely to be indirect and occur through interaction with other drivers, thus counteracting simplistic Malthusian notions of 'population pressure'. Environmental factors (such as access to ecosystem services) can affect migration decisions, although here too interaction effects with other drivers are very important and make it difficult to distinguish a group of people as 'environmental migrants', given the multi-causal nature of migration (Foresight 2011).

It is beyond the scope of this chapter to analyse each of these factors in detail, but there are three key points that can be taken forward. First, underlying patterns of governance, linked closely to the structural features and ideological characteristics of the international political economy, play a key role in constituting international migration. Second, migration governance in EU member-states needs to be located in the context of the broader structures of the international political economy, which are pivotal to its production as a social and political process that becomes visible at the borders and boundaries of governance systems. Third, as we have seen, the EU and its member-states tend to focus on policies to stem migration flows, with more limited involvement in policies affecting the admission of migrants.

The five sets of drivers that we have identified underlie and constitute international migration. It is through their effects and interaction that international migration becomes visible as a social and political issue and is then defined and categorised, primarily at state borders. However, it is very important to note that the presence of a driver does not mean that a person will migrate. Of central importance is the fact that economic inequality, conflict and environmental degradation may actually reduce people's ability to move. Rather than all of these factors leading to 'floods' of migrants at the EU's borders, there may actually be a set of rather different issues associated with poverty, inequality and immobility. It is the relative immobility of large numbers of the world's population in the face of inequality that can get lost in often fevered debate – more usually in receiving countries – about the effects of migration. This does not mean that migration is always and in all circumstances a 'good thing' and must be encouraged, but it is important to understand the ways in which, for those who move, migration can form part of a solution for themselves and their families to the effects of inequalities. Restrictions on movement can exacerbate, rather than reduce, these inequalities.

MIGRATION GOVERNANCE BEYOND THE STATE

This section explores the EU as a regional system of migration governance and the ways in which liberalisation within the EU has been accompanied by 'boundary build-up' at its external borders. This helps to contextualise the subsequent discussion of the key components of the 'internal' and 'external' governance of migration in Europe. If governance beyond the state is to develop, then there are good reasons to assume that it would be more likely to occur at regional level within smaller, more focused organisations within which there can be a degree of shared purpose based on common interests (Hurrell 1995, 2007). The EU is highly relevant in this regard because it has reshaped European politics by achieving high levels of economic and political integration through the creation of a supranational governance system with a common institutional system, possessing both law-making powers and enforcement capacity.

International migration has been seen as an unlikely area of multilateral cooperation because of its close link to national sovereignty and tendencies towards domestic political salience (Keohane et al. 2009). However, there is a powerful tension in international politics between international migration embedded in multifaceted social networks and the laws, policies and institutions developed by states to regulate this movement. This tension has become more acute in the context of EU widening. This can give rise to perceptions that international migration is ungovernable or, at least, significantly stretches the capacity of governing authorities. It also leads to widespread perceptions of policy failure: that governments systematically fail to achieve their (usually restrictive) policy objectives (Castles 2004). It is this complex relationship between migration networks and political authority that defines the contemporary setting for understanding the governance of international migration. It can also help to explain how and why EU member-states have sought to cooperate on measures to stem migration flows while also being reluctant to commit themselves to common approaches that might affect their ability to regulate the numbers of migrants to be admitted to their territories.

As already noted, analysis of European migration governance necessarily hinges on the definition and redefinition of the borders and boundaries of European governance systems. What could be more powerfully symptomatic of EU borders than the electrified fences surrounding the Spanish enclaves in North Africa of Ceuta and Melilla, or Greek plans to build a wall on its land border with Turkey? The location and meaning of state borders and boundaries are also inextricably linked to the organisation of governance systems. The analysis of governance is also a huge field of scholarly enquiry. The provision of conditions for accumulation, welfare, security and continuity are core purposes of governance, but are not necessarily associated with a particular form or location of governmental authority. Governance itself has been taken to signify the 'hollowing out' of state authority in the context of more complex and 'multilevel' politics. The analysis within this chapter focuses on the continued resonance and relevance of states in their various forms within the international system as the key factor that defines and constitutes international migration. While states, and relations between them, have changed – nowhere more so than in Europe – they necessarily remain central to the analysis of international migration.

International migration provides an example of constraints on the sovereign authority of even the most powerful states. Within the EU, complex migration dynamics play out in a politics of migration, rights and security that affects the workplace and gendered employment, as well as asymmetric power relations between states. Andreas (1998: 591) has argued that more general dynamics are in play at the boundaries between developed and less-developed countries, and that these have powerful effects on Europe and North America as key destinations. In turn, this:

> suggest[s] a more complex and paradoxical dynamic: the expansion of cross-border economic activity and the decline of geopolitical tensions are paralleled by a rapid expansion of border policing and rising tensions over prohibited cross-border flows . . . These borders are increasingly protected and monitored, not to deter armies or impose tariffs on trade, but to confront a perceived invasion of 'undesirables', particularly illegal immigrants, drug traffickers, and other clandestine transnational actors.

Regionalisation in its very different forms in Europe (the EU) and North America (the North American Free Trade Area, NAFTA) can be understood as recognition of the reconstitution of state authority in the context of global restructuring, but also as designed to accelerate, modify or occasionally reverse the effects of globalisation. Regional integration seeks liberalisation in movement of goods, capital and services, but has a far more ambivalent relationship to population mobility. Massey and Espinosa (1997: 991–2) identify how:

> the provisions of NAFTA . . . help to bring about the social and economic transformations that generate migrants. The integration of the North American market will also create new links of transportation, telecommunication, and interpersonal acquaintance, connections that are necessary for the efficient movement of goods, information, and capital, but which also encourage and promote the movement of people, students, business executives, tourists, and, ultimately, undocumented workers.

This has clear resonance for the EU that has free movement provisions at its very core, but has encountered a problematic relationship between the extension of the 'four freedoms' (goods, capital, services and people) and the growing unease about international migration in many European countries. This is redolent too of what Purcell and Nevins (2004) refer to as 'boundary build-up', which entails efforts to liberalise free movement of goods, services and capital while simultaneously reinforcing controls to inhibit the movement of people, particularly those types of migrants defined as 'unwanted' by state policies.

THE DEVELOPMENT OF EU MIGRATION GOVERNANCE

The chapter now moves on to assess the European governance of migration, with a focus on developments since 1999. The section is particularly interested in EU policy on labour migration, although there are clear links between labour migration and other important migration flows, such as those by family migrants and asylum-seekers and refugees. Moreover, the EU has been very active in its self-declared 'fight against illegal immigration' (CEC 2006). Migration flows defined as irregular or illegal are closely linked to policies that define other flows as regular. In its Annual Report on Migration and Asylum for 2011, the Commission noted that it is, of course, difficult to give a precise figure for irregular migration, and referred to estimates of between 2.5 million and 4 million irregular migrants in EU member-states (CEC 2012: 4). Irregular and regular migration are, in effect, two sides of the same coin and are closely connected to the underlying economic, social, political, demographic and environmental drivers of migration within sending and destination states. While often mistakenly represented as an issue of desperate people in boats seeking to access the territory of southern member-states such as Malta and Italy, the reality of irregular migration is more complex. There is a shocking loss of life at the EU's southern maritime borders that shames the EU and its member-states, and also evidence of the serious mistreatment of migrants and denial of basic human rights (Stege et al. 2012). However, most irregular migrants do not enter via these dangerous routes, but rather enter by 'regular' routes and then overstay. Moreover, they are often able to find work, particularly in the informal economies of member-states.

EU migration governance thus needs to be related to the key forms of migration, such as for purposes of employment, for family reasons or to seek refuge, and also to the distinction made by states between regular and irregular flows. This is particularly relevant because the categories assigned to individuals ('high-skilled migrant', 'illegal immigrant') are not personal characteristics of individuals, but rather reflect the categorisations that develop at the borders of member-states. Categorisation is of obvious importance in the governance of migration and, as Bowker and Leigh Star (1999: 5) note, 'each standard and each category valorizes some point of view and silences another. This is not inherently a bad thing – indeed it is inescapable. But it *is* an ethical choice, and as such it is dangerous – not bad, but dangerous.'

As Box 22.1 shows, since 1999 there has been significant institutional and policy development encompassing both internal and external aspects of migration governance. The timeline in Box 22.1 shows key developments, particularly an extension of competence linked to constitutionalisation of a legal basis for action through treaties and then the institutionalisation of measures on various types of migration through EU level directives and regulations. As already noted, the application since 2009 of the OLP and a full role for the CJEU are of particular importance.

In addition to these institutional and policy dynamics, there is evidence of the 'multilevelling' of migration governance with power-sharing between institutions and

---

BOX 22.1   TIMELINE OF KEY EU MIGRATION POLICY DEVELOPMENTS, 1999–2012

1999   The Amsterdam Treaty creates a new Title IV of the Treaty dealing with free movement, migration and asylum.

The Tampere Agreement outlines a policy plan for the period until 2004 dealing with key aspects of migration policies including both the internal ('fair treatment of third country nationals') and the external dimensions ('root causes' approaches) of policy.

The High Level Working Group on Migration is established to bring together interior, foreign and development ministries to deal with external aspects of EU migration governance.

2000   Nice Treaty provides for the use of qualified majority voting (QMV) and the application of the co-decision procedure in areas related to irregular immigration and return (attained as of 2004).

Two directives are established seeking to tackle discrimination based on race and ethnic origin.

2003   Directive on the right to family reunification is established (Council Directive 2003/86/EC of 22 September 2003 on the right to family reunification (OJ L 251, 3.10.2003, p. 12)).

Directive on the rights of legally resident TCNs who are long-term residents is established (Directive 2003/109/EC of 25 November 2003 concerning the status of third-country nationals who are long-term residents (OJ L 16, 23.1.2004, p. 44)).

Directive on the rights of legally resident TCNs who are long-term residents is established.

2004 Commission Green Paper is produced on an EU approach to managing economic migration (COM(2004) 811 final).

Directive on student migration is established (2004/114/EC on the conditions of admission for TCNs for the purposes of studies, pupil exchange, unremunerated training or voluntary services).

2005 Policy Plan on Legal Migration is produced (COM(2005) 669 final).

The Hague Programme outlines a programme of work on internal security, including migration and asylum, for the period 2005–09.

Directive on migration by scientific researchers is established (2005/71/EC on a specific procedure for admitting TCNs for the purposes of scientific research).

2006 The Global Approach to Migration is adopted, dealing with both internal and external dimensions of migration governance (CEC 2006).

2007 The financial perspective 2007–13 allocated €4020 million to 'Solidarity and Management of Migration Flows' including €1820 million to external borders, €676 million to a return fund, €699 million to the European Refugee Fund and €825 million to an Integration Fund.

2008 The returns directive establishes common standards and procedures in member-states for returning illegally staying TCNs.

'Mobility Partnerships' are agreed with Moldova and Cape Verde, aiming to link routes for regular migration (particularly temporary forms of migration) to the control of irregular flows.

2009 The Lisbon Treaty comes into force, introducing a new provision on labour migration and expressing the intention to develop a common immigration policy. Article 79(5) states that this objective shall not affect the right of member-states to determine the numbers of labour migrants to be admitted. The Treaty applies the Ordinary Legislative Procedure (OLP) to migration policy and extends CJEU competencies to allow preliminary references to be made from lower courts in member-states. The EU Charter of Fundamental Rights was made binding on member-states (with limitations on its use in the Czech Republic and UK).

Blue card directive (2009/50/EC) creates fast-track and flexible procedures for the admission of 'highly qualified employees' and their family members.

Mobility Partnership is agreed with Georgia.

2010 The Stockholm Programme outlines a policy agenda on internal security for the period 2010–14, including a strong focus on the external dimension of policy in the context of the 'Global Approach to Migration and Mobility' (CEC 2011a).

2011 The single permit directive is adopted (2011/98/EU) that seeks a common basis for the rights of TCNs in all member-states.

Mobility Partnership is agreed with Armenia.

incorporate both internal and external aspects of migration governance and are sympto-matic of the hybrid character of the institutional and policy setting for European migra-tion governance.

'Internal' Migration Governance

The 2000s saw a steady accretion of institutional competencies, albeit within a frag-mented policy system within which member-states have maintained a grip on admis-sions policies, and there has emerged 'variable geometry' (with Denmark, Ireland the UK remaining outside of most measures). The EU has not developed a comprehensive migration policy, but has developed a sectorally focused approach. This has given rise to directives on family migration, the rights of long-term residents who are TCNs, stu-dents and researchers. The returns directive of 2008 applied to the expulsion of irregular migrants and was the first directive in the area of migration policy that was agreed using the co-decision procedure involving the Council and EP as co-legislators.

Of particular significance are the directives on family reunion and long-term resi-dents, as both saw tension during the negotiation process between the Commission (as the originator of the policy proposals) and member-states. This was particularly evident in the provisions within both directives for states to adopt 'integration measures'. These are important because they make a link between admission and integration policies. The family reunion directive of 2003 determined the conditions under which legally resident TCNs could exercise the right to family reunification, but also recognises the rights of member-states to impose conditions on family migration and gives them margin to do so in relation to factors such as the definition of the family, waiting periods and integration measures. It also 'aims to highlight' the need for integration policy to grant TCNs rights and obligations comparable to those of EU citizens. During the negoti-ating period the Commission was forced, in the face of member-state opposition, to temper aspects of the original proposals that would have impinged more directly on member-states' admissions policies. A core group of states – with Austria, Germany and the Netherlands to the fore – insisted on EU measures that did not place additional constraints on their capacity to regulate admission by family members. The directive allowed member-states a significant margin to pursue their own policy objectives, par-ticularly related to integration measures, although this has led to cases being brought to the CJEU where the proportionality of such measures has been contested, as discussed below.

In terms of the involvement of supranational institutions in the development of the family reunion directive, the three-year negotiation process between the Commission's original proposal in 2000 and final agreement in 2003 saw movement away from the Commission's more liberal initial proposals towards a stronger emphasis on integration by migrants and their families. The Commission's original proposals had conceptual-ised 'integration' in relation to the promotion of social stability through, for example, access to training and education for family members. The final directive saw the inclu-sion of integration provisions in accordance with national laws in member-states. In the Netherlands, for example, 'integration abroad' tests require people to demonstrate the capacity (for example, linguistically) to 'integrate' before they migrate. In 2011 a Green Paper produced by the Commission initiated a consultation process and identified weaknesses in the 2003 directive, particularly in respect of the significant discretion given to member-states (CEC 2011b).

The basis for EU action regarding the rights of long-term legally resident TCNs was closely linked to 'market-making' objectives. However, within this directive we also see that member-states insisted on being able to apply integration measures in their national laws. The directive established rights and freedoms for long-term TCNs to be granted after five years of continual residence. These rights include access to employment and self-employed activity, education and vocational training, social protection and assistance, and goods and services. The directive also gives the right to move and reside in another member-state. As with the directive on family reunion, during the Council negotiations a clause was inserted (in Article 5, conditions for acquisition of secure status) to include 'compliance with integration conditions provided for by national law'. Member-states were given wide discretion to use mandatory integration requirements (for example, passing an integration test or covering financial costs) before a person could be granted access to the benefits and rights conferred by the status of a long-term resident.

While measures on family migration and the rights of long-term residents relate to important aspects of migration law and policy, neither relate to the core of migration policy, namely admissions. In fact, both the family reunion and long-term residents' directives make it very clear that admissions remain a matter for member-states, and also introduce into EU-level law the idea that admissions and integration are linked. This reflects a clear preoccupation in national law and policy in sending states with the recruitment of economic migrants, preferably the highly skilled. The rationale for this was captured by ex-French President Nicolas Sarkozy who argued that France preferred immigration that was *choisie* (chosen), such as by the highly skilled, to that which was *subie* (endured), such as by family members (Carvalho and Geddes 2012).

While numbers of migrants to be admitted remains a member-state prerogative, there has been some involvement by the EU in rules related to admission. These take the form of a sectoral approach that focuses on particular kinds of labour migration and tries to connect EU action to arguments about the 'added value' of EU involvement in certain aspects of migration policy for, in particular, economic and demographic reasons. For example, in its 3rd Annual Report on Immigration and Asylum of 2011, the Commission once again sought to make the case for the potential contribution of migration to the EU's growth agenda (CEC 2012: 4) on the basis that even at a time of crisis, 'economic migration . . . remains an important component of efforts to address the challenge of labour shortages, notably in the context of the EU's ageing population and an increasingly competitive international market for talent with other countries outside Europe also experiencing skills shortages'. It also announced the intention to open a consultation by the end of 2012 with member-states, social partners (such as employers and trade unions) and other stakeholders on 'the opportunities of economic migration', although the consultation had only limited effects as the political climate at member-state level was not conducive to Commission measures on economic migration (CEC 2012: 5).

It is in this context that we can consider the EU's 'blue card' directive of 2009. This seeks to approximate rules between member-states on application for the status of highly qualified migrants and the rights associated with this status. The blue card system creates a one-track procedure for non-EU citizens to apply for entry as a highly qualified migrant for a period of up to two years, with scope for renewal. Denmark, Ireland and the UK are not covered by the directive because of their ability to opt out. The directive also seeks to promote mobility of the highly skilled between member-states. The directive does not cover the numbers to be admitted, nor the sectors of employment that would be preferred or prioritised for admission. These remain matters for member-states to decide. There was some criticism from non-EU states that this effort by the EU to involve itself in the 'competition' for highly qualified migrants could contribute to the 'brain drain'. The South African government expressed this concern with regard to recruitment of healthcare professionals. Debate soon shifted to ways in which the blue card scheme could be further developed. For example, Parkes and Angenendt (2010) argued that the EU could involve itself in 'sovereignty-lite' efforts to attract highly qualified migrants and thus create some 'added value' for member-state policies. They contended that efforts needed to be made to develop human capital within the EU through training, as well as opportunities for mobility within the EU. They also suggested that greater efforts needed to be made to exploit the value of higher education, with the possibility for student migrants being encouraged to live and work in the EU after finishing their studies. As with many EU measures, this first initial step does look rather timid. It introduced weak forms of coordination into the area of highly qualified migration, but did not impinge on the ability of member-states to implement the directive as they saw fit and in relation to their own perceptions of labour-market needs. The measures surveyed in this section all relate to the EU's role in 'internal' migration governance. They show efforts to institutionalise and constitutionalise an EU approach to migration policy that draws from broader arguments about economic integration, but also reflects the trend in member-state policies to make connections between admissions policy and integration. The EU thus seeks to position itself in this debate. There is a tendency when surveying such developments to focus on their novelty. Indeed, the role of the EU as a supranational organisation is new and distinct. It is in many ways a remarkable development that a supranational organisation with law-making powers can now involve itself in such core state concerns as migration policy (with the limits that have been discussed). However, it must also be asked whether this changes the content or scope of policy. Here there are grounds to be more sceptical. Indeed, it could be argued that the core dilemmas have remained quite stable and that it is the context within which decisions are made that has changed. For example, writing the late 1980s, Zolberg noted that:

> In recent decades, the capitalist democracies have reaffirmed their long-established immigration policies which, collectively, constitute a protective wall against self-propelled migration, but with small doors that allow for specific flows. One of the doors was provided to allow for the procurement of certain types of labor; and the other to let in a small number of asylum-seekers. The future shape of international migrations depends in large part on how these doors are manipulated. (Zolberg 1989: 406)

The discussion thus far shows that the EU is now involved in collective, EU-level efforts to address the policy dilemma as viewed from the perspective of major destination countries. In the next section, we see how this has also involved the development of an important external dimension to European migration governance, or what could be called 'migration as foreign policy'.

'External' Migration Governance

There is a very different basis in law and policy to the EU's external dimension of migration governance. Here the focus has been on exporting EU measures to non-member-states with a perception on the part of some analysts that this has been motivated by the desire to co-opt non-member-states within the control-oriented EU approach to migration (Lavenex 2006). These efforts have also had a strong bilateral focus with, for example, Italy having close links with Libya (both during the Gaddafi regime and with attempts to maintain agreements with the new government in Libya) and Spain working closely with Morocco. The external dimension of policy has also been central to the GAMM. The GAMM is very clear in its focus on interdependence as the core driver of EU action on migration and on the relevance of both the internal and external dimensions of policy. In its Communication on the GAMM published in 2011, the Commission (CEC 2011a: 2) stated that 'globalisation, demographic change and societal transformation are affecting the EU, its member states and countries around the world'. The Communication refers to the importance of dialogue at global level, but emphasises the centrality of regional, national and local levels. The EU thus positions itself as the key interlocutor between member-states and other countries, with the development of dialogue structures that bring together EU and non-EU states.

There has been a rapid growth in interest in the external dimension of EU migration governance, which is predicated on the development of capacity to control borders and manage migration. There are significant differences in the extent of the leverage that the EU can exert when dealing with non-member-states. For potential member-states there is a far more direct mechanism for transmission of EU priorities into the settings of domestic governance systems. This occurs through the imposition of the requirements of Chapter 24 of the EU *acquis* covering free movement, migration and asylum (see, e.g., Taylor et al. 2012). The EU has also sought to consolidate migration within its relations within the 16 countries that constitute its 'neighbourhood'. Without the 'carrot' of membership, the EU seeks issue linkages to connect migration to other issues, such as economic development. According to the Commission, the GAMM is contextualised by the overarching framework of external migration policy and within the EU's foreign policy framework. The principal mechanism is dialogue on mobility and migration to 'exchange information, identify shared interests and build trust and commitment as a basis for operational co-operation for the mutual benefit of the EU and its partners' (CEC 2011a: 5).

The clearest example of the construction of migration and mobility within the EU's external relations occurs through what are known as Mobility Partnerships (thus far with Moldova, Cape Verde, Georgia and Armenia). These reflect the longer-term development of EU external governance in the area of migration and the focus on ways in which the EU can seek to combine highly selective admissions policies with measures to stem irregular migration. The intentions of Mobility Partnerships are bold in that they seek to develop new forms of international migration relations between the EU and non-member-states. However, as already noted, the decision about the number of migrants to be admitted remains a matter for the member-states. Thus, a non-EU country can reach agreement on a Mobility Partnership with the EU, but for it to have any meaningful effect on opportunities for its citizens to migrate to an EU member-state, agreement would be required from that member-state on, for example, the numbers of migrants who could move and the economic sectors which they could enter. There is little as yet to suggest that Mobility Partnerships have created new opportunities that would not already have existed as a result of national recruitment. Mobility Partnerships also demonstrate the link between the internal and external dimensions of EU migration governance. The basis for them is the pursuit of member-states' policy priorities; that is, seeking to work with sending countries to manage migration and reinforce the selective basis of the admissions policies. In return for some access to routes for labour migration to the EU (although admissions is a matter for the member-states and not for the EU), partner countries are expected to make efforts to ensure that they control irregular flows. Mobility Partnerships are essentially intergovernmental agreements that are not binding on member-states. The Commission's role is limited to coordination, while the European Parliament and CJEU are largely excluded (Carrera et al. 2011).

This external dimension fits within a broader body of work on the external governance of the EU, which occurs when 'the institutional/legal boundary is moved beyond the circle of member states' (Lavenex 2004: 683). Lavenex shows that the institutional and legal boundaries do not necessarily move at the same time and argues that 'the crucial criterion for external governance is the extension of the legal boundary of authority beyond institutional integration. In contrast to cooperation under an international agreement or convention, external governance takes place when parts of the *acquis communautaire* are extended to non-member states.' This occurs largely in the realm of intergovernmental cooperation with a very limited role for supranational institutions. In terms of policy content, Parkes (2009: 328) has observed that, through the development of Mobility Partnerships, the EU is acknowledging that responsibility for the regulation of migration to and from the EU is now shared between the member-states and the EU. The EU is thus a new arena for interstate cooperation on migration and is thus also reflective of a change in the strategic setting for action on migration governance. There is also scope for differences to emerge between member-states in the implementation of Mobility Partnerships. Parkes (2009: 331) also finds Mobility Partnerships to be 'conceptually ambitious but fragmented in their application', as there is scope for conflict with other EU objectives, such as in the field of development policy.

CONCLUSION

This chapter has explored the construction of migration as an issue of European governance with implications for both internal policy and external relations. It has sought to address the issue of how, why and with what effects the EU has now acquired a greater role in the area of migration governance and what this means both for our understanding of governance and also for the constitution of migration policy. The chapter has sought to demonstrate how the EU cuts across the societal and the international levels and to reveal the relevance of beginning a discussion of European migration governance with a prior discussion of the centrality of the border and boundaries of European states in configuring this debate. It argued that, as international migration is made visible by the borders and boundaries of European governance systems, it is crucial to explore the ways in which underlying economic, social, political, demographic and environmental processes can affect international migration, and in turn be affected by it. International migration was thus specified as a challenge of governance and not to governance. This is more than a semantic issue because it means that international migration is related to the underlying conditions that 'produce' it and these are tied to the broader scope and ideational context within which 'the European project' has developed and will develop in the future. International migration thus needs to be linked to a broader debate about the future of Europe. This is not only because migration will continue to play a key role in European societies, but also because it is part of a much broader debate about the future of work and welfare in Europe. International migration does not drive these debates, but the relationship between migration and various types of labour market and welfare state is now a key issue for the EU as it thinks about its economic future in the face not only of economic crisis, but also other factors such as demographic change.

It was in this context that this chapter sought to identify the key drivers of policy, particularly in the area of labour migration policy. The important distinction between migration and mobility was identified and it was argued that the pursuit of 'virtuous' mobility and of new forms of temporary and circular migration has become a key rationale for the development of EU action. Member-states have not been willing to cede responsibility for the numbers of migrants to be admitted, but the EU has developed a sectoral approach that now encompasses highly qualified migrants plus proposals for similar common rules at EU level for seasonal workers and intra-corporate transferees. This does not amount to a common migration policy, but does significantly change the dynamics of migration governance. Not least, it changes the strategic context within which migration policy is understood and made. However, the policy dilemma remains fundamentally similar and can be captured by the 'walls' and 'doors' analogy used by Zolberg (1989). Moreover, the form that this governance takes – namely, the development of transgovernmentalism – helps to circumvent the intergovernmental versus supranational dichotomy and enables us to see how cooperation over time creates hybrid structures containing both intergovernmental and supranational elements.

REFERENCES

Acosta, D. and A. Geddes (2013), 'The development, application and implications of an EU rule of law in the area of migration policy', *Journal of Common Market Studies*, **51** (2), 179–93.

Andreas, P. (1998), 'The escalation of immigration control in the post-NAFTA era', *Political Science Quarterly*, **113** (4), 591–615.

Boswell, C. (2003), 'The external dimension of EU migration and asylum policy', *International Affairs*, **79** (3), 619–38.

Bowker, G. and S. Leigh Star (1999), *Sorting Things Out: Classification and its Consequences*, Cambridge, MA: MIT Press.

Carrera, S., A. Atger, E. Guild and D. Kostakopoulou (2011), 'Labour immigration policy in the EU: a renewed agenda for Europe 2020', CEPS Policy Brief No. 240, Brussels: Centre for European Policy Studies.

Carvalho, Joao and Andrew Geddes (2012), 'La politique d'immigration: la retour à l'identité national', in J. Maillard and Y. Surel (eds), *Politiques publiques. 3. Politiques publiques sous la présidence Sarkozy*, Paris: Presse FNSP, pp. 279–98.

Castles, S. (2004), 'Why migration policies fail', *Ethnic and Racial Studies*, **27** (2), 205–27.

Commission of the European Communities (CEC) (2000), *Communication on a Community Immigration Policy*, COM(2000) 757 final.

Commission of the European Communities (CEC) (2005), *Communication: Policy Plan on Legal Migration*, COM(2005) 669 final.

412   *Handbook of the international political economy of governance*

Commission of the European Communities (CEC) (2006), *Communication on Policy Priorities in the Fight against Illegal Immigration*, COM(2006) 402 final.
Commission of the European Communities (CEC) (2007), *Communication on Circular Migration and Mobility Partnerships between the EU and Third Countries*, COM(2007) 248 final.
Commission of the European Communities (CEC) (2011a), *Communication on the Global Approach to Migration and Mobility*, SEC(2011) 1353 final.
Commission of the European Communities (CEC) (2011b), *Green Paper on the Right to Family Reunification of Third Country Nationals Living in the EU* (Directive 2003/86 EC).
Commission of the European Communities (CEC) (2012), *Communication: 3rd Annual report on Immigration and Asylum* (2011), SWD(2012) 139 final.
European Migration Network (EMN) (2011), *Temporary and Circular Migration: Empirical Evidence, Current Policy Practice and Future Options in EU Member States*, Luxembourg: European Migration Network.
Fargues, P. and C. Fandrich (2012), *Migration After the Arab Spring*, Migration Policy Centre Research Report, 2012/09, Florence: European University Institute.
Foresight (2011), *Migration and Global Environmental Change: Future Challenges and Opportunities*, London: Government Office for Science.
Freeman, G. (1998), 'The decline of sovereignty: politics and immigration restriction in liberal states', in C. Joppke (ed.), *Challenge to the Nation State: Immigration in Western Europe and the United States*, Oxford: Oxford University Press, pp. 96–108.
Geddes, A. (2005), 'Europe's border relationships and international migration relations', *Journal of Common Market Studies*, **43** (4), 787–806.
Geddes, A. and A. Taylor (2013), 'How, why and with what effects EU capacity bargains strengthen states: the case of migration and border security in South East Europe', *West European Politics*, **36** (1), 51–70.
Global Commission on International Migration (GCIM) (2005), *Migration in an Inter-Connected World: New Directions for Action*, Geneva: Global Commission on International Migration.
Guiraudon, V. (2000), 'European integration and migration policy: vertical policy-making as venue shopping', *Journal of Common Market Studies*, **38** (2), 251–71.
Heisler, M. (1992), 'Migration, international relations and the new Europe: theoretical perspectives from institutional political sociology', *International Migration Review*, **26** (2), 596–622.
Hurrell, A. (1995), 'Explaining the resurgence of regionalism in world politics', *Review of International Studies*, **21** (4), 331–58.
Hurrell, A. (2007), *On Global Order: Power, Values and the Constitution of International Society*, Oxford: Oxford University Press.
Keohane, R., S. Macedo and A. Moravcsik (2009), 'Democracy-enhancing multilateralism', *International Organization*, **63** (1), 1–31.
Keohane, R. and J. Nye (1977), *Power and Interdependence: World Politics in Transition*, Boston, MA: Little Brown.
Lavenex, S. (2004), 'EU external governance in "wider Europe"', *Journal of European Public Policy*, **11** (4), 680–700.
Lavenex, S. (2006), 'Shifting up and shifting out: the foreign policy of European immigration control', *West European Politics*, **29** (2), 329–50.
Massey, D. (1990), 'Social structures, household strategies and the cumulative causation of migration', *Population Index*, **56** (91), 3–26.
Massey, D. and K. Espinosa (1997), 'What's driving Mexico–US migration: a theoretical, empirical and policy analysis', *American Journal of Sociology*, **102** (4), 939–99.
Parkes, R. (2009), 'EU mobility partnerships: a model of EU policy co-ordination?', *European Journal of Migration and Law*, **11** (4), 327–45.
Parkes, R. and S. Angenendt (2010), 'After the Blue Card: EU policy on highly skilled migration. Three ways out of the impasse', Heinrich Boll Stiftung, Discussion paper, February.
Pierre, J. (ed.) (2000), *Debating Governance: Authority, Steering and Democracy*, Oxford: Oxford University Press.
Purcell, S. and J. Nevins (2004), 'Pushing the boundary: state restructuring, state theory, and the case of the US–Mexico border enforcement in the 1990s', *Political Geography*, **24** (2), 211–35.
Risse, T. (2011), *Governance without a State: Policies and Politics in Areas of Limited Statehood*, Ithaca, NY: Cornell University Press.
Ruhs, M. (2006), 'The potential of temporary migration programmes in future international migration policy', *International Labour Review*, **145** (1–2), 7–36.
Slaughter, A.-M. (1997), 'The real new world order', *Foreign Affairs*, **76** (5), 183–97.
Stege, U., M. Veglio, E. Roman and A. Ogada-Osir (2012), *Betwixt and Between: Turin's CIE. An Investigation into Turin's Immigration Detention Centre*, Turin: International University College of Turin.

Taylor, A., A. Geddes and C. Lees (2012), *The European Union and South East Europe: The Dynamics of Multi-Level Governance and Europeanisation*, London: Routledge.

Vertovec, S. (2007), 'Circular migration: the way forward in global policy?', International Migration Institute, University of Oxford, Working Paper, 2007, No. 4.

Wallace, H. (2000), 'An institutional anatomy and five policy models', in H. Wallace, W. Wallace and M. Pollack (eds), *Policy-Making in the European Union*, 5th edition, Oxford: Oxford University Press, pp. 49–89.

Zolberg, A. (1989), 'The next waves: migration theory for a changing world', *International Migration Review*, **23** (3), 403–30.

23 The international political economy of governing carbon

Peter Newell

How should 'we' govern carbon? More precisely, how should we govern carbon: in a global world where direct intergovernmental and public control over the actors and processes which extract and burn most carbon is either weak and indirect or often non-existent; in a carbon-constrained world faced with dangerous levels of climate change, but in which political responses to the threat fall well short of what the science suggests is required; and in a world of extreme poverty and inequality in which large increases in carbon associated with energy use will be required to meet the basic needs of millions of the world's inhabitants?

The first point refers to such issues as the weak and fragmented nature of global energy governance, where governments continue to resist the concession of power to regional and global institutions over a sector of such high strategic importance (Florini and Sovacool 2009; Newell 2011). The second refers to the scale of cooperation, political action and finance required to keep temperature increases below 2°C compared with pre-industrial levels (the stated aim of the 2009 Copenhagen Accord), amid calls for US$100 billion to be made available annually by 2020 for mitigation and adaptation actions, and all in the context of a global financial crisis. The third refers to the 1.6 billion people who are still without access to electricity, who are the target of the UN's Year of Sustainable Energy for All. Meeting policy goals associated with climate change, energy security and energy poverty simultaneously implies reconciling a number of potential conflicts where the goals are in tension with one another and compete for prominence. In short, address-ing one can undermine efforts to achieve another. For example, achieving energy security through access to secure supplies of fossil fuels conflicts with the reduction in dependence on fossil fuels that is necessary to tackle climate change. Confronting energy poverty, meanwhile, requires providing access to energy to many millions of the world's citizens. But, if this need is met through a huge increase in fossil fuel use, climate change objec-tives will be undermined. Collective efforts to manage competing uses of, and claims over, carbon mean, in effect, dealing with the everyday governance of the carbon cycle.

All life is based on the element carbon – carbon that is constantly on the move, cir-culating between soil, forest, marine and atmospheric ecosystems. Although global governance since the 1990s has been oriented towards managing that part of the cycle where fossil fuels are burned and the resulting emissions released into the atmosphere, increasingly, as I shall discuss below, soil carbon and carbon absorbed (and released) by forests and oceans are also increasingly subject to governance instruments. These aim to record and value the contribution of these resources to the carbon cycle in monetary terms, because their healthy functioning is critical to avoiding the worst effects of climate change.

Precisely because it is clearly about much more than tackling climate change, the global governance of carbon therefore presents political and economic challenges of dizzying proportions, for which there are few historical precedents or positive examples to imitate. Until the late twentieth century, when a growing scientific consensus and multilateral responses to the threat of climate change forced the issue, carbon has neither been defined as a problem, nor been governed in an explicit, public or purposeful way. This was so, despite carbon's intimate relationship to colonialism, imperialism and war, given the role that oil and coal, in particular, have played in fuelling (literally) such ventures and constituting the *raison d'être* for territorial conquest in the first place (Yergin 1992; Harvey 2003). Climate change, however, has come to be seen as a quintessential 'wicked' problem (Rittel and Webber 1973) in its own right, imbricated as it is in the everyday production and consumption of energy, food and water. Indeed, carbon is embodied (literally) in all human activity, so decisions have to be made about which levels of carbon use are appropriate and legitimate within the thresholds imposed by the Earth's carrying capacity. As Gavin Bridge (2013) has noted, carbon has become:

> a common denominator for thinking about the organization of social life in relation to the environment . . . From fossil-fuel addiction and peak oil to blood barrels and climate change, carbon's emergence as a dominant optic for thinking and writing about the world and human relations within it is tied to the various emergencies with which it is associated.

Power is inevitably exercised in arriving at judgements about legitimate uses of carbon. Chinese steel is targeted by United States proposals for border tax adjustments – which impose tariffs on products not subject to carbon control in the exporting country – so as to ensure it does not enjoy a comparative advantage over products manufactured in the US which have been subject to such control (Cosbey 2008). Yet other countries have not dared to challenge the US about the carbon intensity of its exports (of cars, agricultural produce and the like). Equity-based proposals for 'contraction and convergence', whereby richer countries would have to contract their emissions sharply while poorer countries converge upwards to an agreed per capita entitlement within a carbon budget determined by what is necessary to minimise the threat of dangerous climate change, have struggled to gain traction because of their distributional implications. Most emissions trading schemes to date instead employ an allocation system which distributes permits on the basis of existing levels of use, effectively institutionalising unequal use of the commons. Global responses to the challenge of carbon governance, unsurprisingly, then reflect and reinforce existing social and power relations.

This chapter traces and seeks to explain the governance of carbon by an array of public and private actors operating transnationally and across scales, as befits any attempt to track, monitor and commodify key elements of the carbon cycle. The main focus of the chapter is the rise and evolution of market-based tools to govern carbon by states and business alike, for which high levels of political commitment remain in place notwithstanding plentiful evidence of their shortcomings (Gilbertson and Reyes 2009). This is where the ideological component of carbon governance comes into play – through a commitment to carbon markets over other possible solutions to manage the environmental side-effects of carbon despite their poor performance to date. In part, it is driven by the opportunities presented by carbon commodification, which will be described later in the chapter: 'blue' carbon to value the carbon-absorption properties of oceans and marine ecosystems; 'green' carbon to capture, store and value carbon sequestration in forests; or 'gold' carbon to denote carbon-reduction projects that also deliver higher levels of social benefits. It also reflects the preferences of powerful actors for carbon trading over taxation or regulation as responses to climate change.

The way carbon is governed and ungoverned yields many insights into the international political economy of governance in general. Firstly, we can observe patterns of accommodation and resistance by powerful actors to calls for new or strengthened forms of governance. Powerful states and transnational corporations (TNCs) seek to shape governance in ways which preserve their control over highly profitable sectors and activities responsible for generating the bulk of the world's carbon dioxide emissions. Strategies of resistance have taken a range of forms, from early denial of the scientific case for action on climate change (which continues to be a strategy for some powerful industry bodies and oil-producing states), to questioning the economic case for action (which continues to be a line of resistance for organisations such as the Global Warming Foundation in the United Kingdom and the American Petroleum Institute in the United States), through to accommodation by promoting the least-cost, minimum-change options in the form of voluntary agreements or carbon trading, often in alliance with pro-market civil-society groups (Meckling 2011; Newell and Paterson 1998). The ability of political elites to accommodate pressures to subject carbon to constraints, while resisting demands for policies which would more profoundly upset the existing order, is reflected in the persistence of the ungovernance (neglect) of core areas of economic activity in the world's most powerful states, such as energy and trade. The effect is to reduce the overall impact and effectiveness of concerted efforts to reduce carbon emissions. The implications of increases in carbon associated with new rounds of trade liberalisation are off-limits in terms of policy debate, while the World Bank's ongoing support for fossil fuel infrastructures directly undermines any emissions savings produced by its climate programmes (WRI 2008). The forms of power which operate to accommodate the threat that far-reaching action on climate change poses to the existing organisation of the global political economy operate at an ideological, institutional and material level (Levy and Newell 2002), as will be explained below. What results is the disconnect between regulation of capital, which remains weak and fragmented, and regulation for capital, which establishes rules of the game and property rights necessary for new waves of accumulation – in this case through carbon trading.

Secondly, and relatedly, we can observe a shift over time towards the marketisation of carbon governance (Newell 2008). The observation made by Michael Jacobs (1997: 365) in the late 1990s – that, 'as in other spheres of political and economic life, markets have become a central organising principle of environmental policy' – is even more pertinent today. While the marketisation of environmental governance has perhaps gone furthest in the area of climate change, where 'politics are increasingly conducted by, through and for markets' (Newell and Paterson 2010: 77), the trend has been widespread. This can traced through the creation of permit trading schemes for sulphur dioxide in the US and emissions trading schemes in the European Union (EU), UK and Denmark, tradeable quota systems in fisheries policy in New Zealand and the Renewable Energy Certificate trading schemes that now operate in a number of countries. In the case of carbon, it is also manifested in the rise of private governance and voluntary regulation, public–private partnerships and a plurality of transnational climate governance arrangements

(Hoffman 2011; Bulkeley et al. 2012), as well as attempts to individualise responsibility for collective failures through proposals for tradeable personal carbon allowances.

Thirdly, the evolving nature of carbon governance reflects shifting geometries of power in the global political economy. This is true in terms of realignments of power between the state and capital, in conditions of globalisation in general and with regard to the role of finance capital in particular, which has been one of the main beneficiaries of carbon markets and is central to the financialisation of carbon (Newell and Paterson 2009). It is also true at a geopolitical state level, with the growing economic power and related exponential increase in carbon emissions that has accompanied spectacular growth patterns in China, India and Brazil in particular. The Copenhagen summit in 2009, in which the US considered China, India, Brazil and South Africa above the EU as the central players with which targets and measures had to be discussed, was highly emblematic of the shifting geopolitics of climate change. The enhanced power of these countries has served to raise the profile of the intimate connections between the global economy and responses to climate change around issues such as trade, aid and technology, which are enrolled as bargaining chips in the design of grand strategies for tackling climate change. There are concerns about 'climate protectionism' being used by powerful states to deny access to their markets for products claimed to be carbon intensive (as with the use of border tax adjustments noted above), while at the same time 'kicking away the ladder' (Chang 2002) by denying the use of subsidies, infant industry support and the like to developing countries nurturing 'clean energy' sectors. In 2011, for example, the US threatened to bring a World Trade Organization (WTO) case against China's use of subsidies to its wind energy industry. The issue was the fairness of China's clean technology subsidies and domestic sourcing requirements (so-called import substitution subsidies), and conflict was only narrowly avoided when China agreed to end the use of the subsidies in question (ICTSD 2011).

Fourth, the scalar politics of carbon governance enlist global and regional institutions, cities and local communities, non-governmental organisations (NGOs) and businesses in collective (though often not common) endeavours to tackle climate change and govern carbon in innovative ways (Bailey and Maresh 2009). This has occurred through international public–private partnerships, such as the Renewable Energy and Energy Efficiency Partnership (REEEP), Carbon Rationing Groups of concerned citizens at the local level, and alliances of cities such as the C40 programme supported by the Clinton Foundation (Bulkeley and Newell 2010). In the case of carbon trading, it embodies attempts to capture carbon within global circuits of capital, producing forms of governance which require trans-scalar cooperation between local communities and NGOs, consultants and verification agencies, banks, corporations, governments and the United Nations (UN). This brings together the hosts of carbon offset projects, purchasers and financiers, and public agencies responsible for the approval of projects and the release of carbon credits. This can be described as multilevel governance, since it transcends local to global decision-making and arenas of authority. But it also embodies a spatial element. This refers, for example, to the 'fixes' employed to capitalise on profitable opportunities to govern carbon in a context of uneven development: reducing carbon where it is cheapest to do so and selling it where demand and prices are highest.

These spatial social dynamics are thus international and intra-national. The global spatial organisation of carbon pollution occurs between countries, such as the export of resource-intensive forms of production overseas. These forms of 'ecologically uneven exchange' mean that the responsibility for pollution, as well as the pollution itself, is redistributed globally such that 'emissions are increasing sharply in developing countries as wealthy countries "offshore" the energy and resource intensive stages of production' (Roberts and Parks 2008: 169). Environmental justice literatures, meanwhile, highlight the racial, gender and class politics of the intra-national, as well as global, spatial geographies of contamination: who lives with the burdens of extracting energy and its various side-effects, including carbon emissions, and who captures the benefits of patterns of production organised in this way (Carmin and Agyeman 2011; Newell 2007).

I will illustrate below the importance of each of these dimensions in practice through the governance of carbon through offset mechanisms and emissions trading. The following sections first provide a brief history of carbon trading, which charts the shift from state-led regulation to the embrace of market-based instruments. Secondly, the chapter looks at the development of 'multi-colour carbon': attempts to isolate and valorise the contributions of oceans and forests, for example, to the carbon cycle and therefore to tackling climate change. Their aim is to incentivise their protection by enrolling them in global circuits of capital through carbon trading. Thirdly, the chapter looks at the governance of the carbon economy before offering some overall conclusions.

FROM COMMAND AND CONTROL TO MARKETISATION: A BRIEF HISTORY OF CARBON TRADING

We now have what is commonly called a carbon economy. However, it is, in fact, made up of several, increasingly interconnected, carbon markets. It takes different forms in different parts of the world, but includes emissions trading systems (ETS) in the EU and US, emerging schemes in cities (such as Montreal) and countries such as China and South Korea, and the buying and selling of offsets through the UN's Clean Development Mechanism (CDM) created as part of the Kyoto Protocol, as well as through a voluntary carbon market (VCM). The carbon economy has had a turbulent history since its inception: its monetary value was significantly affected by the global financial meltdown of the late 2000s, which suppressed levels of demand for carbon credits, and its legitimacy questioned amid claims of climate fraud (double-counting of credits), 'toxic' and 'subprime carbon', and acts of (neo)colonial dispossession of communities in the global South, such as areas of forest being acquired for carbon sequestration purposes (Bachram 2004; Lohmann 2006; Friends of the Earth 2009).

Despite its crisis-ridden nature, the importance of the carbon economy should not be underestimated. Interest in the CDM exceeded expectations. The global value of primary offset transactions grew to US$7.2 billion in 2008, more than a tenfold growth from 2004, largely due to the CDM. Under the CDM, Certified Emissions Reductions (CERs) amounting to more than 1.8 billion tonnes of carbon dioxide (CO_2) equivalent were produced in the first commitment period of the Kyoto Protocol (2008–12) (UNFCCC 2012). The revenues of the CDM constitute the largest source of mitigation finance to developing countries to date (World Bank 2010). Over the 2001 to 2012 period, the CDM spurred US$215 billion in investment (UNFCCC 2012). The demand for credits issued by the CDM is dominated by the EU ETS which accounted for 84 per cent of global carbon market value in 2010 (Capoor and Ambrosi 2011). The voluntary carbon market, meanwhile, remains only a fraction of the size of regulated markets. But, while the volumes in the VCM remain very small, at less than 0.3 per cent of the global carbon markets, overall transaction volumes increased 28 per cent between 2009 and 2010, and 2010 was a record year for activity in the VCM. Across carbon markets as a whole, however, after five consecutive years of robust growth, the total value of the global carbon market stalled at US$142 billion (Capoor and Ambrosi 2011). Carbon prices are currently at an all-time low, fluctuating between €4 and €6 per tonne, and have been rocked by corruption scandals, including 'carousel' value-added tax (VAT) fraud (whereby carbon credits are bought and imported tax-free from other EU countries, then sold to domestic buyers, charging them VAT) and allegations of human rights abuses in UN CDM-accredited projects. These markets remain politically and economically important, but very unstable. What is perhaps most notable is that, despite these crises, faith in carbon markets as a key element of global responses to the threat of climate change remains strong, as affirmed by the UN climate change meetings in Durban in 2011 and Doha in 2012.

The world of climate politics was not always thus. In the years up to 1992, being built on foundations similar to those of other Multilateral Environmental Agreements, and particularly coming in the wake of the apparently successful Montreal Protocol to tackle ozone depletion, a 'command and control' process of setting targets globally that countries enforce nationally seemed a logical way to proceed for the climate regime. After all, this was the template for numerous previous regimes aimed at regulating pollutants of one form or another. Yet, even as discussions moved from the United Nations Framework Convention on Climate Change (UNFCCC) to efforts to produce a legally binding emissions-reductions treaty, opposition set in. This was not an issue amenable to convenient techno-fixes, such as the substitution of damaging chemicals (replacing CFCs (chlorofluorocarbons) with HFCs (hydrofluorocarbons), as in the case of ozone), or one that only affected a handful of large TNCs in the core of the global economy (such as ICI and DuPont) for which alternative accumulation strategies could easily be identified. The ramifications of regulating energy supply and use to the world's economy, upon which growth depends, made climate change a far more politically contentious issue to address.

It soon became clear that, if action were to be taken at all, and particularly by those economies contributing most to the problem, markets offered the most politically palatable solution, albeit as part of a suite of measures to bring down the costs associated with reducing emissions and increase flexibility about where emissions reductions take place. Once it became clear that outright opposition to action was no longer tenable, market-based solutions were attractive since they aligned closely with prevailing ideologies hostile to regulation, which emphasised the primacy of 'efficiency' as the policy goal, and which reflected the preferences of powerful factions of capital in leading economies for trading schemes over taxes or regulation. The incorporation of market mechanisms became the *quid pro quo* for the involvement of the US, in particular, in the negotiations on a Kyoto Protocol (notwithstanding the fact that, having insisted on flexible mechanisms, the US then walked away from the Kyoto deal). The US fought hard to project the 'success' of its domestic sulphur dioxide trading scheme as a model for international carbon trading, while domestic industries sought to avoid domestic reduction measures that might drive capital overseas, and had a clear preference for paying others to reduce where it would be cheapest to do so. The prospect of a transfer of resources from the global North to the South through the trading of offsets also provided an incentive for many governments in developing countries to support market-based approaches. Emissions trading and the CDM were what eventually resulted from this confluence of potential beneficiaries from the carbon economy.

The intellectual heritage of the idea of using markets for the provision of environmental goods has a much longer history. It can be traced back to the work of the economists Arthur Pigou (1920) and Ronald Coase (1960), who emphasised the need to internalise costs which producers are able to externalise on to society. However, as Philibert and Reinhaud (2004) suggest in a report for the IEA (International Energy Agency) on emissions trading, 'economists spend much of their time attempting to understand how markets work. In the case of tradeable permit schemes, the reverse is true: these markets have been created from theoretical considerations' (cited in Meckling 2011: 51). Considerable work went into building the political case for them through reports and studies which sought to assemble the evidence base for market-based approaches (Lane 2012). Nevertheless, constructing markets based on these ideas needed agents with power and influence to take them forward. The case for emissions trading was successfully made in the US and then globalised through transnational business coalitions, including alliances with conservative environmental NGOs that advocated market-based carbon governance. At the centre of this initiative was *Project 88: Harnessing Market Forces to Protect the Environment* (Stavins 1988), directed by Robert Stavins, a former economist at the Washington-based NGO Environmental Defense that had embraced market-based tools. The project had as its guiding rationale the desire 'to link environmental protection to the predominant economic logic in the 1980s' (Meckling 2011: 54).

Project 88 is generally credited with developing the political consensus that resulted in the development of the market in sulphur dioxide emissions under the 1990 Clean Air Act Amendments (Lane 2012). Its role was to weaken industry opposition to the Act and create support for a different approach to environmental governance. The Clean Air Act (CAA) had been deeply unpopular with industries that found themselves both newly regulated and under increasing international competitive pressures, which responded to these events by lobbying against both individual pieces of legislation and the increase in regulation as a whole (Meidinger 1985). As part of this response, the CAA came under attack almost immediately from economists who urged that it be recast to 'work more flexibly through market incentives' (Andrews 1984: 58, cited in Lane 2012).

The privileging of efficiency over other policy criteria was crucial for securing a victory for emissions trading in the US and elsewhere and came to trump equity as the other guiding principle in early proposals for international trading made by economists such as Michael Grubb (1989) and Frank Joshua at the United Nations Conference on Trade and Development (UNCTAD 1992). These proposals strongly emphasised the equity benefits of emissions trading, particularly in terms of North-to-South financial transfers. Richard Lane (2012: 584), in his account of the early rise of emissions trading, explains the centrality of 'efficiency' thus:

> this economic concept is taken as the simple, and in a real sense, natural, logic of global greenhouse gas regulation – a 'law' of the social world. In this way, the logic of efficiency is commonly presented as the broader context within which environmental, and specifically climate change regulation has developed. The iron law of efficiency is taken to shape, to frame, to determine the viability of environmental regulation.

In this way, he concludes, 'the efficiency of emissions trading, and the inefficiency of direct controls have been constructed precisely as *natural facts* – non-negotiable laws, silently prescribing certain (market-based) regulatory forms whilst not proscribing others (direct controls, technological standards etc)' (Lane 2012: 584). This helped to prepare the ground for the idea that, if action on climate change was to advance, it had to come in the form of a market-based and business-friendly mechanism.

In the context of global efforts to tackle climate change, the increasing fit between, on the one hand, the flexibility and market-centred nature of the proposed emissions trading, which had been rolled out intra-nationally to tackle acid rain, and on the other, US government priorities in the climate negotiations, gave the idea of carbon trading considerable traction. For the US government, it was vital to enrol industrialising developing countries rapidly in efforts to tackle climate change within a framework that did not prescribe means for achieving targets but was guided only by the most cost-effective options. This led to international efforts to ensure that flexible market mechanisms were included in the UN Kyoto Protocol negotiated in 1997: a *quid pro quo* for the US signing the treaty.

Alongside support for emissions trading as one of these 'flexible mechanisms' proposed in the Kyoto Protocol, another result was a global offset scheme: the CDM, described as the 'Kyoto surprise' because of the rapid and seemingly haphazard way in which it emerged (Werksman 1998). The CDM was a product of an eleventh-hour negotiation at Kyoto. Drawing on Brazilian proposals concerning a Clean Development Fund which would collect revenues from fines imposed on Annex 1 Parties and redistribute them as finance for projects in non-Annex 1 parties, it was reworked in informal contact groups in the final days of Kyoto to become a global carbon market mechanism. The political and commercial drivers for flexible market-based approaches, particularly a mechanism such as the CDM which opened up a global market in lowest-cost emissions reductions, included the desire to avoid imposing costs on powerful nations and sectors that feared loss of competitive advantage if emissions cuts were required of them, but not of their emerging competitors in countries such as India and China. This logic underpinned the subsequent refusal by the US to ratify the Kyoto Protocol, supported by an aggressive lobbying campaign by many US companies, and was embodied in the Byrd–Hagel Senate resolution that prevented the US from ratifying a treaty that did not include binding emissions cuts for leading developing countries.

The UK and the US are home to most of the trading on compliance and voluntary markets respectively. It is perhaps unsurprising that emissions trading has first taken hold in the Anglo-American heartlands of global capitalism, given the presence of powerful financial centres in the US and UK together with strong histories of neoliberal approaches to environmental regulation and resistance to taxation (such as UK hostility to regional carbon taxation in Europe) (Grant et al. 2000). Carbon trading has, however, increasingly been globalised, as multilateral institutions, such as the World Bank, the United Nations Development Programme (UNDP) and regional development banks, and global capital adopt and diffuse this preferred mode of carbon governance. Key corporate actors have played an important role as transmission belts in advocating the adoption of emissions trading as the preferred strategy in the jurisdictions in which they operate (Meckling 2011). The embrace of emissions trading by many leading corporate actors is indicative of a shift in the terrain of struggle from one centred around the merits or otherwise of the scientific case for regulating carbon, which characterised the focus of business lobbying for much of the 1990s, to having to engage in the debate about how best to respond and in that context ensure that the strategies that emerged were business-friendly and created new investment opportunities (Levy 2005). Here, then, the marketisation of governance is understood not just as a product of strategies to deflect attention from regulatory demands which might exact a higher burden, but as a way of trying to reconcile action on climate change with the imperative of growth in a capitalist economy by identifying opportunities for accumulation. Although the emergence of carbon trading is represented as a loss in the 'carbon wars' (Leggett 1999) on the part of big business (Meckling 2011), large sections of which initially opposed any action at all (Newell and Paterson 1998), it is telling that emissions trading only emerged once it had the backing of powerful business actors, such as BP and then Shell and Eurelectric, and could thus be presented to financial actors as an attractive investment opportunity. It presents concessions for incumbent actors, who are permitted to buy their way out of trouble rather than reduce emissions at source, but also creates new opportunities for 'carbon coalitions' (Meckling 2011) directly involved in carbon trading and able to financialise carbon.

Power needs to be exercised to dilute the critique that climate change potentially represents of the growth logic of contemporary capitalism (Kovel 2002). It also needs to be exercised in order to rework responses to climate change as a 'win–win' opportunity to increase efficiencies and therefore save money, as well as make money from buying and selling carbon through sales to corporations that need permits to meet their emissions reduction targets, or from being sold on secondary markets to investors who buy and sell carbon credits according to the best available prices in the market. Facing up to the overall tension between an economy based on expanded use of fossil fuels and the need dramatically to reduce carbon dioxide emissions is, therefore, temporarily put on hold by moving carbon around through trading and achieving some marginal emissions reductions in an economy that continues to be structured along business-as-usual lines. Indeed, capital's constant need for innovation and for the creation of new sites of accumulation has led to a series of experiments in extending the frontiers of commodification of the carbon cycle beyond those covered by the mechanisms described above, which largely address 'black carbon', to incorporate more ecosystem services within global circuits of capital. Some of these attempts are described briefly below.

MULTI-COLOUR CARBON

The view that the best way to protect nature is to place a price on it has also gained powerful backing in recent years, from efforts to lever carbon finance to pay for forest conservation through REDD (Reducing Emissions from Deforestation and Forest Degradation) schemes ('green' carbon), to newer attempts to quantify the benefits that marine ecosystems provide for climate protection ('blue' carbon). Interest in what is generally referred to as 'payments for ecosystem services' (PES) has brought into loose alliance large investors (such as Meryll Lynch and JPMorgan), multilateral and regional development banks (but especially the World Bank which has led on many such efforts, including the Forest Carbon Partnership Facility), international institutions (such as UN-REDD), richer governments keen to pursue options to reduce pollution that require less domestic effort on their part, and many conservative and conservation NGOs with good connections and deep pockets (such as the International Union for the Conservation of Nature, IUCN, and Conservation International) that see carbon sequestration as a new revenue stream for their forestry or marine conservation efforts. The sorts of alliances that are brought into being by such initiatives are themselves indicative of neoliberal modes of governance, given their reliance upon finance capital, their emphasis on public–private networks to implement initiatives, and their ideological preference for market-based and voluntary approaches as opposed to state-based regulation (Newell and Paterson 2010).

Meanwhile, the quantitative governance tools of accountancy, disclosure and audit have provided the means both to create a fungible and commensurate unit that can be commodified and traded, and to generate trust among investors that they are buying a credible product (Lovell and Mackenzie 2011). The attempt is to 'render the messy materiality of life legible as discrete entities, individuated and abstracted from the complex social and ecological integuments' (Prudham 2007: 414). In sum, contemporary forms of carbon governance increasingly link *governance by quantity* – setting emission-reduction targets through caps within which trading can take place (such as occurs with the EU's Emission Trading Scheme); *governance by price* – to shape investor and consumer behaviour which requires rules of trading and linkage; and *governance by information disclosure* – measuring, reporting, monitoring and verifying emissions (Newell and Paterson 2010). Governance systems intended for other purposes also have to be reworked to ensure they can operate in the service of carbon trading. These include the activities of credit rating agencies, the creation of insurance products (such as on volumes of CERs likely to be delivered), and systems of disclosure (such as the Carbon Disclosure Project): what Descheneau and Paterson (2011: 665) refer to as the 'routinization' of financial products in carbon markets. In this way, as they put it, 'carbon market actors borrow from existing financial practices to make the emerging market readily intelligible, to enable it to operate as a matter of financial routine'.

The greatest interest in commodifying multi-colour carbon so far has been in 'green' forestry carbon. REDD's market share has grown by 500 per cent from 2009. The World Bank attributes this meteoric rise to formal international recognition for REDD as part of UN climate change mitigation strategies, as well as interest from California's emerging cap-and-trade programme. REDD project methodologies have also been approved by the sorts of standard-setting bodies discussed below – through the Verified Carbon Standard (VCS) and forest-focused third-party standards such as Brasil Mata Viva (BMV) (Capoor and Ambrosi 2011). With nearly twice as much carbon found in soil as in the atmosphere, and the fact that small changes in the level of carbon in soils can drive large changes in atmospheric carbon concentrations, 'brown' soil carbon has also entered the calculus of carbon capitalists. As the World Bank (Capoor and Ambrosi 2011: 59) claims, 'sustainable land management projects that increase the carbon content of soils represent a "triple win" for society: development, climate change resilience, and climate change mitigation'. The Bank's BioCarbon Fund is involved in one such sequestration project in Kenya to generate soil carbon offsets. Meanwhile, the multi-agency 'Blue Carbon' report in 2009 claimed that an estimated 50 per cent of the carbon in the atmosphere that becomes bound or 'sequestered' in natural systems is recycled into the seas and oceans; 'another example of nature's ingenuity for "carbon capture and storage"' (UNEP et al. 2009). Or, as Achim Steiner, Executive Director of the United Nations Environment Programme (UNEP), puts it:

> if we are to tackle climate change and make a transition to a resource efficient, Green Economy, we need to recognize the role and the contribution of all the colours of carbon. Blue carbon, found and stored away in the seas and oceans, is emerging as yet another option on the palette of promising opportunities and actions, one that can assist in delivering a bright rather than a dark brown and ultimately black future. (UNEP et al. 2009)

As the frontiers of carbon commodification are pushed back, however, so they encounter resistance from community activists, the Climate Justice Movement and watchdog entities such as CarbonTrade Watch and CDM Watch (now renamed Carbon Market Watch), along with others opposed to particular projects or the ideology and practice of carbon markets in general (Bond 2012; Böhm and Dabhi 2009). Much of this has focused on CDM or forestry pilot projects. Protest, media campaigns and lobbying has forced carbon market advocates to introduce safeguards and forms of regulation to protect their legitimacy from critiques of their social and environmental integrity. This has created a wave of private regulation and certification to offer assurances to buyers of carbon credits that the projects they are supporting have environmental integrity and deliver development benefits, as will be described below. It is to issues of governance in the carbon economy that I now turn.

GOVERNING THE CARBON ECONOMY

Critics of carbon markets focus on their weak governance and their unregulated and 'Wild West' nature. This is considered particularly problematic when the system is premised on claims of additionality: having to prove that emissions reductions would not have been achieved without the offset. This is an invitation to make speculative claims that are hard to verify. Others, however, such as the World Bank, talk of a 'flight to quality' as offset providers in voluntary carbon markets increasingly emulate the use of governance and quality assurance tools in compliance markets, such as project design documents, third-party verification and use of voluntary standards. Reviews of carbon markets observe:

> Over the past 2 years numerous writers and analysts have likened the voluntary carbon markets to the 'wild west'. In 2007 market trends highlight that this frontier has become a settlement zone. Customers are increasingly savvy about the opportunities and pitfalls in the carbon offset domain and stakeholders are aggressively working to forge the rules of the game and structures to enable smooth transactions. (Capoor and Ambrosi 2009)

While 50 per cent of the transactions conducted in 2007 involved credits verified to a specific third-party standard, in 2009 the figure was 90 per cent (Carbon Retirement 2009). This is clearly a rapidly evolving market. From being sold as a response to climate change that implied lower transaction costs, it was perhaps inevitable that, as with all markets, rules and institutions were required to bring them into being and ensure their smooth functioning. With echoes of Polanyi (1980 [1944]), laissez-faire approaches to markets have produced demands to re-embed markets in frameworks of social control. Even key participants in carbon markets acknowledge the inevitability of this. Abyd Karmali, Managing Director, Global Head of Carbon Markets, Merrill Lynch, reflects that:

> Those who assume that the carbon market is purely a private market miss the point that the entire market is a creation of government policy. Moreover, it is important to realize that, to flourish, carbon markets need a strong regulator and approach to governance. This means, for example, that the emission reduction targets must be ratcheted down over time, rules about eligibility of carbon credits must be clear etc. Also, carbon markets need to work in concert with other policies and measures since not even the most ardent market proponents are under any illusion that markets will solve the problem. (ClimateChangeCorp 2011)

It would be unsurprising to most scholars of international political economy (IPE) that attempts to create markets for environmental products and services, despite claims, described above, about their ability to bypass institutional conflict, reduce transaction costs and regulatory burden and increase efficiency, often require substantial institutional infrastructures in order to be able to function. Carbon markets require states to negotiate and construct national allocation plans (in the case of emissions trading), and they require agreement on rules of the game: which sectors are in and out of the scheme, and who decides. Other actors have to be enrolled, involving lawyers, consultancy firms, banks and verification agencies, and new state bureaucracies have to be created to approve projects and ensure they align with national priorities. For the governance of market mechanisms to be effective and legitimate, attention needs to be paid to aspects of 'good' governance: transparency of flows; measures for identifying and dealing with evidence of collusion and corruption between a limited range of actors with the necessary expertise and skills; and adequate systems of participation, representation and accountability, especially to actors invoked as the beneficiaries of projects and partnerships (Newell 2009). In reality, few of these checks and balances are in place or operating effectively. My own fieldwork in India, Argentina and South Africa reveals a series of shortcomings, including the simultaneous performance by individuals of the roles of project developer, regulator and auditor; weak capacity at national level to screen projects for their alleged development benefits; and the existence of only token efforts to engage communities expected to host offset projects in discussions about how they will affected (whether positively or negatively) (Newell et al. 2011; Newell and Bumpus 2012).

The breadth and range of networks of public and private actors that have to be enrolled to make the offsets market function creates a series of mutual interdependencies. For example, in the case of the compliance market, the Conference and Meetings of the Parties ultimately exercises authority over the remit of the CDM. The CDM Executive Board (EB), which reports to the Conference and Meetings of the Parties, approves methodologies and accredits private Designated Operational Entities (DoEs) upon which the authority is conferred to assess whether projects have delivered their claimed emissions reductions and should therefore be issued with Certified Emissions Reductions (CERs). With just ten members, the CDM EB has to delegate significant power and authority to DoEs to approve projects and then later to verify that they have achieved the claimed emissions reductions. Given that there are around 40 approved DoEs and far fewer that are approved to operate in each individual sector in which the CDM is active, DoEs inevitably end up having to approve one another's projects. This potentially creates openings for collusion and disincentives to criticise or reject another firm's project for fear they will reciprocate (Green 2008). Nevertheless, to maintain the environmental credibility on which the system notionally rests, sanctions are occasionally applied. Indeed, several DoEs have had their accreditation temporarily suspended for continually proposing projects that do not fulfil the minimum approval criteria. There have also been calls to address potential conflicts of interest between members of the CDM Executive Board, the roster of experts upon which they call for guidance, and the projects they have been involved in developing but are then also charged with assessing.

On the demand side, market actors need strong signals from climate negotiators to create conditions of scarcity by setting targets that are stringent enough to drive demand for the products they are selling (governance by quantity). They also require of public institutions rules of conduct for predictability and credibility. At the same time, businesses often complain about the overly stringent application of additionality criteria and about delays in the approval process. They want maximum flexibility and a more harmonised and scaled-up process, including further moves towards programmatic or sectoral CDMs which open up many more opportunities at lower cost. There are divisions among traders between those anxious to safeguard the environmental integrity of the market on which their profitability rests and those with less at stake in terms of long-term reputation that want to maximise short-term profits. Dubbed 'cowboy capitalists', these actors have tended to be concentrated in the voluntary market and have prompted efforts to provide buyers of offsets with firmer guarantees of their credibility through initiatives such as the Offset Quality Initiative that aims to articulate and promote key principles that ensure the quality of greenhouse gas emission offsets. The balance of power among and between these actors, who share common political ground around the desirability of offsets, but competing commercial interests and preferences, continues to shape the governance of offsets (Bailey et al. 2011).

The shadow of regulation and intervention by public authorities, as well as criticism from activists and negative media exposure, create an incentive for new forms of private and voluntary regulation to protect the credibility of the market as a whole and preserve the autonomy of the network of traders and brokers to set their own modus operandi. It requires them to address the governance problems that arise in relation to quality control, integrity, independence and credibility. For example, the Climate, Community and Biodiversity standards are produced by a partnership of international NGOs, founded in 2003, which accredits land-based carbon projects which demonstrate compliance with the triple goals of mitigating climate change; improving the well-being and reducing the poverty of local communities; and conserving biodiversity. Each of the initiatives set up to address specific concerns about the integrity of offsets and their beneficiaries entails enrolling a broader network of actors in order to lend them credibility and ensure their smooth operation. While CERs are awarded for quantifiable emissions reductions in the compliance (CDM) market, the same is not true for contributions to sustainable development. To capture value associated with those contributions, other forms of private regulation have been developed in carbon markets, such as the CDM Gold Standard and Plan Vivo initiatives.

Many of these standards seek to offer assurances about quality that transcend the spatialities of carbon markets by managing the distance between project host and buyer and the anonymity of the transaction by quantifying and valuing benefits to communities and seeking to guarantee the quality of the product. Governance challenges are inevitably intensified when an attempt is made to govern globally (albeit indirectly, as with the CDM Executive Board) local resource-use decisions around forests, waste and energy, imbued as they are in conflicting systems of value and property rights in diverse settings (Newell and Bumpus 2012). This occurs when the logics of global capital and local socio-ecological systems meet through the new carbon economy. The potential for negative social and environmental consequences is a function of the 'articulation between the abstract representations required of commodification and the socio-ecological complexity of locally produced natures' (Lansing 2011: 732). The UN's EB then is left in the uncomfortable, and ultimately unmanageable, situation of having to operate as the final arbiter of quality control and ensuring projects make a contribution to global mitigation efforts, even though the power to actually demonstrate and oversee this directly is delegated to private verifiers.

CONCLUSIONS

The account provided in this chapter of the IPE of governing carbon, and the constitution and governance of the carbon economy in particular, illustrates clearly several of the defining features of the contemporary IPE of governance identified by the editors of this volume in their Introduction. I conclude the chapter with some reflections on these connections.

Firstly, ideology is apparent in decisions (and non-decisions) about who should govern carbon and how, and about which social and environmental side-effects of carbon and which parts of the carbon cycle are to be governed and on whose behalf. The rise of emissions trading can be explained in part by its fit with prevailing ideological currents (regarding the primacy of efficiency as the guiding policy principle and the importance of pricing public goods) and current configurations of power, given their less disruptive effects, their compatibility with business-as-usual corporate strategy for many key players, and their ability to generate opportunities for new entrants to the market. The importance of ideology is also apparent in debates about how much governance of carbon markets is required. The key issue here has been how to balance environmental integrity with the overwhelming desire to accumulate capital through the investment opportunities created. This plays out in the competing approaches of the International Emissions Trading Association (IETA) pressuring the CDM EB to speed up and streamline its approval procedures on the one hand, while on the other hand groups such as the NGO Carbon Market Watch, informed by a far more sceptical view of the role of carbon markets in response to climate change, resist this on the grounds that environmental integrity will suffer with less scrutiny of individual projects. In short, contests over who and what carbon markets are for are informed by conflicting world-views and interests.

Secondly, whilst public international law and institutions continue to be primary reference points (Kanie and Haas 2004; Young 2010), theory has followed practice in trying to make sense of the plurality of forms of environmental governance that have emerged (Newell et al. 2012). These forms of governance operate at a number of levels and accordingly climate change often features in debates about 'multilevel governance'

(Betsill and Bulkeley 2006). Carbon markets in particular need to enrol diverse ecologies in global commodity circuits and, in so doing, involve elaborate networks of public and private actors to provide finance, assure quality and monitor delivery. This is true from global-level UN oversight and financing from multilateral development banks to project-level consultations organised by municipalities and project developers. We have also observed key roles for states as market-makers and regulators and for regional institutions, in particular the EU. Given the embeddedness of carbon in virtually all aspects of human development, it necessarily transcends the ability of any one governance system, or any governance system at all, to subject it to effective oversight and management.

Thirdly, the observed dependence on the public and private spheres of action is a characteristic common to many forms of governance, especially where governments often only exercise very indirect forms of control over the processes and decisions that manage carbon. As Geoffrey Heal (1999: 222–3) argues:

> carbon dioxide is produced as a result of billions of de-centralized and independent decisions by private households for heating and transportation and by corporations for these and other needs, all outside the government sphere. The government can influence these decisions, but only indirectly through regulations or incentives.

Ironically, governments often have to look to partner with the private sector in seeking to govern carbon because in many cases, through privatisation, they have outsourced the responsibility for the provision of energy. In large parts of the majority developing world, states have either relinquished control over, or been required to liberalise, their energy sectors as part of power sector reform programmes overseen by multilateral development banks and designed to leave large elements of energy provision in private hands (Cho and Dubash 2005). Lack of control over key infrastructure means that the sorts of large-scale changes required to confront a problem such as climate change are that much more difficult to negotiate and enforce as a result.

Equally, we have seen many examples of how private governance, or the creation of market-based forms of governance, still ultimately rely on the state and international institutions (such as the CDM EB) to set the rules, enforce them and oversee some notion of fair play, which at least some private actors recognise is critical to the integrity and effectiveness of those markets. The reflections of Abyd Karmali, cited earlier, bear this out. The dependence of public and private power and authority is mutual; unsurprisingly, perhaps, for critical scholars of IPE who tend to be sceptical in any case about the degree of separation between state and private actors.

Finally, the issue of the complex, transnational, multi-actor base of governance again applies *par excellence* to the governance of carbon where arrangements are both complex, varied and uneven in their make-up, and transnational in their orientation, though often less so in terms of their origins or the groups and actors that are represented within them. For example, a survey of 60 transnational climate change governance initiatives found that the vast majority (87 per cent) were initiated by actors in the global North (Bulkeley et al. 2012). Here there remains a bias towards Europe and North America, in part because of the concentration of leading NGOs and business associations working on climate change in those regions, and in part because of pressure upon those regions to demonstrate leadership on the issue, given their disproportionate historical responsibility for causing the problem. Studies of transnational business coalitions have also concluded that, while presenting themselves as global bodies, many are in fact dominated by US big business (Meckling 2011; Newell 2003).

Indeed, one of the challenges in terms of the future geopolitical geometry of carbon governance, particularly that which is private and voluntary in nature, is where it will come from in a world in which India, China and Brazil for example are more powerful global players but where, especially in the case of China, drivers for corporate environmentalism may be weaker. Fear of loss of competitive advantage to firms from these regions is often invoked by European and North American corporations as a basis for not advancing further with action on climate change, despite claims about the abundance of 'win–win' opportunities to lower emissions and save money. The claim is that, if their competitors are not subject to the same (self-imposed) standards, then they will be faced with higher costs that make them less competitive.

In terms of governance being multi-actor, I take this as almost a given, since governing which only involves one actor would be called something else: government, international law or civil regulation. But, again, the environmental arena, perhaps more than others touched on in this volume, requires the input of a range of actors to shape decisions, incentives and practices across all areas of everyday conduct in relation to food, transportation, housing and heating. Governing carbon implies the governance of water, energy and food, and necessitates, therefore, multilevel, multi-actor governance in the public and private realms given its imbrication in every aspect of the everyday. Strong and effective forms of governance are also required to handle the trade-offs between achieving each of these goals. Attempts to create a new generation of cleaner fuels has seen a boom in biofuel production (Smith 2010), but this, in turn, has increased the prices of basic food commodities, leading to the 'tortilla riots' in Mexico and conflicts over food in other parts of the world. Similarly, the viability of different future options for energy is constrained by the availability of water. An ironic effect of a warming world is that water shortages reduce our ability to generate hydropower in some areas, but also create problems for the envisaged uptake of some forms of renewable and nuclear energy. Likewise, the water and energy inputs required by different forms of agricultural production increasingly affect the sustainability and viability of different ways of producing food. Understanding and acting upon these linkages and complexities presents a test for any governance system, not least one as weak, as under-resourced and as fragmented as that which exists to govern carbon.

REFERENCES

Andrews, R.N. (1984), 'Economics and environmental decisions, past and present', in V.K. Smith (ed.), *Environmental Policy under Reagan's Executive Order: The Role of Benefit–Cost Analysis*, Chapel Hill, NC, USA and London, UK: University of North Carolina Press, pp. 43–85.

Bachram, H. (2004), 'Climate fraud and carbon colonialism: the new trade in greenhouse gases', *Capitalism, Nature, Socialism*, **15** (4), 10–12.

Bailey, I., A. Gouldson and P. Newell (2011), 'Ecological modernisation and the governance of carbon: a critical analysis', *Antipode*, **43** (3), 682–703.

Bailey I. and S. Maresh (2009), 'Scales and networks of neoliberal climate governance: the regulatory and territorial logics of European Union emissions trading', *Transactions of the Institute of British Geographers*, **34** (4), 445–61.

Betsill, M. and H. Bulkeley (2006), 'Cities and the multi-level governance of global climate change', *Global Governance*, **12**, 141–59.

Böhm, S. and S. Dabhi (eds) (2009), *Upsetting the Offset: The Political Economy of Carbon Markets*, Colchester: Mayfly Books.

Bond, P. (2012), *Politics of Climate Justice*, Scottsville: University of KwaZulu Natal Press.

Bridge, G. (2013), 'Resource geographies 1: Making carbon economies, old and new', *Progress in Human Geography*, **35** (6), 820.

Bulkeley, H., L. Andonova, K. Bäckstrand, M. Betsill, D. Compagnon, R. Duffy, A. Kolk, M. Hoffman, D. Levy, P. Newell, T. Milledge, M. Paterson, P. Pattberg and S. Vandeveer (2012), 'Governing climate change transnationally: assessing the evidence from a database of sixty initiatives', *Environment and Planning C: Government and Policy*, **30**, 591–612.

Bulkeley, H. and P. Newell (2010), *Governing Climate Change*, London: Routledge.

Capoor, K. and P. Ambrosi (2009), *State and Trends of the Carbon Market 2008*, Washington, DC: World Bank.

Capoor, K. and P. Ambrosi (2011), *State and Trends of the Carbon Market 2010*, Washington, DC: World Bank.

Carbon Retirement (2009), 'The state of voluntary carbon offsetting in the FTSE 100', http://www.carbonretirement.com/sites/default/files/TheStateofVoluntaryCarbonOffsettingintheFTSE100.pdf, accessed 20 April 2012.

Carmin, J. and J. Agyeman (eds) (2011), *Environmental Justice Beyond Borders: Local Perspectives on Global Inequities*, Cambridge, MA: MIT Press.

Chang, H.-J. (2002), *Kicking Away the Ladder – Development Strategy in Historical Perspective*, London: Anthem Press.

Cho, A. and N. Dubash (2005), 'Will investment rules shrink policy space for sustainable development? Evidence from the electricity sector', in K. Gallagher (ed.), *Putting Development First: The Importance of Policy Space in the WTO and IFIs*, London: Zed Books, pp. 146–79.

ClimateChangeCorp (2011), 'Is carbon trading the most cost-effective way to reduce emissions?', http://www.climatechangecorp.com/content.asp?ContentID=6064, accessed 22 December 2011.

Coase, R. (1960), 'The problem of social cost', *Journal of Law and Economics*, **3** (October), 1–44.

Cosbey, A. (2008), *Border Carbon Adjustment*, Winnipeg: International Institute for Sustainable Development.

Descheneau, P. and M. Paterson (2011), 'Between desire and routine: assembling environment and finance in carbon markets', *Antipode*, **43** (3), 662–81.

Florini, A. and B.K. Sovacool (2009), 'Who governs energy? The challenges facing global energy governance', *Energy Policy*, **37**, 5239–48.

Friends of the Earth (2009), *Sub-Prime Carbon: Re-thinking the World's Largest New Derivatives Market*, Washington, DC: Friends of the Earth.

Gilbertson, T. and O. Reyes (2009), 'Carbon trading – how it works and why it fails', *Critical Currents*, 7, http://www.carbontradewatch.org/articles/new-book-exposes-dangers-of-carbon-market-ahead-of-bolivia-climates.html.

Grant, W., D. Matthews and P. Newell (2000), *The Effectiveness of EU Environmental Policy*, Basingstoke: Macmillan.

Green, J. (2008), 'Delegation and accountability in the Clean Development Mechanism: the new authority of non-state actors', *Journal of International Law and International Relations*, **4** (2), 21–55.

Grubb, M. (1989), *The Greenhouse Effect: Negotiating Targets*, London: Royal Institute of International Affairs.

Harvey, D. (2003), *The New Imperialism*, Oxford: Oxford University Press.

Heal, Geoffrey (1999), 'New strategies for the provision of global public goods: learning from international environmental challenges', in Inge Kaul, Isabelle Grunberg and Marc Stern (eds), *Global Public Goods: International Cooperation in the Twenty-first Century*, Oxford: Oxford University Press, pp. 240–64.

Hoffman, M. (2011), *Climate Governance at the Cross-Roads: Experimenting with a Global Response After Kyoto*, Oxford: Oxford University Press.

ICTSD (2011), 'China to end challenged subsidies in wind power case', *Bridges Trade BioRes*, **11** (11), 13 June.

Jacobs, Michael (1997), 'Sustainability and markets: on the neo-classical model of environmental economics', *New Political Economy*, **2** (3), 365–85.

Kanie, N. and P. Haas (eds) (2004), *Emerging Forces in Environmental Governance*, Hong Kong: United Nations University Press.

Kovel, J. (2002), *The Enemy of Nature: The End of Capitalism or The End of the World*, London: Zed Books.

Lane, R. (2012), 'The promiscuous history of market efficiency: the development of early emissions trading systems', *Environmental Politics*, **21** (4), 583–603.

Lansing, D. (2011), 'Realizing carbon's value: discourse and calculation in the production of carbon forestry offsets in Costa Rica', *Antipode*, **43** (3), 731–53.

Leggett, L. (1999), *Carbon Wars: Global Warming and the End of the Oil Era*, London: Penguin.

Levy, D. (2005), 'Business and the evolution of the climate regime: the dynamics of corporate strategies', in D. Levy and P. Newell (eds), *The Business of Global Environmental Governance*, Cambridge, MA: MIT Press, pp. 73–105.

Levy, D. and P. Newell (2002), 'Business strategy and international environmental governance: toward a neo-Gramscian synthesis', *Global Environmental Politics*, **3** (4), 84–101.

Lohmann, L. (2006), *Carbon Trading: A Critical Conversation on Climate Change, Privatisation and Power*, Sturminster Newton, UK: Corner House.

Lovell, H. and D. Mackenzie (2011), 'Accounting for carbon: the role of accounting professional organisations in governing climate change', *Antipode*, **43** (3), 704–30.

Meckling, J. (2011), *Carbon Coalitions: Business, Climate Politics and the Rise of Emissions Trading*, Cambridge, MA: MIT Press.

Meidinger, E. (1985), 'On explaining the development of "emissions trading" in US air pollution regulation', *Law and Policy*, **7** (4), 447–79.

Newell, P. (2003), 'Globalization and the governance of biotechnology', *Global Environmental Politics*, **3** (2), 56–72.

Newell, P. (2007), 'Trade and environmental justice in Latin America', *New Political Economy*, **12** (2), 237–59.

Newell, P. (2008), 'The marketisation of global environmental governance: manifestations and implications', in J. Parks, K. Conca and M. Finger (eds), *The Crisis of Global Environmental Governance: Towards a New Political Economy of Sustainability*, London: Routledge, pp. 77–96.

Newell, P. (2009), 'Varieties of CDM governance: some reflections', *Journal of Environment and Development*, **18** (4), 425–35.

Newell, P. (2011), 'The governance of energy finance: the public, the private and the hybrid', *Global Policy*, **2** (1), 94–105.

Newell, P. and A. Bumpus (2012), 'The global political ecology of the CDM', *Global Environmental Politics*, 12.

Newell, P. and M. Paterson (1998), 'Climate for business: global warming, the state and capital', *Review of International Political Economy*, **5** (4), 679–704.

Newell, P. and M. Paterson (2009), 'The politics of the carbon economy', in M. Boykoff (ed.), *The Politics of Climate Change: A Survey*, London: Routledge, pp. 80–99.

Newell, Peter and Matthew Paterson (2010), *Climate Capitalism: Global Warming and the Transformation of the Global Economy*, Cambridge: Cambridge University Press.

Newell, P., P. Pattberg and H. Schroeder (2012), 'Multi-actor governance and the environment', *Annual Review of Environment and Resources*, **37**, 365–87.

Newell, P., J. Phillips and P. Purohit (2011), 'The political economy of clean development in India: CDM and beyond', *IDS Bulletin*, **42** (3), 89–96.

Philibert, C. and Julia Reinaud (2004), *Emissions Trading: Taking Stock and Looking Forward*, Paris: IEA.

Pigou, A.C. (1920), *The Economics of Welfare*, London: Macmillan.

Polanyi, K. (1980 [1944]), *The Great Transformation*, Boston, MA: Beacon Press.

Prudham, S. (2007), 'The fictions of autonomous invention: accumulation by dispossession, commodification, and life patents in Canada', *Antipode*, **39** (3), 406–29.

Rittel, H. and M. Webber (1973), 'Dilemmas in a general theory of planning', *Policy Sciences*, **4** (2), 155–69.

Roberts, J. Timmons and Bradley Parks (2008), 'Fuelling injustice: globalization, ecologically unequal exchange and climate change', in Jan Ooshthoek and Barry Gills (eds), *The Globalization of Environmental Crises*, London: Routledge, pp. 169–87.

Smith, J. (2010), *Biofuels and the Globalization of Risk: The Biggest Change in North-South Relationships since Colonialism?*, London: Zed Books.

Stavins, R.N. (1988), 'Project 88: harnessing market forces to protect the environment', http://www.hks.harvard.edu/fs/rstavins/Monographs_&_Reports/Project_88-1.pdf.

UNCTAD (1992), *Combating Global Warming: Study on a Global System of Tradeable Carbon Emission Entitlements*, New York: United Nations.

UNFCCC (2012), 'UNFCCC releases report on the benefits of the Kyoto Protocol's clean development mechanism', 20 November, UNFCCC press office, Bonn.

UNEP, FAO, UNESCO, IUCN, CSIC (2009), 'Blue carbon: the role of oceans in binding carbon', October, http://www.grida.no/files/publications/blue-carbon/BCflyer_screen.pdf.

Werksman, J. (1998), 'The Clean Development Mechanism: unwrapping the Kyoto surprise', *Review of European Community and International Environmental Law*, **7** (2), 147–58.

World Bank (2010), *World Development Report 2010: Development and Climate Change*, Washington, DC: World Bank.

World Resources Institute (WRI) (2008), *Correcting the World's Greatest Market Failure: Climate*

Change and Multilateral Development Banks, Washington, DC: WRI, http://www.wri.org/publication/correcting-the-worlds-greatest-market-failure.

Yergin, D. (1992), *The Prize: The Epic Quest for Oil, Money, and Power*, New York: Free Press.

Young, O. (2010), *Institutional Dynamics: Emergent Patterns in International Environmental Governance*, Cambridge, MA: MIT Press.

24 Global climate governance
Matthew J. Hoffmann

The attempt to govern climate change globally has been a fascinating, if disappointing, endeavour. Deciding on the rules and institutions necessary for decisively decarbonising economies and societies on a global scale, as well as for dealing with the effects of the climate change we are already destined to endure, has to this point eluded the best efforts of the international community to achieve international collective action on a grand scale. For most of the past 20 years the much-maligned United Nations (UN) process that produced the 1992 Framework Convention on Climate Change (UNFCCC), the 1997 Kyoto Protocol and a range of recent agreements intended to move the treaty-making forward past 2012 has been the only global climate governance process in play. The global response to climate change was the UN process, with all the opportunities and challenges a global multilateral process affords.

The single focus of global climate governance has, however, fragmented in the last decade (Biermann et al. 2009; Keohane and Victor 2011; Abbot 2012). Now multiple multilateral fora are also engaged in governing climate change to greater or lesser degrees (though the UNFCCC process retains pride of place multilaterally). Even more significantly in terms of the shape of the global response to climate change, alternative governance mechanisms – which I have called climate governance experiments (Hoffmann 2011) and others have discussed as transnational climate governance (Andonova et al. 2009; Bulkeley et al. 2012) – have begun to emerge, offering new directions for the global response to climate change. These include subnational and municipal networks; non-governmental organisation (NGO)–corporate alliances; and the rise of carbon markets in both the private sector and amongst a variety of governmental units (subnational to supranational). The dominance of the UN negotiations as *the* governance model is eroding and the shape of global climate governance is rapidly changing. There are now available two fundamentally different models of climate governance: the traditional, centralised, top-down UN process; and a decentralised and bottom-up mechanism that engages diverse actors at multiple levels. How these mechanisms develop and interact will have profound implications for how the world addresses this most pressing of issues.

The main thrust of this chapter is to examine these two governance models. It begins by exploring the essence of the multilateral response to climate change and briefly details the challenges that it has endured since the Kyoto Protocol came into force in 2005 and work began on its replacement. The chapter then discusses the emergence and shape of the alternative, experimental model of global climate governance, briefly assessing its potential. It closes with a discussion of the politics between the models and what is now necessary to understand global climate governance.

THE MULTILATERAL RESPONSE TO CLIMATE CHANGE

To understand where the international community has come to in the global response to climate change – a limping multilateral system that is consistently criticised for failing to seriously address the problem of climate change – we must first understand the scope and source of climate governance. That means it is imperative that we begin with mega-multilateralism (Hoffmann 2011). This is a governance process whereby the entire international community participates in the negotiation of treaties and agreements designed to address problems of common interest. This form of governance – one dominated by the principle of universal participation (Hoffmann 2005) – saw numerous expressions, beginning in the 1970s. From the Law of the Sea negotiations, to global trade treaties and the mega-conferences around human rights in the 1990s, this means of governance became a key tool for the international community.

Mega-multilateralism perhaps reached its pinnacle in climate governance. From its beginning in the late 1980s, climate governance was conceived of as a problem requiring a universal, multilateral response (Hoffmann 2005; Bodansky 1994). The mantra in the international community was that climate change is a global problem that requires a global response. This makes a great deal of sense. Climate change is a profoundly global problem in a number of ways. The climate system is global. Carbon dioxide emissions, which are a key cause of the greenhouse effect that leads to climate change, arise from almost all industrial, agricultural, energy production and transportation processes. Further, because of atmospheric mixing, emissions anywhere are essentially emissions everywhere: there are no local emissions and there is no local greenhouse effect. The impacts of climate change, while variable, are also global.

Yet mega-multilateralism, however much sense it makes, was not merely a natural or the only possible choice for managing climate change. This means of multilateral cooperation was substantially conditioned by norms of universal participation that prevailed in the 1980s and 1990s, as well as by the political choices of major actors (actors in the global South were attracted by the legitimacy of universal negotiations and actors in the global North by a desire to spread responsibility for the problem) (Hoffmann 2005). Whatever its origins, pursuing climate governance through this taken-for-granted mechanism has had profound political implications and many of the challenges of climate governance can be laid at the initial choice of this governance model.

THE DESCENT OF MULTILATERAL CLIMATE GOVERNANCE[1]

The Kyoto Protocol was the high-water-mark for mega-multilateral climate governance. Its signing in 1997 represented the first time that the international community had agreed to binding restrictions on greenhouse gases. It contained mechanisms, especially carbon-market mechanisms such as cap-and-trade and offsetting, which have since become standard tools in addressing climate change. It engaged the global North in reducing emissions and the global South in measuring emissions and in the offsetting process through the Clean Development Mechanism (CDM). Ironically, given the overwhelmingly negative perception of the Kyoto Protocol, it achieved its goal of a 5 per cent reduction of 1990 greenhouse gas emission levels by 2012 amongst signatories with a reduction commitment (an achievement blunted by the withdrawal of the United States and Canada and the lack of reduction commitments from the states in the global South).

Despite all this 'success', the Kyoto Protocol is widely viewed as a failed climate treaty. Global emissions have continued to rise unabated, except by the ravages of global financial crisis. The largest contributors to the problem (China and the United States) have assiduously avoided taking on binding emission reduction commitments, either within the confines of the Kyoto Protocol or in the negotiations to replace it. The last seven years of UN negotiations have been substantially geared towards negotiating a replacement for the Kyoto Protocol, which expired in 2012, and the lack of progress on the problem highlights the challenges of governing climate change through the mega-multilateral model.

From the very initiation of the multilateral climate governance process, the challenges have remained relatively stable. The political economy of state-centric, multilateral climate governance looks pretty much the same today as it did when the negotiations began in 1990 for the UNFCCC (Sell 1996; Victor 2011; Barrett 1992, 2003). First, there are fundamental challenges involved in collective action (especially with universal participation), precisely because of the structure of the climate change problem. Addressing climate requires that the international community impose near-term and concentrated costs in order to secure long-term and diffuse benefits. This is a recipe for difficult negotiations. Second, the scope of the problem augurs against effective mega-multilateralism. Fully addressing climate change requires decarbonisation of the world's energy, economic and transportation systems. The entrenched interests in the status quo are formidable.

Third, and perhaps most importantly, the diversity of interests across the international community with regard to climate change makes it nearly impossible to find practical zones of agreement (other than a zone of agreement on doing nothing). Briefly, because of its pre-eminent position as an energy consumer and carbon dioxide producer, the US does not want to incur what would be significant costs to its economy to deal with the problem, especially in the absence of action by major economic competitors such as China. Large developing countries, which have rapidly grown in terms of energy consumption and carbon dioxide emissions (in absolute if not per capita terms), prioritise development over action on climate change and also argue that a problem historically caused in the North should be dealt with by Northern states first. The US is reluctant, at best, to take significant action. China, India, Brazil and other developing states are reluctant, at best, to take significant action. The European Union, which has taken significant action, has not been able to convince either side to make significant concessions.

The end result of these political-economic realities is stalemate. European and small island nations want to move forward quickly. The United States, under both the Bush and the Obama administrations, has not shown an interest in moving quickly on significant binding reduction. India and China and other large Southern nations continue to tie their action to Northern states leading with bolder moves (though some signs of movement in this position were evident in recent negotiations). This has been the consistent story since the Kyoto Protocol was signed. The Europeans and major Southern states push for significant actions by Northern states, whilst the United States, and to a lesser extent Japan, Russia and Canada, work both to reduce and slow the response to climate change, as well as push for concomitant Southern actions. While states were able to agree to modest emissions reductions for the Global North at Kyoto, since then the reality is that the international community has been unable to overcome the obstacles to collective action.

Bali 2007 to Cancún 2010: From Road Map to Accord

After agreeing to begin discussing a replacement for the Kyoto Protocol at the Montreal Conference of the Parties (COP) in 2005, there was muted hope that the international community would move forward at the 2007 Bali negotiations. The US reluctantly agreed to the goal of negotiating a new agreement (after unsigning the Kyoto Protocol in 2001) after being uncharacteristically bluntly confronted in a plenary session by developing countries. An angry delegate from Papua New Guinea famously chastised the US, saying: 'if you cannot lead, leave it to the rest of us. Please get out of the way' (Revkin 2008). Getting the US to sign up to the 'Bali Roadmap' was, however, a hollow victory. All that was agreed after acrimonious negotiations was to begin a two-year process of negotiating a post-Kyoto Protocol agreement, essentially from scratch, by the 2009 Copenhagen COP (UNFCCC 2008).

The hopes for Copenhagen proved to be unfounded. Even with the new Obama administration in power and China signalling willingness to consider significant action, the international community was not able to achieve a legally binding replacement for the Kyoto Protocol. In fact, what the parties agreed in the Copenhagen Accord was a significant departure from the Kyoto Protocol style of agreement. The Copenhagen Accord was largely negotiated by the US and China (with some additional influence by other larger developing countries) and was thus largely viewed as non-transparent and thereby in violation of the universal participation norm and spirit of the COPs. In fact, the final COP result only 'took note' of the Accord, rather than adopting it officially. In addition, the Copenhagen Accord moved the international community away from collective, and towards individualised, emissions reductions goals. Up to this point, the UN negotiations had been focused on negotiating a collective goal and allowed flexible mechanisms for achieving it. At Copenhagen, an agreed collective target was not attainable. Instead, the Copenhagen Accord enshrined a pledge-and-review style of global response. Each country pledged a reduction level and baseline and would submit their pledges and work towards the pledges for review (for instance, the US pledged to achieve 17 per cent below 2005 levels by 2020). This is a relatively radical departure from the kind of collective action attempted up to this point in the UN negotiations (UNFCCC 2009).

On the heels of the disappointment in Copenhagen, the 2010 Cancún negotiations were initially seen as a success. The 'Cancún Agreements' were endorsed by nearly 200 nation-states (UNFCCC 2010). They purported to enshrine efforts to reduce emissions of greenhouse gases aggressively, lay out a goal of stabilising global warming below a 2 degree temperature rise, provide billions of dollars to developing countries for adaptation to the ravages of climate change, shore up the climate for investment in climate-friendly technology and carbon markets, and reaffirm the global commitment to the CDM and the process of Reducing Emissions from Deforestation and Forest Degradation (REDD), both of which are tools that facilitate the development of low-carbon economies and forest protection in the Global South (UNFCCC 2010). It appeared as though the COP process had got back on track.

Unfortunately, lost in the mild euphoria that an agreement was reached in Cancún was the fact that, substantively, the Copenhagen Accord and the Cancún Agreements were actually quite similar. Both allowed developed countries to set their own emission reduction targets and methods. Both committed developed countries to provide US$100 billion per year by 2020 for adaptation efforts in developing countries. Both called on developing countries to begin nationally appropriate mitigation efforts and move away from business-as-usual. Both called for holding warming under 2 degrees. There are small, but important, differences in the two agreements. For example, there is more consensus on monitoring and verification of commitments and a reaffirmation of major market mechanisms such as the CDM and REDD in the Cancún Agreements. But, on balance, the two results are functionally similar. Perhaps most significantly, the pledge-and-review nature of the global response to climate change was maintained in Cancún.

The features that set the Cancún Agreements apart from the Copenhagen Accord were not a matter of detail, but of process. The Copenhagen Accord was widely perceived as being a backroom deal, with the US and China colluding and usurping the ideals of transparency and consultation that have come to be cherished in a multilateral process that has engaged virtually the entire world for the last two decades. The Cancún Agreements, on the other hand, were developed through the traditional negotiating process and transparency was stressed from the outset and throughout the meeting. Instead of countries 'taking note', almost in protest, of a Copenhagen Accord that they had no hand in devising, the last plenary session erupted in applause as nearly 200 nation-states committed to the Cancún Agreements.

Back to Collective Goals?

The Cancún Agreements set out the commitments of signatory states through 2020. This did not address the problem of the expiring Kyoto Protocol, or the fact that many in the international community wanted more than a pledge-and-review system: they wanted collective targets for emissions reductions. This desire was the focus of the 2011 Durban and 2012 Doha negotiations. Whereas the worries heading into Durban and even the trends from late in the final week of the negotiations pointed to an epic disaster for the multilateral negotiations, the international community managed to eke out agreement on a number of issues that may portend success in the future. The most important point from this chapter's perspective is that all countries attending the negotiations (194) agreed to 'launch a process to develop a protocol, another legal instrument or an agreed outcome with legal force under the Convention applicable to all Parties' (UNFCCC 2011). These negotiations began in 2012 in Doha, but no substantive progress was made, which means that the work of coming up with the new multilateral agreement by 2015 will fall on the 2013 and 2014 negotiations.

In 2006 one observer of the multilateral governance process lamented that the Kyoto process 'has not only got "stuck" but is digging itself into ever deeper holes of rancorous relationships, stagnating issues, and stifling debates', concluding that this 'ossifying' regime cannot produce the rules and innovations necessary to meet the climate challenge (Depledge 2006: 1, 3; see also Victor 2011). What is remarkable is how stable this governance model has been. The obstacles to collective action and thus an effective multilateral response have essentially remained the same for two decades. Yet, for the vast majority of these last 20 years, there has been no significant questioning of the basic assumption that brought us the UNFCCC and the Kyoto Protocol – which has been the appropriateness and efficacy of mega-multilateralism. Much of the governance reform literature centres on how to do multilateralism better (see, e.g., Aldy and Stavins 2007; Victor 2011). Critics decry the lack of progress and criticise the results of the negotiations, but this model, until very recently, remained synonymous with global climate governance. Ironically, then, the Kyoto Protocol may mark both the high point of universal, multilateral mechanisms for addressing global climate change and the onset of the demise of this mechanism. For all the efforts of negotiators and the undoubted urgency surrounding this issue, multilateral treaty-making has consistently failed to produce treaties and agreements that effectively address climate change.

AN ALTERNATIVE GOVERNANCE MODEL[2]

Since 2006, however, there has been more questioning of the fit between the multilateral governance model and the problem of climate change, especially when one considers that truly addressing climate change requires societal and economic transformation that might not be achievable through global treaty-making (Prins and Rayner 2007). The issue may simply be too complex and the negotiating process simply too unwieldy and fraught with competing interests to produce the kind of legally binding, comprehensive and effective treaty that has been the ultimate goal since the early 1990s when global warming first became a prominent global issue.

Accompanying and perhaps motivating the questions about the multilateral governance model is the emergence of a range of initiatives and activities that have been seeking to fill the void of a breakdown in the multilateral treaty-making process (Andonova et al. 2009; Bulkeley et al. 2012; Bulkeley and Newell 2010). Global networks of cities are working to alter municipal economies, transportation systems and energy use. Corporations are forming alliances with environmental NGOs to devise major and small ways to deliver climate-friendly technology and move towards a low-carbon economy. States, provinces, environmental organisations and corporations are engaged in developing carbon markets that promise low-cost means of reducing emissions. These climate governance experiments are shaping how individuals, communities, cities, counties, provinces, regions, corporations and nation-states now respond to climate change. They are more than lobbying efforts looking to shape the multilateral process. On the contrary, they are explicitly engaged in making rules (broadly conceived as including principles, norms, standards and practices) and entail a conscious intention to create, shape and alter behaviour for a community of implementers (whoever and whatever they may be) to follow.

This is a new mode of climate governance: a decentralised, self-organised approach that is at once more circumscribed and more expansive than the multilateral approach. It is more circumscribed because the individual initiatives that comprise the model of experimental governance are all small relative to the global treaty-making effort. They deal with pieces of the climate change issue, rather than attempting a central unified global response. Yet it is also more expansive, because the range of actors engaged in the response is truly multilevel and, collectively, climate governance experiments have a broader goal of transformation. Further, while there now exist numerous climate governance experiments, they are patterned and comprise a nascent and organised model of climate governance. In the next section, I describe the emergence and organisation of this experimental governance.

The Rise of Experimentation

The key elements in the emergence of the experimental model of governance were diverse actors coming to see themselves as authoritative responders to climate change and those actors becoming motivated to take action. We first need to look beyond climate change itself to explain the conditions of possibility. Globalisation – the erosion of the competence and authority of nation-states (individually and collectively) – has had a profound effect on the way in which a range of actors see themselves and thus on their relationship with the dominant context of multilateral governance. We are, by many accounts, in the midst of a general global shift toward the fragmentation of governing authority. The ability of nation-states, on the one hand, to manage transnational issues, and on the other, to command authority, what Rosenau (2003: 281) called 'readiness to comply with directives', have both been compromised by globalisation. Saskia Sassen (2006: 2) argues that 'a good part of globalization consists of an enormous variety of micro-processes that begin to denationalize what had been constructed as national'. Actors other than nation-states thus increasingly take on the role of 'governors' of transnational issues (Avant et al. 2010): political authorities able to design and make rules themselves, rather than merely complying with the directives of nation-states or the results of cooperation among nation-states (treaties and intergovernmental organisations). In climate change, this means that cities, states and provinces, corporations and more have begun to see themselves as authoritative actors.

The signing of the Kyoto Protocol in 1997 catalysed the emergence of the experimental model of climate governance by motivating possible governors of climate change to take action. The Kyoto Protocol made clear the challenge of reducing carbon dioxide emissions at various scales and, as importantly, the potential profit to be made, thereby motivating innovation. An example of this process was the emergence of the Greenhouse Gas Registry (now the American Carbon Registry). When the Environmental Defense and the Environmental Resources Trust observed the importance of market mechanisms such as emissions trading in the Kyoto Protocol negotiations (an option they strongly advocated throughout the negotiation process), they identified a need for infrastructure. A significant part of this task was to get companies ready to calculate their carbon footprints, as well as measure and account for emission reductions that would eventually be traded amongst regulated entities. They took it upon themselves to devise rules to guide corporate measurement and trading by launching the Greenhouse Gas Registry in 1997 (author interviews).

If the signing of the Kyoto Protocol served to enhance the prospects for experimentation, the stalemate in the UN process that developed in the 1990s and early 2000s significantly accelerated the pace of innovation. Actors outside the UN process reacted strongly to both the US withdrawal and the overall malaise in the negotiations, with the result that experimentation took off significantly after 2001. In one particularly visible example, the US Mayors Climate Protection Agreement was an outright repudiation of the US withdrawal from the Kyoto Process (US Mayors 2005). More broadly, both the US withdrawal and the stalemate that characterised most of the 2000s led many actors to conclude that the multilateral process was finally broken or at least that momentum would need to come from outside the process.

The result was the emergence of dozens, if not hundreds, of innovative initiatives, engaging every kind of political actor, working on different aspects of the climate change problem, undertaking a whole range of activities, at multiple scales. Table 24.1 presents a list of 59 such experimental initiatives and gives a sense of the diversity of approaches to climate governance. Table 24.2 describes the kinds of activities that these initiatives now undertake.

Organisation and Functions of Experimental Governance

The existence of these multiple and diverse climate initiatives would be an interesting footnote to the global governance of climate change if they were merely a series of disorganised, random attempts at doing something to address climate change. However, upon examination of these experiments collectively, it becomes clear that experimental governance activity is actually relatively patterned, even while it is not centrally organised.

At a broad level, a shared philosophical world-view of liberal environmentalism underpins the experimental system of governance (Bernstein 2001). Climate governance experimentation, in the main, entails a voluntary, market-oriented approach that is focused on mitigation, rather than adaptation. Market mechanisms (pricing carbon, emissions trading, economic incentives, and the joint pursuit of greenhouse gas emissions reductions and profit) dominate the ways experiments answer the question of how climate change should be appropriately addressed. Climate governance experiments are, for the most part, advocating climate action by making the case that such action is or will be economically beneficial.

Beyond generally sharing an orientation, the collection of experiments also exhibits both functional differentiation and thematic clustering. Experiments can be readily grouped into four archetypes or governance models on the basis of how they are seeking to respond to climate change:

1. Networkers such as the Climate Group and 2degrees respond to climate change by fostering information exchange, undertaking educational activities, meeting to discuss best practices, or even just putting actors interested in climate change together.
2. Infrastructure builders such as the Climate Registry, which does carbon accounting, and the Carbon Disclosure Project, which facilitates corporate reporting of exposure to climate change, see their role as building the capacity of diverse actors to engage in the global response to climate change, thereby facilitating the measurement of carbon footprints, certification of carbon credits and development of climate action plans.
3. Voluntary actors such as the C40 group of large cities ask implementing actors to take direct action to reduce greenhouse gas emissions, but have little in the way of accountability or oversight over their members.
4. Accountable actors such as the Western Climate Initiative, which is organising a

Table 24.1   Climate governance experiments

Experiment name	Description
2degrees	Social networking platform for actors working in corporate environmental sustainability, climate change and green technologies.
Alliance for Resilient Cities	An Ontario-based network of municipalities focused on adaptation to climate change.
American Carbon Registry	Apparently the world's first private emissions registry started in 1997 as the Greenhouse Gas Registry.
American College and University Presidents Climate Commitment	Pledge and programme to eliminate greenhouse gas emissions at US colleges and universities.
Asia Pacific Partnership on Clean Development and Climate	Voluntary partnership among select countries to cooperate on technological development and implementation in a number of sectors.
Australia's Bilateral Climate Change Partnerships	Agreements and partnerships signed between Australia and other countries (developed and developing) to take action on climate change.
Business Council on Climate Change	Partnership of San Francisco Bay Area businesses committed to reducing their greenhouse gas emissions.
C40 Cities Climate Leadership Group	A network of the world's largest cities created to share best practices and develop collaborative initiatives to do with city-specific issues.
California Climate Action Registry	Voluntary greenhouse gas registry now operating under the Climate Action Reserve.
Carbon Disclosure Project	Resource/database for institutional investors to inform their investment choices based on emissions reported by the world's largest corporations.
Carbon Finance Capacity Building Programme	Partnership to encourage the use of Carbon Finance to reduce greenhouse gas emissions in cities, in particular emerging mega-cities of the South.
Carbon Rationing Action Groups	Network of local groups to support and encourage one another in reducing individual carbon footprints.
Carbon Sequestration Leadership Forum	Framework agreement between governments to promote and develop carbon capture and storage technology.
CarbonFix	Both a labelling standard setter and greenhouse gas offset supplier.
Chicago Climate Exchange	Private cap-and-trade system whose members make a legally binding emission reduction commitment.
Climate Alliance of European Cities with Indigenous Rainforest Peoples	Association of European cities and municipalities that have entered into a partnership with indigenous rainforest peoples.
Climate, Community, and Biodiversity Alliance	Partnership between companies, NGOs and research institutes to create a certification standard to evaluate land-based carbon mitigation projects.
Climate Neutral Network	A web-based platform for networking and the sharing of best practices on reducing and offsetting greenhouse gas emissions.

Table 24.1   (continued)

Experiment name	Description
Climate Saver	Corporate partnership between major corporations, organised by the World Wildlife Fund, to increase efficiency in operations/products to voluntarily reduce their greenhouse gas emissions.
ClimateWise	An association of insurance-related companies/organisations established to collaborate on climate issues.
Clinton Climate Initiative	Programme of the Clinton Foundation that seeks to provide direct assistance to individual cities and facilitating the sharing of best practices to do with climate.
Community Carbon Reduction Project	A UK-based network of local community partners that engage in education, research, and outreach to cut their CO_2 emissions to meet a target of 60% reduction by 2025.
Conference of New England Governors and Eastern Canadian Premiers Climate Change Action Plan	Voluntary agreement to pursue coordinated actions on climate change in the region.
Connected Urban Development	Partnership programme between Cisco and cities to create urban communications infrastructures to reduce carbon emissions.
Cool Counties Climate Stabilization Initiative	Network of counties created to address climate change.
Covenant of Mayors	Commitment by European cities to go beyond the objectives of the European Union energy policy in terms on reduction of CO_2 emissions through enhanced energy efficiency and cleaner energy production and use.
e8 Network of Expertise for the Global Environment	Non-profit international group of nine major electricity companies from Group of Eight (G8) countries, promoting sustainable development through electricity sector projects and activities worldwide.
Edenbee	Web-based social network (such as Facebook) designed to encourage users to reduce their carbon footprints.
Eurocities Declaration on Climate Change	Agreement by European cities to fight climate change at the local level.
Evangelical Climate Initiative	An agreement by evangelical leaders to motivate their followers to protect the climate.
Global Greenhouse Gas Registry	A global, corporate-wide emissions registry for companies based in developing or other countries (i.e. US) not subject to Kyoto Protocol obligations (now defunct).
ICLEI Cities for Climate Protection Campaign	Campaign that seeks to promotes the development and implementation of greenhouse gas emission reduction strategies among local and municipal governments.
Institutional Investors Group on Climate Change	A forum for collaboration between pension funds and other institutional investors to address the investment risks and opportunities associated with climate change.

Table 24.1   (continued)

Experiment name	Description
International Climate Action Partnership	International forum of governments and public authorities that are engaged in the process of designing or implementing carbon markets.
Investors Group on Climate Change	Collaboration of Australian and New Zealand investors focus climate-related investment risk.
Investor Network on Climate Risk	A US$7 trillion network of investors geared toward integrating climate risks into investment decisions.
Klimatkommunerna	Association of Swedish municipalities, counties and regions working actively on climate issues.
Major Economies Forum on Energy and Climate	A 'complementary' process to Kyoto Framework that brings together leaders of the world's 17 largest economies to discuss climate.
Memoranda of Understanding on Climate Change initiated by the State of California	Memoranda between California and various international states and subnational units/states/provinces for joint efforts on climate change.
Methane to Markets	A framework agreement between countries to promote methane recovery internationally.
Midwestern Greenhouse Gas Reduction Accord	Policy framework to develop a market based cap-and-trade mechanism amongst Midwestern US states and Canadian provinces.
National Association of Counties County Climate Protection Program	Project to provide US counties with best practices, tools and resources to assist them in developing and implementing successful climate change programmes.
Network of Regional Governments for Sustainable Development	International network of subnational regional governments based on partnerships and bilateral cooperation agreements among members.
North South Climate Change Network	Network of an NGO, university, and local communities with the goal of improving Ontario's knowledge of, and response to, climate change.
Ontario–Quebec Provincial Cap-and-Trade Initiative	Inter-provincial cap-and-trade programme (now folded into the Western Climate Initiative).
Regional Greenhouse Gas Initiative	Regional cap and trade programme among Northeast and Mid-Atlantic states in the US.
Renewable Energy and Energy Efficiency Partnership	International NGO that works in partnership with business, civil society, and government actors to reduce the barriers to the uptake of renewable energy and energy efficiency technologies and projects.
Southwest Climate Change Initiative	Framework agreements between two Southwest US states to coordinate emissions reductions.
The Climate Group	An independent, non-profit organisation dedicated to advancing business and government leadership on climate change.
The Climate Registry	A collaboration between US states, Mexican and Canadian provinces, and Native American organisations aimed at developing and managing a consistent North American greenhouse gas emissions reporting system.

Table 24.1   (continued)

Experiment name	Description
Transition Towns	Network/set of principles that encourages communities to 'relocalise' all essential elements that the community needs to sustain itself.
Union of the Baltic Cities Resolution on Climate Change	Resolution among Baltic cities to combat climate change and make plans for adaptation.
US–China Memorandum of Understanding to Enhance Cooperation on Climate Change, Energy and the Environment	Bilateral climate change MOU between the US and China.
US Mayors Climate Protection Agreement	Agreement by US Conference of Mayors to advance the goals of the Kyoto Protocol in the US.
UK Bilateral Climate Change Agreements with US States	Formal agreements between UK government and various US states.
West Coast Governors' Global Warming Initiative	Collaboration between three Western US states that produced a set of recommendations on cooperative strategies.
Western Climate Initiative	Network of states and provinces in the United States, Canada, Mexico to cooperate on climate action and a regional cap and trade system.
World Business Council for Sustainable Development	Chief executive officer (CEO)-led, global association geared toward sharing of best practices and knowledge on climate change.

Source: Hoffmann (2011: Chapter 1).

Table 24.2   *Experimental governance activity*

Activity	Number of initiatives
1. Catalogue emissions/undertake inventory	20
2. Set targets/formulate action plan/do risk assessment	32
3. Efficiency measures or offsetting	15
4. Education/information and best practice exchange/regular meetings	49
5. Set certification standards/funding criteria	4
6. Mandate emissions reductions	7
7. Emissions trading	8
8. Monitoring (of implementing actors)	16
9. Enforcement	7
10. Technology development	7

Source: Hoffmann (2011: Chapter 2).

carbon trading scheme in the US and Canada, take action, but include provisions for oversight and accountability.

Each experiment plays one of these roles in the nascent experimental governance system. The world of climate governance experiments is thus far from a random assortment of initiatives and is actually quite structured, with clear functional differentiation on top of a common philosophical foundation. Instead of thinking of experiments as idiosyncratic, we should think of them as playing specific roles or embodying specific identities in the global response to climate change.

The differentiation is indeed functional, not just because it is a matter of different functions, but also because it facilitates the emergent functioning of the experimental system. Specifically, clusters of experimental activity have emerged as sites where experiments interact and build relationships with each other, as well as with other participants in the global response to climate change. Climate governance experiments are not isolated initiatives. On the contrary, relationships within the experimental world are now evident, including networking, a combination of competition and cooperation between initiatives, the emergence of communities of practice, and the development of redundancy in the system facilitated by functional differentiation.

For example, the recently conceived alliance between the Cisco-initiated Connected Urban Development (CUD) programme and the Climate Group illustrates the complex connections that can emerge amongst experiments. In late 2009 these two experiments announced their forthcoming alliance to much (internal) fanfare:

> Over the coming months, the Climate Group will reach out to its extensive global network of corporate partners, cities and states to develop the CUD Alliance and scope a new program to further advance its existing cities-focused work it currently delivers under the five-year HSBC Climate Partnership. Once the Alliance is in place, a new program – to be formally launched next year [2010] – will deploy urban demonstration projects in transformational technical areas such as smart connected buildings, smart transportation and smart grid. (Climate Group 2009)

The Connected Urban Development programme is a voluntary actor experiment initiated by Cisco that focuses on reducing emissions from the use of information and communications technology and using those technologies to reduce emissions (and enhance economic growth) in a number of other areas within cities. It grew into a global pilot project that demonstrates the ways in which cities can reduce their emissions from their own information and communication technology (ICT) infrastructure and use ICT to reduce emissions and enhance economic growth in other areas. From its initial work in San Francisco, Amsterdam and Seoul, it has expanded to numerous pilot projects in seven cities (Lisbon, Birmingham in the UK, Hamburg and Madrid joined the original three in 2008).

At the same time as the Connected Urban Development programme was emerging, the Clinton Climate Initiative and C40 were developing their own technology deployment programmes for cities (Clinton Climate Foundation n.d.). In addition, the Eurocities experiment relatively recently introduced (December 2009) a 'Green Digital Charter' which, much like the Connected Urban Development programme, asks cities to work together to use ICT in the service of climate change goals through specific projects and partnerships (Eurocities n.d.-a). In other words, multiple experiments are working in overlapping areas, forming linkages at times and working independently at others.

What results is both a web of relationships and redundancy in the experimental system. Currently 34 cities have signed on to the Eurocities Digital Charter (as of January 2013), including three Connected Urban Development cities: Amsterdam, Birmingham and Lisbon (Eurocities n.d.-b). A policy officer with Eurocities reported that the Digital Charter emerged from the European Commission's reaction to the SMART 2020 report put out by the Climate Group, noting that the report had a big effect in raising the awareness and visibility of the role of information technology in cities in addressing climate change (author interview).

The SMART 2020 programme itself is a key piece of the Climate Group's work on cities and technology. Coming full circle, the new alliance between the Climate Group and Cisco's Connected Urban Development programme should be seen in this light. Though Cisco had kicked off the Connected Urban Development programme, it had not been able to involve other companies in its work or to make much headway into city networks (author interview). The Climate Group's network of cities, subnational governments and corporations was thus an ideal match. Cisco was involved in the research for the SMART 2020 report and was simultaneously considering what kind of partnerships, especially with NGOs, would allow it to scale up and expand its programme (author interview). The Climate Group wanted to transform SMART 2020 from a report into projects, and the Connected Urban Development programme was looking for a platform from which to expand its projects (author interview).

The combined strengths provided a foundation for the alliance. The Climate Group will bring its networking (corporate and governmental) to bear as a platform for advancing the aims of the Connected Urban Development programme. It additionally sees a role for itself in the Alliance in setting performance standards for the pilot projects and assessing their benefits (author interview). By tracking them independently and bringing some consistency to the reporting, the alliance will be better able to make claims about the results of the projects (author interview). The goal of the alliance is to facilitate the transition from pilot programmes, independently observed, into business opportunities that enhance the municipal and global response to climate change. This kind of scaling-up has the potential to catalyse much wider transformation if adoption in multiple cities and across multiple corporations can be achieved.

Implications of the Experimental Governance Model

Collective action looks very different in the experimental model than it does in the multilateral governance model. First, collective action is at two levels. The individual experiments need to form. These are, for the most significant part, voluntary associations, but the initiating actors are finding implementing actors willing to join and follow the rules of the experiments. Collective action is facilitated by the relatively small size of most experiments and by the common purpose that brings the actors together in the first place. The experimental governance system is another level of collective action and it is more amorphous. Here we see self-organisation and clustering, rather than a conscious attempt to have a centrally oriented and driven single response to climate change.

Collective action is thus not an obstacle to moving ahead on climate change in the experimental governance model, but it is an open question as to whether this model can produce an effective response. On the one hand, climate governance experiments are operating on many levels and addressing multiple aspects of the problem, perhaps catalysing the kind of transformation necessary. On the other hand, climate governance experiments are small in scale and there is no central purpose driving their collective activities and no oversight exercised over the collection of experiments.

WHERE TO FROM HERE?

If climate scientists are correct about the urgency of the problem, we have little time to change course and avoid the worst effects of climate change. We have two operative models of climate governance, both of which present challenges and opportunities for effectively governing climate change. The multilateral approach to climate change is familiar and offers the hope of an explicit and conscious global response that draws on the conventionally legitimate authority of states, but it has been unable to overcome the enormous challenges to collective action that have been readily apparent for the last two decades. A global, comprehensive treaty may be the best and most effective response to climate change and capable of engendering the kind of transformation we need in the economy and energy system, but the stalemate seems unlikely to let up in the near to medium term.

The experimental system provides dynamism. There is lots of activity going on, lots of movement in different directions. The vignette described above paints a somewhat rosy picture of a budding division of labour amongst experiments and the ways in which different experiments can interact and cooperate to exploit synergies in their mutual quests for addressing climate change. Different experiments are bringing their different strengths and skill-sets together in order to pursue common goals. Yet some relatively large challenges to expanding the influence of these projects are still looming. It is not yet clear how scaling-up and catalysing transformation in the absence of a centralised governmental approach can be accomplished quickly. We may have the illusion of movement and progress, but little actual effective response.

Fortunately, the choices are not mutually exclusive and scholarship should now turn to examining how the traditional multilateral model and the experimental model interact. Climate governance experiments may not constitute a full global response to climate change on their own, but activity in the experimental governance system may be able to alter the political conditions that have hampered collective action in the multilateral arena. By building coalitions that are supportive of broader action on climate change, climate governance experiments have the potential to break the deadlock in the multilateral process. Similarly, it may be that the best course of action multilaterally in the near term would be to refocus on achieving agreements where that is possible and on providing coordination for experimentation. The goals should include provision of global-level support for and enhancement of city networks, global pilot projects, the multiple carbon markets that are emerging, and regional initiatives.

The situation in climate governance is not unique. Across multiple global issues we are seeing the fragmentation of once unitary multilateral processes and the emergence of new governors. The key, analytically, is to understand how both systems emerge and function and to avoid falling into the trap of considering a particular model as the natural one. In addition, the key scholarly challenge we still have to face is to understand better how conventional and alternative global governance models can and will coexist and interact.

NOTES

1. Parts of this section are drawn from Hoffmann (2011: Chapter 1).
2. This section is drawn from Hoffmann (2011: Chapters 3 and 5).

REFERENCES

Abbott, K.W. (2012), 'The transnational regime complex for climate change', *Environment and Planning C: Government and Policy*, **30**, 571–90.
Aldy, Joseph and Robert Stavins (eds) (2007), *Architectures for Agreement: Addressing Global Climate Change in the Post-Kyoto World*, Cambridge: Cambridge University Press.
Andonova, Liliana, Michele Betsill and Harriet Bulkeley (2009), 'Transnational climate governance', *Global Environmental Politics*, **9** (2), 52–73.
Avant, Deborah, Martha Finnemore and Susan Sell (2010), *Who Governs the Globe?*, Cambridge: Cambridge University Press.
Barrett, Scott (1992), *Convention on Climate Change: Economic Aspects of Negotiations*, Paris: OECD.
Barrett, Scott (2003), *Environment and Statecraft*, Oxford: Oxford University Press.
Bernstein, Steven (2001), *The Compromise of Liberal Environmentalism*, New York: Columbia University Press.
Biermann, F., P. Pattberg, H. van Asselt and F. Zelli (2009), 'The fragmentation of global governance architectures: a framework for analysis', *Global Environmental Politics*, **9**, 14–40.
Bodansky, Daniel (1994), 'Prologue to the Climate Change Convention', in Irving Mintzer and J.A. Leonard (eds), *Negotiating Climate Change: The Inside Story of the Rio Convention*, Cambridge: Cambridge University Press, pp. 45–74.
Bulkeley, Harriet, Liliana Andonova, Karin Backstrand, Michele Betsill, Daniel Compagnon, Rosaleen Duffy, Matthew Hoffmann, Ans Kolk, David Levy, Peter Newell, Matthew Paterson, Phillip Pattberg and Stacy VanDeveer (2012), 'Governing climate change transnationally: assessing the evidence from a database of sixty initiatives', *Environment and Planning C*, **30**, 591–612.
Bulkeley, Harriet and Peter Newell (2010), *Governing Climate Change*, London: Routledge.
Climate Group (2009), 'Cisco and the Climate Group to develop new Connected Urban Development Alliance', http://www.theclimategroup.org/what-we-do/news-and-blogs/Cisco-and-The-Climate-Group-to-develop-new-Connected-Urban-Development-alliance/.
Clinton Climate Foundation (n.d.), 'C40-CCI Cities', http://www.clintonfoundation.org/main/our-work/by-initiative/clinton-climate-initiative/programs/c40-cci-cities/expanding-climate-change-knowledge.html.
Depledge, Joanna (2006), 'The opposite of learning: ossification in the climate change regime', *Global Environmental Politics*, **6** (1), 1–22.
Eurocities (n.d.-a), 'Green Digital Charter', http://eurocities.wordpress.com/eurocities%E2%80%99-green-digital-charter/.
Eurocities (n.d.-b), 'Green Digital Charter Signatories', http://www.greendigitalcharter.eu/signatory-cities.
Hoffmann, Matthew J. (2005), *Ozone Depletion and Climate Change: Constructing a Global Response*, Albany, NY: State University of New York Press.
Hoffmann, Matthew J. (2011), *Climate Governance at the Crossroads: Experimenting with a Global Response after Kyoto*, New York: Oxford University Press.
Keohane, Robert and David Victor (2011), 'The regime complex for climate change', *Perspectives on Politics*, **9** (1), 7–23.
Prins, Gywn and Steve Rayner (2007), 'The wrong trousers: radically rethinking climate policy', Joint Research paper of James Martin Institute for Science and Civilization and MacKinder Centre for the Study of Long-Wave Events, Oxford: James Martin Institute.
Revkin, Andrew (2008), 'Issuing a bold challenge to the US over climate', *New York Times*, 22 January, http://www.nytimes.com/2008/01/22/science/earth/22conv.html.

Rosenau, James N. (2003), *Distant Proximities: Dynamics Beyond Globalization*, Princeton, NJ: Princeton University Press.

Sassen, Saskia (2006), *Territory, Authority, Rights: From Medieval to Global Assemblages*, Princeton, NJ: Princeton University Press.

Sell, Susan (1996), 'North–South environmental bargaining: ozone, climate change, and biodiversity', *Global Governance*, **2**, 93–116.

United National Framework Convention on Climate Change (UNFCCC) (2008), 'Report of the Conference of the Parties on its thirteenth session, held in Bali from 3 to 15 December 2007', http://unfccc.int/resource/docs/2007/cop13/eng/06a01.pdf.

United Nations Framework Convention on Climate Change (UNFCCC) (2009), 'Report of the Conference of the Parties on its fifteenth session, held in Copenhagen from 7 to 19 December 2009', http://unfccc.int/resource/docs/2009/cop15/eng/11a01.pdf.

United Nations Framework Convention on Climate Change (UNFCCC) (2010), 'Report of the Conference of the Parties on its sixteenth session, held in Cancún from 29 November to 10 December 2010', http://unfccc.int/resource/docs/2010/cop16/eng/07a01.pdf.

United Nations Framework Convention on Climate Change (UNFCCC) (2011), 'Report of the Conference of the Parties on its seventeenth session, held in Durban from 28 November to 11 December 2011', http://unfccc.int/documentation/documents/advanced_search/items/3594.php?rec=j&priref=600006771

US Mayors (2005), 'The US Mayors Climate Protection Agreement', http://www.usmayors.org/climateprotection/documents/mcpAgreement.pdf.

Victor, David (2011), *Global Warming Gridlock*, Cambridge: Cambridge University Press.

25 Governing the international political economy of transnational environmental crime

Lorraine Elliott

Transnational environmental crime (TEC) involves the trading or smuggling across borders of species, resources and pollutants in violation of prohibition or regulation regimes established by multilateral environmental agreements (MEAs) and/or in contravention of national law. This includes the trafficking of illegally logged timber (sometimes called 'stolen' timber); the illegal trade in endangered, threatened and some protected species; the black market in ozone-depleting substances (ODS) and other prohibited or regulated chemicals; and the transboundary dumping of toxic and hazardous waste, including electronic waste (e-waste).

The expansion of TEC black markets is a consequence, albeit an unintended one, of a globalised liberal political economy. Globalisation, Peter Andreas (2002: 40) has argued, 'creates a new opportunity structure for those involved in criminalized markets'. As with other forms of criminal endeavour, crimes associated with illegal extraction, harvest and waste have become increasingly transnationalised as those involved take advantage of freer trade, increases in the frequency and volume of commodity shipments, fewer border controls, and easier transfers of funds through global financial and banking systems that offer more opportunities to launder profits into 'legitimate' enterprise. TEC is also, somewhat paradoxically, a function of the growth in global environmental governance. The entry into force of a series of multilateral environmental agreements designed to regulate activities which generate negative environmental externalities, or in some cases to prohibit the transboundary movement of the products of that activity, has created incentives for increasingly profitable black markets.

The first section of this chapter introduces the main forms of transnational environmental crime: wildlife smuggling, timber trafficking, black market in ozone-depleting substances and the illegal trade in hazardous waste. The second section focuses on 'relationships of exchange between traders [and] markets' (Edwards and Gill 2002: 204) as a form of enterprise crime that operates through transnational networks. Those networks function within the illicit space and across the boundaries between illicit and licit economies. The third section examines the form and function of TEC governance as a response to that illicit form of transnational political economy. As explained there, 'governing' TEC has been driven by the need to combat public 'bads' (rather than provide public goods) through regulating or preventing trade and pursuing illegal profits. The processes by which this arena of illicit international political economy is governed reach deep into law enforcement and transnational crime prevention. They rely on public and private spheres of action and a complex, transnational multiple-actor base. The governance complex is fragmented, but also increasingly (perhaps somewhat counter-intuitively) focused, given form through multilevel partnerships and networks that seek to enhance governance capacity, disrupt criminal activity and protect the environment. The final section draws conclusions.

TRANSNATIONAL ENVIRONMENTAL CRIME

The UN Convention against Transnational Organised Crime has a rather tortuous definition of what makes criminal activity transnational. A crime is transnational if it is committed in more than one state; is committed in one state but a substantial part of its preparation, planning, direction or control takes place in another state; or is committed in one state but has substantial effects in another state (UNGA 2000: article 3). André Bossard, former Secretary General of the International Criminal Police Organization (Interpol), has a much simpler definition: the activity must be recognised as a criminal offence in at least two countries as a result of international or national law and a border must be crossed (cited in Friman and Andreas 1999: 5). In the case of transnational environmental crime, this border-crossing can involve the perpetrators, the products and/or the illegal profits.

This illegal trade relies on a political economy of 'lootable commodities' – those that are 'high in value but have low economic barriers to extraction' (Farah 2010: 2) – and 'uncritical markets [that] ensure that there are buyers for goods at the right price, regardless of how they are obtained, processed or transported' (Nellemann et al. 2010: 34). As with all other forms of illegal trade, figures on the exact size and value of transnational environmental crime markets rely partly on extrapolation from actual seizures and partly on speculation and guesswork. These markets are driven by both price and cost differentials: when expected returns (price) are higher than for analogue legal trade, when 'demand exceeds the supply of legal products' (in the case of timber, for example) (OECD 2011: 7), and when compliance with regulations (cost) can be avoided through illegal practices, as is the case in the black markets in ODS and hazardous waste.

The Illegal Wildlife Trade

Wildlife smuggling constitutes a serious threat to species and biodiversity. Between 2003 and 2005 more than 60 per cent of the rhinoceros populations in Kenya and Somalia were killed by commercial poachers (Sims 2006). Rhino poaching in South Africa has increased almost 25-fold, from 13 animals killed in 2007 to 330 in 2010 (CITES 2012). The numbers of tigers has been so severely reduced by the demand for skins and traditional Asian medicines that fewer than 3200 are estimated to remain in the wild (TRAFFIC 2011: 4). The profits can be high even for small-scale operators. Cut pieces of illegal ivory have been reported to sell in Vietnam for the equivalent of close to US$1900 a kilo (WWF 2009). Rhino horn is said to be more valuable than gold and can exceed the price of class A drugs (Gwin 2012). An individual endangered Lear's Macaw can sell for US$60000 on the illegal market (Giovanini 2006: 26).

As much as 25 per cent of the international trade in wildlife and plants is thought to be illegal. While supply and the pursuit of profit is clearly a factor in this trade, which is conservatively valued at US$10 billion a year (CAWT 2007; Haken 2011: 11), the chains of custody are primarily demand-driven. Private collectors and zoos clamour for rare and unusual species of birds, animals, reptiles and plants; research facilities want laboratory animals; and niche consumer markets create demand for traditional Asian and African medicines and exotic foods, such as reef fish and bushmeat. The trade is also driven by a far more mundane demand for unusual pets, such as Chinese three-striped turtles and the slow loris; and for fashion items, such as ivory, tortoise-shell and luxury shahtoosh shawls made from the down hair of the critically endangered Tibetan antelope (which has to be killed for its wool). Developing countries are not the only ones vulnerable to the illegal wildlife trade. Wild birds of prey are smuggled from the United Kingdom for the falconry market in the Middle East. Countries such as Australia and New Zealand are prime targets for poachers and smugglers seeking wild birds, reptiles and native insects for sale to international collectors.

Timber Trafficking

The trade in illegally logged timber – described by one observer as being of 'industrial scale' (Lawson 2004a: 1) – is a significant component of what is an otherwise legal, although often unsustainable, global industry. Illegal logging, which takes place in some of the world's most vulnerable forests, is an umbrella term for a range of activities: extraction crimes, such as logging without a licence or logging inside protected areas or national parks; transportation crimes, involving the smuggling across borders of illegally logged or stolen timber and timber products, or timber species that are protected from trade under the Convention on International Trade in Endangered Species (CITES); and processing crimes, such as the fraudulent labelling of timber destined for export (timber laundering). It is a major driver of deforestation, habitat destruction and species endangerment.

While not all illegally logged timber is destined for transnational trade, there is almost certainly a close relationship between the extent of illegal logging and the extent of timber trafficking. Illegal logging is reported to account for 50 to 90 per cent (by volume) of forest output in tropical producer countries, and between 15 and 30 per cent of global output (Nellemann 2012: 6). In Indonesia, for example, where at its height somewhere between 51 per cent and 80 per cent of timber cut was thought to be illegally logged (UNODC 2010: 167), the equivalent of 300 000 million cubic metres of illegally harvested timber is smuggled out of the country each month (WWF, n.d.).

The illegal timber trade is also sustained by the ease of commodity displacement with loggers and traffickers turning to new and more profitable timber species – or to manufactured products – as other species attract (unevenly implemented) protection status under international or domestic law. This form of TEC is driven in part by a market for cheap timber and timber products. But the trade also reflects demand for high-value species. Five hundred rosewood logs seized by Thai customs in August 2010 were estimated to be worth US$1.5 million on the Chinese market (EIA 2012: 3). Illegally sourced mahogany can fetch more than US$1700 a cubic metre (Urrunaga et al. 2012: 3). The market might generate profit for timber traffickers, but it is costly for governments and legitimate industry. The World Bank (2006) conservatively estimates the cost to timber-producing countries in lost government revenue at about US$5 billion a year. The trade in illegally logged timber depresses world timber prices by something between 7 and 16 per cent because the companies and agents involved pay no taxes, fees or other forms of licence and use cheap and often vulnerable sources of labour (*The Economist* 2006: 74).

The Black Market in Ozone-depleting Substances

The ODS black market is a direct consequence of international agreement on targets to reduce and phase out the production and consumption of such substances as the most effective way to reverse the destructive depletion of the ozone layer. The trade initially focused on developed countries where demand for cheap ODS, in service industries in particular, went 'underground' as production and consumption became effectively illegal in those countries and the cost of retrofitting equipment rose. In the mid 1990s, according to the United Nations Environment Programme (UNEP), between 16 000 and 30 000 tonnes of illegal CFCs (chlorofluorocarbons) – equivalent to more than 10 per cent of global production – was traded annually, with a black market value estimated at something in the vicinity of US$300 million a year (Brack 2001: 5).

The market has now shifted to developing countries – the so-called Article 5 countries – which have benefited from a longer phase-out period. The Asia Pacific, which accounts for over 80 per cent of the world's CFC production and consumption, is a major hub for smuggled ODS, particularly CFCs and halons. As with other illegal environmental commodities, the profits can be substantial. Cylinders of HCFC-22 imported illegally into the United States in 2007 were estimated to have been likely to fetch US$70 each had they entered the black market (Gatica 2011). Despite improved surveillance and tighter restrictions, the illegal trade in the latter half of the first decade of this century was still thought to constitute between 7000 and 14 000 tonnes of ODS a year, about 10 to 20 per cent of the legitimate trade (Clark 2007: 1). Regulatory advances under international law, particularly the Montreal Protocol on Substances that Deplete the Ozone Layer, have created incentives for commodity displacement. As the implementation of phase-out agreements has made it harder to launder ODS through practices such as the use of fraudulent documentation, there is evidence of a growing black market in HCFCs (hydrochlorofluorocarbons), which are now also subject to accelerated phase-out targets.

Transboundary Dumping of Hazardous Waste

Hazardous waste, banned from international trade under the Basel Convention except in very specific circumstances, can take a number of forms: material waste of various kinds; componentry that contains or releases toxic chemicals; electronic waste; and decommissioned ships that contain hazardous products, such as asbestos or polychlorinated biphenyls (PCBs).[1] Given the vast range of substances and products that might qualify as 'hazardous' in some form under international law, the extent of the illegal trade is unclear. However, the results of a joint enforcement operation carried out in 17 European seaports in 2005 give some idea of what the level might be. Of 140 waste shipments inspected, 68 – or some 48 per cent – turned out to be illegal (reported in UNEP 2006).

In contrast with the sectors explored above, the illegal trade in hazardous waste is explicitly supply-driven, mobilised by a desire on the part of waste producers to avoid high disposal costs and by the profit motive on the part of those who are able to sell on the waste for illegal disposal. The waste is often dumped in the world's poorest countries, with consequences that include the non-remediable pollution of water tables, river systems and local ecosystems and damage to animal, plant and human health, sometimes to the extent of extreme disability and even death.

DOING BUSINESS: THE POLITICAL ECONOMY OF ENTERPRISE CRIME AND BLACK MARKETS

TEC is reputed to be one of the fastest-growing areas of criminal activity, globally worth many billions of dollars to criminal syndicates around the world. Estimates have ranged from US$31 billion a year (Lauterback 2005) to US$40 billion or more (Hayman, cited in Lovell 2002). While some forms of TEC are opportunistic, occasional and informal, this area of illegal trade has become increasingly systematic, well financed and highly organised. These are not occasional movements of goods. Large quantities of environmental contraband are daily moved across borders, sometimes by individual smugglers and via rather ordinary forms of concealment (in cars, luggage, express post bags and, as with drugs, hidden on the person), but also in bulk consignments by ship, barge, truck and plane.

As with other forms of transnational crime, transnational environmental crime can be characterised as enterprise crime or, in what Phil Williams (2002: 164) calls the 'neo-Clausewitzian' approach, as 'simply the continuation of business by other means'. The attractions are obvious. Compared with other forms of smuggling and illegal trade, the risks are low and the profits are high; 'the very essence of rational profit maximizing entrepreneurs described in neo-classical economics' (Geopolicity 2011: 10). Fewer resources are given to the suppression, interdiction and prosecution of such crimes. Law enforcement and customs officials are not only less aware of and less interested in environmental crime, but they are often poorly trained to look for or recognise illegal environmental goods.

Some of this enterprise is managed by commodity-specific smuggling syndicates; a kind of illicit market specialisation. But well-known organised crime groups have also become actively involved in the most lucrative areas of transnational environmental crime, a strategy of diversification that Mackenzie (2002) refers to as 'multiple competences' and David Luna calls 'poly-crime' (2008: 2). The trade in endangered species, for example, is reported to constitute part of what Williams (2001: 70) refers to as a 'diverse portfolio of criminal activities' in which Russian and Chinese crime groups, African-based smuggling rings, Asian crime groups and even South American drug traffickers are now involved (see, e.g., Europol 2011: 30–31; Milliken and Shaw 2012).

TEC also goes hand in hand with other kinds of illegal commodities, such as drugs and arms. This kind of parallel trafficking involves moving environmental contraband along the same smuggling routes used for other illegal commodities, combining illegal shipments, or using ostensibly legal shipments to conceal other forms of illegally sourced or traded goods and resources. Protected turtles, for example, have been found in the same shipments as marijuana (Cook et al. 2002). A seizure of CFCs in the Gambia also uncovered 2 tonnes of cocaine smuggled from South America (WCO 2010: 2). Evidence from seizures suggests that illegal environmental goods have been used in barter trade. Protected birds have been smuggled from Australia and exchanged for heroin in Thailand (Cook et al. 2002: 15). Reports suggest that Chinese crime groups have exported the raw ingredients for methamphetamine to South African drug dealers in exchange for illegally harvested abalone which can fetch up to US$200 a pound in Asian retail markets (Schoofs 2007).

The most recent manifestation of this kind of 'venture capital' model of TEC has brought militia groups into illegal environmental activity in search of quick and substantial profits to fund political causes. The Sudan-based Janjaweed militia is involved in elephant poaching in Chad. Rebel groups in the Democratic Republic of Congo have become actively involved in the illegal ivory trade (Felbab-Brown 2011: 7) and the Kenyan Wildlife Service has identified armed groups from Somalia as the cause of an increase in elephant poaching within Kenya. Illegal logging and gun smuggling go hand-in-hand in places such as Liberia (Farah 2010). Recent evidence even hints at the possible involvement of groups with links to terrorist organisations (Levy and Scott-Clark 2007).

Transnational environmental crime also creates opportunity structures for legal companies to engage in shadow enterprise and for front or shell companies to be used to hide illegal connections and practices. This arises because, in contrast to drugs, for example, illegal environmental trade sits alongside a legal one: in timber, in wildlife and even in chemicals and waste. Black markets, according to Naylor (2002: 3, 4), have become 'institutionally embedded in the legal economy' and, in some sectors at least, legal businesses use 'ever shadier methods'. Commodities and profits are laundered with the assistance of delinquent professionals and 'shadow facilitators' (Farah 2010). Environmental goods and resources are moved in and out of the licit economy through the use of counterfeit or falsified documentation. Legitimate companies process fraudulent permits and lend their infrastructure to facilitate transportation in sectors such the illegal timber trade.

Networked TEC Markets

The market functions of exchange and distribution – of illicit goods in this case – persist and flourish through networks. In simple terms, networks are 'actors . . . linked to each other through stable formal or informal relationships of communication and exchange' (Sangiovanni 2005: 7). They rely on horizontal, decentralised, fluid and sometimes transitory arrangements that are assumed to be more resilient and flexible than hierarchical and centralised institutions in responding to changing circumstances. Much of the work on networks in global governance has focused on the licit sphere of activity. But, as Phil Williams (2001: 4) observes, 'organised crime is increasingly operating through fluid network structures rather than formal hierarchies'.

The concept of a 'networked market' describes the chains of custody through which illegally sourced or produced commodities are physically located and then moved to their destination. The nodes in the network are designed to manage illicit trade flows. The links between the nodes consist of relationships of (illegal) commercial exchange. Some TEC market networks are simple, even amateur or opportunistic attempts that involve a small number of people, uncomplicated smuggling routes and unsophisticated forms of concealment. The market networks that underpin or manage the movement of large quantities of illegal environmental products, commodities or wastes are likely to involve multiple sources of goods, multiple participants in the chain of custody and the use of sophisticated methods to conceal either the goods or their true nature or origin. To make detection more difficult, illicit environmental goods are often moved along complex routes through more than one transshipment point where enforcement is lax and where goods can easily be repackaged, relabelled and given fraudulent documentation before being moved on.

A few examples will give a flavour of what we know about TEC market networks in practice. Intelligence on merbau smuggling syndicates in Southeast Asia shows that they involve timber brokers in Jakarta, companies and individuals in Malaysia that oversee the actual logging, companies in Singapore which charter cargo vessels and arrange false documentation, and brokers in Singapore and Hong Kong who connect sellers in places such as Papua with buyers in India and China (Newman and Lawson 2005: 9). Timber logged illegally in the Congo Basin, most often under the control of militia groups, is moved through local front companies to companies in and through Burundi, Rwanda and Uganda, exported globally to the European Union, the Middle East, China and other Asian countries, with support from financiers in the US (Nellemann et al. 2010: 6). The illegal trade in elephant tusks into Asia is reported to involve interlocking webs of shell companies, South-East Asian and African nationals, and a complex smuggling route that trades from Africa across multiple borders and through several Asian ports before reaching its final destination (*Agence France Presse* 2007; Banks et al. 2007). For example, ivory that ends up in China or Japan may have come from the Democratic Republic of Congo, Cameroon and Nigeria, through ports including Hong Kong, Macau and Taiwan. Jernelov (2005) also reports a complicated distribution line in CFCs from Spain via Singapore or Dubai, through India to Nepal or Bangladesh and then back again to the market in India, often relabelled or with fraudulent documentation.

Illicit networks of this kind also derive operational advantages from the inbuilt redundancy that comes from having few critical nodes – those without which the network would cease to function. As with licit markets, critical nodes exist at the point of production, harvest or capture; at the point of export and import; and at the point of retail or final use. But, with multiple actors filling or able to fill any one role, lines of communication and exchange can (easily) be repaired if any one node is removed through interdiction or prosecution. This 'makes it difficult for law enforcers to pinpoint and unravel them' (Sangiovanni 2005: 9).

The networks that sustain illicit transnational markets also require effective mechanisms of social control. As well as the kinds of efficient communication and transfer that sustain transnational market exchange in the licit economy, TEC networks are likely to place a high value on concealment. This demands that personal contact across a network is limited or controlled, especially if participants in illicit markets are likely to cooperate in 'complex and [often] unpredictable ways' (Williams and Godson 2002: 323). Doing business in the illicit economy influences the ways in which intermediaries in the network establish and maintain contacts, the ways in which bonds of trust are sustained in the absence of formal hierarchy and, as Edwards and Gill (2003: 62) point out, the ways in which 'criminal expertise is transferred'. The more effective these webs of affiliation and mechanisms of social control are, the less likely is the risk of exposure and the more resilient a network will be in maintaining illicit markets.

Local communities who provide labour for illegal logging, timber processing or wildlife poaching are often integrated into criminal networks through patron–client relationships. These are likely to involve semi-feudal connections to local timber barons or local officials who control aspects of criminal activity, or through social coercion that takes advantage of economic vulnerability in situations where alternative livelihoods are not available. Local communities are sometimes also 'bought off' to minimise protests in areas where resource extraction is known to be illegal (see, for example, the case-studies of Cameroon in Van Oijen and Angerand 2007). Those engaged in illicit TEC market activity have also moved to take advantage of the 'upperworld' of corrupt officials and politicians, enabling them to evade control mechanisms and protect illegal chains of custody. Indeed, some commentators suggest that corruption should best be understood not as a pathology of the state, but rather as an instrument of risk management – a strategy for doing business – for criminal groups (Williams 2002: 174–5). Local officials, customs officers, police and the judiciary are bribed to overlook illegal shipments, to assist with false paper trails and forged documentation, to help evidence disappear during prosecutions, to delay or drop prosecutions, and even to return no convictions when cases are brought to trial. Syndicates running timber smuggling enterprises in Indonesia, for example, have 'bought off local Indonesian customs officials and harbour masters' and used their influence to 'have any attempted shipments by competitors stopped' (Lawson 2004b: 13). Companies in Ukraine have 'negotiated' with customs officers to facilitate the importation of 'uncontrolled' ODS (Demkine 2001: 10) and companies involved in timber theft in Papua are reported to be 'aided every step of the way by officials from the military, police and forestry departments, as long as the requisite bribe is paid' (Newman and Lawson 2005: 7).

In their most extensive form, TEC networks integrate criminal actors fully into the economic and political institutions of the state, often delivering them significant power and even, as Serrano (2002: 18) suggests, consolidating 'exclusive governing authority'. Rather than being just the recipients of bribes, government officials, protection and enforcement officers, and politicians can take key roles as the organisers, facilitators and beneficiaries of illicit market networks. The Environmental Investigation Agency reports cases of park wardens contracting poachers in Zambia's South Luangwa National Park, and government vehicles being used in Tanzania to transport poached ivory, coordinated by a former game ranger who acts on behalf of senior members of the government (Banks et al. 2007: 6). Police and military officers are known to be heavily involved in organising and coordinating illegal logging in a number of countries in South-East Asia or providing security for logging operations (Noor and Syumanda 2006; Goncalves et al. 2012).

As with other forms of systematic criminal activity, these kinds of bribery and corruption undermine attempts to instill good governance. They corrode the institutions of the state and compromise core values, such as the rule of law. In the most extreme cases of high-level corruption and personal patronage, the state itself no longer functions in the Weberian sense as a provider and guarantor of public goods, but more as a 'protection racket', or kleptocracy, that sustains private appropriation, resource 'asset stripping' and rent-seeking.

GLOBAL GOVERNANCE AND/OF TEC

Disrupting criminal networks, even informal and opportunistic ones, is difficult. The most sophisticated smuggling networks in TEC are often better resourced than law enforcement and border control agencies. Penalties are often minimal. Intelligence on TEC activities is generally limited compared with what is known about other illicit markets, such as drugs or arms, and inter-agency arrangements within countries, let alone between them, for exchange of information, joint operations or mutual assistance are often uneven.

One of the challenges for governments in dealing with TEC is finding the right regulatory mix across prevention, detection, apprehension and prosecution. This involves the use of economic incentives, command-and-control strategies and law enforcement practices to contain relationships of exchange along the TEC chain of custody, restrict both supply-side and demand-side activity, interdict illegal trade, seize goods, pursue and punish perpetrators, and use surveillance of corruption, fraud and money-laundering to gather and act on financial intelligence. However, this regulatory mix – which captures policy instruments at a domestic level – is only one component of the 'systems of [authoritative] rule-making, political coordination and problem-solving' (Rosenau 2002: 8) that constitute and define the reach of global TEC governance.

At a more complex level, responses to TEC on the part of government agencies and other actors are informed by the variable forms of institutional geometry that Biermann et al. (2009) call 'governance architectures'. As this section of the chapter demonstrates, at its core the governance architecture for TEC is a fragmented one. There is no single instrument or institution whose sole or primary purpose is to establish norms, policies and procedures for combating transnational environmental crime. Rather, the governance of TEC is articulated through the apparently discrete international and transnational dimensions of environmental policy on the one hand, and border control, crime prevention and enforcement on the other.

This fragmentation of governance across multiple scales and multiple actors is not, however, fundamentally conflictive. It is not intentional, except to the extent that different institutions and sites of authority have different mandates to deal with either the environmental or the criminal side of the policy challenge. Rather, drawing on the typology developed by Biermann and colleagues, it reflects a state of affairs that sits somewhere between cooperative and synergistic fragmentation. The former situation is marked by 'different institutions and decision-making procedures that are loosely integrated', an ambiguous relationship 'between norms and principles of different institutions' and core institution(s) that do not 'comprise all countries that are important in the issue area' (Biermann et al. 2009: 20). The latter – synergistic fragmentation – 'provides for effective and detailed general principles that regulate . . . policies in distinct yet substantially integrated institutional arrangements' (Biermann et al. 2009: 20).

The Multilateral Core

The multilateral environmental agreements that are most relevant to TEC – the 1973 Convention on International Trade in Endangered Species, the 1987 Montreal Protocol on Ozone Depleting Substances and the 1989 Basel Convention on the Transboundary

Movement of Hazardous Waste – are neither transnational crime nor law enforcement agreements.[2] Their purpose is to enhance conservation and environmental protection efforts through guidelines for the harvesting, production, use of and trade in particular substances or species. The Montreal Protocol commits parties to protecting the ozone layer through the control and, ultimately, the elimination of the production and consumption of chemicals that deplete it. The objective of CITES is to protect species that are endangered or threatened as a consequence of international trade. The Basel Convention was negotiated to manage the movement of hazardous wastes between countries and to ensure their environmentally safe disposal. Given that restrictions on trade, even for environmental purposes, remain controversial under General Agreement on Tariffs and Trade (GATT)/World Trade Organization (WTO) rules, the MEAs reflect a preference for trade regulation rather than prohibition, except where a ban on trade can be agreed in accordance with consent-based principles of international law.[3] Each agreement establishes schedules of which species, chemicals and wastes may and may not be traded across state borders, the conditions under which trade may occur (including restricting trade with non-parties) and the various forms of licensing, control and consent procedures that are required to manage that trade.

Of the three conventions, only Basel refers specifically to illegal traffic, calling it 'criminal' (article 4(3)) and requiring parties to 'introduce appropriate . . . legislation to prevent and punish such traffic' (article 9). Article VIII of CITES also requires parties to penalise trade that violates the Convention, but does not specifically describe such violations as criminal or illegal. The Montreal Protocol itself says nothing about illegal trade and it is generally accepted that the Parties were ill-prepared for the possibility that the Protocol could generate such outcomes.

Transnational crime agreements – such as the UN Convention against Transnational Organized Crime (TOC) and the UN Convention against Corruption – pay little attention to environmental crime as a serious crime. The preamble to the UN TOC Convention suggests (in effect) that it should constitute an effective tool against criminal activities such as illicit trafficking in endangered species of wild flora and fauna, but this is the only TEC-relevant reference in the treaty. Transnational environmental crimes generally fall outside the serious crimes framework defined in the Convention. National legislation rarely imposes the penalties of four or more years of imprisonment for activity such as timber trafficking or wildlife smuggling that would identify them as 'serious crimes' under the Convention.

Despite the lack of either a core institution or a clearly articulated normative structure in international law, TEC has nevertheless achieved a growing policy salience. Indeed, the issue area has become increasingly congested with activity. Some of this has happened under the auspices of the key TEC conventions. CITES has adopted a series of resolutions on illegal wildlife trade and has, in some cases, declared all trade in a particular species (sturgeon) or product (bear gall) to be effectively illegal. Parties are exhorted to strengthen controls on illegal trade, 'not to encourage illegal trade',[4] and to enhance their efforts to combat illegal trafficking across the full enforcement spectrum. The Meeting of the Parties under the Montreal Protocol has similarly adopted a series of decisions on illegal trade – though the Parties conspicuously avoid using the terms 'crime' or 'criminal' – with calls for more effective tracking and reporting systems. The United Nations Environment Programme (UNEP), which hosts the Montreal Protocol

Secretariat, has worked extensively through its regional offices and its Division of Technology, Industry and Economics, to develop Regional Networks of Ozone Officers and the OzonAction programme on capacity-building and training for implementing the Protocol and dealing with problems of illegal ODS trade. The Basel Convention secretariat has established procedures for reporting illegal traffic of hazardous wastes and the Conference of the Parties has adopted 'guidance elements' and a training manual for the detection, prevention and control of illegal trade.

Multilevel Governance

These distinct institutional processes are characteristic of multilevel governance, which is generally defined as decision-making within a common governance arrangement but dispersed across multiple jurisdictions or sites of authority, above, below and, in some cases, alongside states (see Jordan 2001; Zürn et al. 2010). The key MEAs described above now sit amidst governance and rule-making efforts that involve multiple actors, rely on a range of modalities including markets, regulation, monitoring, and intelligence-sharing, and have various degrees of formality and informality. TEC features on the policy agenda of non-environmental international agencies, such as the UN Office of Drugs and Crime (UNODC), the UN Commission on Crime Prevention and Criminal Justice (CCPCJ), the Regional Intelligence Liaison Offices (RILO) of the World Customs Organization (WCO), and Interpol. The UNODC, which hosts the secretariat for the UN TOC Convention, includes environmental resources in its Transnational Organized Crime Threat Assessment (TOCTA). In South-East Asia the Office has expanded the work of its Border Liaison Office network to include wildlife and timber trafficking. International cooperation on illicit international trafficking in forest products (including wildlife) is now a regular item on the agenda of the CCPCJ, a functional commission of the United Nations Economic and Social Council (ECOSOC) with the mandate to guide the UN on its crime prevention and criminal justice agenda.[5] The World Customs Organization proclaims its front-line role in protecting borders against illegal environmental trade, Council sessions have adopted a number of recommendations on TEC, and the Customs Enforcement Network is being used to assist TEC enforcement efforts.[6] Interpol's Environmental Crime programme dates to 1992. It is supported by an Environmental Crime Committee and working groups on pollution crime, wildlife crime and (since 2012) fisheries crime. Although the programme remains 'extra-budgetary', Interpol has an increasingly clear mission to dismantle environmental crime networks, strengthen operational capacity and mobilise political support for environmental law enforcement. The 79th session of Interpol's General Assembly in November 2010 recognised a 'vital need for a global response to combating environmental crime' (Interpol 2010: 1) and, in March 2012, the organisation held the first ever International Chiefs of Environmental Compliance and Enforcement summit.

TEC governance also involves a plethora of activity outside this international and intergovernmental space. Bilateral and regional agreements bring governments together in arrangements such as Wildlife Enforcement Networks (ASEAN-WEN providing the model here), the European Union (EU)'s Voluntary Partnership Agreements, which address issues of forest governance and law enforcement, and the Lusaka Agreement Task Force, which implements cooperative enforcement commitments among governments in

Eastern and Southern Africa on illicit wildlife trade. Key non-governmental organisations (NGOs) – TRAFFIC, the Environmental Investigation Agency, International Fund for Animal Welfare and a range of others – have a long history of working independently to monitor environmental crime, conduct investigations, gather and share intelligence, and provide training and capacity-building. NGOs whose mandate is not specifically environmental, such as Global Witness and Transparency International, have also established an active profile on TEC issues. Corporate engagement is less well developed than in other spheres of activity that cross over into the illicit space – there is, for example, no equivalent of the Kimberley Process on conflict diamonds – but is reflected in commitments to sustainability and verification under private authority arrangements such as those managed by the Forest Stewardship Council, the Tropical Forest Trust and the World Wide Fund for Nature (WWF)'s Global Forest and Trade Network.

The state is not irrelevant in this governance mix. As Andreas (2004: 642) points out, the state itself 'defines the boundaries of illegal market activities'. This occurs through processes of commission and omission. States – or governments in practice – are central to the form and function of relevant treaty law as negotiators and as responsible implementers of that law through domestic legislation and regulation. Yet the involvement of organised criminal groups brings the monopoly claims of the sovereign state into conflict with the shadow area of illegality that functions beyond or as a challenge to sovereign space and authority. Weak states, and those characterised by 'socio-economic destitution', are more likely to offer the kinds of 'commercial opportunities' that attract criminal groups (Wennmann 2004: 105). At the same time, efforts to control borders and reassert the role of the state in the face of both licit and illicit market liberalisation can have the unintended consequence of encouraging criminal groups to develop more innovative concealment and avoidance strategies. Finally, as Kahler (2009: 3) notes, 'governments may also choose to delegate to networks . . . or use them as a new form of collaboration'. In the context of TEC, networks can function as enforcement strategies as well as instruments to enhance negotiation and cooperation.

Indeed, 'networked threats' of the kind associated with TEC, and explored in the second section of this chapter, are argued to 'require a networked response' (Slaughter 2004a: 2). This is because the hierarchical structures associated with (state) bureaucracies are assumed to be not much good at fighting networks as a consequence of what Sheptycki (1995: 618) some while ago called 'linkage blindness' – a lack of information networking and exchange that can result in inefficient and ineffective 'overlap and duplication of functions and expertise'. As a United Nations Environment Programme report on combating the illegal trade in ozone-depleting substances put it, 'networking counts' (UNEP 2002).

Networking Counts

Global governance networks can be described as 'non-hierarchical forms of policy-making . . . which involve public authorities as well as private actors' (Kohler-Koch and Rittberger 2006: 34). They are assumed to be more efficient and effective in dealing with complex coordination and deliberation problems – and therefore in overcoming problems of fragmentation – for three reasons that address the challenges of governance failure identified by Dixon and Dogan (2002: 175): 'knowledge problems (lack of governance knowledge), capability problems (lack of governance instruments) [and] implementation problems (lack of governance effectiveness)'. First, networks that involve public and private actors are argued to facilitate and improve the quality and depth of cooperation between countries, enhance compliance with international treaties and facilitate 'more effective and timely adoption of national legislation' (Töpfer 2002: 3). They not only 'expand regulatory reach', but also 'build trust and establish relationships among their participants . . . [and] establish the conditions essential for long-term cooperation' (Slaughter 2004b: 162). Raustiala further argues that the 'existence of a network strengthens incentives to seek convergence [of policies, regulations and operational practice] because convergence allows for deeper and broader cooperation' (cited in Slaughter and Zaring 2006: 215).

Second, transnational networks are expected to enhance problem-solving capacities and reduce transaction costs, improve data collection, facilitate the flow of information, and support coordination among multiple agencies. Powell argues that network forms of organisation should be 'more effective than either markets or hierarchies in situations requiring know-how [and] demanding speed' (cited in Slaughter and Zaring 2006: 218). Third, networks can help to enhance institutional 'learning' through what Sheptycki (1995: 617) called the 'transnational trade in criminological knowledge'. UNEP (2002: 4, 10) refers to this as 'collective learning by sharing while doing' and 'peer-to-peer problem solving'. Networks, in theory at least, enable actors and agencies to share policy tools more effectively and quickly than hierarchical arrangements and institutions, to 'exchange regular information about their own practices and develop databases of best practice' (Slaughter 2004b: 162) and to 'brainstorm innovative . . . solutions' (UNEP 2002: 5).

Specific partnerships lie at the core of some components of policy and governance convergence. The MEAs, the institutions that host them and other key intergovernmental organisations have developed a series of overlapping bilateral Memoranda of Understanding (MoUs) and other agreements to strengthen the depth and quality of cooperation on various TEC sectors. The World Customs Organization has concluded MoUs with (among others) UNEP (2003), the CITES Secretariat (1997), the Basel Convention (1997) and the Lusaka Action Task Force. The LATF has established MoUs with the CITES Secretariat (2000), the Interpol Secretariat (2006) and the Commission for Central African Forests (2010). Interpol has negotiated MoUs with the CITES Secretariat (1998) and the Basel Convention (1999), as well as those mentioned above. These partnership arrangements have also become cross-sectoral. In 2002 the secretariats of CITES, the Basel Convention and the Montreal Protocol (bringing together wildlife, waste and ODS) signed an MoU to strengthen cooperation among them. Many of these MoUs focus on mutual consultation, information exchange (including secure information and joint databases where appropriate), reciprocal representation and technical cooperation, ranging from joint training materials through to enforcement action including strategies such as controlled deliveries and joint operations. Their objective, whether explicit or not, is to enhance problem-solving capacities and institutional learning, as well as to strengthen cooperation.

This patchwork of bilateral and trilateral partnerships (of which only a small selection is identified above) has become increasingly networked as governments, international organisations, NGOs and the corporate sector have begun to explore more innovative ways of working together to govern and combat transnational environmental crime. The Green Customs Initiative, operational since 2003, is a cooperative partnership of 11 MEA secretariats and international organisations to detect and prevent the illegal trade in environmentally sensitive commodities at the same time as facilitating the legal trade. The iPIC network, initially established to bring together governments in South Asia, South-East Asia and the Pacific to strengthen cooperation on the application of prior informed consent strategies for ODS, has expanded to include the EU, as well as countries in Europe, Central Asia, and Latin America and the Caribbean. The International Consortium on Combating Wildlife Crime (ICCWC – pronounced 'eye-quick') brings together CITES, Interpol, the UNODC, UNEP and the World Bank to provide coordinated support to national wildlife law enforcement agencies and to relevant sub-regional and regional networks.

Kahler (n.d.: 4) reminds us that the emergence of networks in global governance 'does not mean that governments have been evicted from their traditional roles'. But while some TEC governance arrangements remain more firmly under the auspices of government networks than others – in effect, constituting transgovernmental networks of national officials and intergovernmental secretariats – others function as variations of global public policy networks that bring together government, non-state and private sector actors. TEC networks involving NGOs are more likely to function as coordination and knowledge networks than implementation networks. This is perhaps not surprising. TEC governance spans the boundary between environmental protection, in which transnational non-state agency is increasingly accepted, and the making and implementation of rules on crime prevention, enforcement and border protection over which sovereign states claim and seek to retain individual and collective authority.

It is notable too that NGOs and scientific bodies have become increasingly important components of the networked and multilevel architecture that characterises TEC governance, often as key partners in formal arrangements and active partners in informal arrangements. The wildlife NGO TRAFFIC (itself a network) is, for example, a formal partner with CITES under an MoU adopted in 1999 to strengthen capacity building, communication and liaison. This relationship now includes TRAFFIC acting as a mandated collection point for data from the Parties (on the killing of elephants, for example) and a formal requirement for TRAFFIC to report its analysis to each CITES Conference of the Parties. The Coalition against Wildlife Trafficking (CAWT), a US government initiative which describes itself as 'voluntary public–private coalition of like-minded governments and organizations sharing a common purpose',[7] includes a range of NGOs in partnership with like-minded governments. NGOs are partners with governments and international organisations in so-called 'Track II' arrangements, such as the Asia Regional Partners' Forum on Combating Environmental Crime (ARPEC) and the International Network on Environmental Compliance and Enforcement (INECE). The dependence on public and private spheres of action, and the frequent blurring of the two, is reflected also in the extent of undercover and intelligence-gathering operations that track and report on criminal activity undertaken as much by key NGOs, such as TRAFFIC and the Environmental Investigation Agency, as by governments or international enforcement and policing agencies, such as Interpol and the World Customs Organization.

CONCLUSION

As the Environmental Investigation Agency (2008: 2) puts it, environmental crime is 'serious, transnational and organized'. Crimes associated with illegal extraction, harvest and waste are serious because of their environmental consequences; because of the ways that they undermine the rule of law and good governance at local, national and global levels; and because of their links with violence, corruption and a range of crossover crimes, such as money-laundering. They have become increasingly transnationalised through the involvement of criminal actors in more than one country (and often many countries) linked together through networks of illegal trade and illicit finance to move goods across borders. Indeed, this area of criminal activity is sufficiently systematic and organised that it now merits consideration alongside other forms of transnational organised crime. The criminal networks that sustain larger-scale TEC are professional and well organised with complex transnational relationships of communication and exchange that span the illicit and licit economies and link local harvest, extraction and waste production to a global marketplace.

In simple terms, transnational environmental crime could be understood as a problem of the kind of regulatory failure that occurs when there is insufficient regulation, or when regulatory systems are based on outdated or insufficient knowledge, or when domestic agencies 'inadequately fulfill their oversight, supervisory and enforcement functions' (Kaufmann and Penciakova 2011). The Director of the UN Interregional Crime and Justice Research Institute (UNICRI) has argued that the fight against TEC is complicated (and compromised), not just by 'scarce awareness and knowledge of the problem, [and] insufficient regulation', but also by 'scarce international cooperation' (Calvani 2009: 14). It is perhaps more accurate to suggest that global governance responses to TEC have been characterised not so much by 'scarce' cooperation as by 'fragmented' cooperation. For much of its history the global architecture of TEC governance has been the product of independent policy spheres rather than of specific design, resulting in a 'patchwork of . . . institutions that are different in their character . . . their constituencies . . . [and] their spatial scope' (Biermann et al. 2009: 16).

Yet, as this chapter has demonstrated, TEC governance architectures have come to display an increasing degree of convergence in purpose and, more particularly, in practical strategies for political coordination and problem-solving. This convergence can be explained by two related factors. First, the epistemic community – those with authoritative claims to policy-relevant knowledge and expertise who are actively engaged in action on TEC – is actually quite small. In the TEC space, this includes government officials, law enforcement officers, criminal investigation and border control agencies, environmental NGOs, scientific and research bodies, and the private sector. Second, the kinds of partnerships and networks that have come to characterise TEC governance help to facilitate knowledge transfer and strengthen policy coherence. Those networks function at and across multiple levels and sites of authority, providing opportunities to bring together international organisations, non-governmental organisations and government (state) agencies in the fight against transnational environmental crime. Yet the chapter has also hinted at factors that can serve to constrain those opportunities for better and more effective global (TEC) governance: limited resources, weak coordination and poor strategies for managing intelligence, on the one hand; and the continuing problems of weak states, government corruption and the integration of illicit with licit economies, on the other.

NOTES

1. One of the most extensive forms of waste trade is electronic waste or e-waste. Trade in e-waste is not necessarily illegal: trade in used computers and other high-tech electronics for appropriate and safe reuse or recycling into the secondhand market is permitted under international law although domestic regulatory structures are often fairly permissive.
2. Two further conventions – the 1998 Rotterdam Convention on the Prior Informed Consent Procedure for certain Hazardous Chemicals and Pesticides in International Trade and the 2001 Stockholm Convention on Persistent Organic Pollutants – have been brought into the TEC governance architecture because of their own trade restrictions and through the development of a single integrated secretariat.
3. The Basel Parties have agreed to a ban on the trade in hazardous waste for final disposal between Organisation for Economic Co-operation and Development (OECD) and non-OECD countries and a ban on the export of wastes intended for recovery or recycling, although at the time of writing (October 2013) this was not yet in force.
4. Conf. 6.4 (REV), Controls on illegal trade, adopted at the Sixth Meeting of the Conference of the Parties, Ottawa (Canada), 12–24 July 1987 and amended at the Ninth Meeting of the Conference of the Parties, Fort Lauderdale (United States of America), 7–18 November 1994.
5. The challenges posed by environmental crimes constituted the key thematic focus for the Commission's 22nd session in April 2013. The Commission adopted a resolution encouraging member-states to make the illicit trafficking in wild fauna and flora a serious crime under the terms of the UN Convention Against Transnational Organized Crime.
6. The Customs Enforcement Network is an internet-based system that provides secure access to seizure data, alerts, intelligence and secure communications.
7. See http://www.cawtglobal.org/about/.

REFERENCES

Agence France Presse (2007), 'Wildlife smuggling in Asia still a roaring trade', 2 June, http://news.sawf.org/LifeStyle/38061.aspx.

Andreas, Peter (2002), 'Transnational crime and economic globalization', in Mats Berdal and Mónica Serrano (eds), *Transnational Organized Crime and International Security*, Boulder, CO: Lynne Rienner Publishers, pp. 37–52.

Andreas, Peter (2004), 'Illicit international political economy: the clandestine side of globalization', *Review of International Political Economy*, **11** (3), 641–52.

Banks, Debbie, Justin Gosling, Julian Newman, Rachel Noble and Mary Rice (2007), *Upholding the Law: The Challenge of Effective Enforcement*, London: Environmental Investigation Agency.

Biermann, Frank, Philipp Pattberg, Harro van Asselt and Fariborz Zelli (2009), 'The fragmentation of global governance architectures: a framework for analysis', *Global Environmental Politics*, **9** (4), 14–40.

Brack, Duncan (2001), 'The scope of the problem: and overview of the illegal ODS trade', *OzonAction Newsletter*, Special Supplement no. 6, 4–7.

Calvani, Sandro (2009), 'Transnational organized crime: emerging trends of global concern', NATO Defense College, Rome, 26 November.

Clark, Ezra (2007), 'Ozone depleting substances – the global illegal trade: history and current trends', paper presented to the Meeting of the Regional Ozone Network for Europe and Central Asia, Ashgabat, Turkmenistan, 26 February to 2 March.

Coalition Against Wildlife Trafficking (CAWT) (2007), 'Countering multi-billion dollar illegal wildlife trade focus of government backed coalition', Press Release, 20 February.

Convention on International Trade in Endangered Species (CITES) (2012), 'CITES to explore new financial sources to tackle the decline in wildlife', Press Release, 16 August, http://www.cites.org/eng/news/pr/2011/20110816_SC61.php.

Cook, Dee, Martin Roberts and Jason Lowther (2002), *The International Wildlife Trade and Organized Crime: A Review of the Evidence and the Role of the UK*, Godalming, UK: WWF-UK.

Demkine, Volodymyr (2001), 'Facing the challenge in countries with economies in transition', *OzonAction Newsletter*, Special Supplement no. 6, 9–12.
Dixon, John and Rhys Dogan (2002), 'Hierarchies, networks and markets: responses to societal governance failure', *Administrative Theory & Praxis*, **24** (1), 175–96.
The Economist (2006), 'Down in the woods', 25 March, 73–5.
Edwards, Adam and Peter Gill (2002), 'Crime as enterprise: the case of 'transnational organised crime'', *Crime, Law and Social Change*, **37** (3), 203–23.
Edwards, Adam and Peter Gill (2003), 'Measurements and interpretations', in Adam Edwards and Peter Gill (eds), *Transnational Organised Crime: Perspectives on Global Security*, London: Routledge, pp. 59–64.
Environmental Investigation Agency (EIA) (2008), *Environmental Crime: A Threat to Our Future*, London: EIA.
Enviromental Investigation Agency (EIA) (2012), *Rosewood Robbery*, London: EIA.
Europol (2011), *EU Organised Crime Threat Assessment*, The Hague: Europol.
Farah, Douglas (2010), *Transnational Crime, Social Networks and Forests: Using Natural Resources to Finance Conflicts and Post-Conflict Violence*, Washington, DC: Program on Forests (PROFOR).
Felbab-Brown, Vanda (2011), 'The disappearing act: the illicit trade in wildlife in Asia', Working Paper no. 6, Washington, DC: Brookings Institution.
Friman, H. Richard and Peter Andreas (1999), 'Introduction: international relations and the illicit global economy', in H. Richard Friman and Peter Andreas (eds), *The Illicit Economy and State Power*, Lanham, MD: Rowman & Littlefield, pp. 1–23.
Gatica, Staci (2011), 'US licensing system and enforcement activity', Meeting of Ozone Action Networks from Latin America and the Caribbean, 5 October, http://www.pnuma.org/.../oct%205-stacy-USA_ODS_Licensing_System_Ill.
Geopolicity (2011), *The Economics of Piracy: Pirate Ransoms and Livelihoods off the Coast of Somalia*, Dublin: Geopolicity Europe.
Giovanni, Dener (2006), 'Taking animal trafficking out of the shadows: RENCTAS uses the internet to combat a multi-billion dollar trade', *Innovations*, **1** (2), 25–35.
Goncalves, Marilyne Pereira, Melissa Panjer, Theodore S. Greenberg and William B. Magrath (2012), *Justice for Forests: Improving Criminal Justice Efforts to Combat Illegal Logging*, Washington, DC: World Bank.
Gwin, Peter (2012), 'Rhino wars', *National Geographic*, March, http://ngm.nationalgeographic.com/2012/03/rhino-wars/gwin-text/1.
Haken, Jeremy (2011), *Transnational Crime in the Developing World*, Washington, DC: Global Financial Integrity.
Interpol (2010), *Resolution: Sustainable Environmental Crime Programme*, AG-2010-RES-03, adopted at the 79th INTERPOL General Assembly, Doha, 8–11 November.
Jernelov, Arne (2005), 'The ozone mafia', Project Syndicate Print Commentary, http://www.project-syndicate.org/print_commentary/jernelov6/English.
Jordan, Andrew (2001), 'The European Union: an evolving system of multi-level governance . . . or government?', *Policy and Politics*, **29** (2), 193–208.
Kahler, Miles (n.d.), 'Networked politics: agency, power and governance', School of International Relations and Pacific Studies, University of California San Diego, http://irps.ucsd.edu/assets/014/6727.pdf.
Kahler, Miles (2009), 'Networked politics: agency, power and governance', in Miles Kahler (ed.), *Networked Politics: Agency, Power and Governance*, Ithaca, NY: Cornell University Press, pp. 1–20.
Kaufmann, Daniel and Veronika Penciakova (2011), 'Preventing nuclear meltdown: assessing regulatory failure in Japan and the United States', Opinion, 1 April, Brookings Institution, http://www.brookings.edu/research/opinions/2011/04/01-nuclear-meltdown-kaufmann.
Kohler-Koch, Beate and Berthold Rittberger (2006), 'The "governance turn" in EU Studies', *Journal of Common Market Studies*, **44** (Supplement 1), 27–49.
Lauterback, Andrew (2005), Statement by the Chair, Interpol Environmental Crimes Committee to the 5th International Conference on Environmental Crime, Lyon, 2–3 June.
Lawson, Sam (2004a), *The Ramin Racket: The Role of CITES in Curbing Illegal Timber Trade*, London: Environmental Investigation Agency.
Lawson, Sam (2004b), *Profiting from Plunder: How Malaysia Smuggles Endangered Wood*, London, UK and Bogor, Indonesia: Environmental Investigation Agency/Telapak.
Levy, Adrian and Cathy Scott-Clark (2007), 'Poaching for Bin Laden', *The Guardian*, 5 May, http://www.guardian.co.uk/world/2007/may/05/terrorism.animalwelfare (accessed 21 February 2010).
Lovell, Jeremy (2002), 'Eco-crooks outwitting law agencies', Reuters News Service, http://www.planetark.org/dailynewsstory.cfm/newsid/16164/newsDate/28-May-2002/story.htm.
Luna, David (2008), 'Overview: dismantling illicit networks and corruption nodes', presentation at the 13th International Anti-Corruption Conference, Athens, 2 November.

Mackenzie, Simon (2002), 'Organised crime and common transit networks', Trends and Issues in Crime and Criminal Justice working paper no. 233, Canberra: Australian Institute of Criminology.

Milliken, Tom and Jo Shaw (2012), 'The South Africa – Viet Nam Rhino horn trade nexus: a deadly combination of institutional lapses, corrupt wildlife industry professionals and Asian crime syndicates', Johannesburg: TRAFFIC.

Naylor, R.T. (2002), *Wages of Crime: Black Markets, Illegal Finance and the Underworld Economy*, Ithaca, NY: Cornell University Press.

Nellemann, C. (2012), 'Green carbon, black trade: illegal logging, tax fraud and laundering in the world's tropical forests', Norway: INTERPOL/United Nations Environment Programme, GRID-Arendal.

Nellemann, C., I. Redmond and J. Refisch (2010), 'The last stand of the gorilla: environmental crime and conflict in the Congo basin', Norway: UNEP, GRID-Arendal.

Newman, Julian and Sam Lawson (2005), *The Last Frontier: Illegal Logging in Papua and China's Massive Timber Theft*, London, UK and Bogor, Indonesia: Telapak/Environmental Investigation Agency.

Noor, Rivani and Rully Syumanda (2006), 'Social conflict and environmental disaster: a report on Asia Pulp and Paper's operations in Sumatra, Indonesia', Moreton-in-Marsh, UK: World Rainforest Movement.

Organisation for Economic Co-operation and Development (OECD) (2011), 'Illegal trade in environmentally sensitive goods: draft synthesis report', COM/TAD/ENV/JWPTE(2011)45, Paris: OECD Trade and Agriculture Directorate/Environment Directorate.

Rosenau, James N. (2002), 'Governance in a new global order', in David Held and Anthony McGrew (eds), *Governing Globalization: Power, Authority and Global Governance*, Cambridge: Polity Press, pp. 70–86.

Sangiovanni, Mette Eilstrup (2005), 'Transnational networks and security threats', *Cambridge Review of International Affairs*, **18** (1), 7–13.

Schoofs, Mark (2007), 'Traffic jam: as meth trade goes global', *Wall Street Journal*, 21 May, http://www.aegis.com/news/wsj/2007/WJ070506.html.

Serrano, Mónica (2002), 'Transnational organised crime and international security: business as usual?', in Mats Berdal and Monicá Serrano (eds), *Transnational Organised Crime and International Security*, Boulder, CO: Lynne Rienner Publishers, pp. 13–36.

Sheptycki, J.W.E. (1995), 'Transnational policing and the makings of a post-modern state', *British Journal of Criminology*, **35** (4), 613–35.

Sims, Josh (2006), 'Illegal trading: follow that badger!', *The Independent*, 2 November, http://environment.independent.co.uk/wildlife/article1948975.ece.

Slaughter, Anne-Marie (2004a), *A New World Order*, Princeton, NJ: Princeton University Press.

Slaughter, Anne-Marie (2004b), 'Disaggregated sovereignty: towards the public accountability of global government networks', *Government and Opposition*, **39** (2), 159–90.

Slaughter, Anne-Marie and David Zaring (2006), 'Networking goes international: an update', *Annual Review of Law and Social Science*, **2**, 211–29.

Töpfer, Klaus (2002), 'Foreword', in United Nations Environment Programme, *Networking Counts: Montreal Protocol Experiences in Making Multilateral Evironmental Agreements Work*, Paris: UNEP Division of Technology, Industry and Economics, p. 2.

TRAFFIC (2011), 'World leaders aim for deal to save the tiger', *Asia Wildlife Trade Bulletin*, **11** (May), 3–4.

United Nations Environment Programme (UNEP) (2002), *Networking Counts: Montreal Protocol Experiences in Making Multilateral Environmental Agreements Work*, Paris: UNEP Division of Technology, Industry and Economics.

United Nations Environment Programme (UNEP) (2006), 'Liability for Côte D'Ivoire hazardous waste clean-up', News Release 2006/58, http://www.unep.org/Documents.Multilingual/Default.asp?DocumentID=485&ArticleID=5430&l=en.

United Nations General Assembly (UNGA) (2000), *Convention against Transnational Organised Crime*, A/RES/55/25.

United Nations Office of Drugs and Crime (UNODC) (2010), *The Globalization of Crime: A Transnational Organized Crime Threat Assessment*, Vienna: UNODC.

Urrunaga, Julia M., Andrea Johnson, Inés Dhaynee Orbegozo and Fiona Mulligan (2012), *The Laundering Machine: How Fraud and Corruption in Peru's Concession System are Destroying the Future of its Forests*, Washington, DC: Environmental Investigation Agency.

Van Oijen, Danielle and Sylvain Angerand (2007), *Illegally Logged Wood from Cameroon on the Dutch Market*, Amsterdam, The Netherlands and Paris, France: Milieudefensie/Les Amis de la Terre.

Wennmann, Achim (2004), 'The political economy of transnational crime and its implications for armed violence in Georgia', *CP 6: The Illusions of Transition: Which Perspectives for Central Asia and the Caucasus*, Geneva: Graduate Institute of International Studies/CIMERA.

Williams, Phil (2001), 'Transnational criminal networks', in John Arquilla and David Ronfeldt (eds), *Networks and Netwars: The Future of Terror, Crime and Militancy*, Santa Monica, CA: RAND, pp. 61–97.

Williams, Phil (2002), 'Transnational organized crime and the state', in Rodney Bruce Hall and Thomas

J. Biersteker (eds), *The Emergence of Private Authority in Global Governance*, Cambridge: Cambridge University Press, pp. 161–82.

Williams, Phil and Roy Godson (2002), 'Anticipating organized and transnational crime', *Crime, Law and Social Change*, **37** (4), 311–55.

World Bank (2006), 'Weak forest governance costs $US 15 billion a year', Press Release No. 2007/86/SDN, 16 September.

World Customs Organization (WCO) (2010), 'Project Sky-hole Patching II', 10 November, http://www.green-customs.org/docs/Sky_Hole_Patching_BKK.pdf.

WWF (n.d.), 'Country Profile: Indonesia', http://gftn.panda.org/gftn_worldwide/asia/indonesia_ftn/indonesia_profile/, accessed 17 July 2012.

WWF (2009), Elephants under threat as illegal ivory price soars in Viet Nam', 16 February, http://wwf.panda.org/?156422/Elephants-under-threat-as-illegal-ivory-price-soars-in-Viet-Nam, accessed 10 February 2012.

Zürn, Michael, Sonja Wälti and Henrik Enderlein (2010), 'Introduction', in Henrik Enderlein, Sonja Wälti and Michael Zürn (eds), *Handbook on Multi-Level Governance*, Cheltenham, UK and Northampton, MA, USA: Edward Elgar, pp. 1–13.

Conclusion: the governance of the international political economy
Anthony Payne and Nicola Phillips

We observed in the Introduction to this volume that, during the 1990s and early 2000s, we thought that we knew what we were dealing with in terms of the core structural, ideological and political forces at play in relation to the governance of the international political economy, and openly acknowledged that these moorings had been loosened by a range of trends and events experienced since 2007–08. By implication at least, we offered up the contents of this book as a means to reach that firmer ground on which the field could perhaps again rest for a period. To that end, a large number of thorough, detailed studies of important aspects of the governance of the international political economy have been gathered together in the preceding pages. They represent the best of current research and draw on the knowledge and insights of some of the most promising and most experienced political economists presently working in the global academy. And yet it has to be conceded that we are not at all sure that we have collectively succeeded in charting a way to the firmer understanding that we sought. We readily make this admission, but in fairness we move on quickly to say that we do not think this is due to shortcomings in our collective analytical powers in this volume.

Why do we forgive ourselves in this way? The answer is that we can now see more clearly that we are living through a period of considerable uncertainty in the evolution of the contemporary international political economy. In such circumstances many critical thinkers are content to fall back on Gramsci, reach for their copy of *The Prison Notebooks* and quote the passage where he writes that 'the crisis consists precisely in the fact that the old is dying and the new cannot be born', noting that 'in this interregnum a great variety of morbid symptoms appear' (Gramsci 1971). However valid the call for hesitancy might seem, we ought to try to respond to Gramsci's implicit challenge and identify the key elements of the confusion and contradiction that characterise so many attempts to assess the current condition of the international political economy. Colin Hay and Anthony Payne (2013) have recently tried to do this by suggesting that the present conjuncture is being shaped by a remarkable, and hugely challenging, coalescence of three major processes of structural change occurring simultaneously and interacting in all manner of complicated ways. They can be distinguished analytically as follows:

- financial crisis: a largely Western crisis brought about by neoliberal excess and now rendering the resumption of economic growth a severe conundrum for the United States, Japan and nearly all major European economies and a problem at least for the rest of the global economy;
- shifting economic power: the recent intensification of longstanding movements in the locus of economic power in the world characterised by the rise of countries like China, India, Brazil and several others too; and

- environmental threat: the eventual realisation that climate change is both real and accelerating and is now asking the most serious questions about the ongoing viability of traditional notions of economic growth, the ways we are governed and indeed the good society itself.

The key point, though – and the reason this all adds up to what Hay and Payne have called the 'Great Uncertainty' – is that these processes of change are all taking place concurrently and arguably will come to a head at broadly the same time. They also feed off each other in extraordinary and unexpected ways, with the politics flowing both through and between them in highly complex fashion.

This formulation is but one way to catch the core elements of the current condition of the international political economy. But it has the merit of seeing the links and interactions that connect apparently disparate phenomena and is actually not far away from other attempts to frame where we are presently. Barry Gills (2010: 169), for example, talked quite early on of the emergence of a challenging combination of 'capitalist crisis, systemic crisis [and] civilisational crisis'. The truth is that there is absolutely nothing to be gained by asserting conclusions aggressively and overconfidently, just for the sake of form, when more mature counsel suggests that this is a moment for caution and acceptance that an era of transition for the international political economy is under way, with the eventual outcome still unknown. Of course, the problem with transitions is that it is usually easier (although not easy) to see when they begin than when they end, and even harder to see when they might end when the transition is still unfolding. Here it is important to remind ourselves that getting from the Wall Street crash of 1929 to the Bretton Woods conference of 1944 took 15 years. The other great recent period of shift – the 'long 1970s' – is even harder to date with precision. But, again, it took a lot of pounding by the neoliberal right to move us from the first signs of the crisis of 'embedded liberalism' (Ruggie 1982) in the late 1960s to the heyday of Reaganism and Thatcherism in the early 1980s. So perhaps 15 years is about standard for these sorts of transitions? If so, and if the destabilising financial events of 2007–08 do mark the significant beginning of this transition, then we all have a long haul to live through – and many other edited books will no doubt appear – before any kind of end-game is reached.

In short, the international political economy has experienced tension and is manifestly in flux. But it has not collapsed or, as yet, become unrecognisable from what it was at, say, the turn of the century. There exists a lot of continuity, as well as much change, as always, perhaps, even in eras of acknowledged transition. As with all forms of instability, we suggest that the best way to proceed is to re-examine as carefully as possible the foundations of the structure in question. We do that here by going back to the four themes that we argued in the Introduction are foundational to the study of the governance of the international political economy. These were: the ideologies that underpin this governance; the levels at which it is articulated and practised; the actors involved in the various systems of governance; and the ethical questions that are generated by human experience of the whole process of governance. Drawing on the collective findings of our many contributors, we now offer an editorial reflection on these four organising aspects of the process of governance by seeking to assess how each seems to be working itself out at this uncertain moment.

HOW NEOLIBERALISM GOES ON AND ON

We certainly still take it as foundational to the study of governance that all modes of governance are distinguished by their differing ideological assumptions. Governing involves making ideological choices and ideologies can make governing seem like common sense. There is no need at all to adjust this broad perspective. The more difficult task is to judge exactly where the dominant form of global ideological consensus of the last three decades, namely, neoliberalism, now stands in the minds of the world's elites and its many citizens. In his chapter in Part I of the book Andrew Gamble showed that 'neoliberalism as the latest ideological form of economic liberalism has been adapted to different contexts for the governance of the international system'. He thus noted that the Washington Consensus in the 1980s was succeeded by the Post-Washington Consensus in the 1990s, and then in turn by 'the present period of policy inertia and political grid-lock after the financial crash'. But, interestingly and importantly, he does not think that this current period is without ideological character: indeed, he refers explicitly to a 'third phase of neoliberalism' opening in 2008. Admittedly, leading states did intervene decisively to prevent a complete collapse of the global financial system, but they generally presented their actions as temporary measures that did not signal a break with neoliberal orthodoxy. Gamble concedes that a fierce ideological battle has broken out since then about who was most to blame for the financial crash and he acknowledges that new proposals have been tabled, and some implemented, that seek to build a more resilient financial architecture. All that said, his overall conclusion is arresting: that the power of the broad ideology of neoliberalism, although 'not monolithic' and possessing 'many internal contradictions', is 'undeniable' and 'seen at its strongest in times of economic downturn and austerity', precisely because it has come to be 'embedded at many different levels and in many different institutions'. This, he suggests, is 'what makes radical alternatives to it seem so futile and utopian, because it is hard to imagine such a large overturning of the commonsense assumptions that underpin governance' in so many of the arenas of the international political economy.

The case-study chapters in Part II of the book largely support this perhaps unexpected conclusion. We have had highlighted for us many examples of how, at the micro level, market thinking has penetrated the mind-sets and thus the behavioural patterns of all varieties of apparently non-commercial organisations. This is an important finding, because we generally focus in the study of international political economy on what is prominent, visible and self-evidently political, rather than on the 'everyday' (but see Hobson and Seabrooke 2007). But, of course, at the macro level as well we have seen that some of the major governmental institutions of governance, such as the International Monetary Fund (IMF) and the World Bank at the global level, the European Commission and the European Central Bank (ECB) at the regional level, and myriad departments of state in various countries managing policy at the national level in spheres as diverse as healthcare and the environment as well as finance and trade, have all continued in fundamental ways and at key moments to favour the 'story' of the market. No arena of public policy-making demonstrates this fact more starkly than that supposedly pertaining to the 'development' of the poorest countries and peoples of the world. It has been suggested in several of the chapters that the whole mainstream development debate since 1945, and still very much so today even after 2007–08, has been shaped by a systemic ideological bias towards a vision of development as essentially technocratic, as a problem that can be 'fixed' provided that resources and appropriate institutions are brought to bear upon the various domestic obstacles that repeatedly get in the way. It is true that throughout this period the United Nations, and most especially the United Nations Development Programme, has consistently articulated an alternative vision grounded in a notion of 'human development', and done so not without impact. But it remains the case that this has amounted ultimately to little more than a 'credible critique' that gains a hearing but does not generally shape the dominant practices of governance.

   Why, then, does neoliberalism seem to go on and on, even if in so doing it remakes itself into a subtly adjusted new variant of its core form? Part of the answer is that challenges to ideological orthodoxy tend to get absorbed unless marginalised actors deliberately choose to make the unthinking commonsense assumptions of a particular field of policy the explicit object of their challenge. We saw this in the discussion of the attempt to insert a 'development agenda' into the work of the World Intellectual Property Organization (WIPO). Although led by Argentina and Brazil and supported by a number of civil-society actors, this radical push for change has been steadily 'reframed' into a reformist call for better balance in the current intellectual property regime. Bourdieu (1992) was tellingly drawn upon to suggest that political challenges are likely to be successful only when they question the legitimacy of, and then sever adherence to, the dominant categories of perception of the social order. This argument also highlights one of the many problems with the 'rising powers' thesis that has been so prominent of late in international political economy and which again several of the chapter authors in Part II consider. The point is that it will not be enough for China, India, Brazil or any other 'rising' country merely to assert their national interests within the halls of governance of the international political economy. They can with increasing ease block outcomes by this means; but, if they want to modify existing governance regimes beyond marginal adaptation to their presence and new power, they will necessarily have to find and promulgate a new global ideology of governance. This is hard to do and, notwithstanding passing references to the existence of a 'Beijing Consensus' (Ramo 2004) or a new Latin American 'post-neoliberalism' (Grugel and Rigarozzi 2012), there is, as Gamble himself says, 'little sign as yet that the era of economic liberalism is drawing to a close'.

HOW GOVERNING ACROSS LEVELS DOES (BUT OFTEN DOES NOT) TAKE PLACE

We also accept, and indeed have long accepted, that governance is both articulated and practised at a number of levels within the international political economy. This insight goes beyond the widely acknowledged interplay between the domestic and the international and has lately come to be addressed analytically by means of the lens of 'multilevel governance' (Hooghe and Marks 2001; Bache and Flinders 2004). But, again, more is at stake here in the argument than just the claim that governance has moved upwards, downwards and sideways and now occurs on multiple levels. In his chapter in Part I Colin Hay invited us to think about this issue in an even more complex way by interrogating the concept of interdependence. In particular, he highlighted for our attention the notion of 'spatial interdependence' (as distinct from 'domain interdependence'). By the former, he refers to 'the interconnectedness (for some, the growing interconnectedness) of political and economic processes on different spatial scales; and, typically, to the idea that domestic dynamics are shaped (again, for many, increasingly) by transnational or global factors and that transnational or global dynamics are shaped (increasingly) by domestic dynamics'. But, as he went on to argue, 'as soon as we acknowledge that actions motivated by the desire to realise an intention at a specific spatial scale are likely to have consequences at other spatial scales, we become aware of the need for governance across levels'. Hay prefers this phrase to the more familiar notion of multilevel governance because he argues that it is precisely this capacity to operate across levels that is made necessary by a world of spatial interdependence. He cited the highly relevant problem of debt and suggested that it is no longer enough to forego at the national level the repayment of debt whilst growth is being resuscitated (the classical Keynesian position) because global financial market actors ('bondholders') might demand a higher rate of interest on debt denominated in the currency of the more intransigently indebted country. The solution, or, as he says, at least the potential solution, is governance across levels; specifically, 'a combination of transnational coordination and national action' whereby a community of indebted national states adopt a collective transnational position by means of which to ward off global market pressures.

But, as again Hay observed, 'such governance across levels is not something we are very good at'. Once more, many of the case-study chapters in Part II of the book sustain this judgement. The best exemplars probably come in the environmental sphere of policy-making and with particular relation to the problem of managing climate change. We saw the argument made that the attempt to manage all of the actors, interests and, above all, levels of action involved in this issue via the 'mega-multilateralist' process that has come to be called Kyoto has not only failed, but was almost bound to fail. It was just too complex an array of factors and dimensions to be able to be coordinated at transnational level within a single diplomatic regime. The same point can also be made about the working of the World Trade Organization (WTO), which has lately come under criticism because of its decade-long failure to bring to fruition the 'Doha development round' it inaugurated in 2001. Again, although this is often presented as a failure of leadership by critics of such big, institutional, global processes, it might just be that the necessary governance across levels cannot be put together on such a sensitive issue of perceived direct relevance to the national interests when so many countries (presently 159) are involved. The extent of the coordination required is manifestly huge. Given these various and obvious problems encountered in reaching global decisions, one conclusion that could be drawn is that the international political economy needs a coordination agency with a remit to play the key, apparently missing, networking function. Here the irony is that it has actually recently created one, namely the Group of 20 (G20). But, as again we have seen, the constituent states of the G20 have only allowed the organisation to play that role at fleeting crisis moments. Although it arguably has the informality and versatility that is required, it has nevertheless not yet become a fully operational part of global governance, resulting in the continuing absence of effective policy coordination across levels, as identified.

The interesting test-cases where coordination has worked better have come at the regional level, although it has to be admitted that by that we mean only to refer to the

European Union (EU). No other regional governance system possesses anything like the sophistication of EU decision-making. Of late, with the 'Eurocrisis' unfolding before our eyes, it has become conventional to lament the weaknesses of the internal govern-ance of the EU. We certainly saw plenty of evidence of that in the discussion presented earlier of the collective muddle over currency management that has been generated by the various states, regional bodies and international institutions involved. It looks to have been a major error not to have designed in advance some sort of 'crisis work-out mechanism' (an error, though, recalling our previous thematic argument, that was at least in part brought about because advocates of the euro were so confident of the pros-pects of market stability that they thought this would simply not be necessary). We saw here too that, in the absence of effective regional coordination, decisions always tend to get dragged down to national level. But, if given enough time by the bond markets, who is to say that the EU's leaders might not eventually come up with some workable decision-making framework for handling across the necessary levels the asymmetries of power and position that are at the root of the 'Eurocrisis'? The resulting arrange-ments would no doubt be the opposite of neat; they might even look ugly; but it would be a strong argument that asserts that the task could not be done. After all, as other chapters showed, the EU has succeeded, albeit on less high political terrain, in govern-ing across levels in areas such as migration and even, to some extent, in climate policy too.

HOW TRANSNATIONAL PLURALISM WORKS IN PRACTICE

We continue to argue as well that a further foundational dimension of the contemporary governance of the international political economy is its openness to, and thus by exten-sion dependence upon, the activities of multiple actors operating from many institutional bases. Indeed, if that was not the case, we would be operating analytically in a simpler world composed merely of governments pursuing rival goals. We deploy the notion of 'transnational neopluralism', as advanced by Philip Cerny (2010), to catch the essence of the multiple-actor claim. Cerny concisely reiterated the central hypothesis of this approach in his chapter in Part I of the book, arguing that in the contemporary era 'those actors who will be most effective at influencing and shaping politics and policy outcomes are those who possess the most transnationally interconnected resources, power and influence in a globalising world'. In the main, they would be actors who:

> perceive and define their goals, interests and values in international, transnational ands translo-cal contexts . . . are able to build cross-border networks, coalitions and power bases among a range of potential allies and adversaries . . . and . . . are able to coordinate and organise their strategic action on a range of international, transnational and translocal scales in such a way as to pursue transnational policy agendas and institutional *bricolage*.

Globalisation in this sense not only constitutes a set of permissive conditions for the operation of transnational pluralism; according to Cerny, 'it also is itself increasingly constituted by the very political processes identified here'. In short, 'the strategies and tactics adopted by actors to cope with, control, manage and restructure political institu-tions, processes and practices determine what sort of globalisation we get'.

This is a notably agency-based perspective, but it serves to give a valuable dynamism to our understanding of the governance of the international political economy. However, the analytical challenge to which it gives rise is to go beyond the broad brush and explore in greater detail precisely how transnational pluralism currently works itself out in the many day-to-day practices of governance. On this front our case-study authors in Part II have responded very effectively, bringing vividly into their accounts of different policy domains all manner of different types of political actor. We can, however, immediately draw an important conclusion, which is that, although transnational pluralism is genuinely pluralist, it is at the same time deeply unequal in respect of the capacities, both ideational and material, that actors bring to bear upon the governance agendas with which they engage. As we have repeatedly seen in the chapters, multinational corporations, financial market actors, consumers, epistemic communities of scientists and experts – all are much better positioned to organise their activities on a transnational basis than, say, trade unionists, workers or even nationally organised forms of business. By comparison with this latter grouping, civil-society networks and 'transnational' advocacy coalitions (by definition) have done much better in catching on to the new rules of the globalisation game and have made their presence felt in several important policy arenas discussed in the chapters. Moreover, as again Cerny noted in his contribution, '"Left" and "Right" are not opposites today, but are characterised by new forms of overlap and fragmentation', largely shaped by disagreements about how first to interpret and then respond to the ongoing narrative of neoliberalism. The result is that 'Long-term left/right blocs are giving way to mixed, complex and looser coalitions'.

A further consideration that flows from detailed pluralist analysis is whether or not the governance of the international political economy has, to some extent, been 'privatised'. Several previous analyses (see, e.g., Cutler et al. 1999; Nölke and Graz 2008) have picked up the growing presence of powerful private actors in what once would have been judged properly to be public arenas of decision-making, and our chapter authors frequently discuss this issue. Their problem lies in finding a pattern beyond a broad trend in the direction of greater private involvement in governance compared to, say, the classical Bretton Woods period. Some contributors prefer to highlight the role of private actors; others report the continuing centrality of states. Often the difference is only the relative weight of the presumption from which the analysis starts. Some also stress the fact that private actors, even when fully engaged within the governance of a particular policy area, necessarily still rely on the framework of rules and resource capabilities laid down by public authorities. Something of a tug of war was also frequently observed between public authorities and private actors, or between regulation and the market, in which 'victories' are notched at various points by both sides, as seen lately, for example, in the politics surrounding the regulation of banks under the terms of Basle 3. It is also important, as argued more than once in the chapters, not to approach this discussion from entrenched (positive or negative) positions in the debate: what matters most is perhaps the balance of efficacy between public and private action. Most complex governance arenas inevitably require that both types of actor are comprehensively engaged if progress towards solutions to policy dilemmas is to be achieved.

A final question raised by this book's investigation of how transnational pluralism works in practice in finance, trade, development, migration, the environment and other issue areas is arguably the most worrying of all. It is the suggestion, once more raised by

Cerny in his chapter in elaborating possible broad 'scenarios of change', that actually 'no group or group of groups will be at the steering wheel of change in the international system, and competition between different groups will in turn undermine the capacity of any one of them to exercise control'. According to this vision the eventual outcome would be something close to that predicted some while ago now by Alain Minc (1993) when he talked of the emergence of 'the new Middle Ages', characterised not by the exercise of clear political authority defined through sovereignty and territoriality but rather by the contestation, often without legitimacy, of a confusing mosaic of overlapping, competing networks of public and private players. We may be much closer to this reality today, 20 years after he first published this analysis, than perhaps even he thought likely.

HOW A DEEPER ENGAGEMENT WITH ETHICS COULD HELP

Finally, we still think that it is vital always to probe the ethical dimension of all forms of governance of the international political economy. In his contribution to Part I, James Brassett provided an overview of the literature that has thus far been developed on the matter of global governance as an ethical question. He began by addressing a range of traditional political theory approaches, including liberal cosmopolitan, deliberative and critical democratic modes of thinking, and noted how a number of authors emphasised the need to rethink 'scale, inclusion and legitimacy in a global context'. Yet, in the end he acknowledged that we still face what he called 'the traditional question of democratic theory', namely: 'what to do in cases of radical disagreement?' As he went on to ask, 'what if humans will not renegotiate property rights to land, if the wealthy will not redistribute, if different cultures wish to remain exclusivist, and if analytically weak conceptions of global governance continue to prevail (as they do)?' Looking to widen his lens, he then proceeded to draw into the discussion some more 'performative' propositions associated with the work of post-structural scholars who draw variously on Nietszche, Foucault and Derrida. For such thinkers, 'ethics can take on a wholly different guise, less a realm of thought capable of reflexively "improving" the world, and more an already existing constituent element in that world'. From this perspective, ethics is global governance. Brassett rejects the familiar critique that post-structural thought is essentially nihilistic and precludes by its nature agendas of improvement. Instead, he highlights and accepts 'the responsibility to imagine new, less violent forms of ethical relation'; in other words, he endorses the case for 'thinking differently, about how everyday global governance can be imagined otherwise'. In sum, he proposes a 'better conversation', wherein 'we might start to see ethical approaches to global governance rather like "attempts", among many others, to engage the world in less harmful ways'.

In good part, the many chapter authors in Part II of the book have responded to this injunction positively and have engaged with ethical issues in their analyses. Various illustrations can be easily provided. We heard that the IMF, for example, lacks a legitimate mandate for its adoption of a more intensive systemic surveillance of national financial systems, post-crash. We saw reference made to the inadequacy of attempts to constrain the private power of United States financial actors in the context of the existence of a corrupt, money-driven political system in that country. We were reminded of the disjunction that has sat at the heart of the 'Eurocrisis' between the designers and main beneficiaries of the single currency and those who have been required to pay up when the system goes wrong, namely, its citizen guarantors. We were exposed to the thought, completely heretical in the context of the dominant ethical framework shaping the Millennium Development Goals, that 'harms' deriving from the unequal structure of the international political economy might actually bear significantly and negatively upon the development prospects of a number of the world's poorest countries. We could go on. What is not in doubt is that issues of representation, inclusion and exclusion, equity, legitimacy of decision-making and yawning democratic deficits do very much belong in the discussion of the governance of the international political economy. It is pleasing, moreover, that they have been amply raised throughout this book.

Indeed, we end on an ethical note. As we said at the beginning of the Introduction, we have sought in this book to refresh the academic study of the governance of the international political economy and we hope that we have succeeded to some degree in that aim. But the reality that has been revealed along the way is that we still await the impact of the effort of all of us, as global citizens, to refresh the actual governance of the international political economy. The truth is that we are not well governed globally; in fact, we are often misgoverned or governed badly. We remain prey to the power of a dominant ideology that does not serve the interests of even the majority of the world's peoples, let alone all of them. We have not put in place consistently effective mechanisms for bringing off the complex coordination needed to advance solutions to the most 'wicked' of global problems. We tolerate the unequal access of different types of actors to the main sources of power and decision-making in the international political economy and we do not subject the resulting arrangements to sufficient, rigorous, ethical interrogation. Regardless of how well we think we do as academic analysts, we ought to be honest enough to recognise that our collective record as citizens of a troubled and threatened world needs, very quickly, to become a lot better.

REFERENCES

Bache, Ian and Matthew Flinders (eds) (2004), *Multi-Level Governance*, Oxford: Oxford University Press.
Bourdieu, Pierre (1992), *Language and Symbolic Power*, Cambridge: Polity Press.
Cerny, Philip (2010), *Rethinking World Politics: A Theory of Transnational Neopluralism*, Oxford: Oxford University Press.
Cutler, Claire A., Virginia Haufler and Tony Porter (eds) (1999), *Private Authority in International Affairs*, Albany, NY: SUNY Press.
Gills, B.K. (2010), 'Going South: capitalist crisis, systemic crisis, civilisational crisis', *Third World Quarterly*, **31** (2), 169–84.
Gramsci, Antonio (1971), *Selections from The Prison Notebooks*, ed. Geoffrey Nowell-Smith and Quintin Hoare, London: Lawrence & Wishart.
Grugel, Jean and Pia Rigarozzi (2012), 'Post-neoliberalism in Latin America: rebuilding and reclaiming the state after crisis', *Development and Change*, **43** (1), 1–21.
Hay, Colin and Anthony Payne (2013), 'The Great Uncertainty', *SPERI Comment*, 30 January, available at: http://www.sheffield.ac.uk/speri.
Hooghe, Liesbet and Gary Marks (2001), *Multi-Level Governance and European Integration*, Lanham, MD: Rowman & Littlefield.
Hobson, John M. and Leonard Seabrooke (eds) (2007), *Everyday Politics of the World Economy*, Cambridge: Cambridge University Press.
Minc, Alain (1993), *Le nouveau moyen âge*, Paris: Gallimard.

Nölke, Andreas and Jean-Christophe Graz (eds) (2008), *Transnational Private Governance and its Limits*, London: Routledge.
Ramo, J.C. (2004), *The Beijing Consensus*, London: Foreign Policy Centre.
Ruggie, J.G. (1982), 'International regimes, transactions and change: embedded liberalism in the postwar economic order', *International Organization*, **36** (2), 379–415.

Index